Bioethics and Human Rights

Bioethics and Human Rights

Contemporary Issues at Home and Abroad

Third Edition

Edited by Wanda Teays
and Alison Dundes Renteln

ROWMAN & LITTLEFIELD
Lanham • Boulder • New York • London

Published by Rowman & Littlefield
An imprint of The Rowman & Littlefield Publishing Group, Inc.
4501 Forbes Boulevard, Suite 200, Lanham, Maryland 20706
www.rowman.com

86-90 Paul Street, London EC2A 4NE

British Library Cataloguing in Publication Information Available

Library of Congress Cataloging-in-Publication Data

Names: Teays, Wanda, editor. | Renteln, Alison Dundes, editor.
Title: Bioethics and human rights : contemporary issues at home and abroad / Wanda Teays, Alison Dundes Renteln.
Description: Third edition. | Lanham : Rowman & Littlefield, 2023. | Includes bibliographical references and index.
Identifiers: LCCN 2023035449 (print) | LCCN 2023035450 (ebook) | ISBN 9781538188590 (cloth) | ISBN 9781538188606 (paperback) | ISBN 9781538188613 (ebook)
Subjects: LCSH: Medical ethics. | Civil rights. | Human rights. | MESH: Bioethics. | Human Rights.
Classification: LCC R724 .B46 2023 (print) | LCC R724 (ebook) | DDC 174.2—dc23/eng/20231017
LC record available at https://lccn.loc.gov/2023035449
LC ebook record available at https://lccn.loc.gov/2023035450

We dedicate this volume to all those
working to protect human rights and challenge global injustice.

Acknowledgments

Thank you, Rowman & Littlefield, for supporting a third edition of this text. The new and updated chapters have made for wider coverage of the issues—topics as timely as climate change, the Havana Syndrome, pandemic ethics, health care for migrants in detention centers, and reproductive justice in light of the *Dobbs* decision. Given that human rights are inherently global in scope, we have adopted a new title: *Bioethics and Human Rights: Contemporary Issues at Home and Abroad.*

We are most grateful to our editor, Natalie Mandziuk, whose guidance helped shape the direction of this new edition. We so appreciate your insights and encouragement. Thank you, Natalie. Thanks also to the reviewers for their helpful suggestions and enthusiasm, and the production team for their high-quality work in putting this book together.

We also want to thank our contributors, whose excellent essays will be appreciated by readers, researchers, faculty, and students. And, finally, thanks to all of you whose interest in bioethics and human rights makes this volume possible.

Contents

Introduction

Wherever we turn we confront ethical dilemmas. Some are personal—our own issues to resolve. Should I stop eating animals? How honest should I be with my ailing mother? Should I turn in my friend who cheated on the exam?

Some dilemmas are those facing friends, family, or acquaintances seeking our advice, for example, about dropping out of school, choosing chemo over radiation, joining a political protest group, or becoming a subject in a pesticide experiment to make some extra cash.

Some dilemmas face people far removed from our own lives, but whose decisions reverberate, setting a precedent for others to follow or to contest. For instance, is it wrong of doctors to refuse to perform an abortion or treat a child suffering from monkeypox, a relative of smallpox? Do medical personnel have a duty to treat in a pandemic? Is it right of rich patients to buy a kidney from a poor person? Should doctors participate in lethal injections?

The issues range all over the map in terms of diversity and complexity. Take the man, identity unknown, who has been on life support for nearly 17 years, going in and out of consciousness. No one knows whether he has a family looking for him and what sort of care they would want him to receive. What do we owe him?

Then there's the detainee held at a CIA Black Site who may or may not have known anything useful to his interrogators. Should it have been permissible to slam his head into a wall or confine him to a box with holes drilled in it for air? Is it humane to lock someone in solitary confinement for days, months, years, or decades? Are there exceptions to professional duties, regulations, and principles?

Consider also the dilemma facing a victim of an IVF mistake resulting in a pregnancy with the wrong embryos and whose genetic parents want "their" baby. What should she do? Decisions, decisions. Few are easy. The factors brought to bear are shaped by the context in which they arise, and the values rooted in a culture or religion.

In order clear the path for defensible moral reasoning, we should start with our objectives, what we are seeking to achieve, what questions we want answers to. If we are to be guided by what is sought, we need to set goals and keep our perspectives in mind. We can't just assert truisms. We must show the way from moral shortcomings to virtue and from ideas to policies. To accomplish that goal, the boots have to be on the ground, as they say. Abstract principles can be inspiring. But effecting change means *doing* something, tackling ethical issues head-on, and arriving at defensible decisions that are just and fair.

We are pleased to have a third edition of this book and the opportunity to expand its coverage. We are also pleased that most of the chapters in this volume are original essays written by some of the top ethicists in the field. Their ideas and insights make clear the importance of creating a solid foundation for Bioethics. Readers will also appreciate the new chapters—which include essays on pandemic ethics, the "Havana Syndrome," vaccinations, the *Dobbs* decision on abortion, vulnerable populations in human experimentation, and the bioethical issues of climate change.

The diverse perspectives underscore the significance of values and beliefs on our decision-making. Justice concerns extend around the world, with individuals and communities responding differently to these challenges. We see this with the Western emphasis on patient autonomy, which is at odds with family-centered decision-making that health caregivers often face.

With more frequent migration, medical professionals are confronted with moral and cultural conflicts that are frequently unfamiliar or multilayered. This requires us to delve into policies and differing world views, leading us to ask how many, if any, ethical principles are universal. Authors in Part I tackle this issue and examine the ways theoretical perspectives frame the inquiry and shape the direction of our moral reasoning.

The point of view can make all the difference. This is the case both in the framing of problems and the very concepts that are used. For example, look at the interpretation of truth-telling. When an individual is diagnosed with a health problem, it is generally thought that medical professionals must inform the patient regarding treatment options. However, that presumption is not shared worldwide, as some cultures leave the patient out of the equation, particularly if the prognosis is grim. Families and acquaintances may then play a pivotal role in the patient's treatment.

As the chapters in Part II indicate, Bioethics is fundamentally about human rights and the fiduciary duties of doctors and researchers. This includes such issues as patient rights, medical tourism, solitary confinement, informed consent, the rights of human subjects, and protections against exploitation and invasive procedures.

Another focus of Bioethics centers on such life-and-death issues as pediatric genomics, abortion, euthanasia, and doctor involvement in lethal injections. This we examine in Part III. We need only look at the social, political and medical issues around abortion and, with that, the moral status of the fetus. Is it a *person*? What rights does it have? How do we resolve conflicts between the rights of the fetus and those of the woman in whose body it is gestating? We need to decide what factors should be taken into consideration and if the best resolution is found in the political or judicial arenas. What is permitted prior to conception, much less afterward, has generated ethical conflicts that are ongoing.

A major concern is the boundary of personal autonomy and the limits of personal liberty. Think about all the ways these issues arise. That the procreation market includes people who sell their own gametes or who gestate the genetic children of others merits scrutiny. Moreover, both reproductive autonomy and autonomy at the end of life put self-determination at center stage. What duties do others have in upholding personal autonomy? Can I ask you to take my life when I want to die? What are the limits of self-determination when others are asked to play a part? Should children be able to participate in medical decision-making? To what degree can women determine their reproductive freedom over their own bodies when it comes to pregnancy and abortion? And how far do fathers' rights extend? Clearly these are controversial issues that warrant our attention.

The ethical concerns go beyond what we do to our own bodies to how others are used to accomplish our ends. Our contributors tackle these issues. For instance, Cecilia Wee discusses active and passive euthanasia from the perspective of Confucianism. Her explication helps us see how morality, culture, and religion can intersect and impact attitudes regarding killing versus letting die. And Cher Weixia Chen turns the spotlight on doctor's participation in lethal injections and the harvesting of organs from prisoners being executed.

The range of public health concerns is both deep and wide. Bioethics is inherently about health—our bodies, procreation and birth, disease and suffering, pain and death. It is about access to health care, the allocation of resources, and just medical practices. It is about vulnerable populations used in research and experimentation, as sources of human organs, or as "gestational carriers" bearing children for others.

We are not immune to its reach. Just one traveler from China brought SARS to the West. And we saw how quickly COVID-19 spread from one country to the next. Whether the source was a lab leak or transmission from an animal, there are serious concerns to consider. Health issues are often human rights issues affecting the principles and policies that guide us. Throughout this book, we see that is the case.

In the Preamble of the Constitution of the World Health Organization (WHO), health is defined as "a state of complete physical, mental and social well-being, and not merely the absence of disease or infirmity." The WHO further asserts that governments are responsible for providing "adequate health and social measures."

We might ask if access to health care is a fundamental right. A great deal follows from the answer to that question. The WHO's definition of health has brought with it considerable debate, given the social and ethical implications. In addition, it provides neither a discussion of the nature of mental or social well-being nor guidelines as to how they might be achieved. The very generality of the definition, as Daniel Callahan (1973) observes, has resulted in a concept that may be too far-reaching. His recommendation is to pull in the reins, and so he asserts that "Health is a state of physical well-being." That state need not be "complete," he argues, but it must be adequate.

When looking at public health on an international scale, it is easy to see why the WHO suggested a broader approach to health. In many cases, physical well-being, mental well-being, and social well-being are intertwined. Assumptions, culture, traditions, and values, as well as biases and prejudices, transform what each person considers good health. They also affect who has moral standing or whose health concerns are considered most pressing. This can result in disparities regarding access to resources and personnel, treatment options, decision-making, and policy considerations. The valuable insights gathered in this anthology further our understanding of bioethics and deepen our appreciation for the global impact of the issues examined.

Organization of This Book

This text is set out in four parts. They are as follows:

PART I: THEORETICAL PERSPECTIVES

This first unit presents key approaches to bioethics, starting with Bernard Gert's inquiry as to whether there can be a global ethical framework. This leads to the issue Tom L. Beauchamp considers; namely, whether a universal morality is compatible with multiculturalism. A central issue has to do with truth-telling and what sort of assumptions and principles should guide us. Ilhan Ilkilic takes this up in the third chapter. Another perspective discussed in Part I links back to the opening question; namely does a global bioethics require a global moral language? Søren Holm offers his analysis in Chapter 4. In the next chapter Udo Schüklenk examines key issues in global health ethics—including central issues about justice. And in the last chapter of Part I Akiko Ito gives us an overview of the UN Convention on the rights of persons with disabilities. Together, these essays lay a foundation for our inquiry. We then turn to applications. In Parts II, III, and IV, the authors examine key concerns and cases that merit our consideration and put our moral reasoning skills to work.

PART II: HUMAN RIGHTS

This second unit focuses on human rights and its importance in bioethics. We begin with an historical overview by Robert Baker that grounds the discussion and shows how widespread are the concerns. The next two chapters illustrate the ways bioethics put human rights under the spotlight; as shown in Virginia Warren's focus on medical tourism and Wanda Teays' critique of solitary confinement. Each issue asks us to consider the right to be treated with dignity and respect, and what we owe one another in protecting that right. In Chapters 10 and 11 Peter F. Omonzejele (on research-related injuries, especially of unmarried African women) and Marlene Brant Castellano (on aboriginal research) turn the spotlight to vulnerable populations in human experimentation. In the last chapter of this unit Alison Dundes Renteln discusses virginity restoration surgery. She calls us to look at the role of cultural traditions and self-determination—which links back to the theoretical perspectives raised in Part 1.

PART III: LIFE AND DEATH

The third unit focuses on life and death. The opening chapter by Maya Sabatello looks at pediatric genomics, zeroing-in on adolescents' participation in decision-making. Their engagement and power to decide about genomic testing and use of genomic data in such settings has been limited; thus, calling for a reconsideration of who decides what in treatment matters. We then turn to reproductive freedom, with two chapters examining one of the most controversial issues, that of abortion. Michael Boylan looks at the abortion debate in the 21st century in Chapter 14 and Kimberly Mutcherson examines reproductive justice in light of the *Dobbs* decision in Chapter 15. The debate rages on, making it clear that a resolution is not yet within reach. The next three chapters focus on euthanasia—another crucial life and death issue. Carlos Verdugo-Serna considers whether euthanasia could be a medical duty on the part of doctors, especially in light of unnecessary pain and suffering. Scott Stonington and Pinit Ratanakul consider what bioethical principles and framework should guide us. One issue is whether the presumed universality of values applies to non-Western societies. In Chapter 18, Cecilia Wee turns the focus to Confucian views on killing versus letting die. She argues that the distinction between act and omission doesn't carry the same moral weight in Confucianism and this may factor into end-of-life decisions. In the final chapter in Part III Cher Weixia Chen examines lethal injection in China and discusses whether it should be permissible to harvest organs from executed prisoners. As these chapters demonstrate, the perspective and underlying values can make all the difference.

PART IV: PUBLIC HEALTH

The fourth and last unit of the text examines public healthcare. We start with Zenon Culverhouse's discussion of mental health utilizing a framework of epistemic injustice. We then turn in Chapter 21 to Rosemarie Tong's explication of feminist perspectives on the problem that caring for the elderly mostly falling on women. Neither topic has received much attention from bioethicists, making these two essays all the more timely. In Chapter 22 Alison Dundes Renteln discusses the use of sound as a weapon and the implications for international law and for bioethics. She examines such acoustic attacks as the "Havana Syndrome" and considers whether a new treaty is needed to control the consequences of sonar warfare. The next chapter by Peter Tagore Tan also examines a controversial issue; namely, the public health concerns raised by climate change. In recent years there have been life and death struggles resulting from climate change, so it is prudent for bioethicists to turn their attention to this matter. In Chapter 24 Rita Manning looks at those held in immigration detention and the significant issues they face regarding healthcare. She highlights our obligation to the vulnerable population housed in ICE detention, most recently in light of the COVID-19 pandemic. The last three chapters continue the spotlight on pandemics. Chapter 25 presents an overview by Edward H. Spence of issues and policies using Gewirth's Positive Rights. He argues that we have an obligatory duty to help those who cannot help themselves and that duty applies to both individuals and institutions. In Chapter 26, Wanda Teays considers whether there is a duty to treat in a pandemic given the risks go beyond patients and doctors. We need to examine how far "duty" extends. Part IV ends the text with a discussion by Bradley P. Stoner about the vaccination controversy—all too relevant in an age where pandemics are a vital concern.

Key Features of This Book

- International cases that offer a wider and deeper understanding of bioethics
- Original essays by experts in the field offer vital insights for both healthcare professionals and academics
- Exercises that help develop critical thinking and moral reasoning skills
- Thoughtful pieces for professional development clarify our obligations and duties as ethicists, professors, and medical caregivers to those who depend on us for guidance
- Accessible chapters that will inspire students to reflect on moral dilemmas and the relevance of ethics to their lives
- Real-world cases and interesting discussion topics for each unit of the book—perfect for classroom activities, group projects, or essay assignments
- Additional resources, including Internet resources, essay questions, case analyses, group topics, and bioethics in the movies
- Chapters that widen the playing field beyond Western assumptions and values by recognizing other cultures, values, and religions
- It is suitable for both graduate and undergraduate classes
- It includes voices not often heard, resulting in a broader range of readings than commonly found in bioethics texts
- Chapters and units work together but are independent of one another, giving faculty flexibility in setting out the course

New to This Edition

We have reshaped the second edition and expanded the coverage of issues for this third edition with new and updated readings. These include:

UPDATES:

- Udo Schüklenk's update to his chapter on global health
- Akiko Ito's update to her chapter on disability rights
- Michael Boylan's update on the abortion debate
- Cher Weixia Chen's update to her chapter on lethal injection in China
- Rita Manning's update on the healthcare of migrants being held in ICE detention facilities

NEW CHAPTERS:

- Peter F. Omonzejele's essay on human experimentation and the bride-price tradition in Africa
- Kimberly Mutcherson's essay on reproductive justice in light of the *Dobbs* decision

- Alison Dundes Renteln's essay on acoustic attacks and the "Havana Syndrome"
- Peter Tagore Tan's discussion of the bioethical issues related to climate change
- Edward H. Spence's overview of obligatory duties in pandemic ethics
- Wanda Teays' essay on whether there is a duty to treat in a pandemic
- Bradley P. Stoner's examination of the vaccination controversy

As you can see, this third edition includes chapters on important issues facing us. The abortion debate has resulted in more restrictions as well as tighter laws and policies. And the COVID-19 pandemic with the widespread loss of life has brought to the fore pressing concerns—concerns that are not easily resolved. The additions, combined with the excellent readings from the first and second editions, make this book a most appealing resource—as a primary text, reference book, or a supplement.

References

Callahan, Daniel. 1973. "The WHO Definition of 'Health.'" The Hastings Center Studies 1 (3): 77–78.

Part I

THEORETICAL PERSPECTIVES

CHAPTER 1

A Global Ethical Framework for Bioethics

Bernard Gert

Abstract

Although morality is universal, it allows for some significant variations because of cultural differences. Bioethics is morality applied to medicine and medical research, so a global bioethics should be thought of as an application of the common moral system to medicine and medical research that allows for significant variations in different cultures or societies. Common morality has rules that prohibit killing, causing pain or disability, deceiving and breaking promises, but there is some variation in the interpretation of these rules, as well as in what counts as an adequate justification for violating them. Different societies also have some significant differences in their laws and in the duties that they regard physicians as having. There are also differences in whom they hold as fully protected by the moral rules. These societal variations have significant effects on what morality encourages, prohibits, and requires physicians to do.

Introduction[1]

Different cultures give different answers to some of the questions with which bioethics is concerned. This much seems obvious, and it has led many to conclude that there is no universal morality, while leading others to conclude that where there is disagreement, one of the disagreeing cultures must be mistaken. In this chapter I describe what I believe is the universal moral system and explain how its universality is consistent with limited but true moral disagreement.

To begin, I distinguish the claim that morality is universal both from the claim that it always provides a unique correct solution and from the claim that it is explicitly recognized by every (or any) culture. As with grammatical rules, the moral system is normally followed without conscious reflection.

I next present the ten moral rules that I believe constitute the core of the universal moral system. One source of moral disagreement arises from different interpretations of these rules themselves. For instance, although the rule prohibiting killing is universal and cultures normally agree on when an action is a killing, certain actions (removing from a ventilator) may constitute killings in some cultures but not in others.

In every culture, violations of the moral rules require moral justification; thus, universal morality includes not only rules but also a procedure for justifying violations of these rules. I next introduce a two-step procedure for justifying violations of moral rules and consider how, using the identical procedure, members of different cultures can come to different conclusions about whether a particular violation is morally permissible.

In the last section, I discuss moral disagreements arising from differences of opinion regarding who or what is fully protected by this moral system, an issue the system itself cannot resolve. In all cultures, moral agents must be treated morally, but some cultures include others within morality's sphere of protection as well. And, finally, I note that, although a certain amount of disagreement is consistent with our universal morality, that morality itself puts substantial limits on the permissible ways of resolving the disagreements it sanctions.

Morality, Or the Moral System

Morality is a public system that is known by all those who are held responsible for their actions (i.e., all moral agents). A public system is a system that has the following two characteristics. In normal circumstances: 1) All persons to whom it applies (i.e., those whose behavior is to be guided and judged by that system) understand it (i.e., know what behavior the system prohibits, requires, discourages, encourages, and allows); and 2) It is not irrational for any of these persons to accept being guided and judged by that system.

The clearest example of a public system is a game, such as bridge or football. A game has an inherent goal and a set of rules that form a system that is understood by all of the players (i.e., they all know what kind of behavior is prohibited, required, discouraged, encouraged, and allowed by the game), and it is not irrational for all players to use the goal and the rules of the game to guide their own behavior and to judge the behavior of other players by them. Although a game is a public system, it applies only to those playing the game, and, if one does not want to abide by the rules, one can quit playing the game. No one can quit being governed by morality. Morality is a public system that applies to all people who understand it and can guide their behavior accordingly. Moral agents are subject to moral judgments simply by virtue of being rational persons who are responsible for their actions.

Although there is general agreement about who is subject to moral judgment, there is considerable disagreement about who is protected by morality. Some—for example, Kant—hold that only moral agents are fully protected, whereas others—for example, Bentham—hold that all beings who can suffer pain are protected. Morality has the inherent goal of lessening the amount of harm suffered by those included in the protected group, either all moral agents or a more inclusive group.

It contains rules that prohibit some kinds of actions, such as killing, and require other kinds, such as keeping promises, and moral ideals that encourage certain kinds of actions, such as relieving pain. It also contains a procedure for determining when it is justified to violate a moral rule, such as when a moral rule and a moral ideal conflict. Morality does not provide unique answers to every question; rather, it sets the limits to legitimate moral disagreement. It is important to realize that unresolvable moral disagreement on some important issues, such as abortion, is compatible with total agreement in the overwhelming number of situations where moral judgments are made.

A useful analogy to morality or the moral system is the grammar or grammatical system used by all competent speakers of a language. Almost no competent speaker can explicitly describe the grammatical system that she uses, yet all competent speakers know the grammar of their language in the sense that they use it when speaking and in interpreting the speech of others. If presented with an explicit account of the grammatical system, competent speakers have the final word on its accuracy.

They should not accept any description of the grammatical system if it rules out speaking in a way that they regard as acceptable or allows speaking in a way that they regard as completely unacceptable. Morality or the moral system requires consistency in a way that grammar does not; so moral agents should not accept any description of morality if it conflicts with the overwhelming set of their considered moral decisions or judgments that are consistent.

There is such overwhelming agreement in most moral matters that we do not even make conscious moral judgments about them; for example, causing pain to someone simply because one feels like doing it. But morality involves one's emotions and interests far more than grammar, so people sometimes make moral decisions and judgments that are inconsistent with the vast majority of their considered moral judgments because they are distorted by their emotions or interests. This has the result that sometimes even competent moral agents can be shown that some of their moral decisions or judgments are mistaken.

Common Morality[2]

When some people claim that there is a common morality, they sometimes mean that there is a universal moral system that provides a unique correct answer to every moral question. Those who deny that there is a common morality sometimes mean that there is not a unique correct answer to any moral problem.

Not surprisingly, both of these extreme views are mistaken. To claim that there is a common morality is to claim that there is a universal moral system that provides a global framework for all acceptable moral decisions and judgments, but it does not mean that there is a unique correct solution to every moral problem.

There are, of course, unique correct answers to many moral questions, but these are usually moral questions that no one ever asks, such as "Is it morally acceptable to torture someone because I enjoy seeing someone in pain?" Even in most situations where one might be tempted to do an immoral action, no one consciously deliberates about what is the morally right thing to do, such as keeping an important promise that it is inconvenient for one to keep. Similarly, in most situations, no one consciously makes a judgment about someone who does not do a morally wrong action—for example, refrains from cheating in a game.

Bioethics is a field in which people often do consciously deliberate about what is the morally right thing to do, such as whether to perform an abortion. Physicians also sometimes consciously make judgments about someone who does not give in to the temptation to do the morally wrong action—for example, does not give an unnecessary antibiotic to a patient who requests it. In what follows, I shall provide a brief description of the common morality that provides a global framework for bioethics, but I shall also show that, even when there is complete agreement on the facts, including probabilities of future harms and benefits, there can be unresolvable differences in the decisions and judgments that people make.[3]

Moral Rules

There is universal agreement that actions such as killing, causing pain or disability, and depriving of freedom or pleasure are immoral unless one has an adequate justification. Similarly, there is universal agreement that deceiving, breaking a promise, cheating, violating the law, and neglecting one's duties also need justification in order not to be immoral.

When I say that all societies have moral rules that prohibit such actions, all I mean is that doing these kinds of actions is immoral unless one has an adequate justification for doing them. Although there are alternative ways of formulating the moral rules, following is a list of moral rules that includes all of the kinds of action that need justification. Although these rules are subject to some variation in interpretation, they can be understood by all those who are held responsible for their actions.

1. Do not kill.
2. Do not deceive.
3. Do not cause pain.
4. Keep your promises.
5. Do not disable.
6. Do not cheat.
7. Do not deprive of freedom.
8. Obey the law.
9. Do not deprive of pleasure.
10. Do your duty.

The rule prohibiting causing pain prohibits causing not only physical pain but also mental pain; the rule prohibiting causing disabilities prohibits causing not only physical disabilities but also mental and volitional disabilities; the rule prohibiting depriving of freedom includes prohibiting the depriving of opportunities and resources; and the rule prohibiting the depriving of pleasure includes prohibiting depriving of future pleasure as well as present pleasure. The rule prohibiting deceiving can be broken by withholding information, as well as by lying; and the rule requiring one to keep one's promises requires keeping informal agreements as well as formal contracts.

Finally, "duty," in the rule requiring one to do one's duty, is meant in its everyday sense, where duties are determined by one's social role, job or profession, or special circumstances. Someone who takes a job is often told what duties are involved. "Duty" is not used as philosophers customarily misuse it, to mean whatever one morally *ought* to do. We are morally required to obey all of the moral rules unless we have an adequate justification for not doing so, but in the everyday sense of "duty," it is a misuse to say we have a duty to obey these rules (e.g., not to kill) or to do our duties.

Duties in this everyday sense are not derived from our common morality, but in each society duties develop from social roles and from the history and practice of the professions in that society. Knowing about social roles and the practices of a field or profession in a particular society is not only necessary for understanding what duties people have in that society, but it is sometimes also necessary for understanding the interpretation of the moral rules in that society.

In many societies, these rules are understood to prohibit not only actual violations but also attempts to violate them, even if the attempt is unsuccessful. They are also often understood to prohibit not only intentional violations but also violations done knowingly but not intentionally. They can even be understood to prohibit some unknowing violations if the person should have known that his action was a violation of a moral rule, or that he was likely to cause harm to someone. But what it means "to cause harm to someone" is not as simple and straightforward as it initially seems. Although one can take "Do not kill" to mean "Do not cause death," causing death, like causing pain or disability, does not mean simply doing an intentional act that you know will result in a person's death, pain, or disability.

Consider a physician who is deciding whether to comply with a competent ventilator-dependent patient's refusal to be stay on the ventilator. If the physician does decide to disconnect the patient from the ventilator, does that count as killing him, or even as assisting his suicide? For most people in American society, complying with a competent patient's refusal to stay on the ventilator when one knows that disconnecting the patient from the ventilator will result in the patient's death does not count as either killing the patient, or even as assisting his suicide.

This is also the legal view in this society. In every state of the United States, physicians are legally required to take a competent patient off of the respirator if the patient refuses to be on it any longer, yet in every state, physicians are prohibited from killing patients, even competent patients who have requested to be killed. Further, although all states require complying with a competent patient's refusal to continue on a ventilator, almost all states do not even allow physician-assisted suicide.

However, some religious people in the United States regard taking a competent patient off of a respirator, even if the patient refuses to be on it any longer, as interfering with the will of God—and hence, as killing the patient—and they do not sanction it. This may also be the view of those societies in which religion has a greater influence on the interpretation of the moral rules than is the case in the United States.

Although no society denies that when physicians comply with a terminal patient's request to be given a lethal injection, they are killing that patient, some more secular societies, such as the Netherlands, consider it morally justified for a physician to kill a patient in these circumstances. Thus, societies can differ from one another not only in their interpretation of the rule prohibiting killing; they can also differ from each other in what they consider to be morally justified cases of killing. These differences do not conflict with all societies accepting that violating the moral rule that prohibits killing needs moral justification.

Like "cause," "deprive" is also not as simple as it initially seems. "Do not deprive of freedom" does not mean simply do not intentionally do any act that you know will have the result that someone does not have the freedom or opportunity to do something he would have had if you had not done that act. For example, in every country with automobiles and parking lots, if, in the normal course of affairs, you arrive at a parking lot before another person, you do not deprive him of the opportunity to park in that lot if you take the last parking place. You do not even need to justify parking in the last space. Further, no one in any country holds that someone who wins a race fairly has deprived the other runners of the pleasure of winning the race.

However, there may be societal differences concerning whether a teacher who grades a student's exam fairly and gives it a very bad grade has broken the rule prohibiting causing pain. Some might say that she has broken the rule but that she is justified in doing so because it is her duty to grade exams fairly, but others might say that she has not broken the rule at all. Similarly, some might claim that a physician who tells a patient about his very poor prognosis, even if she does so in a very compassionate manner, is still violating the rule against causing pain.

However, similar to what some would say about the teacher, some might claim that the physician is justified in violating the rule because it is her duty to tell her patient the truth about his prognosis, while others might claim that telling the patient the truth does not even violate the rules against causing pain and so does not need to be justified at all. But in some societies, doctors do not regard it as necessary to tell a patient the unpleasant truth in order to proceed with treatment. If the physician only has a duty to tell a member of the patient's family, she is not justified in causing pain to the patient.

Deciding whether to tell a patient bad news can also be influenced by a society's interpretation of the rule prohibiting deceiving. Although every society regards a physician lying to a patient as deceiving, one society may also regard a physician as deceiving a patient if she withholds unpleasant information about the patient's medical condition, because doctors have a duty to tell their competent patients about their diagnosis and prognosis. However, another society—which does not regard a doctor as having a duty to tell patients bad news, such as Russia—may not regard withholding unpleasant information as deceiving at all.

Given this wide variation in the interpretation of the rules, some based on the differences in the duties doctors have in that society, it may seem as if talking about a common morality or a global framework for bioethics is a sham. That is because we are discussing interesting cases, where there are legitimate differences in the interpretation of a moral rule. Most cases are not interesting; in fact, in the overwhelming majority of cases, all societies agree on when a given moral rule has been violated, and also agree on whether the violation is justified.

Disagreements Based on Different Interpretations of a Moral Rule

Different interpretations of a moral rule can lead to unresolvable moral disagreement not only between different societies, but also within a given society. I include in the category of disagreements based on different interpretations of the rules only those different interpretations that do not involve deciding who is impartially protected by the moral rules.

Even when there is no doubt that all involved are impartially protected by the moral rules, there is sometimes disagreement on what counts as breaking the rule (e.g., what counts as killing or deceiving). Even people who agree that complying with a competent patient's refusal to continue on the respirator is not killing sometimes disagree on whether discontinuing food and fluids counts as killing. In addition to the disagreement about whether withholding information counts as deceiving, there is also disagreement about whether dyeing one's hair counts as breaking that rule.

Some of these disagreements can be resolved, but some cannot. And often some institution will have to make a decision that settles the matter for the people governed by that institution. Hospitals may adopt rules determining when it is allowed to discontinue life-sustaining treatments, and those physicians that follow those rules are not regarded as having killed their patients but only as having allowed them to die.

Because different societies have different legal systems and impose different duties on physicians, the moral rules prohibiting violating the law and neglecting one's duties will differ in the actions that they prohibit and require. For example, in the United States, doctors have a duty to tell their competent patients about their diagnosis and prognosis, but, in many countries in South America, Israel, and Russia, doctors may tell family members rather than the patient. A universal morality allows for significant cultural or societal variation.

Although there is overwhelming agreement on the moral status of the vast majority of actions, these kinds of actions are those about which no one consciously makes moral decisions and judgments. Normally, we consciously make moral decisions and judgments only on actions about which there is some controversy. With regard to these kinds of situations, morality often does not provide a unique solution to every moral problem, even within a particular society.

Moreover, because their legal systems differ and different duties are assigned, societies may differ in the judgments that are made about particular actions, even when these judgments are uncontroversial within each society. But the differences in laws and duties do not affect the universality of morality any more than the fact that people make different promises affects the universality of morality. And just as promises can sometimes be justifiably broken, so laws can sometimes be justifiably violated and duties can be justifiably not performed. Morality places significant limits on legitimate moral variation between societies, as well as within societies.

Morally Relevant Features and the Two-Step Procedure for Justifying Violations

In addition to the agreement about the kinds of actions that need moral justification, there is general agreement about the way in which violations of moral rules can be justified. There is overwhelming agreement that what counts as an adequate justification for one person must be an adequate justification for anyone else in the same situation. However, since no two situations are exactly alike in all respects, each society must have some way of determining what counts as the same situation.

When it is said that morality requires impartiality, what should be meant is that the same situation does not change simply because the identity of the persons involved in that situation changes. This does not mean that everyone must agree about whether a violation of a moral rule is justified. Impartiality does not require uniformity; impartiality is compatible with disagreement about what counts as an adequate moral justification for any particular violation (e.g., killing or deceiving).

For the same reason, the judges on the US Supreme Court can agree completely on the facts, be impartial, and yet come to different conclusions. It is also important to realize that morality requires impartiality only when one is concerned with the violation of a moral rule; morality does not require impartiality when following a moral ideal (i.e., doing something morally good, such as aiding the needy or relieving pain). Morality allows people to give to whatever charity they prefer; morality does not require impartiality when giving to charities.

One of the most important differences between moral rules and moral ideals is that it is possible for moral rules to be impartially obeyed all of the time. That is why, unless they have an adequate justification for not doing so, people can be required to obey the moral rules all of the time. People are only encouraged, not required, to follow the moral ideals, and no one can even favor following moral ideals all of the time because it is humanly impossible to do so. The moral rules set constraints on one's behavior regardless of what one's goals are, and it is possible for these constraints to be obeyed all of the time. The moral ideals provide goals for one's behavior, but there is a limit on how much time it is possible to spend trying to achieve these goals. Nonetheless, moral ideals express the point of morality more clearly than moral rules, for following them is directly acting to achieve the goal of morality, which is the lessening of suffering harm by all those protected by morality.

Although obeying the moral rules is required and following the moral ideals is only encouraged, when following a moral ideal conflicts with obeying a moral rule, it is sometimes justified to violate the moral rule in order to follow the moral ideal. When there is a conflict between two moral rules or between obeying a moral rule and following a moral ideal, there is a two-step procedure for deciding what one morally ought to do.

This two-step procedure is employed in all societies, though usually not consciously, to determine whether a violation of a moral rule is justified. As stated above, when we are talking about impartiality, everyone agrees that what counts as an adequate justification for one person must be an adequate justification for anyone else in the same situation. But for this statement to serve any purpose or have any force, there must be a specification of what counts in the same situation.

For the purposes of justifying a violation of a moral rule, two situations count as the same situation when all of their morally relevant features are the same. A morally relevant feature is a feature such that, if it changes, it can change whether a rational person would regard that violation of a moral rule as justified. In ordinary circumstances, the day of the week, the time of the day, and the season of the year are not morally relevant features. Unless the day, time, or season are related to some other feature, a change in them cannot change whether a violation of a moral rule is justified.

I have compiled a list of ten questions, the answers to which are morally relevant features. I do not claim that any change in any of these features would lead a rational person to change his position concerning whether a particular violation is justified. I do claim that, for a rational person who does not use any idiosyncratic beliefs (i.e., beliefs that are not shared by all rational persons), only a change in these features can change whether that person regards the violation as justified.

Two violations count as being in the same circumstances or as the same kind of violation if all of the following questions have the same answers. The answers to these questions are the morally relevant features of the violation.

1. What kind of act is it (i.e., what moral rule is it a violation of)?
2. What harms are caused, avoided (not caused), and prevented?
3. What are the relevant beliefs and desires of the person harmed?
4. What is the relationship between the parties?
5. What goods are being gained?
6. Is a violation of a moral rule being prevented?
7. Is a violation of a moral rule being punished?
8. Are there alternative actions that will not violate a moral rule or cause less harm?
9. Is the action being done intentionally or only knowingly?
10. Is the situation an emergency?

When serving on the ethics committee of a hospital, I found that, if one did not recognize all of these morally relevant features, one was quite likely to make a moral judgment that no one, including oneself, would accept. For example, an unacceptable moral judgment could result from a failure to recognize that it is a morally relevant feature that two situations differ in that in one situation there is an alternative action that would result in less harm. Similarly, a seriously mistaken moral judgment may result from a failure to recognize that it is a morally relevant feature if two situations differ in that one situation is an emergency situation. I cannot show that all of the morally relevant features are answers to just these ten questions.

Perhaps in some other society, or even in my society, some other morally relevant features may be discovered. But, in each society, there must be some way of identifying what counts as the same situation or the same kind of violation. Describing a situation in terms of its morally relevant features is the first step in the two-step procedure that all people in all societies must employ to guarantee that what counts as an adequate justification for one person counts as an adequate justification for anyone else in the same situation.

The second step in the two-step procedure is estimating the results of everyone knowing that they are allowed to violate the rule in these circumstances. If one estimates that *less* harm would result from everyone knowing that they are allowed to violate the rule in these circumstances than from everyone knowing that they are *not* allowed to violate the rule in these circumstances, then one is acting impartially in violating that rule. If everyone would make the same estimate, then the violation is strongly justified; if not everyone would make the same estimate, then the violation is only weakly justified. Weakly justified violations involve serious moral disagreement.

If everyone would estimate that *more* harm would result from everyone knowing that they are allowed to violate the rule in these circumstances than everyone knowing that they are *not* allowed to violate the rule in these circumstances, then the violation is unjustified. What one estimates about the harms and benefits of everyone knowing that violating a rule in the specified situation is allowed is shown by whether one would favor everyone knowing that they are allowed to violate the rule in these circumstances. This has a superficial resemblance to Kant's categorical imperative, but both its foundation and its results are significantly different.

Disagreements Based on Differences about When a Violation of a Moral Rule is Justified

In addition to the unresolvable disagreements that arise from differences in the interpretation of the moral rules, there are two other kinds of differences that can lead to unresolvable disagreements between different societies, or even between persons in the same society, about whether a violation of a moral rule is justified. The first is a difference in the ranking of the harms and benefits, although not in what counts as harms. Everyone agrees on what the harms are (i.e., death, pain, disability, loss of freedom, and loss of pleasure). All rational persons try to avoid these harms unless they have an adequate reason for not avoiding them (e.g., to avoid what they take to be a greater harm or to gain a compensating benefit for themselves or someone else).

This may not be obvious because sometimes one may not appreciate the benefit involved (e.g., some cultures require suffering pain in order to gain the status necessary for being a full member of the society, a practice not unlike fraternity hazing). Also, for some religious people, the harm they will avoid is based on religious belief. For example, a Jehovah's Witness may refuse a blood transfusion that will save his life because he believes that having a blood transfusion violates the biblical prohibition against eating blood and so will result in the loss of eternal bliss.

Although there is universal agreement on what counts as harms, people do not all agree on the ranking of these harms. Further, pain, disability, loss of freedom, and loss of pleasure have degrees, and even death occurs at very different ages, so that there is no agreement that one of these harms is always worse than the others. Some people rank dying several months earlier as worse than a specified amount of pain and suffering, while other people rank that same amount of pain and suffering as worse. Thus, for most terminally ill patients, it is rationally allowed either to refuse death-delaying treatments or to consent to them.

Most actual moral disagreements (e.g., whether to discontinue treatment of a terminally ill incompetent patient) are based on disagreements about the facts of the case (e.g., how painful the disease is, how painful the treatment is, and how long the treatment would prolong the patient's life). Differences in the rankings of the harms account for much of the rest of the moral disagreements (e.g., how much pain and suffering it is worth to prolong life for three months).

Often, the factual disagreements about prognoses are so closely combined with different rankings of the harms involved that they cannot be distinguished. Further complicating the matter, the probability of suffering any of the harms can vary from very low to almost certain, and people can differ in the way that they rank a given probability of one harm against a different probability of another harm. Disagreement about involuntary commitment of people with mental disorders that make them dangerous to themselves involves a disagreement about both what percentage of these people would die if not committed, and whether a significant probability of death within one week (e.g., 2 percent) compensates for a 100 percent probability of three to five days of a very serious loss of freedom and a 30 percent probability of long-term mental suffering.

Actual cases usually involve much more uncertainty about outcomes, as well as the rankings of many more harms. Thus, complete agreement on what counts as a harm or evil is compatible with considerable disagreement on what counts as the lesser evil or greater harm in any particular case. It should be apparent that there is also considerable disagreement concerning the rankings of the benefits or goods (i.e., consciousness, abilities, freedom, and pleasure), but the rankings of the benefits play a much smaller role in justifying violations of moral rules than the rankings of harms.

Obviously, if people rank the harms differently, even when they agree on all of the facts, they will disagree in their estimates of whether more harm would result from everyone knowing that they are allowed to violate the rule in these circumstances than from everyone knowing that they are not allowed to violate the rule. Hence, they will differ in whether they favor everyone knowing that they are allowed to violate the rule in these circumstances. Suppose that two people agree that legalizing active euthanasia will result in the same reduction in the amount of pain and suffering of terminally ill patients and that they also agree that, due to mistakes and pressure, it will result in the same increase in people dying somewhat earlier than they might want to die. If they rank pain and death differently, they may disagree about whether one should legalize active euthanasia. One may hold that death is such a serious evil that avoiding quite a large amount of pain and suffering does not justify any significant increase in the number of earlier deaths, wanted or unwanted, whereas another may hold that death for a terminally ill patient is not as serious as the pain and suffering that results from living longer. Different societies may differ in the rankings that most of their members hold, and many different rankings seem acceptable.

But even if they rank the reduction of pain and suffering and the increase in somewhat earlier deaths exactly the same, they may still disagree because of their differing views of human nature. This difference may be most marked when one is considering people in different societies. People in a relatively homogeneous society may have a different estimate concerning what would be the result of everyone knowing that they can violate the rule against killing terminally ill patients in clearly specified circumstances than people living in a quite heterogeneous society, like the United States. People in a homogeneous society may believe that there will be relatively few cases of unwanted earlier deaths due to mistakes and pressure, whereas those in a heterogeneous society may believe that there will be far more unwanted earlier deaths due to mistakes and pressure.

But, even within a particular society, people can have different views about what would happen if everyone knows that they are allowed to break a moral rule in the same circumstances. For example, some people hold that, when asked about how you like someone's clothes or hair, it is justifiable to deceive them in order to avoid hurting their feelings. They would favor allowing deception in this kind of situation because they believe that everyone knowing that this kind of violation is allowed would result in significant harm being avoided with only a minimal loss of trust. Others would not favor allowing deception in this kind of situation because they believe that the loss of trust would be significant and would outweigh the amount of harm avoided.

This ideological difference concerning human nature may also involve a different ranking of the harms involved, and there may be no way to decide which of these estimates is correct. It may be that one estimate is shared by most in one society and another by most in another society, but there may be no way to decide which of these estimates is correct even in a particular society.

Disagreements Based on Differences on Who Is Impartially Protected by the Moral Rules

The debates about abortion and animal rights are best understood as debates about who is included in the group that is impartially protected by the moral rules. However, there is no way to resolve this issue, for it makes sense to talk of impartiality only when the group toward which one is supposed to be impartial has been specified. Fully informed rational persons who hold that animals are not protected as strongly as moral agents can disagree about how much they should be protected (i.e., they can disagree about how strong a reason has to be to be an adequate reason to justify killing or causing pain to an animal). People can also disagree about whether fetuses are protected as strongly as moral agents and, if they are not, how much they are protected. They may even disagree about whether a fetus is protected to the same degree at all stages or whether the fetus deserves more protection as it develops. Some societies do not even hold that neonates are protected as strongly as moral agents and so allow infanticide with no justification, or much less than is needed to justify killing a moral agent.

That there is no unique correct answer to the question about who is protected as strongly as moral agents is why discussions of abortion and animal rights are so emotionally charged and often involve violence. Morality, however, does set limits to the morally allowable ways of settling unresolvable moral disagreements. These ways cannot involve violence or other unjustified violations of the moral rules, but must be settled peacefully. Indeed, one of the proper functions of a democratic government is to settle unresolvable moral disagreements by peaceful means.

As mentioned at the beginning of this chapter, some maintain that morality is only, or primarily, concerned with the suffering of harm by moral agents, while others maintain that the harms (e.g., death, pain, and loss of freedom) suffered by those who are not moral agents is as important, or almost so, as the harms suffered by moral agents. But, even if one regards animals as not included in the group impartially protected by the moral rules, this does not mean that one must hold they should receive no protection. There is a wide range of morally acceptable options concerning the amount of protection that should be provided to those that are not included in the group toward which morality requires impartiality.

Many hold that, although the reasons that are adequate to justify killing or causing pain to animals do not have to be as strong as the reasons that are adequate to justify killing or causing pain to moral agents, some reasons are needed. Few hold that it is morally justifiable to cause pain to animals just because one feels like doing so. Many states have laws prohibiting cruelty to animals to enforce this moral position. Yet many hold it is justifiable to use animals in painful medical experiments that will help provide treatments for important human maladies. Many also hold that it is justifiable to kill animals for food, even when alternative vegetarian alternatives are available. Many also hold that it is justifiable to deprive animals of their freedom so that people can enjoy seeing them in zoos, but many now feel that they should be put in larger, more comfortable surroundings than the small cages that have been commonly used.

Regardless of the cultural variations in morality, the similarity in the content of morality is sufficiently great that there is general agreement that the world would be a better place if everyone acted morally, and that it gets worse as more people act immorally more often. This explains why we teach children to act morally and why every society has laws that prohibit serious immoral actions. A complete account of morality would discuss the moral virtues, but, simply from the account of morality presented, it is obvious why the moral virtues connected with the second five rules—truthfulness, trustworthiness, fairness, honesty, and dependability—are those traits of character that all rational people want others to have, and at least pretend to have themselves.

Rational persons favor others acquiring the moral virtues in order to lessen their own risk of suffering harm and, since they know that other rational persons also want them to act morally, they must, at least, pretend to cultivate these virtues in themselves. This explains the truth of La Rochefoucauld's saying, "Hypocrisy is the homage that vice pays to virtue."

Conclusion

In conclusion, the fact of disagreement between cultures over issues in bioethics does not force us to choose between the idea that one party to any disagreement must always be acting immorally and the idea that there is no universal morality. For the reasons I have given, a universal moral system does not mean universal agreement. But it does limit legitimate disagreement.

Where a culture allows the violation of moral rules in such a way that, even by its own lights, it would not do to have everyone know that actions with the same morally relevant features are permissible, that culture permits actions that are immoral. Thus, for instance, no culture could allow everyone to know that actions with the same morally relevant features as Nazi medical experiments were permissible. No one in any culture could want everyone to know that it was generally permissible to cause death, terrible pain, and disability to many persons to satisfy the curiosity and sadistic impulses of a few. Nor, I expect, could any society accept the consequences of everyone knowing that actions with the same morally relevant features as assisting in involuntary female circumcision were permissible.

Nonetheless, as in some of the examples discussed above, there are times when each party to a disagreement can present a sound moral argument for its own moral position. Recognition and careful application of this distinction between morally defensible disagreement and indefensible disagreement certainly has implications for how practitioners should engage with those with whom they disagree. When the other side advocates what is clearly in conflict with morality, sanctioning their customs may be inappropriate.

In other cases, however, cases where we must admit that morality itself makes no distinction between our own position and the position of those with whom we disagree, nothing more forceful than discussion, or perhaps a vote, is an appropriate way of resolving the disagreement. We may also find that an understanding of how legitimate moral disagreement is possible makes it easier, in appropriate circumstances, to truly respect moral positions that are contrary to our own.

Notes

1. The editors would like to thank Heather Gert, the author's daughter, for graciously supplying this introduction and conclusion after Bernard's untimely death.
2. The phrase "common morality" is explicitly used by Tom Beauchamp and James Childress in later editions of their text, *Principles of Biomedical Ethics*. In that book, they contrast their understanding of common morality with the one presented in this chapter. However, in a recent paper, Tom Beauchamp acknowledges that the account of common morality presented here is superior to the account provided in *The Theory of Morality* by Alan Donagan, which they used to support their four principles.
3. For a full account of this common moral system, see *Morality: Its Nature and Justification* (revised edition, 2005, Oxford University Press). For a shorter account, see *Common Morality: Deciding What to Do* (paperback edition, 2007, Oxford University Press). For applications of the common moral system to bioethics, see *Bioethics: A Systematic Approach* (Bernard Gert, Charles M. Culver, and K. Danner Clouser, 2006, Oxford University Press).

CHAPTER 2

The Compatibility of Universal Morality, Particular Moralities, and Multiculturalism

Tom L. Beauchamp

Abstract

Topics addressed in this chapter are moral relativism, the objectives of morality, universal morality, particular moralities, multiculturalist theory, and cultural moral imperialism. I argue that cultural relativism is an untenable theory and that a universal common morality transcends all cultural standards. The norms of universal morality are not thick in moral content, but they afford a starting framework that we can use to construct thick, action-guiding norms. The common morality allows for moral disagreement and legitimate differences of opinion about how to best specify universal norms, and thus it supports the development of particular moralities that differ from other particular moralities. However, the common morality does not allow for the so-called multicultural world, which some writers in ethics take to mean a world void of universal moral norms. Yet their views misrepresent even the commitments of multiculturalist theory. Multiculturalism is the theory that respect is owed to cultural traditions because morality itself demands this form of respect. Multiculturalism asserts that, universally, it is morally wrong to not acknowledge the moral rights of persons merely because their beliefs descend from different cultural histories.

Do all moral beliefs derive from cultural standards, or are there moral standards that transcend cultures and conventions? In one type of theory, morality is relative to cultural arrangements and aspirations. The notion of an objective principle or universal morality has no place in this theory. In another type of theory, universal moral standards, such as human rights and basic moral rules, are independent of particular cultures, nations, and organizations. I will present a version of the second type of theory. In addressing this problem, I will consider the subjects of moral relativism, the objectives of morality, universal morality, particular moralities, multiculturalism, and cultural moral imperialism. I will argue both in opposition to a relativism of basic moral standards and in support of a universally valid common morality.

The Untenability of Cultural Relativisms

INTRODUCTION

Moral relativism is an ancient problem about cultural differences that remains vibrant today. Two types of relativism are examined in this section: descriptive cultural relativism and normative cultural relativism. There are many species of relativism, but these are the two most prominent forms.

DESCRIPTIVE CULTURAL RELATIVISM

Defenders of descriptive relativism regard many discoveries in the social sciences as constituting evidence of an extensive diversity of moral practices across cultures. This work has cataloged and described many cultural differences, but these differences do not demonstrate that morally committed people in diverse cultures disagree about universal moral standards that underlie and justify their particular moral beliefs and practices. Simple examples are principles of honesty and truth-telling, virtues of caring and trustworthiness, and ideals of charity and friendliness.

Consider the vast similarity, in virtually every nation, in codes and regulations governing research involving human subjects. There are understandable and justifiable differences from country to country, but the differences pale in comparison to the sea of similarity in the norms governing how this research can and cannot be conducted. A few dozen principles are globally accepted as canonical for research ethics. Here are a few (steeply abridged) examples:

- Disclose all material information to subjects in medical research.
- Obtain an individual, voluntary, informed consent to biomedical interventions.
- Maintain secure safeguards for keeping personal information about subjects private and confidential.
- Receive surrogate consent from a legally authorized representative for incompetent subjects.
- Protect subjects in research against excessive risk.
- Ethics review committees must scrutinize and approve research protocols.
- Research cannot be conducted unless its risks and intended benefits are reasonably balanced and risks are minimized.
- Special justification is required if proposed research subjects are vulnerable persons.

Several global organizations and many governments have officially supported these norms in codes and regulations, but the force and authority of the norms themselves are not contingent on any particular form of agreement. As the World Medical Association says of its "Declaration of Helsinki" and as the US government says of its *Belmont Report*, the "ethical principles" governing research involving human subjects are valid independently of any state of cultural belief or law.[1] Scandals in the history of research involving human subjects have occurred precisely when people in cultures neglected these principles in their laws and practices.

True cultural relativists reject these claims. They subscribe to the thesis that no moral principles of any sort, general or particular, are valid independent of the cultural contexts in which they have arisen and shaped to their present form. Relativists regard the relevant social science data as indicating that moral rightness and wrongness vary from place to place and that there are no absolute or universal moral standards that apply across all societies. Even the concepts of rightness and wrongness themselves are meaningless apart from the specific cultural contexts in which they arise, and patterns of culture can be understood only as unique wholes. In a much quoted statement, anthropologist Ruth Benedict once expressed the thesis as being that the term "morality" *means* "socially approved habits" and that the expression "It is morally good" is *synonymous* with "It is habitual."[2]

There is no need to question the anthropological reports on which cultural relativism is erected. Many are informative, solid scientific studies. However, these studies do not show that there are no basic universal moral principles. More importantly, these descriptive reports of what people in fact believe do not support any normative position about what is right and wrong or about what any person or culture ought to believe. This takes me to the second type of relativism.

NORMATIVE CULTURAL RELATIVISM

Though descriptive cultural relativism contains no normative content about how one ought to behave, the theory can be altered and given normative content. In this theory the statement "What is right at one place or time may be wrong at another" is interpreted to mean that *it is right* in one context to act in a way that *it is wrong* to act in another context. According to cultural normative relativism, one ought to behave in the ways one's culture determines to be correct and not behave in ways one's culture determines to be incorrect.

Cultural normative relativism is usually expressed as a theory based on cultural group beliefs and institutions, not merely on beliefs that appear only within the borders of nation-states. Accordingly, normative relativism does not merely say that when one is in Japan one should act as the Japanese do or when in the United States as the Americans do. It is a cultural, not a geographic, theory about the source of moral correctness.

Normative group relativists hold both that there is no criterion independent of one's culture for making a judgment that a practice is right or wrong or to assess whether the standards of one's social group are the standards one ought to uphold. More generally, normative relativism is the theory that a form of moral conduct is right or wrong for persons if and only if their culture holds that it is right or wrong.

One weakness in this theory is that it is often difficult to determine which group, society, or institution constitutes the culture that should be followed. For example, in pre-Taliban Afghanistan women were often well educated and worked in professions, but under the Taliban-imposed culture they were not allowed to work or to seek an education beyond the age of eight. Should we say that women should be governed by either of these conflicting sets of norms? Can one ever be bound by a coercively imposed culture? What from a moral point of view are one's obligations under these circumstances? Do any of the series of controlling groups in Afghanistan give any of its citizens the normatively correct set of beliefs and action guides? This is not a problem about Afghanistan and its history. Determining how to identify an appropriate cultural group is a serious theoretical problem for normative relativism.

A bigger problem is that, however precisely formulated, normative relativism has no justification for its view that a norm is acceptable merely because the members of a cultural group believe it in a certain way—or because individuals or the members of a religious group believe it in a certain way. This commitment to being morally bound by group norms is at the heart of the theory of normative cultural relativism and cannot be eliminated without abandoning the theory. But the idea that the slave trade, sexual harassment under a severe threat by a superior, excluding women from training as physicians, and denying human rights to "foreigners" ought to be practiced merely because a group believes in the practice has no moral justification or credibility. It is no more than a justification of tradition by appeal to tradition (or of culture by appeal to culture), a clear case of begging the question of moral justification.

Normative relativism has other problems as well. If right and wrong are entirely relative to a culture's standards, no person could ever maintain that his or her culture's standards are wrong or seek any kind of reform. Rejection by individuals of the culture's standards is wrong in this theory, no matter what the standards are. Similarly, if there are no moral norms about exposing research subjects to high risks, about coercion and exploitation of nursing home populations, about unacceptable occupational risks to health, or about unethical billing for health reimbursements, then normative relativism implausibly maintains that the absence of such standards is morally normative in these situations. No reasonable person would accept such a view.

The unacceptability of descriptive cultural relativism and normative cultural relativism does not mean that a multicultural theory is unacceptable. I will later argue that multiculturalism is no relativism at all, and is actually an important defense of universal morality and human rights.

The Objective of Morality

I now turn to a thesis about what I will call the objective of morality.[3] This objective is that of promoting human flourishing by counteracting human circumstances in interactions with others that cause the quality of people's lives to worsen. The objective is to prevent or limit problems of indifference, conflict, suffering, hostility, scarce resources, limited information, and the like. This thesis has notable similarities to, though it is broader than, what Bernard Gert, in chapter 1 in this volume, described as the goal of morality: "Morality has the inherent goal of lessening the amount of harm suffered by those included in the protected group."

Following in the path of Thomas Hobbes and David Hume, I accept the following as the background circumstance of morality: From centuries of experience we have learned that the human condition tends to deteriorate into misery, confusion, violence, and distrust unless certain norms are enforced through a public system of norms.[4] When complied with, these norms lessen human misery and foster cooperation. These norms may not be necessary for the *survival* of a society, as some have maintained,[5] but they are necessary to ameliorate or counteract the tendency for the quality of people's lives to worsen and for social relationships to disintegrate. In every well-functioning society, norms are in place to prohibit lying, breaking promises, causing bodily harm, stealing, fraud, the taking of life, the neglect of children, and failures to keep contracts. These norms, when socially enforced, achieve the objective of morality.

Many philosophers with different conceptions than the one I just presented nonetheless do not significantly disagree about the general norms that comprise morality. That is, philosophers from many different theoretical standpoints converge on the principles, virtues, rights, and responsibilities that are central to morality and in doing so converge on essential conditions of any system of belief that deserves to be called morality.[6] They also agree on paradigm cases such as the judgment that rules legitimating the slave trade are morally unacceptable no matter what a culture might think about the legitimacy of these rules.

The universal character of the human experience and of social responses to threatening conditions (by formulating norms that are suitable for the moral life) helps *explain* why there is a common morality, but it does not *justify* the norms.[7] What justifies the norms of the common morality, in the pragmatic theory I accept, is that they are the norms best suited to achieve the objectives of morality. Once the objective(s) of morality have been identified, a set of standards is pragmatically justified if and only if it is the best means to the end identified when all factors—including human limitations, shortcomings, and vulnerabilities—are taken into consideration. If one set of norms will better serve the objective of morality than a set currently in place, then the former should displace the latter.

This account is my own preferred strategy for the justification of moral norms, but I appreciate that others prefer a different justification, such as a contractarian one or the full account and justification of morality found in Gert's *Morality: Its Nature and Justification*.[8] However, I will not further pursue these theoretical matters because they would make no difference to the arguments I provide hereafter.

The Common Morality as Universal Morality

What are the principal cross-cultural norms of the common morality?[9] The common morality comprises *rules*, *virtues*, *ideals*, and *rights*—each of which I briefly discuss in this section.

Gert and I both understand the common morality as universal morality. It is not relative to cultures or individuals and is to be distinguished from norms that bind only members of particular groups. Gert views the nature and number of the moral rules in the common morality as precisely determinable,[10] whereas I regard these matters as less cleanly demarcated. I will not address this issue here, but I emphasize that it is of the highest importance in the interpretation of both Gert's theory in chapter 1 of this volume and my account that the focus not be exclusively on moral principles or rules of obligation. "Common morality" references the entire "moral system," to use Gert's preferred language.

I will now outline what I see as the main constituent elements in the system (elements that Gert and I catalog somewhat differently, but not in a way that compromises the core of the common morality).

UNIVERSAL RULES OF OBLIGATION

Here are a few examples (not a complete catalog) of rules of obligation in the common morality: 1) Do not kill; 2) do not cause pain or suffering to others; 3) prevent evil or harm from occurring; 4) rescue persons in danger; 5) tell the truth; 6) nurture the young and dependent; 7) keep your promises; 8) do not steal; 9) do not punish the innocent; and 10) obey the law. These norms have been justified in various ways by various philosophical theories, but I will not treat this problem of justification here. These cross-cultural norms obviously are implemented in different ways in different cultural or group settings, a matter I will later discuss when treating the topic of specification.

UNIVERSAL VIRTUES

The common morality also contains standards that are *moral character traits*, or virtues. Here are a few examples: 1) honesty; 2) integrity; 3) nonmalevolence; 4) conscientiousness; 5) trustworthiness; 6) fidelity; 7) gratitude; 8) truthfulness; 9) lovingness; and 10) kindness. These virtues are universally admired traits,[11] and a person is deficient in moral character if he or she lacks these traits. Negative traits amounting to the opposite of the virtues are *vices* (malevolence, dishonesty, lack of integrity, cruelty, etc.). They are substantial moral defects, universally so recognized by persons committed to morality.

UNIVERSAL IDEALS

Moral ideals such as charitable goals, community service, dedication to one's job that exceeds obligatory levels, and service to the poor are also a part of the common morality. These aspirations are not *required* of persons, but they are universally *admired* and *praised* in persons who accept and act on them.[12] Here are four examples that can be interpreted both as ideals of virtuous character and ideals of action: 1) exceptional forgiveness; 2) exceptional generosity; 3) exceptional compassion; and 4) exceptional thoughtfulness.

UNIVERSAL RIGHTS

In addition to the basic obligations, virtues, and ideals just mentioned, human rights form an important dimension of universal morality. Rights in general are justified claims to something that individuals or groups can legitimately assert against other individuals or groups. Human rights in particular are those that all humans possess.[13]

Many philosophers, political activists, lawyers, and framers of political declarations now regard rights theory as the most important type of theory for expressing a universal moral point of view. Human rights language easily crosses national boundaries and supports international law and policy statements by international agencies and associations. Although human rights are, for this reason, often interpreted as legal rights, this interpretation does not properly capture their status. They are universally valid moral claims, and they have been so understood at least since early modern theories of rights were developed in the seventeenth century.[14]

The point of human rights language is to provide standards that transcend norms and practices, in particular, cultures that conflict with human rights. However, as James Griffin has rightly pointed out, we are sometimes satisfied that a basic human right exists, yet we are uncertain about what precisely the basic right gives us a right to.[15] This problem should be handled through what I will refer to in the next section as *specification*—the process of reducing the indeterminate character of abstract norms and giving them specific action-guiding content, often in the context of what I will call particular moralities.

Particular Moralities

It might be thought, given my emphasis on universal morality, that I do not allow for any form of pluralism or for local moral viewpoints—as if morality were a monolithic whole that does not permit disagreements and differences of approach. However, this is a misunderstanding of the connection between universal morality and the many moral norms that are particular to cultures, groups, and even individuals. Unlike the common morality, with its notably abstract and therefore content-thin norms, particular moralities present concrete, nonuniversal, and content-rich norms.

Particular moralities include the many responsibilities, ideals, attitudes, and sensitivities found in, for example, cultural, religious, and professional guidelines. Nonetheless—and this is a key matter in understanding why relativism is an unacceptable theory—*all justified particular moralities share the norms of the common morality with all other justified particular moralities.*

In order to have a practical, action-guiding morality, the norms of the common morality must be made specific in content. We cannot erect policies and practices on vague notions such as "respect for persons." All abstract norms must be carefully defined and then carefully fashioned as specific, well-crafted norms that give specific guidance to actions such as truthful disclosure, maintenance of confidentiality, obtaining an informed consent, providing access to medical care, and the like. These more concrete norms often must be made more concrete still for certain contexts. For example, the requirement of obtaining informed consent will be fashioned somewhat differently for contexts of research and contexts of medical practice.

Consider an example of a rule that sharpens the requirements of a more general norm of avoiding conflicts of interest. The rule to be specified is, "Avoid conflicts of interest in making treatment recommendations" (which itself is a specification of a more general principle of avoiding conflicts of interest). This rule might be specified as follows: "When physicians prescribe pharmaceutical products, they must avoid favoring products in which they have a financial relationship if this financial interest influences their judgment." The initial norm of avoiding conflicts endures, even though it is now a more specific rule.

Specification is a process of reducing the indeterminate character of abstract norms and generating more specific norms.[16] Specifying the norms with which one starts, whether those in the common morality or norms from a source such as a professional code, is accomplished by *narrowing the scope* of the norms, not by explaining what the general norms *mean*. As Henry Richardson puts it, specification occurs by "spelling out where, when, why, how, by what means, to whom, or by whom the action is to be done or avoided."[17] All norms are subject to specification, and many already specified rules will need further specification to handle new circumstances of conflict. Progressive specification can continue indefinitely.

To illustrate progressive specification, consider an additional specification that can be made to the rule already specified above, namely, "When physicians prescribe pharmaceutical products they must avoid favoring products in which they have a financial relationship if this financial interest influences their judgment." To this proscription we can add the following words shown in italic type: "When physicians prescribe pharmaceutical products they must avoid favoring products in which they have a financial relationship if this financial interest influences their judgment *and they must avoid prescribing products if their judgment is influenced by a personal relationship they have with a representative of a company that distributes the product(s).*" These specified rules can be indefinitely specified and turned into a whole policy governing this type of conflict of interest.

Very commonly, more than one line of specification is available when confronting practical problems and moral disagreements, and different persons or groups will offer conflicting specifications. For any moral problem several competing specifications may be offered by thoughtful and fair-minded parties, and thereby many different provisions in particular moralities are coherent ways to specify the common morality. This latitude must be permitted in practical moral thinking. We cannot demand more of people than that they faithfully specify norms with an eye to the overall coherence of the resulting particular morality while ensuring that their specifications do not violate the norms of universal morality.

Good examples of particular moralities that contain at least some specifications are *professional moralities* in biomedical research, medical practice, nursing practice, veterinary practice, and the like. These moral codes, declarations, and standards of practice often legitimately vary from other moralities in the ways they handle justice in access to health care, human rights, justified waivers of informed consent, government oversight of research involving human subjects, privacy provisions, and the like.

Multiculturalism as a Universalistic Theory

It is an undisputed fact that multiple cultures have constructed unique particular moralities. This fact suggests to several writers in ethics that it is likewise an undisputed fact that morals are relative to cultures, or "pluralistic," the word now commonly heard in bioethics. Some writers in bioethics insist that we live in a multicultural world in which many moral cultures can live together peacefully, without need for the outmoded notion of universal, basic norms.

This characterization has matters upside down. In this section, I argue that multiculturalism requires and insists on universal norms. Multiculturalism is not a pluralism or relativism. Multiculturalism is a universalistic theory to the effect that particular moralities are owed respect because morality itself demands it. The term "multicultural world" has been hijacked by various writers in bioethics to suggest the reverse, and especially to suggest that there is no universal morality and no commonly held morality.[18]

The Universal Norms in Multiculturalism

The term *multiculturalism* refers to theories that support the moral principle that cultural or group traditions, institutions, perspectives, and practices should be respected and should not be violated or oppressed as long as they do not themselves violate the standards of universal morality. The objective of multiculturalism is to provide a theory of the norms that should guide the protection of vulnerable cultural groups when threatened with marginalization and oppression caused by one or more dominant cultures.

Resistance to forceful dominance and cultural oppression drive multiculturalist theory, which holds that respect is owed to people of dissimilar but peaceful cultural traditions because it is unjust and disrespectful to marginalize, oppress, or dominate persons merely because they are of an unlike culture or subculture. The moral notions at work in this account are universal theses about rights, justice, respect, and nonoppression.[19]

The major demand in multiculturalism is that people of one culture are morally obligated to tolerate and not interfere with the views of those in other cultures (as long as those views are themselves not in violation of universal moral norms). This universally valid demand is independent of any particular culture's values and is not valid *because* a culture accepts it.[20] These are matters of human rights, not of human contracts or cultural arrangements or the current state of national or international law. Without universal norms of toleration, respect, restraint, and the like, a multiculturalist could neither explain nor justify multiculturalism.

In short, the moral obligation to respect the views of people from other cultures is not confined to people in cultures that *recognize* this obligation. By design of multiculturalism as a moral theory, moral obligations of respect and tolerance apply to all cultures whether or not they recognize these norms. Harvey Siegel puts it accurately when he says "multiculturalism is itself a culturally transcendent or universal moral, educational, and social ideal in the sense that it is applicable to all cultures . . . and rests upon other equally transcendent, moral imperatives and values."[21]

Cultural Imperialism

Some seem to think that my support of transcendent, universal moral standards is merely a disguised form of cultural imperialism. Persons outside of a given culture who press for recognition within that culture of the human rights of women, minorities, children, the ill, the disabled, the oppressed, the marginalized, the economically disadvantaged, and other vulnerable groups have been denounced in some literatures as cultural imperialists who incorporate "Western values" that are uncritically assumed to be universally valid, but that—beneath the veneer of fairness, equity, and respect—simply camouflage the continuance of Western dominance.

These charges of cultural imperialism have understandable roots in hundreds of years of colonial political and economic domination. Despite this perplexing history, threats of "cultural imperialism" today have nothing to do with so-called Western values or with any history of moral imperialism emanating from the Western world or from any history of imperialism from any particular region of the world. Virtually every region of the world has a horrid history of imperialistic control extending from one people to another.

Numerous cultural traditions, past and present, and in all parts of the world, have held that their cultural values are universal values to which everyone should conform. This claim might be correct in the sense that one culture might have understood and insisted on universal norms not recognized by some other culture(s). However, the concern here is the *imposition* of norms by one culture on another.

The Practical Importance of Controlling Cultural Oppression by Universal Norms

There is today a convergence of global opinion that cultural differences must not be allowed to obscure the conditions of injustice and oppression that are presented by despotic rulers as nothing more than ways of protecting a culture's traditional values.[22] There are no more important human rights than rights against oppression—a broad category, but today the most consequential form of human rights violation.

Even the governments of many nations that are signatories to the UN Universal Declaration of Human Rights do not protect the basic human rights of women and children, or at least they have an unduly narrow vision of what those rights are. When complaints and resistance movements arise, governments often claim that they are treating women and children in accordance with *their* cultural traditions, but here is a true case in which forms of oppression are being disguised by dominant powers that have no respect for universal values.

Susan Okin has justly argued that conflict between traditional cultural practices and persons subordinated to those practices cannot be resolved by the theory that regional control, based on some tradition, may legitimately be asserted over persons in the local region who do not come from or follow the dominant tradition. She argues that, when these conflicts arise, they ought always to be resolved in terms of the rights of the oppressed, never resolved merely in terms of cultural practices or some kind of balancing of competing interests. Neither tradition nor a balancing of interests should be given priority when there are serious human rights violations. The enforcement of human rights that override even long-standing traditional values ought, in this account, to be the primary consideration.[23]

We are often told in writings in ethics that there are important East–West moral differences and that Western values should not be imposed on Eastern nations. However, these alleged differences are virtually never explained in detail and documented. The available empirical literature on the subject often does not support the claims. Amartya Sen points out that the idea of "Asia as a unit" with a set of Asian values different from those of the West makes no sense despite its frequent mention. He notes that about 60 percent of the world lives in Asia, with virtually nothing to solidify it as a uniform moral culture (other than universal morality, which simply solidifies it with the rest of the world): "There are no quintessential values that apply to this immensely large and heterogeneous population, that differentiate Asians as a group from people in the rest of the world."

Sen notes that violations of basic rights of freedom occur routinely in many parts of Asia and that dictatorial heads of state use the excuse that "Asian nations" do not accord the same value to personal autonomy and political freedom as do Western countries; therefore, the human rights to freedom extolled in the West are either irrelevant or objectionable. Sen rightly sees such claims as morally unacceptable while noting an interesting piece of history: The idea of "Asian values" and "the Orient" were originally the products of a Eurocentric perspective that regarded the whole of the Asian region as united by a body of non-Western standards. Sen briskly criticizes Western governments, including those in the United States and European nations, for indirectly backing this unfounded idea of Eastern values and allowing such a specious conception to serve as an excuse for not giving primacy to human rights.[24]

Conclusion

The arguments in this chapter all move to the conclusion that a universal set of moral norms comprises the common morality. Although these norms are thin in their abstract moral content, they are far from empty, and they afford a starting point for the specification of action-guiding norms, in particular, moralities and practical ethics. They constitute a wall of moral standards that cannot justifiably be violated in any culture or by any group or individual.

Notes

1. See the 2008 revision of the World Medical Association's "Declaration of Helsinki: Ethical Principles for Medical Research Involving Human Subjects," Part B, "Basic Principles for all Medical Research" (first adopted 1964); *The Belmont Report: Ethical Guidelines for the Protection of Human Subjects of Research* (Washington, DC: DHEW Publication OS 78-0012, 1978). It first appeared in the *Federal Register* on April 18, 1979.

2. Ruth Benedict, "Relativism and Patterns of Culture," in *Value and Obligation*, ed. Richard B. Brandt (New York: Harcourt Brace and World, 1961), 457.

3. The term and much of my understanding of the issues derive from G. J. Warnock's similar language in *The Object of Morality* (London: Methuen & Co., 1971), esp. 15–26.

4. Cf. Bernard Gert, *Morality: Its Nature and Justification*, revised ed. (New York: Oxford University Press, 2005), 11–14.

5. See the sources referenced in Sissela Bok, *Common Values* (Columbia: University of Missouri Press, 1995), 13–23, 50–59 (citing several influential writers on the subject).

6. Cf. Tom L. Beauchamp and James F. Childress, *Principles of Biomedical Ethics*, sixth ed. (New York: Oxford University Press, 2009), 260–61, 361–63.

7. John Mackie, *Ethics: Inventing Right and Wrong* (London: Penguin, 1977), 22–23, 107ff.

8. Gert, *Morality: Its Nature and Justification.*

9. Although there is only one universal common morality, there is more than one *theory* of the common morality. For the theories pertinent to this volume, see Bernard Gert, *Common Morality: Deciding What to Do* (New York: Oxford University Press, 2004, paperback edition, 2007); and Tom L. Beauchamp and James F. Childress, *Principles of Biomedical Ethics*, sixth ed. (New York: Oxford University Press, 2009), chaps. 1, 10.

10. See, in the present volume, Gert's list of ten moral rules. Gert readily acknowledges that there is disagreement among philosophers on the matter and says that there is not even "complete agreement concerning what counts as a moral rule." Gert, *Morality: Its Nature and Justification*, 13.

11. See Martha Nussbaum's assessment that, in Aristotelian philosophy, certain "nonrelative virtues" are objective and universal: "Non-Relative Virtues: An Aristotelian Approach," in *Ethical Theory, Character, and* Virtue, ed. Peter French et al. (Notre Dame, IN: University of Notre Dame Press, 1988), 32–53, esp. 33–34, 46–50.

12. See Gert, *Common Morality: Deciding What to Do*, 20–26, 76–77; Richard B. Brandt, "Morality and Its Critics," in *Morality, Utilitarianism, and Rights* (Cambridge: Cambridge University Press, 1992), chap. 5.

13. Cf. Joel Feinberg, *Rights, Justice, and the Bounds of Liberty* (Princeton, NJ: Princeton University Press, 1980), esp. 139–41, 149–55, 159–60, 187. See also Alan Gewirth, *The Community of Rights* (Chicago: University of Chicago Press, 1996), 8–9.

14. Pioneering theories of international rights and natural rights—now generally restyled as *human* rights—first prospered in philosophy through the social and political theories of Hugo Grotius, Thomas Hobbes, and John Locke. See Anthony Pagden, "Human Rights, Natural Rights, and Europe's Imperial Legacy," *Political Theory* 31 (2003): 171–99.

15. James Griffin, *On Human Rights* (Oxford: Oxford University Press, 2008), 97, 110.

16. Henry S. Richardson, "Specifying Norms as a Way to Resolve Concrete Ethical Problems," *Philosophy and Public Affairs* 19 (Fall 1990): 279–310; and "Specifying, Balancing, and Interpreting Bioethical Principles," in *Belmont Revisited: Ethical Principles for Research with*

Human Subjects, ed. James F. Childress, Eric M. Meslin, and Harold T. Shapiro (Washington, DC: Georgetown University Press, 2005), 205–27.

17. Richardson, "Specifying, Balancing, and Interpreting Bioethical Principles," 289.

18. Examples are H. Tristram Engelhardt Jr., *The Foundations of Bioethics*, second ed. (New York: Oxford University Press, 1996); Robert Baker, "A Theory of International Bioethics: Multiculturalism, Postmodernism, and the Bankruptcy of Fundamentalism," *Kennedy Institute of Ethics Journal* 8 (1998): 201–31; Leigh Turner, "Bioethics in a Multicultural World: Medicine and Morality in Pluralistic Settings," *Health Care Analysis* 11 (2003): 99–117.

19. Compare the arguments in the essays in Robert K. Fullinwider, ed., *Public Education in a Multicultural Society* (Cambridge: Cambridge University Press, 1996).

20. See the essays by Charles Taylor, Amy Gutmann, Steven C. Rockefeller, Michael Walzer, and Susan Wolf, in *Multiculturalism and "The Politics of Recognition,"* ed. Amy Gutmann (Princeton, NJ: Princeton University Press, 1992).

21. Harvey Siegel, "Multiculturalism and the Possibility of Transcultural Educational and Philosophical Ideals," *Philosophy* 74 (1999): 387–409.

22. See Martha Nussbaum and Jonathan Glover, eds., *Women, Culture, and Development* (Oxford: Oxford University Press, 1995); and Marcia Angell, "The Ethics of Clinical Research in the Third World," *New England Journal of Medicine* 337 (1997): 847–49.

23. Susan Moller Okin, "Is Multiculturalism Bad for Women?" in *Is Multiculturalism Bad for Women?*, published as an anthology, ed. Joshua Cohen, Matthew Howard, and Martha C. Nussbaum (Princeton, NJ: Princeton University Press, 1999), 20–24.

24. Amartya Sen, *Human Rights and Asian Values* (New York: Carnegie Council, 1997). The quote is on page 13.

CHAPTER 3

Culture and Ethical Aspects of Truth-Telling in a Value Pluralistic Society

Ilhan Ilkilic

Abstract

Advances in medical science and technology offer us not only new diagnostic measures and possibilities but also allow us to make better prognoses in terminal disease stages. As a consequence, physicians can work out more precise diagnoses, enabling them to inform their patients about the expected future course of their condition. Under these circumstances, truth-telling as a classical issue of medical ethics remains a highly charged problem. The concept of truth-telling has become controversial in multicultural societies because of the differences in attitude toward this practice, based on diverse cultural value systems and preferences. The demographic changes effected by migrant groups, especially in Western European countries, mean that truth-telling will be an ever more common problem in everyday medical practice, posing serious challenges for health-care professionals.

This chapter describes some arguments pertinent to this issue and discusses a real case history recorded at a German hospital. Telling the truth about a diagnosis in an intercultural setting and the participation of family members in the decision-making process in a multicultural society are identified as the key ethical points of this case. It also discusses some metaethical issues, such as the universal applicability of the ethical principle of "respect for autonomy" with regard to truth-telling. Some practical suggestions for everyday medical practice in a multicultural society are developed, and, in the conclusion, some ethical theses are proposed.

Introduction

Rapid developments in medicine enable us not only to produce better diagnoses but also to make more accurate predictions about the future development of illnesses. As a result of these developments, unfavorable diagnoses, such as malignant cancer, are made more frequently, and infaust (dire) prognoses are to be communicated to patients. Thus, the standard question of medical ethics concerning the morally correct way of handling the disclosure of unfavorable diagnoses and prognoses persists. It is even more complicated given the existence of different values among patients and caregivers. Ethical questions in medical practice have increased as a consequence of pluralistic value systems and demographic changes associated with new migrants in Western European countries.

The first part of this chapter discusses arguments in the context of the communication of an unfavorable diagnosis and prognosis. The second part provides a concrete case in an intercultural setting recorded in a German hospital, involving a patient and his family coming from a Muslim country. The central problems included the demand of family members to be involved in the decision-making process, identifying the appropriate mode of communication, and the general search for an ethically acceptable way of dealing with a patient from a foreign culture. Because the patient and his family were Muslims, I consider Islamic principles relevant to truth-telling. The third part discusses two ethical approaches associated with possible options for action in such a conflict situation and evaluates them. Finally, I offer practical recommendations for dealing with such conflicts in a pluralistic society in an ethically appropriate way.

Part 1: Arguments in the Context of Communicating an Unfavorable Diagnosis and Prognosis

In industrial countries, well into the 1960s, the disclosure of an unfavorable diagnosis and infaust prognosis to patients was considered to contravene the Hippocratic principle of "doing no damage" (*nil nocere*). Empirical studies from the early 1960s made in the United States show that 90 percent of doctors were against informing their patients of a diagnosis of cancer (Oken 1961). Physicians, on their own, chose to withhold information from patients ostensibly to save them from fear and desperation so as not to weaken their powers of recovery (Van de Loo 2000).

This attitude changed somewhat in the 1970s when the self-determination and responsibility of the patient in the relationship between doctor and patient were deemed more important (Steinhart 2002). In another study from the United States, conducted in 1977, only 2 percent of American doctors spoke out against informing a patient of an unfavorable diagnosis and prognosis (Novack et al. 1979). Eventually, informing the patient about the diagnosis, therapy options, and prognosis became an integral part of a doctor's responsibilities (Brown 1995). The historical analysis of this development, in particular in the European and Western world, indicates that the moral assessment of this practice is closely tied to the value placed on the autonomy of the patient (Faden and Beauchamp 1986, Tuckett 2004, Surbone 2006).

Truthfulness in conversations with a patient is crucial for establishing a relationship of trust between patient and doctor. It represents the indispensable basis for any ethically acceptable medical intervention and cannot be established without honesty on the part of the doctor. This implies being informed of any illness, even if it is difficult or impossible to cure (Jameton 1995, Van de Loo 2000, Salomon 2003).

In addition to the issue of truthfulness, there are other substantial arguments in favor of communicating a negative prognosis (Sullivan et al. 2001). Rapid developments in biomedicine have created new diagnostic and therapeutic measures allowing for better treatments and sometimes even healing diseases previously considered incurable. There are also increasingly more options for treating an illness with various impacts on a patient's quality of life. For this reason, being informed enables patients to weigh their options, according to their values and preferences, thereby being involved in determining their own futures (Jameton 1995).

Receiving information about a serious illness allows the patient to contemplate the serious side effects of, for example, chemotherapy, on an adequate informational basis; one cannot expect a patient left with the impression that he or she has only a harmless illness to agree to a therapy with serious side effects (Salomon 2003). The patient can evaluate such a therapy appropriately only if he or she is in a position to perceive the benefits offered and to decide about them on the basis of the required information. Only if the danger of a disease becomes more evident is one prepared to undergo a long and unpleasant therapy. Communicating the gravity of a condition can thus support patient compliance.

Besides the ethical arguments, there are also legal norms that determine the framework for medical decision-making and action. In the German legal system, every medical intervention for diagnostic and therapeutic purposes is seen as a potential personal injury and can be legitimated only by gaining the patient's informed consent (Walter 2000). The validity of such consent presupposes the patient's ability to understand the planned intervention and thus his or her being appropriately informed by the doctor. It follows from these premises that the doctor is obligated, in all but a few exceptional cases, to communicate unfavorable diagnoses to the patient. These legal regulations and the guidelines of professional institutions in Germany are based on specific ethical norms, including the concepts of human well-being and human dignity. A contravention of these regulations and guidelines leads to sanctions or criminal proceedings (Ulsenheimer 2008).

Despite these arguments, one can imagine situations in which withholding an unfavorable diagnosis would be legitimate and even ethically desirable. The central paradigm "respect for the autonomous decision of the patient" implies not only the right to know but also the right not to know (Macklin 1999, 100; Chadwick 1997). Consequently, withholding medical information could be ethically allowed if the patient wants to make use of his or her negative rights and refuses to receive relevant information.

In addition, withholding information can also be ethically justified if the information to be communicated would harm the patient seriously without benefiting him or her in any way. In this case, the doctor, not the patient, decides because of the professional scientific expertise and experience with the procedure. A perceived risk of suicide or a serious depression after being informed of the diagnosis can legitimate such medical decisions. For good reason, this procedure requires a very sensitive investigation of the situation and a critical approach to the case on the part of the doctor in charge (Brody 1997).

Withholding an unfavorable diagnosis does, however, bring up numerous ethical problems. Regardless of whether this withholding of information has been requested by the patient or contemplated by the doctor, it must not lead to refusing therapy, as a patient might refuse to hear the true diagnosis ("right not to know") but nevertheless wants an appropriate therapy. But this poses a problem: How can necessary chemotherapy with its serious side effects be carried out legitimately without the patient suspecting a cancer diagnosis? In a case like this, one wonders if it is reasonable to expect a desirable degree of compliance at all.

The communication of such information is also *lege artis* of central importance. A quiet place without time pressure or the presence of others is certainly more appropriate for the communication of a negative diagnosis and prognosis than a crowded ward (Pilchmaier 1999, Salomon 2003). It is desirable to create suitable circumstances for answering patients' questions. The use of easy-to-understand language and an appropriate tone of voice is bound to have a positive effect on the communication. Providing for professional psychological counseling of the patient following the conversation is equally important.

Part 2: Truth-Telling in an Intercultural Context

In a multicultural society characterized by the existence of different cultures and value systems, truth-telling gives rise to several ethical questions. First, it may be difficult for the physician to understand the values of a patient from another culture (or family members' attempts to influence the doctor's procedure in communicating an unfavorable diagnosis and prognosis), which can cause ethical conflicts. Legal regulations, codes of conduct established by professional institutions, and procedural conventions can limit the options for dealing with actual problems. As an example, let us consider some ethical problems that arose in an actual case in a German hospital. My colleagues Prof. Dr. Abdullah Takim and Asst. Prof. Dr. Rainer Brömer informed me about this case:

> A twenty-three-year-old Turkish man was diagnosed with malignant cancer. Several cycles of chemotherapy achieved no success in treatment. The patient's state of health deteriorated progressively, making his imminent death more and more likely. The patient was transferred to a palliative ward. Both the patient and his parents had only rudimentary knowledge of the German language, which did not allow for an adequate communication with the medical team. With the help of an interpreter, who was a member of their wider family, the doctor in charge informed the parents about their son's hopeless situation; the son was also partly involved in this talk.
>
> A nurse of Turkish descent happened to overhear the conversation and later informed the doctors that the interpreter had not passed on to the patient the information about his expected imminent death, probably on the request of his parents. The doctors considered this a clear contravention of the patient's "right to know." With the help of a different interpreter, they arranged another conversation with the patient during which he was informed of the possibility that he might soon die. Two days later the patient

passed away. The parents later accused the doctors of being responsible for their son's death: They had contributed to the worsening of his condition and thus hastened his demise.

Here, there is a conflict of opinion between the patient's parents and the medical team regarding disclosure to the patient of an unfavorable diagnosis and prognosis. In this ethical conflict, the medical team believes that the patient himself should decide whether he wants to receive the full information about his condition. The balance between the *right to know* and the *right not to know* should be made by the patient himself, out of respect for the patient's autonomous decision-making. Among the other norms, autonomy is accorded the highest priority in the medical team's decision-making process. As an adult and autonomous human being, the patient should decide, through an individual evaluation of his various options. Withholding requisite information would mean disenfranchising the patient and violating his right to self-determination.

The starting point for the parents' decision and attitude is, however, a different one. Their approach may be described as caring and consequentialist. In their decision-making process, patient autonomy does not play a central role. For the parents, the issue is primarily whether the disclosure of the infaust (dire) prognosis will affect their son's well-being. They expect that the medical team's course of action will upset their son and thus weaken his regenerative powers. This approach is regarded as harmful in preference to one of withholding the diagnosis and prognosis. In this case, the patient died two days after receiving the information. His parents therefore felt that their decision had been vindicated, and they accused the medical team of having acted wrongly.

COMMUNICATION AND DEALING WITH THE FAMILY

Communication difficulties often play a decisive role in the processes leading up to clinical–ethical conflicts in medical practice. Linguistic and cultural barriers in an intercultural setting increase those difficulties, further complicating the conflict (Ilkilic 2002, 2007; Hancock et al. 2007). Since the solution of such conflicts initially requires the clarification of the conflicting parties' different interests, overcoming these barriers is of central importance (Krakauer et al. 2002; Valente 2004; Volker 2005). In an intercultural context, a linguistic understanding of the patient's wishes and preferences is necessary but often not sufficient to guarantee an ethically appropriate way of dealing with a given problem. Rather, the significance and sometimes the background of these wishes in a given culture should be clarified in writing, as well as verbally (Kagawa-Singer and Blackhall 2001). Only then can one hope for an appropriate ethical evaluation of goods.

In the case described above, it is striking to observe that no conversation took place between the two conflicting parties after the patient's death, that is, the medical team and the parents. Neither party really knew why the other acted the way it did, nor did they grasp the different sets of values brought to bear on the decision-making. The medical team probably saw in the family's position a clear violation of the patient's autonomy and self-determination and considered it to be ethically unacceptable. The family members, on the other hand, believed that the patient must be protected at all costs from the damage that his being informed about his unfavorable diagnosis would presumably cause. They did not understand why the medical team would want to harm him in such a way.

In this case, it would have been sensible for the responsible doctor to take the initiative in a conversation with the parents. Such a conversation could have provided both parties more information about the backgrounds of the other's position, opening a broader access to the culturally alien motivation, possibly enabling a reflective attitude to their own positions. A better understanding of one another based on such a conversation, even though it cannot guarantee consensus in such cases, seems to be an indispensable instrument—particularly in an intercultural setting.

In such a conversation, the family members could have informed the medical team from their own cultural perspective about the normative meaning of withholding an unfavorable diagnosis and prognosis, to be understood, in their culture, as a moral imperative based on the conviction that the communication of such information directly harms the affected person and is therefore to be avoided. Disclosure would also destroy the hope of healing, which would create, according to this anthropology, an unacceptable situation. In addition, this knowledge would be a burden for the patient and thus decrease his quality of life. Not to know about one's imminent death is considered beneficial for the patient's well-being and is therefore a desirable condition.

On the other hand, the medical team could have informed the family about the legal constraints of which they probably were unaware. This information would have given the family a better idea of the range of options for decision-making and action available to the medical team and thus perhaps created a basis for understanding the chosen action. Further, ethical arguments and their backgrounds could have been presented, including the conviction that a person as a self-determined and thus responsible being has a right to make decisions about his current state. This presupposes, further, the doctor's responsibility to provide information about the medical conditions of this state (Van de Loo 2000, 284).

In medical ethical terms, the communication of an unfavorable diagnosis and infaust prognosis is not to be viewed as direct harm. Such harm arises only through the perception and reflection of the affected person. From this understanding, the wishes and preferences of the family members cannot be allowed to guide the attitude of the doctors—unless, that is, they can provide information about the presumed will of the patient. This aspect is, however, irrelevant in this case, since the patient himself was competent to express his own opinion and make his own decisions.

Even though it is not to be expected that this comprehensive exchange of views will lead directly to consensus, it would contribute significantly to preventing an escalation.

THE ACTIONS OF THE MEDICAL TEAM

The German Medical Association (*Bundesärztekammer*) prescribes in its guidelines for medical treatment of the terminally ill that the information given to a dying person about his or her condition and treatment options must be truthful. This information and the way it is delivered "must however take account of the dying person's situation and present fears" (*Bundesärztekammer* 2004, 1).

The doctor in charge may withhold information about the hopeless situation of his or her patient if she is convinced that this would clearly and unequivocally cause damage to the patient. He or she should withhold an unfavorable diagnosis 1) if the patient himself explicitly asks the doctor to do so; 2) if the doctor is convinced that such information would lead to a suicide attempt; or 3) if this information would cause serious psychological disturbance. Family members may be informed about such a diagnosis only with the permission of the patient (*Bundesärztekammer* 2004, 1).

These principles are firmly based on the respect for the patient's personal rights, particularly the right of self-determination. Medical treatment therefore requires a patient to be informed before having to consent to any intervention (*Bundesärztekammer* 2007). The patient needs to be given information not only about the therapy to be carried out but also about the critical reasons for the specific therapeutic measures chosen. In our example, the reasons for stopping conventional cancer therapy and shifting to palliative care should be explained to the patient, requiring him or her to be informed of the infaust prognosis.

The position of the family members in the decision-making process, scarcely attended to by the medical team, can also be traced back to the patient-centered attitude described here. This attitude is based on an anthropocentric individualistic concept of the human being. The procedure adopted by the medical team also implies a cultural invariance claim as if in no culture the family had normative significance for decision-making unless explicitly desired by the patient. It should be noted that this attitude led to the escalation of the conflict.

Medical guidelines and legal regulations allow medical practice to be performed more simply and, in the course of time, lead to a certain routine. This routine is based on well-considered ethical arguments; it is, however, easily interrupted as soon as culturally conditioned ethical problems arise. The way the medical team acted may be viewed as a conventional attitude based on the ethical norms and legal regulations described above. It remains to be considered, though, whether there could be further pragmatic reasons for this attitude.

One reason for the behavior of the medical team could be wanting to stay on the right side of the law. Following the parents' wishes without the consent of the patient could have legal consequences. Legal sanctions now increasingly play a major role in the decisions and actions of doctors, especially those with less professional experience. Critical discussions and concerns debated among academics and the public produce headlines such as "the making of medicine into law" or "the dictatorship of legal constraints" (Ulsenheimer 2008).

A further reason can be a lack of time for a detailed conversation with family members or with the patient (Hancock et al. 2007). Time pressure has long been a phenomenon in everyday medical practice and may present a barrier to an ethically appropriate delivery of medical care. One example is the decrease in time devoted to informing patients or discussing treatment options in detail. Despite this situation, it is necessary to find an appropriate context for longer conversations, not only with the patient, but also with family members. "Time pressure must play no role," says the training brochure for further education that is published by the German Medical Association (*Bundesärztekammer* 1998, 114).

An additional problem can arise from a lack of *intercultural competence*. Intercultural competence means the ability to discern and analyze the basic elements of an intercultural conflict and to integrate them into the medical and ethical decision-making process (Ilkilic 2008). In the absence of this competence, the reality of cultural components in a conflict might initially be overlooked. In this case, the integration of culture-specific values and connected wishes into the decision-making process is prevented.

It is also difficult to clarify the normative significance of culture-specific attitudes and preferences for practice. One cannot, of course, expect such a difficult achievement from a medical team; nevertheless, there should be some sensitivity to the cultural phenomena in everyday life. In complex cases where the team faces a challenge for which it feels unprepared, outside experts can be called upon, and the clinical ethics committee or clinical ethics consultants can be involved (Paul 2008; Gordon 2010).

ESTABLISHING THE WILL OF THE PATIENT

Finding out the patient's actual will to be informed of an unfavorable diagnosis and prognosis and the parents' attitude(s) is of central importance. In an intercultural setting of this kind, it is difficult for the doctor to "take account of [the patient's] present fears" (*Bundesärztekammer* 2004, 1). It is conceivable that a conversation with family members might be able to clarify the patient's attitude to being informed about an unfavorable diagnosis and prognosis. It is more likely that an appropriate approach could be found on this basis; however, this requires a certain degree of caution.

There is no reason to expect from the outset that the family members will communicate this information perfectly. Given a conflict of interests, the patient's real attitude may be concealed or misrepresented. Here, a relationship of trust between the family members and the medical team is necessary. In certain circumstances this information could be checked against statements made by acquaintances or friends of the patient. However, this may be impossible because of the lack of time or personnel.

Finding out the will of the patient directly by means of a conversation between the patient and his doctor may be difficult because of the linguistic and cultural barriers. The presence of an interpreter creates another barrier to a direct conversation. Sensitive nuances and subtle formulations can be lost in translation. Similarly, the doctor will be unable to interpret certain gestures and expressions of the patient's body language because, first, she might not know the meaning of the patient's movements in his cultural context and, second, the content transmitted by emphasis is easily lost in the interpreter's rendition. Thus, access to the patient's will is filtered through multiple layers of mediation. These difficulties can be minimized by use of interpreters specifically trained for such situations.

In any case, gaining an adequate understanding of the patient's preferences requires an optimized strategy. The difficulty in choosing such a strategy consists, among other things, in the alien appearance of the patient's culture. For this reason, a preliminary conversation can be helpful to allow access to the patient's personality. In a conversation of this kind, one can discuss the patient's current knowledge of his or her condition and possibly also ask about any expectations regarding treatment options or the course of the medical condition. The significance and value of his family can also be addressed in this conversation. One can even ask directly whether a direct involvement of family members in the decision-making process would be in accordance with his wishes.

The information and impressions gained in the initial conversation can be helpful for determining the strategy for the second talk. They can also help to eliminate strategies found to be inappropriate. Sensitivity and caution should accompany the doctor's actions in these conversations. "The question about the truth about the seriousness of the illness is therefore ultimately a question about the appropriate truth" (*Bundesärztekammer* 1998, 114).

FAMILY AND TRUTH-TELLING

Withholding an unfavorable diagnosis or prognosis on the request of family members is not a rare occurrence in some countries in the world. Such a practice is often encountered outside the Western world, in particular in Asian and South American countries, but also in the Near East and Muslim countries (Berger 1998; Mobeireek et al. 2008). The medical ethicist Yali Chong, from the Peking University Health Care Center, emphasizes the importance of the family in decisions about informing the patient of his condition. He even speaks of the model of family–patient–doctor in the Chinese–Confucian culture (Cong 2004).

Here, the seriousness of the illness also determines the influence of the family on the procedure to be adopted. "If the illness is very easy to cure, the family member will directly disclose all the information to the patient or allow the patient to do so. Otherwise, the family member offers only partial information or lies to the patient" (Cong 2004, 152). Jotkowitz and his colleagues argue similarly on this topic and speak of a similar reserve with respect to informing a patient fully about a bad diagnosis and prognosis in the Jewish tradition (Jotkowitz et al. 2006).

In Turkey, family members' desire to be involved in determining medical treatment is also strong if the illness is incurable and terminal (Ozdogan et al. 2006; Aksoy 2005). It is common for family members to express to the doctor their wish that the patient is not informed of a bad diagnosis, often before the diagnosis has even been made. It is also not rare for the doctor, in the case of an unfavorable diagnosis, to discuss the further procedure with family members first. The attitude of the parents in the case described above can be viewed as a typical instance of such cases.

It would certainly be wrong to see this attitude as a merely cultural attitude without any moral foundations. Two forms of argumentation can be constructed from the perspective of the Turkish–Islamic culture that is rarely made explicit in practice. The first one assumes that informing patients about an incurable disease or imminent death would upset them and thus cause a psychological burden. This action is to be viewed as unequivocally harmful and hence to be avoided.

Here, the classical medical–ethical principle of avoiding harm comes to the fore. This form of argumentation is not foreign to Western European medical ethics and also not insignificant in common practice. The important difference consists in the normative interpretation of the individual assessment of this practice. In the Turkish–Islamic culture, this principle of doing no harm is initially independent of an individual attitude. Family members are involved in the decision-making process on this basis. The central importance accorded to the family in social life generally makes this involvement easier. Even from an individualist perspective, this action is not *eo ipso* to be seen as detrimental to the patient's well-being. Whether this action is harmful can be decided only on the basis of the patient's own attitude to this practice.

The attitude of the family members in the above-mentioned case can also be justified by Islamic belief. In Islamic thought, the time of death is set by God and remains hidden from human beings (Quran Sura 56: 60). Humans can speculate about it with the means at their disposal, but they cannot predict this moment with absolute certainty. A predictive statement about end of life is viewed critically from this religious perspective. "One is ultimately not God" is the reaction to such statements. It is worth noting that such reactions more frequently follow negative prognoses. Such an assertion is also seen as an open attack on the theological concept of hope.

To take away the hope of healing would contradict the implicit attributes of God in Islamic belief, since this attitude would deny God's omnipotence. This theological foundation would also make the family's attitude in the situation described above plausible, from the perspective of their religious beliefs, even if it was not made explicit at the time.

Part 3: Universalistic and Particularistic Approaches to Truth-Telling

When it comes to medical–ethical conflicts in an intercultural setting, such as those discussed and analyzed above, the conceptualization of the cultural phenomena, their ethical evaluation and integration into the decision-making process take on central importance. As the example has shown, cultural phenomena are often given little attention in the procedure followed by the medical team.

At this point, it is important to ask whether the approach adopted in this conflict is the only ethically legitimate course of action or whether a different procedure might provide a better way of dealing with the conflict. In other words, is an anthropocentric, individualistic ethical approach, based on human dignity, personal rights, and the right to self-determination, able to take account of cultural phenomena and to integrate them into the decision-making process? The latter question is directly connected with the ethical assessment of culturally specific values. This and similar questions have already been addressed by medical ethicists in discussions about the universality of the principle of respect for patient autonomy. In what follows, two basic positions on the topic of truth-telling will be examined.

American bioethicist Ruth Macklin argues that established fundamental ethical principles can adequately address cultural phenomena in medical care and integrate them into the decision-making process in an appropriate way. She distinguishes between the principles of "respect for the person" and "respect for autonomy" and subordinates the latter principle to the former (Macklin 1998). Autonomy, a self-evident consequence of the principle of respect for the person, does not in her opinion exclude withholding an unfavorable diagnosis and taking family members' choices into account during the decision-making process.

Provided the patient agrees, family members can contribute to the health-care team's deliberations. In the same way, the patient's wish not to be informed about an unfavorable diagnosis can be honored by the physician (Macklin 1998, 7). Note that this approach claims universal validity and is thought capable of resolving conflicts in an intercultural physician–patient relationship.

Chinese medical ethicist Ruiping Fan denies the universally binding character of "Western bioethical principles" and questions their "abstract content," which would offer a basis for the moral evaluation of medical practices in all cultures (Fan 1997). He argues his position, taking the principle of autonomy as an example and discussing two forms of determination that can be derived from it, namely, self-determination and determination by the family.

In his opinion, the Western principle of autonomy leads to self-determination where the starting point is individual free will and the subjective determinability of moral goods. Determination by the family can be derived, on the other hand, from the East Asian principle of autonomy. This form of determination claims an objective understanding of moral goods and emphasizes the value of harmonious dependency within the family. These two concepts of autonomy cannot, according to Fan, be equated with each other, as they imply different moral actions.

Fan illustrates these theoretical discussions with instances of truth-telling in the case of an unfavorable diagnosis and prognosis. From the Chinese or Confucian perspective, withholding a diagnosis and prognosis can be ethically justified. First, the family members should be informed and, subsequently, the further procedure should be decided upon in consultation with the family. If the family decides to withhold information from the patient, the doctor should respect this decision (Fan and Li 2004). According to Fan and Li's particularistic approach, this procedure rests on the following conditions:

1. The physician finds evidence of manifest mutual concern of the family members for the patient.
2. The family's wishes are not egregiously in discord with the physician's professional judgment regarding the medical best interests of the patient.

If either or both of the two necessary conditions are not met, the physician should communicate directly with the patient (Fan and Li 2004, 189).

Critical Discussion of Universalistic and Particularistic Approaches

A major concern of the universalistic approaches argued by Macklin and others is the prevention of harm, which can reach the degree of a violation of human rights. For this reason, every medical action must first be examined to assess whether it represents a violation of human rights. In a second step, the intervention should be evaluated from the patient's perspective. Only then can it be ethically legitimated in medical practice.

This approach presupposes a hierarchy among ethical principles, according to which patient autonomy is most important (Macklin 1998). To argue for the universal application of this approach assumes the validity of this hierarchy among ethical principles. Yet, as long as such a hierarchy in the form just described is not accepted in a given culture, this approach cannot be applied ("unbridgeable moral gap between Western individualism and non-Western communalism"; Baker 1998, 212).

A further deficiency of the universalistic approach is its inability to ethically assess culturally dependent moral phenomena like family autonomy. It is not able to ascribe a normative value to such phenomena. This approach is always dependent from the individualistic understanding of the human being. Therefore, this ascription of ethical value thus has a *hypothetical* character and not an *a priori* one.

If one applies the entire approach to our case study, the attitude of the medical team can be ethically legitimated on its basis. The medical team deliberately ignored the wishes of the family and instead turned to the patient himself. The reason given was the patient's autonomy. As long as the patient does not assent, no normative value can be ascribed to the wishes of the family. It is obvious that this ignorance of the cultural phenomena led to the escalation of the conflict.

In addition, this approach presupposes a responsible adult and informed patient with whom one can communicate perfectly without linguistic or cultural barriers. A further difficulty comes in when the patient is not able to express himself, as is the case, for example, with an incompetent or comatose patient, infant, or fetus.

Despite these difficulties, this approach possesses an important strength for a multicultural society, the constituent groups of which are by no means homogeneous. It is ethically unjustifiable to decide about the treatment given to a patient merely on the basis of his (perceived) membership in a religious or ethnic group. An indiscriminate application of the knowledge gained about the patient's culture or the extrapolation from previous individual experiences can turn out to be mistaken in a current case. For this reason, it is always important to uncover the individual patient's attitude to a specific practice.

The normatively relativist or particularistic approach promises a better account of cultural phenomena in making ethical judgments than universalistic ones. Particularists can derive moral maxims for actions from culturally specific phenomena. Because the moral judgments within a culture are affected by other cultural phenomena, they receive as such a normative value—without being examined according to fundamental ethical principles. Thus, withholding an unfavorable diagnosis, for example, is morally right if this practice is morally accepted within a certain culture. This position is clearly supported, especially by cultural anthropology.

Unfortunately, this approach implies a *culturalistic fallacy*. I understand under the culturalistic fallacy that the ethical justification of a moral practice or attitude is only through its existence in a certain group. According to this attitude, a reflection upon or criticism of a culture's moral practice is impossible.

A comprehensive application of this approach is not only problematic because of the culturalistic fallacy but also because of its prerequisite moral homogeneity within a given ethnic group. In the age of globalization, a profound change in values is taking place, even in societies considered closed to the outside world, so that disparate values emerge within each culture. If the members of a certain culture live in another country, the influence of the dominant values in the host country would be strong and thus support the heterogeneity of values within this ethnic group.

If one applies this approach to our case study, the relatives' wish attains normative value and can under certain circumstances be acted on. If the patient's expectations agree with those of the family, this approach is better able to take account of the cultural phenomena. If the patient does not agree with the family's wishes, however, the patient could then be restrained in his decisions, even disenfranchised. An insoluble problem is also presented by the juridical justification of the medical team's actions. Withholding medical information without the patient's assent can have legal, as well as moral, repercussions for the doctor.

Conclusion

The disclosure of an unfavorable diagnosis and infaust prognosis to a patient, communicating essential (and existential) information to the person most immediately concerned, has historically been a controversial topic. Today, it has lost nothing of its controversial status. On the contrary, we encounter this question in medical practice much more frequently and with a growing complexity. Truth-telling in the intercultural setting of a value pluralistic society requires a better founded and more comprehensive discussion of the problem than has hitherto taken place.

From the comprehensive discussion and analysis presented above, the following conclusions on a practical and theoretical level can be developed:

- An ethically appropriate way of handling the disclosure of an unfavorable diagnosis and infaust prognosis in an intercultural setting requires first of all culturally sensitive and successful communication, especially in case of a conflict of preferences and interests, in order for the conflicting parties to reach a mutual understanding of their values and of the specific reasons for their attitude. Translation by relatives or hospital staff has often proven counterproductive and ethically problematic; hence, communication should be mediated by professional interpreters trained for medical practice.
- An ethically legitimate resolution of such conflicts often requires intercultural competence, to be understood as the ability to recognize and analyze the goods at stake

in an intercultural conflict and to integrate them into medical–ethical decision-making. The availability of such competence cannot, however, be taken as a given. It should be imparted during medical studies and supported in professional life by means of further training. Intercultural competence must also be recognized as an important competence for members of ethics committees in a value pluralistic society.

- The decisions and actions of doctors must be taken within the limits of the law and conforming to the regulations of professional institutions. These regulations should be laid down in such a way as to leave sufficient space for taking account of cultural phenomena. Equally, in a culturally determined medical–ethical conflict, it should be investigated whether a procedure diverging from the conventional practice is possible. For reasons presented above, it often happens that options that are in principle available for medical decision-making are not pursued. With a culturally sensitive attitude and intercultural competence, additional options can be better integrated into medical decision-making.
- The ethical problems that arise in applying the universalistic and particularistic approaches were discussed in detail above. A rigid application of any of these approaches appears to be problematic in many respects. Instead, an integrative procedure should be followed. This procedure entails taking account of the ethical goods at issue in the conflict from the perspective of the conflict parties. This does not mean prioritizing either patient autonomy or family autonomy but, rather, contextualizing these forms of autonomy sensitively in concrete terms.

Only then can both the wholesale application of patient autonomy often found in conventional practice and the overruling of the individual patient's wishes based on his presumed belonging to a certain culture be prevented. This process of argumentation and reflection, however, presents a challenge for the medical team, which should therefore in complex situations have access to expertise from a competence center or to ethical consultancy by a clinical ethics committee or clinical ethics consultant.

Acknowledgment

The author would like to thank Dr. Rainer Brömer for his important comments and critical perusal of this manuscript.

References

Aksoy, S. 2005. "End-of-Life Decision-Making in Turkey." In *End-of-Life Decision-Making: A Cross-National Study*, edited by R. H. Blank and J.C. Merrick, 183–95. Cambridge, MA: MIT Press.

Baker, R. 1998. "A Theory of International Bioethics: Multiculturalism, Postmodernism, and the Bankruptcy of Fundamentalism." *Kennedy Institute of Ethics Journal* 8, no. 3: 201–31.

Berger, J. T. 1998. "Culture and Ethnicity in Clinical Care." *Archives of Internal Medicine* 158, no. 19: 2085–90.

Brody, H. 1997. "The Physician-Patient Relationship." In *Medical Ethics*, second edition, edited by R. W. Veatch, 75–101. Boston: Jones and Bartlett Publishers.

Brown, K. H. 1995. "Information Disclosure." In *Encyclopedia of Bioethics*, edited by W. Reich, 1221–24. New York: The Free Press.

Bundesärztekammer. 1998. *Gesundheit im Alter. Texte und Materialien der Bundesärztekammer zur Fortbildung und Weiterbildung*. Köln.

———. 2004. Grundsätze der Bundesärztekammer zur ärztlichen Sterbebegleitung. *Deutsches Ärzteblatt* 19: 1–2.

———. 2007. *Berufsordnung für die deutschen Ärztinnen und Ärzte.*

Chadwick, R. 1997. "Das Recht auf Wissen und das Recht auf Nichtwissen aus philosophischer Sicht." In *Perspektiven der Humangenetik*, edited by F. W. Silvia Petermann and Michael Quante, 195–207. Paderborn: Ferdinand Schöningh.

Cong, Y. 2004. "Doctor-Family-Patient Relationship: The Chinese Paradigm of Informed Consent." *Journal of Medicine and Philosophy* 29, no. 2: 149–78.

Faden, R. R., and T. L. Beauchamp. 1986. *A History and Theory of Informed Consent.* New York: Oxford University Press.

Fan, R. 1997. "Self-Determination vs. Family-Determination: Two Incommensurable Principles of Autonomy: A Report from East Asia." *Bioethics* 11, no. 3–4: 309–22.

Fan, R., and B. Li. 2004. "Truth Telling in Medicine: The Confucian View." *Journal of Medicine and Philosophy* 29, no. 2: 179–93.

Hancock, K. et al. 2007. "Truth-Telling in Discussing Prognosis in Advanced Life-Limiting Illnesses: A Systematic Review." *Palliative Medicine* 21, no. 6: 507–17.

Ilkilic, I. 2002. "Der muslimische Patient. Medizinethische Aspekte des muslimischen Krankheitsverständnisses in einer wertpluralen Gesellschaft." Diss., Münster London: Lit.

———. 2007. "Medizinethische Aspekte im Umgang mit muslimischen Patienten." *Deutsche Medizinische Wochenschrift* 132, no. 30: 1587–90.

———. 2008. "Kulturelle Aspekte bei ethischen Entscheidungen am Lebensende und interkulturelle Kompetenz." *Bundesgesundheitsblatt Gesundheitsforschung Gesundheitsschutz* 51, no. 8: 857–64.

Jameton, A. 1995. "Information Disclosure: Ethical Issues." In *Encyclopedia of Bioethics*, edited by W. Reich, 1225–332. New York: The Free Press.

Jotkowitz, A. et al. 2006. "Truth-Telling in a Culturally Diverse World." *Cancer Investigation* 24, no. 8: 786–89.

Kagawa-Singer, M., and L. J. Blackhall. 2001. "Negotiating Cross-Cultural Issues at the End of Life: 'You Got to Go Where He Lives.' " *JAMA* 286, no. 23: 2993–3001.

Krakauer, E. L. et al. 2002. "Barriers to Optimum End-of-Life Care for Minority Patients." *Journal of the American Geriatric Society* 50, no. 1: 182–90.

Macklin, R. 1998. "Ethical Relativism in a Multicultural Society." *Kennedy Institute of Ethics Journal* 8, no. 1: 1–22.

———. 1999. *Against Relativism: Cultural Diversity and the Search for Ethical Universals in Medicine.* New York: Oxford University Press.

Mobeireek, A. F. et al. 2008. "Information Disclosure and Decision-Making: The Middle East versus the Far East and the West." *Journal of Medical Ethics* 34, no. 4: 225–29.

Novack, D. H. et al. 1979. "Changes in Physicians' Attitudes toward Telling the Cancer Patient." *JAMA* 241, no. 9: 897–900.

Oken, D. 1961. "What to Tell Cancer Patients: A Study of Medical Attitudes." *JAMA* 175: 1120–28.

Ozdogan, M. et al. 2006. "Factors Related to Truth-Telling Practice of Physicians Treating Patients with Cancer in Turkey." *Journal of Palliative Medicine* 9, no. 5: 1114–19.

Paul, N. W. 2008. "Klinische Ethikberatung: Therapieziele, Patientenwille und Entscheidungsprobleme in der modernen Medizin. In *Grenzsituationen in der Intensivmedizin*, edited by T. Junginger, 208–17. Berlin: Springer.

Pilchmaier, H. 1999. "Wahrheit und Wahrhaftigkeit am Krankenbett." *Deutsches Ärzteblatt* 96, no. 9: 536–37.

Salomon, F. 2003. "Wahrheit vermitteln am Krankenbett." *Deutsche Medizinische Wochenschrift* 128, no. 23: 1307–10.

Steinhart, B. 2002. "Patient Autonomy: Evolution of the Doctor–Patient Relationship." *Haemophilia* 8, no. 3: 441–46.

Sullivan, R. J. et al. 2001. "Truth-Telling and Patient Diagnoses." *Journal of Medical Ethics* 27, no. 3: 192–97.

Surbone, A. 2006. "Telling the Truth to Patients with Cancer: What Is the Truth?" *Lancet Oncology* 7, no. 11: 944–50.

Tuckett, A. G. 2004. "Truth-Telling in Clinical Practice and the Arguments for and Against: A Review of the Literature." *Nursing Ethics* 11, no. (5): 500–13.

Ulsenheimer, K. 2008. *Arztstrafrecht in der Praxis*. Heidelberg: C. F. Müller.

Valente, S. M. 2004. "End of Life and Ethnicity." *Journal for Nurses in Staff Development* 20, no. 6: 285–93.

Van de Loo, J. 2000. "Aufklärung / Aufklärungspflicht." In *Lexikon der Bioethik*, edited by W. Korff, 284–7. Gütersloh: Gütersloher Verlagshaus.

Volker, D. L. 2005. "Control and End-of-Life Care: Does Ethnicity Matter?" *American Journal of Hospital Palliative Care* 22, no. 6: 442–46.

Walter, U. 2000. "Aufklärung / Aufklärungspflicht: Rechtlich." In *Lexikon der Bioethik*, edited by W. Korff, 287–88. Gütersloh: Gütersloher Verlagshaus.

CHAPTER 4

Lost in Translation

Søren Holm

Abstract

This chapter will analyze the question of whether a global bioethics can be established if we do not have a prior common moral language. The first part will analyze two contenders for a global moral language: 1) human rights; and 2) a set of core principles (looking closely at Ruth Macklin's work). It will argue that neither constitute a shared moral language, and will identify the reasons they don't. The second part will then discuss whether a hybrid approach involving core human rights interpreted in the light of core moral principles can form the basis for a global bioethics. It will again be argued that such an approach is problematic. The third part will then consider whether we are not better off by accepting that there are irresolvable moral differences at both theoretical and practical levels and accepting that the real moral task is to mediate between these differences in concrete situations.

Introduction

It is a trite platitude that we live in a connected global world where the consequences of our actions may spread far and wide and where perhaps, more importantly, we are aware that the consequences of our actions may spread far and wide. How are we to deal with the global moral problems that occur in such a world? One suggestion is that because the problems are global they should be analyzed and resolved within an agreed-upon global moral framework. It is this suggestion that will be analyzed critically in this chapter. I will outline the epistemic and social conditions necessary for convergence on a common position and apply this analysis in relation to convergence on a common set of core or fundamental moral principles. I will also consider the use of human rights as the common minimal framework.

In the analysis I will use the principle of "respect for persons" as the main example of a potentially universal moral principle and the important 1998 book *Against Relativism: Cultural Diversity and the Search for Ethical Universals in Medicine*, by Ruth

Macklin, as the main source of examples. I have chosen to use Macklin's book in this way because I take it to be one of the strongest, best, and clearest defenses of an unabashed universalist position in bioethics.

I furthermore agree with Macklin's universalism at the theoretical level but disagree with her concerning the conditions under which theoretical universalism can be converted into concrete ethical judgments. This makes her book and analysis an appropriate touchstone for the more skeptical view I develop here.

The analysis will mainly relate to the possibility of a global ethics, but many of the arguments are also relevant to the possibility of a common ethics within a single multicultural society. But, before proceeding any further, it is important briefly to make the case for why a common, global ethics might be considered desirable. The world in which we live is not "the best of all worlds." The rights of millions of people are breached without justification, unjustifiable resource inequalities are perpetuated and widened, and the strong are often allowed to prey on the weak with impunity.

There are thus many ways in which the world could be made a better place, ethically speaking. Although each of us can do much on our own to make the world a better place, there are also many things that can be changed only if individuals or states work together. The necessary cooperation will plausibly be easier if it is possible to reach agreement on what features of the world we ought to change and why we ought to change them. And this agreement might be believed to require a common set of ethical principles. If we, for instance, want to identify unjustifiable resource inequalities that ought to be rectified, this seems to presuppose agreement on some account of what justice requires. We may be able to proceed some of the way in the absence of a common global ethics, but getting all the way seems to require one. And it would therefore be a major achievement if we could agree on one.

Conditions for Convergence

Under what general conditions can we reasonably expect convergence on a common moral framework, in a situation where moral agents 1) start from radically different positions; 2) are able to communicate with each other and engage in moral discourse; and 3) are willing to engage in moral discourse in good faith?[1]

Let us first note that the answer to this question is independent of whether we assume a foundationalist or a coherentist account of moral justification. On either of these accounts, the process by which convergence is achieved in discourse between real moral agents is going to be a coherence-seeking process involving all the elements of wide reflective equilibrium as inputs (i.e., beliefs and facts about the world, considered moral judgments, and moral theories) (Daniels 2008). We will never be in a situation where we try to agree on our common moral principles without any prior moral commitments. Agreeing on foundationalism or coherentism will be an outcome of the process, not an initial assumption, and it might not even be a necessary outcome.

As a starting point in a convergence-seeking process, the participants will need to try to reach agreement on the ground rules for the process. Here, there are major stumbling blocks. The one that is commonly discussed is whether considered moral judgments that are based on (religious) comprehensive worldviews are admissible in the process (Audi and Wolterstorff 1997; Rawls 1996). Robert Audi, for instance, proposes two principles of secular reason and motivation as side constraints on interventions in public political debates.

THE PRINCIPLE OF SECULAR RATIONALE

"One has a prima facie obligation not to advocate or support any law or public policy that restricts human conduct, unless one has, and is willing to offer, adequate secular reasons for this advocacy or support" (Audi and Wolterstorff 1997, 25).

THE PRINCIPLE OF SECULAR MOTIVATION

"One has a (prima facie) obligation to abstain from advocacy or support of a law or public policy that restricts human conduct, unless one is sufficiently *motivated* by (normatively) adequate secular reason" (Audi and Wolterstorff 1997, 28).

Admitting moral judgments based on religious worldviews will make it more difficult to reach consensus, but not admitting them is also problematic. There are no participants in the process who do not hold a comprehensive worldview that influences their concrete judgments. Only some of these comprehensive worldviews are religious,[2] but a specific nonreligious worldview can be as idiosyncratic, held as strongly, and influence concrete judgments as much as a religious one (e.g., a Marxist–Leninist worldview) (Luther 1986).

If nonshared components of comprehensive worldviews are excluded *ab initio*, it is likely to have one of two effects. It will either mean that those who are strongly committed to their comprehensive worldview will be less interested in engaging with the process, or it will mean that they cannot engage in good faith. They will not be able to state their views in what they see as the strongest possible way, but rather will be forced to find ways of stating them that are less satisfactory from their point of view.

Here, we seem to be between a rock and a hard place, philosophically speaking. Either we complicate our coherence-building process by letting participants state their initial ethical views clearly and with their own justification, or we run the risk of making it impossible for some participants to engage in the process in good faith. If we choose to exclude nonshared components of comprehensive worldviews, we further have the problem that it becomes unclear how the persons who hold these views should view the outcome of the process.

Let us imagine that wide reflective equilibrium has been obtained around a set of global ethical principles. It then seems possible to claim that participants in the process should accept these principles because they are a way of making their own moral views more coherent and thereby, presumably, more justifiable. But, if the input is not "their own moral views," it is difficult to see why they should have any commitment to accepting the outcome.

A slightly different issue that is often confused with the religion issue is the issue of nonnegotiable commitments. If any party in the process has nonnegotiable commitments, it may block the achievement of coherence, and it may therefore be a necessary component of good faith that everything is up for grabs. But nonnegotiable commitments can be held for a variety of reasons, not only religious ones.

The other stumbling block is that real-life coherence seeking does not take place behind a veil of ignorance. All participants are aware of who they are and of what consequences a given set of common ethical principles will have for them and their descendants. In an ideal world where everyone is motivated by ethical concerns, only this would not matter, but it will matter for real-world consensus building.

We can therefore not expect agreement on common, global ethical principles to be reached quickly or without contention. What we can expect is a slow process moving forward in a piecemeal fashion, and maybe not even always moving forward. We may be able to reach agreement that a specific ethical construct is a fundamental ethical principle and part of a common global ethics, whereas other constructs still have only the status of plausible candidates or still have vague scope and content.

What we cannot expect, even if we are committed theoretical universalists, is that agreement on the universal principles is reached quickly or easily.

How Precise a Consensus Can We Reach?

Let us, despite the problems alluded to above, assume that we have reached a consensus that "respect for persons" is a fundamental and universal ethical principle[3] that should guide our global ethics. Are we then in a position to make concrete ethical judgments?

Let us first consider a case where "respect for persons" is the only moral consideration that is engaged. No other principles are in play, and it is clear that everyone involved falls within the scope of the principle[4] (i.e., that they are persons). In such a case, we would still need to specify the content of the principle in order to form a judgment. It is a well-known and often repeated criticism of Beauchamp and Childress's principlist approach that, whereas we might be able to agree on the importance of the four principles when they are fairly content-less labels, it is much more difficult to agree on their precise content (e.g., how much beneficence is required). And the same question must be raised here: What does "respect for persons" actually mean? A brief survey of the literature makes it clear that this is a highly controversial question.

John Harris argues that respect for persons has two distinct aspects:

> Respect for persons requires us to acknowledge the dignity and value of other persons and to treat them as ends in themselves and not merely instrumentally as means to ends or objectives chosen by others. Respect for persons has two distinct dimensions:
>
> 1. Respect for autonomy.
> 2. Concern for welfare.

> When I suggest that these elements are crucial to any conception of respect for persons I mean simply that no one could claim to respect persons if their attitude to others failed to take account of, and indeed exhibit, these elements. (Harris 2003, 10)

But respect for autonomy and concern for welfare seem to be two very different things. Macklin explicates respect for persons primarily as respect for personal autonomy that avoids many interpretative problems, being primarily a negative condition and therefore a potential candidate for a strict and complete duty.

If, however, Harris is right, and respect for persons also encompasses concern for welfare, we are left with the further problem of how to explicate welfare.[5] Is the welfare of a person a purely subjective matter to be decided only from the first-person perspective, or is it (at least partly) an objective matter? To agree on this will be important in order to come to concrete judgment in cases where a person wants to perform actions that will negatively affect some objective assessment of their welfare or interest. But are we likely to reach consensus on the explication? Or likely to reach consensus on what should be incorporated in a list of objective goods conducive to welfare?

This might, initially, seem not to matter if we take the more restrictive Macklin line equating respect for persons with respect for autonomy, and relegating welfare considerations to some other fundamental ethical principle. But thinking that this move will solve the problem is partly an illusion, because welfare ceases to matter only if we take respect for autonomy to be absolute in the sense that paternalistic action is never justifiable. If we accept that there are instances where paternalism in respect of a competent person is justified, the question of our account of welfare again raises its head. And, given that no philosophical agreement has yet been reached on this issue, we would surely expect too much of our consensus process if we believed it would give us a firm answer.

A more complicated problem occurs when we have more than one fundamental moral principle in play and where they are in potential conflict.[6] This is a very old problem, and most moral systems have ways of dealing with it (e.g., the processes of specification and balancing in Beauchamp and Childress's work) (2009).

But, in the global context, what sometimes happens is that someone brings a moral consideration to the table that is new in the sense that it is outside of the moral system of the other participants in the discourse. This would still happen even if we had an agreed-upon set of global moral principles because, unlike in ideal philosophy, not everyone will have been at the discourse where these principles were agreed.

Let me illustrate this problem with an extended example from Macklin's book. In a chapter on death and birth, she discusses organ transplantation in the Philippines and the role of traditional Filipino morality in shaping the practice:

> The dead person whose organs are removed is not in a position to make a proper "donation" in an act that stems from the right sort of moral motivation. The relevant concept in the traditional Filipino value system is known as *kusang loob*. For an act to have moral worth it must be done out of *kusang loob*, an idea similar to free will but not exactly the same. If a person needs to be told what to do, or is coerced into performing an action, the act does

> not come out of *kusang loob*. To have moral worth, an action must also be done without anticipation of reward or personal gain and not purely out of a sense of duty.
>
> The implications for the morality of organ donation are rather straightforward. If a person is not in a position to act from the proper moral motivation, that is, out of *kusang loob*, it is better for the action not to have been done at all. Presumably, then, only if a person had signed an organ donation card, done so in an uncoerced manner and not purely out of a sense of duty, would the donation qualify as being done out of *kusang loob*. [. . .]
>
> What follows from this picture for ethical relativism? Should we conclude that the medical practice of organ transplantation is ethically wrong in the Philippines because of the value attached to the concept of *kusang loob* but ethically right elsewhere as long as the proper safeguards are followed? [. . .]
>
> The Filipino concept of *kusang loob* is a feature of a moral system in that culture that does not appear to have an exact counterpart in our own society, at least not with respect to organ donation. *Kusang loob* falls under the category of moral motivation, an aspect of ethical behavior that may legitimately differ from one society to another and is therefore an example of one of the things that turns out to be relative. The application of this concept to organ donation yields the result that organ donation itself is neither morally right nor morally wrong, but its rightness or wrongness depends (among other things) on the moral motivation of the individual whose organs are harvested for transplantation. This marks a cultural and ethical difference from organ donation in other cultures where a donation need not stem from a particular moral motivation. This difference is not at the level of fundamental ethical principles, so it does not confirm the proposition that ethical principles vary from one culture to the next with no deeper underlying principles. (Macklin 1998, 143–44)

I agree with Macklin that nothing in this account of the implications of traditional Filipino values for organ transplantation confirms "the proposition that ethical principles vary from one culture to the next with no deeper underlying principles," but I disagree with the way she justifies this conclusion.

Believing that moral motivation is important in deciding whether an act is morally right or wrong is not a peculiar Filipino concern. The non-Filipino philosopher Immanuel Kant famously argued that motivation in the form of a good will was the only thing that decided rightness and wrongness:

> Nothing can possibly be conceived in the world, or even out of it, which can be called good, without qualification, except a good will. [. . .]
>
> A good will is good not because of what it performs or effects, not by its aptness for the attainment of some proposed end, but simply by virtue of the volition; that is, it is good in itself, and considered by itself is to be esteemed much higher than all that can be brought about by it in favor of any inclination, nay even of the sum total of all inclinations. (Kant 1985)

And the characteristics that make an action problematic in the Filipino case have some overlaps with what makes an action heteronomous and therefore without value in Kantian philosophy.

Similar concerns related to motivation or intention can also be found in many other ethical systems. It is therefore impossible to drive a wedge between fundamental ethical principles and concerns with motivation in the way Macklin does. That the right motivation matters in the moral assessment of actions may eventually be one of the fundamental ethical principles that emerge from a consensus process.

There is nothing inherent in the concept of a "fundamental ethical principle" that precludes this. A fundamental ethical principle does not have to be about rights or duties. But if we can't just discount *kusang loob* as a particular Filipino ethical value that can never count as a fundamental ethical principle, how are we to deal with it? If we are really committed to universalism and to moral discourse in good faith, it seems that we will minimally have to consider whether we need to augment our set of fundamental ethical principles with a principle about right, ethical motivation. This will not be necessary if we can plausibly claim that our current set of fundamental ethical principles already contains all the principles that can count as fundamental ethical principles. But it is difficult to see how such a claim can be sustained, at least at the present stage of the discourse, where we are still moving forward toward a global, common ethics.

So the introduction of *kusang loob* into the debate as a possible important ethical consideration will, at least temporarily, destabilize our set of fundamental ethical principles. It is only after we have seriously considered whether *kusang loob* or some suitable modification can make our set of principles even more coherent that we can make a concrete judgment concerning Filipino as well as non-Filipino organ donation.

This is not a problem if *kusang loob* is an isolated instance of a prima facie valid ethical consideration found in a specific culture, but there are, of course, likely to be many such examples—and therefore, many circumstances—where concrete judgment might elude us because our set of global common ethics cannot be claimed to be complete.

Human Rights as the Common Framework

But is the analysis above not far too complicated and hairsplitting? Could we not simply sidestep the philosophical issues and seek convergence in the area of international human rights law?

The link between public health, medicine, ethics, and human rights was first analyzed in detail by Jonathan Mann, and a turn toward human rights has been prominent in recent developments in "global ethics" (Mann 1997). Most have argued that ethics and human rights are complementary, but at least some commentators foresee a development where human rights law will eventually subsume bioethics and make bioethics more or less redundant (Faunce 2005).

Roberto Andorno furthermore argues that human rights are best understood as a result of a consensus-seeking process that allows consensus on principles without requiring consensus on justifications. The agreed-upon set of human rights may not be the result of wide reflective equilibrium, but they are nevertheless agreed:

> The global success of the human rights movement in contemporary society is probably due to the fact that a practical agreement about the rights that should be respected is perfectly compatible with theoretical disagreement on their ultimate foundation (14). The Universal Declaration of Human Rights of 1948 is the best example of this phenomenon, because it was drafted by representatives of particularly diverse, even opposed, ideologies. Upon this strong legislative foundation has been built an extensive network of human rights mechanisms designed to develop international standards, monitor their implementation and investigate violations of human rights. (Andorno 2002, 960)

The advantages of moving to a human rights arena are many, according to proponents of such a move: 1) States voluntarily agree to be bound by human rights, and such rights therefore have undisputed normative force; 2) Human rights jurisprudence provides an interpretative system for determining the scope and meaning of human rights; and 3) Specific institutions (e.g., the European Court of Human Rights [ECHR]) can provide authoritative interpretations with legal force. Therefore, if we, as an example, want to know the scope and meaning of the right to private and family life enunciated in Article 8 of the European Convention of Human Rights, we can look at ECHR jurisprudence. Article 8 states that:

1. Everyone has the right to respect for his private and family life, his home and his correspondence.
2. There shall be no interference by a public authority with the exercise of this right except such as is in accordance with the law and is necessary in a democratic society in the interests of national security, public safety or the economic well-being of the country, for the prevention of disorder or crime, for the protection of health or morals, or for the protection of the rights and freedoms of others.

In relation to sexual matters, we would find that the Article 8 rights in general protect against discrimination because of sexual orientation or activity, but also that not all kinds of sexual activity are protected. In the judgment in *Laskey, Jaggard and Brown v. the United Kingdom* (judgment of February 19, 1997), the ECHR, for instance, found that the organized, consensual sadomasochistic activities carried out by a group of men were not protected by Article 8.

The human rights framework thus specifies the rights of individuals and provides mechanisms for authoritative interpretation. These rights are furthermore universal in scope and consensually agreed upon, at least within the relevant set of jurisdictions (member states of the Council of Europe, in the case of the ECHR). It thus seems that human rights give the universalists everything they could reasonably want, and that they circumvent all of the problems about agreement on precise content discussed above because of the existence of authoritative interpretations.

One possible criticism of this positive picture is that there are problems with our current enumerations of human rights and that we should add some—and perhaps also remove some—from our lists of binding human rights. I think this a valid criticism (Holm 2009), but not one that I will pursue here.

The criticism that I want to pursue here is based on the fact that the precise content of specific human rights is an area of huge contestation. The lawyers for Laskey, Jaggard, and Brown argued that their activities were protected by Article 8, and many commentators have agreed with them, but the ECHR disagreed. It is a standard legal fiction that courts interpret laws; they do not make them. Or, to put it differently, when a court makes a decision on a point of law, it simply states what the legal position is; it does not change the legal position. According to this fiction, the lawyers for Laskey et al. simply made a legal mistake.[7] Article 8 did not protect these kinds of sexual activities, and it had never done so.

But, given recent changes in sexual mores, it is quite likely that the *Laskey* judgment will one day be overturned. This will be of no help to Laskey et al., who have long since served their prison sentences. But it will mean that Article 8 suddenly protects activity that the court had previously denied it protected. Or, to put it differently, if *Laskey* is overturned, it will illustrate that the content of human rights is much more fluid and malleable than we might initially believe. It will also illustrate that the initial, voluntary consent of states is almost completely irrelevant to the normative force of their current human rights commitment. The rights that the original signatories signed up to in 1950 when the European Convention on Human Rights and Fundamental Freedoms was signed was a set of rights with very different content than the rights in 2010.

Human rights do give us legal enforceability in some regions of the world, but they do not substitute for a common global ethics. They are a parallel normative system with as many interpretative problems and as much vagueness of content.

The Dismal Conclusion?

In this chapter, I have argued for the conclusion that the likelihood that we will be able to agree on a global moral framework that is sufficiently specific to lead to concrete judgment concerning global moral problems is very small indeed. The justification for this conclusion is not that moral relativism is true. I believe there are compelling arguments showing moral relativism to be unsustainable as a theoretical position; there are also good arguments for accepting moral universalism, but that is a matter for another discussion.

Alas, the falsity of moral relativism does not guarantee actual convergence on one commonly accepted moral framework. In this chapter, I have presented arguments showing that there are very large epistemic and social obstacles standing in the way of actual moral convergence, and that we should not expect overall convergence to happen. Even if we could achieve convergence on principles like "respect for persons," it is unlikely that we could converge on the precise interpretation of that principle.

This may sound like a dismal conclusion, but one way of seeing it in a more positive light is by realizing that it is essentially the position we have taken since the inception of philosophical ethics among the pre-Socratics. Agreement has rarely been achieved in the theoretical realm, but that has not precluded genuine moral progress and agreement on concrete judgments. We may still not agree on exactly why chattel slavery is wrong, but is it not a sufficient cause for joy that most of us now have an unshakable belief that it is wrong, that laws are in force banning it, and that these laws are almost universally enforced?

In one sense, it would be strange indeed if we, at this precise moment in time, achieved what has eluded all of our philosophical forerunners—that is, an agreed-upon set of universal, content-full ethical principles.

Notes

1. The good-faith requirement is necessary, but, unfortunately, often absent from real-life moral discourse where participants often expect other people to change their views without themselves being willing to change.
2. We will here sidestep the issue of trying to define *religion* or *religious*.
3. Without necessarily assuming foundationalism.
4. In reality, we know that reaching agreement on the scope of the person concept at the beginning and end of life is highly contentious.
5. This is, of course, a quite general problem in ethics.
6. I here assume that there is more than one fundamental moral principle, although that is, of course, disputed.
7. As did Laskey et al. themselves if they thought that their actions were protected.

References

Andorno, R. 2002. "Biomedicine and International Human Rights Law: In Search of a Global Consensus." *Bulletin of the World Health Organization* 80: 959–63.

Audi, R., and N. Wolterstorff. 1997. *Religion in the Public Square*. Lanham, MD: Rowman & Littlefield.

Beauchamp, T., and J. Childress. 2009. *Principles of Biomedical Ethics*, sixth ed. New York: Oxford University Press.

Daniels, N. 2008. "Reflective Equilibrium." In *The Stanford Encyclopedia of Philosophy*, Fall 2008 ed., edited by Edward N. Zalta. Published April 28, 2003. http://plato.stanford.edu/archives/fall2008/entries/reflective-equilibrium/.

Faunce, T. A. 2005. "Will International Human Rights Subsume Medical Ethics? Intersections in the UNESCO Universal Bioethics Declaration." *Journal of Medical Ethics* 31: 173–78.

Harris, J. 2003. "Consent and End of Life Decisions." *Journal of Medical Ethics* 29: 10–15.

Holm, S. 2009. "Global Concerns and Local Arguments: How a Localized Bioethics May Perpetuate Injustice." In *The Philosophy of Public Health*, edited by A. Dawson, 63–72. Farnham: Ashgate.

Kant, I. 1985. *Fundamental Principles of the Metaphysics of Morals*. Translated by Thomas Kingsmill Abbott. http://en.wikisource.org/wiki/Groundwork_of_the_Metaphysics_of_Morals.

Luther, E. 1986. *Ethik in der Medizin*. Halle: Martin Luther Universität.

Macklin, R. 1998. *Against Relativism: Cultural Diversity and the Search for Ethical Universals in Medicine*. New York: Oxford University Press.

Mann, J. M. 1997. "Medicine and Public Health, Ethics and Human Rights." *The Hastings Center Report* 27, no. 3: 6–13.

Rawls, J. 1996. *Political Liberalism (With a New Introduction and the "Reply to Habermas")*. New York: Columbia University Press.

CHAPTER 5

Issues in Global Health Ethics

Udo Schüklenk

Abstract

This chapter provides a brief overview of major ethical challenges in international health. This overview aims to demonstrate that current health inequities are not simply an unfortunate incident, but that they are unjust and ought to be addressed. Among the issues reviewed is the question of whose moral responsibility global health resourcing is. What are the moral obligations, if any, of nation-states, international institutions, transnational NGOs, and large multinational corporations in this context?

Infectious disease control poses its own ethical challenges. HIV/AIDS and influenza will be used as examples of paradigmatic pandemic diseases that require a concerted global response. The next section of this chapter provides an overview of some of the salient ethical issues in infectious disease control, focusing initially on HIV/AIDS, before investigating the issues of standard of care in clinical trials in the Global South, as well as the question of access to experimental drugs in public health emergencies, such as the 2014–2015 Ebola virus disease outbreaks in West Africa.

This chapter will also take a closer look at the morality of health workers' migration issues. It is well known, for instance, that more Malawi trained health-care workers work in other countries than in Malawi itself. What are the moral obligations of health workers to the societies that enabled their training? What are the obligations of net recipient countries (usually located in the Global North)? Is free-riding on developing countries' training of health-care professionals ethically acceptable?

This chapter will conclude with a cursory discussion of at least some of the pertinent issues in international multicenter clinical research studies. Questions to be addressed include standards of care in a trial, as well as post-trial care with regard to both therapeutic and nontherapeutic clinical research.

Preventable Suffering and Global Health

Gross inequities in health treatment and health outcomes exist throughout the world. These inequities are determined by a complicated combination of local circumstances and international policies, and it is beyond the scope of this chapter to examine in detail the evidence relating to them. However, there is a clear geographic pattern: Health outcomes, health-care systems, and access to health care in the Global South fall far below the standards that are enjoyed by the Global North. This triggers important questions for all manner of academic disciplines, from economics to immunology to anthropology to public policy and beyond.

Many of the issues that arise have clear ethical dimensions, and I will consider some of the most relevant. Inequities between countries are inevitable. Some countries are stronger than others in terms of geographic area, natural resources, location, and population size. Such differences are unavoidable, and in broad terms are morally neutral. However, inequities in health outcomes and access to health care do not necessarily fall into the same category. Many, if not all, are the direct or indirect products of historical and/or contemporary exploitation in the form of colonialism and global economic policies.[1]

Why should we be concerned about health in the first place? Why does health matter? Even though having good health is not synonymous with living a happy or worthwhile life, there is a strong link between good health and the ability to pursue one's preferences: the satisfaction of preferences is made easier by good health and more difficult by illness. Improving health and access to health care, therefore, must be one priority for any initiative designed to prevent suffering and improve the quality of people's lives.

Those living in the Global South are disadvantaged in comparison to those living in the Global North. This is typically characterized by poorer health generally and worse morbidity and mortality.[2] However, it must be borne in mind that these suboptimal health outcomes are not simply a symptom of substandard health-care systems; they are typically also indicative of extreme poverty. Social inequality in societies with two-tier health-care systems or private health-care delivery infrastructure translates into significant differences in terms of health outcomes, and these differences are usually to the detriment of the poorer members of society.

Similarly, while investment in health services is obviously crucial to improving health outcomes, interventions in other policy areas can also lead to dramatic health improvements. For example, education, social inclusion, and safe and sanitary built environments have beneficial impacts on individual and public health. In some circumstances, these can improve health outcomes to a greater degree than clinical interventions. Basic primary care facilities in many developing countries can be more effective in terms of health outcomes than state-of-the-art facilities, such as high-tech transplant centers. When adjustments are made to account for population size and cost of living, developed countries spend approximately thirty times more per person on health care than developing countries.[3]

It is arguable that these international disparities are largely a consequence of the global economic system. A minority of the world's population lives with material abundance while a significant proportion suffer severe harm as a result of extreme poverty. It is morally significant that this harm—of which poor health outcomes is only one manifestation—is preventable: If the necessary resources to address global poverty were made available, much of this suffering could be avoided.

The relationship between global economics, poverty, and suffering was brought into sharp focus by the events following the earthquake that struck Haiti in January 2010. This earthquake caused devastating damage to towns, villages, and cities, and more than 150,000 Haitians were killed.[4] Much of the destruction, death, and suffering was preventable. Due to the extreme poverty in Haiti, its building safety standards are much lower than in the developed world, and buildings are therefore less resilient. If an earthquake of the same magnitude had struck Japan, for example, less damage would have been done to the built environment, and fewer people would have died or been injured.

The poverty in Haiti is preventable. At its root is interference by its formal colonizers and the United States.[5] When seen in this light, much of the suffering caused by the earthquake was not merely unfortunate; it was unjust. It was not so much a result of the—unavoidable—earthquake, but of the poverty that meant building safety standards in Haiti were as low as they were.

There is now widespread acceptance that the developed world has a moral obligation to address the suffering caused by extreme poverty by providing (health) aid to the developing world. As we shall see later in this chapter, different models of moral reasoning support this conclusion. There is disagreement about the nature and extent of this obligation—which specific harms should be addressed, and how aid interventions ought to be prioritized. Competing answers to these questions can translate into enormously divergent policy solutions. But before we take a closer look at these policy issues, it will be useful to examine and discuss the competing theoretical frameworks that underpin them.

Political Versus Humanitarian Rationales

A large proportion of aid to the developing world is delivered by means of intergovernmental transactions. These transactions involve the transfer of money, resources, or expertise by a government or intergovernmental organization in the developed world to governments in the developing world. The actors involved in delivering this type of aid are governments, but there is continuing disagreement among political philosophers about the question of whether the obligation to provide aid has its roots at the governmental level or whether this obligation actually belongs to individual citizens in the developed world. These competing ideas take a variety of forms, and they have been loosely categorized into two discrete strands.[6]

The first line of reasoning is the *political rationale*, which holds that the obligation to provide aid lies essentially with governments or nation-states. Pogge has suggested that governments or nation-states are responsible for providing aid as a form of reparation or compensation for historical wrongs.[7] This can be taken to mean, for example, that certain European countries have an ethical obligation to provide assistance to certain West African countries due to the manifold social, economic, and environmental harms inflicted on one country by another during colonialism. The political rationale goes beyond just compensation for past wrongs. It also addresses ongoing wrongs, such as foreseeable extreme poverty caused in the developing world by present global economic arrangements.

Some objections to the political rationale have been made. Firstly, the idea of international aid as reparation for specific, definable harms, if applied strictly, might unduly reduce the obligations of some nations in the developed world. That is, while some developed countries have a clear history of colonialism or exploitation, others do not. This latter group, with no clear history of exploitation, could claim that they are therefore not morally required to provide aid to the developing world.

Secondly, major changes to geopolitics mean that some of the nation-states involved in historical injustices no longer exist. This raises the problem of how aid transactions should be carried out on behalf of now-nonexistent developed countries, or as compensation to now-nonexistent countries in the developing world.

Thirdly, it might be possible to define some countries as being both the victims and the perpetrators of exploitation. This is particularly relevant in the case of countries with rapidly growing economies, such as China or South Korea, which once were part of the developing world but whose status in the global economy is now more accurately defined as "emerging" or "developed."

The political rationale is laudable in its intention to provide a theoretical basis upon which affluent governments in the developed world could be persuaded to alleviate suffering by providing support to under-resourced governments in the developing world. If accepted by developed governments, the political rationale would yield overseas aid policies that could have an enormous impact on the well-being of people living in the developing world, and this would undoubtedly be desirable. However, although the political rationale is capable of producing favorable outcomes, its scope is necessarily limited by its premises, and this is probably the most serious objection to it.

The political rationale holds that aid transactions should be seen as compensation for historical malfeasance on the part of developed world governments, but while it is true that there are good reasons for governments in the developed world to adopt this attitude, the political rationale alone cannot provide a sound theoretical basis for the type of aid necessary to alleviate suffering effectively.[8] For example, some preventable suffering has not come about as a result of colonialism or subjugation on the part of countries in the developed world. There are numerous instances in which developing countries have been devastated by natural disasters, civil war, or gross political mismanagement.

While it could be argued that the causes of some of these might actually be traced back to the developed world—climate change or oppressive foreign and economic policies, for instance—the causes of at least some of them are well and truly local. Earthquakes, tsunamis, volcanic eruptions, civil wars, and failed political systems can all result in extremely poor health conditions and desperate but preventable suffering. However, the political rationale states that, unless these conditions are linked to the behavior of developed world governments, there is no justice-based obligation to provide aid or assistance in such circumstances.[9] Consequentialists might beg to differ.

The governments of developed countries, according to the political rationale, have an obligation to provide aid to the developing world because of what has caused people's suffering, not simply by virtue of the fact that they are suffering. Those people who are starving as a result of political subjugation or military occupation should be afforded medical aid, but those who are starving because their crops have been obliterated by an earthquake should not. This picture seems incomplete, and indicates that the political rationale alone cannot provide a sufficiently plausible theoretical basis for the provision of medical aid to those who need it most. It requires that injustices should only be addressed when their causes can be traced to the behavior of governments in the developing world. But frequently the circumstances that are arguably most deserving of aid have no such cause. Moreover, the political rationale fails to offer any kind of guidance for the crucial task of prioritizing health aid. Severe health inequities exist within countries, as well as between them. Even in developed countries, there can be vast differences in health outcomes and health conditions between citizens. For example, the average life expectancy at birth of a man living in Kensington, an affluent area in London, is 84.3 years, whereas a man living in Glasgow, also in the United Kingdom, can on average expect to live 70.7 years.[10]

Since the central tenet of the political rationale is that governments have an obligation to address the inequities brought about by their behavior, domestic inequities must also be considered. The political rationale offers no guidance on how competing domestic and overseas demands on public funds should be resolved, and therefore leaves an important policy question unanswered. It is possible that the political rationale could require the prioritization of domestic needs ahead of overseas needs, perhaps even to the outright exclusion of any overseas interventions. It is probably fair to suggest that, although the suffering prevalent in developed countries can be serious and should be addressed, it is rarely as serious as the suffering experienced by those in absolute poverty in the developing world.[11]

The scope of the political rationale is far narrower than that which can reasonably be expected of a comprehensive approach to global health ethics. It provides no satisfactory answers to the question of how aid should be prioritized. The *humanitarian rationale*, on the other hand, sees individual citizens as the relevant moral agents in obligations to provide overseas aid. At first glance, this approach might seem counterintuitive: Although individuals can and do make contributions to charities, currently the main actors in the provision of global aid are governments. But perhaps this is simply a matter of practicality. The size and complexity of overseas aid payments means that they ought to be decided and negotiated by governments and the transactions involved should be carried out by governments, but this does not mean that the relevant moral actors are governments. The humanitarian rationale argues this very point, and suggests that governments are acting as a necessary proxy for transactions between the morally responsible individual citizens in the countries involved.

According to this logic, when the Australian government makes an aid payment to support a public health initiative in Sudan, for example, this is a manifestation of a payment by the citizens of Australia to the citizens of Sudan. The obligation to provide aid in this scenario does not belong to the Australian government but to the Australian people, and the obligation requires that aid is provided to the people of Sudan, not to the Sudanese government. The fact that the transaction is carried out by governments is merely a matter of expediency.

The humanitarian rationale has at its root the principle of moral equivalence, or "universal undifferentiated moral standing."[12] This principle, simply put, asserts that every person has an equal claim to moral consideration. This thought is at the heart of the liberal tradition and has been central to many civil rights agendas. The humanitarian rationale asserts that in principle, each person has a moral relationship with every other person, regardless of nationality or country of residence. This notion is strongly associated with the utilitarian tradition. It sees suffering or the prevention of the pursuit of preferences as harmful, and therefore as having negative moral value.

We have a moral obligation to relieve suffering or barriers to preference satisfaction whenever doing so does not involve comparable risks to ourselves. When applied to the issue of global suffering, this view argues that those living in the developed world are morally obliged to prevent harm to those living in the developing world until the point that by doing so they would cause greater harm to themselves. However, the present distribution of resources is so distorted that such a tipping point is very unlikely to come about anytime soon. Interestingly, some empirical estimates assert that sufficient resources could be diverted to address global poverty without bringing about any appreciable difference to the quality of life of those living in the developed world.[13]

It has been argued that geographic or political borders provide useful and ethically significant demarcations in deciding the boundaries of moral groups.[14] This view is supported by the fact that evolutionary pressure seems to support a preference for assisting members of one's family or one's immediate community over assisting strangers or people living on the other side of the world. However, although there are undoubtedly strong evolutionary reasons for human beings holding this kind of instinctive attitude, it does not stand up to much ethical scrutiny; good ethics does not always conform to our moral instincts, but explores them and sometimes requires us to act in opposition to them.

Some of the greatest ethical triumphs in recent history were cases in which the instinct to attribute special moral status to those in our immediate social groups was overcome: the abolition of slavery, universal franchise, and the vast majority of civil rights movements. Our moral group is expanding and becoming more inclusive; people who were historically excluded because of sex, skin color, sexual orientation, or worldview have been gradually admitted to the group. The rationale used for making these changes is applicable to those who as yet are not part of the established moral group. In the case under consideration, it is an argument against exclusion based on geographic location, and requires that we do not recognize geographic or political borders as having special moral relevance.

Poor access to health resources, prolonged sickness, and premature death are very common phenomena in the developing world, and clearly these involve preventable suffering and lost quality life years. They also constitute important hindrances to economic development. In the developing world, much sickness and premature death is easily preventable. It is caused by treatable conditions, many of which are very effectively contained in the developed world. The question of providing aid to the developing world is therefore largely one of resource allocation priorities: Could the developed world provide health-care assistance to the developing world without incurring a comparable risk to itself? I have no doubt that it could.

As has been established, the political rationale cannot quite provide a sufficient theoretical basis for the type of interventions required to address global suffering satisfactorily. A reconceptualization of the nature of the moral obligation based on the humanitarian rationale yields more plausible results. The humanitarian rationale proposes that inhabitants of the developed world have an obligation to provide aid to the peoples of the Global South who are suffering preventable harm regardless of the particular political or economic explanations for the suffering in question. Importantly, this approach also requires that those in the Global South who have the means to reduce preventable suffering also act on their moral obligations.

But the humanitarian rationale is faced with a challenge concerning scope. For example, how much aid is the developed world obliged to provide to the developing world? An initial response might be to consider calculating the degree of need in each case. The obligation then would be to provide as much aid as is necessary to alleviate the problem, based on need, so long as doing so does not create a comparable disadvantage to those living in the developed world.

Given how overwhelming the need is, it might be a more defensible approach to focus instead on doing maximal good—that is, to focus on achieving the best possible health outcomes with the limited resources available. This may well mean that those with the greatest needs might not be served first. If the needs-based, or the health-outcomes-based models were to become policy in the developed world, it would yield overseas aid interventions on a far larger scale than anything that has been implemented to date. Despite the persuasive case for this type of reallocation of resources, it is difficult to see an immediate radical change to overseas aid. In the case of government spending, for example, even the most generous nations currently allocate only a tiny proportion of their GDP to overseas aid.[15]

International Financial Arrangements

Aid payments to the developing world must be considered in the global economic context. Of particular significance is a system of governmental loans that was implemented in the 1970s and 1980s, ostensibly to help developing world countries to alleviate acute health and wider social problems by investing in their domestic infrastructure. A number of countries in Latin America and the Caribbean took substantial loans from various international financial organizations, such as the World Bank and the International Monetary Fund, for this purpose, but there were specific conditions attached to the loans that affected the ways in which they could be used. These conditions were primarily concerned with policy reforms in the recipient countries and required them to adopt neoliberal economic policies and to implement corresponding political and economic instruments. These conditions, attached to the World Bank loans, have in many cases crippled health-care services in the recipient countries and have prevented the kind of reform and investment for which the loans were initially intended; in fact, in some cases the current system is no better than the old system.

While it might in some circumstances be desirable to attach such conditions for structural or policy reform to aid payments, these conditions must be sensitive to existing local cultural and political systems.

Perhaps the most damaging consequence of these conditions was the requirement that health services in the recipient countries became privatized. This undid much of the good work that had previously been done, particularly in containing endemic diseases. Furthermore, recipient governments were required to employ expensive overseas consultants in order to establish and manage the new privatized health systems, which was a particularly inefficient use of the loans. In certain countries, a long-term effect of the privatized health-care requirement imposed by the loans has been the emergence of vastly unequal multitiered systems, in which all patients must pay for health care. In such systems, the rich minority of the population have access to health resources that are far superior to those available to the poor majority. It is difficult to see how such situations—or the policies underpinning the loans that created them—can be ethically justified, although there have been various unsuccessful attempts to do so.[16]

Access to Treatment

While differences in terms of health outcomes and provision exist both between and within countries in both the developing world and the developed world, there is a clear division between even the best-performing developing countries and the worst-performing developed countries. It is possible to make a few general observations about the differences between the two.

The average life expectancy of someone living in the developing world is shorter than that of a person living in the developed world. A person living in the developing world is more likely to spend a greater proportion of his or her life in ill health. Medical conditions that are easily treatable in the developed world go untreated in the developing world, and access to vaccines, medicines, and other medical treatment is worse, in comparison. The types of illnesses encountered and the particular social contexts in which they exist make approaches to health policy in the developing world different from approaches in the developed world, in significant respects. Easily preventable diseases, such as diarrhea and influenza, kill millions of people every year in the developing world. So why are vaccines and medicines not made available to those who need them in the developing world?

The answer to this question has two parts. The first part has to do with affordability. Some treatments are simply too expensive for those living in the developing world. Governments cannot afford to purchase enough drugs for their citizens, and the citizens themselves cannot afford to pay for their own treatment. The second part of the answer has to do with logistics: In many cases the health-care infrastructure required to distribute medicines and organize mass vaccinations does not exist. Poor people in under-resourced countries either have no access to or cannot afford the simple treatments taken for granted in more affluent countries. Infectious diseases that are controlled or effectively eradicated in the developed world are rampant in the developing world because vaccines are too expensive and vaccination programs are not in place.

Drug prices are set by the pharmaceutical companies that develop and eventually sell the drugs. When a successful drug has been developed, it is protected by a patent that prevents the drug from being copied or produced by others. This system is designed to ensure that the company responsible for investing in the research and development of a drug can recoup the investment necessary to bring the drug to market and make a profit. For a pharmaceutical company to survive, its profits must at the very least cover the costs of all of its research and development programs, including those that are ultimately unsuccessful. In fact, it is the incentive of substantial profits that motivates the pharmaceutical companies to undertake expensive research and development in the first place. Predictably, the pharmaceutical industry defends the system of patents and pricing by arguing that it serves the public interest: The development of new and better medical products depends upon commercial incentives for pharmaceutical companies to undertake drug research and development in the first place. While this might seem reasonable at first glance, the idea that pharmaceutical companies are motivated by the public interest does not bear much scrutiny.

Pharmaceutical companies that hold patents on new medicines refuse to supply customers who cannot afford to pay their prices, thus effectively precluding access in much of the developing world. Furthermore, patent holders frequently refuse to grant licenses to other companies that would produce and supply the same drugs at a reduced cost and aggressively pursue legal action against companies that breach patents.[17] The result is usually that a new drug does not become available in the developing world until after the patent has expired, normally ten or more years after it has been granted. The patent holders cannot expect to make much profit from sales in large parts of the developing world while they hold the patent, and they certainly will not do so once the patent has expired. The profit on a new medicine comes almost exclusively from its sale in the developed world; making patented drugs available in the developing world could harm the profit margins of its developer.

Perhaps the pharmaceutical industry has reason to be concerned that forgoing the patents in the developing world might mean that unlicensed versions of a drug become available in the developed world, thus impacting on profits. However, strict regulation of production and supply could prevent this from occurring. Pharmaceutical companies genuinely motivated by notions of public interest might reasonably be expected to make patented drugs available in the developing world, albeit under strict regulatory conditions. But it would be unreasonable to expect pharmaceutical companies to act altruistically. It is not trivially true that shareholders of pharmaceutical companies should subsidize research that, according to both the humanitarian and political models, is the responsibility of all well-off citizens in the developed world. Pharmaceutical companies have fiduciary responsibilities to their shareholders to maximize profits, and to prioritize the public interest ahead of commercial interest might conflict with these responsibilities. If pharmaceutical companies were concerned more with the public interest than with profits, shareholders might prefer to invest in other industries, thus inhibiting the pharmaceutical industry's research capability, with harmful consequences for drug research and development.

Perhaps we should not expect them to undertake drug research on diseases most prevalent in the developing world unless those diseases are also prevalent in wealthy markets, or unless there are clear advance purchase commitments from motivated buyers. The lesson to be drawn from this analysis is this: If we think medicines ought to be developed for diseases prevalent in the developing world, then we should consider paying for these drugs in order to incentivize that research is undertaken on them. An argument can legitimately be had about the degree to which profits are derived from such drugs, but we cannot reasonably expect pharmaceutical companies to undertake this work purely altruistically.

The nature of existing health-care infrastructures in many developing countries would make large-scale treatment or vaccination initiatives very difficult and perhaps in some cases impossible. The establishment of working health-care infrastructures would go some way toward allowing the kinds of preventive and reactive treatment programs that could make a significant contribution to addressing persistent health problems in the developing world. However, some governments in the developing world consistently fail to invest in health care, and often prioritize military spending ahead of health-care spending.

This practice is going on at the time of writing in Zimbabwe, North Korea, and Myanmar, among others. This behavior is sometimes used as an argument against providing medical aid to these countries: If their own governments choose not to prioritize health spending, the developed world has no reason to step in to assist. However, as we have seen, the obligation to provide aid exists between individuals, and the humanitarian rationale, while condemning the prioritization of military spending over health spending, would require the developed world to provide health aid to people living in those countries whose governments neglect to do so.

Infectious Disease Control

Infectious diseases pose a direct threat to individuals as well as, if they spread efficiently, to the functioning of society at large. In the Global North, health-care systems are generally quite efficient in managing and controlling the spread of common infectious diseases. However, in the Global South, where health-care systems are less well developed and less comprehensive in their coverage, infectious diseases are more difficult to control.

HIV/AIDS is a paradigmatic example of this, and we need only compare the historical infection rates in Western and Central Europe with those in sub-Saharan Africa to see the extent of this problem.[18]If HIV/AIDS is permitted to continue to spread unchecked in the Global South, its already harmful consequences will worsen. The natural spread of HIV/AIDS has been reinforced in some parts of the Global South by unhelpful government interventions, such as the disastrous treatment and education policies of the HIV/AIDS–denying Mbeki administration in South Africa.[19] In the absence of a preventive vaccine for HIV, any successful initiative to control the disease would involve testing populations, treating those who are HIV-positive and taking measures to prevent further infections. Incidentally, treating those who are HIV-positive with highly active antiretroviral medicines would have another desirable effect: For all intents and purposes they would be rendered noninfectious. AIDS treatment would not only provide them with the means necessary to survive, it would also have effects comparable to a preventive vaccine in terms of the effective protection it provides to the sexual partners of the infected person, because they could not be able to acquire the virus from their infected sex partner.

Of course, implementing successful treatment initiatives requires both money and knowledge of one's infection. As far as the latter issue is concerned, such initiatives could potentially require significant infringements on the autonomy of those who get tested. Historically, these violations of individual autonomy were considered too severe to seriously consider the option of mandatory HIV testing.

Part of the rationale at the time was that even if those who were affected could have been identified, there was no effective treatment to reduce the fatalities caused by the disease.[20] However, today's treatments for HIV/AIDS are capable of preserving the lives of people with HIV/AIDS and eliminating the risk that they would infect others. The existence of these treatments casts serious doubt on the autonomy objection. Identifying those who are infected by HIV/AIDS and treating them could bring about enormous health benefits, and this might well be sufficient to override concerns about the potential violation of infected individuals' autonomy.

Let us consider a more complex version of this scenario, namely, the question of whether or not it might be good policy to introduce mandatory HIV testing for pregnant women in areas where there is a high prevalence of HIV. There is a 35 percent chance that an infant born to an HIV-positive woman will also be HIV-positive. The number of children infected during pregnancy by their mothers, worldwide, was estimated to be between 2.1 and 2.8 million in 2004.[21] However, a fairly simple treatment program for the mother and child exists that results in a reduction in mother-to-child transmission of 67.5 percent.[22]

Unfortunately, in many parts of the world where this type of intervention would be most effective due to a high prevalence of HIV, such as Botswana, being HIV-positive carries a stigma that can have fairly severe social consequences. It is conceivable that pregnant women in these circumstances would feel sufficient social pressure that they would avoid attending clinics where they would be mandatorily tested for HIV, thus defeating the purpose of mandatory testing. These social and cultural phenomena might make a policy of mandatory testing difficult, but not impossible, to deliver. For example, a mandatory testing program could aim to guarantee the confidentiality of the HIV status of mothers and newborns in an attempt to minimize such stigmatization and its concomitant negative consequences. Unfortunately, on current treatment modalities it would be difficult for those women who are HIV-positive to preserve their anonymity while undergoing treatment.

While such operational challenges are certainly important, there is a prior debate regarding the ethical acceptability of mandatory HIV testing for pregnant women. A rigorous set of conditions has been proposed[23] that must be met in order for mandatory testing to be ethically justifiable. A pregnant woman must have voluntarily decided to carry her fetus to term, in full knowledge of available alternatives including abortion. A pregnant woman is not morally obliged to carry and deliver a fetus that she does not want.

However, when a pregnant woman does voluntarily decide to carry a fetus to term, she arguably accepts an obligation not to injure the fetus and to take reasonable steps to prevent it from being subjected to serious risk of bodily harm, such as a life-threatening HIV infection. Pregnant women therefore could be seen to have an obligation to ensure that they do not transmit HIV to their fetus, and this would require that the HIV status of the mothers is established.

Poor health resources and fragmented medical advice and treatment might make such a policy difficult to implement in the developing world. Pregnant women in developing countries might not have sufficient access to alternatives to pregnancy, and therefore a decision to carry a fetus to term might not always be voluntary. The obligations that apply to genuinely voluntary pregnancies would not apply in such cases. Substandard health care in the developing world could mean that pregnant women engage with health professionals too late in their pregnancies for abortion to be viable. This, again, might alter the voluntariness of a pregnancy and therefore any obligations that it implies.

The second condition for justifiable mandatory testing is that HIV-positive women who undergo mandatory testing and successfully deliver their children must be given access to life-preserving antiretroviral medication for themselves. This would mean that the mothers would be more likely to be well enough to look after their children, considerably improving the children's chances of survival. Furthermore, it would reduce the pressure on developing countries that are already struggling to cope with huge numbers of AIDS orphans.

However, participation in such an initiative would have to be voluntary since it would be impractical to enforce or supervise the women's adherence to antiretroviral treatment. Women who undergo some antiretroviral treatment but who do not continue to receive it can develop drug-resistant strains of HIV. This could have serious health consequences not only for the women concerned, but also for any future children that they may choose to have, and indeed, for their sexual partners if they practice unsafe sex. Likewise, there are significant societal-level health implications of introducing drug-resistant strains of HIV.

The third condition is that the anonymity of pregnant women and their children should be maintained throughout and after the pregnancy, for the reasons outlined above. This would likely constitute a formidable operational challenge to health authorities.

Antiretroviral treatment has the potential to make a significant impact not only on MTCT (mother-to-child transmission of HIV), but also on the global spread of HIV/AIDS. Enormous amounts of time and resources have been invested in trying to develop a preventive vaccine for HIV, but to no avail. However, as mentioned already, as well as preserving the lives of those who are HIV-infected, long-term treatment with modern antiretroviral medications can render patients effectively noncontagious.[24]

The combination of better health and a reduced chance of infecting others is likely to provide a strong incentive for at-risk individuals to seek testing and, for those who are HIV-positive, treatment. This incentive would be stronger still if it was accompanied by changes to the legality of unsafe sex and a shift in the cultural attitudes toward HIV-positive individuals in both the developed and the developing world. By removing these legal and cultural barriers, at-risk individuals would be more willing to get tested. This in turn would allow health-care agencies to quantify and track the incidence of HIV/AIDS, and to contain it by rigorous treatment with antiretroviral medication.

Medical Research and Care for Research Participants

A substantial amount of research into the development of new medical products takes place in the Global South and involves citizens of developing countries as research participants. Such research is most often carried out by pharmaceutical companies based in the Global North, and the imbalance in power between these countries and the communities and individuals involved in research raises a number of ethical concerns about the potential exploitation of research participants in the Global South.

One of the most controversial issues in international research ethics concerns the standard of clinical care that should be afforded to research participants. The central issue is whether participants in the control arms of an international, multicenter trial should be given the same treatment, regardless of their geographic location, or whether they should be given the best locally available treatment. This issue has triggered more than a decade of heated debate among the international bioethics community, following ACTG 076, an AIDS clinical trial that set out to establish whether an affordable treatment that would reduce the incidence of MTCT could be developed for use in the developing world.

Previous trials in the Global North had demonstrated that pregnant mothers who used particular treatment regimens were much less likely to pass HIV on to their offspring than those pregnant women who took no medication. At the time of ACTG 076, therefore, a successful gold standard of care had been established in the Global North, but it was unaffordable to most pregnant women in poorer countries. The investigators in ACTG 076 tested a lower, less expensive, dosage of the drug. The trial sought to find out whether a lower dosage was more effective than no treatment at all, not whether it was more effective than the higher dosage used in the developed world. Those in the treatment arm of the trial received the lower dosage while those in the control arm received a placebo. The trial design was heavily criticized by medical scholars and ethicists,[25] because it contravened what was at the time one of the basic proscriptions of the World Medical Association's Declaration of Helsinki,[26] which required that those in the control arm of clinical trials are given access to the best available therapeutic and diagnostic techniques. This would have required that everyone in the control arm, regardless of their geographic location, should receive the gold standard treatment; only in the absence of a gold standard does a placebo control become acceptable, as a means to test the null hypothesis.

However, some defended the trial methodology and suggested that the Declaration of Helsinki was mistaken and should be revised to allow this type of trial. They pointed out that since pregnant women in the developing world had no access to the gold standard drug, the women in the control arm were no worse off than they would have been if they had not participated in the trial, while those in the treatment arm were likely to be better off. However, this justification is problematic. It makes little sense in clinical terms, since the purpose of most drug trials is to see how the trial drug performs against the gold standard drug, not poorer or no treatments.

Critics of the Helsinki Declaration argue that, if it were followed strictly, all new treatments would have to be tested against the best medication available anywhere in the world, even if such a medication was unaffordable for a large proportion of the global population. This would effectively prohibit trials designed to develop treatments that would be affordable in poorer countries. However, both of these defenses rely on a controversial premise—that drugs are by some law of nature too expensive for people in the developing world to afford them. The reality, however, is that they are only too expensive because of the high prices demanded by pharmaceutical companies. The distinction between local and global standards of care is artificial, and any argument based on it is arguably flawed.[27] The proposition here really is that it is justifiable to design clinical trials that provide knowingly suboptimal care to participants because of economic considerations. The trial is not motivated primarily by a scientific question; rather, it hopes to address an economic question.

A related issue concerns the post-trial clinical care that should be provided to research participants in the developing world. After all, part of the ethical rationale of clinical research in developed countries is that patients, including those enrolled in the trial, would be able to access the drug that was tested successfully in a trial. Due to the cost issues mentioned earlier in this chapter, the same cannot be said for trial participants in the developing world. This raises the possibility of exploitation, as well as the question of whether special provisions ought to be made with regard to post-trial access to medicines.

The Declaration of Helsinki requires that any benefits resulting from clinical research should be made available to the individuals and communities that are involved in the research. This could be taken to mean that research participants should remain on that medication that the trial finds is the most effective, whether it is the trial drug or the best existing alternative. However, it has been argued that such a policy would be unaffordable in the Global South, and that it might prevent valuable research from taking place. Trial sponsors might be unwilling to undertake a whole range of research projects if they can foresee that they would be burdened with such high post-trial care costs. The economics involved are complicated, but there is reason to believe that this argument is inaccurate.[28]

It perhaps says something about the motivations of global pharmaceutical companies that the debates about standards of care can often—if not always—be reduced to calculations of profitability. But, as we have seen, it would be difficult to expect the pharmaceutical industry to stop behaving in accordance with profit motives. They have their own fiduciary obligations vis-à-vis their shareholders to contend with.

Medical Research in Infectious Disease Outbreaks

The issue of placebo controls in clinical research returned with a vengeance during the 2014–2015 Ebola virus disease (EVD) outbreak in Liberia, Sierra Leone, and Guinea. At the time, no successful therapeutic means existed to treat people with high-viral-load EVD. The infection resulted in a fast-acting catastrophic illness, rendering patients during the final stages of disease progression highly infectious. Unlike in the case of the HIV-infected pregnant women in sub-Saharan Africa, a placebo control in clinical trials involving such patients is more readily defensible given that no gold standard of care exists. One would need to find out initially whether a particular unregistered medical intervention that is tested is better than doing nothing, achieves the same, or might even be worse than doing nothing. Catastrophically ill patients could still be harmed by a drug that does more harm than good to them.

A contested ethical issue has been whether it is ethically defensible to offer patients access to experimental agents as a last attempt at preserving their lives. The stakes are high, and the odds are also high that such drugs will fail.[29] A panel convened by the World Health Organization (WHO) during the EVD outbreak agreed that it would be ethically justifiable to use such drugs.[30] However, it is one thing to argue that it would be justifiable to *offer* such drugs to patients, provided they gave true first-person voluntary consent as an indication of their willingness to take their chances with such agents. It is quite another thing to claim that such patients also have a moral claim to access such experimental drugs.

Some authors have argued that catastrophically ill patients have a moral claim right to such drugs because in the absence of such a claim right, they could not be considered true volunteers in placebo-controlled trials. The ethical argument here, much abbreviated, goes like this: It is a cornerstone of research ethics (and research regulations the world over) that patients, if they have the capacity to do so, must be asked for their first-person voluntary informed consent to trial participation. If the only way for catastrophically ill patients to access an experimental—last chance—agent is in a placebo-controlled clinical trial, they are arguably made this coercive offer: If you want a 50/50 chance of accessing the experimental agent tested in this trial, you must accept the randomization procedure that is part of the trial design.

This offer is arguably coercive because patients are unable to access the experimental drug without trial participation. Many patients would likely not wish to be randomized into the placebo arm, knowing what essentially amounts to nontreatment for the underlying infection will mean for their survival probabilities. To ensure that those patients who opt to participate in the trial are true volunteers, it has been argued, it is necessary to provide them with an alternative access route to the experimental agent.[31]

Against such a view count several considerations, chief among them that medical progress would likely be delayed, because it would take longer to recruit a sufficient number of patient volunteers for trial participation. Of concern is also the fact that such experimental drugs are typically in short supply, unless they are off-label uses of existing cheap medicines, so if a drug manufacturer had to produce additional quantities to provide to non-trial participants, they might decide that the costs are too high for such an endeavor, given the high probability that the drug will fail.

Migrant Health-Care Workers

As we have seen, the problem of global health inequities is largely one of affordability and resource allocation. Developing world governments usually do not have the fiscal resources to provide health care that is comparable to wealthier countries like Canada or the United Kingdom, whose public health-care systems are able to provide a higher standard of health care for their citizens. Sometimes it is the case that these governments could deploy additional resources toward their health-care systems, but they choose to prioritize spending in other areas like national defense or infrastructure development.

A significant part of the problem is that developing countries do not have enough health-care workers to be able to deliver the requisite services. Of course, since the COVID-19 pandemic, the scarcity of health-care workers is also a growing phenomenon in the Global North. This has significant consequences for countries in the Global South that try to maintain a well-staffed local workforce. The market for health-care workers is global, after all, much like in other areas of the economy.

It is here where the widespread migration of health workers from developing countries to developed countries comes into play. This is unsurprising. Even the United States does not train a sufficient number of nurses to cover its needs, but relies on recruiting nurses from other parts of the world. Nurses, doctors, and other health professionals who train in the developing world frequently go on to spend the majority of their career working in developed countries. Fewer than one-fifth of the total number of doctors and nurses in the world work in developing countries, and one in five doctors who received their training in the developing world works in the developed world.[32]

The incentives for health-care workers are clear: Global North countries promise an overall better standard of living for them and their family members. Higher wages mean that they can send a proportion of their salary back home to support their wider family. Furthermore, a large proportion of health spending in the developed world focuses on the control of HIV/AIDS and other infectious diseases, so health-care workers whose specialty is not infectious disease management have a better chance of finding work overseas than at home. When viewed in a global context, this situation is harmful; it exacerbates rather than mitigates the disparities in global health.

One proposed solution to the problem of the migration of health-care workers places an obligation on three distinct groups: recruiters and policymakers in the developed world; international medical aid organizations; and health-care workers from the developing world themselves.[33] Each of these groups has voluntarily contributed to the problem and is therefore morally responsible for addressing it. The contribution of Global North governments and policymakers lies both in their willingness to freeload by accepting cheap skilled labor from the Global South, and in allowing shortages of health-care professionals in their labor markets.

Responsible governments in the Global North should train enough health-care professionals to staff their own health-care systems, thus removing the need to source labor from the Global South. Arguably, the Global North should compensate nations of the Global South for the health-care workers poached from them—for example, by supporting an educational infrastructure that produces an oversupply of health-care workers. While some governments in the Global North recognize this moral responsibility and have taken steps to address it,[34] the problem remains. The obligation of recruiters operating in the Global South lies in not contributing to the overall harmful consequences already caused by the migration of health care workers. Responsible recruitment policies would rule out proactively recruiting from countries with critically low numbers of health-care professionals. Rather, recruitment should be limited to recruiting individuals only when there is a surplus of professionals with comparable skills or specialisms in their home countries.

To suggest that health-care workers themselves have an obligation not to migrate seems at first glance problematic, placing a moral restriction on their ability to pursue a better life for themselves and their families. However, perhaps migration should be allowed only after health-care workers have spent a reasonable amount of time working in their home countries, perhaps giving enough service to pay back some or most of the cost of their training. Such policies exist in some countries, such as South Africa, and are similar to those that operate in some European countries, whose armed forces pay for the training of doctors in return for a period of military service when they qualify.

A sensible system of migration for health-care workers would ensure that there was a net gain, at least in the short and medium terms, to the Global South. It would also incorporate a system of compensation, whereby the countries that benefit from migration provide financial or in-kind reparations to Global South countries that provide the workers. This might include exchange programs for students and early-career professionals; access to equipment, facilities, training, and scholarly resources; and a commitment to direct more research into those medical issues affecting the developing world.

Conclusion

This chapter has covered some of the most challenging issues in global health ethics. However, it should not be seen as an exhaustive. Space constraints have forced me to omit some very important issues, such as transplant tourism and resource prioritization during global pandemics. I have highlighted that numerous injustices exist in global health-care resourcing, and that they are characterized by a clear and consistent recurring division between the resource-poor world and the more affluent world. These problems are not simply accidents of nature. They are to a large extent the product of the historical exploitation of the peoples of the Global South that is reinforced by unfair current global economic policies.

This is not to deny that globalization has also brought benefits to people living in the Global South. It seems clear, however, that whatever ethical analysis one wishes to avail themselves of, people in the Global North—and this now includes large numbers of well-off citizens in countries such as India and the People's Republic of China—have moral obligations to assist those in the developing world by providing health aid and, arguably, by restructuring global trade and financial arrangements.

Notes

1. T. W. Pogge, *World Poverty and Human Rights*, 2nd ed. (Cambridge: Polity, 2008).
2. C. Mather, et al., "Global Patterns of Healthy Life Expectancy in the Year 2002," *BMC Public Health* 4 2004: 66, doi:10.1186/1471-2458-4-66.
3. G. J. Schreiber, P. Gottret, L. K. Fleisher, and A. A. Leive, "Financing Global Health: Mission Unaccomplished," *Health Affairs* 26(4) 2007: 921–34, doi:10.1377/hlthaff.26.4.921.
4. "Haiti Capital Earthquake Death Toll 'Tops 150,000,' " *BBC News*, January 25, 2010, http:// news.bbc.co.uk/2/hi/americas/8477770.stm.
5. P. Farmer, M. C. Smith, and P. Nevil, "Unjust Embargo of Aid for Haiti," *Lancet* 361 (2003): 420–23.
6. C. Lowry and U. Schüklenk, "Two Models in Global Health Ethics," *Public Health* 2(3) 2009: 276–84, doi:10.1093/phe/php032 global bioethics.indb 267.
7. Pogge, *World Poverty and Human Rights.*
8. Lowry and Schüklenk, "Two Models in Global Health Ethics."
9. J. Narveson, "We Don't Owe Them a Thing! A Tough-Minded But Soft-Hearted View of Aid to the Faraway Needy," *The Monist* 86(3) 2003: 419–33.
10. Office For National Statistics, "Big Variation in Life Expectancy," modified October 21, 2009, http://news.bbc.co.uk/1/hi/health/8317986.stm.
11. P. Singer, *The Life You Can Save: Acting Now to End World Poverty* (London: Picador, 2009), 8, 12.
12. Lowry and Schüklenk, "Two Models in Global Health Ethics."
13. Singer, *The Life You Can Save: Acting Now to End World Poverty*, chapter 10.
14. P. Collier, "A New Alms Race to Help the World's Poor," *Observer,* March 15, 2009, http://www.guardian.co.uk/books/2009/mar/15/poverty-life-save-peter-singer.
15. Singer, *The Life You Can Save: Acting Now to End World Poverty*, chapter 10.
16. U. Schüklenk, M. Kottow, and P. A. Sy, "Developing World Challenges," in *A Companion to Bioethics*, edited by H. Kuhse and P. Singer, 404–16 (Oxford: Wiley-Blackwell, 2009).
17. G. Anand, "Drug Makers Decry Indian Patent Law," *Wall Street Journal*, modified February 11, 2010.
18. UNAIDS, AIDS Epidemic Update 2009, November 2009, http://data.unaids.org/pub/Report/2009/JC1700_Epi_Update_2009_en.pdf.
19. P. Chigwerdre, G. R. Seage III, S. Gruskin, T.-H. Lee, and M. Essex, "Estimating the Lost Benefits of Antiretroviral Drug Use in South Africa," *Journal of Acquired Immune Deficiency Syndrome* 49(4) 2008: 410–15; U. Schüklenk, "Professional Responsibilities of Biomedical Scientists In Public Discourse," *Journal of Medical Ethics* 30 (2004): 53–60.
20. U. Schüklenk, "AIDS as a Global Health Emergency," in *A Companion to Bioethics*, edited by H. Kuhse and P. Singer, 441–54 (Chichester: Wiley-Blackwell, 2009).
21. UNAIDS, AIDS Epidemic Update 2005.
22. E. M. Connor, R. S. Sealing, R. Gelber, et al., "Reduction of Maternal Infant Transmission of Human Immunodeficiency Virus Type 1 with Zidovudine Treatment," *New England Journal of Medicine* 331 1994: 1173–80.
23. U. Schüklenk and A. Kleinsmidt, "Rethinking Mandatory HIV Testing during Pregnancy in High HIV-Prevalence Regions: Ethical and Policy Issues," *American Journal of Public Health* 97(7) 2007: 1179–83.
24. P. Vernaza, B. Hirschel, E. Bernasconi, and M. Flepp, "Les Personnes Séropositives Ne Souffrant D'aucune Autre Mst Et Suivant Un Traitement Antiretroviral Efficace Ne Transmettent Pas Le Vih Par Voie Sexuelle," *Bulletin des Médecins Suisse* 89(5) 2008: 165–69.

25. P. Lurie and S. M. Wolfe, "Unethical Trials of Interventions to Reduce Perinatal Transmission of the Human Immunodeficiency Virus in Developing Countries," *New England Journal of Medicine* 337(12) 1997: 853–56; U. Schüklenk and R. Ashcroft, "International Research Ethics," *Bioethics* 14(2) 2000: 158–72.

26. World Medical Association, "World Medical Association Declaration of Helsinki," 2008, http://www.wma.net/en/30publications/10policies/b3/17c.pdf.

27. U. Schüklenk, "The Standard of Care Debate: Against the Myth of an 'International Consensus Opinion,'" *Journal of Medical Ethics* 30 2004: 194–97.

28. Schüklenk, "AIDS as a Global Health Emergency."

29. M. Hay, D. W. Thomas, and J. L. Craighead, "Clinical Development Success Rates for Investigational Drugs," *Nature Bio-Technology* 32(1) 2014: 40–51; J. Arrowsmith, "Trial Watch: Phase 3 and Submission Failures 2007–2010," *Nature Reviews: Drug Discovery* 10(2) 2011, February: 87.

30. WHO, "Ethical Considerations for Use of Unregistered interventions for Ebola Virus Disease (EVD)," August 12, 2014, http://www.who.int/mediacentre/news/statements/2014/ebola-ethical -review-summary/en/. See also WHO, "Ethical Considerations for Use of Unregistered Interventions for Ebola Virus Disease (EVD): Report of an Advisory Panel to WHO," accessed August 7, 2017, http://apps.who.int/iris/bitstream/10665/130997/1/WHO_HiS_KER_GHE_14.1_eng.pdf.

31. U. Schüklenk and R. Smalling, "The Moral Case For Granting Catastrophically Ill Patients the Right to Access Unregistered Medical Interventions," *Journal of Law, Medicine & Ethics* 45(3) 2017: 382–91.

32. M. A. Clemens and G. Pettersson, "New Data on African Health Professionals Abroad," *Human Resources for Health* 6(1) 2008, doi:10.1186/1478-4491-6-1, http://www.human-resources-health .com/content/pdf/1478-4491-6-1.pdf.

33. Schüklenk et al., "Developing World Challenges."

34. Department of Health, Guidance on International Nursing Recruitment (London: department of Health, 1999), http://www.dh.gov.uk/prod_consum_dh/groups/dh_digitalassets/@dh/@en/documents/ digitalasset/dh_4034794.pdf.

CHAPTER 6

Rights of Persons with Disabilities from a Global Perspective

Akiko Ito

Abstract

This chapter provides an overview of the implementation phase of the United Nations Convention on the Rights of Persons with Disabilities (CRPD). It discusses the issues most pertinent for policymaking to support national implementation of the CRPD, with a focus on cultural rights. I draw from my involvement in the UN processes as chief of the secretariat for the Convention on the Rights of Persons with Disabilities at the UN to demonstrate how the conception of disability rights is part of international human rights law and policy.

Introduction

In this chapter, I analyze divergent constructions of disability and diverse approaches to equalizing opportunities for persons with disabilities. There has been an important shift in conceptualizing disability from the medical model to the socioeconomic/minority rights model (Hahn 1997); this latter model recognizes principles of bioethics. This reformulation of disability is one of the key driving forces behind the development of conceptual frameworks, and the establishment of the significant legal mechanisms related to disability and human rights.

The Convention on the Rights of Persons with Disabilities (CRPD) is a new and groundbreaking human rights tool that was designed to change society. The treaty, as will be discussed below, clearly applies to emerging issues such as mental health and psychological aspects of disability, as well as bioethics concerns related to disabilities. It is imperative that we pay more attention to cross-cultural or global dimensions of disability rights (Chen and Renteln 2023). I conclude with recommendations regarding the implementation of the CRPD, including mainstreaming disability rights into global priorities.[1]

Disability, Culture, and Emerging Issues

Prior to 1970, the United Nations approached disability issues from the perspective of a social welfare model. In its first ten years of work, the United Nations focused on promoting the rights of persons with physical disabilities. Its primary concern was the establishment of international bodies and the development of suitable operational programs to deal with disability issues in cooperation with non-governmental organizations. In the period from 1955 to 1970, the emphasis was on the goals of prevention and rehabilitation, but little attention was paid to obstacles created by specific institutions and society in general (UN Secretariat 1997, 14–15; Degener and Koster-Reese 1995; Kanter 2014).

The social welfare perspective emphasized helping those with disabilities fit into general societal structures. For example, a deaf person might only be taught how to read lips. New approaches stress modifications to the environment to promote the equalization of opportunities for persons with disabilities, e.g., providing sign language interpreters at public events. This new formulation emphasizes society's responsibility to remove barriers that underpin the exclusion of persons with disabilities and denial of their basic citizenship rights (Finkelstein 1980; Oliver 1983, 1990).

This approach sees persons with disabilities as constituting a minority group. According to Harlan Hahn, discrimination has historically isolated persons with disabilities as a minority group. In his view, "people with disabilities are a minority group because they have been the objects of prejudice and discrimination" (Hahn 1997, 47). Because discrimination occurs over time, it reinforces attitudes that, in turn, reinforce discrimination, thus becoming a vicious cycle. He considers *public attitudes* rather than physical limitations to be the primary source of difficulties facing persons with disabilities.

The minority-group model specifies that public policy shapes all facets of the environment. It considers government policies to be reflecting societal attitudes and values. As a result, existing features of architectural design, job requirements, and daily life that have a discriminatory impact on disabled citizens can't be viewed merely as happenstance or coincidence (Hahn 1997, 46).

Other scholars contend that a true human rights approach toward the issue of disability differs from approaches focusing on the environment (e.g., Rioux 1997).[2] In contrast to the environmental adaptation approach, which looks at ecological barriers, human rights approaches look at the rights to which all people, regardless of disability status, are entitled. It analyzes how society marginalizes people with disabilities and considers ways that the social environment can be changed (Oliver 1992).

Given these different perceptions of disability, the CRPD establishes a major conceptual break from earlier approaches, as seen in the World Programme of Action as well as the Standard Rules. It exclusively focuses on guaranteeing the human rights of persons with disabilities.[3] The CRPD addresses disability prevention and rehabilitation as an aspect of full and comprehensive *human rights protection* for persons with disabilities. As a result, prevention and rehabilitation are directed at ensuring equal access and making all public health programs accessible to persons with disabilities.

Drafters of the CRPD signaled that public health issues are not appropriately addressed within the framework of disability rights. The framework of disability rights would thus exclude public health issues, such as protecting the general population from infectious diseases, or implementing public safety policies, like road safety or industrial accident prevention. This tension is particularly pronounced in view of the CRPD. For that reason, its drafters explicitly adopted a comprehensive, rights-based understanding of disability rooted in the social context. The Convention wants to address the long-standing challenge of defining disability within a human rights and social model framework. Consequently, it does not specifically define disability.[4]

The CRPD Preamble took a different approach, by asserting that:

> Disability is an evolving concept and that disability results from the interaction between persons with impairments and attitudinal and environmental barriers that hinders their full and effective participation in society on an equal basis with others[5] . . . Persons with disabilities include those who have long-term physical, mental, intellectual or sensory impairments which in interaction with various barriers may hinder their full and effective participation in society on an equal basis with others[6] (see Article 1).

The Convention thus adopts a broad categorization of persons with disabilities. This moves away from the World Health Organization's more *medical orientation* and embraces a *social model* of disability, within which civil, political, economic, social, and cultural rights are enumerated and elaborated. Clearly, this is a major shift, with broad implications. In the next section, I will discuss cultural aspects that should be considered.

Cultural and Related Emerging Dimensions in Disabilities

Disability is closely associated with the environment according to the *social model*, as we saw in the discussion above. It is important to pay attention to cultural and anthropological aspects of disability, since they play key roles in the environment for persons with disabilities. This includes culturally sensitive implementation of the CRPD.

The United Nations has facilitated the implementation of regional years and decades on disability mechanisms—as seen in Europe's Year of the Disabled, the Asian and Pacific Decade of Disabled Persons, and the African Decade of Disabled Persons. These mechanisms can be more culturally sensitive than those at the international level. They also provide culturally appropriate opportunities for intraregional cooperation and technical assistance.

The CRPD recognizes the right of persons with disabilities to take part on an equal basis with others in cultural life (Article 30). This called for measures to ensure that persons with disabilities have access to: a) cultural materials in accessible formats; b) TV programs, films, theater, and other cultural activities, in accessible formats; c) places for cultural performances or services, such as museums, cinemas, libraries, and tourism services; and, as much as possible, d) monuments and sites of national cultural importance.

The CRPD calls for appropriate measures to enable persons with disabilities to have the opportunity to develop and utilize their creative, artistic, and intellectual potential. This is not only for their benefit, but also for the enrichment of society. In addition, the CRPD calls for States Parties to ensure that laws protecting intellectual property rights do not pose an unreasonable or discriminatory barrier to access by persons with disabilities to cultural materials (Lazar and Stein 2107). Persons with disabilities are entitled, on an equal basis with others, to the recognition and support of their specific cultural and linguistic identity, including sign languages and deaf culture. This chapter plays a key role in promoting culturally sensitive mainstreaming of disability into development priorities.

In the future, the mental, psychological, and emotional aspects of disability will be a key issue in development processes. Paying more attention to cultural, anthropological, and environmental determinants of disability will play a crucial role in determining the quality of life of persons with disabilities, as well as the effectiveness of policy implementation. Because persons with mental, psychosocial, or intellectual disabilities are often much marginalized, it is critical that we attend to these aspects of disability.

Bioethics in the Convention on the Rights of Persons with Disabilities

The CRPD asserts that "States Parties undertake to collect appropriate information, including statistical and research data, to enable them to formulate and implement policies to give effect to the present Convention." The process of collecting and maintaining this information "shall comply with internationally accepted norms to protect human rights and fundamental freedoms and ethical principles in the collection and use of statistics" (see Article 31.1.b). Given the importance of research and the protection of human subjects, not to mention the importance placed on the Nuremberg Code and the Declaration of Helsinki, attention needs to be directed to this area of the CPRD.

Similarly, the CPRD's position on respect for the family, the right to decide freely and responsibly on the number and spacing of their children and to have access to age-appropriate information, reproductive and family planning education are recognized. Moreover, the means necessary to enable them to exercise these rights are provided; and the right to retain their fertility on an equal basis with others is also specifically addressed (see Article 23).

Finally, the CPRD's statement on health holds that States Parties shall provide persons with disabilities with the same range, quality, and standard of free or affordable health care and programs as provided to other persons, including in the area of sexual and reproductive health and population-based public health programs (see Article 25). It is clear that the relationship between bioethics and disability requires greater attention (Ouellette 2011).

Implementation: Culturally Sensitive Mainstreaming into Millennium Development Goals

Prior to the successful adoption of the CRPD, the UN put other instruments into effect. At the global level, the UN has adopted the World Programme of Action as an international policy framework for disability-inclusive development. It has also adopted the Standard Rules for the equalization of opportunities, reaffirming the principles of inclusive policies, plans, and activities in development cooperation and providing further guidance on disability-inclusive measures.

The World Programme of Action, marking a "slow shift towards a rights-based model" of disability, is a hybrid instrument utilizing a human rights–oriented approach. It clearly articulates some of the core human rights issues of concern for persons with disabilities. At the same time, it reflects some of the more traditional conceptions of disability by focusing on disability prevention and rehabilitation. That said, it captures the social context of disability in observing that "It is largely the environment which determines the effect of an impairment or a disability on a person's daily life."[7]

The Standard Rules, while not legally binding, remain a practical framework in defining obstacles and barriers to equal opportunities for person with disabilities. It also helps target areas of action. These rules should serve as a guide to States that have not yet signed and ratified the CRPD. They could also be used to foster further integration of disability with the United Nations system against the fuller framework of the CRPD. This could then be used as an additional mandate for inclusion within and across the United Nations system.

Significance of the Convention on the Rights of Persons with Disabilities

The CRPD promotes both human rights and development, and is legally binding. It provides a comprehensive normative framework for mainstreaming disability in the development agenda, with new opportunities (Flynn 2011). Mainstreaming disability in development policies, processes, and mechanisms has been on the United Nations agenda for more than a quarter of a century. Since the mid-1990s, many development agencies, funds, and programs have taken significant steps to mainstream disability at the policy level. The Convention recognizes the importance of international cooperation and its promotion for the realization of the rights of persons with disabilities and their full inclusion into all aspects of life (see Article 32).

In particular, Article 32 stipulates that international cooperation measures should:

a. be inclusive of and accessible to persons with disabilities;
b. facilitate and support capacity-building, including through the exchange and sharing of information, experiences, training programs, and best practices;

c. facilitate cooperation in research and access to scientific and technical knowledge; and
d. provide technical and economic assistance, including by facilitating access to and sharing of accessible and assistive technologies, and through the transfer of technologies.

As the president of the General Assembly noted, the CPRD represents "a great opportunity to celebrate the emergence of comprehensive guidelines the world so urgently needs" (Al Khalifa 2006).[8] The World Programme of Action and the Standard Rules were important milestones toward developing a legally binding human rights convention that would apply human rights to persons with disabilities.

The Standard Rules contributed to the development of the CRPD in articulating accessibility as a priority area for targeted reforms. They also serve as a core component in achieving rights for persons with disabilities. The CRPD takes these and other concepts further, situating them within a framework that is comprehensive in its coverage of specific substantive rights and providing principles and obligations applicable to the achievement of civil, political, economic, social, and cultural rights.

Following these significant advances, the United Nations agencies, funds, and programs have started to mainstream disability in their development policies. For example,

- The UN Population Fund (UNPF; formerly the UN Fund for Population Activities) and WHO developed guidance notes on the sexual and reproductive health of persons with disabilities for their headquarters and regional and country offices, after UNPF's integration of disability in its Strategic Plan 2008–2013, as a cross-cutting issue that cut across most aspects of development.
- The Joint UN Programme on HIV/AIDS (UNAIDS) developed a policy brief on HIV and disability along with its ten co-sponsors.
- The UN Development Programme (UNDP) has started developing guidance notes on integrating disability into its development activities.

The development of processes and mechanisms to implement these policies is still underway. In addition, some United Nations agencies have yet to fully address the policy and implementation issues of mainstreaming disability, so there is still more work to be done.

The mainstreaming of disability in development cooperation is relatively new to most development partners. The Nordic countries and the United States (through the US Agency for International Development [USAID]) began the process of mainstreaming disability into their development cooperation during the 1990s. Australia, Austria, Canada, the European Union, Japan, New Zealand, and the United Kingdom have also started the integration of development in its policies. However, there has not been extensive experience in mainstreaming disability at the program level, so there has been little opportunity to evaluate best practices or share information on implementation.

Persons with disabilities comprise an estimated 10 percent of the world's population, with 80 percent living in developing countries. It is therefore an urgent priority to mainstream disability as a cross-cutting issue in development policies, and in processes and mechanisms at the global, regional, subregional, and national level. In order to achieve this, it is necessary to pay more attention to the emerging aspects of disability, such as culture and mental well-being.

The CRPD approach to disability and human rights is not a simple addition to international human rights mechanisms. It is groundbreaking in changing the global society with its social model perspective, its attention to accessibility for all, and its inclusion of persons with disabilities in all the processes of decision-making and implementation. Together with gender equalization efforts, and efforts to mainstream mental, psychological, and emotional aspects of development, the CRPD will play a key role in forming a new sustainable community and better quality of life for all people.

For more information, see https://www.un.org/development/desa/disabilities/about-us.html.

Notes

1. For United Nations reports and policies, see http://www.un.org/disabilities/default.asp?id=23. See also the appendix to this text on Human Rights and Disability Rights.
2. Marcia H. Rioux, "Disability: The Place of Judgement in a World of Fact," *Journal of Intellectual Disability Research* 41, no. 2 (1997), 102–11.
3. The CRPD in art. 1 provides: "The purpose of the present Convention is to promote, protect and ensure the full and equal enjoyment of all human rights and fundamental freedoms by all persons with disabilities, and to promote respect for their inherent dignity. . . ."
4. *See* CRPD, *supra* note 1 at Preamble, para. (e) and art. 1.
5. *Id.* at preamble, para. (e).
6. CRPD, *supra* note 1 at art. 1.
7. World Programme, para. 21.
8. Statement by H. E. Sheikha Haya Rashed Al Khalifa, President of the United Nations General Assembly, at the Adoption of the Convention on the Rights of Persons with Disabilities (December 13, 2006), *available online at* <http://www.un.org/ga/president/61/statements/statement20061213.shtml>.

References

Al Khalifa 2006 Statement by H. E. Sheikha Haya Rashed Al Khalifa, President of the United Nations General Assembly, at the Adoption of the Convention on the Rights of Persons with Disabilities (December 13, 2006), *available online at* <http://www.un.org/ga/president/61/statements/statement20061213.shtml>.

Chen, Cher Weixia, and Alison Dundes Renteln. 2023. *International Human Rights: A Survey.* Cambridge: Cambridge University Press. See chapter 10, "The Rights of Persons with Disabilities."

Finkelstein, Victor. 1980. *Attitudes and Disabled People.* New York: World Rehabilitation Fund.

Kanter, Arlene. 2014. *The Development of Disability Rights under International Law: From Charity to Human Rights*. London: Routledge.

Lazar, Jonathan, and Michael Ashley Stein (eds.). 2017. *Disability, Human Rights, and Information Technology*. Philadelphia: University of Pennsylvania.

Oliver, Michael. 1983. *Social Work with Disabled People*. Basingstoke, UK: Macmillan.

———. 1990. *The Politics of Disablement: Social Work with Disabled People*, Basingstoke, UK: Macmillan.

Ouellette, Alicia. 2011. *Bioethics and Disability: Toward a Disability-Conscious Bioethics*. Cambridge: Cambridge University Press.

Rioux, Marcia H. 1997. "Disability: The Place of Judgement in a World of Fact." *Journal of Intellectual Disability Research* 41, 2, 102–11.

Part I Internet Resources

THEORETICAL PERSPECTIVES

Moral Theory | Stanford Encyclopedia of Philosophy
https://plato.stanford.edu/entries/moral-theory

Bioethics | UNESCO
https://en.unesco.org/partnerships/partnering/bioethics

What Are the Most Common Ethical Theory Examples
https://overtimephilosophy.com/the-many-meanings-of-ethical-theories-and-principles

AMA Principles of Medical Ethics | American Medical Association
https://code-medical-ethics.ama-assn.org/principles

The 9 Nursing Code of Ethics Every Nurse Must Adhere To
https://www.nursingprocess.org/nursing-code-of-ethics-and-interpretive-statements.html

Principles of Clinical Ethics and Their Application to Practice
https://pubmed.ncbi.nlm.nih.gov/32498071

A Quick Guide to Ethical Theory in Healthcare: Solving Ethical Dilemmas
https://pubmed.ncbi.nlm.nih.gov/16556920

A Framework for Making Ethical Decisions | Science and Technology Studies
https://www.brown.edu/academics/science-and-technology-studies/framework-making-ethical-decisions

20 Most-Common Examples of Ethical Dilemmas in Nursing | Nursingprocess.org
https://www.nursingprocess.org/ethical-dilemma-in-nursing-examples.html

Stafford Library | Ethics Resource Guide: Ethical Theories
https://library.ccis.edu/ethics/theories

Thinking Ethically | Markkula Center for Applied Ethics
https://www.scu.edu/ethics/ethics-resources/ethical-decision-making/thinking-ethically

Applied Ethics
https://iep.utm.edu/applied-ethics/

Nuffield Council on Bioethics
https://www.nuffieldbioethics.org

United Nations World Enable
https://www.un.org/development/desa/disabilities/about-us.html

Part I Discussion Topics

THEORETICAL PERSPECTIVES

1. How can we bring in a range of voices and concerns to address injustice in health care?
   - What kinds of changes should occur in the training of doctors, nurses, and other caregivers to be more inclusive of different ethnicities and socioeconomic groups?
2. In chapter 1, Bernard Gert sets out the following moral rules that he thinks are universal: 1) Do not kill; 2) Do not deceive; 3) Do not cause pain; 4) Keep your promises; 5) Do not disable; 6) Do not cheat; 7) Do not deprive of freedom; 8) Obey the law; 9) Do not deprive of pleasure; and 10) Do your duty.
   - What do you think of his list? Would you make any additions or changes?
3. Gert argues that "Duties in [the] everyday sense are not derived from our common morality, but in each society, duties develop from social roles and from the history and practice of the professions in that society." This statement ties "duty" to social roles (which affect individuals) and professional roles (for medical personnel, researchers, etc.).
   - Are there any other things that shape our sense of duty?
4. In chapter 2 on universal morality, Tom L. Beauchamp notes: "True cultural relativists . . . subscribe to the thesis that no moral principles of any sort, general or particular, are valid independent of the cultural contexts in which they have arisen and shaped to their present form." Consider this: When there are language barriers, we turn to translators to ensure channels of communication are in place.
   - Should there be something like culture translators to enable better communication in the health-care setting? Share your thoughts and offer three to four recommendations as to how this might be achieved.
5. Tom L. Beauchamp points out that "It is often difficult to determine which group, society, or institution constitutes the culture that should be followed." For example, in pre-Taliban Afghanistan women were often well educated and worked in professions, but under the Taliban-imposed culture, they were not allowed to work or to seek an education beyond the age of eight. He then asks: "Should we say that women should be governed by either of these conflicting sets of norms?"
   - What do you think?

6. How much truth should doctors and nurses share with patients? To what degree should cultural values shape truth-telling?
7. The notion of the duty to inform usually focuses on diagnosis. The California case of *Arato v. Avedon* (1993) raised the issue of whether a doctor has to inform the patient of a dire prognosis. Mark A. Rothstein (2011) pushes the issue further, arguing that access to information is not as burdensome as it once was. He thus asserts that doctors have a duty to notify patients of new medical information. Share your thoughts as to whether we should change doctors' duties to inform, in light of Rothstein's observations:

    > Physicians generally have had no ethical or legal duty to notify patients about new medical information discovered after a visit, notwithstanding the health care benefits to patients that might flow from receiving the information. The rule was based on the relatively high burdens that notification would impose on physicians compared with the likelihood of benefits to patients. This established view, however, no longer may be appropriate in light of new physician–patient relationships and the reduced burden of patient notification using new types of health information technology (HIT). As a result, there is a duty to inform patients and former patients about relevant, medical development subsequent to their episode of care. ("Physician's Duties to Inform Patients of New Medical Discoveries: The Effect of Health Information Technology," *Journal of Law, Medicine, and Ethics* 39, 4, 2011)

8. Is there a way to mediate disputes around bioethical issues to go beyond the traditional debate (or adversarial) model? Not all moral problems have a clear "winner."
    - Offer two or three ideas for constructing or applying a mediation model.
9. Søren Holm asks if global bioethics requires a global *moral* language. What do you think? Would that help address cultural or other obstacles we might face?
10. When looking at theoretical perspectives of health care, we need to consider how we define our terms. Look, for example, at the controversy over the eighteen-year-old Montreal swimmer Victoria Arlen, a Paralympic gold medalist in the 100-meter freestyle. Arlen spent almost two years in a coma and is now confined to a wheelchair. On August 10, 2013, she was disqualified from the Paralympic Swimming World Championships in Montreal due to "insufficient evidence to suggest there was a permanent impairment," according to Craig Spence, the Paralympic committee spokesperson (see Rachel Lau, "Swimmer and Olympic Gold-Medalist Disqualified for Not Being 'Disabled' Enough," *Global News*, August 14, 2013).
    - Share your thoughts on whether Arlen should have been disqualified.
    - Offer a working definition of disability for swimmers in the Paralympics.

Part II

HUMAN RIGHTS

CHAPTER 7

Bioethics and Human Rights: A Historical Perspective

Robert Baker

> The sacred rights of Mankind are not to be rummaged for among old parchments or musty records. They are written, as with a sunbeam, in the whole volume of human nature by the hand of Divinity itself, and can never be erased or obscured.
>
> —Alexander Hamilton, 1787[1]

Bioethics and human rights were conceived in the aftermath of the Holocaust, when moral outrage reenergized the outmoded concepts of "medical ethics" and "natural rights," renaming them "bioethics," and "human rights," to give them new purpose. Originally, principles of bioethics were a means for protecting human rights, but through a historical accident, bioethical principles came to be considered as fundamental. In this chapter I reflect on the parallel development and accidental divorce of bioethics and human rights to urge their reconciliation.

The 1948 UN Declaration: From the Rights of Man to Human Rights

The immediate precursor to "human rights" are the *droits de l'homme*, the "natural, inalienable, and sacred rights of man" to "liberty, security, property, and resistance to oppression" declared by the French Republic in 1789.[2] The rights, in turn, derive from the God-given inalienable rights to life, liberty, and the pursuit of happiness in the 1776 American Declaration of Independence. Yet, despite this heritage, the rights of man were moribund in the first part of the twentieth century:

> All . . . attempts to arrive at a bill of human rights were sponsored by marginal figures—a few international jurists without political experience or professional philanthropists supported by the uncertain sentiments of professional idealists. The groups they formed, the declarations they issued, showed an uncanny similarity in language and composition to that of

> societies for the prevention of cruelty to animals. No . . . political figure of any importance could possibly take them seriously; and none of the liberal or radical parties in Europe thought it necessary to incorporate into their program a new declaration of human rights.[3]

Individual human rights began to receive attention only after the failure of the system of ethnically based *group* rights negotiated at the end of World War I. One of Woodrow Wilson's war aims had been to "make the world safe for democracy by render [ing] it a secure habitation for the fundamental right of man to be governed by rulers accountable to him."[4] Ethnic groups were to rule themselves.

In the treaties drawn up after World War I, the multinational Austro-Hungarian and Turkish empires and various Middle Eastern colonies were dissolved and reconstructed as ethnically and religiously cohesive nation-states. This process of nation creation inevitably stranded some ethnic and religious minorities in the new nation-states—Muslims in Europe, Christians in the Middle East, and Jews everywhere. These minorities, however, were recognized and protected in the treaties that created the new nation-states.

The nature of "human rights" was left unspecified until the 1948 Universal Declaration of Human Rights. Specification was prompted by the 1947 Nuremberg trials, at which doctors, lawyers, scientists, and soldiers were indicted for "crimes against humanity." The trials taught the world what it meant to strip a human of rights. Shortly after the Nuremberg trials commenced, Eleanor Roosevelt convened a committee to draft a declaration of human rights. Thus, Jews in Nazi Germany became surrogates for all humans without rights, and the details revealed daily at Nuremberg gave content to the rights recognized by Articles 4 through 20 of the Declaration.

Articles 4, 5, and 9 prohibit the "slavery or servitude," "arbitrary detention or exile," and "torture, or cruel, inhuman, or degrading treatment or punishment" that was concurrently on display at Nuremberg. Articles 6, 8, 10, and 11 ensure that never again would Nazi-style laws strip individuals of citizenship: "everyone has a recognition everywhere as a person before the law."

Article 12 prohibits a future *Kristallnacht*, yellow Stars of David, and other stigmatizing actions by protecting individuals' privacy, family, and home against attacks on honor and reputation. Mindful of the Nazi Racial Purity laws and the laws stripping Jews of their nationality and their property, Article 16 declares that everyone has a right to marry freely and to found a family "without any limitations due to race, nationality, or religion."

Article 15 states that everyone has a right to a nationality, and Article 17 affirms that everyone has a right to own property. Article 13 guarantees that, unlike the Jews of the 1930s and 1940s, victims of human rights abuse would have the right to flee from persecution. Finally, Article 14 grants a right of asylum. The Declaration proclaims nine additional rights—rights of participation, rights to social security, rights to education, and so forth—but the first twenty declarations of human rights were designed to prevent anyone from ever undergoing the treatment accorded to the Jews by the Nazis.[5]

The Universal Declaration of Human Rights was shaped not only by the failure of minority rights and by outrage at the discovery of the Holocaust, but by the need, underlined by the events unfolding at Nuremberg, to make transcultural, transnational, and transtemporal moral and legal judgments. Unlike their precursors, the *droits de l'homme* and the God-given natural rights of Jefferson and Hamilton, human rights *had* to be globally acceptable.

They had to be neutral between all religious and secular worldviews. Individuals might still subscribe to Hamilton's view that rights are "written, as with a sunbeam, in the whole volume of human nature by the hand of Divinity itself," but, in laying claim to universality, the UN Declaration abandoned all claims to religious authority.

To protect an individual's right to practice religion, the emerging human rights culture had to be neutral about religion. As philosopher Charles Taylor has observed, "the concept of human rights could travel better if separated from some of its underlying justifications."[6]

The Nuremberg Code and the Principlist Precedent in American Bioethics

The Preamble to the Universal Declaration of Human Rights reminds the world that it originates as a reaction to "barbarous acts which have outraged the conscience of mankind." The same has been said of the Nuremberg Code: It is "impossible to analyze the origins of the Nuremberg Code apart from the historical setting of atrocities and murders committed in Nazi Germany."[7] Like the Declaration, the Code is a post-Holocaust document.

Why did the tribunal need to *invent* a code of ethics to condemn the Nazi researchers? To quote the defense for the Nazi doctors, at that time there was "an almost complete lack of written legal norms"[8] on human-subjects research. There were two notable exceptions: the 1931 German Health Ministry regulations, and the 1946 American Medical Association (AMA) research principles.

The Ministry regulations prohibited research on German *patients* without their informed consent. The AMA principles prohibited research on *persons* without their consent; it thus anticipated the bioethical turn by using the language of principles to expand the traditional protections of medical ethics from "patients" to "persons."[9]

Read literally, however, neither the regulations nor the principles were applicable to the German researchers. Physicians and scientists working at the camps dealt with *inmates*, not with *patients* covered by the German health insurance,[10] and, as *Germans*, they were not answerable to *American* ethics principles. The researchers' conduct thus seemed to elude the scope of extant medical ethical principles, legal standards, and applicable regulations.

To deal with these problems, the prosecution turned to two American physicians: Colonel Leo Alexander, a psychiatrist who had treated concentration camp survivors, and Professor Andrew Ivy, former scientific director of the Naval Medical Research Institute at Bethesda—and the official observer for the AMA. Both argued that unconsented human experimentation was impermissible, appealing to Hippocratic tradition.[11]

Ivy, however, also appealed to the "*laws of humanity* and the *ethical principles* of the medical profession."[12] The expression "laws of humanity" was the language of the Nuremberg indictment; "ethical principles" was the language of the AMA, which had parsed ethics as "principles" since its 1903 "Principles of Medical Ethics."[13] Ivy went further than the AMA, however, by grounding his principles in human rights: "The involved Nazi physicians and scientists ignored . . . ethical principles and rules . . . which are necessary to insure the *human rights* of the individual" (emphasis added).[14] Ivy's conception of ethical principles as mechanisms for protecting human rights circumvents the defense arguments about the time and place at which specific rules were formulated.

Human rights are inviolable irrespective of any principle, rule, or law stating their inviolability. Thus, even if no ethical principle or law accepted in Germany in the 1930s and 1940s was violated, "physicians and scientists whose conduct is contrary to the laws of humanity and human rights . . . should be prosecuted as criminals."[15] For, to reiterate, unlike laws and principles, human rights are inviolable regardless of whether a rule, principle, or law was formulated prohibiting a specific act of violation.

The Nuremberg judges incorporated aspects of both Alexander's and Ivy's testimonies into their judgment condemning the Nazi doctors. They accepted Ivy's principlist discourse but ignored his elegant suggestion that transcultural ethics could be grounded in human rights. Instead, they fabricated a fiction, or, if one prefers, a myth.

They claimed that, "*All agree*, that certain *basic principles* must be observed in order to satisfy moral, ethical, and legal concepts." Consequently, they argued, because the Nazi experiments were contrary to "the principles of the law of nations as they result from the usages established among civilized peoples, from the laws of humanity, and from the dictates of public conscience,"[16] the Nazi doctors were guilty of crimes against humanity.

Because the Tribunal grounded its case on the myth of converging civilized opinion, the Nuremberg Code should be regarded conceptually, as well as chronologically, as an artifact of the pre–human rights era. This historical accident is significant because the research ethics decalogue promulgated at Nuremberg was appropriated by the American bioethics movement of the 1970s as a foundational document. Its *universally agreed basic principles* thus set a precedent for the language and justifications offered in American bioethics—and rights discourse was ignored.

The Rebirth of Human Rights and Bioethics in the 1970s

It was an accident of history that human rights and the principles of bioethics were reborn in the 1970s in government documents (The Final Declaration of Helsinki, *The Belmont Report*) in which they were presumed to serve symbolic functions—which is to say, no real function at all.

The Final Declaration of Helsinki was intended to legitimate the Soviet Empire . . . yet, as political theorist Michael Ignatieff notes, the human rights movements legitimated by the Declaration of Helsinki would eventually bring "the Soviet system crashing down."[17] For, unlike its precursor, "minority rights," "human rights" discourse served to unify. Appeals to "minority rights" tended to imply rights for *my* minority, not for yours; by contrast, no one's human rights came at the expense of anyone else's.

By 1966, evidence of the abuse of human subjects was apparent enough to prompt the National Institutes of Health (NIH) to mandate a system of peer review to protect research subjects.[18] In that same year an article published in the *New England Journal of Medicine* by Henry Beecher himself found that twenty-two research papers published in such leading journals as *JAMA* and the *New England Journal of Medicine* between 1948 and 1965 were morally questionable.[19]

In the absence of substantive guidelines, however, peer review alone did not prevent research abuses. In 1973 Senator Edward Kennedy investigated a study by the US Public Health Service on untreated syphilis in African American males, which was conducted without their informed consent. The public was outraged, and federal response was swift.

On July 12, 1974, President Nixon signed the National Research Act (NRA), forming a National Commission for the Protection of Human Subjects of Biomedical and Behavioral Research to develop substantive rules for protecting the human subjects of federally funded research. In the next four years the National Commission published several reports recommending regulations to protect research subjects. Internationally, there was a parallel move, starting with Helsinki II (Tokyo, 1975).

The most influential report issued by the National Commission concerned *principles*. In 1978, it issued the three-volume *Belmont Report*,[20] in which it asserted that three basic ethical principles should regulate research on human subjects—the principles of respect for persons, beneficence, and justice. Following the Nuremberg precedent, the commissioners justified these principles in terms of convergence: The principles were deemed binding because "all agreed" that they ought to be binding.[21]

Convergence was a liberating concept. Tom Beauchamp and James Childress were perhaps the first to appreciate this point. In *Principles of Biomedical Ethics* (first published in 1979),[22] they construct bioethics[23] in terms of four "basic" principles—autonomy, beneficence, nonmaleficence, and justice—one more than the three used in *The Belmont Report*. These principles, in turn, are justified by a presumed *convergence* of reflective ethical thought.

By placing convergence at the level of principles, Beauchamp and Childress liberated bioethics from the ethical theories that happened to be in vogue, philosophically. By so doing, it not only unified the ethical analysis of researcher and clinician conduct, it also deprofessionalized medical ethical discourse. Thus, just as human rights discourse could become a public discourse only if freed from conceptions of divine and human nature, so too, bioethics discourse could serve as a public discourse only if freed from conceptions of the medical profession, its nature, and mission.

The new discourses open the domain of diplomats and doctors to ordinary people, who have no professional pretensions whatsoever. Bioethics and human rights are thus kindred democratizing and deprofessionalizing public discourses that transform the ethics of elites into everyday ethics.

Bioethics and Human Rights: Some Parallels

The parallels between bioethics and human rights as concepts, discourses, movements, and fields are striking. Both were conceived out of the horror of the Holocaust; both draw strength from the resolve that "never again" would any vulnerable population be treated as the Nazis had treated the Jews; both support respect for persons; both stake claims to universality; both were born in governmental documents that explicitly justify transnational, transtemporal, and transcultural moral judgments; both became unfashionable in the era of Cold War realism; both are international, and thus (perhaps not surprisingly) both refer to Helsinki declarations; both were resurrected in the mid-1970s; both are supported by an unusual alliance of governmental and nongovernmental organizations; both became widely disseminated by disassociating themselves from earlier metaphysical and philosophical moorings; and both use a public discourse to democratize the domain of professional elites, although, ironically, both are supported by professional groups who consider themselves expert in the domain of the discourses. Yet, despite these similarities—and even though one of the progenitors of the Nuremberg Code, Andrew Ivy, envisioned principles as mechanisms for protecting human rights—American bioethics has been ill at ease with the idea of human rights.

It is time to reconsider. Pandemics leap from continent to continent, companies peddle their cures around the world, biomedical experiments sponsored in the developed world are conducted in the developing world, and, in all corners of the globe, the new biology foments culture shock. Bioethical issues do not stop for border crossings. Thus, we need global bioethics. But the principlism that has served American bioethics so well is too parochial to play on an international stage, and so to meet the challenges of global bioethics, we need to turn to the more cosmopolitan concept of human rights.

Once bioethics enters the international stage, the ideal of converging principles becomes unsustainable. Different cultures embrace different principles and differ in their interpretations of common principles. If principlism is to function internationally, it must be reconceptualized to shed its parochialism.

Reconciling Bioethics with Human Rights

It is time to reconsider Ivy's proposal that we construe the principles of international bioethics as mechanisms for protecting human rights. Rights discourse is already the accepted language of international ethics. As members of the United Nations, virtually all the nations on Earth have pledged themselves to accept as "a common standard," that "all human beings are born free and equal in dignity and rights." As philosopher Richard Rorty has observed, ours is already a human rights culture.

A global bioethics that envisions principles as mechanisms for protecting human rights will thus inherit an internationally accepted ethical discourse.[24] Rights discourse is the best means available for achieving the shared goal of both bioethics and human rights theory: the moral demand that never again will anyone be treated in the manner that Nazis treated Jews.

An international bioethics based on respect for human rights will also be free from the feckless dispute over whose principles are preferable. Principles are preferable insofar as they effectively protect human rights. Because effectiveness is partially a function of cultural experience, different societies may properly employ different principles—respect for persons, respect for families, solidarity—insofar as they effectively protect human rights in the culture in question. The proposed reconciliation of human rights and bioethics thus recognizes cultural variation in principles and does not challenge American principlism within its home cultural sphere.

Grounding international bioethics discourse in human rights will not be a panacea. Human rights discourse may be the lingua franca of the international community, but the scope and limits of human rights should properly be subject to intense debate, as should the principles and rules that we create to protect these rights. The depth of the dilemmas that we must address will not dissipate merely because we use a common mode of moral discourse to address them. The transcultural scope of human rights discourse can, however, dissipate problems of moral parochialism.

Each culture has a deeply rooted predilection to treat its own conception of morality, its own moral concepts and principles, as primary. Human rights discourse was designed to be as cosmopolitan and international as the United Nations itself; it permits us to transcend our parochialism and thus to focus on the substance of the profound moral challenges that we face.

Acknowledgments

I should like to thank Joseph d'Oronzio for inviting me to compare the historical development of bioethics and human rights, thereby providing me with an excuse to engage in an exceptionally illuminating exercise. This chapter draws on my earlier work on human rights, which has been enriched by discussions at the International Association of Bioethics (Tokyo), The Hastings Center, New York University, the Mount Sinai Medical Center (especially with Rosamond Rhodes and Stephen Baumrin), and by critiques by Tom Beauchamp and Ruth Macklin.

Notes

1. A. Hamilton in *Nonsense upon Stilts: Bentham, Burke and Marx on the Rights of Man*, edited by Jeremy Waldron (London: Methuen, 1987), 18.

2. French Assembly, "Declaration of the Rights of Man and the Citizen, 1789," in *Nonsense upon Stilts: Bentham, Burke and Marx on the Rights of Man*, edited by Jeremy Waldron (London: Methuen, 1987), 26.

3. H. Arendt, *The Origins of Totalitarianism* (New York: Meridian Books, 1958), 292.
4. E. Schwelb, *Human Rights and the International Community: The Roots and Growth of the Universal Declaration of Human Rights, 1948–1963* (Chicago: Quadrangle Books, 1964), 24.
5. J. Morsink, *The Universal Declaration of Human Rights: Origins, Drafting, and Intent* (Philadelphia: University of Pennsylvania Press, 1999).
6. C. Taylor, "Conditions of an Unforced Consensus on Human Rights," in *The East Asian Challenge for Human Rights*, edited by J. R. Bauer and D. A. Bell (London and New York: Cambridge University Press, 1999), 126.
7. M. Grodin, "The Historical Origins of the Nuremberg Code," in *The Nazi Doctors and the Nuremberg Code*, edited by G. A. Annas and M. Grodin (London and New York: Oxford University Press, 1992), 135–36.
8. J. Katz, *Experimentation with Human Beings* (New York: Russell Sage Foundation, 1972), 300.
9. The AMA adopted this principle, but only in 1946—that is, only at Ivy's insistence, and only after the Nazi researchers were indicted.
10. Although this point was not raised at the trial, Romany, Jews, and homosexuals had been stripped of German citizenship and were considered *Untermenschen*, subhumans, and thus were not protected by regulations covering *Menschen*, humans. For the 1931 regulations in English and German, see H. M. Sass, "Reichrundschreiben 1931: Pre-Nuremberg German Regulations Concerning New Therapy and Human Experimentation," *The Journal of Medicine and Philosophy* 8 (1983): 104–9.
11. L. Alexander, "Ethics of Human Experimentation," *Psychiatric Journal of the University of Ottawa*, 1 (1976): 40–46. See also Grodin, "The Historical Origins of the Nuremberg Code."
12. M. Grodin, ed., *The Nazi Doctors and the Nuremberg Code* (London and New York: Oxford University Press, 1992), 134–35.
13. A. C. Ivy, "Report on War Crimes of a Medical Nature Committed in Germany and Elsewhere on German Nationals and the Nationals of Occupied Countries by the Nazi Regime during World War II," Document JC 9218, American Medical Association Archives, 1946: 9.
14. American Medical Association, "Principles of Medical Ethics (1903)," in *The American Medical Ethics Revolution*, edited by R. Baker, A. Caplan, E. Emanuel, and S. Latham (Baltimore: Johns Hopkins Press, 1999).
15. Ivy, "Report on War Crimes of a Medical Nature," 11.
16. Ibid., 13–14.
17. Katz, *Experimentation with Human Beings*, 305.
18. M. Ignatieff, "Human Rights: The Midlife Crisis," *The New York Review of Books* 46 (1999): 59.
19. W. J. Curran, "Governmental Regulation of the Use of Human Subjects in Medical Research: The Approach of Two Federal Agencies," *Daedalus* 92 (1969): 576–78.
20. H. Beecher, "Ethics and Clinical Research, *New England Journal of Medicine* 274 (1966): 1354–60; National Commission for the Protection of Human Subjects of Biomedical and Behavioral Research, *The Belmont Report* (Washington, DC, 1978).
21. For a detailed critique of the convergence justification and replies, see R. Baker, "Multiculturalism, Postmodernism, and the Bankruptcy of Fundamentalism," *Kennedy Institute of Ethics Journal* 8 (1998): 210–31; R. Baker, "A Theory of International Bioethics," *Kennedy Institute of Ethics Journal* 8 (1998): 233–74; R. Baker, "Negotiating International Bioethics: A Response to Tom Beauchamp and Ruth Macklin," *Kennedy Institute of Ethics Journal* 8 (1998): 423–55; T. L. Beauchamp, "The Mettle of Moral Fundamentalism: A Reply to Robert Baker," *Kennedy Institute of Ethics Journal* 8 (1998): 423–55; R. Macklin, "A Defense of Fundamental

Principles and Human Rights: A Reply to Robert Baker," *Kennedy Institute of Ethics Journal* 8 (1998): 403–22.

22. T. L. Beauchamp and J. F. Childress, *Principles of Biomedical Ethics* (London and New York: Oxford University Press, 1979, 1983, 1989, 1994).

23. Ironically, Beauchamp and Childress tend to avoid the term *bioethics*. The term was coined in the early 1970s perhaps by Sargent Shriver, or by André Hellegers, or by Van Rensselaer Potter. It achieved canonical status when the Library of Congress entered it as a subject heading, citing as its authority an article, "Bioethics as a Discipline," published by Daniel Callahan in the first volume of the *Hastings Center Report*. Callahan can thus also be credited with coining the term. See A. R. Jonsen, *The Birth of Bioethics* (London and New York: Oxford University Press, 1998), 26–27; and W. T. Reich, "The Word 'Bioethics': The Struggle for Its Earliest Meanings," *Kennedy Institute of Ethics Journal* 4 (1994): 319–36; 5 (1995): 19–34.

24. Transnational medical ethics has already done this: thus, the Preamble to the Convention for the Protection of Human Rights and Dignity of the Human Being with Regard to the Application of Biology and Medicine: Convention on Human Rights and Biomedicine, adopted by Council of Europe in 1997, the term "rights" or "human rights" appears eight times—no mention is made of "principles." "Convention for Protection of Human Rights and Dignity of the Human Being with Regard to the Application of Biology and Biomedicine: Convention on Human Rights and Biomedicine," *Kennedy Institute of Ethics Journal* 7 (1996): 277–90.

CHAPTER 8

Medical Tourism: Justice, Autonomy, and Power

Virginia L. Warren

Abstract

"Medical tourism" refers to patients traveling across national borders for medical treatment. My primary focus is on patients living in the United States who travel to low-income countries for medical care. The main reasons for medical tourism include—above all—saving money, cutting waiting time, and getting medical treatment unavailable at home. I consider traveling for major surgery, for kidney transplants from poor people who illegally sell a kidney, and for experimental treatment not yet available in the United States. The principal moral concerns I discuss are based on patient autonomy, harms to the patient and to others back home (such as drug-resistant infections), and harms to poor people in the destination country—including injustice due to "brain drain" when international patients come for medical treatment.

Many solutions to these objections to medical tourism have been offered, and more could be devised. However, a fundamental problem works against their being tried or fully enforced: the power of money and its impact on politics. I close by offering an approach to bioethics that directly addresses power in health care. I expand the discussion of autonomy, as usually understood, to include empowering patients, health-care professionals, and the general public—both individually and in partnership with others. I then advance the following principle: *the duty to confront power, often in coordination with others, in order to further other important moral principles and values.* It is not free-standing; it concerns how and when one should act to carry out other moral duties. It is the duty that whistle-blowers follow, although I have expanded it—in the age of #MeToo—to accentuate the power of working together. Confronting power may help more people to fulfill their right to basic health care—both in the United States and in destination countries—and help justice be better served.

Introduction

Medicine has become a global market, with a growing number of patients traveling to other countries for medical treatment. In the biomedical literature, "medical tourist" is the commonly used name for patients who travel across national borders for medical treatment. Glenn Cohen (2015, xv) writes: "I will define them as individuals who travel abroad for the primary purpose of getting health care (as opposed to expatriates who receive care while living abroad, or individuals who get sick on vacation)." Peta Cook et al. (2013, 63) rely on a similar definition: "We view medical tourism as the phenomenon of patients travelling to foreign or international locales with the motivation to receive invasive medical treatment, usually because cost or availability confers some financial or personal advantage."

While I also adopt this narrower interpretation of medical tourism, some sources consider broader ones. For example, Halina Kotikova and Eva Schwartzhoffova (2013) write about traveling to health spas and other health care–related businesses. Cook et al. (2013, 63) note that when the medical treatment is less burdensome, "medical tourism" is sometimes used to "include the practice of packaging together holidays with medical treatments. The marketing of medical tourism often concentrates on nearby attractions and/or vacation packages" for the patient and family or other caretakers. In these two examples, the "tourism" label seems a felicitous match.

Discussions of medical tourism refer to the *home* (or source) country in which patients live and the *destination* country and/or specific medical center to which they travel for medical care. Cohen (2015, 1–37) offers a comprehensive overview of medical and legal terms, along with occupations and groups, related to medical tourism. "While medical tourists come predominantly from the developed world, medical-tourist sites are found globally, with many medical tourists flowing to world-class facilities in the developing world" (Cook et al. 2013, 61–62).

My primary focus is on patients living in the United States who travel to low-income countries for medical care. Reasons for medical tourism include—above all—saving money, as well as cutting waiting time, and getting medical treatment unavailable at home. The principal moral concerns I discuss are the patient's autonomy (avoiding coercion and having sufficient correct information to make an informed decision), harms to the patient (due to poor medical quality) and to others back home (such as drug-resistant infections), and possible harms to poor people in the destination country—especially, if they suffer injustice because their right to basic health care is undermined when international patients come for medical treatment. As we will see, some moral issues raised about medical tourism mirror issues raised when patients stay in the United States.

A Toolbox of Moral Principles for Bioethics

The field of bioethics began its modern development with the Nuremberg Code (1947) on human experimentation, which was signed by many nations after World

War II in response to the horrors of experiments forced on human subjects by the Nazis. It emphasizes autonomy and begins: "The voluntary consent of the human subject is absolutely essential."

The moral framework of bioethics further developed during the 1960s and 1970s. After a period of wide-ranging exploration of how to approach ethical issues in medicine and biology, a short list of moral principles (which were put forth by, among others, Tom L. Beauchamp and James F. Childress [1979] in the first edition of their basic textbook) gained prominence: autonomy, nonmaleficence, beneficence, and justice. Also considered are the value of life and other rights and utilitarianism. Later, virtue ethics and to some degree feminist ethics have been added.

I will examine three reasons US patients might choose to get medical care in other countries and a possible objection based on treating poor people in destination countries unjustly. I close by offering an approach to bioethics that addresses the impact of economic and political power on health care. I expand the discussion of autonomy, as commonly understood, to include empowering patients, health-care professionals, and the general public—both individually and in partnership with others. I then advance the following principle: *the duty to confront power, often in coordination with others, in order to further other important moral principles and values.*

First Reason for Medical Tourism: Patients Save Money

Without question, saving money is the principal reason many US patients travel to other countries for medical care. Comparing prices in the United States with those in destination countries is eye-opening. Neil Lunt et al. (2011) produced an influential report—with a chart (included by Cohen [2015, 4] and Lunt et al. [2013, 34]) comparing the costs of medical procedures in the United States with nine other countries where medical tourism is common—including India, Thailand, Singapore, Malaysia, and Mexico. Rounding off, hip or knee replacement surgery may cost about one-quarter as much as in the United States, heart bypass surgery may cost about one-tenth as much, and heart valve replacement surgery may cost somewhat over one-twentieth as much. Even after adding in travel and temporary living expenses, the savings for patients can be considerable. The evidence of cost saving for medical tourists living in the United States (and in many other high-income countries) for many medical procedures is well established.

Compared with other high-income countries, the United States on average spends considerably more per capita on health care and a larger percent of its GDP, and gets poorer health outcomes; among the higher expenses paid in the United States are physician services, drugs, and administrative costs (Papanicolas et al. 2018). In the United States, the practice of medicine has much less government regulation than in other high-income countries, where governments hold down prices, and, alone among those countries, many in the United States have no health insurance at all. Medical debt is a significant problem in the United States, even for those who are insured (Hamel et al. 2016).

Several moral objections may be raised to US medical tourists seeking less expensive medical care elsewhere, including based on patient autonomy, quality of care, harm to others, and injustice to poor people in the destination country.

Medical tourists from the United States may have their autonomy compromised in several ways. They may feel forced to travel by the burden of high medical costs at home; they may even face bankruptcy. However, patients will find it difficult to get reliable information to make the decision to go to a specific country. Comparing medical costs of a procedure in the United States with those in various destination countries is difficult, in part, because US medical prices—which should be transparent and available—may be as opaque as cement.

According to Cohen's (2015, 76) careful research,

> Quality of care remains one of the—and probably *the* most—frequently cited concern about medical tourism. Although one can find many anecdotal instances of poor care being delivered as part of medical tourism, the kind of data one would need to make a full-fledged assessment is currently largely absent. . . . At the same time, the existing often-touted signals of high quality—JCI [Joint Commission International] accreditation, number of Western-trained physicians [a kind of reverse brain drain going toward destination countries, but Lunt et al. (2011, 35–36) question its significance], partnerships with prestigious facilities in the developed country—seem more about branding and less about rigorous measures of quality.

Hence, medical tourists may be harmed by inferior medical care, and making a truly informed choice based on quality is, once again, quite difficult.

Justice may also be a concern. Below, I will discuss possible injustice done to poor people in some destination countries where US patients go as medical tourists. It may be that injustice in the United States—where many are denied the right to basic, affordable health care—could lead to poor people in destination countries receiving even worse health care as a result.

Second Reason for Medical Tourism: Avoiding Long Wait Times

In some countries, long wait lines for nonemergency medical care can be a significant problem, making faster care one reason patients travel to other countries. For example, patients in European Union countries may travel to other EU countries that have less waiting time for a specific procedure, and Canadians may travel to the United States (Cohen 2015, 6, 9–10). Moreover, saving time for patients may also save money for insurers. For example, Lunt et al. (2011, 31) cite evidence that, if the UK's health service sent patients to India for total hip and knee replacement surgeries, the health service might save over a hundred million pounds a year, in addition to reducing the waiting lists with tens of thousands of UK patients.

While avoiding long wait lines is not a main factor leading US patients to travel to other countries, there is a major exception. In the United States, there is a long wait to receive kidneys for transplantation. There are simply not enough donated kidneys for all who need them. Most are from deceased donors who register to have their organs removed upon their death, and some are from volunteer living donors. Many on dialysis die before receiving a kidney.

Among the moral objections to medical tourism for kidney transplants raised below, the first two concern how the kidneys are obtained: they are bought and sold. It is illegal to pay people to donate organs in the United States, and worldwide only Iran has legalized selling organs (and Iran regulates it); still, black markets for buying organs exist in many places in the world (Cohen 2015, 263).

First, it can be objected that using purchased kidneys is intrinsically wrong because selling an organ debases the seller's human dignity. Nikola Biller-Andorno and Zumrut Alpinar (2014, 773–74) consider this line of argument unhelpful. They argue that the concept of human dignity is either too vague to be helpful, or—if based on Kantian ethics or the values of specific religions—not widely enough shared to persuade people generally. They find autonomy a more convincing objection. I am sympathetic to the human dignity objection, although I agree that it is philosophically intricate.

Second, it can be objected that kidney sellers are not acting autonomously. To begin with, they are desperate for money, or they would not be selling parts of their body. Further, "The brokers who manage the trade are often affiliated with organized crime and rely on misinformation, pressure, and sometimes threats to recruit sellers" (Cohen 2015, 313). Sellers are regularly lied to about how long and difficult recovery is and then cheated out of much of their promised payment. They often regret their decision (Cohen 2015, 300, 313) because they are worse off physically and financially than before the surgery. Given real-world conditions, this objection is conclusive against medical tourists receiving purchased kidneys.

Third, the quality of medical care for medical tourists may be questioned: Are medical outcomes worse in the destination country than if patients had transplant surgery and follow-up care in the United States? While reliable data from destination countries is hard to come by since the procedure is illegal (Cohen 2015, 281), we may surmise that the quality is generally low. However, if patients are quite *un*likely to receive a donated organ in the United States, then their comparison with transplant surgery elsewhere would be to continue their poor quality of life at home without the surgery—which is an easier comparison to beat.

Fourth, the autonomy of kidney transplant tourists may also be examined. Again, because the procedure is illegal—and patients are not discussing medical tourism with their home physicians—it is unlikely that kidney transplant tourists are fully and correctly informed about the quality, conditions, and cost of the medical treatment elsewhere.

So far, I am following the way patient autonomy is usually construed in bioethics: compare the risks and benefits *for the patient* of different alternatives. However, we may wonder whether the kidney recipients were informed, more broadly, about the true situation for kidney *sellers* in that destination country: their likely medical results, whether they would probably be lied to or cheated out of money, and whether afterward they would likely suffer greatly, leaving them awash with regret. I think we know the answer, and not only because the brokers from destination countries lie to medical tourists as well. For the information that patients are usually deemed to require—in order to make an autonomous medical decision—does not include whether others may suffer a harm or injustice as a result, or whether there is a serious environmental impact, or a host of other possible effects. We will return to possible injustice caused to others when discussing brain drain below.

There is general agreement that buying kidneys for transplant in the black market is morally wrong, and I concur. Responses offered by Biller-Andorno and Alpinar (2014, 781) and Cohen (2015, 314) include shutting down organ trafficking in destination countries, through monitoring by international bodies and/or through having better police enforcement of existing laws prohibiting such sales; increasing the supply of donated kidneys in home countries by passing laws that presume consent for organ donation at death; and lessening demand by preventing kidney failure. For many in the United States who currently face kidney failure, focusing on long-term supply and demand for donated kidneys will leave their dreams of a healthier life to fade and die. However, for the foreseeable future, that is all we have.

Third Reason for Medical Tourism: Experimental Procedures Not Legally Available in the Home Country

Currently, patients living outside the United States may become medical tourists for abortions or physician-assisted suicide if they are unavailable where they live. In the case of finding surrogate mothers willing to be pregnant (usually with an embryo from the sperm and/or egg of the adopting parents) and to relinquish that child for adoption—a type of fertility tourism—people may come from other countries to the United States, where surrogacy is legal (Cohen 2015, 372–73).

I focus here on experimental drugs, medical devices, and procedures that are not legally available for patients in the United States because the Federal Drug Administration (FDA) has not yet approved them. Current examples include stem cell therapy (Cohen 2015, 421–78; Hall 2013b, 12–16; Hall 2013a, 204), and transplanting parts of animals into humans, such as cells from the pancreas of pigs to potentially help patients with type 1 diabetes (Cook et al. 2013, 65).

Regarding drugs, the FDA approval process in the United States takes many years. "It has been estimated that, from start to finish, the FDA approval process can take up to ten years for a successful drug. Until a drug is approved, it is illegal to sell the drug to willing patients, unless the drug qualifies for one of FDA's narrow exceptions" (Cohen 2015, 422). Even with recent attempts to fast-track some potentially life-saving drugs, the average approval time of eight years has been reduced to about seven (Healy 2017). Relatively few patients are accepted into clinical trials, and, even then, one has a 50 percent chance of being randomly assigned to a placebo (or, in cases where there is already an established treatment, to that existing treatment). Patients in the United States who want access to unapproved drugs or medical devices may seek them elsewhere.

Moral objections to medical tourism for unapproved experimental drugs and procedures include, above all, risk of harms to the patient that are not balanced by the chance of compensating benefits for the patient (weighing nonmaleficence against beneficence). Human stem cell therapy, for example, is of unproven value (Lunt et al. 2013, 42–43). Moreover, harm may be done to others in the United States upon return. Drug-resistant bacteria may be transported back, after infections are caught in destination hospitals (Hall 2013a, 207–9). Cook et al. (2013, 65) warn that experimental surgeries using parts of nonhuman animals are especially risky since viruses completely new to humans could be introduced from other species. Further, financial burdens may be placed on the US health-care system if patients return in need of significant follow-up treatment after poorly done procedures. Of these objections, the risk of overall harm to the patient is viewed as the greatest concern by medical tourists, the risk depending on the specific procedure and place. Whether the patient can get reliable information upon which to base a decision also varies.

Objection: Injustice—Including from Brain Drain—to Those in the Destination Country

An important and frequently discussed objection to medical tourism concerns justice. That poor people in the destination country may be treated unjustly rests on a general claim about human rights: Everyone has a right to the basic necessities of life, including food, clothing, shelter, and health care. One specific version of this objection concerns brain drain. In general, brain drain occurs when professionals choose not to work in areas where patients are most in need in order to work elsewhere—usually to be paid more, although getting higher status or better working conditions may also be involved. Poor people in a destination country may have their health unjustly harmed when medical professionals—and medical centers and equipment—are allocated away from serving their health needs to those of incoming medical tourists. The argument is as follows:

1. Poor people in a destination country for medical tourism have a right to basic health care, and in many countries this right is not, in general, being fulfilled.
2. [*causal connection*] If medical tourists come to a destination country for medical treatment and doing so *causes* many poor people there (who may already have inadequate health care) to have health care that is both worsened *and* less than what they have a basic right to, then an injustice is done to those poor people.
3. [*specific case*] Specific evidence must support the claim that medical tourists to *this* destination country for *this* medical treatment cause such an injustice.

4. Therefore, it is unjust for there to be medical tourism to *this* destination country for *this* medical treatment.
   a. [*specific responsibility*] Therefore, it is unjust for medical tourists to choose to go to *this* destination country for *this* medical treatment.
   b. [*specific responsibility*] Therefore, it is unjust for physicians and other medical professionals in *this* destination country to work in medical centers within this country that actively serve—and advertise to attract—medical tourists from other countries, when they could serve poor people in the United States instead.
   c. [*specific responsibility*] Therefore, it is unjust for physicians and other medical professionals in *this* destination country to leave to work in *other* countries that actively serve patients who can pay more, when they could stay and serve poor people in *this* country instead.

Cohen (2015) carefully underscores that evidence is needed to prove the causal connection (premise 2) between medical tourists traveling for a specific treatment and poor people of a specific country having worse health care as a direct result (premise 3). After painstaking analysis of available data from a range of destination countries, both Cohen (2015, 210–26) and Lunt et al. (2011, 35–36) arrive at conclusions that are equivocal. They agree that, in a number of countries, there is anecdotal evidence that medical tourism causes poor people in the destination country to have worse medical care as a result; for example, when there is brain drain of medical professionals—plus reallocation of money, medical centers, and equipment—to serve medical tourists instead. However, they determine that the best available evidence is as yet inconclusive. Even if poor people's medical care is getting worse, other factors may be the cause—such as medical resources and personnel being "drained" away to serve the wealthy of their own country. Cohen (2015, 226) ultimately concludes that while he "cannot prove" the causal connection in any country, there is "sufficient evidence" to show "that the claim is plausible enough" to examine the moral objection to medical tourism based on injustice.

I distinguished different versions of the conclusion (4a, 4b, 4c) since, even if poor people in destination countries are suffering an injustice because their right to basic health care has been eroded due to medical tourism, it can still be debated exactly who—or what institution—is morally responsible for that injustice. The more we ponder specific responsibility for such injustice, the more complexities emerge, as follows.

Regarding (4a), deciding whether it is unjust for *medical tourists* from the United States to choose to go to countries where poor people are caused to have worse health care as a result is complicated. US medical tourists, in particular, may have extreme financial problems that prevent them from getting good medical care at home (Cohen 2015, 257). They may have no health insurance, or they may be underinsured—with high copays and annual deductibles, especially for a family. While US patients are not often as poor as poor people in low-income destination countries, it is hard to find them guilty of injustice if medical bankruptcy looms or their medical condition is life-threatening (e.g., requiring heart surgery). Arguably, the wealthier or better insured that US patients are, the more blameworthy they may be (Cohen 2015, 259). While the Affordable Care Act (ACA) greatly improved access and lowered costs for many in the United States, much more must be done to guarantee the right to basic health care for all.

This remaining injustice in the US health-care system may contribute to injustice in destination countries. Overall, it is necessary to confront the economic and political power affecting health-care systems in order to help more people to fulfill their right to basic health care—both in the United States and in destination countries—thereby helping justice be better served.

Regarding (4b), the situation for *physicians*, *nurses*, and *other medical professionals* who grew up—and often trained—*in destination countries* with significant poverty is difficult to unravel, as well. These professionals' decisions about where to work, whether to specialize, and which patients to serve are often freer choices than those of the medical tourists we just discussed. Of course, destination countries (and medical centers) could give inducements for medical professionals to serve more of their own poor. We miss the big picture if we look only at individuals and not at the policies and practices of institutions—including financial rewards for general practice versus various specialties; the funding sources for major hospitals that influence where they locate; money donated to politicians who vote on health-care policies; and policies about medical student debt. An example of the latter comes from California, which has begun a program for medical school loan forgiveness for physicians who serve low-income California patients (Gutierrez 2019).

I added (4c) to ask whether, if *medical professionals* opt out of serving poor patients in their own country, there is a moral difference that depends upon where they practice. That is, is there a moral difference between medical professionals staying in their own country to serve medical tourists (4b) and leaving to work in another country (4c)—as long as the patients they serve are similarly well off? Either way, it is brain drain away from serving their poor. While admittedly unlikely, medical professionals in destination countries might leave to serve poor people in another country.

That brain drain does not strike me as wrong overall. To press the point further, if they left their country to work at the world-renowned Mayo Clinic in Minnesota in order to do research on a disease affecting poor people in their own country (again unlikely), that decision strikes me as praiseworthy. In the Mayo Clinic case, the "brain" has not drained away; it has relocated in order to help from afar. We can also imagine that they chose to work at the Mayo Clinic in order to do more total good for the entire world's poor by researching a disease that does not affect their country of origin. This case, although brain drain, seems praiseworthy too. At issue may be a mixture of moral considerations: one's motive (self-regarding or altruistic), commitment to one's country (if one judges this morally relevant), the degree of harm to the health care of poor individuals, and other moral factors (including other justice issues) that may outweigh brain drain.

In sum, even if a country's poor people are treated unjustly because of medical tourism—due, in particular, to brain drain of medical professionals—assigning moral responsibility for that specific injustice is complex. And similar moral issues arise in the United States. Brain drain of medical professionals within the United States—away from poorer areas toward wealthier areas or specialized medical centers—should elicit similar debate.

Confronting Power in Health Care

I was initially put off by the "medical tourist" label. I preferred "cross-border medical traveler" or "international medical traveler." However, since reconciling economic interests with the well-being of patients is one of the larger issues in US health care, I have come to view the term "medical tourist" as a helpful reminder of the general conflict between money and the best interests of patients.

Money from drug, medical device, and private insurance companies infiltrates US health-care decisions, sometimes with disastrous results. For example, physicians freely prescribe pain-killing opioids, but most have little or no training in how to get patients safely off them (Rieder 2019). Drug companies get rich, patients get addicted and die at alarming rates, and federal reporting law is ignored. "For years, long after the opioid crisis began, the giant pharmacy chains, including Walgreens and CVS, and Walmart did almost nothing to fulfill their legal duty to monitor suspicious orders, the plaintiffs' lawyers claim. While they were supposed to block such orders and alert the Drug Enforcement Administration, they did so rarely" (Hoffman et al. 2019).

Another big problem is that transparency of US health-care prices is often woefully lacking (Lazarus 2019). Knowing more about costs would help patients save money by knowing their options, and at least some pressure might be exerted to lower prices. A study showed that almost 70 percent of patients who tried to get cost information ahead of time from providers had trouble doing so (Hamel et al. 2016, 26–28). Even medical bills received afterward are designed to be difficult to decipher. Could the US government force transparency and require lower health-care prices? Certainly—as governments in many other countries do; but it appears unlikely now. Money's influence on health care and US politics will remain until power is met with power.

In response to the objections raised above to medical tourism—including when patient autonomy is undermined, when patients and others risk harm from lower-quality medical treatment and from drug-resistant bacteria, and when poor people are treated unjustly—many solutions have been offered, and more could be devised.

Let us take determining the quality of health care in destination countries as an example. As we saw above, Cohen (2015, 76) conclude that attempts at accreditation, such as through the JCI, do not guarantee rigorous quality internationally. Cook et al. (2013, 65) concur: "Despite the interest in accreditation, however, there is no effective global regulation of the medical industry," and individuals are largely left to fend for themselves when trying to assess the quality of medical care abroad.

Cook et al. (2013) then recommend seeking institutional support outside of the medical world—both to raise the quality of health care for medical tourists and to give them more reliable information upon which to base their decisions. They speculate that NGOs might help medical tourists to become more effective consumers: "It is possible to imagine that in a context of lax global regulation, non-governmental organizations (NGOs) will take on a global quasi-regulatory role. Being unencumbered by the market forces to which national medical and regulatory actors are subject, . . . NGOs will become the 'global police' of risky biomedicine" (71–72). Perhaps so, but only if these NGOs can remain uncorrupted by market forces in the long run.

Cohen (2015, 71–77) offers a different way for medical tourists to lower their risk of getting poor-quality medical care, while retaining much of their autonomy. He proposes that patients' choices be "channeled" by their private health insurance companies. Well-researched, safer options of destination countries (or specific medical centers) would be designated as the default (or cheaper) choice for medical tourists. Thus, patient autonomy would be respected as much as possible, consistent with protecting both patients and the general public from harm (e.g., from drug-resistant bacteria). Again, I wonder whether those devising and implementing the channeling protocol will remain uncorrupted over time.

I am less fond of another of Cohen's (2015, 134) proposals. Instead of making it illegal for US physicians to get referral fees from medical tourist destinations—a clear conflict of interest—Cohen (2015, 134) proposes that these fees must simply be disclosed to patients considering medical tourism. Even if paid trips to that country and other inducements were also disclosed, unconscious bias is real, and patient trust may erode.

In sum, these solutions and others run the risk of corruption. A fundamental force works against these solutions being made into policy or law or later being fully enforced: the power of money, which also impacts political power. Little will change until power is met with power.

Expanding the Moral Toolbox: From Autonomy to Empowerment

I offer an approach to bioethics that directly addresses power in health care in two ways. In this section, I expand the discussion of autonomy to include empowerment and later advance this principle: *the duty to confront power, often in coordination with others, in order to further other important moral principles and values.*

Bioethics literature shines a light on respecting the right of individual patients to make decisions that are autonomous, to be fully informed and neither pressured nor coerced. Before patient autonomy gained widespread acceptance in US health care in the 1970s, the term "following doctor's orders" was commonplace. And families of terminal patients were often encouraged not to tell their dying relatives that they were terminal in order not to ruin that person's last days on Earth. Patient autonomy was always about power: The power of physicians (and family members) was significantly reined in by competent patients' right to make informed decisions for themselves. A historical note: A secondary, self-interested, financial motive helped propel patient autonomy into its current pivotal place in medical practice. Since the patient, once informed of the risks and alternatives, chose this treatment, then, if the medical results went badly, the threat of a medical malpractice suit being brought against the physician was reduced. Physicians present: patients choose.

While recognizing patient autonomy as a massive, positive cultural shift that does empower patients in some basic respects, I claim that we need to debate how bioethics might go further. I propose expanding the discussion of autonomy, as usually understood in health care, to include empowering patients—as well as health-care professionals and the general public—both individually and in partnership with others. A familiar example of empowerment is when patients and their families are encouraged to join support groups around specific medical issues in order to share practical information and give emotional support.

I maintain that the practice of medicine—including, but not limited to, medical tourism—would be enhanced by considering other ways, besides autonomy, of empowering individuals, setting up a wide variety of supportive frameworks for them to develop their skills, confidence, and even courage (hence, there may be some overlap with virtue ethics' concentration on character traits). To advocate for empowerment—of patients, physicians, nurses, and other allied health professionals, and to some degree the general public in one's country and beyond—is paradigmatically a social enterprise. This social component is exemplified by many social movements, such as the civil rights struggle for racial equality and the recent #MeToo movement on sexual abuse. Empowerment typically involves changes in the decision-maker, as well as forging connections with people, and striving over time to change institutional policies, laws, and prevailing attitudes and norms.

I offer this *definition of empowerment*: One is empowered when one is a) involved in long-term projects; b) during which one develops skills and character traits that contribute to shaping one's life and/or furthering social change; c) often while being supported by—and supporting—others in a group or community effort with which one identifies; d) thus changing one's view about one's identity and abilities (Warren 2019, 54–55).

In short, autonomy changes what you know; empowerment changes who you are. Autonomy keeps others from interfering with you; empowerment seeks strength through relationships in order to make systemic change over time.

Becoming empowered may help you to act more autonomously—by more assertively requesting information and better resisting outside pressure. However, autonomy—as it is commonly employed in bioethics, and I think of as "tamed autonomy"—is narrower than empowerment, which centrally includes changes to your character traits, skills, self-concept, and relationships over time.

Becoming empowered is explicitly advocated by physicians in a National Public Radio (NPR) essay titled, "Be a Powerful Patient: Take Control of Your Care When You're Seriously Sick" (Schumann et al. 2019). They exclaim: "Figure out what matters to you, and fight for it. . . . Have a frank conversation with your doctor about *your* values and what you want (and don't want!) and you'll be an empowered patient with a doctor as your advocate, not your adversary." A companion NPR essay by Mara Gordon (2019) advocates standing up to a surgeon who pushes you toward surgery before you have fully researched it. She explains how to shop for the best surgeon and how to find out whether a physician is taking money from drug or device companies. You do not simply receive information; you seize power and act to protect yourself from the influence of money.

I would add that setting up actual support groups to empower patients in these ways would jump-start change, reminiscent of feminist conscious-raising groups in the 1960s. Further, we should not only ask how to empower people, but also ask how people are currently *dis*empowered—and then change it.

Money is conveniently hidden from view in many discussions of autonomy. The autonomy perspective focuses narrowly on the physician–patient relationship; seeking significant institutional, social, and political change is usually brushed aside. It regularly fails to shine light on the flagrant, intentional, and systemic lack of transparency in US medical costs—including the costs of specific procedures (and how some costs might be reduced), information that autonomous agents certainly need (Lazarus 2019). In the United States, the high cost of medical care is the prime motive for medical tourism.

Expanding the Moral Toolbox: The Duty to Confront Power

Having explored how the concept of empowerment might change health care for the better, I advance the following principle: *the duty to confront power, often in coordination with others, in order to further other important moral principles and values.* It is not free-standing; it concerns how and when one should act to carry out other important moral duties and values. It is the duty that whistle-blowers follow, although I have expanded it—in the age of #MeToo—to accentuate the power of working together, sustained over time, perhaps building a movement to change public opinion or specific policies and laws.

The duty to confront power concerns more than achieving an end. As with empowerment, the process matters: Typically, one is changed through carrying out this duty. One stands up and becomes a whistle-blower. If others join in, each gathers strength from the other, as the risk lessens of being attacked or disbelieved. There may be progress toward action within small groups, then professional organizations, including political action.

The key questions then become deciding which specific moral principles or values to promote, and how. A concern for justice might lead to advocating for health insurance for all.

A truly global health concern is mitigating the effects of climate change. Martha Bebinger (2019) reports that the World Health Organization called climate change "the greatest health challenge of the 21st century" and that

> the American Medical Association, American Academy of Pediatrics and American Heart Association were among 70 medical and public health groups that issued a call to action asking the US government, business and leaders to recognize climate change as a health emergency. "The health, safety and wellbeing of millions of people in the United States have already been harmed by human-caused climate change, and health risks in the future are dire without urgent action to fight climate change," the coalition statement said.

In addition to direct political advocacy, what else can be done? Bebinger titles her essay, "Has Your Doctor Talked to You about Climate Change?" She considers whether and how physicians should discuss with their patients the ways climate change specifically affects their health. For example, "heat waves, more pollen, longer allergy seasons" worsen symptoms for patients with allergies, asthma, and COPD. We have returned to autonomy: What information should a patient know? Bebinger adds that medical and nursing schools should do better at teaching how the environment—including climate change—impacts patients' health.

Conclusion

I examined three reasons for US patients to become medical tourists: to save money, to cut waiting time (in particular for kidney transplants), and to get experimental medical treatment as yet unavailable in the United States. Cutting waiting time is rarely a motive for medical tourism from the United States, except to obtain kidneys that are illegally sold by poor people in other countries. Since the people selling are overwhelmingly pressured, lied to, and frequently regret their decision later, this category is ruled out as immoral.

Getting experimental treatment in other countries poses risks to patients over and above the risks of an unproven treatment. The general quality of surgery or postoperative care may be less than in the United States, and it is difficult to get reliable evidence of quality upon which to base an informed decision. Also, both patients and the general public risk drug-resistant bacteria being brought back home. Balancing overall risks and benefits of choosing unproven experimental treatment is based on weighing risks and benefits for the patient, as well as for the public—thus weighing nonmaleficence against beneficence. Moral acceptability will vary with the reliability of the evidence of quality medical treatment in a destination country, how desperate the patient's situation is without the experimental treatment, risk of infection to the general public, and risk of incurring extra costs for follow-up treatment in the United States (which may be borne by others, rather than the patient) from poor-quality treatment.

The primary reason for US patients to become medical tourists is to save money, and the savings can be considerable. However, the indicators of quality medical care in other countries are not reliable, including attempts at accreditation. Again, quality may be less than in the United States, and patients may not have reliable information upon which to base comparative judgments. Regarding US patients who are financially desperate, the possible link between injustice in the United States leading to greater injustice in destination countries was considered. That is, when many in the United States who are denied the right to basic, affordable health care become medical tourists, that might lead to poor people in destination countries receiving worse health care—through brain drain of their medical professionals (or draining away other medical resources) in order to treat medical tourists instead. While the causal connection is far from proven, the concern remains.

What is needed? First, there should be lower demand in the United States for medical tourism based on cost—especially for the 27 million people who are uninsured (Kaiser Family Foundation 2018) and millions more who are underinsured. This is a matter of justice. Second, greater efforts should be made to improve the quality of medical care in destination countries, and to gather and widely release more reliable data, so that patients' decisions are better informed.

The big picture is clear. There is an elephant in the room, and bioethics should be vigilant in calling attention to it: the power of money. Money affects health care throughout the world, and confronting its power should be more central in bioethical discussions.

Many solutions have been offered—and more could be—for raising the quality of medical care in destination countries, for disseminating that information widely, and for treating poor people in destination countries more justly. However, these solutions are, under current conditions, vulnerable to corruption by economic interests and are either not attempted or not carried out effectively.

For example, while destination countries could tax medical tourism and use the money to give their poor people better medical care, no such policies exist to remedy injustice (Cohen 2015, 224–25). As we saw above, the JCI—which accredits the quality of many international medical centers—economically benefits from approving medical centers too easily. I contend that Cohen's (2015) proposal—to channel US patients who are privately insured into better-quality destination sites through default selections and rewards—has promise but would work well only if health-care insurers could be trusted to overlook what would benefit them financially. Cook et al. (2013, 71–72) advocate for NGOs to "quasi-regulate" the quality of health care globally precisely because they are not influenced by monetary gain. But I question whether that insulation would long endure if they did begin to regulate.

I propose that we make economic power more central to bioethical debates of all kinds, asking new questions and reframing old ones. We need to empower patients and health-care professionals to stand up individually and through professional and political organizations. And the duty to confront power in health care should be actively debated: What is most in need of change, and how can it be accomplished, including through political action. Under the right conditions, medical tourism from the United States can be a valuable and morally justified option. Consider the adjoining sister cities of Calexico in California and Mexicali in Mexico. "It is common for residents of Calexico to get dental and medical care in Mexicali, which has first-rate hospitals and a large number of doctors and dentists. Insurance companies routinely send their American patients to Mexicali for care," which is much less expensive (Abcarian 2019).

Where we go from here? Remember the elephant.

References

Abcarian, R. 2019. "Trump's Threat Roils Calexico, Where a Border Closure Could Spell Disaster." *Los Angeles Times*, April 6, 2019. https://www.latimes.com/local/abcarian/la-me-abcarian-calexico-20190406-story.html.

Beauchamp, T., and J. F. Childress. 1979. *Principles of Biomedical Ethics.* 1st ed. New York: Oxford University Press.

Bebinger, M. 2019. "Has Your Doctor Talked to You about Climate Change?" NPR. Published July 13, 2019. https://www.npr.org/sections/health-shots/2019/07/13/734430818/has-your-doctor-talked-to-you-about-climate-change.

Biller-Andorno, N., and Zumrut Alpinar. 2014. "Organ Trafficking and Transplant Tourism." In *Handbook of Global Bioethics*, edited by Henk A. M. J. ten Have and Bert Gordijn, 771–83. Dordrecht: Springer.

Cohen, I. G. 2015. *Patients with Passports: Medical Tourism, Law, and Ethics.* New York: Oxford University Press.

Cook, P. S., G. Kendall, M. Michael, and N. Brown. 2013. "Medical Tourism, Xenotourism and Client Expectations." In *Medical Tourism: The Ethics, Regulation, and Marketing of Health Mobility*, edited by C. M. Hall, 60–74. New York: Routledge.

Gordon, M. 2019. "Do You Need That Surgery? How to Decide, and How to Pick a Surgeon If You Do." NPR. Published July 19, 2019. https://www.npr.org/sections/health-shots/2019/07/19/743248074/do-you-need-that-surgery-how-to-decide-and-how-to-pick-a-surgeon-if-you-do.

Gutierrez, M. 2019. "California Doesn't Have Enough Doctors. To Recruit Them, the State Is Paying Off Medical School Debt." *Los Angeles Times*, July 16, 2019. https://www.latimes.com/politics/la-pol-ca-california-doctor-shortage-medical-debt-20190716-story.html.

Hall, C. M. 2013a. "The Contested Futures and Spaces of Medical Tourism." In *Medical Tourism: The Ethics, Regulation, and Marketing of Health Mobility*, edited by C. M. Hall, 203–16. New York: Routledge.

———. 2013b. "Medical and Health Tourism: The Development and Implications of Medical Mobility." In *Medical Tourism: The Ethics, Regulation, and Marketing of Health Mobility*, edited by C. M. Hall, 3–27. New York: Routledge.

Hamel, L., M. Norton, K. Pollitz, L. Levitt, G. Claxton, and M. Brodie. 2016. "The Burden of Medical Debt: Results from the Kaiser Family Foundation/New York Times Medical Bills Survey." https://www.kff.org/wp-content/uploads/2016/01/8806-the-burden-of-medical-debt-results-from-the-kaiser-family-foundation-new-york-times-medical-bills-survey.pdf.

Healy, M. 2017. "FDA's Program to Speed Up Drug Approval Shaved Nearly a Year Off the Process." *Los Angeles Times*, December 5, 2017. https://www.latimes.com/science/sciencenow/la-sci-sn-fda-expedited-drugs-20171205-story.html.

Hoffman, J., K. Thomas, and D. Hakim. 2019. "3,271 Pill Bottles, a Town of 2,831: Court Filings Say Corporations Fed Opioid Epidemic." *New York Times*, July 19, 2019. https://www.nytimes.com/2019/07/19/health/opioids-trial-addiction-drugstores.html.

Kaiser Family Foundation. 2018. "The Number of Uninsured People Rose in 2017, Reversing Some of the Coverage Gains Under the Affordable Care Act." December 10, 2018. https://www.kff.org/uninsured/press-release/the-number-of-uninsured-people-rose-in-2017-reversing-some-of-the-coverage-gains-under-the-affordable-care-act/.

Kotikova, H., and E. Schwartzhoffova. 2013. "Health and Spa Tourism in the Czech and Slovak Republics." In *Medical Tourism: The Ethics, Regulation, and Marketing of Health Mobility*, edited by C. M. Hall, 109–22. New York: Routledge.

Lazarus, D. 2019. "Column: Insured Price: $2,758. Cash Price: $521. Could Our Healthcare System Be Any Dumber?" *Los Angeles Times*, July 30, 2019. https://www.latimes.com/business/story/2019-07-29/column-could-our-health care-system-be-any-dumber.

Lunt, N., R. Smith, M. Exworthy, S. T. Green, D. Horsfall, and R. Mannion. 2011. "Medical Tourism: Treatments, Markets and Health System Implications: A Scoping Review." http://www.oecd.org/els/health-systems/48723982.pdf.

Lunt, N., S. T. Green, R. Mannion, and D. Horsfall. 2013. "Quality, Safety and Risk in Medical Tourism." In *Medical Tourism: The Ethics, Regulation, and Marketing of Health Mobility*, edited by C. M. Hall, 32–46. New York: Routledge.

Nuremberg Code. 1947. In *Trials of War Criminals before the Nurernberg Military Tribunals under Control Council Law No. 10*. Volume II. Washington, DC: US Government Printing Office, 1949, 181–182. https://www.loc.gov/rr/frd/Military_Law/pdf/NT_war-criminals_Vol-II.pdf. Reprinted in *Journal of the American Medical Association* 276 (1961).

Papanicolas, I., L. R. Woskie, and A. K. Jha. 2018. "Health Care Spending in the United States and Other High-Income Countries." *Journal of the American Medical Association* 319, 10: 1024–39. doi:10.1001/jama.2018.1150.

Rieder, T. 2019. *In Pain: A Bioethicist's Personal Struggle with Opioids*. New York: Harper.

Schumann, J. H., M. Gordon, and C. Weiner. 2019. "Be a Powerful Patient: Take Control of Your Care When You're Seriously Sick." NPR. July 10, 2019. https://www.npr.org/2019/07/09/739927857/take-control-of-your-care-when-youre-seriously-sick.

Warren, V. 2019. "Intellectual Disability, Sexual Assault, and Empowerment." In *Analyzing Violence against Women*, edited by W. Teays, 51–61. Cham, Switzerland: Springer Nature Switzerland AG.

CHAPTER 9

Solitary Confinement[1]

Wanda Teays

Abstract

In this chapter I discuss what many consider the worst form of torture: solitary confinement. A disaster in terms of a method of rehabilitation (as intended by the Quakers, who put it to use years ago), solitary confinement has brought about any number of harms and no apparent benefits. The days of the Quakers thinking solitary confinement purifies the soul are long gone. In its place we find a practice that causes both mental and physical suffering, with long-term damage. We will look at five cases to get a sense of the potential harm of solitary. They include a lawyer, a detainee, two hostages, three prisoners, and three men on death row. The picture that they present is truly alarming. Each of these cases indicates why solitary confinement should be banned or restricted to a matter of hours, if absolutely necessary. We then look at the examples of countries that have made changes and, within the United States, the actions of Rick Raemisch, the Colorado governor who put an end to long-term solitary in his state.

Introduction

It is no mistake on Nel Noddings' part to consider isolation a manifestation of evil. The utter cruelty of confining another person to a cell, cage, or box boggles the mind. That it can go on for years—or even decades—is unimaginable. Where was the outcry when Zacarias Moussaoui was sentenced to life in prison in solitary confinement with no possibility of parole for his role in the attacks on 9/11? "It's an awful thing, solitary," Sen. John McCain wrote of his time as a prisoner of war. "It crushes your spirit and weakens your resistance more effectively than any other form of mistreatment" (Marcus 2012).

The fantasy of the Quakers, who thought solitary confinement would purify the soul and be an effective form of rehabilitation, has been shown to be groundless. That it has continued to the present day and is commonly used in prisons and detention centers indicates how misguided is this policy, and how urgent is the need to put an end to it.

Let's assume for the moment that there could be therapeutic benefits to a short period of isolation. If that were the case, we would need to clarify what they are and whether they outweigh the long-term risks. The practice needs to be assessed by medical professionals to fully grasp the potential harms and consider the alternatives.

Cyrus Ahalt and Brie Williams (2016) are right on track in raising this concern: "Aside from conducting some important studies that have linked even relatively brief isolation to worsening mental health, the medical community has been largely absent from the national debate over solitary confinement. That absence is conspicuous."

It's conspicuous and it needs to change. This is particularly so, given the rampant misuse of the practice. We see this with the number of minor infractions that result in "segregation" (= solitary).

The Misuse of Solitary

Joshua Manson cites examples from a United Nations' report.

> In both the U.S. immigration and detention and federal prison systems, for example, people can be held in solitary confinement for the sole reason that they will be released, removed, or transferred within 24 hours. Also under U.S. federal law, people can be held in solitary confinement if they are HIV-positive and there is "reliable evidence" that they may "pose a health risk" to others.
>
> In California, people may be subject to isolation just because they are "a relative or associate of a staff member." In Pennsylvania, people may be subject to solitary confinement, against their will and consent, because they are "at a high risk of sexual victimization" if there exists no "alternative means of separation from the likely abuser." Also in Pennsylvania, people may be subject to solitary confinement simply because "there is no other appropriate bed space." (Manson 2016)

And so on. You don't have to be a danger to others to end up in solitary confinement, contrary to what we might think. This is particularly disturbing in light of the potential harms of being placed in solitary for even short periods. It can cause long-lasting trauma, mental suffering, and psychological harm.

Solitary can also heighten the risk of suicide. We see this, for example, with the case of Jack Letts. A British Canadian man who went off to Syria to join ISIS, Letts was captured and held in prison by Kurdish authorities. He ended up in solitary.

> He told the [Canadian] consular official that he had attempted suicide after his first month in solitary confinement but was found in time by his Kurdish guards. "I started to go insane and talk to myself and I thought dying was better than my mother seeing me insane," Letts said. "So I tried to hang myself." He has since been allowed to live in a cell with other prisoners. (Brewster 2018)

Jack Letts's reaction to solitary matches the experience of one after another after another. We can see this in the following five cases—the use of solitary on a lawyer, a detainee, two hostages, three prisoners, and three on Death Row. Each case paints a bleak picture of the use of solitary confinement.

FIRST CASE: LAWYER XIE YANYI

Xie Yanyi had spent much of his career in China representing clients in sensitive legal cases involving victims of official corruption, police violence, or religious persecution. John Sudworth (2017) of the BBC reports on China's "war on law":

> The crackdown on China's already beleaguered human rights field began in mid 2015, halfway through Xi Jinping's first term. Now, anointed in office for a second term by the Communist Party Congress that ended this week, it stands as one of his most gloomy legacies. In total, more than 300 lawyers, legal assistants and activists have been brought in for questioning, with more than two dozen pursued as formal investigations.

Xie Yanyi, one of those arrested, said he didn't see sunlight for six months and that he was kept in a stress position and crouched on a low stool from 6:00 in the morning until 10:00 at night. He elaborates:

> After 15 days like this, [he said], his legs went numb and he had difficulty urinating. At times he was denied food and was beaten. . . . But harder to bear was the time spent in solitary confinement, he asserts. "I was kept alone in a small room and saw no daylight for half a year. I had nothing to read, nothing to do but to sit on that low stool." In his view, "People could go mad in that situation. I was isolated from the world. This is torture—the isolation is more painful than being beaten." (Sudworth 2017)

SECOND CASE: DETAINEE JOSE PADILLA

Detainee and American citizen Jose Padilla was held over three years in solitary confinement. The conditions were harsh: his windows were blacked out; there was no clock or calendar; and only a steel platform to sleep on (no mattress) before having access to legal counsel (Sontag 2006).

Two psychiatrists and a psychologist who conducted examinations of Padilla contend that both his extended detention in solitary and interrogation left him with severe mental disabilities. All three say he may never recover. In their opinion, "Padilla's ordeal in the brig was so psychologically unsettling that it has left him terrorized. Any reminder of the ordeal through questions by his lawyers or others triggers a recurrence of the disorganizing terror Padilla experienced" (Richey 2007).

THIRD CASE: HOSTAGES TERRY ANDERSON AND FRANK REED

Journalist Terry Anderson was covering Lebanon's civil war of 1975–1990 when he was kidnapped along with other foreigners. He was released in 1991 after being held prisoner in an underground dungeon for six and a half years (History.com 2009).

Fellow hostage Frank Reed, an American private-school director, was held in solitary confinement for four months before being put in with Anderson. Surgeon and public health commentator Atul Gawande reports on Reed's condition: "By then, Reed had become severely withdrawn. He lay motionless for hours facing a wall, semi-catatonic. He could not follow the guards' simplest instructions. Released after three and a half years, Reed ultimately required admission to a psychiatric hospital" (2016).

Anderson didn't fare so well either:

> He missed people terribly, especially his fiancée and his family. He was despondent and depressed . . . A month into his confinement, he recalled in his memoir, "The mind is a blank. Jesus, I always thought I was smart. Where are all the things I learned, the books I read, the poems I memorized? There's nothing there, just a formless, gray-black misery. My mind's gone dead. God, help me." One day, three years into his ordeal, he snapped. He walked over to a wall and began beating his forehead against it, dozens of times. His head was smashed and bleeding before the guards were able to stop him. (Gawande 2009)

FOURTH CASE: PRISONERS ROBERT KING, HERMAN WALLACE, AND ALBERT WOODFOX, AKA, "THE ANGOLA THREE"

The three Black Panther activists were convicted in the early 1970s of a prison guard's murder (they claimed they were framed). Each spent decades in solitary—King, twenty-nine years; Wallace, forty-one years; and Woodfox, forty-three years, the longest in US history. King commented on the conditions:

> The cells were pretty bare, and they were maybe about . . . 3 feet wide and about 6 feet long. It was almost like it was in a tomb, and there was a slab of concrete that you slept on. You ate three meals a day—you had two slices of bread each meal. During the wintertime, you froze, and during summertime, you were overheated. But in any event, you were starved. (Kennedy 2016)

Wallace died three days after his release in 2013. Woodfox was freed February 19, 2016, and died on August 4, 2022, from complications of COVID-19. In a February 2016 interview with *The Guardian* (UK), Woodfox remarked on the brutality of solitary:

> Some of the guys found the pressure so great that they just laid down in a fetal position and stopped communicating with anybody. I've seen other guys

> who just want to talk and make noise, guys who want to scream. Breaking up manifests itself in any number of ways in individuals. (Pilkington 2016)

As for himself, Woodfox observed that

> The panic attacks started with sweating. You sweat and you can't stop. You become soaking wet—you are asleep in your bunk and everything is soaking wet. Then when the claustrophobia starts it feels like the atmosphere is pressing down on you. That was hard. I used to talk to myself to convince myself I was strong enough to survive, just to hold on to my sanity until the feeling went away. (Pilkington 2016)

FIFTH CASE: DEATH ROW CONVICTS MARCUS HAMILTON, WINTHROP EATON, AND MICHAEL PERRY

Convicted of first-degree murder in Louisiana and sentenced to death, all three men have been in solitary confinement for over twenty-five years. They aren't the only ones: According to Liam Stack (2017), seventy-one prisoners sentenced to death in Louisiana are being held in solitary confinement at the Angola state penitentiary.

> They spend 23 hours a day in windowless concrete cells that measure 8 by 10 feet. They are allowed to leave the cell for one hour each day to shower, make phone calls or walk along the tiered walkway beside their cells. Three times a week, they can use that hour to go outside to sit in a small outdoor cage. (Stack 2017)

Evidently "a lot, if not most" of the states that have the death penalty house their death row inmates in solitary confinement, according to Betsy Ginsberg, the director of the civil rights clinic at the Benjamin N. Cardozo School of Law (Stack 2017).

The damaging effects of prolonged solitary confinement on the mental and physical health of prisoners have been well established, as Stack points out. Social psychologist Craig Haney notes that even those with no history of mental illness were engaged in a "constant, ongoing struggle to maintain their sanity." In addition, "These conditions predictably can impair the psychological functioning of the prisoners who are subjected to them," he [observed]. "For some prisoners, these impairments can be permanent and life-threatening" (Stack 2017).

Overview of Issues

On any given day, approximately 80,000 prisoners are being held in solitary confinement in the United States alone. That's not all. According to the Bureau of Justice Statistics, over the course of a year, nearly 1 in 5 (= 20 percent) US prisoners spent time in solitary confinement. This adds up to 400,000 people who are incarcerated and are also in solitary during a given year (Ahalt and Williams 2016). With such staggering numbers, a lot more needs to be done to justify this practice.

Others convey similar sentiments and raise important concerns. For instance, it's not only prisoners who are subjected to solitary confinement. Immigrants in detention facilities are also at risk.

John V. Kelly, acting inspector general of the US Department of Homeland Security, points out that, "Staff did not always treat detainees respectfully and professionally, and some facilities may have misused segregation" (Sacchetti 2017). He cites the example of a detainee who reported being locked down for multiple days for sharing coffee with another detainee (Office of Inspector General, Homeland Security 2017). This is clearly an overreaction to a minor offense.

The Harms of Solitary

Misuse is one concern. So are the extreme conditions and the resulting psychological effects. Social scientist Craig Haney undertook a two-year study of inmates who were subjected to prolonged use of solitary confinement at Pelican Bay prison in California. He states that,

> Sealed for years in a hermetic environment—one inmate likened the prison's solitary confinement unit to "a weapons lab or a place for human experiments"—prisoners recounted struggling daily to maintain their sanity.
>
> They spoke of longing to catch sight of a tree or a bird. Many responded to their isolation by shutting down their emotions and withdrawing even further, shunning even the meager human conversation and company they were afforded. (Goode 2015)

Haney said that after months or years of complete isolation, many prisoners begin to lose the ability to initiate behavior of any kind. In extreme cases, "prisoners may literally stop behaving [at all]," thus becoming "essentially catatonic" (Gawande 2016).

In addition, almost 90 percent of these prisoners had difficulties with "irrational anger," as Terry Anderson notes about his own experience. In contrast, only 3 percent of the general population are said to suffer extreme anger. Not surprising, Haney claims that many prisoners in solitary become consumed with revenge fantasies.

This is a far cry from the rehabilitation that Quakers sought in turning to solitary confinement. Rather than a time to cool off, solitary seems more likely to bring emotions to the boiling point. Just look at some of the harms that have been documented.

Atul Gawande (2016) reports that studies show diffuse slowing of brain waves after a week or more of solitary confinement. He cites the 1992 case of fifty-seven prisoners of war whose EEGs showed brain abnormalities months after a six-month detention in Yugoslavia. Such evidence indicates solitary confinement has both physical as well as psychological harms.

ABUSIVE AND AGGRESSIVE FORMS OF SOLITARY

If things aren't bad enough when people are confined to eight-by-ten-foot cells, there have been even more alarming cases. A macabre turn of events has been the practice of cramming suspected terrorists into boxes (for example, Abu Zubaydah). Yes, boxes. Presumably this is to encourage them to be more forthcoming— as if subjecting them to such miserable conditions would inspire them to divulge useful information. The result is that their confinement is more physically taxing than it would be with the use of rooms or prison cells.

Such an extreme has been accepted if not sanctioned at the highest level. In fact, psychologist-masterminds Drs. Mitchell and Jessen recommended using such "aggressive techniques" as part of the interrogation process on so-called high-value captives. This included detainees Abu Zubaydah and Mohamed Ben Soud being placed in wooden boxes with holes poked in them to allow airflow (Fink and Risen 2017). They were then forced into crouched positions, unable to stand up or move about. The Senate Intelligence Committee Report details Zubaydah's confinement to a box:

> He spent a total of 266 hours (11 days, two hours) in the large (coffin-size) confinement box and 29 hours in a small confinement box, which had a width of 21 inches, a depth of 2.5 feet, and a height of 2.5 feet. . . . According to the daily cables . . . Abu frequently "cried," "begged," "pleaded," and "whimpered," but continued to deny that he had any additional information. (2014, 52–53)

To add to the pressure, then US district attorney Jay Bybee authorized via a memo the use of insects placed in the box to exploit the victim's phobias and fears. The memo permitted Zubaydah to be kept in a dark, confined space small enough to restrict his movement (CNN 2009).

> In addition, putting a [so-called] harmless insect into the box with Zubaydah, who "appears to have a fear of insects," and telling him it is a stinging insect would be allowed, as long as Zubaydah was informed the insect's sting would not be fatal or cause severe pain. "If, however, you were to place the insect in the box without informing him that you are doing so . . . you should not affirmatively lead him to believe that any insect is present which has a sting that could produce severe pain or suffering or even cause his death," the memo said. (CNN 2009)

Descriptions and Denials

The five cases of solitary confinement are disturbing enough when looking at the individuals affected, not to mention those like Abu Zubaydah and Ben Soud, who were crammed into boxes. It is also important to consider the scope of the use of solitary and how it can be obscured or hidden by the way it is described. We see this in the following mixture of linguistic manipulation and denial:

> "The Bureau [of Prisons] does not recognize the term solitary confinement. Therefore, the Bureau does not have a definition or reference to provide," the BOP told investigators with the DOJ [Department of Justice] Office of the Inspector General.
>
> One former BOP official told investigators that "solitary confinement does not exist" within the federal prisons system. But the inspector general's office said the Bureau of Prisons is just arguing semantics. (Reilly 2017)

Moreover, as law professor Joseph Margulies points out, there is no upper bound on holding a detainee in solitary confinement or being subjected to interrogations (2006, 107). To get a sense of the enormity of the problem in the United States, look at the numbers reported in July 2017 by the US Department of Justice on the Federal Bureau of Prisons:

> As of June 2016, of the 148,227 sentenced inmates in the BOP's [Federal Bureau of Prisons'] 122 institutions, 9,749 inmates (7 percent) were housed in its three largest forms of Restricted Housing (RHU). . . . Although the BOP states that it does not practice solitary confinement, or even recognize the term, we found inmates, including those with mental illness, who were housed in single-cell confinement for long periods of time, isolated from other inmates and with limited human contact.
>
> Although the BOP generally imposes a minimum amount of time that inmates must spend in RHUs, it does not limit the maximum amount of time. . . . As a result, inmates, including those with mental illness, may spend years and even decades in RHUs. (Office of the Inspector General, DOJ 2017)

The Use of Euphemisms

One of the ways that solitary confinement has been made more palatable is through distorting language. Whitewashing it with euphemisms like "disciplinary segregation," "administrative segregation," or "Segregated Housing Units (SHU)" does not alter the fact that such isolation is harmful and its extensive use alarming. With such labeling, they can avoid admitting that they practice solitary confinement. To what advantage? Colin Dayan asserts, "Since prison officials claim that these units are non-punitive, they are difficult to fight" (2007, 54).

The *Washington Post* editorial board (2017) responded to the Department of Justice report by declaring solitary confinement to be torture. "Restrictive housing placement is the bureau's preferred terminology," they stated, "but the report released last week made clear that is a semantic dodge." The *Post* pointed out that:

> Among those forced to languish alone were inmates with serious mental illness, some of whom were isolated for more than five years. A number of state prison systems have taken steps to limit or end their use of solitary confinement because of mounting evidence of its detrimental effects.

> The Inspector General cited research that isolation can cause anxiety, depression, anger, paranoia and psychosis among prisoners. "You have no contact, you don't speak to anybody, and it's a form of torture on some level," a psychologist at one prison told investigators.

Where Is the Outrage?

Given this is the case, it is puzzling how little outcry there is among medical personnel and the general public. The solution? The *Post* (2017) calls it:

> Ending such barbarity is not only morally correct but also has practical benefits in improving public safety. Prisoners subjected to solitary confinement have difficulty reentering society and are more likely to re-offend.

Colin Dayan observes that solitary confinement was once considered the most severe deprivation, and now its use is normalized (2007, 54). However, change is finally afoot. We see this in the practice of solitary confinement being banned in the state of Colorado. Rick Raemisch, the executive director of the Colorado Department of Corrections, explains:

> Long-term solitary was supposed to be rehabilitative, but it did not have that effect. Studies have found that inmates who have spent time in solitary confinement are more likely to reoffend than those who have not. Data shows that prisoners in solitary account for about half of all prison suicides; self-harm is also more common in solitary units than in less-restrictive ones.
>
> One social psychologist even found that the degree of loneliness experienced by people in solitary is matched only by that of terminal cancer patients. In addition, solitary confinement was intended to be a last resort for those who were too violent to be in a prison's general population. But then we gradually included inmates who disrupted the efficient running of an institution. In other words, inmates could be placed in solitary for almost any reason, and they were. (Raemisch 2017)

Working for Change

Raemisch came to see that major changes were in order. He noted how he benefited from listening to the perspectives of others. This came about in 2015 when he assisted the State Department with other United Nations countries in modernizing international standards for the treatment of prisoners—known as the Nelson Mandela Rules. It was decided, Raemisch (2017) reports, that keeping someone for more than fifteen days in solitary was torture.

This conclusion was echoed in a report of the Human Rights Clinic at the University of Texas School of Law. "Its authors concluded," reports Jacey Fortin, "that solitary confinement in Texas violates international human rights standards and amounts to a form of torture" (2017). The bottom line is that:

> We agree that if somebody commits a crime, they should receive a punishment . . . But we say, at the same time, that once you impose a punishment on a person, you need to keep treating that person with humanity and with dignity. (Fortin 2017)

Raemisch would concur. As he puts it, "There now is enough data to convince me that long-term isolation manufactures and aggravates mental illness. It has not solved any problems; at best it has maintained them. That's why, in September, Colorado ended the practice" (2017).

This decision is significant; others should follow their example. We need to recognize that its widespread use in the United States doesn't make it right. Many other countries are in the same boat in the use and misuse of solitary.

> In an October 17, 2016, [meeting], UN Special Rapporteur on Torture, Juan E. Méndez, presented a report to the General Assembly detailing and comparing solitary confinement practices around the world. He declared that solitary confinement may amount to cruel, inhuman, or degrading treatment and in some cases torture, and may thus, under certain conditions, be prohibited under international law.
>
> In that 2011 report, Méndez further called for a categorical ban on subjecting juveniles and people with mental illness to solitary confinement, and to end the practice of prolonged and indefinite solitary confinement. (Solitary Watch 2016)

In contrast, Norway is at the other end of the spectrum in its use of solitary confinement. As Ahalt and Williams (2016) indicate, Norwegian leaders realized that the old model simply did not work—that it did more harm than good, and the time had come for its replacement. Norway's approach stands in dramatic contrast with the systemic overuse of solitary.

What Role Can Doctors Play?

Doctors have a role to play in this. The Norwegian model is worth serious consideration. Ahalt and Williams (2016) offer their recommendation—one it behooves health professionals to take. "We believe the health professions have a responsibility to work with criminal justice policymakers to assess the risk of health-related harm underlying correctional practices such as solitary confinement. Fortunately, a compelling model for such a partnership exists." This they saw practiced at a Norwegian maximum-security prison. At the time, it housed 250 men, many serving long sentences for violent crimes.

> We asked the warden how many prisoners were being held in isolation and were surprised to hear his answer: one. That morning, a prisoner had trashed his cell. Guards, using motivational interviewing strategies, tried unsuccessfully to defuse the situation. The man was now cooling off in isolation under the close supervision of a health care team. "As soon as he

> calms down," the warden told us, "He will return to the general population." We asked how long that might take. "Tonight?" the warden guessed. "Tomorrow, certainly." (Ahalt and Williams 2016)

In comparison:

> In a U.S. prison of the same size, we would expect to find 25 prisoners in solitary, and roughly half of them would be confined for more than a month. But here there was only one serving less than 1 day, with enhanced attention rather than minimal human contact.
>
> The Norwegian criminal justice leaders we spoke with told us that 20 years ago their correctional system resembled ours: overcrowded and violent, with frequent use of solitary confinement. Then, motivated by prison riots, Norwegian leaders undertook broad reform. (Ahalt and Williams 2016)

Norway is not alone in casting a critical eye on solitary, in an attempt to make changes with this outdated and harmful model. What is going on in Britain also deserves our attention. Jean Casella (2015) of Solitary Watch reports on controls that have been put in place:

> Britain has a long history of using solitary confinement. In 1842, it mimicked the United States in opening a prison, . . . devoted to isolating prisoners so they could contemplate their sins. The practice was largely abandoned on both sides of the Atlantic once it became clear that solitary led to madness, not penitence. Prison isolation was revived in the late twentieth century, but never on the scale seen in the United States.
>
> Today, a series of rules allow the short-term use of solitary confinement but are meant to check its overuse and abuse. Prison governors (wardens) may place individuals in what are officially called "care and separation" units to preserve the "good order and discipline" of the prison. But after 72 hours, their continued segregation requires the approval of not only the governor, but—as confirmed in a recent court decision—the Cabinet Secretary for Justice. With the necessary approvals, terms in solitary can stretch longer, but must be reviewed and renewed every 14 days.

With the additional oversight and a high-level approvals process, the abuse of solitary confinement should be curtailed. Moreover, this model allows for more transparency and thus has less likelihood of misuse.

Conclusion

There is little doubt that solitary confinement is cruel and unusual punishment and, for any extended period, is a form of torture. It has virtually no value as an instrument of rehabilitation. That it has not yet been banned or subjected to strict limitations in terms of use and duration is simply deplorable.

Both Norway and Britain have moved to a different model of addressing behavioral or other issues that made solitary seem a legitimate option. We need to give close attention to the approaches they have taken and consider the range of alternatives to solitary.

Although it seems unreasonable to have oversight by a governor, a director of justice, or the like, an oversight committee could be employed to help end the abuses taking place with solitary confinement.

One option might be to use a review board such as a bioethics committee or a variation thereof, drawing upon medical professionals, clergy, and members of the community. In other words, we need more transparency about what is taking place and more controls on what is being done.

Note

1. © Springer Nature Switzerland AG 2019. Wanda Teays, "Doctors and Torture: Medicine at the Crossroads,"International Library of Ethics, Law, and the New Medicine 80: 95–107. Used with permission.

References

Ahalt, Cyrus, and Brie Williams. 2016, May 5. "Reforming Solitary-Confinement Policy—Heeding a Presidential Call to Action," *New England Journal of Medicine*; 374:1704–6. http://www.stopsolitaryforkids.org/wp-content/uploads/2016/05/NEJM-Solitary-May-2016-p1601399.pdf. Retrieved June 5, 2018.

Brewster, Murray. 2018, February 8. "Alleged ISIS Operative 'Jihadi Jack' Begs Canada to Let Him Come Here," CBC News, http://www.cbc.ca/news/politics/jihadi-jack-isis-consular-1.4526882. Retrieved June 5, 2018.

Casella, Jean. 2015, October 21. "Off the Block," Solitary Watch, http://solitarywatch.com/2015/10/21/off-the-block/. Retrieved June 5, 2018.

CNN. 2009, April 17. "2002 Memo: Had to Be Intent to Inflict 'Severe Pain' to Be Torture," CNN, http://www.cnn.com/2009/POLITICS/04/16/us.torture.documents/. Retrieved June 5, 2018.

Dayan, Colin. 2007. *The Story of Cruel and Unusual*. Boston: MIT Press.

Fink, Sheri, and James Risen. 2017, June 20. "Psychologists Open a Window on Brutal C.I.A. Interrogations," *New York Times*, https://www.nytimes.com/interactive/2017/06/20/us/cia-torture.html. Retrieved June 5, 2018.

Fortin, Jacey. 2017, April 26. "Report Compares Texas' Solitary Confinement Policies to Torture," *New York Times*, https://www.nytimes.com/2017/04/26/us/texas-death-row-torture-report.html. Retrieved June 5, 2018.

Gawande, Atul. 2009, March 30. "Hellhole," *The New Yorker*, https://www.newyorker.com/magazine/2009/03/30/hellhole. Retrieved June 5, 2018.

Goode, Erica. 2015, August 3. "Solitary Confinement: Punished for Life," *The New Yorker*, https://www.nytimes.com/2015/08/04/health/solitary-confinement-mental-illness.html. Retrieved June 5, 2018.

History.com. 2009, December 4. "1991: Hostage Terry Anderson freed in Lebanon," https://www.history.com/this-day-in-history/hostage-terry-anderson-freed-in-lebanon. Retrieved June 5, 2018.

Kennedy, Merrit. 2016, February 19. "Last of 'Angola 3' Released After More Than 40 Years in Solitary Confinement," NPR, https://www.npr.org/sections/thetwo-way/2016/02/19/467406096/last-of-angola-3-released-after-more-than-40-years-in-solitary-confinement. Retrieved June 5, 2018.

Manson, Joshua. 2016, October 28. "UN Report Compare Solitary Practices in the US and Around the World," Solitary Watch, http://solitarywatch.com/2016/10/28/un-report-compares-solitary-confinement-practices-around-the-world/. Retrieved June 5, 2018.

Marcus, Ruth. 2012, October 16. "The Cruelest Punishment," *Washington Post*, https://www.washingtonpost.com/opinions/ruth-marcus-why-are-we-subjecting-our-youths-to-solitary-confinement/2012/10/16/76a7bc50-17b6-11e2-9855-71f2b202721b_story.html.

Margulies, Joseph. 2006. *Guantánamo and the Abuse of Presidential Power*. New York: Simon & Schuster.

Office of the Inspector General. 2017, July. "Review of the Federal Bureau of Prisons' Use of Restrictive Housing for Inmates with Mental Illness," US Department of Justice. https://oig.justice.gov/reports/2017/e1705.pdf#page=1. Retrieved June 5, 2018.

Office of the Inspector General. 2017, December 11. "Concerns about ICE Detainee Treatment and Care at Detention Facilities," Homeland Security, https://www.oig.dhs.gov/sites/default/files/assets/2017-12/OIG-18-32-Dec17.pdf. Retrieved June 5, 2018.

Pilkington, Ed. 2016, February 20. "Albert Woodfox Speaks After 43 Years in Solitary Confinement: 'I Would Not Let Them Drive Me Insane,'" *The Guardian* (UK), https://www.theguardian.com/us-news/2016/feb/20/albert-woodfox-angola-3-first-interview-trump-confinement. Retrieved June 5, 2018.

Raemisch, Rick. 2017, October 12. "Why We Ended Long-Term Solitary Confinement in Colorado," *New York Times*, https://www.nytimes.com/2017/10/12/opinion/solitary-confinement-colorado-prison.html. Retrieved June 5, 2018.

Reilly, Ryan J. 2017, July 12. "Federal Prisons Officials Claim Inmates Aren't Held in Solitary. DOJ Watchdog Says They Are," *Huffington Post*, https://www.huffingtonpost.com/entry/federal-prison-solitary-confinement-mental-illness_us_59664623e4b005b0fdca5f85?nf5. Retrieved June 5, 2018.

Richey, Warren. 2007, August 13. "US Terror Interrogation Went Too Far, Experts Say," *Christian Science Monitor*. Retrieved June 5, 2018.

Sacchetti, Maria. 2017, December 17. "Watchdog Report Finds Moldy Food, Mistreatment in Immigrant Detention Centers," *Washington Post*, https://www.washingtonpost.com/local/immigration/watchdog-report-finds-moldy-food-mistreatment-in-immigrant-detention-centers/2017/12/15/c97b380a-e10d-11e7-89e8-edec16379010_story.html?utm_term=.1bc140373121. Retrieved June 5, 2018.

Solitary Watch. 2016, October 28. "UN Report Compares Solitary Confinement Practices in the U.S. and Around the World," http://solitarywatch.com/2016/10/28/un-report-compares-solitary-confinement-practices-around-the-world/. Retrieved June 5, 2018.

Sontag, Deborah. 2006, December 4. "Video Is a Window into a Terror Suspect's Isolation," *New York Times*, http://www.nytimes.com/2006/12/04/us/04detain.html. Retrieved June 5, 2018.

Stack, Liam. 2017, March 30. "3 Men on Death Row in Louisiana Sue Over Solitary Confinement," *New York Times*, https://www.nytimes.com/2017/03/30/us/3-men-on-death-row-in-louisiana-sue-over-solitary-confinement.htm. Retrieved June 5, 2018.

Sudworth, John. 2017, October 25. "China Lawyer Recounts Torture Under Xi's 'War on Law,'" BBC News, Beijing, BBC, http://www.bbc.com/news/blogs-china-blog-41661862. Retrieved June 5, 2018.

Washington Post Editorial Board. 2017, July 15. "Solitary Confinement Is Torture. Will the Bureau of Prisons Finally Stop Using It?," *Washington Post,* https://www.washingtonpost.com/opinions/solitary-confinement-is-torture-will-the-bureau-of-prisons-finally-stop-using-it/2017/07/15/f719de20-68c6-11e7-8eb5-cbccc2e7bfbf_story.html?utm_term=.adc722effac4. Retrieved June 5, 2018.

CHAPTER 10

Compensation for Research-Related Injury for a Typically Ignored Social Harm

Peter F. Omonzejele

Abstract

This chapter acknowledges that unanticipated injury could occur in the medical research setting, and in many cases, pharmaceutical companies compensate affected subjects for such injury. It is for this reason that pharmaceutical companies such as Pfizer developed a research policy document, which includes compensation for research-related injury. The argument in this chapter is that compensation policies in research-related injury that constitutes social harm—especially where it involves young unmarried African women—cannot be redressed by current policies. This is because such social harm could adversely impair such women's potential to benefit from the bride-price tradition due to stigma. The consequence for the deprivation of the bride-price tradition for those young women is far-reaching, as it defines their status and place in their local communities. Although the author does not support the bride-price tradition based on associated human rights issues, the aim of this chapter is to show that compensation for research-related injury as found in current policy documents is deficient in redressing certain social harms in some cultures. The author demonstrates how with the use of the non-pecuniary compensation-in-community framework, such social harms could be mitigated.

Introduction

Medical research, like other human activities, can inadvertently go wrong. In some cases, the wrong could be catastrophic, and even fatal. In fact, investigators undertake medical research on humans because they do not know for certain the effect the study will have. This means that medical research may be a risky enterprise that could potentially lead to injury for research subjects. To address the possibility of injury in the medical setting, Pfizer, for instance, developed a compensation policy document entitled "Compensation to Research Subjects in Clinical Studies" (Pfizer, February 15, 2017) for its sponsored research. According to Pfizer (2017):

> The purpose of this clinical and medical controlled document (CMCD) policy is to describe the requirements for the compensation, expense reimbursement, and post-study transitional care of the research subject (including both patients and healthy volunteer subjects) who participate in the conduct of Pfizer-sponsored studies.
>
> In regard to research-related injury:
>
> Pfizer offers reasonable compensation for time and effort to healthy volunteer subjects and, depending upon study design, may also provide reasonable compensation to other study subjects when health benefits from study participation are remote or non-existent. In addition, reasonable compensation may be provided to parents, guardians, or caregivers of minor children or incapacitated subjects. (Pfizer 2017)

There is no need to reproduce Pfizer's entire policy document here, since we have captured the relevant aspect above, which is compensation for research-related injury.

Let me state *ab initio* that I am mindful of the debate over whether research subjects should be compensated for research-related injury, since they voluntarily consented to participate in the study. In general, the argument for non-compensation for research-related injury goes thus: When subjects freely consent to participate in a study, they incur whatever risk and potential harm that might be associated with the study (Grant and Sugarman 2004, 717–38).

On the other hand, it has been argued by bioethicists, such as Munshi and Thatte (2013, 61–69), that not to compensate subjects for research-related injury because they voluntarily consented to participate negates the principles of justice and respect for persons. They further argue that, in the conduct of medical research, risk and harm are often unknown and unexpected, and so it is wrong to invoke the concept of "no fault" compensation for research-related injury.

In line with this argument, Chapman et al. (2020, 732–47) reviewed the moral justifications for research-related injury on the basis of justice, and advised the US government to develop a national compensation system for research-related injury, which would co-opt the beneficiaries of research to bear the burden of compensation for such injury.

I do not intend to dwell much on the debate, since my focus is on the effectiveness of policy documents, such as Pfizer's, to compensate for all research-related injury, particularly where it states that: "Pfizer generally covers the cost of protocol-required treatments and procedures. Pfizer covers the cost for medical treatment for any injury or illness that occurs as a direct result of taking part in a Pfizer-sponsored study at no cost to the research subject."

I will consider how well Pfizer's compensation policy effectively addresses research-related injury that culminates in social harm among unmarried African women, especially where the harm deprives participants of the benefits of the bride-price tradition. (For clarification: The argument about the possible commodification and objectification of persons based on the bride-price tradition is beyond the scope of this chapter. While I do not support the tradition, nonetheless, it is a way of life that is cherished in most African countries.) This means that the gap I aim to fill in this chapter is pertinent if a study design must include participants from the category of young unmarried African women. For example, it appears Pfizer's compensation policy is incapable of redressing this sort of potential risk and social harms in the medical research setting, as such social harm cannot be remedied by medical treatment or by pecuniary compensation in research regulatory documents.

At this point, let us examine the nature of risk in medical research, as we can then appreciate the depth of social harm in the conduct of medical research.

Risks in Medical Research

Research-related injury in most cases is unanticipated; since "research is inherently uncertain, unintended harm is an inevitable part of the research enterprise" (Larkin 2015, 309). This implies that healthy research subjects potentially incur risk the moment they consent to participate in a study. Such potential risk could translate into injury, and "such injuries may range from relatively minor harms (such as bruises due to a study procedure or vomiting due to a new drug) to major injuries (such as organ damage or temporary physical disability) to catastrophic injuries (such as permanent disability or death)" (Larkin 61). In some cases, research guidelines take into account possible injuries and determine the circumstances in which research should be undertaken to limit harm in the research setting. This is not to imply that there hasn't been research in which harm was an anticipated outcome. In fact, such cases abound, which I have previously exemplified (Omonzejele 2012, 47–50).

For example, within the period between 1932 and 1945, Japanese doctors conducted abusive medical research among Chinese, Russians, Mongolians, Koreans, and other nationalities (Nei et al. 2003, 106). Japanese doctors carried out vivisections on Chinese prisoners for the purpose of training newly employed army surgeons. Furthermore, Japanese doctors deliberately infected prisoners of war with infectious diseases such as cholera, typhoid, and plague, and carried out "unusual and non-established treatments" (Nei et al. 2003, 106) in order to study the tolerance of the human body under extraordinary circumstances. In the infamous Unit 731 in Japan, approximately three thousand human beings were killed by Japanese medical researchers in the course of various types of medical study (Nei et al. 2003, 106).

Another case involved women in New Zealand with cervical cancer who were left untreated for their condition. These women were neither told of their diagnosis nor informed that they were involved in a study. Instead, they were regularly invited to the hospital for the purpose of observation. Most of them died due to lack of medical intervention for their condition (Schüklenk 2000, 967–70).

In the United States during the 1930s through the 1970s, four hundred poor Black men were diagnosed with syphilis, but left untreated, as researchers wanted to know the natural progression of the disease. It is now known as the Tuskegee Syphilis Study. This case "has been described as an egregious case of blatant racism" (Paul and Brookes 2015, 12). Though there was standard treatment (penicillin) for the condition, the subjects were placed on a placebo. This study has been condemned by most ethicists and by the lay public.

The above-mentioned research abuses with anticipated injury and harm is not the focus of this chapter, as such research should never have been undertaken in the first place. The examples were given to show that not all investigations are well intentioned. The aim of this chapter is to consider compensation for unintended and unforeseen injury or harm incurred by subjects based on their participation in research, as it is generally understood that research subjects concede to possible risks the moment they consented to participate in the study. Risk, unfortunately, is an inherent part of research.

As I have previously shown and discussed (Omonzejele 2012, 82–85), Levine (1988, 37) explained that "risk entails prediction of some future occurrence of harm. Risk may be expressed in terms of probability that certain harm will occur." In medical research, risks could be described as probable hazards that a subject or patient may incur in the course of participating in a study.

Diagram One: Types of Risk in the Medical Research Setting

Risks in the research and care settings are classified as physical, psychological (Levine 1988, 42–48), and social risks (Barber 1978, 1–19, 21). In clinical and care studies, there is always the possibility that research subjects could incur tangible harms (physical harm); this is particularly true in the early stages of clinical trials, or in the course of invasive care. One would reasonably expect that researchers would do all they can to prevent foreseeable harms to their subjects.

However, despite efforts by researchers to prevent harm, clinical trials can never be risk-free, as subjects will always bear the physical risk of unpredictable harms. For instance, some harm associated with the research may come about many years after their participation in a study. In the same way, some harms incurred in the course of treatment could come much later, such as psychological harm. This is because "physical risks might be totally unknown while an intervention is in its investigational phases, owing to a long period of latency between the intervention and the development of the adverse effect" (Levine 1988, 43).

In some studies, potential physical risks/harms connected to a study hold indirect risks for those not involved in the study (Levine, 44). Holder (1980, 5–7) indicates an instance of indirect physical risks to non-research subjects based on their association with research subjects. According to Holder, when children are inoculated with rubella (German measles) vaccines in a trial, it could result in the transmission of the virus to a pregnant woman with whom the child has had close contact. This could cause the woman to give birth to a severely deformed baby, despite the fact that the pregnant woman did not participate in the rubella vaccine trials. This sort of risk is incurred by association.

Other than physical risks associated with enlisting in research as a subject, risks can also be psychological or social. Psychological risks are related to situations where the mental well-being of a subject is affected as a result of participation in a study.

According to Levine (1988, 45), such studies constitute "threats to the psychological integrity of the subject." For instance, Katz (1972, 365–69) states that "in a study to understand how humans would behave in an environment with sensory deprivation," healthy subjects were induced into a state of traumatic neurosis, and long after the studies, the research subjects still suffered from "lingering disturbances." Of course, such research might be borderline in terms of ethical acceptability, and one would therefore address the problems potentially generated through the topic of favorable versus unfavorable risk/benefit ratio.

In addition to physical and psychological risks, research subjects may be subjected to social risks. This is the case, for instance, when enlisting participants in the research leads to stigmatization within one's family or community. Social risks have far-reaching implications in the African context, sometimes long after studies have taken place. Such risks could prevent a woman from getting married (meaning her bride-price would not be paid), even though she was merely an infant when her family was stigmatized as a result of their participation in research. As already stated, the focus of this chapter is on young unmarried African women who participated in research and suffered social harm, making it impossible for them to benefit from the bride-price tradition.

The question then is: How does Pfizer's policy document on compensation for research-related injury redress this sort of injury? To understand the enormity of this sort of harm, it is important to shed light on the African bride-price tradition, its implication for African women, and the consequences of its deprivation, for whatever reason.

The African Bride-Price Tradition

As already mentioned, I do not necessarily support the bride-price tradition based on human rights issues. Despite this view, the bride-price tradition in most African countries is cherished as a rite with profound implications. It is for this reason that young women and their families look forward to it. In most African countries, marriages are only recognized upon the payment of the so-called "bride price," known as *labola* in South Africa, *roora* in Zimbabwe, *mahari* in East Africa, and generally referred to as "head-money" in West African countries (Omonzejele 2008, 121). The African bride price is the payment either in cash or in-kind, which family members of the groom make to the family members of the bride in order for the groom to marry the latter's daughter. According to Mbaye and Wagner (2017, 893):

> Before the actual marriage celebration, several consultative visits and mutual invitations take place between the future spouses and/or close family members. To conclude this period of negotiations, the bride's parents have to choose a date for the marriage ceremony and announce the desired value of the bride price. This bride price can be composed of cash and material goods such as furniture and jewels.

The bride price is the last and most important marriage rite, which takes place only after all other rites (such as consultations, "wine carrying," etc.) have been performed to the satisfaction of both families (Omonzejele 2012, 29–33).

Marriage for women as derived from the bride-price tradition in Africa has social implications, as oftentimes unmarried mature women are not accorded respect, and such women are often referred to derogatorily as women "without anchor" (Omonzejele 2012, 29–33). In many cases, landlords would often not rent out their property to single women, to give just one example of the associated disadvantages. Though it is possible for an unmarried woman to ignore the negative social implications associated with her marital status when living in urban areas, it is impossible to ignore such restrictions in her ancestral community, especially as such restrictions relate to one's association.

When a woman reaches a certain age, she is expected to be married; when this is not the case, she can no longer belong to her relevant age-grade. Let me explain: African communities are divided into associations, and one's age determines to a large extent the association one belongs to. This means that a woman who chooses not to get married (or due to stigma, no one was willing to pay the bride price for her) might find it difficult to function in her ancestral community. Marriage is the only way to join the higher association of married women in her community, or in any other community she might have married into. In summary, one could even say that an unmarried woman disconnects herself from her community, since she is unlikely to find an appropriate functional role in her community.

Apart from the above, a point will be reached where family members of an unmarried mature woman will be embarrassed by their daughter's marital status. In light of this, African women are pressured into marriage, even if they would prefer not to, and marriages in Africa are contracted on the payment of the bride price. Based on this, it is a rarity to find an African woman who does not desire to benefit from the bride-price tradition. It is only when a man (or man's family) has paid the bride price for a woman that he can lay claim to her as his "own." The same applies to any offspring from the union, which can only be legitimately considered as his after the bride price has been paid.

There have been cases in the past (and this still applies in many ethnic groups in Africa) where offspring from unions where the bride price has not been paid retained the woman's family name. This is because the children's biological father has no rights of claimant over such children, as their father never paid the bride price for their mother. Likewise, women who live with their men in a "marriage-type" union without the payment of the bride price are regarded as concubines to such men. Their families do not consider themselves as in-laws. And neither are such women treated respectfully, i.e., they are usually not invited to partake in traditional functions, at least not in the capacity of a married woman.

The payment of the bride price is taken so seriously that, where a couple lived together (and perhaps had children), and where the woman died before the payment of her bride price, this price has to be paid even in death; otherwise, she will not receive befitting burial rites as accorded to married women.

The relevance of this extensive survey is to establish the importance of the bride price to African women, which is the foundation of marriage rites in most African countries. It is also to enable those not conversant with the issue of the African bride price to understand the level of social harm it constitutes when deprived of it due to stigma.

Redressing Research-Related Injury Culminating in Social Harm Which Causes the Deprivation of Bride Price

What has been shown above is that the bride-price tradition is crucial to a woman's life in Africa—a tradition most, if not all, young women look forward to benefiting from. It bestows privileges on them that cannot be replaced by monetary (or provision of care) compensation, as indicated in the Pfizer policy document for research-related injury. The fact remains that it might be necessary to recruit this category of research participants—for instance, in research exclusively pertaining to unmarried teenage African girls. Since we cannot entirely stop research among this category of subjects—especially where there are potential benefits for them and their communities—then we must devise alternate ways to mortify any harm suffered in the course of the study. Since this challenge is cultural and cannot be addressed using the Pfizer injury redress system, it makes sense to seek an Indigenous mortification system for this sort of harm.

I suggest the compensation-in-community framework (hereafter referred to as the C-in-C framework). This system was previously suggested as a way of avoiding undue inducement in the conduct of medical research undertaken in African countries (Omonzejele 2012, 117–19). The C-in-C framework is a non-pecuniary two-tiered system of compensation where investigators or research companies negotiate the modality of compensation with host communities, while research subjects are compensated by their communities. The suggested compensation framework requires two modes of consent: community consent, and individual, voluntary, first-person consent. Compensation negotiations for potential involvement in medical research takes place between traditional/community leaders and investigators, as the framework does not allow for direct negotiation between researchers and potential subjects. Although it was suggested as a way of avoiding undue inducement for research protocols designed to be undertaken in African countries, it could also be used to mortify research-related injury, which constitutes social harm, culminating in depriving subjects who typically benefit from the bride-price tradition due to stigma. Let me demonstrate with an example.

Let us assume Esther participated in research that makes it impossible for her to benefit from the bride-price tradition. As already mentioned, it is most unlikely that Pfizer's policy on research-related injury (or any such Western-based redress policy) could mitigate her harm/injury, insofar as Pfizer's redress policy cannot arrange for her bride price to be paid. On the other hand, the Indigenous C-in-C framework could be used to address Esther's circumstances; for instance, by invoking the custom of "stay-at-home daughters," known as the Aireuwa custom.

Before I shed more light on what is meant by the Aireuwa custom, it is important to state that local communities could decide what is appropriate according to their own circumstances. I will use just one community to explain my point; as Tangwa (2000, 39–43) has correctly explained, ethical themes and values in Africa are similar in their essentials. Against this background, I have decided to situate my example among the Irrua people of Edo State, Nigeria.

Irrua is made up of the Esan-speaking people in Edo State, Nigeria. According to a report published by the National Archives of Nigeria (1984, 143) the "vast majority of the people are animists and ancestor worshippers." The people are "said to have migrated from Uhe near Ife at about the same time as the Bini (Edo) left that part of the country" (Ibid., 147). Geographically, Irrua is:

> situated in a narrow strip of high ground running South West from the boundary of the Kukuruku Division near Agbede. The North and North Western boundary is the Divisional boundary, while the District of Ewu lies to the West. Ekpoma borders the area to the South West and Uromi to the South and East. The area of the district is approximately 50 square miles, and the population is estimated at 12,000. The density is therefore 240 to the square mile (Ibid., 146).

At the economic level, the people are mostly farmers. The topography "forms part of a fairly level plateau, but falls away steadily to the North and North West. The soil is sandy and appears fertile. The area is thickly wooded and has a plentiful supply of oil and coconut palms" (Ibid., 146). My rationale for choosing this community as an example is that it is my ancestral village, and I am conversant with how the community functions in terms of decision-making. Because of my ancestral affinity with Irrua, it is easy for me to know how the suggested C-in-C framework works in that setting in mitigating social harm suffered by a female research subject, which makes it impossible for her to benefit from the bride-price tradition.

The Aireuwa custom among the Irrua people of Nigeria is normally invoked by families with the support of the community when a man has sired only daughters. The Aireuwa custom is different from the slightly similar custom known as the Arebhoa. According to Okojie (1960, 115):

> Arebhoa is usually a man's first daughter (his Ehale). She was not married out to a man. When she came of age she lived in her father's house where anyone who chose could keep her as a lover. All the issues of the association belonged to the girl's father. The natural father of the issues had one reward: uninhibited companionship at the girl's father's compound. Only the well-to-do men could afford to have daughters and not make money out of them, for in Esan custom, the suitor paid the bride price popularly called dowry to the girl's father. In the case of Arebhoa, no such price was demanded or paid; hence, the natural father was merely a biological donor.

Although the Arebhoa custom is similar to the Aireuwa custom, it is different in the following aspects:

a. The Arebhoa custom pertains to a man's first daughter, whereas in the case of the Aireuwa custom, any of the daughters may have chosen to undertake the tradition. In fact, it is a custom of sacrifice for sustaining her father's name after his death.
b. A woman under the Arebhoa custom—who must be a man's first daughter—has siblings of both sexes, whereas an Aireuwa only has sisters as siblings.
c. Arebhoa may be considered a customary choice; on the other hand, the Aireuwa is a customary necessity.

For the purpose of this chapter, our focus is on the custom of Aireuwa, and effort was made to differentiate it from a similar custom to avoid confusion.

In the customary practice of Aireuwa, one of the daughters remains in her father's house and is not expected to get married. This means no bride price will be paid on her. In our example, Esther in this case could have sexual relations with a man of her choice, most preferably from within her immediate community, to prevent future disputes. Children from such unions belong to Esther, and they bear Esther's family name. A man who is from that community and understands the tradition will not normally challenge the decision that the child or children belong to Esther. Unlike in the West, where children are had "with," in Africa, children are had "for." Let me explain.

Let us assume that Paul and Pauline are Canadians who met and fancied each other. They went either to a church or the courthouse to have their wedding. Within a year, they had a son, christened Jacob. In a manner of speaking, in the West, Paul had Jacob *with* Pauline. This is most probably because marital unions in Western countries are considered as contractual partnerships.

On the other hand, back in Africa, Andrew and Angela met and fancied each other. Luckily for them, both parents supported their intention to get married. I say "luckily," because where parents do not support a potential marital union, it is almost impossible to go forward with it. The negotiation of the bride price is exclusively between families and kinfolk, with no input whatsoever from the couple. Andrew's and Angela's parents arrived at the amount of the bride price to be paid, and they tied up the marriage. If Angela goes on to have a child, in Africa, it will be said that she had a child *for* Andrew, not *with* Andrew. This is because a marital arrangement in Africa is primarily undertaken for the purpose of procreation; it is a duty-based relationship rather than a partnership or a love-based union. Love is only considered as an added benefit to marriage. (A further discussion on this arrangement is beyond the scope of this chapter.)

Returning to Esther, according to the Aireuwa custom—and this should be understood carefully—unlike usual marital arrangements in African countries, where a wife bears children *for* her husband, any children brought forth by Esther belong to *her*, and not to the man who had sexual relations with her. This is because a woman who falls under the Aireuwa custom does not also fall under the bride-price tradition.

Nevertheless, a woman who is granted the Aireuwa dispensation is accorded the same level of respect, status, and seniority as a woman whose bride price has been paid.

This is important, as previously discussed, because among married women in Africa, seniority is not determined by age as such, but rather is calculated according to the time elapsed since a woman married into that community. For instance, a thirty-year-old woman is considered junior to a twenty-year-old woman who got married into that community before her. This means that in their meetings, she (the twenty-year-old) is accorded more respect, and comes before the thirty-year-old in the order of hierarchy.

This means that if the status of Aireuwa was bestowed on Esther by her family and community at the same time as the above-mentioned twenty-year-old got married, through the bride-price tradition, both are accorded the same respect and status by that community. This is how a community with the use of the C-in-C framework could compensate a subject who suffered social harm that deprived her from participating in the bride-price tradition.

This is just one example. Communities are at liberty to decide how to mortify social harm suffered by members of their communities, especially where the research benefited said community—for instance, in promoting reproductive health for teenage girls.

I assume that because of the novelty of this form of mortification for (social) harm in the research setting, certain concerns will be raised, which I address below.

Potential Criticism

Before I address potential criticism that might be raised with the Aireuwa custom as compensation for research-related injury, it is important to state once again that the Aireuwa custom is just one of the possible compensation systems to be derived from the C-in-C framework. As previously mentioned, communities can decide for themselves what they deem to be appropriate compensation for one of their members who suffered social harm in the course of her participation in medical research.

Following is a list of possible criticisms and my responses:

Why would a community as represented by the elders not stigmatize research subjects based on the social harm suffered by the victim(s)?

They would not participate in the stigmatization of the victim of social harm, since with the use of the C-in-C framework, they provided community consent for the study to take place. Since it is not possible for them to compel any man through his family to pay a bride price on the victim of social harm, the burden of care is on the community to mitigate the harm suffered by their member. It is for this reason that the community would take responsibility for the care of the victim of social harm, which deprives her of benefiting from the bride-price tradition, by using the Aireuwa custom to grant her a special dispensation.

What happens to the woman's father who missed out on his daughter's bride price, which would have brought him cash or an in-kind payment?

It makes sense to assume that the community could compensate him as it deemed fit—for instance, with a plot of land.

What happens when a woman under the Aireuwa dispensation gets involved sexually with a man outside her community and the man wishes to claim paternity for their child?

A woman under the Aireuwa custom will ensure that she does not fall pregnant if she's in a relationship with an "outsider," in order to avoid paternity and custody disputes.

Someone might argue that the Aireuwa dispensation cannot be said to constitute appropriate compensation for research-related injury incurred, as it does not in a concrete sense redress the social harm, since the victim still did not get a man to pay her bride price, which would have enabled her to get married in a proper way.

This may be true to some extent. However, we have to understand that there is some harm that cannot be fully mortified. For instance, let's say a man named John was wrongly accused of murder and was given a jail term of sixty years. After thirty years in jail, the actual murderer was caught. John was released from jail and was compensated monetarily for miscarriage of justice. Despite the monetary compensation paid to John, it cannot make up for the unjust denial of his freedom and the psychological trauma he suffered for thirty years. The fact remains, however, that the State cannot undo the thirty years he spent in jail.

In the same vein, unanticipated and unintended research-related injury (such as social harm, which impairs the ability to access the bride-price tradition) cannot be mortified by sponsors of research; likewise, communities cannot entirely mitigate it, either. But the community can still redress the harm with the Aireuwa custom, which bestows the same level of respect and status accorded to women who benefited from the bride-price tradition. It is making the best of a bad—albeit, unintended and unforeseen—consequence of research.

Conclusion

Without doubt, research holds many benefits for society. But the conduct of research depends on the availability of research subjects. Unfortunately, when subjects voluntarily consent to participate in research, in the same breath, they have also consented to possible risks associated with the research that could culminate in physical, psychological, and social harms.

One such possible injury is social harm, which holds the potential to deprive unmarried African woman of the benefits of the bride-price tradition. Unfortunately, Pfizer's policy document for research-related injury—which states that "Pfizer covers the cost for medical treatment for any injury or illness that occurs as a direct result of taking part in a Pfizer-sponsored study at no cost to the research subject"—cannot redress social harm suffered by such victims. It is for this reason that I employed the C-in-C framework, where compensation for research participants is through the community and not directly from investigators. Based on the C-in-C framework, the Aireuwa custom was suggested as a community-based compensation that enables the injured party to enjoy the same respect and acceptance accorded to those who participate in the bride-price tradition.

References

Barber, B. 1978. "Some Perspectives on the Role of Assessment of Risk/Benefit Criteria in the Determination of the Appropriateness of Research Involving Human Subjects." In *The National Commission for the Protection of Human Subjects of Biomedical and Behavioural Research: The Belmont Report: Ethical Principles and Guidelines for the Protection of Human Subjects of Research.* Washington, DC: *DHEW Publications* 78-0014, 1–19, 21.

Chapman, C. R., S. Sukumaran, G. T. Tsegaye, Y. Shevchenko, and A. L. Caplan. 2020. "The Quest for Compensation for Research-Related Injury in the United States: A New Proposal." *Journal of Law, Medicine and Ethics* 47 (4): 732–47.

Grant, R.W., and J. Sugarman. 2004. "Ethics in Human Subjects' Research: Do Incentives Matter? *Journal of Medicine and Philosophy* 29 (6): 717–38.

Holder, A. 1980. "Job Applicants as Research Subjects: The Case of Rubella Vaccine Trial." In Robert Levine, 1988, *Ethics and Regulation of Clinical Research*, 2nd ed. New Haven, CT: Yale University Press.

Katz, Jay. 1972. *Experimentation with Human Subjects.* New York: Russell Sage Foundation.

Larkin, M. E. 2015. "Defining Compensable Injury in Biomedical Research." *Health Matrix C Level* 25: 309.

Levine, Robert. 1988. *Ethics and Regulation of Clinical Research*, 2nd ed. New Haven, CT: Yale University Press.

Mbaye, L. M., and N. Wagner. 2017. "Bride Price and Fertility Decisions: Evidence from Rural Senegal." *Journal of Development Studies* 53 (6): 893.

Munshi, R., and U. Thatte. January–March 2013. "Compensation for Research-Related Injury," *Perspective in Clinical Research* 4 (1): 61–69.

National Archives of Nigeria. 1982. *Intelligence Report on the Irrua Clan in the Ishan Division.*

Nei, J., T. Tsuchiya, H. M. Sass, and K. Tsuneishi. 2003. "A Call for Further Studies on the Ethical Lessons of Japanese Doctors' Experimentation in Wartime China for Asian and International Bioethics Today." *Eubios Journal of Asian and International Bioethics* 13 (3): 106.

Okogie, Christopher. 1960. *Ishan Native Laws and Customs.* Lagos: Nigeria National Press.

Omonzejele, Peter. 2008. "African Women as Clinical Research Subjects: Unaddressed Issue in Global Bioethics. *Studies in Ethno-Medicine* 2 (2): 121.

———. 2012. *The Ethics of Medical Research in Africa.* Saarbrücken, Germany: LAP Lambert Academic Publishing.

Paul, C., and B. Brookes. 2015. "The Rationalization of Unethical Research: Revisionist Accounts of the Tuskegee Syphilis Study and the New Zealand "Unfortunate Experiment." *American Journal of Public Health* 105 (10): 12.

Pfizer. February 15, 2017. "Compensation to Research Subjects in Clinical Studies." https://www.pfizer.com/research/research_clinical_trials/compensation_trial_participants (accessed June 13, 2019).

Schüklenk, Udo. 2000. "Protecting the Vulnerable: Testing Time for Clinical Research." *Social Science & Medicine* 51 (6): 969–77.

Tangwa, G. 2000. "The Traditional African Perception of a Person: Some Implications for Bioethics." *The Hastings Center Report* 30 (5): 39–43.

CHAPTER 11

Ethics of Aboriginal Research

Marlene Brant Castellano

Abstract

This chapter proposes a set of principles to assist in developing ethical codes for the conduct of research within the Aboriginal community or with external partners. It places the discussion of research ethics in the context of cultural worldview and the struggle for self-determination as peoples and nations. It affirms that Aboriginal Peoples have a right to participate as principals or partners in research that generates knowledge affecting their culture, identity, and well-being. To provide context and rationale for the principles presented, the chapter outlines features of the current public dialogue on research ethics, how ethics are framed in Aboriginal cultures, and how Aboriginal perceptions of reality and right behavior clash with norms prevailing in Western research. Current initiatives of Aboriginal communities and nations, research-granting councils, and institutions to establish ethical guidelines for Aboriginal research are highlighted as evidence that the development of workable ethical regimes is already well begun.

Introduction

In September 1992, the Royal Commission on Aboriginal Peoples (RCAP) brought together about eighty Aboriginal Peoples who were involved in research as academics, lawyers, graduate students, project staff and consultants, community leaders, and Elders. We met at a workshop at Nakoda Lodge in Alberta to shape the emerging research agenda of RCAP. As co-director of research, I was the chairperson of the initial session in which numerous participants voiced harsh criticism of past research and serious skepticism that RCAP research would serve them any better. "We've been researched to death!" they protested. The workshop was not off to a promising start, until an Elder who had opened the meeting spoke quietly from a corner of the room. "If we have been researched to death," he said, "maybe it's time we started researching ourselves back to life."

That piece of wisdom has been repeated often in the past ten years. It was prophetic of the change that would gather remarkable momentum in just a decade. Aboriginal knowledge has always been informed by research, purposeful gathering of information, and thoughtful distillation of meaning. Research acquired a bad name among Aboriginal Peoples because the purposes and meanings associated with its practice by academics and government agents were usually alien to the people themselves, and the outcomes were, as often as not, misguided and harmful. Aboriginal Peoples in organizations and communities, as well as universities and colleges and some government offices, are now engaged in transforming Aboriginal research into an instrument for creating and disseminating knowledge that once again authentically represents us and our understanding of the world.

Researching ourselves may mean self-initiated action, or it may mean entering into effective partnerships. In either case, the ground rules that should guide new practices are not immediately evident. Where Aboriginal expectations diverge from past practice, resistance from the academic research establishment is to be expected.

This chapter proposes a set of principles to assist in developing ethical codes for the conduct of research internal to the Aboriginal community or with external partners.[1] The context and rationale for these principles is developed in early sections outlining the current dialogue on research ethics, how ethics are framed in Aboriginal cultures, and how Aboriginal perceptions of reality and right behavior clash with prevailing norms of Western research. Efforts of Aboriginal communities and nations, as well as research-granting councils and institutions, to establish ethical guidelines for Aboriginal research, are highlighted as evidence that the development of workable ethical regimes is already well begun.

In this chapter: "Research" means activity intended to investigate, document, bring to light, analyze, or interpret matters in any domain, to create knowledge for the benefit of society or of particular groups. "Aboriginal" refers to First Nations, Inuit, and Métis Peoples as referenced in the Canadian Constitution. "Indigenous" is used interchangeably with Aboriginal, usually in international contexts. Where sources refer to specific groups, such as First Nations, the terminology of the source is retained.

"Aboriginal research" means research that touches the life and well-being of Aboriginal Peoples. It may involve Aboriginal Peoples and their communities directly. It may assemble data that describes or claims to describe Aboriginal Peoples and their heritage. Or, it may affect the human and natural environment in which Aboriginal Peoples live. "Ethics" refers to rules of conduct that express and reinforce important social and cultural values of a society. The rules may be formal and written, spoken, or simply understood by groups who subscribe to them.

The language, images, and perspectives in this chapter are those of a Mohawk woman and academic of a certain generation. I suggest that the principles I articulate are relevant more broadly to Aboriginal research, though readers from other cultures, particularly Métis and Inuit colleagues, will undoubtedly need to do some translation to connect my words with their own worldviews and experiences.

An Active Discourse on Research Ethics

International concern about research ethics arose from revelations in the Nuremburg trials of atrocities committed in experimentation on humans by the Nazis during World War II. To prevent future violations of human rights in the name of science, Western nations developed the Nuremburg Code representing broad international agreement on ethical standards in medical research. The Nuremburg Code was replaced by the Helsinki Declaration, which was adopted in 1964 and subsequently updated.[2] Ethical codes place emphasis on informed consent and are intended to strike a balance between the risk incurred by participants and the potential benefit of the research to society.

The federal government is a major funding source, directly and indirectly, of research involving human subjects. It relies on other agencies to ensure that an ethical balance between benefit and risk is maintained in much of the research that it funds. This leaves open questions about the adequacy of safeguards of the public interest.

Aboriginal Peoples interested in research share the concerns cited above and welcome the current review of principles and processes for governing research involving human subjects. However, even if ethical oversight of research sponsored by public institutions is made more consistent, up-to-date, and enforceable, there is a danger that concerns particular to Aboriginal Peoples will be neglected or made subject to inappropriate regulation.

It is essential that Aboriginal Peoples and their organizations put forward not only concerns but also solutions to the ethical problems that too often have made research affecting them inaccurate and irrelevant. Reframing ethical codes and practice is necessary to ensure the social benefit that motivates research also extends to the Aboriginal Peoples whose universe is being studied.

An Aboriginal Perspective on Ethics

Descriptions of Aboriginal societies seldom speak of the ethics that support order, cohesion, and personal responsibility in those societies. Anthropological studies document customs that sometimes have the character of law. Dr. Clare Brant, a Mohawk physician who became the first Aboriginal psychiatrist in Canada, wrote an influential paper entitled "Native Ethics and Rules of Behavior." In it, he used the language of ethics to illuminate some powerful, unspoken assumptions that guide behavior he observed in his Iroquoian, Cree, and Ojibway patients.

Brant's elaboration of the ethic of noninterference, which inhibits argument and advice-giving as normal means of communication, is particularly relevant for researchers and professionals offering services to Aboriginal Peoples. While noninterfering behavior may be perceived as passive and irresponsible, Brant points out that it is consistent with teaching based on nonintrusive modeling rather than direct instruction that attempts to shape the behavior of the learner.[3] Elder Peter Waskahat speaks of the foundations of knowledge and the connections between land, family, spirituality, values, and everyday living:

> We had our own teachings, our own education system, teaching children that way of life was taught by the grandparents and extended families; they were taught how to view and respect the land and everything in Creation. Through that the young people were taught how to live, what the Creator's laws were, what were the natural laws, what were these First Nations' laws, and so on; the teachings revolved around a way of life that was based on their values.[4]

When Aboriginal Peoples speak about maintaining and revitalizing their cultures, they are not proposing to go back to igloos and teepees and a hunter-gatherer lifestyle. They are talking about restoring order to daily living in conformity with ancient and enduring values that affirm life. The relationships between individual behavior, customs and community protocols, ethics, values, and worldview are represented by the symbol of a tree.

The leaves represent individual behaviors. Protocols and community customs are small branches, while ethics—the rules governing relationships—are the large branches. Values—deeply held beliefs about good and evil—form the trunk of the tree. The worldview or perception of reality underpinning life as it is lived, like the roots of the tree, is not ordinarily visible. The whole of the tree is rooted in the earth that supports us. In this symbolic representation, I suggest that the earth is like the unseen world of spirit—vast, mysterious, and friendly, if we learn how to respect the laws that govern it.

Some nations have codified their ethical systems. The Iroquois Great Law of Peace teaches the importance and the requirements of cultivating a "good mind" in order to live well and harmoniously in the world. The potlatching ceremonies of West Coast nations were public means of validating genealogies, family responsibilities, inheritance rights, and land tenure. Many other nations transmitted their ethical codes orally and nonverbally through family and community relationships. Public ceremonies reinforce the community's worldview and provide instructions for living. Skills for decoding complex messages from the social and natural environment are embedded in traditional languages.

The persons most knowledgeable about physical and spiritual reality, the teaching and practice of ceremonies, and the nuances of meaning in Aboriginal languages, are Elders. Elders typically have been educated in the oral tradition, apart from the colonizing influence of the school system. They carry credentials that are recognizable within Aboriginal society, but invisible to those who assess expertise on the basis of formal education. They enjoy respect as sources of wisdom because their way of life expresses the deepest values of their respective cultures. In many cases, they have exceptional skills in transmitting these values to those who seek their counsel.

Within Aboriginal communities, the struggle has gone beyond survival as small enclaves set apart from non-Aboriginal Canada. The struggle now extends to applying cultural ways in the management of lands and economic activity; the structures of governance; the provision of health, education, justice, and other human services;

and relations with the larger Canadian society and the world community. The struggle is to live and thrive as peoples and nations maintaining and expressing distinctive worldviews and contributing uniquely to the Canadian federation. In the language of the United Nations Working Group on Indigenous Populations, this is the pursuit of self-determination.

Indigenous peoples have the right of self-determination. By virtue of that right they freely determine their political status and freely pursue their economic, social, and cultural development.[5] Fundamental to the exercise of self-determination is the right of peoples to construct knowledge in accordance with self-determined definitions of what is real and what is valuable. Just as colonial policies have denied Aboriginal Peoples access to their traditional lands, so also colonial definitions of truth and value have denied Aboriginal Peoples the tools to assert and implement their knowledge. Research under the control of outsiders to the Aboriginal community has been instrumental in rationalizing colonialist perceptions of Aboriginal incapacity and the need for paternalistic control.

Aboriginal scholars who have been educated in Western universities and who are conversant with Aboriginal ways of knowledge-seeking are challenging Western assumptions and methodologies of research. In the study of Elders' language referred to earlier, the authors explain:

> The Elders' comments allude to formal and long-established ways, procedures, and processes that First Nations persons are required to follow when seeking particular kinds of knowledge that are rooted in spiritual traditions and laws. The rules that are applied to this way of learning are strict, and the seekers of knowledge are required to follow meticulous procedures and processes as they prepare for and enter the "quest for knowledge journey."

In the world of Aboriginal knowledge, a discussion of ethics cannot be limited to devising a set of rules to guide researcher behavior in a defined task. Ethics—the rules of right behavior—are intimately related to who you are, the deep values you subscribe to, and your understanding of your place in the spiritual order of reality. Ethics are integral to the way of life of a people.

The fullest expression of a people's ethics is represented in the lives of the most knowledgeable and honorable members of the community. Imposition of rules derived from other ways of life in other communities will inevitably cause problems, although common understandings and shared interests can be negotiated. This is the ground on which Aboriginal Peoples stand as they engage in dialogue about research ethics that will limit the risks and enhance the benefits of research affecting their lives.

"Jagged Worldviews Colliding"

Leroy Little Bear coined the phrase "jagged worldviews colliding" to describe the encounter of Aboriginal philosophies and positivist scientific thought.[6] Aboriginal worldviews assume that human action, to achieve social good, must be located in an ethical, spiritual context as well as its physical and social situation. Scientific research is dominated by positivist thinking that assumes that only observable phenomena matter.

Little Bear points out that much externally sponsored research has documented customs, but missed the deeper significance of those customs: Anthropologists have done a fairly decent job of describing the customs themselves, but they have failed miserably in finding and interpreting the meanings behind the customs. The function of Aboriginal values and customs is to maintain the relationships that hold creation together.[7]

Research was defined earlier in this chapter as knowledge creation for social benefit. If researchers and those researched have vastly different notions of what constitutes social benefit and how it is achieved, the research is unlikely to satisfy the needs and expectations of participants on both sides of the divide. This section outlines some of the issues that arise in devising ethical regimes that are appropriate for Aboriginal research.

Should Ethics Be Restricted to Research on Human Subjects?

In Aboriginal knowledge systems, the boundary between material and spiritual realms is easily crossed. Similarly, the boundaries between humans, animals, plants, and natural elements are also permeable. This is represented in traditional stories of communication between humans and other beings and transformation of persons into animals and sea creatures, or vice versa.

Because many Aboriginal societies maintain primary dependence on a healthy natural environment to meet their needs, industrial development that sacrifices environmental values directly infringes on their well-being and human rights. Ethical regimes for Aboriginal research must therefore extend beyond current definitions of research involving human subjects to include research that affects Aboriginal well-being. This includes environmental research that will impact their physical environment or archival research that may perpetuate negative or inaccurate representations of Aboriginal Peoples.

Maintaining a Balance between Reductionist Analysis and Holistic Vision

The prevailing model of scientific inquiry reduces the scope of analysis to smaller bits of reality that can then be analyzed with greater specialization. This is referred to as a reductionist approach. Research that takes measures to exclude variables or influences from the environment that might contaminate cause-effect sequences is applauded as more reliable than data about complex and unexplainable lived experience.

Social sciences exploring human experience have adopted scientific method as the hallmark of their credibility, even though human behavior is subject to many variables that interrupt linear cause-effect sequences. The science of ecology has emerged as an approach to understanding the interdependence of elements and processes in the natural world, to some extent countering the dominance of reductionist research. However, the role of intuitive insight or vision in scientific breakthroughs is regularly downplayed in Western disciplines and institutions.

In contrast, the heart of Aboriginal science acknowledges the spirit of the plant, animal, or the land and the importance of relationships in supporting life. Gregory Cajete, a Tewa educator, writes:

> Native peoples through long experience and participation with their landscapes have come to know the language of their places. In learning this language of the subtle signs, qualities, cycles, and patterns of their immediate environments and communicating with their landscapes, Native people also come to know intimately the "nature" of the places which they inhabit. Learning the language of place and the "dialects" of its plants, animals, and natural phenomena in the context of a "homeland" is an underlying foundation of Native science.[8]

Aboriginal science does not ignore analysis of the particular. In fact, the perception of patterns is synthesized from multiple keen observations. Holistic awareness and highly focused analysis are complementary, not contradictory. There are examples of effective partnership between communities and scientists. The Sandy Lake Health and Diabetes Project in northwestern Ontario has brought together clinical treatment, community-based prevention strategies, and participation in genetic studies.[9]

The Akwesasne Mohawk community enlisted scientists from Cornell University to assist in verifying the nature and degree of pollution that was destroying the health of their crops and animals. Too often, however, perceptions and concerns at the community level are dismissed as anecdotal while priority-setting for research proceeds on a different track. The Aboriginal ethic is that all aspects of the world we know have life and spirit, and that humans have an obligation to learn the rules of relating to the world with respect. We enter into mutual dialogue with the many people and other beings with whom we share the world.

Knowledge is not a commodity that can be purchased and exploited at will. Information can be gathered by individuals to shape personal perceptions. Aboriginal societies traditionally were respectful of the unique vision of individuals. However, individual perceptions had to be validated by community dialogue and reflection before they became collective knowledge, the basis of collective action. This was the function of the many councils responsible for family, clan, village, or nation affairs. Research that seeks objectivity by maintaining distance between the investigator and informants violates Aboriginal ethics of reciprocal relationship and collective validation.

If the researcher assumes control of knowledge production—harvesting information in brief encounters—the dialogical relationship with human and nonhuman sources is disrupted and the transformation of observations or information into contextualized knowledge is aborted. Attempts to gain an understanding of Aboriginal life and concerns from an objective, short-term, outsider vantage point have produced much research that Aboriginal Peoples reject as distortions of their reality.

Where Aboriginal Peoples control access to research sites—for example, research on First Nations territories—organizations and local governments are increasingly insisting on community control. This may mean assuming full responsibility for conducting the research, or it may mean collaborative research, in which the respective responsibilities of community and outside researchers are set out in a contract. Some initiatives to achieve balanced, mutually respectful partnerships between Aboriginal communities and researchers are described later in this chapter.

Voluntary Consent

In many cases, research in Aboriginal communities and on Aboriginal matters is initiated by agencies that Aboriginal Peoples receive essential services from. The research is often funded by governments that control the resources on which the community depends. Rightly or wrongly, many Aboriginal Peoples fear that refusing to consent to research may result in loss of funding for essential needs. They are at a disadvantage in negotiating conditions that would alter the imbalance in power between researchers and the community and give adequate recognition to community priorities and approaches to knowledge creation.

Privacy of health data collected routinely in the delivery of services has become a major concern in health research, especially with the possibility of sharing masses of data electronically across borders. Once information is transferred, it becomes difficult to monitor the secondary or tertiary purposes for which it is used.

From Guidelines to Governance

The discussion on ethics of Aboriginal research over the past decade has clearly demonstrated that more appropriate and enforceable protection of Aboriginal Peoples' interests in research activities is required. Aboriginal Peoples are wary, however, of regulations that seek to include them as an addendum to protocols based on Western assumptions about the construction and distribution of knowledge. This section proposes some principles flowing from the previous discussion that could guide the development of appropriate ethical regimes.

Creating Knowledge: An Aboriginal Right

Aboriginal Peoples in Canada enjoy constitutional protection of rights to maintain their identity and participate as collectives in Canadian society. Creating and sharing knowledge that authentically represents who you are and how you understand the world is integral to the survival of a people's identity. The Royal Commission on Aboriginal Peoples, in its analysis of the foundations and exercise of self-government, proposed that, "All matters that are of vital concern to the life and welfare of a particular Aboriginal people, its culture and identity" fall within the core of Aboriginal jurisdiction.[10]

The government of Canada has acknowledged the inherent right of self-government, although the substance of the right has not been defined. This leads to the first principle in devising an ethics regime for Aboriginal research.

Principle 1: Aboriginal Peoples have an inherent right to participate as principals or partners in research that generates knowledge affecting their culture, identity, and well-being. This right is protected by the Canadian constitution and extends beyond the interests that other groups affected by research might have.

Fiduciary Obligations

The restricted capacity of Aboriginal nations and communities to protect their interests and rights in the face of more powerful governments and institutions has led to case law defining fiduciary obligations of Canadian governments. A duty to consult, which could affect how research is conducted, has been recognized in decisions of the British Columbia Court of Appeal. The National Aboriginal Health Organization (NAHO) is currently preparing a paper exploring related issues in federal government fiduciary obligations to Aboriginal Peoples and health.[11]

Principle 2: The government of Canada has a fiduciary obligation to guard against infringement of Aboriginal rights in research activities, particularly in institutions and activities for which it is responsible. The appropriateness of particular safeguards must be endorsed by Aboriginal Peoples through their representative organizations.

Diversity of Aboriginal Cultures

In the speech from the throne on September 30, 2002, Governor General Adrienne Clarkson announced the government of Canada's intent to "work with provinces to implement a national system for the governance of research involving humans, including national research ethics and standards." Ethical codes developed by Aboriginal Peoples recognize the diversity of Aboriginal communities and the primacy of community authority in deciding what matters are appropriate for research, the protocols to be respected, and how resulting knowledge should be distributed.[12]

The situation of the Métis deserves specific attention. Although they are recognized in the constitution as one of the Aboriginal Peoples of Canada, they are excluded from federal and most provincial legislation protecting their Aboriginal rights and access to culturally specific services. They generally lack resources to develop organizational and governance infrastructure and to conduct or partner in research undertakings. A search for examples of community-based research protocols did not turn up examples of Métis-specific documents.

Principle 3: Action by the government of Canada to establish ethical standards of research should strike a balance between regulations that restrict infringement of

Aboriginal rights and those that respect the primacy of ethical codes originating in affected communities, including Métis communities.

The Scope of Ethics Regimes

Ethics that govern research only on human subjects is too restricted to provide the protections sought by Aboriginal Peoples. The report to the Commission on Human Rights from the seminar on draft principles and guidelines for the protection of the heritage of Indigenous People provides a useful model for defining the scope of ethical regulation. The report proposes that "heritage," broadly defined, should be the object of protective measures.

Principle 4: Ethical regulation of research affecting Aboriginal Peoples should include protection for "all knowledge, languages, territories, material objects, literary or artistic creations pertaining to a particular Aboriginal People, including objects and forms of expression which may be created or rediscovered in the future based upon their traditions," as cited in emerging international norms.

Harmonization of Ethical Protection and Intellectual Property Law

A study of intellectual property and Aboriginal Peoples sponsored by Indian and Northern Affairs Canada underlines the inadequacy and inappropriateness of existing intellectual property regimes in protecting traditional Aboriginal knowledge. National and international rules governing copyright, trademarks, patents, and licensing procedures consistently conflict with Aboriginal culture norms, or are practically inaccessible. Canadian rules are designed to conform to international standards.

Principle 5: "The federal government, in collaboration with Aboriginal Peoples, should review its legislation on the protection of intellectual property to ensure that Aboriginal interests and perspectives, in particular collective interests, are adequately protected."[13]

Administrative Infrastructure

Implementation of an ethics regime in Aboriginal research requires more than the clear statement of principles. Legislation at best sets out boundaries for protection of heritage rights. As noted earlier, the administration of existing guidelines is in the hands of research ethics boards (REBs) located in universities and research institutes, from which Aboriginal communities are generally distant, socially and culturally. The Indian Act, which sets parameters for program funding for registered Indians, makes no provision to support research administration or ethics enforcement in its administrative regimes.

In its submission to Health Canada on Governance of Research Involving Human Subjects, NAHO recommended the creation of a system of Aboriginal research ethics boards (AREBs) to address local, regional, and national Aboriginal concerns. The brief further recommended that a national committee be formed consisting of Aboriginal experts who would develop ethical standards that could provide a reference point for AREBs and minimum standards for institutional REBs.[14]

Principle 6: Development and implementation of ethical standards for Aboriginal research should be in the hands of Aboriginal Peoples, as experts in devising minimum standards for general application and as majority members on Aboriginal-specific research ethics boards serving local, regional, and national communities.

Costs of Implementing an Ethical Regime

Briefs submitted in 2002 noted that establishing the relationships and ground rules for research in Aboriginal communities required time and effort prior to finalizing a research proposal.[15] Granting councils generally do not fund up-front costs of developing a research plan, thereby placing serious limitations on respectful—that is, ethical—research practice in or with Aboriginal communities.

Aboriginal involvement in research to support evidence-based decision-making in service planning is generally not recognized in the administration budgets of Aboriginal communities and organizations.

Principle 7: The costs of community consultation, development of research plans, negotiation and implementation of ethical protocols, and skills transfer should be recognized in budget formulas for research grants and project planning, whether conducted by researchers internal or external to Aboriginal communities.

Education for Ethical Practice

Ethics of consent, safety, and social benefit in research has evolved over decades. Ethical practice is advanced through a combination of institutional regulation, peer monitoring, and communication in the venues where researchers meet and confer with one another. Establishing research practices that respect Aboriginal worldviews, priorities, and authority will also be an evolving process.

Aboriginal communities that have taken up the challenge of conducting and monitoring research have promoted a broad base of local involvement in field research, management committees, and board governance. By their actions, they have demonstrated that research is too important to be left to a small group of academics, even if the experts are Aboriginal. Aboriginal community researchers, in concert with their peers in graduate schools and universities, are now talking about reinstating Aboriginal research methodologies to explore processes that have been neglected or poorly represented in past research. The terminology used for this process is "community control," borrowing the language that has driven parallel moves to assert Aboriginal authority over government institutions, education, health, and social services.

Aboriginal initiative is essential to reform research practice and bring it into conformity with Aboriginal notions of ethical behavior. Aboriginal assertiveness is already evident in the surge of activity devising community research codes and the demands for effective partnership in major research undertakings.

Principle 8: Responsibility for education of communities and researchers in ethics of Aboriginal research rests with Aboriginal communities and organizations, government funders, granting agencies, professional associations, research institutions, and individual researchers working collaboratively.

Conclusion

This chapter places the discussion of ethics governing Aboriginal research in the context of cultural worldview and the struggle for self-determination as peoples and nations. Self-determination has been seen as a political goal expressed most notably in self-government that recognizes a degree of autonomy in relation to Canadian state institutions. The language of self-government has obscured the reality that Aboriginal Peoples are engaged in a struggle to reestablish ethical order in their communities and nations.

This order reaffirms fundamental values that are rooted in their traditional construction of reality, sometimes called a worldview. Efforts to regain control of education, health, justice, etc., are only in part about the power to govern. They are fundamentally about restoring order to daily living in conformity with ancient and enduring principles that support life.

Aboriginal Peoples are digging deep into their traditional teachings, reviving their ceremonies, and working to conserve their languages. As they take control of community services and institutions, they are proving that traditional teachings offer a sturdy ethical framework for restoring vitality to community life. Aboriginal academics, professionals, service providers, and political leaders are rediscovering and updating traditional values in the practice of education, the arts, health services, justice, and government. They are also challenging the assumptions of research rooted in a scientific worldview that clashes with their concepts of reality and right relationships.

It would be wrong to suggest that all Aboriginal Peoples hold traditional worldviews with the same degree of tenacity. However, applied research, going on spontaneously and autonomously in Aboriginal communities and organizations, is demonstrating that when learning, healing, or rehabilitating is aligned with traditional ethics and values, it takes on astounding energy. The leaves of a tree, connected to their vital source, display health and vigor.

The active discussion of research ethics now going on in government and in granting councils opens up an opportunity for Aboriginal Peoples to engage in dialogue on how research can be adapted to achieve social benefit as they define it. The principles proposed in this chapter start with an affirmation of the right of Aboriginal Peoples to generate and disseminate knowledge for and about themselves. This is not to say that all dialogue should halt until complex questions about rights and responsibilities are definitively resolved. Starting with such an affirmation simply underlines that governance of research touches on fundamental issues of Aboriginal culture, identity, and well-being.

Establishing and enforcing ethical practice in Aboriginal research will require a continuing commitment to implementing protective legislation, administrative infrastructure, and education of the many participants in research. It is my hope that the articulation of issues and principles in this chapter will advance the dialogue that is already under way.

Update (Wanda Teays)

At the author's request, we have added an update on recent changes.

In December 2010, three major research agencies of the Canadian federal government adopted an updated policy statement, *The Tri-Council Policy Statement: Ethical Conduct for Research Involving Humans* (TCPS).[16] The revised guidelines include a chapter titled "Research Involving the First Nations, Inuit and Métis Peoples of Canada."

Aspects of this policy statement are relevant to the discussion on research protocol involving Aboriginal Peoples and are worthy of mention. From what is set out below, we can see that steps have been made to address the concerns raised in this chapter, and to better appreciate the concerns Marlene Brant Castellano has raised.

The key points of the TCPS guidelines for research involving the First Nations, Inuit, and Métis People of Canada include the following:

- The *Principle of Concern for Welfare* is broader, requiring consideration of participants and prospective participants in their physical, social, economic, and cultural environments, where applicable, as well as concern for the community to which participants belong.
- This policy acknowledges the important role of *Aboriginal communities* in promoting collective rights, interests, and responsibilities that also serve the welfare of individuals.
- Aboriginal Peoples are particularly concerned that research should enhance their *capacity to maintain their cultures, languages, and identities* as First Nations, Inuit, or Métis peoples, and to support their full participation in, and contributions to, Canadian society.
- The interpretation of *Concern for Welfare* in First Nations, Inuit, and Métis contexts may therefore place strong emphasis on *collective welfare* as a complement to individual well-being.
- *Justice* may be compromised when a serious imbalance of power prevails between the researcher and participants.
- In the case of Aboriginal peoples, *abuses stemming from research* have included misappropriation of sacred songs, stories, and artifacts; devaluing of Aboriginal Peoples' knowledge as primitive or superstitious; violation of community norms regarding the use of human tissue and remains; failure to share data and resulting benefits;

and dissemination of information that has misrepresented or stigmatized entire communities.

The TCPS guidelines acknowledge that mutual trust and communication take time, not to mention mutually beneficial research goals, collaboration in research, and the assurance "that the conduct of research adheres to the core principles of Respect for Persons, Concern for Welfare—which in this context includes welfare of the collective, as understood by all parties involved—and Justice."(Chapter 9 Introduction B: Interpreting the Ethics Framework)

Among the new requirements is the "Recognition of the Role of Elders and Other Knowledge Holders." Such knowledge holders should participate in the design and execution of research and the interpretation of research results. In this way, research will be understood within the context of cultural norms and traditional knowledge. Moreover, "Community advice should also be sought to determine appropriate recognition for the unique advisory role fulfilled by these persons" (Article 9.15).

The TCPS guidelines also recognize the importance of privacy and confidentiality. Article 9.16 sets out the specifics and emphasizes that "Researchers shall not disclose personal information to community partners without the participant's consent." To examine the entire document to get a more detailed presentation of the changed policies, see the Tri-Council Policy Statement: ethical conduct for research involving humans - TCPS2 (2022) available online at https://ethics.gc.ca/eng/policy-politique_tcps2-eptc2_2022.html. The policy is updated periodically and prior versions are archived.

Acknowledgment

I wish to thank the National Aboriginal Health Organization (NAHO) for providing the stimulus and the forum for exploring these important matters.

Notes

1. This chapter was commissioned in 2002 by the National Aboriginal Health Organization to assist in developing an organizational position on research ethics. Documentary research and conceptual development were substantially advanced by conversations with NAHO staff, particularly Richard Jock, Yvonne Boyer, and Gail McDonald. Analysis and interpretation and errors and omissions are entirely the responsibility of the author.

2. Yvonne Boyer, "Aboriginal Health: A Constitutional Rights Analysis," *Ottawa: National Aboriginal Health Organization*, 2003. Available online at: http://www.naho.ca/documents/naho/english/publications/DP_rights.pdf.

3. Clare C. Brant, "Native Ethics and Rules of Behavior," *Canadian Journal of Psychiatry* 35 (August 1990): 534–39.

4. Harold Cardinal and Walter Hildebrandt, *Treaty Elders of Saskatchewan* (Calgary: University of Calgary Press, 2000), 6.

5. United Nations, Economic and Social Council, Draft Declaration on the Rights of Indigenous Peoples (1994), E/CN.4/Sub.2/1994/2/Add.l.

6. Leroy Little Bear, "Jagged Worldviews Colliding," in Marie Battiste, ed., *Reclaiming Indigenous Voice and Vision* (Vancouver: UBC Press, 2000), 77.

7. Ibid., 81.

8. Gregory Cajete, *Native Science, Natural Laws of Interdependence* (Santa Fe, NM: Clear Light Publishers, 2000), 284.

9. National Council on Ethics in Human Research (NCEHR), "Research Involving Aboriginal Individuals and Communities: Genetics as a Focus," Proceedings of a Workshop of the Consent Committee, November 19–21, 1999 (Ottawa: NCEHR, 2001), 51.

10. Royal Commission on Aboriginal Peoples (RCAP), *Report of the Royal Commission on Aboriginal Peoples, Vol. 2: Restructuring the Relationship* (Ottawa: Canada Communications Group, 1996), 215.

11. Yvonne Boyer, "Aboriginal Health: A Constitutional Rights Analysis" (Ottawa: National Aboriginal Health Organization, 2003). Available online at http://www.naho.ca/documents/naho/english/publications/DP_rights.pdf.

12. Mi'kmaw Ethics Watch, "Principles and Guidelines for Researchers"; Kahnawake Schools Diabetes Prevention Project, Code of Research Ethics; and Schnarch, "Ownership, Control, Access and Possession (OCAP)."

13. Royal Commission on Aboriginal Peoples (RCAP), *Report of the Royal Commission on Aboriginal Peoples, Vol. 3, Gathering Strength* (Ottawa: Canada Communications Group, 1996), 601.

14. National Aboriginal Health Organization (NAHO), "Governance of Research Involving Human Subjects, Research Brief" (Ottawa: National Aboriginal Health Organization, 2000).

15. Social Sciences and Humanities Research Council (SSHRC), "A Discussion Paper for the Roundtable Consultation" (Ottawa: SSHRC, November 29, 2002).

16. Canadian Institutes of Health Research, Natural Sciences and Engineering Research Council of Canada, and Social Sciences and Humanities Research Council of Canada, "Tri-Council Policy Statement: Ethical Conduct for Research Involving Humans -TCPS2 (2022). Available online at https://ethics.gc.ca/eng/policy-politique_tcps2-eptc2_2022.html

CHAPTER 12

The Human Rights Dimensions of Virginity Restoration Surgery

Alison Dundes Renteln

Abstract

This chapter considers the ethical issues that arise when women seek revirgination surgeries to avoid "honor"-related violence. The preoccupation with virginity in many societies exerts tremendous pressure on women to be—or at least appear to be—"pure" on their wedding nights. Sometimes the cultural imperative is so serious that women fear for their lives. Although many consider this social control—the fact that women should feel compelled to undergo these procedures—so objectionable that they would ban the surgeries, the question is whether the principle of autonomy should empower women to seek whatever type of medical treatment they wish, particularly if their lives are at stake. While in an ideal world hymenoplasties would be unnecessary, surgeons' refusal to perform this surgery arguably violates women's human rights.

> A woman's honor is like a match. It can only be lit once.[1]
>
> —Arab proverb

Introduction

Although health is often treated as a neutral concept that can be analyzed in objective terms, in reality, cultural context shapes the interpretation of what constitutes beneficial medical practices.[2] Women may sometimes find themselves at the mercy of medical professionals who question their motivations for seeking surgical procedures. This is particularly the case regarding "elective" surgery not deemed necessary by "cosmopolitan" medicine. One such operation is hymenoplasty (also known as hymenorrhaphy), a type of reconstructive or cosmetic procedure to repair a woman's hymen (the thin membrane that stretches across the vagina). While a number of activities can cause the hymen to break, it is most commonly ruptured when a girl or woman has sexual intercourse for the first time. A ruptured hymen is, therefore, often presumed to be evidence of past sexual activity, and for a variety of reasons some women want to avoid that presumption.

Taking the hymenoplasty debate as a starting point, in this chapter I consider whether physicians should have the power to refuse women access to surgery based on their possibly misguided concern for their patients' presumed lack of autonomy, or the presumption that they suffer from "false consciousness."[3] Denying adult women access to elective procedures in the name of women's rights or on the basis of other justifications raises serious questions about whether they enjoy genuine autonomy in liberal democracies.

The anatomical status of unmarried girls is a concern across the globe. According to customary law in many societies, their condition affects family honor because premarital sex is often thought to bring shame on the family.[4]

Sexual activity before marriage may be dangerous for women in countries with strict codes of sexual morality, and the problem is exacerbated when women from these societies move to countries with more sexual freedom. Differing moral codes concerning sexual conduct inevitably complicate the lives of young women who move from Islamic polities to European countries.[5]

Many have to maneuver in new social worlds where more liberal attitudes toward sexual activity exist, while at the same time having to adhere to the more conservative rules of their families and communities. To function as required in both realms, some women ask surgeons to repair their hymens in order to conceal their past sexual activities.[6] While the question of whether a type of sexual behavior alters virginity may appear to be relatively trivial, for these women it can be a matter of life and death.[7] They fear that if they do not appear to be virgins on their wedding night, they may become victims of honor killings.[8]

In this context, one asks whether women seeking hymen reconstruction should be legally guaranteed access to this surgical procedure, despite the well-intentioned objections of surgeons, especially when denial of "revirgination" could result in death. In deciding how to formulate public policy regarding hymenoplasty, one should take into account the serious qualms doctors have about performing this surgery, including the commonly expressed view that hymen reconstruction perpetuates sexist attitudes toward women.[9] For surgeons, the basic question is whether performing a hymenoplasty is consistent with domestic law and international human rights standards; for women seeking the surgery, the question is whether the denial of the surgery violates their fundamental human rights.

In what follows, I assess the debate about hymen restoration. This study of a controversial surgical practice, complicated by cultural conflicts regarding its necessity, affords insight into biases inherent in the medical profession.[10] The analysis of this operation requires consideration of the motivations of those seeking it, as well as a brief assessment of the social value of virginity. Most importantly, this study demonstrates the necessity of having a realistic understanding of the consequences of defloration for women in particular cultural communities.

The Cultural Significance of Virginity

In some societies women are expected to be virgins when they marry;[11] this is ostensibly to ensure the paternity of future offspring.[12] Although this expectation of virginity on the wedding night was prevalent in European countries and North America in the not-so-distant past, it has ceased to play as crucial a role since the mid-twentieth century and the advent of the sexual revolution.[13] Virginity continues to be an important requirement for individuals in some communities, including Islamic societies.[14] A study of South Asian women in Ontario, for instance, emphasizes the importance of the norm of virginity in the context of explaining the cultural motivation for domestic violence.[15]

Although many assume there is a single understanding of "virginity," its meaning has changed over time and varies in different parts of the world. Scholarship about the historical significance of virginity usually associates it with an intact hymen.[16] For the purposes of this analysis, that definition is the relevant one—although it should be noted that relying on the hymen as the indicator of virginity is misleading. Not only can the appearance of an intact hymen vary considerably,[17] but, as mentioned above, its rupture can occur for reasons other than sex.

Moreover, the breaking of the hymen does not always result in bleeding. Indeed, studies indicate that only half of women observed blood during their first sexual experience.[18] This matters, because traditionally, in societies in which the virginity of the bride had to be demonstrated, the presence of blood on the sheets was crucial. It is also erroneous to presume that virginity is necessarily related to what Westerners might call chastity, or purity. For instance, an ethnographic study of the sexual experience of young adults in Morocco noted that while young women accept the proposition that they should be virgins when they marry, they enjoy sexual intimacy without vaginal penetration.[19] The pressure to find alternative ways to have sexual experience without risking the loss of virginity, as understood in the community, has also intensified because the age of marriage has risen.

As virginity plays a significant role in marriage negotiations, families in many countries have been known to require virginity testing of their daughters. This practice has been strongly condemned by human rights organizations such as Human Rights Watch because it is regarded as an affront to women's dignity.[20] Moreover, as virginity testing is often compelled as a prerequisite to a forced marriage, it is considered even more reprehensible.[21]

In some societies rituals are performed to celebrate the virginal status of girls. For instance, regions in South Africa, such as the province of KwaZulu-Natal, have experienced a revival of *umhlanga*—a Zulu reed dance ceremony celebrating virginity—despite vociferous protests against virginity testing.[22] To take part in *umhlanga*, girls must be "certified" virgins. Although some fear the certification may put girls at risk because it may attract men who want a virgin in order to avoid contracting AIDS, others contend that the virginity testing is actually beneficial, because it protects young girls. So, despite trenchant criticisms of virginity testing,[23] some commentators defend the practice because it is accepted by the communities.[24]

While many people assume that there is no longer a preoccupation with virginity in modern societies in the twenty-first century, wedding customs in modern societies reflect the continuing importance of this "virtue," even though it is conveyed in symbolic terms. For instance, at American weddings the bride typically wears a white gown that ostensibly signifies her pure state. Before she departs for her honeymoon, it is customary for the bride to throw her bouquet, which symbolically represents her "defloration." Another wedding ritual that arguably reflects the cultural value attached to virginity is the breaking of glass. For example, at Jewish weddings after the bride and groom drink out of the same glass, the groom breaks it under his foot.[25] While it is unlikely that those participating in such rituals are deliberately perpetuating sexist or misogynistic attitudes requiring the purity of women at the time of marriage, they nevertheless reinforce these societal understandings.

The Demand for Hymenoplasty

One should not conflate virginity testing of young girls with the quite distinct debate about adult women requesting hymen restoration surgery to avoid honor-related violence.[26] An adult woman's decision to undergo a reconstructive surgery that does not involve any serious risk of physical harm has nothing to do with the question of the best interests of the child, nor does it necessarily involve duress.

In Europe and North America women have been requesting hymenoplasty for the past few decades.[27] According to one study, "Hymenoplasty has proliferated in various parts of Europe,"[28] and the American Society of Plastic Surgeons says vaginal surgery, including hymenoplasty, is one of the industry's fastest-growing segments.

The increase in demand for "revirgination" surgeries in European countries and North America may be a consequence of increased migration, the reality that young women are caught between two cultures, and the fact that they marry at a later age. Underlying it all, however, is women's need to avoid honor-related violence, or at least allay their fears that it might occur.

As hymen repair seems to be occurring more frequently, the medical profession is addressing the question of its legitimacy with a sense of urgency.[29] The pressure on surgeons to perform hymenoplasties led to an intense discussion about the ethical challenges they face: On one hand is the possibility that performing the surgery simply reinforces gender inequities in certain cultural milieus; on the other hand is women's fear that they will be subjected to honor-related violence and even death if the procedure is not performed.

Such ethical dilemmas regarding hymen restoration surgery are not limited to liberal Western countries. In Iran, for example, where hymenoplasty is illegal and doctors can be prosecuted for performing it, Ahmadi remarks that some doctors nevertheless have gone to great lengths to do the surgery in order to protect women from honor-related violence:

> The physicians seemed to assume the moral burden of protecting these women's welfare, suggesting they would have felt morally culpable if some-

> thing were to happen to them, when knowing that performing a simple medical procedure may have prevented reprisal. Perceiving the risk of not performing hymenoplasty as too great, the physicians respect the autonomy of those requesting . . . the surgery.[30]

Social science supports the claim that adult women in Europe also seek hymen repair because they fear they will be victims of honor-related violence if they are discovered not to be virgins on their wedding night.[31] Research is available on the plight of young Muslim women in Spain, Sweden, and the Netherlands.[32] In light of past research on the importance of marriage traditions to immigrants, enforcement of norms regarding sexual morality may take on a special significance for migrants to ensure the maintenance of cultural identity.[33] Scholars contend that young women caught between Islamic and European norms concerning "sexuality, virginity and marriage exposes these young women to very specific and severe forms of acculturative stress."[34] They also point out that keeping secrets from their families may result in "feelings of guilt and anxiety."[35]

Medical professionals, however, tend to handle questions of the proper nature of surgeries without adequate consideration of the consequences for their female patients, revealing the paternalism of medicine. Rather than allowing medical elites to decide a question on their own that affects the well-being of many women, it would be preferable to weigh the arguments for and against hymenoplasty.

Objections to Hymenoplasty

The primary argument against hymen restoration is that it perpetuates sexist attitudes toward women. In essence, surgeons performing the procedure would be reinforcing the patriarchal notion that women must be virgins, or at least must appear to be, on their wedding night. Even though women are the ones requesting the surgery, its performance has the effect of undermining the dignity of women. Professor Jacques Lansac, president of the National College of Gynecologists and Obstetricians of France comments: "The surgery is an attack on women's dignity . . . [and] liberty."[36]

This argument is reminiscent of the position taken by the Human Rights Committee when it rejected the contention by Manuel Wackenheim, a man with dwarfism, that he had the right to employment in dwarf-tossing competitions.[37] France banned the contests because they allegedly undermined the dignity of persons with disabilities. According to this line of argument, a paternalistic approach to human rights is justifiable because the state has an obligation to protect the dignity of members of a group even if particular individuals fail to appreciate how their choices and actions undermine their own self-interest.[38]

A second objection is the "virginity fraud" involved. As the purpose of the surgery is to deceive a future husband about the status of his wife's hymen and thereby create the illusion of virginity, some surgeons find the fraud involved objectionable; they regard their involvement as a form of complicity in the deceit.[39] According to this line of argument, they owe a duty not only to the woman who is the patient, but also to the husband and family.[40] This deceit is not new; for centuries women have used a number of circumvention techniques to fool their grooms on their wedding nights.[41] One trick was to ensure that the groom was sufficiently inebriated that he would not notice the difference in the bride's condition.

Techniques discussed in the literature include having midwives repair the broken hymen with needle and thread and animal membrane;[42] using a vial (or sponge or capsule) of animal's blood and surreptitiously spreading it in the appropriate place; concealing a small blade in the wedding dress to make a small cut; and substituting already bloodied sheets. Another more contemporary option is the use of kits available online; some produced in China cost as little as $30. They involve the insertion of red substance that mimics blood. A company in Germany, Virginia Care, also claims to sell artificial hymens that are basically pouches of bovine blood.[43]

But it is the relatively new use of surgery that implicates the medical profession in the wedding night schemes and may partly explain their reluctance to perform the surgery.[44] The fact that some physicians have conscientious objections to performing the procedure should not constitute a reason for disallowing the surgery altogether, provided another surgeon can be found to operate.

A number of professional associations have taken a position opposing the surgery on the grounds that "refusal to do a hymenoplasty represented the best practice and current standard of medical care."[45] Physicians opposed to the surgery referred to a policy statement from the American College of Obstetricians and Gynecologists, "Vaginal Rejuvenation and Cosmetic Vaginal Procedures', which officially discouraged the procedure 'because of a paucity of information about their safety and efficacy'.[46]

The mostly consistent rejection of hymenoplasty by medical professional organizations—including the Royal College of Obstetricians and Gynaecologists and the [leave as is] National College of French Gynecologists and Obstetricians—reflects a genuine desire to undermine the patriarchal ideology that women must be virgins at the time of marriage.[47] The policy of the UK-based Royal College of Obstetricians and Gynaecologists states explicitly

> that cultural or religious norms which place women in positions of vulnerability or subservience are unacceptable. This includes cultures in which women fear for their safety if it is discovered that their hymen is perforated.
> . . .
> While the Standards Board supports the concept of patient and professional autonomy, it believes that any decision to provide cosmetic genital surgery should be based entirely on clinical grounds.[48]

While this position of trying to reject patriarchal logic by refusing to perform hymen repair is not without merit, it is an approach that may prove short-sighted if it winds up sacrificing the very individuals that the policy is designed to save.

Principles of biomedical ethics also enter into the debate. The key principle is nonmaleficence, or do no harm. Some doctors consider the procedure unjustifiable because the women are not "sick"; the procedure is not "medically necessary"; and it appears to be a type of harm or mutilation.[49] Although hymenoplasty is usually a minor surgery lasting thirty to forty-five minutes, performed under either local or general anesthesia, it does involve some risk, as do all surgical procedures.[50] The recovery may take four to six weeks, although innovations may reduce that.[51] As a matter of principle, there is a question as to whether doctors are required to perform surgeries that may be regarded as "self-mutilation" or "self-harm" when there is no medical reason for it.[52] On this basis, surgeons might decline to operate.

Moreover, if the women who were their patients are attacked or killed and family members are prosecuted, the physicians worry that they might be required to testify in court, which may be another disincentive to performing the surgery. Even more worrisome may be the possibility that the doctors themselves could be subject to retaliation if the family members discover that they have performed the surgery. The experience of doctors running abortion clinics in the United States surely demonstrates the possibility that communities can show their extreme displeasure when they disagree with a specific type of surgery.

Another major concern of surgeons is the legal status of the practice. As various countries have enacted laws that ban genital surgeries, medical personnel have expressed concern about the legally ambiguous status of the procedure.[53] They contend that European laws that ban female genital mutilation (FGM) are broad in scope and appear to apply to genital cosmetic surgery and hymen repair. Although there may not yet exist a definitive interpretation of relevant statutes, the vagaries of the laws may also discourage surgeons from operating.

The high-profile prosecution of a physician in the United Kingdom suggests that this concern is not unfounded.[54] The doctor delivered a baby to a woman who had undergone female genital cutting in her homeland in Somalia. After the delivery, he stitched the area to repair tearing she had experienced during labor. To his surprise, he was prosecuted under the national law prohibiting surgery of the female genitalia. This charge was absurd, insofar as the law was designed to prevent *removal* of parts of the female anatomy of little girls who lack legal capacity to consent; it was not intended to prevent surgeons from performing reconstructive surgery on consenting adult women. Fortunately, the doctor was acquitted.[55]

This case indicates that legal officials may see fit to prosecute doctors for "revirgination" under statutes that do not clearly distinguish among different types of surgeries. That surgeons must operate in the shadow of the vague laws may, in fact, discourage them from providing reconstructive surgery that adult women urgently request and actually need.

Arguments in Favor of Allowing Hymenoplasty

THE PRINCIPLE OF PATIENT AUTONOMY

The most significant argument in favor of hymen repair is the autonomy interest of women. Simply put, women as patients should have the ability to decide what types of surgical procedures they wish to have, whether they are medically necessary or not. That patients who are in control of their mental faculties and have legal capacity should make decisions about surgery is hardly controversial. Patient autonomy, while admittedly not an absolute principle that should be limited in extreme cases of self-harm, is a well-established principle in medical ethics.

Even if one does not subscribe to full autonomy and supports the prohibition of some procedures, women should at least be able to have reconstructive surgery. The hymenoplasty debate emerged following heated public discussion of female genital mutilation, a surgery that has been designated as a criminal offense in many jurisdictions because it is considered a form of mutilation.[56] Yet it is unclear why some types of operations are condemned as "mutilation" while others are accepted as elective procedures. Although many people in modern societies condone the pervasive trend toward "flesh wounds,"[57] FGM has usually been condemned as an extreme form of violence against women.

A new double standard has emerged, which becomes particularly evident when one considers that certain types of genital surgeries are treated as permissible, while hymenoplasties to avoid "honor"-related violence are not. In Western societies adult women are increasingly opting for genital surgeries for aesthetic reasons,[58] giving rise to a new field called "cosmetogynecology." According to the American Society for Aesthetic Plastic Surgery, 400 girls age eighteen and younger had labiaplasty in 2015—an 80 percent increase over the previous year—and a 2013 British report noted a fivefold increase over ten years.[59] These cosmetic genital surgeries as of yet have not been subject to regulation, nor have they generated much public debate about their legitimacy. This constitutes selective enforcement of laws that apply to female genitalia.

It is worth emphasizing here the major difference between FGM and hymenoplasty. Unlike female genital cutting, which involves the permanent removal of parts of the body, hymen restoration is a reconstructive surgery. Also, whereas female genital cutting is generally performed on very young girls, those seeking hymenoplasties are predominantly adult women. While some might question their judgment, it seems perfectly reasonable for the women to request the surgery when they face a credible threat of honor-related violence. Given that the surgery is restorative and requested by adults, women should be entitled to have it performed.

HUMAN RIGHTS AS A BASIS FOR HYMENOPLASTY

Not only does the principle of patient autonomy support the argument in favor of hymenoplasty, but the framework of human rights law also offers some basis for requiring that states ensure the availability of the procedure. A growing body of literature and global policies support the proposition that there is a right to health.[60] Even without such an explicit right, women arguably have a right of access to health care and medical services under existing instruments, particularly the International Covenant on Economic, Social, and Cultural Rights. Article 12 stipulates that there is a human right to the highest attainable standard of health. This provision has been elaborated in General Comment Number 14 (2000), which calls for paying attention to women's right to health in particular.[61]

Although the right to health is considered a well-established human right, whether it applies to the right to surgery is not an entirely settled question. While some scholars regard it only as an "emerging" norm, others support an expansive interpretation of the right to health that includes a right to essential surgery.[62] This logic is convincing: If the International Covenant of Economic, Social, and Cultural Rights guarantees a right to the highest attainable standard of health, then this right should be construed as encompassing the right to surgery.

If such a right to surgery is accepted, there would have to be further debate about whether hymenoplasty constitutes an essential surgery. It stands to reason that this relatively innocuous procedure should be covered as essential surgery if it can spare women from violence or death. In addition, the fact that women live in fear of honor-related violence serves as a mental health argument in favor of interpreting the surgery as essential.

Another relevant human right is the right to culture. Here the argument is that women may choose to remain a part of their cultural communities despite certain oppressive, patriarchal practices, and this choice is protected by international human rights law.[63] The right to culture guarantees the right to participate in the cultural life of the community, even if the relevant moral code is inconsistent with views of external observers. Hence, women should be guaranteed access to the surgery so they can continue to take part in the major activities of their communities. Although it may seem peculiar that deceit should be authorized as part of cultural rights, it may be a necessary means by which participation can be maintained.

The right to bodily integrity is another argument women could invoke in support of access to hymenoplasty. Although usually employed as part of campaigns against surgeries such as male circumcision and FGM, there is no reason why bodily integrity must necessarily be interpreted as *prohibiting* certain forms of surgery. After traumatic and disfiguring injuries, some people might argue that they have a right to reconstructive surgery in order to *restore* their bodily integrity. In a similar vein, women can justifiably argue that they want to restore the hymen because they consider it essential for their understanding of bodily integrity and their sense of well-being.

Feminists take differing positions on the propriety of this surgery. While some oppose it because it reflects patriarchal values, others champion it as an expression of autonomy. Although it would be preferable to live in a world that no longer valued virginity and used it as a cruel means of social control, the question is whether adult women should have the right to a reconstructive procedure in the interim.

Weighing the Arguments

In the previous sections I considered arguments for and against hymenoplasty. Ultimately I conclude that women should have the right to undergo the procedure if they choose to do so.[64] Patient autonomy is important and should be recognized in legal systems as a general matter, and certainly with regard to reconstructive surgery. If autonomous decision-making is to be protected, then the autonomy of physicians should be protected as well. If surgeons have objections to the surgery, whether based on feminist principles, a judgment that it is medically unnecessary, or other grounds, they ought to have the right to decline to do so.

The law as it is currently designed in some jurisdictions may not afford protection to doctors who perform the surgery. The fact that adult women elect to have the procedure may be insufficient to protect doctors again prosecution; the statutes may stipulate either that culture cannot justify the performance of the surgery, or that consent is not a defense when the operation represents a form of mutilation.

Recognizing these risks, what policy changes should be implemented? For surgeons willing to perform hymen reconstruction, the question is whether the laws ought to be modified to address the ambiguous status of this procedure. That would at least avoid the worry that the surgery constituted a crime. For those who do not wish to perform the hymenoplasty, the code of medical ethics should permit an opt-out policy.

Questions also arise about whether doctors who do not wish to perform the procedure should be ethically required to refer women to other doctors or to other sources of counseling.[65] When young women migrate to new lands from countries that require virginity at the time of marriage, they often lack the mentoring of older women about how to handle their precarious situation. As a consequence, some medical professionals have suggested that counseling young immigrant women about possible alternatives to hymenoplasty might reduce the number of requests for this type of surgery.[66] According to one scholar, in the absence of mentors, surgeons in the Netherlands who declined to perform the surgery recommended use of the circumvention techniques mentioned earlier in the chapter.[67] Establishing more extensive counseling programs with absolutely strict confidentiality could yield real benefits for both the young women and surgeons.

Autonomy in the Medical Context

In the field of biomedical ethics, the principle of autonomy is ordinarily of paramount importance. This means in practical terms that patients should be treated with dignity and that they are entitled to decide whether or not to accept medical treatment. Leading texts emphasize that as long as patients possess legal capacity and are informed of the potential risks of medical procedures, they should be able to make their own decisions about taking drugs, having surgeries, or making changes to their lifestyles.[68] With respect to surgical ethics, the conventional wisdom is that patients should be able to choose whether or not to undergo surgeries, even if the procedures are not medically necessary. Autonomy also requires that medical professionals operate in the best interests of their patients.[69]

Interestingly, recent studies of hymenoplasty regard the decision to undergo the surgery as an act of resistance. It demonstrates that women recognize the constraints of their social environment and cleverly find means to function within that reality. Those who conduct ethnographic research increasingly highlight the "empowering" nature of the decision to "medicalize" the procedure. One study concludes with the nuanced argument that "women seeking HR [hymen reconstruction] are both victims and agents: They cannot realistically hope to be completely free of coercive patriarchal attempts to control their bodies, but they may resist such attempts by seeking HR."[70] Nevertheless, it is still possible that by acting in this manner they reinforce patriarchal norms that demand "purity" of women.[71] Future research will reveal whether this procedure serves the interests of women or not.

Conclusion

In an ideal world there would be no double standard regarding premarital sex for men and women, and women would not need to deceive their husbands. Until such time as women enjoy the same liberties as men, they will have to maneuver within patriarchal systems. As they strive to circumvent the sexist customs that limit their activities, the medical profession must reconsider its ill-conceived policies recommending that surgeons refuse to provide the "revirgination." Even if one wishes that women did not have to resort to surgery to avoid serious threats to their well-being, in democratic systems the possibility of requesting reconstructive surgery should be available to them.

The empowerment of patients should mean that they can choose to have elective surgeries, whether physicians are eager to perform them or not. Surgeons' refusal to operate on women seeking hymenoplasty who believe it is necessary to save their lives clearly interferes with their autonomous decision-making. They should consider the possible consequences for their patients. Whether the state is obligated to fund the surgeries is another matter, but the absence of government financing would most likely result in the further victimization of poor women if they cannot obtain hymenoplasties.

While many types of cosmetic and reconstructive surgery could be condemned as reflecting self-hatred on the part of women,[72] only some types of surgical procedures seem to attract widespread condemnation. Despite the possible negative aspects of allowing hymenoplasty, it is ultimately better to empower women to make their own health-care decisions. Instead of assuming that the choice to undergo the knife reflects a lack of agency, a feminist reconsideration could regard this choice as one that is strangely empowering.

Notes

1. K. Shaheen, "Hymenoplasty: Why Do Women Get Virginity Back?," *The Daily Star* (Beirut, October 8, 2013) <www.dailystar.com.lb/News/Lebanon-News/2013/Oct-08/233897-hymenplasty-why-do-women-get-virginity-back.ashx>, accessed April 24, 2017.
2. C. O. Airhihenbuwa, *Health and Culture: Beyond the Western Paradigm* (Sage, 1995); S. Johnsdotter and B. Essén, "Genitals and Ethnicity: The Politics of Genital Modifications" (2010) 18 *Reproductive Health Matters*, 29.
3. Some see this rather as a form of "relational autonomy," whereby individuals willingly allow their choices and decision-making to be constrained by their social settings. See J. Nedelsky, *Law's Relations: A Relational Theory of Self, Autonomy, and Law* (Oxford University Press. 2011); in this volume. see also Deveaux (chapter 5), Johnson (chapter 15), Benda-Beckmann (chapter 16), and Ali and Kazmi (chapter 19).
4. F. H. Stewart, *Honor* (University of Chicago Press, 1994); A. Agarwal, *Crimes of Honor: An International Human Rights Perspective on Violence against Women in South Asia* (PhD dissertation, University of Southern California, 2008). Fatima Mernissi asserts that "The concepts

of honour and virginity locate the prestige of a man between the legs of a woman. It is not by subjugating nature or by conquering mountains and rivers that a man secures his status, but by controlling the women related to him by blood or by marriage, and forbidding them any contact with male strangers." F. Mernissi, "Virginity and Patriarchy" (1982) 5 *Women's Studies International Forum*, 183. See also R. Husseini, *Murder in the Name of Honour: The True Story of One Woman's Heroic Fight Against an Unbelievable Crime* (Oneworld Publications, 2009), 83.

5. A. Steigrad, "Muslim Women in France Regain Virginity in Clinics" (Reuters, April 3, 2007) <www.reuters.com/article/us-muslimwomen-europe-virginity-idUSL25320251 20070430>, accessed April 24, 2017; S. Meichtry and M. Colchester, "Secular, Muslim Culture Clash Ensnares French Doctors. Hymenoplasty Spotlights Debate Over Repression," *Wall Street Journal* (New York, June 10, 2008), A11; E. Sciolino and S. Mekhennet, "In Europe, Debate Over Islam and Virginity," *New York Times* (New York, June 11, 2008) <www.nytimes .com/2008/06/11/world/europe/11virgin.html>, accessed April 24, 2017; "More Women Becoming Virgins Again with Hymen Replacement Operations on the NHS," *Daily Mail* (London, July 30, 2010) <www.dailymail.co.uk/news/article-1298684/Surge-virginity-repair -operations-NHS.html>, accessed April 24, 2017.

6. The status of this tissue is of such monumental significance that women in some societies worry about participating in athletic activities such as cycling, which can, in rare cases, result in the rupture of the hymen.

7. N. Shalhoub-Kevorkian, "Imposition of Virginity Testing: A Life-Saver or a License to Kill" (2005) 60 *Social Science & Medicine*, 1187, 1190.

8. T. T. Pham, *Moroccan Immigrant Women in Spain: Honor and Marriage* (Lexington Books, 2014), 113.

9. G. Heinrichs, "Is Hymenoplasty Anti-Feminist?" (2015) 26 *Journal of Clinical Ethics*, 158.

10. Among important considerations of this practice, see, e.g., A. Longmans et al., "Ethical Dilemma: Should Doctors Reconstruct the Vaginal Introitus of Adolescent Girls to Mimic the Virginal State?" (1998) 361 *British Medical Journal*, 459; R. J. Cook and B. M. Dickens, "Hymen Reconstruction: Ethical and Legal Issues" (2009) 107 *International Journal of Gynecology and Obstetrics*, 266.

11. There is a double standard in that there is no such expectation for men.

12. D. Holtzman and N. Kulish, "Nevermore: The Hymen and the Loss of Virginity" (1996) 44 (suppl) *Journal of the American Psychoanalytic Association*, 303; H. Blank, *Virgin: The Untouched History* (Bloomsbury, 2007); T. T. Dao Jensen, "Visions of Virginity in the Abstinence-Only Curriculum" (PhD dissertation, Arizona State University, 2008). For rules governing how to evaluate paternity in light of the length of gestation, see I. Ghanem, *Islamic Medical Jurisprudence* (Arthur Probsthain, 1982), 30. DNA tests would provide a reliable method instead.

13. Evidence of continuing concern with virginity is reflected in US practices such as abstinence, virginity pledges, and the "true love waits" movement. Controversies over "slut walks" suggest that there continues to be a preoccupation with virginity in the United States; see A. North, "Should 'Slut' be Retired?," *New York Times* (New York, February 3, 2015) <https:// op-talk.blogs.nytimes.com/2015/02/03/should-slut-be-retired/?_r=0>, accessed April 24, 2017. A sensational televised story of a few young women auctioning off their virginity for hundreds of thousands of dollars to pay for their college education and help support their families also suggests its enduring value in North America; see A. B. Wang, " 'It's my decision.' This Woman Is Auctioning Off Her Virginity to Help Her Family," *Washington Post* (Washington, DC, October 25, 2016) <www.washingtonpost.com/news/wonk/wp/2016/10/25/its-my-decision

-this-woman-is-auctioning-off-her-virginity-to-help-her-family/?utm_term=.6c1caa84dc6d>, accessed April 24, 2017.

14. B. R. van Moorst et al. contend that virginity is important in the religious ethics of many groups; see "Backgrounds of Women Applying for Hymen Reconstruction: The Effects of Counselling on Myths and Misunderstandings about Virginity, and the Results of Hymen Reconstruction" (2012) 17 *The European Journal of Contraception and Reproductive Health Care*, 93, 94. It also is used metaphorically to signify a lack of (business) experience, as with Richard Branson's Virgin Atlantic Airlines, and high quality, as with extra virgin olive oil. For a famous essay analyzing the trauma associated with the loss of virginity, see . Freud, "The Virginity Taboo" in S. Whiteside (trans.), *The Psychology of Love* (Penguin Classics, 2006 [1918]), 262.

15. S. Hunjan and S. Towson, " 'Virginity Is Everything': Sexuality in the Context of Intimate Partner Violence in the South Asian Community," in S. D. Dasgupta, ed., *Body Violence: Intimate Violence against South Asian Women in America* (Rutgers University Press, 2007), 53, 59. See also Husseini (n. 4), 83: "So much of the problem of violence against women in general, and specifically in so-called honour crimes, revolves around the hymen—the proof of virginity; a literal seal of virtue. It represents the 'honour' of the girl and, more importantly, of her family."

16. J-J Amy provides a definition: "*Virginity* could be defined as the *absence of any prior sexual intercourse with penetration of the vagina that caused an identifiable lesion of the hymen.*" J-J Amy, "Certificates of Virginity and Reconstruction of the Hymen" (2008) 12 *European Journal of Contraception and Reproductive Health Care*, 111; see also D. Pollack, "Virginity Testing: International Law and Social Work Perspectives" (2008) 51 *International Social Work*, 262–67; J. Awwad et al., "Attitudes of Lebanese University Students Towards Surgical Hymen Reconstruction" (2013) 42 *Archives of Sexual Behavior*, 1627. In Christianity some struggle to explain the status of the Virgin Mary, because although conceived through the Immaculate Conception, baby Jesus arrived through vaginal birth; see M. Mayblin, "People Like Us: Intimacy, Distance, and the Gender of Saints" (2014) 55 (suppl. 10) *Current Anthropology*, 271.

17. Amy (n. 16).

18. This fact is widely known (see, e.g., Pham [n. 8] 100). Nevertheless, it seems not to have obviated the need for women to produce blood on their wedding night.

19. F. Bakass, M. Ferrand, and the ECAF team, "Sexual Debut in Rabat: New 'Arrangements' between the Sexes" (2013) 68 *Population*, F 37. Surprisingly, this empirical study makes no reference to hymenoplasty. Likewise, a study of Lebanon also mentioned that "more than half of Lebanese female university students approved premarital sexual contact without vaginal penetration." The researcher concludes: "This finding underpins the fact that sexual taboos seem to relate more to the physical state of virginity than to the virtue of chastity." See Awwad et al. (n. 16), 1633.

20. Human Rights Watch, see <www.hrw.org/news/2014/12/01/un-who-condemns-virginity-tests>, accessed April 24, 2017.

21. Parents sometimes take their minor daughters to doctors for testing and possible hymen restoration, if necessary, before marrying them off. L Kopelman, "Make Her a Virgin Again: When Medical Disputes about Minors are Cultural Clashes" (2013) 39 *Journal of Medicine and Philosophy*, 8.

22. L. Vincent, "Virginity Testing in South Africa: Re-Traditioning the Postcolony" (2006) 8 *Culture, Health & Sexuality*, 17. For a comparative analysis of testing in Brazil and South Africa, see L. B. Brown, "Abject Bodies: The Politics of the Vagina in Brazil and South Africa" (2009) 56 *Theoria*, 1.

23. For oppressive use of virginity tests, see, e.g., K. Engelhart, "Brides Forced to Take Tests for Virginity," *Maclean's* (Toronto, July 27, 2009) <www.macleans.ca/news/world/brides-forced-to-take-tests-for-virginity/>, accessed April 24, 2017.

24. While Vincent concedes that some may object to the testing as a violation of the privacy rights of girls, her article (n. 22) questions why it is treated differently from male circumcision under the Children's Rights Bill. For a defense of the testing as beneficial to girls, see A. Wickström, "Virginity Testing as a Local Public Health Initiative: A 'Preventive Ritual' More than a 'Diagnostic Measure' " (2010) 16 *Journal of the Royal Anthropological Institute*, 532.

25. For the association between unbroken glass and virginity, see A. Dundes, "The Psychoanalytic Study of Folklore" in A. Dundes, *Parsing Through Customs: Essays by a Freudian Folklorist* (University of Wisconsin Press, 1987), 32. It is probably no coincidence that the barrier to women's success in the workplace is usually called the "glass ceiling."

26. Although it is difficult to know whether the restoration surgery succeeds in protecting women from honor-related violence, there is some evidence in this direction. In Egypt hymen restoration was considered responsible for reducing the rate of honor killings by 80 percent. See P. Kandela, "Egypt's Trade in Hymen Repair" (1996) 347 *Lancet*, 1615; M. O'Connor, "Reconstructing the Hymen: Mutilation or Restoration?" (2008) 16 *Journal of Law and Medicine*, 164.

27. M. H. J. Bekker et al., "Reconstructing Hymens or Constructing Sexual Inequality? Service Provision to Islamic Young Women Coping with the Demand to be a Virgin" (1996) 6 *Journal of Community & Applied Social Psychology*, 329; A. Chozick, "Virgin Territory: U.S. Women Seek a Second First Time. Hymen Surgery Is on the Rise and Drawing Criticism," *Wall Street Journal* (New York, December 15, 2005), A1.

28. Pham (n. 8), 106; B. Crumley, "The Dilemma of 'Virginity' Restoration," *Time* (New York, July 13, 2008) <http://content.time.com/time/world/article/0,8599,1822297,00.html>, accessed April 24, 2017.

29. L. Seng Khoo and V. Senna-Fernandes, "Hymenoplasty and Virginity—An Issue of Socio-Cultural Morality and Medical Ethics" (2015/2016) 3 *PMFA News*, 1.

30. A. Ahmadi, "Ethical Issues in Hymenoplasty: Views from Tehran's Physicians" (2014) 40 *Journal of Medical Ethics*, 430.

31. See Steigrad (n. 5).

32. See especially B. Essén, A. Blomkvist, L. Helström, and S. Johnsdotter, "The Experience and Responses of Swedish Health Professionals to Patients Requesting Virginity Restoration (Hymen Repair)" (2010) 18 *Reproductive Health Matters*, 38; see also S. Ayuandini, "How Variability in Hymenoplasty Recommendations Leads to Contrasting Rates of Surgery in the Netherlands" (2017) 19 *Culture, Health, & Sexuality*; Pham (n. 8); Bekker et al. (n 27).

33. F. Strijbosch, "The Concept of the Pela and Its Social Significance in the Community of Immigrant Moluccans in The Netherlands" (1985) 17 *Journal of Legal Pluralism*, 177.

34. Ibid., 331.

35. Ibid., 333.

36. Steigrad (n. 5). A judgment in Lille where a judge annulled a marriage because a woman had lied about being a virgin sparked great controversy.

37. *Wackenheim v. France*, Communication No 854/1999: France, 26/07/2002, CCPR/C/75/D/854/1999 (Jurisprudence).

38. For a thoughtful consideration of this decision, see E. Stamatopoulou, *Cultural Rights in International Law* (Martinus Nijhoff, 2007), 118.

39. Insofar as all cosmetic surgery involves deceit, taken to its logical extreme, this argument would require rejection of all such procedures. P de Lora, "Is Multiculturalism Bad for Health Care? The Case for Re-Virgination" (2015) *Theoretical* Medicine and Bioethics, 141, 154.

40. D. D. Raphael, "Commentary: The Ethical Issue is Deceit" (1998) 316 *British Medical Journal*, 460.

41. C. Addison, "Enlightenment and Virginity" (2010) 2 *Inkanyiso: Journal of Humanities and Social Sciences*, 71, 77; "Virginity for Sale" (*Marie Claire*, January 20, 2010) <www.marieclaire.com/politics/a3809/fake-hymens-for-sale/>, accessed April 24, 2017; see also R. Evelth, "Artificial Hymens Have Come a Long Way Since Blood-Filled Fish Bladders," *Smithsonian* (Washington, DC, August 12, 2013) <www.smithsonianmag.com/smart-news/artificial-hymens-have-come-a-long-way-since-blood-filled-fish-bladders-27752278/>, accessed April 24, 2017.

42. This is according to a former director of the Kinsey Institute for Research in Sex, Gender, and Reproduction, quoted in Chozick (n. 27).

43. R. Gert, "Women Simulate Virginity with Artificial Hymens. German Company Sells Easy-to-Use Product Ensuring Blood on Wedding Sheets" (*The Times of Israel*, December 18, 2015) <http://www.timesofisrael.com/women-simulate-virginity-with-artificial-hymens/>, accessed April 24, 2017.

44. People were concerned about fake or "falsified" virginity in earlier centuries. Tassie Gwilliam provides an interesting analysis comparing faked virginity to counterfeit money, implying that the fraud devalues virginity just as "fake money devalues coinage." It also suggests women's bodies are comparable to commodities for exchange. Male authors have written at length in novels about virginity fraud or counterfeit maidenhead; see T. Gwilliam, "Counterfeit Maidenheads in the Eighteenth Century" (1996) 6 *Journal of the History of Sexuality*, 518. In an influential essay, Fatima Mernissi refers to the phenomenon as "artificial virginity" (n. 4).

45. Kopelman (n. 21), 10.

46. Despite the declared "paucity of information," the committee that issued the policy warned that the surgery "could cause scarring, pain, altered sensation, and sexual dysfunction"; see Kopelman (n. 21), 10.

47. See Royal College of Obstetricians and Gynaecologists, Statement No. 6, "Hymenoplasty and Labial Surgery" (July 2009) 1–3, and a subsequent position paper. This document lists the organizations in other countries opposed to hymenoplasty, such as France, New Zealand, and Malaysia. But see the Swedish National Board of Health and Welfare's Ethical Committee's Protocol No. 43 (March 19, 2004) (discussed in Essén et al. [n. 32], 42–43), which allows the surgery if a woman's life is in danger.

48. See Royal College of Obstetricians and Gynaecologists, Statement No. 6, "Hymenoplasty and Labial Surgery" (July 2009), 1–3.

49. For a discussion of whether consent should be treated as a defense to self-harm, see A. D. Renteln, "Cutting Edge Debates: A Cross-Cultural Consideration of Surgery" in W. Teays et al., eds., *Global Bioethics and Human Rights: Contemporary Issues* (Rowman & Littlefield, 2014), 220, and D. J. Baker, *The Right Not to Be Criminalized: Demarcating Criminal Law's Authority* (Ashgate, 2011).

50. Amy (n. 16), 112; Steigrad (n. 5).

51. D. Shaw and B. M. Dickens, "A New Surgical Technique of Hymenoplasty: A Solution, but for Which Problem" (2015) 130 *International Journal of Gynecology and Obstetrics*, 1.

52. For a discussion of the ethics of amputation for individuals who want to have certain body parts removed when there is no medical necessity, see D. Patrone, "Disfigured Anatomies and Imperfect Analogies: Body Integrity Identity Disorder and the Supposed Right to Self-Demanded Amputation of Healthy Body Parts" (2009) 35 *Journal of Medical Ethics*, 541. This topic is beyond the scope of this analysis, and has little bearing on my argument inasmuch as the operation central here is *reconstructive* surgery.

53. O'Connor (n. 26), 16.

54. S. Laville, "First FGM Prosecution: How the Case Came to Court," *The Guardian* (London, February 14, 2015) <www.theguardian.com/society/2015/feb/04/first-female-genital-mutilation-prosecution-dhanuson-dharmasena-fgm>, accessed April 24, 2017.

55. S. Laville, "Doctor Found Not Guilty of FGM on Patient at London Hospital," *The Guardian* (London, February 4, 2015) <www.theguardian.com/society/2015/feb/04/doctor-not-guilty-fgm-dhanuson-dharmasena>, accessed April 24, 2017.

56. See, e.g., M. Mabilia, "FGM or FGMo? Cross-Cultural Dialogue in an Italian Minefield" (2013) 29 *Anthropology Today*, 17.

57. See, e.g., V. Blum, *Flesh Wounds: The Culture of Cosmetic Surgery* (University of California Press, 2005).

58. Johnsdotter and Essén (n. 2); B. J. Hill, *Supra-Natural: Genderventions and Genitalia* (PhD dissertation, Indiana University, 2013), 101.

59. R. C. Rabin, "A Baffling Trend in Surgery: More Teenage Girls are Seeking Cosmetic Changes to Genitalia," *New York Times* (New York, April 26, 2016), D4.

60. B. C. A. Toebes, *The Right to Health as a Human Right in International Law* (Intersentia/Hart, 1999). Toebes discusses women's health issues but makes no mention of hymenoplasty.

61. See <www.refworld.org/pdfid/4538838d0.pdf>, accessed April 24, 2017.

62. See, e.g., K. A. McQueen et al., "Essential Surgery: Integral to the Right to Health" (2010) 12 *Health and Human Rights*, 137; Renteln (n. 49).

63. L. L. Veazey, *A Woman's Right to Culture: Toward Gendered Cultural Rights* (Quid Pro, LLC, 2015).

64. For an argument in favor, see de Lora (n. 39), 141.

65. S. Bastami, "When Bleeding Is Vital: Surgically Ensuring the 'Virginal' State" (2015) 26 *Journal of Clinical Ethics*, 154. In the United States, a survey of one thousand physicians showed they were divided over the question of referral.

66. S. Ayuandini, "Finger Pricks and Blood Vials: How Doctors Medicalize 'Cultural' Solutions to Demedicalize the 'Broken' Hymen in the Netherlands" (2017) 177 *Social Science & Medicine*, 61, 64.

67. Ibid.

68. R. Young, "Informed Consent and Patient Autonomy," in H. Kuhse and P. Singer, eds., *A Companion to Bioethics* (2nd ed., Wiley-Blackwell, 2009), 530; T. L. Beauchamp and J. F. Childress, *Principles of Biomedical Ethics* (6th ed., Oxford University Press, 2009), 99.

69. A. McLean, *Autonomy, Informed Consent and Medical Law: A Relational Challenge* (Cambridge University Press, 2009).

70. V. Wild et al., "Hymen Reconstruction as Pragmatic Empowerment? Results of a Qualitative Study from Tunisia" (2015) 147 *Social Science & Medicine*, 54, 60.

71. M. Kaivanara, "Virginity Dilemma: Re-Creating Virginity Through Hymenoplasty in Iran" (2016) 18 *Culture, Health & Sexuality*, 71, 81.

72. V. Pitts-Taylor, "Becoming/Being a Cosmetic Surgery Patient" (2009) 10 *Studies in Gender and Sexuality*, 119.

Part II Internet Resources

HUMAN RIGHTS

Human Rights | United Nations
https://www.un.org/en/global-issues/human-rights

Universal Declaration of Human Rights | United Nations
https://www.un.org/en/about-us/universal-declaration-of-human-rights

Human Rights Watch | Defending Human Rights Worldwide
https://www.hrw.org

What Are Human Rights? | UNICEF
https://www.unicef.org/child-rights-convention/what-are-human-rights

What Are Human Rights? | Equality and Human Rights Commission
https://www.equalityhumanrights.com/en/human-rights/what-are-human-rights

Human Rights | Stanford Encyclopedia of Philosophy
https://plato.stanford.edu/entries/rights-human

Human Rights: A Brief Introduction | Harvard University
https://dash.harvard.edu/bitstream/handle/1/23586712/Human Rights-A Brief Introduction, 2014 ed.pdf?sequence=1

Anti-Slavery International
https://www.antislavery.org/

Council on Foreign Relations
https://www.cfr.org/article/changing-landscape-global-lgbtq-rights

Disabled Persons International
https://disabledpeoplesinternational.org/

Equality Now (Women's Rights)
https://www.equalitynow.org/

Minority Rights Group International
https://minorityrights.org/new/

Redress (Anti-Torture)
https://redress.org/

Survival International
https://www.survivalinternational.org/

Part II Discussion Topics

HUMAN RIGHTS

1. In setting out a historical perspective on human rights, Robert Baker asserts that "Pandemics leap from continent to continent, companies peddle their cures around the world, biomedical experiments sponsored in the developed world are conducted in the developing world, and, in all corners of the globe . . . Thus, to meet the challenges of global bioethics, we need to turn to the more cosmopolitan concept of human rights."
   - State four or five examples of biomedical issues that are fundamentally international.
2. In its code of ethics, the AMA asserts that physicians "should only treat individuals when it is in the patient's best interest, and not to verify health so that torture can occur; and should help provide support for victims of torture" (https://www.empr.com/home/news/drug-news/ama-reminds-physicians-of-ethical-obligations-regarding-torture/).
   - What should professional organizations like the AMA do when physician members violate this code and enable torture or "harsh interrogation"? Set out your policy recommendations.
3. Nurses as well as doctors have participated in force-feeding—for example, at Guantanamo Bay. It has been described as brutal and painful and violates the informed-consent right of refusal under patient autonomy.
   - When a hunger striker is close to death, is life-saving intervention via force-feeding morally acceptable?
4. "A black market has emerged as an alternative way to acquire an organ, and one kidney can sell for upwards of $200,000. The World Health Organization estimates that at least 10 percent of kidney transplants are as a result of a black-market transactions" (https://www.pulj.org/the-roundtable/should-it-be-legal-to-sell-your-organs).
   - Do you think it should be morally acceptable to trade, purchase, or barter organs like kidneys that are needed for transplant? Share your thoughts.
   - What might be done to protect people from being exploited by international organ brokers?

5. Do you think scientists should use data obtained from experiments considered immoral, unjust, or exploitative—for example, the Nazi hypothermia studies, the Tuskegee Syphilis Study, the Guatemalan studies, the Human Radiation Studies, and so on?
   - Share your thoughts about using information obtained by means that violate human rights.
6. Peter F. Omonzejele argues that vulnerability to harm and exploitation in the research setting is more pronounced in developing (African) countries often occasioned by social, cultural, and economic circumstances.
   - What should Western researchers and pharmaceutical companies do to better protect vulnerable research subjects?
7. Native Americans, members of the First Nation, and other Indigenous groups have raised issues around the Human Genome Project, other DNA research of Native peoples, and the patenting of genetic material obtained from these research projects.
   - In her chapter Marlene Brant Castellano looks at significant issues in researching Aboriginal people. How might institutional review boards (IRBs) help address policies and practices involving the use of DNA from Indigenous people?
8. Should children be allowed to be human subjects in nontherapeutic experimentation?
   - Are there societal or medical benefits that would justify the use of children?
   - Are there any restrictions that should be put in place if children are to be used as research subjects? Share your recommendations.
9. When the Environmental Protection Agency planned a two-year environmental study using infants and children up to three years old, they offered the families $970, children's clothes, and a camcorder in exchange for using pesticides in their homes (see https://ahrp.org/us-gov-pesticide-exposure-experiments-target-children-970-per-child-wash-post-2/).
   - State your major concerns.
   - Respond to this argument for using children in pesticide studies: "It is crucial to study small children because so little is known about how their bodies absorb harmful chemicals."

Part III

LIFE AND DEATH

CHAPTER 13

Pediatrics Genomics: Current Dilemmas and a Messy Future

Maya Sabatello

Abstract

Children and adolescents are increasingly exposed to genomic data in nonclinical settings. However, their engagement and power to decide about genomic testing and use of genomic data in such settings is limited. Following the traditional conceptualizations of children as incapable of making medical decisions and the parental prerogative to do so on their behalf, children, and especially adolescents' views, are understudied. In this chapter, I begin with a brief historical summary of the genomic revolution and its scientific challenges. I then explore three key nonclinical settings in which children and adolescents' genomic data are likely to be introduced—genomic research, education, and judicial proceedings—and consider the ethical, legal, and social issues that arise. I argue that the risks associated with such exposure of children's genomic data merit that children, especially adolescents, engage in genomic conversations; indeed, adolescents challenge us to rethink the arbitrariness of age as a determinative factor in genomic decisions, and their exclusion from such conversations runs the risk of betraying the preventive goals of the genomic revolution.

Introduction

Advances in genomic sequencing technologies and knowledge are developing exponentially—and are entering ever more spaces that are relevant for children. Moving away from the traditional focus on medical settings and diagnosis of genetic conditions among children with disabilities, children today may be exposed to genomic data in a myriad of other nonclinical settings, from research and recreational genomics to education and judicial proceedings.

Whether this knowledge will improve children's well-being is unclear, yet the introduction of genomic data in nonclinical settings raises ethical, legal, and social issues (ELSI) that will need to be addressed. To what extent should children be involved in genomic decisions? For what purposes? What are the acceptable uses of children's genomic data? Who is to determine? Who stands to benefit (or not) from the increased genomic knowledge? And how are we to balance the potential benefits and costs?

This chapter will explore these questions, taking a child-centered perspective; namely, its starting point is of children as subjects of the law, as bearers of human rights, and as rising genomic citizens (Sabatello and Appelbaum 2016). It will start with a brief discussion of the rise of genomic data and technologies, and then consider key ELSI challenges in three nonclinical contexts: translational genomic research settings, education, and judicial proceedings. Although pediatrics in its medical connotation applies to all children under the age of eighteen, particular attention will be given to adolescents (ages greater than thirteen). No longer children but not yet adults, this age group challenges us to rethink the boundaries of decision-making and abilities in the genomic era.

The Genomic Revolution Is Here . . . and It Is Here to Stay

The completion of the Human Genome Project in 2003 marks a historical moment, moving from the pre- to the post-genetic revolution. This international effort has been described as "one of the great feats of exploration in history . . . an inward voyage of discovery . . . to sequence and map all of the genes—together known as the genome—of members of our species, *Homo sapiens*" (NHGRI, https://www.genome.gov/human-genome-project). With this salutary node and a promissory message of conquering knowledge of nature's genetic blueprint, for a time it seemed as though the world's ills would soon be behind us. Of course, this did not happen. Although the number of genetic tests that are performed in clinical and research settings has since increased (American Academy of Pediatrics 2013), it became increasingly clear that the knowledge gained from the Human Genome Project was only the beginning.

Two key forces played a role in this process. First, the increasing knowledge of genetics showed only how much there is yet to learn. As researchers became acutely aware, the common focus on Mendelian inheritance patterns, whereby health conditions are the result of single-gene mutations (e.g., Huntington's disease), is not applicable to most common disorders, such as diabetes, cardiovascular disorders, and most of the psychiatric conditions (McCabe and McCabe 2007). These latter conditions are often genetically complex, involving interaction among multiple genes, with each gene having only a small effect on the outcome, as well as interactions between these genes and environments. The realization of the genomic complexity of health conditions called for increased genomic research, development of sophisticated technologies that allow generating extensive genomic data, and ongoing efforts to shift emphasis from treatment to prevention by quantifying health predictions based on genetic data (Katzmarzyk et al. 2014; Lazaro-Munoz et al. 2015).

Another factor that has impacted the scientific revolution is the growing private sector of genomics. Since the completion of the Human Genome Project, direct-to-consumers (DTC) genetic testing companies have sprung up in the United States, offering "off the counter" testing for an array of genetic-based health conditions and lifestyle advice (Caulfield et al. 2015). Despite criticism of the dubious scientific value of their genetic tests (Evans 2008), DTC companies have aggressively marketed "recreative genomics" as a way of "finding ourselves" and as an integral part of the democratization of genomic information (Lee and Crawley 2009). With a strong grounding in individualism, DTC companies have further constructed genomic data as key for consumers' empowerment (Nordgren and Juengst 2009), shifting the responsibility for a healthier future from states to consumers, and successfully pushing to the fore personalized or stratified medicine (so-called "Me Medicine") as the ultimate path forward (Dickenson 2013) while they engage in a profitable business of selling and conducting research with genomic data of consumers (Niemiec and Howard 2016; Grand View Research 2019).

Discussions about these developments have largely occurred in the adults' world. The focus on autonomy in medical, research, and familial settings has allowed sidestepping the question of whether the underpinning justifications for parents' (and other adults') power over children stands in nonclinical genomic settings. The next sections consider three emerging contexts in which children's genomics data are becoming increasingly important—that is, translational genomic research, education, and judicial proceedings—and highlight the ethical, legal, and social issues that arise.

Pediatric Participation in Translational Genomic Research

Children are increasingly participating in genomic research (Henderson et al. 2013; Borry et al. 2010); indeed, including them in research is necessary if they are to reap the benefits of genomic research. But children's participation in genomic research evokes ethical and policy dilemmas that are markedly different from those encountered with adults. Below, I discuss two key dilemmas: consent and translational genomics, that is, the application of advances in information technologies and genomic data to improve clinical care and public health.

Informed consent is widely accepted as an ethical and legal requirement of biomedical research, including genomic research (e.g., Nuremberg Code 1949; ICCPR 1968; *Belmont Report* 1972). In contrast, children—including adolescents—do not provide consent to participation in genomic research. Rather, their parents are the ones who provide consent on their behalf, while children are only requested to provide an assent (Clayton 2015). Historically, the rationales for this parental prerogative were grounded in the notion of family autonomy and the assumption that parents are better equipped to make informed decisions about their child's best interests (Capron 1982; King 1984–1985). Although the "best interests" standard does not provide a clear formula, it had been commonly interpreted to mean parents' superior ability to weigh the risks and benefits involved in genomic (and other) research.

Yet these rationales require a pause in the genomic era. With the rise of children's rights worldwide, children can no longer be viewed merely as their parents' passive property. This would apply also in the United States—the only country in the world that has not ratified the Convention on the Rights of the Child—given its commitment, as a signatory to this treaty, to follow its spirit. Moreover, although the justifications for parental medical decision-making power may be appropriate for young children, it is unclear that they are as relevant for adolescents in genomic research. Studies indicate that adolescents' (greater than thirteen years old) medical decision-making capacity is comparable to adults' (Weithorn and Campbell 1982; Santelli et al. 2003), and that their genomic literacy is at least as good as adults' (Rew, Mackert, and Bonevac 2010; Sabatello et al. 2019). And, while adults, including health-care providers, have a hard time keeping up with the pace of genetic tests and genomic knowledge (Secretary's Advisory Committee on Genetics, Health, and Society 2011; Genomic Literacy, Education, and Engagement 2017), adolescents may be particularly equipped for the role of informed decision-makers. They are more likely than any other age group to be exposed to genomic data in school (McQueen, Wright, and Fox 2012), online (Borzekowski and Rickert 2001), and through regular use of mobile devices that offer genomic apps (Sabatello and Appelbaum 2016). As the ethical underpinning of consent and ambiguity of assent are increasingly being questioned (Wilfond and Diekema 2012; Alderson 2007), it will be key for researchers and policymakers to consider what role adolescents should have in genomic research.

A further complicating factor is that genomic research programs increasingly offer return of individualized results. This possibility opens the door for the disclosure of extensive information about children's genomic makeup, including immediately relevant medical information to findings about children's carrier status (e.g., cystic fibrosis), data about preventable adult-onset genomic predispositions (e.g., BRCA 1/2), genomic findings about adult-onset untreatable conditions (e.g., Huntington's disease), as well as (in the future) personal behavioral and other traits.

Whether—and which—results from pediatric genomic research should be returned to parents and children has been the focus of heated debates (e.g., Abdul-Karim et al. 2013; Hens, Levesque, and Dierickx 2011; Hens et al. 2009). Studies indicate that parents and health-care professionals often disagree about this question, especially when there is no near-future urgency in knowledge of these data. Parents tend to view access to their children's genomic data as part of their parental responsibility to care for them (Rew, Mackert, and Bonevac 2010; Levenseller et al. 2014; Kaufman et al. 2008; Sapp et al. 2014), whereas health-care professionals worry that overdisclosure of children's genomics data would violate children's "right to an open future," that is, the power to decide whether and when they want to know about their genetic makeup (Strong et al. 2014; Appelbaum et al. 2014). Regardless, one consequence of the possibility of return of results from pediatric genomic research is that it brings us closer to clinical settings (Berkman and Hull 2014), where the parental prerogative of providing consent has been largely solid.

Nonetheless, there are several reasons as to why increasing children's—especially adolescents'—involvement in genomic decisions is important. First, pediatric engagement in genomic decisions has a legal and philosophical grounding. Although countries and cultures vary in the way they construct childhood and adulthood (Helman 2000), there is a general agreement that a minor's age and maturity are important factors (Levenseller et al. 2014). It is explicitly recognized in Articles 5 and 12 of the Convention on the Rights of the Child and a recommended practice in clinical genomics settings (Holm et al. 2014). A categorical exclusion of children and adolescents from genomic conversations thus not only disregards minors' competence (Borry et al. 2009), but also treats them as a group, rather than as subjects of the law as envisioned in international human rights law.

Second, the goals of the genomic revolution are unlikely to succeed without active engagement of pediatric research participants in the discussion. Although the clinical aspects of genomic data—that is, genomic-based individualized treatment for rare conditions—often receive the spotlight, the deeper promise for genomic research lies in the goal of prevention. That is, the idea that health predictions based on genetic data would allow developing tailored, genomic-based, risk-reducing interventions for healthy populations (Meagher et al. 2017). To date, the rhetoric of "precision prevention" (Meagher et al. 2017) has focused primarily on empowering adult patients and research participants to mitigate their health risks through knowledge of their genetic predispositions. However, disregard for the empowerment of healthy, pre- and asymptomatic children and adolescents is counterintuitive to achieving the desired outcome. Many common disorders have pediatric and juvenile onset (e.g., obesity, depression, and schizophrenia) (Katzmarzyk et al. 2014; Salagre et al. 2018; Wilde et al. 2011) but may be averted or mitigated through early preventive intervention, including by increased knowledge of genetic risks and provision of appropriate supports (Rew, Mackert, and Bonevac 2010; Ryan, Virani, and Austin 2015).

Moreover, although studies have shown that genetic information alone has had no impact on risk-reducing health behaviors among adults (Austin 2015; Hollands et al. 2016), childhood, especially adolescence, offers a unique window of opportunity to develop long-term health behaviors that take into account individualized genomic risks. Because adolescents are less ambiguity-averse than adults (Blankenstein et al. 2016), they may be better positioned than adults to receive genomic results indicating an increased risk for a condition (rather than a diagnostic value), without this information leading to anxiety, which is a common concern raised in studies with adults (Hollands et al. 2016; Wilhelm et al. 2009; Semaka, Balneaves, and Hayden 2013). Adolescents may also be more amenable to changes in health practices than adults, who need to alter long-standing behaviors (Sabatello and Appelbaum 2016). Indeed, studies of healthy adolescents found that many are willing to make behavioral changes in light of genetic data indicating increased risk for breast cancer, heart disease, hypercholesterolemia, and psychiatric conditions (Harel, Abuelo, and Kazura 2003; Bradbury et al. 2009; Ryan, Virani, and Austin 2015; Sabatello et al. 2021a).

Whether the "precision prevention" goal of the genomic revolution can materialize will thus largely depend on the extent to which *healthy* children and adolescents are empowered to be involved in genomic decisions. However, providing genetic counseling and appropriate social supports to children and adolescents raises unique challenges that mirror and are connected with the traditional focus on adults. Studies indicate that parents and teachers play an instrumental role in developing children's and adolescents' sense of empowerment in health-related decisions (Simonsen et al. 2018), but also that parents may be reluctant or not know how to discuss such information with their children (Levenseller et al. 2014; Bernhardt et al. 2003; Metcalfe et al. 2008), and that the genomic knowledge of both parents and teachers may be limited (Johnson et al. 2019; Dougherty 2009). Health-care professionals may equally have difficulty empowering children in genomic conversations. It's not only potentially challenging to mitigate the parent–child relationship (Levenseller et al. 2014; Townsend et al. 2012), but studies also indicate that health-care professionals, including genetic counselors, are insufficiently trained in adolescent medicine (Duncan and Young 2013). Finally, it is unclear how inclusive pediatric empowerment will be in a society that is marked by increasing health disparities, including lack of consistent access to health-care providers, socioeconomic deprivation that is concentered in racial/ethnic minorities (Bentley, Callier, and Rotimi 2017; Sabatello 2017), and human biorepositories that are overwhelmingly composed of European-ancestry samples and thus are inappropriate for accurate, race-sensitive genomic risks assessment to occur (Popejoy and Fullerton 2016; Palk et al. 2019). Larger systemic changes are urgently needed for the genomic revolution to be implemented for all children.

Precision Education

Another nonclinical setting on the horizon for children's genomic makeup to play a role is education. Of course, there is a long (ugly) history to this development. Genetic research relating to IQ and the idea that educational attainment (and other social success) is only the outcome of "inborn ability" have served to justify eugenic practices and racial/ethnic segregation policies in the twentieth century (King 1992; Martschenko, Trejo, and Domingue 2019). Yet genomics is increasingly making its way back into schools.

Since the 1970s, genetic screening programs have begun to spread. Emerging, initially, among Jewish Orthodox communities in Canada to inform future reproductive decisions by identifying carrier status of Tay-Sachs disease (Gason 2006), such programs have expanded over time to other countries and encompass a growing number of genetic conditions for which students are tested (e.g., cystic fibrosis) (Ross 2006). In line with the agenda of precision prevention (see above), more recent efforts have further shifted to focus on genetic *susceptibility* testing of high school students for hereditary hemochromatosis, a preventable and treatable adult-onset disorder (Delatycki et al. 2010). Concurrently, ongoing research is conducted to identify the complex genetic underpinning of a variety of conditions associated with educational attainment, from dyslexia and attention deficit hyperactivity disorder (ADHD) to autism, intelligence, learning disabilities, and behavioral and personality traits, with some researchers explicitly calling for incorporating these data, at some point, into the classroom (Bouregy et al. 2017).

The rationales for the use of genetic data in schools vary. Insofar as genomic screening programs are viewed as promoting public health, school settings are ideal. From a practical perspective, schools provide an opportunity to reach out to a large number of children who are clearly connected with adults' communities (parents, teachers, and the larger community) in ways that can promote awareness and preventive efforts (Gason et al. 2006). The introduction of a diagnostic genomic test in schools may also support a claim for eligibility and facilitate access of children with disabilities for special services, a process that is often contested, time-consuming, and cumbersome on parents (Borgelt et al. 2014). Others argue that genomic data may allow for better tailoring of educational interventions to the needs of children with disabilities (e.g., instructing teachers to respond to students with Fragile X syndrome in ways that take into account the possible heightened anxiety among such students) (Reilly 2012).

More generally, proponents of precision education suggest that understanding the genetic bases of abilities and behaviors that impact learning-related processes will enable identification of environmental and pharmacological interventions that may enhance students' educational attainment (e.g., Grigorenko 2007; Reilly, Senior, and Murtagh 2015). Thus, although the notion of precision education emerged in the context of children with disabilities, some proponents further suggest that precision education could benefit *all* students (Plomin and Ashbury 2014), indeed, that a genomically tailored approach to education would reflect an up-to-date concept of equality (Rothstein 2007).

Although proponents of precision education have cushioned the issue in concepts of the child's best interests, there are several issues that merit attention. First, who should decide about children's genetic testing in schools? Current approaches to children's genetic testing in connection with schools have generally relied on parental consent, even as there have been concerns about the possible peer pressure for testing in this environment (Gason et al. 2006; Frumkin and Zlotogora 2008). However, this was not always the case. For example, in the early 1970s, twelve states in the United States enacted laws mandating African Americans to undergo genetic screening for sickle cell disease, and untested children were denied access to school (Reilly 2000). Although these laws were repealed in 1972 and it is now well accepted that these laws were mobilized by genetic misperceptions, genetic discrimination, and genetic racism (Fulda and Lykens 2006; King 1992), it is unclear that mandatory screening of *all* students would have a similar fate.

Indeed, with the Child Find Mandate requiring schools to identify, locate, and evaluate *all* children who are eligible for special services, regardless of the severity of their disabilities (IDEA 2004), it seems plausible that increased genomic knowledge about conditions associated with educational outcomes will translate into efforts—even a requirement—that students will be tested or that their genomic data be provided in schools. And while a study of the general public in the United States found disapproval of mandatory genetic testing by school authorities (Sabatello et al. 2021b), the expansion of newborn screening using next-generation genomic sequencing (Knoppers et al. 2014), along with stakeholders' attitudes that espouse the use of genomic data in a variety of settings (Collins 2014), are indicative of what the future may hold.

For instance, studies found that teachers support knowing of, and adjusting their educational styles to, students' genetic-influenced learning difficulties (Walker and Plomin 2005; Gason et al. 2005). Studies of parents and potential parents indicate high interest in genetic testing of their children for conditions that are associated with educational attainment, such as ADHD (Sabatello et al. 2021b), and use of such data to support a claim for their child's eligibility for special services (Borgelt et al. 2014), as well as support for preventive behavioral, environmental, and therapeutic interventions on the basis of children's genetic susceptibility for such disorders (Wilde et al. 2011; May, Brandt, and Bohannan 2012). And, as the scientific community marches ahead with expanding the knowledge of the impact of children's genomic makeup on their educational achievements (Bouregy et al. 2017), there are concurrent efforts to incorporate genetic experts in education-related decisions (Grigorenko 2007), along with calls to enhance the involvement of educational psychologists in deciding how genomic knowledge can inform educational interventions in the classroom (Haworth and Plomin 2012).

Children's voices have been largely absent from these discussions. On the one hand, the seemingly high uptake of genetic testing in schools for carrier status and susceptibility screening may suggest high interest among teenagers. In the aforementioned study of high school students and their parents about genetic susceptibility testing for hereditary hemochromatosis, the researchers found that students' positive views about such screening even exceeded those of parents (Gason et al. 2005; Delatycki et al. 2010).

On the other hand, no study to date has explored whether children and teenagers would support testing in schools for learning and behavioral-related genetic conditions. The latter conditions are more genomically complex (as explained above) and have fewer well-established interventions than other medical and physical conditions (e.g., preimplantation genetic testing to avoid conception of a child with Tay-Sachs). Nor is it clear that children and adolescents would support the use of such data by nonmedical professionals, such as educators and educational staff. Learning, and, especially, behavioral and psychiatric, conditions are highly stigmatized in society (Mueller et al. 2012; O'Driscoll et al. 2012; Kinnear et al. 2016), and given conventional misperceptions about genomic determinism—the idea that there is an unbreakable, causative one-sided relationship between genes and behavioral outcomes (Wachbroit 2000)—there is a risk that sharing of such data will lead to biases in assessment of a student's educational capabilities and in decisions about educational placement (Sabatello 2017).

The possible testing and use of children's genetic data in school further raises unique privacy concerns. Teachers' knowledge of students' genetic makeup raises the possibility of their (at least perceived) knowledge of the genetics of the student's family members, thus extending the potential bias to a student's siblings and other relatives (Sabatello 2017). Privacy issues also arise in the relationship between children and their parents, especially with regard to behavioral traits. Even if parents' knowledge of their children's behavioral disorders is acceptable, it is unclear whether parents' knowledge of their children's behavioral genetic *predispositions* fit the criteria of "best interests," nor which predispositions parents should know about (consider, e.g., athletic and musical talent versus risk for schizophrenia). Indeed, as a Belgian study of children ages fifteen to nineteen found, although they approve of sharing "medically important information" with parents, they are more reluctant to share data about behavioral predispositions (e.g., alcoholism) when no medical necessity exists (Hens et al. 2011).

These concerns are all the more acute given the limitations of the Genetic Information Nondiscrimination Act (GINA). This law prohibits the use of genetics in determining health insurance eligibility and employment decisions, but does not extend to school settings or to situations in which individuals voluntarily shared their genomic data (e.g., posted it online). Insofar as teachers and parents may disclose students' genomic information, the protections afforded by GINA will be lost. Before moving ahead with precision education, there is a need to think about how to balance children's legitimate genomic privacy concerns, as well as adults' (i.e., parents, teachers, and scientists) responsibilities in protecting children's interests in both better educational achievements and other important goals.

Children's Genetic Makeup in Judicial Proceedings

Although children cannot generally file an independent claim in courts, children's genetic makeup is increasingly introduced in judicial proceedings. Historically, children's genetic testing was sought predominantly in paternity cases, where a litigant (the mother and a putative father) aimed to establish whether an individual was the biological parent of a child (Uniform Parentage Act 2002). Genetic testing for identification purposes has obtained a high level of accuracy—it can confirm father–child genetic relationships with 99.9 percent probability—and has been initially viewed as divulging important data to improve the child's financial and emotional future.

In past decades, however, children's genetic data have been entering into other judicial proceedings, and entering with a twist. Rather than testing children for identification purposes, genetic tests are increasingly aimed to determine health status. So far, children's genetic data have been used particularly to rebut causation of injury in medical malpractice and toxic tort litigation, where genetic evidence may elucidate whether a child's medical condition is due to genetic causes or medical malpractice (e.g., Marchant and Robert 2009; Brice and Christian 2017). There is yet indication that such data are likely to enter other judicial proceedings as well.

First, studies have found that judges are receptive to genetic data and that they are willing not only to admit such evidence, but also to compel testing (Hoffmann and Rothenberg 2007). This receptiveness may fit with common views of genomics as "hard evidence" (John 2015), even as genomics—especially in the context of complex conditions—are often far from being deterministic.

Second, the blooming market of DTC genetic testing companies further facilitates (and will likely continue to facilitate) the introduction and use of children's genomic data in courts. Such companies have not only adjusted their genomic services to assure that, for example, their paternity tests can meet judicial admissibility criteria (for additional costs), but also their home kits have enabled and are likely to continue to enable an easy process for adults to test their children for a growing number of conditions (Phillips 2016) and genomic predispositions that, notwithstanding the testing's questionable scientific value (Evans 2008), may impact litigants in judicial proceedings.

Finally, it is likely that information about *adults'* genetic predisposition that has begun to enter the courts will, in the future, expand to children who are embroiled in judicial proceedings. For instance, a few defendants in criminal courts have already requested to be tested or to have admitted their genetic test results showing low activity of the MAOA gene, to mitigate judicial decisions of culpability and punishment (Denno 2009; Denno 2011; McSwiggan, Elger, and Appelbaum 2017). The MAOA gene has been associated with impulsive behavior among individuals who experienced childhood adversity, and its introduction in juvenile criminal proceedings may gain similar traction, especially because some scholars advocate for early testing of children for this gene (Marchant 2012). Indeed, the use of genomic data in criminal proceedings may further extend in the future to other behavioral traits or conditions that have juvenile onset, such as opioid addiction (Eitan et al. 2017). With a growing number of studies to identify genetic markers associated with a propensity to addiction (Randesi et al. 2019; Crist, Reiner, and Berrettini 2019) and developing pharmacogenomic treatment options to improve clinical outcomes, the introduction of such data may have significant impact on judicial determination of responsibility and rehabilitation options.

Similarly, information about children's behavioral and psychiatric genetic makeup will likely make its way to child custody proceedings. Such proceedings—including termination of parental rights, adoption, and determination of primary custody of children—revolve around future predictions of both parents' fitness and children's psychosocial adjustment. In the absence of genetic tests to diagnose or confirm common psychiatric conditions (e.g., depression), existing court cases have largely been made on the basis of family history or in the abstract. For example, in *William S. v. State, Dept. of Health & Social Services* (2014; WL 199882, Supreme Court of Alaska), parents appealed a decision to terminate their parental rights, claiming that their child's psychiatric conditions (including depression, ADHD, and oppositional defiant behavior) were the result of his genetics rather than their neglect and family home environment, as determined by the court. Yet, as knowledge of psychiatric genetics and advanced sequencing technologies continues to emerge, it is likely that, once available, genetic tests showing children's predispositions for behavioral and psychiatric conditions will be used in family courts.

Whether the use of children's genomic data in courts will positively facilitate judicial resolution is open for debate (Sabatello and Appelbaum 2016; Sabatello and Appelbaum, 2017). Insofar as genomic data will provide a more accurate prediction about the child's future well-being, judicial actors may find them useful. Conversely, there is a concern that genomic data may introduce biases into the decision-making process. Studies indicate that the general public has only limited understanding of how genetic risk factors affect multifactorial diseases (Etchegary 2014), and tends to view genetics through essentializing frames and as immutable characteristics (Heine et al. 2017).

Although no study has explored judicial genomic literacy, it is likely that judges and other judicial actors are prone to similar conceptualizations of genomics. Even as the public's endorsement of genomic determinism may be overrated (Condit 2011), a study of the use of psychiatric genetic evidence in child custody proceedings found that the general public often conflates psychiatric genetic predisposition and the presence of symptoms (Sabatello et al. 2021c). The introduction of children's genomic data in court may thus lead to increased medicalization of children who are involved in judicial proceedings, also in the absence of symptoms. Concurrently, studies indicate that the public's understanding of genomic data is often strategic (Condit 2019). That is, people interpret genomic data in light of other social constructs that they hold and which they use as they see fit to advance their interests. When considered in light of the heightened racism, sexism, ableism, and other social ills that differentiate groups, rather than uniting them, this finding of biased interpretation should be a cause for concern, all the more so when they may negatively impact the administration of justice.

Conclusion

The genomic train has left the station and children are increasingly taking the ride. Whether they should be tested, for what conditions or predispositions, who is to determine, and how their data should be used in nonclinical settings are issues that we should all consider—and be aware of the risks.

Whether the historical justifications for children's relative passive involvement in medical settings are still applicable to genomic research and other geneticized settings such as schools and courts is open for debate. The possible costs of such uses are not negligible. They involve core values in American society, including autonomy, capacity, and privacy, as well as key challenges within it, namely, stigma against racial/ethnic minorities and bias against other historically marginalized groups (e.g., people with behavioral and psychiatric conditions). Ultimately, however, all of these issues touch upon social, political, and judicial justice, and thus require ongoing engagement and regulations to ensure that *everyone* can enjoy the benefits of scientific progress.

The questions above are all the more pivotal for adolescents—an age group that is uniquely positioned in the genomic era but often remains in the shadow. Their exposure to genomic data and expertise in technology not only surpasses that of adults, but may have significant impacts on both their and society's health. Further research with this population is needed. and we shouldn't miss the opportunity for engaging this population in genomic conversations.

Acknowledgment

This work was supported by grant funding from the National Institute of Health (NIH), K01HG008653 and RM1HG007257.

References

Abdul-Karim, R., et al. 2013. "Disclosure of Incidental Findings from Next-Generation Sequencing in Pediatric Genomic Research." *Pediatrics* 131, no. 3: 564–71.

Alderson P. 2007. "Competent Children? Minors' Consent to Health Care Treatment and Research. *Social Science & Medicine* 65: 2272–83.

American Academy of Pediatrics. 2013. "Ethical and Policy Issues in Genetic Testing and Screening of Children." *Pediatrics* 131, no. 3: 620–22.

Appelbaum, P. S., et al. 2014. "Researchers' Views on Informed Consent for Return of Secondary Results in Genomic Research." *Genetics in Medicine* 17, no. 8: 644–50.

Austin, J. 2015. "The Effect of Genetic Test-Based Risk Information on Behavioral Outcomes: A Critical Examination of Failed Trials and a Call to Action." *American Journal of Medical Genetics Part A* 167a: 2913–15.

Bentley, A. R., S. Callier, and C. N. Rotimi. 2017. "Diversity and Inclusion in Genomic Research: Why the Uneven Progress?" *Journal of Community Genetics* 8, no. 4: 255–66.

Berkman, B. E., and S. C. Hull. 2014. The "Right Not to Know" in the Genomic Era: Time to Break from Tradition? *American Journal of Bioethics* 14, no. 3: 28–31.

Bernhardt, B. A., et al. 2003. "Parents' and Children's Attitudes toward the Enrollment of Minors in Genetic Susceptibility Research: Implications for Informed Consent." *American Journal of Medical Genetics Part A* 116a, no. 4: 315–23.

Blankenstein, N. E., E. A. Crone, W. van den Bos, and A. C. van Duijvenvoorde. 2016. "Dealing with Uncertainty: Testing Risk- and Ambiguity-Attitude across Adolescence." *Developmental Neuropsychology* 41: 77–92.

Blum, K., L. Lott, D. Siwicki, L. Fried, and M. Hauser. 2018. "Genetic Addiction Risk Score (GARS™) as a Predictor of Substance Use Disorder: Identifying Predisposition Not Diagnosis." *Current Trends in Medical Diagnostic Methods* CTMDM-101.

Borgelt, E. L., D. Z. Buchman, M. Weiss, and J. Illes. 2014. "In Search of 'Anything That Would Help': Parent Perspectives on Emerging Neurotechnologies." *Journal of Attention Disorders* 18: 395–401.

Borry, P., et al. 2009. "Genetic Testing in Asymptomatic Minors: Background Considerations towards ESHG Recommendations." *European Journal of Human Genetics* 17, no. 6: 711–19.

———. 2010. "Health-Related Direct-to-Consumer Genetic Testing: A Review of Companies' Policies with Regard to Genetic Testing in Minors." *Familial Cancer* 9: 51–59.

Borzekowski, D. G., and V. I. Rickert. 2001. "Adolescent Cybersurfing for Health Information: A New Resource That Crosses Barriers." *Archives of Pediatrics & Adolescent Medicine* 155, no. 7: 813–17.

Bouregy, S., E. Grigorenko, M. Tan, and S. Latham, eds. 2017. *Genetics, Ethics and Education.* Cambridge: Cambridge University Press.

Bradbury, A. R., et al. 2009. "Learning of Your Parent's BRCA Mutation during Adolescence or Early Adulthood: A Study of Offspring Experiences." *Psychooncology* 18, no. 2: 200–208.

Brice, S. E., and W. V. Christian. 2017. "The Use of Genetic Evidence to Defend against Toxic Tort Claims." *Intellectual Property & Technology Law Journal* 29, no. 3: Parts I & II. https://www.bclplaw.com/images/content/9/6/v2/96913/genetic-evidence-defend-against-toxic-tort-parts1and2.pdf.

Capron, A. M. 1982. "The Authority of Others to Decide about Biomedical Intervention with Incompetent." In *Who Speaks for the Child?: The Problems of Proxy Consent,* edited by Willard Gaylin and Ruth Macklin, 115–52. New York: Plenum Press.

Caulfield, T., et al. 2015. "Marginally Scientific?: Genetic Testing of Children and Adolescents for Lifestyle and Health Promotion." *Journal of Law and Bioscience* 2, no. 3: 627–44.

Clayton, E. W. 2015. "How Much Control Do Children and Adolescents Have over Genomic Testing, Parental Access to Their Results, and Parental Communication of Those Results to Others? *Journal of Law, Medicine & Ethics* 43, no. 3: 538–44.

Collins, F. S. 2014. "Francis Collins Says Medicine in the Future Will Be Tailored to Your Genes." *Wall Street Journal,* July 7, 2014. https://www.wsj.com/articles/francis-collins-says-medicine-in-the-future-will-be-tailored-to-your-genes-1404763139.

Condit, C. M. 2011. "When Do People Deploy Genetic Determinism?: A Review Pointing to the Need for Multi-Factorial Theories of Public Utilization of Scientific Discourses." *Sociology Compass* 5, no. 7: 618–35.

———. 2019. "Laypeople Are Strategic Essentialists, Not Genetic Essentialists." *Hastings Center Report* 49, no. S1: S27–S37.

Crist, R. C., B. C. Reiner, and W. H. Berrettini. 2019. "A Review of Opioid Addiction Genetics." *Current Opinion in Psychology* 27: 31–35.

Delatycki, M. B., et al. 2010. "Implementation of IronXS: A Study of the Acceptability and Feasibility of Genetic Screening for Hereditary Hemochromatosis in High Schools." *Clinical Genetics* 77, no. 3: 241–48.

Denno, D. W. 2009. "Behavioral Genetics Evidence in Criminal Cases: 1994–2007." In *The Impact of Behavioral Sciences on Criminal Law*, edited by N. A. Farahany. New York: Oxford Press, 317–54, 465–98.

———. 2011. "Courts' Increasing Consideration of Behavioral Genetics Evidence in Criminal Cases: Results of a Longtitudinal Study." *Michigan State Law Review* 2011: 967–1047.

Dougherty, M. J. 2009. "Closing the Gap: Inverting the Genetics Curriculum to Ensure an Informed Public." *American Journal of Human Genetics* 85, no. 1: 6–12.

Duncan, R. E., and M.-A. Young. 2013. "Tricky Teens: Are They Really Tricky or Do Genetic Health Professionals Simply Require More Training in Adolescent Health?" *Personalized Medicine* 10, no. 6: 589–600.

Eitan, S., M. A. Emery, M. S. Bates, and C. Horrax. 2017. "Opioid Addiction: Who Are Your Real Friends?" *Neuroscience & Biobehavioral Reviews* 83: 697–712.

Etchegary H. 2014. "Public Attitudes toward Genetic Risk Testing and Its Role in Healthcare." *Personalized Medicine* 11, no. 5: 509–22.

Evans, J. P. 2008. "Recreational Genomics; What's in It for You?" *Genetics in Medicine* 10, no. 10: 709–10.

Frumkin, A., and J. Zlotogora. "Genetic Screening for Reproductive Purposes at School: Is It a Good Strategy?" *American Journal of Medical Genetics Part A* 146a, no 2 (2008): 264–69.

Fulda, K. G., and K. Lykens. 2006. "Ethical Issues in Predictive Genetic Testing: A Public Health Perspective." *Journal of Medical Ethics* 32: 143–47.

Gason, A. A., et al. 2005. "Genetic Susceptibility Screening in Schools: Attitudes of the School Community towards Hereditary Haemochromatosis." *Clinical Genetics* 67, no. 2: 166–74.

———. 2006. "It's 'Back to School' for Genetic Screening." *European Journal of Human Genetics* 14, no. 4: 384–89.

Genomic Literacy, Education, and Engagement (GLEE) Initiative. 2017. "Community-Public Working Group." March 2017. https://www.genome.gov/Pages/About/OD/ECIB/GLEE/GLEE_white_paper_CmtyPublic_WG.pdf.

Grand View Research. 2019. "Predictive Genetic Testing & Consumer/Wellness Genomics Market Size, Share & Trends Analysis Report by Test Type (Population Screening, Susceptibility), by Application, by Setting Type, and Segment Forecasts, 2019–2025." Published June 2019. https://www.grandviewresearch.com/industry-analysis/predictive-genetic-testing-consumer-wellness-genomics-market.

Grigorenko, E. L. 2007. "How Can Genomics Inform Education?" *Mind, Brain and Education* 1, no. 1: 20–27.

Harel, A., D. Abuelo, and A. Kazura. 2003. "Adolescents and Genetic Testing: What Do They Think About It?" *Journal of Adolescent Health* 33, no. 6: 489–94.

Haworth, C. M. A., and R. Plomin. 2012. "Genetics and Education: Toward a Genetically Sensitive Classroom." In *APA Educational Psychology Handbook*, edited by K. R. Harris et al., 529–59. American Psychological Association.

Heine, S. J., et al. 2017. "Essentially Biased: Why People Are Fatalistic about Genes." In *Advances in Experimental Social Psychology*, edited by J. M. Olson, 137–92. Academic Press.

Helman, C. G. 2000. *Culture, Health and Illness*. Oxford: Butterworth.

Henderson, G. E., et al. 2013. "Characterizing Biobank Organizations in the U.S.: Results from a National Survey." *Genome Medicine* 5, no. 1: 1–12.

Hens, K., et al. 2009. "Genetic Research on Stored Tissue Samples from Minors: A Systematic Review of the Ethical Literature." *American Journal of Medical Genetics A* 149a, no. 10: 2346–58.

———. 2011. "The Storage and Use of Biological Tissue Samples from Minors for Research: A Focus Group Study." *Public Health Genomics* 14, no. 2: 68–76.

Hens, K., E. Levesque, and K. Dierickx. 2011. "Children and Biobanks: A Review of the Ethical and Legal Discussion." *Human Genetics* 130, no. 3: 403–13.

Hoffmann, D. E., and K. H. Rothenberg. 2007. "Judging Genes: Implications of the Second Generation of Genetic Tests in the Courtroom." *Maryland Law Review* 66: 858–922.

Hollands, G. J., D. P. French, S. J. Griffin, et al. 2016. "The Impact of Communicating Genetic Risks of Disease on Risk-Reducing Health Behaviour: Systematic Review with Meta-Analysis." *BMJ* 352: i1102.

Holm, I. A., et al. 2014. "Guidelines for Return of Research Results from Pediatric Genomic Studies: Deliberations of the Boston Children's Hospital Gene Partnership Informed Cohort Oversight Board." *Genetics in Medicine* 16, no. 7: 547–52.

John, P. 2015. "When Neurogenetics Hurts: Examining the Use of Neuroscience and Genetic Evidence in Sentencing Decisions through Implicit Bias." *California Law Review* 103: 1019–45.

Johnson, L. M., et al. 2019. "Speaking Genomics to Parents Offered Germline Testing for Cancer Predisposition: Use of a 2-Visit Consent Model." *Cancer* 125, no. 14: 2455–64.

Jones, S., and S. Fox. 2009. "Generations Online in 2009." Pew Research Center. Published January 28, 2009. http://www.pewinternet.org/2009/01/28/generations-online-in-2009/.

Katzmarzyk, P. T., S. Barlow, C. Bouchard, et al. 2014. "An Evolving Scientific Basis for the Prevention and Treatment of Pediatric Obesity. *International Journal of Obesity (London)* 38: 887–905.

Kaufman, D., et al. 2008. "Ethical Implications of Including Children in a Large Biobank for Genetic-Epidemiologic Research: A Qualitative Study of Public Opinion." *American Journal of Medical Genetics Part C* 148c, no. 1: 31–39.

King, P. A. 1992. "The Past as Prologue: Race, Class, and Gene Discrimination." in *Gene Mapping: Using Law and Ethics as Guides*, edited by G. Annas and S. Elias, 94–111. New York: Oxford University Press.

———. 1984–1985. "Treatment and Minors: Issues Not Involving Lifesaving Treatment." *Journal of Family Law* 23: 241–65.

Kinnear, S. H., et al. 2016. "Understanding the Experience of Stigma for Parents of Children with Autism Spectrum Disorder and the Role Stigma Plays in Families' Lives." *Journal of Autism and Developmental Disorders* 46, no. 3: 942–53.

Knoppers, B. M., et al. 2014. "Whole-Genome Sequencing in Newborn Screening Programs." *Science Translational Medicine* 6, no. 229: 229cm222.

Lazaro-Munoz, G., et al. 2015. "Looking for Trouble: Preventive Genomic Sequencing in the General Population and the Role of Patient Choice." *American Journal of Bioethics* 15, no. 7: 3–14.

Lee, Soo-Jin S., and L. Crawley. 2009. "Research 2.0: Social Networking and Direct-to-Consumer (DTC) Genomics." *American Journal of Bioethics* 9, no. 6-7: 35–44.

Levenseller, B. L., et al. 2014. "Stakeholders' Opinions on the Implementation of Pediatric Whole Exome Sequencing: Implications for Informed Consent." *Journal of Genetic Counseling* 23, no. 4: 552–65.

Marchant, G. 2012. "Should We Screen Kids' Brains and Genes to ID Future Criminals?" *Slate*. Published October 17, 2012. https://slate.com/technology/2012/10/should-kids-brains-and-genes-be-screened-to-detect-future-criminals.html.

Marchant, G., and J. Robert. 2009. "Genetic Testing for Autism Predisposition: Ethical, Legal and Social Challenges." *Houston Journal of Health Law and Policy* 9: 203–35.

Martschenko, D., S. Trejo, and B. W. Domingue. "Genetics and Education: Recent Developments in the Context of an Ugly History and an Uncertain Future." *AERA Open* 5, no. 1 (2019): 2332858418810516.

May, M. E., R. C. Brandt, and J. K. Bohannan. 2012. "Moderating Effects of Autism on Parent Views of Genetic Screening for Aggression." *Intellectual and Developmental Disabilities* 50, no. 5: 415–25.

McCabe, E., and L. McCabe. 2007. "Genomic Medicine: A Future Flooded with Risk Information." *Minnesota Journal of Law, Science and Technology* 8, no. 2: 429–39.

McQueen, J., J. Wright, and J. A. Fox. 2012. "Design and Implementation of a Genomics Field Trip Program Aimed at Secondary School Students." *PLoS Computational Biology* 8, no. 8: e1002636.

McSwiggan, S., B. Elger, and P. S. Appelbaum. 2017. "The Forensic Use of Behavioral Genetics in Criminal Proceedings: Case of the MAOA-L Genotype." *International Journal of Law and Psychiatry* 50: 17–23.

Meagher, K. M., et al. 2017. "Precisely Where Are We Going? Charting the New Terrain of Precision Prevention." *Annual Review of Genomics and Human Genetics* 18: 369–87.

Metcalfe, A., et al. 2008. "Family Communication between Children and Their Parents about Inherited Genetic Conditions: A Meta-Synthesis of the Research." *European Journal of Human Genetics* 16, no. 10: 1193–2000.

Mueller, A. K., et al. 2012. "Stigma in Attention Deficit Hyperactivity Disorder." *Attention Deficit Hyperactivity Disorder* 4, no. 3: 101–14.

Nordgren, A., and E. T. Juengst. 2009. "Can Genomics Tell Me Who I Am? Essentialistic Rhetoric in Direct-to-Consumer DNA Testing." *New Genetics and Society* 28, no. 2: 157–72.

O'Driscoll, C., et al. 2012. "Explicit and Implicit Stigma towards Peers with Mental Health Problems in Childhood and Adolescence." *Journal of Child Psychology and Psychiatry* 53, no. 10: 1054–62.

Palk, A. C., et al. 2019. "Potential Use of Clinical Polygenic Risk Scores in Psychiatry: Ethical Implications and Communicating High Polygenic Risk." *Philosophy, Ethics, and Humanities in Medicine* 14, no. 1: 4.

Phillips, A. M. 2016. "Only a Click Away: DTC Genetics for Ancestry, Health, Love . . . and More: A View of the Business and Regulatory Landscape." *Applied & Translational Genomics* 8: 16–22.

Plomin, R., and K. Ashbury. 2014. *G is for Genes: The Impact of Genetics on Education and Achievement*. Chichester, UK: Wiley Blackwell.

Popejoy, A. B., and S. M. Fullerton. 2016. "Genomics Is Failing on Diversity." *Nature* 538, no. 7624: 161–64.

Randesi, M., W. van den Brink, O. Levran, P. Blanken, J. M. van Ree, et al. 2019. "VMAT2 Gene (SLC18A2) Variants Associated with a Greater Risk for Developing Opioid Dependence." *Pharmacogenomics* 20, no. 5: 331–41.

Reilly, C. 2012. "Behavioural Phenotypes and Special Educational Needs: Is Aetiology Important in the Classroom?" *Journal of Intellectual Disability Research* 56, no. 10: 929–46.

Reilly, C., J. Senior, and L. A. Murtagh. 2015. "A Comparative Study of Educational Provision for Children with Neurogenetic Syndromes: Parent and Teacher Survey." *Journal of Intellectual Disability Ressearch* 59, no. 12: 1094–107.

Reilly, P. R. 2000. "Ethical and Legal Issues in Genetic Testing to Predict Risk of Heart Disease." *American Heart Journal* 140, no. 4: S6–S10.

Rew, L., M. Mackert, and D. Bonevac. 2010. "Cool, But Is It Credible? Adolescents' and Parents' Approaches to Genetic Testing." Western Journal of Nursing Research 32: 610–27.

Ross, L. F. 2006. "Heterozygote Carrier Testing in High Schools Abroad: What Are the Lessons for the U.S.?" *Journal of Law, Medicine and Ethics* 34, no. 4: 753–64.

Rothstein, M. 2007. "Legal Conceptions of Equality in the Genomic Age." *Law and Inequality* 25: 429–71.

Ryan, J., A. Virani, and J. C. Austin. 2015. "Ethical Issues Associated with Genetic Counseling in the Context of Adolescent Psychiatry." *Applied & Translational Genomics* 5: 23–29.

Sabatello, M. 2018. "A Genomically Informed Education System? Challenges for Behavioral Genetics." *Journal of Law, Medicine and Ethics* 46, no. 1: 130–44.

———. 2017. "Psychiatric Genomics and Public Mental Health in the Young Mind." *American Journal of Bioethics* 17, no. 4: 27–29.

Sabatello, M., and P. S. Appelbaum. 2016. "Psychiatric Genetics in Child Custody Proceedings: Ethical, Legal, and Social Issues." *Current Genetic Medicine Reports* 4, no. 3: 98–106.

———. 2017. "Behavioral Genetics in Criminal and Civil Courts." *Harvard Review of Psychiatry* 25, no. 6: 289–301.

Sabatello M, Chen Y, Herrera CF, Brockhoff E, Austin J, Appelbaum PS. *Teenagers and Precision Psychiatry: A Window of Opportunity.* Public Health Genomics. 2021;24(1-2):14-25. doi: 10.1159/000512475. Epub 2021 Jan 27. PMID: 33503628; PMCID: PMC7920903. Sabatello, M., Y. Chen, S. C. Sanderson, W. K. Chung, and P. S. Appelbaum. 2019. "Increasing Genomic Literacy among Adolescents." *Genetics in Medicine* 21, no. 4: 994–1000.

Sabatello M, Insel BJ, Corbeil T, Link BG, Appelbaum PS. *The double helix at school: Behavioral genetics, disability, and precision education.* Soc Sci Med. 2021 Jun;278:113924. doi: 10.1016/j.socscimed.2021.113924. Epub 2021 Apr 20. PMID: 33895581; PMCID: PMC8314166. Sabatello M, Insel BJ, Link BG, Phelan JC, Appelbaum PS. *The Psychiatric Genetic Data of Children in Proceedings to Terminate Parental Rights.* J Am Acad Psychiatry Law. 2021 Jun;49(2):166-178. doi: 10.29158/JAAPL.200066-20. Epub 2021 Feb 12. PMID: 33579734; PMCID: PMC8217070. Salagre, E., S. Dodd, A. Aedo, et al. 2018. "Toward Precision Psychiatry in Bipolar Disorder: Staging 2.0." *Frontiers in Psychiatry* 29, no. 9: 641.

Santelli, J. S., et al. 2003. "Guidelines for Adolescent Health Research: A Position Paper of the Society for Adolescent Medicine." *Journal of Adolescent Health* 33, no. 5: 396–409.

Sapp, J. C., et al. 2014. "Parental Attitudes, Values, and Beliefs toward the Return of Results from Exome Sequencing in Children." *Clinical Genetics* 85, no. 2: 120–26.

Secretary's Advisory Committee on Genetics, Health, and Society. 2011. "Genetics Education and Training: Report of the Secretary's Advisory Committee on Genetics, Health, and Society." Genetics Education and Training. February 2011. https://www.genome.gov/Pages/Careers/HealthProfessionalEducation/SACGHS-EducationReport2011.pdf.

Semaka, A., L. G. Balneaves, and M. R. Hayden. 2013. " 'Grasping the Grey': Patient Understanding and Interpretation of an Intermediate Allele Predictive Test Result for Huntington Disease. *Journal of Genetic Counseling* 22: 200–17.

Simonsen, N., A. Lahti, S. Suominen, et al. 2018. "Empowerment-Enabling Home and School Environments and Self-Rated Health among Finnish Adolescents." *Health Promotion International.* Published December 24, 2018.

Strong, K. A., et al. 2014. "Views of Primary Care Providers Regarding the Return of Genome Sequencing Incidental Findings." *Clinical Genetics* 86, no. 5: 461–68.

Townsend, A., et al. 2012. "'I Want to Know What's in Pandora's Box': Comparing Stakeholder Perspectives on Incidental Findings in Clinical Whole Genomic Sequencing." *American Journal of Medical Genetics A* 158a, no. 10: 2519–25.

Uniform Parentage Act (amended 2002), 9B U.L.A. 4, 2002.

Wachbroit, R. 2000. "Genetic Determinism, Genetic Reductionism, and Genetic Essentialism." In *The Encyclopedia of Ethical, Legal and Policy Issues in Biotechnology*, Vol. 1, edited by T. H. Murray and M. J. Mehlman, 352–56. Canada: Wiley-Interscience.

Walker, S. O., and R. Plomin. 2005. "The Nature–Nurture Question: Teachers' Perceptions of How Genes and the Environment Influence Educationally Relevant Behavior." *Educational Psychology* 25: 509–16.

Weithorn, L. A., and S. B. Campbell. 1982. "The Competency of Children and Adolescents to Make Informed Treatment Decisions." *Child Development* 53, no. 6: 1589–98.

Wilde, A., et al. 2011. "Community Attitudes to Genetic Susceptibility-Based Mental Health Interventions for Healthy People in a Large National Sample." *Journal of Affective Disorders* 134, no. 1–3: 280–87.

Wilde, A., P. B. Mitchell, B. Meiser, P. R. Schofield. 2013. "Implications of the Use of Genetic Tests in Psychiatry, with a Focus on Major Depressive Disorder: A Review." *Depression and Anxiety* 30: 267–75.

Wilfond, B. S., and D. S. Diekema. 2012. "Engaging Children in Genomics Research: Decoding the Meaning of Assent in Research." *Genetics in Medicine* 14: 437–43.

Wilhelm, K., B. Meiser, P. B. Mitchell, et al. 2009. "Issues Concerning Feedback about Genetic Testing and Risk of Depression." *British Journal of Psychiatry* 194: 404–10.

CHAPTER 14

The Abortion Debate in the Twenty-First Century and Substantive Due Process

Michael Boylan

Abstract

Part one of this chapter seeks to formulate a structure by which people might more profitably discuss abortion. This structure is tied to a conception of both personal worldview and a practical linking principle connected with the vocabulary of maternal threat vs. fetal respect. This structure does not create a firm line to cross, but instead suggests a continuum by which various arguments can be made that differ only through their various emphases. In part two, the discussion moves to the legal parameters of the United States and a reaction to *Dobbs v. Jackson Women's Health Organization*. It is argued that the concept of substantive due process along with a notion of autonomy, backed by a conception of action-theory, refutes *Dobbs* and supports the civil right of abortion subject to some restrictions, which are set out in part one.

Introduction

There are very few conversations in the public square that have had such a long life with so little agreement to show for it as the abortion debate. This chapter does not intend to "settle" the issue in a manner that everyone will accept, but outlines a way each person may decide how a universal moral theory, along with a "linking principle," can resolve this problem (Deryck Beyleveld and Shaun Pattinson). It is suggested that the means for doing so will lie in the personal worldview imperative (PWI): "All people must develop a single comprehensive and internally coherent worldview that is good and that we strive to act out in our daily lives" (Boylan, 2020, p. 22).

To this end, I will present my argument in the following way. First, I will review some of the history of the debate. Second, I will critically examine the key premises in a version of the arguments from each side. Finally, I will suggest a way of thinking about the problem that does not force a single solution upon the reader, but rather suggests a way to frame the problem so that each reader might legislate his or her own "universal maxim."

Part One: The History of the Debate

One can summarize the debate over abortion as being between two camps:

A. The Pro-Abortion Position (a prominent version)
1. A woman's body is her own. *Assertion*
2. Whatever is one's own is under her discretion to dispose of at will. *Fact*
3. A woman's body is under her discretion to dispose of at will. *1 and 2*
4. The fetus is wholly dependent upon the woman's body (at least, through most of the first two trimesters of pregnancy). *Fact*
5. That which is wholly dependent upon one's body is (barring any other intervening duties) wholly under one's discretion to dispose of at will. *Assertion*
6. The fetus inside a woman is hers to dispose of at will. *3 through 5*
7. To "abort" a fetus is to remove it from one's body. *Fact*
8. Removing a fetus from a mother's body will, in most cases, cause it to be biologically nonfunctional. *Fact*
9. To abort a fetus is to cause it to be biologically nonfunctional. *7 and 8*
10. Removing something from one's body (which is at one's disposal, at will) is permissible. *2 and 3*
11. Removing the fetus from a woman's body is permissible even if such removal renders the fetus biologically nonfunctional. *6, 9, and 10*

B. The Anti-Abortion Position (a prominent version)
1. From the moment of conception, there is a person. *Assertion*
2. All persons should be accorded full human rights. *Fact*
3. To kill an innocent human agent, at will, is impermissible. *Fact* (generally accepted by most moral theories)
4. A fetus is an innocent human agent. *Assertion*
5. To kill a fetus is impermissible. *1 through 4*
6. All morally impermissible acts should be sanctioned by society as impermissible. *Fact*
7. Abortion kills the fetus. *Fact*
8. Abortion is impermissible and should be sanctioned by society as impermissible. *5 through 7*

Obviously, there is a tremendous gap between these two arguments.

Let's examine some aspects of the worldviews that drive each side, and then turn to key premises in the above arguments, as well as other classic renditions of the argument.

To make the worldview of each group seem understandable and sympathetic, I will adopt the persona of an advocate to encourage you to explore these worldviews and evaluate what positive and negative points they each have to offer.

THE WORLDVIEWS OF POSITION A

In order to properly review an ethical argument, one must assess the worldview(s) of those who make such arguments. I believe that much of the power of Position A's argument is tied to 1) the unequal consequences that women face in sexual relations; 2) the issue of personal autonomy; and 3) the general societal repression of women.

Let's examine these in order.

1. **Unequal consequences:** The consequence of a woman engaging in sexual intercourse is (among other things) the possibility of a pregnancy. A man can engage in intercourse as often as he chooses and he will never become pregnant. He can (if he is a purely egoistic sort of fellow) walk away when his sexual partner becomes pregnant. Though the consequence of their action is just as much *his* fault as it is *hers*, only she will have to bear the physical debt of their joint behavior. This is unfair. If both the man and woman *jointly* engage in an action, then they should jointly have to bear the consequences. But history has shown that this has never been the case. In fact, some have speculated that the entire institution of marriage evolved solely to protect the woman from this brute inequality.

   Why should men get off without consequence? The large number of single mothers who must raise families around the world is a testament to the brute inequality of the biological scenario that some sociobiologists have termed "a battle of genetic strategies." Within this scenario, all organisms have a single biological imperative: to send their genes into future filial generations.

   The best strategy for a man is to inseminate as many women as possible, in hopes that some of these forays may result in pregnancies and thus fulfill his biological imperative.

   The best strategy for a woman is to be very selective and to try to get a commitment from the biological father to assist in raising their child. This is because a woman when pregnant loses a proverbial "step or two" in her ability to compete for food and shelter. Also, when the child is born, the woman needs to nurse it for at least six months, and will need some protection. (Some have also theorized that this protection can come from a grandmother; hence, the notion that menopause may also be biologically adaptive.)

   If this scenario has any truth to it, the brute biological reproductive strategies of men and women differ. For thousands of years a mistake on the part of women in the execution of their strategy has had far more deleterious consequences than any failures on the part of men.

   It is often seen as a curiosity among many women that some of the most vocal critics of women and their reproductive decisions are men (who bear no brute biological consequences for their actions, i.e., "It's easy for *you* to say . . ."). Thus, I believe it is fairly clear why women would aspire for their gender to have the *option* to be able to walk away from an unfortunate sexual relationship in the same way men have always had.

   Some critics say that men as well as women ought to face equal consequences. This is a rejoinder that meets this argument at its essence. However, how are such consequences to be enforced? Even in the United States (which aspires to be a nation under law), we cannot make divorced fathers and those who abandon their reproductive partner pay legally sanctioned child support. How can we ever realistically aspire to make men pay the same price that women pay for the consequences of sexual intercourse?

2. **Personal autonomy:** The issue of autonomy relates to the ownership of one's own body. All things being equal, it is difficult to know who would own your body except yourself. This means that whatever you own is yours (unless some intervening duty can be proven). If you want to tattoo yourself, put piercings in various places, or cut off a limb, it is your privilege, because whatever is entirely yours is at your disposal. Thus, if you don't choose to use your body as a "growth chamber" for an embryo, you needn't. It is your body to do with as you wish (cf. Thomson).

   There are at least two objections to Position A, the Pro-Abortion Position:

   a. To say that one "owns" one's body splits the person in two. There is no proper distinction between one's self and one's body. They are one and the same. Thus, all metaphors of "ownership" are faulty and do not fit legal notions of ownership. (For a statement of this position, see McLachlan, "Bodies, Rights and Abortion.")
   b. Of course, those who accept a theology that posits an all-powerful creator God—such as Judaism, Christianity, and Islam (a sizable portion of the world's population)—will demur on this point, since it is dogma that God created everything and therefore "owns" what s/he/it has created. In this case, one's body is not one's own, but God's. This tenet can have an effect upon the argument.

3. **General societal repression:** The general station of women in this society, as well as most societies in history, has been as a repressed and enslaved group. This is a broad, sociological statement. This does not mean that there are not individual men who are sensitive and nurturing of their spouses, daughters, and women in general. But one need only engage in some volunteer work with women's shelters and other facilities that deal with those in need to know the truth of this generalization. Despite all of our laws and aspirations as a society, women are treated differently than men. And this difference *is* an added hurdle that women must overcome, which is not present for men.

   To make the point rather sharper, women are the oppressed gender. For men to say to them that they must abide by laws enacted by men that constrict their reproductive freedom (so that they might not be as free as men) is an act of political enslavement. In this way it is the *freedom of choice* that is essential—not the actual execution of an act of abortion.

   Most women will never have an abortion. Most women would never want to have an abortion. Many women will carry an impaired infant to term rather than abort it. Nonetheless, despite the fact that most women will never avail themselves of the political right of abortion (within the United States and a number of other countries), it is still important to maintain the freedom of choice.

   This is because this freedom of choice is a cornerstone in the edifice that stands against gender enslavement. The struggle of oppressed women demands that they not be subjected to the brute will of men on something so close to their biological nature, viz., their reproductive equality. The *choice* for pregnancy termination is merely one part of a very large structure. However, it is symbolically a very important part. It was not very long ago that women who had to pay for the outcomes of their loving relationships were relegated to disbarred physicians who used dirty tools and whose rate of sepsis was only exceeded by their blood-alcohol ratio (see Reagan).

This image of a woman alone, abandoned by her partner and society, resonates with most women (even if they feel that such a situation will never happen to them). It is sort of a "there but for the grace of God, go I" scenario. For this reason, most women feel solidarity for their sisters in need and strive to protect them from a solitary journey into hell.

The freedom of choice is importantly symbolic as a balance against gender oppression.

THE WORLDVIEWS OF POSITION B

The second group views reality in a much different fashion. To begin with, there is a very strong belief in relatively unencumbered free will. Each person can act as she pleases without much real perturbation. The perception of one gender being oppressed is viewed in several ways, including being seen as a lot of bellyaching by a sex that is already protected and given more than ample opportunities; "Why, a woman today has it so much easier than a man; all she has to do is be close to a man in skill, and she will automatically be hired."

Another view sees sexual intercourse as an activity given by God for the creation of children. When people go against the laws of God, then they must be prepared to "face the music." Abortion is the "easy way out." "Living with a few more unfortunate consequences in life would be good for most of these unregulated young people, anyway."

A third perspective is more profound. It asserts that human life is precious. We should do everything in our power to preserve the life of someone unable to protect him/herself, viz., the unborn. We have so much empathy in society for those with disabilities—and rightly so. What is the basis of this empathy? It is because they need the protection and support of others. When someone is impaired, s/he needs the protection and support of others. A fetus is in a similar position as one impaired. This impairment is not due to a defect in the genotype or in development, but is a natural consequence of the biological stage of this individual. All other things being equal, this embryo will become a human agent capable of reason and of action.

According to the doctrine of *novus actus interveniens*, the normal process of nature is taken to be the standard. This doctrine is well entrenched in the law (Hart and Honoré). The idea is this: If you interfere with the normal operation of nature as a new intervening action, then you are responsible for all the ensuing consequences. For example, let's say John is robbing a bank and says to the teller, "If you move, I'll shoot." Say the teller moves slightly as she presses the alarm button with her foot. The bank robber shoots, and his bullet ricochets off one of the iron bars of the teller's cage and lodges in the neck of a person standing in line behind the gunman.

Now, who "caused" the person to be shot? If one takes an "inciting incident" theory of causation (often taken as definitive in the philosophy of science), then the teller is to blame. But this is ridiculous. The teller was put in an abnormal situation by the gunman. The natural order had been changed by the gunman, with his gun and his demands. Thus, according to the doctrine of *novus actus interveniens*, it is the gunman who is at fault for the bullet in the customer's neck, and not the teller. This is because the gunman changed the natural order, and thus all ensuing events (in an appropriately fashioned action description) can be attributed to him.

How does this apply to abortion?

The natural order would have the fetus grow and develop as it normally would. Any event that intervened to stop this process would be considered to be causally responsible for the fetus's demise. If the fetus is a person, then the intervening party is a murderer. Thus, abortion is murder.

Now, if you were a part of a society that institutionalized murder, and you did nothing about it, then you would be some sort of accessory to the murder. Thus, to live in a society that permits abortion and to do nothing about it would be tantamount to someone turning a blind eye to Hitler, Stalin, or Pol Pot (if you lived in their societies or in the world at large, and could have reacted in some meaningful way). Despite societal acceptance you must do everything you can to stop it.

We have created a society that legalizes the continual killing of thousands of fetuses every year. If these fetuses are children, then aren't we guilty of mass murder? Aren't we to be compared to the great murdering societies of history? Isn't this cause enough to prohibit abortion now?

A Critical Examination of the Premises of Each Side

The last section dealt with a version of the pro and con arguments, per se, and explored in brief the worldviews of each side. Let us begin this section by defining some key terms.

"Abortion" is the removal of a fetus from the female by natural or artificial means.

A "natural abortion" is called "spontaneous abortion," and occurs in 20 to 25 percent of all pregnancies (depending upon how one frames the data). Most spontaneous abortions occur during the first trimester of pregnancy. They are called miscarriages. Miscarriages generally occur because the developing embryo is malformed. It is nature's way of ensuring that potential children with no real chance of survival are given an exit at the beginning of life's journey.

An "artificial abortion" is the removal of a fetus from the female by medical means. Abortion is *not* the killing of that fetus. As a matter of fact, many embryos removed from the female do die. They don't die because they are removed from the mother, as such. For example, one might imagine a time in which there might be an artificial womb in the laboratory. In this case an embryo might be removed from a woman at any time and it would not necessarily result in its death. All this is to say that if there is a right to abortion, it is a right to remove the fetus from your body. This is not a right to kill the fetus.

If the fetus, for example, were able to be preserved, then it would be a separate question of what to do with that fetus. In this case the state would enter the equation as an interested party in order to govern the interests of the newly born, premature infant. This, of course, follows the *viability* approaches of the court in *Roe v. Wade.*

The right to abortion, *simpliciter*, is a right to remove a fetus from one's body. This follows from the sample argument and the worldview enhancement of the same. Therefore, the abortion question changes drastically after the point of viability. In principle one might be able to remove the fetus from the female and raise it separately in some sort of nursery. In these cases, removing a fetus would not be tantamount to causing it to die. One could remove the fetus and allow it to develop without any further contact with its biological mother.

Having clarified this, let's turn to a few key premises in the arguments on each side.

PREMISES OF PRO-ABORTION POSITION

First, let's examine the pro-abortion position as represented by the generic argument as I presented it. Given the worldview background, the argument is persuasive. Detractors are likely to focus upon premise 5: "That which is wholly dependent upon one's body is (barring any other intervening duties) wholly under one's discretion to dispose of at will." *Assertion.* The move is from autonomy over one's own body parts to sovereignty over entities dependent upon one's body. This is an argument that Judith Jarvis Thomson elaborates in her famous article (see contemporary discussion on this: Wennberg, Wilcox, Warren, Pavlischek, and Boonin).

Deontologists might object to a blanket endorsement of this position. It seems to violate the "duty to rescue." This duty is a moral obligation that is supported by Kant, Gewirth, and Donagan. In the duty to rescue, one is obliged to aid another whenever that other person's basic goods of agency are threatened, so long as doing so does not entail that one risks his or her own basic goods of agency.

The reason for this caveat is that one is never *obliged* to risk his or her own basic goods of agency for the sake of another. To do so would be to admit that the other person has more of a right to the basic goods of agency than I do. This would entail that the other person is better qua being an agent than I am. There is no support for such an assertion under the deontological theories I am citing, since all agents are equally entitled to the basic goods of agency simply by being human beings alive on this Earth. Those who choose to risk their own basic goods of agency for the sake of others go "above and beyond" their moral duty, i.e., they are heroes. But one who only fulfills his or her duty to save another when his or her basic goods of agency are not at risk is only an ordinary person doing his or her duty.

For example, in the case of Kitty Genovese (which Thomson cites), the apartment dwellers could have screamed from their window at the attacker or called the police, or both. I can attest from personal experience that this is an effective way to thwart a criminal in the inner city. Thus, if one can aid another whose basic goods of agency are being threatened without risking one's own basic goods of agency, then one is obliged to do so. This is a little different than the depiction given by Thomson. She says we are not obliged to go out and confront the mugger ourselves, and that one who does so is a Good Samaritan. But this implies that there are only two sorts of responses to the Kitty Genovese case—either fight or flight. However, this is too simple. Surely everyone is obliged to aid another when it does not risk one's own basic goods of agency.

But what of abortion?

Is abortion properly analogous to one of these options cited in the above example? Calling the police and yelling from one's window; or leaving the apartment complex to do physical battle with the assailant? In the first case one is merely fulfilling a moral duty. This does not deserve praise but merely a statement of gratitude. In the second case one has risked their basic goods of agency. They might also have been killed. This person is a hero.

Is the woman who chooses to carry a fetus to term more like the person doing her duty or more like the hero? This can be an important component in evaluating this argument.

Returning to premise 5 of the pro-abortion position, we can also note that there is a difference between what one does to one's own body and what one does to entities that are not of one's body. In the case of bacteria, viruses, cysts, and growths, we pay no mind to eliminating them. They are not of our body, and they have no intrinsic worth—nor would a reasonable interpretation of precautionary reasoning dictate that they have any worth (Beyleveled and Pattinson).

A fetus is certainly different. A fetus will, all things being equal, develop into a moral agent who has absolute rights to freedom and well-being. Thus, the argument for potentiality is not wholly without merit. Though the fetus is not *actually* a person in the strong sense of the word, it is still a *potential* person. This potentiality of personhood is not trivial and cannot be dismissed.

PREMISES OF ANTI-ABORTION POSITION

Next, let's examine the anti-abortion position as represented by the generic argument as I presented it. Again, given the worldview background, the argument is persuasive. Detractors are likely to focus upon premise 3: "To kill an innocent human agent, at will, is impermissible. *Fact* (generally accepted by most moral theories).

Now, some would want to discuss the nature of the word "innocent" in this context. Is it meant to be some sort of absolute term, i.e., "in no way deserves to die," or relative to the action description at hand, i.e., "is in no way threatening the life of any other agent (knowingly or unknowingly)." I sharpen this via the methodology of "action description" in the introduction of Boylan (2020) and in Boylan (2004, chapter 2). The first sense is rather silly as depicted because it presupposes so many unstated propositions that need to be argued and defended. The second, on the other hand, has merit. "Innocent" with this reading implies that one is not materially involved in the loss of fundamental rights of agency for another (intended or otherwise).

Take the example of the deer hunter who begins firing at another person, thinking s/he is a deer. That other person could justifiably kill the one firing at him or her. (We assume that the person firing thinks s/he is firing at a deer. We also assume that the only way to stop the gunman is to use lethal force.) The proportionality of "threat" to "minimal response necessary to alleviate the threat" is very important in cases of self-defense. However, in the instance of abortion, the response (abortion) will have a fixed effect (the death of the fetus), until near the end of the second trimester. In this case the only variable is the level of threat. After viability, of course, the situation changes if there is a policy to use an abortion procedure that seeks to preserve the fetus's life. With this reading, the unwitting gunman is not innocent. S/he is materially guilty because s/he jeopardizes the life of another. By this definition, a person may be innocent only if s/he is not materially threatening the life of another (Donagan, 87ff., makes a similar distinction). Thus, a fetus that threatens the life of a mother and is killed as a result is not a case of killing an "innocent."

But let's explore further the sense of "threatens." There are certainly many senses of this word. The most severe is to kill the mother. A fetus (without motive) may be the cause of a mother's death. There are other senses; one identifies "threatens" as ripping apart the worldview in which the pregnant woman lives. This threatens her because it challenges everything that she holds as precious in her life plan (stated or only imagined). This is not trivial. People kill themselves for as much. Where does one draw the line at delineating harm? Is this a question of balancing?

It is always a question of balancing.

The difference between theories that explicitly balance—such as utilitarianism, intuitionism, and virtue ethics—is that they balance on the "back end." They balance at the moment of decision.

Deontological theories balance, too. But they aspire to balance at the front end, i.e., in the depiction of the act to be judged. One balances in judging what *sort* of action is being depicted. The operation of forming an action description is not value-neutral. It involves balancing competing understandings of what is happening—i.e., what is relevant. Thus, there is always balancing. The question is, what drives the decision?

In this case, I am suggesting that it ought to be the personal worldview imperative (PWI). The "consistency" portion of this imperative requires that one treat all cases alike, and create rules (whatever they are) that do not contradict each other and fulfill the aspirations of that moral theory. Thus, there have to be some boundaries as to what should be regarded as "threatening" to one's worldview.

For example, when I used to be a track runner, we had a very talented runner in our club who had the potential to be an Olympic runner. He had joined the club because we had four other runners who were favorites to make the 1976 Olympic team. The only problem was that this runner never finished a race in the four years I ran with the club. Something would always get in the way. Either his splits were not exactly as he had wanted them to be, or a black bird flew over the track (he hated black birds), or he thought he heard someone yelling something at him, or the humidity suddenly changed, *et aliud.* Surely, these distractions, while real and important to him, would be viewed by the rest of us as ultimately trivial. So it is with some senses of "threaten." What should count as a legitimate sense of the word?

To make this point more starkly, let me contrast seven motivations for an abortion that women might bring forward as instances of being threatened. These cases are not meant to be comprehensive, but merely suggestive of certain levels of threat. They only deal with those who have engaged in sexual intercourse willingly and are faced with the resulting pregnancy. I would characterize all nonvoluntary acts of sexual intercourse (such as rape or incest) as creating a very high sense of threat for the woman, which might be characterized as between "A" and "B" in the list below. In this case, the carrying of the fetus (as innocent as s/he may be) constantly reinforces the horror and degradation of the initial act. This humiliation is a primary threat to human action and well-being, so the woman would be fully within her rights to remove the fetus from her body at any time.

Seven Possible Motivations for an Abortion

A. Ms. A is pregnant and it has been determined that if she were to bring this fetus to term, she will die. Ms. A feels threatened because her life is in danger.

B. Ms. B is pregnant. She is a married mother of five other children and of very modest financial means. If she carries this fetus to term, her other five children will be pushed over the edge of starvation. There are not enough resources for six children. Ms. B feels threatened because the lives of her other children are at stake.

C. Ms. C is pregnant. She is married and her obstetrician has told her that the baby she is carrying has a fatal disease that will kill the child by the age of six. It will be a painful death. Maybe medical science will find a cure for this disease, but probably this will not occur. Ms. C feels threatened on behalf of her unborn child.

D. Ms. D is pregnant. She is a thirty-something single person and in a career that is just about to take off. Her profession is so competitive that it's reasonable to assume that if she muffs this opportunity, she will never have another chance. Ms. D feels threatened because her career and personal life plan are at stake.

E. Ms. E is pregnant. She is a high school senior who has been admitted to a very selective college. Her parents would be furious if they knew she was pregnant. Her college admission might not be renewable if she does not attend this fall. Her whole future is in front of her. Her life plan did not include a pregnancy. There is no way that she could be a good mother at this point in her life. It wasn't supposed to work out this way. Ms. E feels threatened because her future and her reputation are at stake.

F. Ms. F is pregnant. She is married and has decided that she would like to have a boy and a girl. They already have the girl, and amniocentesis has indicated that the fetus within her will be a girl, too. They do not want to have more than two children because it is not part of the life plan they have created for themselves. Ms. F feels threatened because she has a girl within her when she wanted a boy.

G. Ms G. is pregnant. She is married and has decided that she would like a male child who is very intelligent and fits the profile of physical features that she feels represents the perfect child: blond hair, blue eyes, six feet tall, 1500+ on the SATs.

> Assume that there is some battery of tests that pretends to predict a genotype that is most compatible with the desired phenotype / developmental end product. Ms. G's test results indicate that her fetus is deficient in several areas: not perfectly blond hair (severalshades of brown seem more likely); predicted height of five-foot-eleven; probable SAT score of just 1200. Ms. G feels threatened because she has a fetus that will not meet her standard for the child she really wants.

Each of these scenarios illustrates on a sliding scale relative senses of being threatened. If one is entitled to kill an otherwise innocent agent who is materially guilty because s/he threatens you, then it is important to create a "floor" that demarcates what is a suitable ground of threat.

In case A, we have a pure sense of self-defense. In B, one may be said to be acting in self-defense on behalf of another (in this case, the other children; though it's more difficult because there are more contingencies). In C, the question transforms into a structure that is similar to those found in active euthanasia. One is paternalistically acting on behalf of another's best interest. The mother thinks, "I know that this child will not want to die so early and with so much suffering." She may also think, "I cannot face the trial of caring for another knowing that the future is both fixed and fatal."

Cases D and E are similar except for the age of the parties. The age issue can work both ways. One might give greater latitude to the younger person because she is not fully mature and responsible for her actions. Or one might give greater latitude to the older person because as one ages, doors of opportunity close. The consequences to the older woman are probably more severe than to the younger. In each case, we have "threaten" in the context of "very disruptive to my life plan."

Cases F and G are also similar because they indicate a sense of eugenics. It is a fact that a great number of abortions that are performed in the world revolve around the sex of the fetus. Thousands of female fetuses have been aborted because the mother desired a son. In Case G we have a science-fiction scenario in which people desire to have designer babies. To some, this is a desirable future. To others, it is a nightmare.

More will be said about these senses of "threaten" in the last section of this chapter.

The other aspect of premise 3 of the anti-abortion position concerns the definition of an agent. This issue has been much discussed in the literature, with little to show for it (Steinbock). I would like to preface my remarks by referring to Beyleveld's and Pattinson's essay on precautionary reasoning. They make the point that *full human rights,* viz., those which confer absolute respect for freedom and well-being, only become operative when there is an agent who clearly meets the criteria of being a prospective, purposive agent.

In a strong sense, this would not be evident without objection until sometime in the child's second year of life. This is a troubling point, because it invokes both methodologies and measurements. Some may want to push the point back a bit, but the ultimate measure in this case is whether the child has shown that s/he has a sense of self, and, that the sense of self deliberates and carries out action. Thus, walking might count, or beginning to speak. *Wherever* one wishes to set this point, it will be well past birth. If we grant this, everyone under the age of thirty months or so has no dialectically necessary claim to agency, then *quod erat demonstrandum*, s/he has no dialectically necessary claim to life (one of the goods of well-being).

This is certainly a very high standard. Does this mean that we are entitled to kill at will all those under the age of thirty months? Surely not. Precautionary reasoning indicates that various actions, such as walking and feeding oneself, indicate that the infant may be more cognizant than we can scientifically document. In these cases, the infant is doing no more than what many other animals also do.

In most cases, human infants go through developmental stages more slowly than do other species. Thus, based on this alone, one would afford more proportional status to puppies or to baby lizards than to humans. Obviously, this is not the way we act, because we employ precautionary reasoning. We do not ascribe to other species the sorts of rights afforded to human agents. Why?

To answer this, we need to examine the personal worldview imperative.

The Personal Worldview Imperative and Abortion

The personal worldview imperative says: "All people must develop a single comprehensive and internally coherent worldview that is good and that we strive to act out in our daily lives." The PWI enjoins each of us to create both a comprehensive and internally coherent vision of life. One aspect of this is to be able to will oneself to have an action performed upon him/herself without violating the laws of nature as the s/he understands them. This interpretation of the PWI comes about through the sense of consistency. It would be inconsistent to view oneself as being outside nature's laws (see Boylan, forthcoming). Therefore, to will exceptions for yourself is irrational (because it is inconsistent). This is similar to the Kantian notion of imperfect duties.

In the case of a fetus, no one could will his/her own demise (i.e., being aborted) without contradicting the natural law that says that *ceteris paribus*, we all act for our own preservation and happiness. But what if we could not will? Certainly, this situation may exist when we are at the beginning of life. In these cases, the fetus does not act (and since "willing" is a precondition to action), the fetus does not will. This would seem to be an exception to the Kantian interpretation of the PWI, above. However, some might claim that such situations should be judged like we would assess a person who is asleep (to use Aristotle's example), i.e., the fetus is not willing *now*, but will be in the position to will in the near future. Such an argument is a form of precautionary reasoning.

The essence of this doctrine (as I choose to use it) is to make precautionary reasoning a form of Aristotelian potentiality that holds open the possibility that the individual in question may be more empowered than we can scientifically determine. At some point we must "draw a line" and say that past that point, it is impossible (from the worldview perspective of the speaker) that the individual in question should be afforded the moral rights of agency—even using precautionary reasoning.

Does this mean that past the point of affording the fetus proportional rights through precautionary reasoning we are entitled to give the fetus no consideration at all, and thus be entitled to kill it "at will"? The notion of proportional rights stems from the individual's best assessment of the possible degree of agency that *may* exist. This goes well beyond any demonstrated agency (which may be as late as thirty months after birth). This attribution of rights is given not because of demonstrated capacity on the part of the fetus, but because it seems possible that an individual may possess attributes that confer agency, viz., a sense of inductive and deductive logic along with the capacity to deliberate about action (even in a very minimal way) *before* this is operationally evident to some observer. Therefore, out of precaution, we act *as if* the individual has these capacities (even though there is no demonstrable evidence for this). As a result, we confer precautionary rights of agency. These differ from full rights of agency only in the fact that they are not *dialectically necessary* (Gewirth) or *apodeitically necessary* (Kant). They are, in fact, contingently necessary (contingent because they are based upon the assessment of that person who is making the attribution).

The answer to this query is "No," because I have linked "precaution" with a sense of Aristotelian potentiality. This interpretation of cautionary reasoning will give some level of respect to any fetus, no matter how immature. On the principle of proportionality I have been exposing, one would give more respect to a thirteen-week fetus than to a four-week fetus. This is because the thirteen-week fetus is closer to enjoying precautionary reasoning than a four-week fetus is. Just how much respect, vis-à-vis various threats that face the mother, must be determined by the agent.

The process goes like this. First, one must establish for him- or herself the floor of precautionary reason. This requires judgment. Personally, I would put the floor at the end of the first trimester of pregnancy (thirteen weeks). Before this point the brain and spinal cord are not connected; therefore, according to my own best understanding, it would be impossible for the fetus to deliberate, plan, and act. Others may disagree with me moving in either direction (i.e., earlier or later in pregnancy).

Second, one must determine the limit of respect one will accord to a fetus who is not a) an actual agent, nor b) a possible agent (even under a liberal sense of precautionary reasoning). The agent in question is *potentially* a *possible* agent. As a potentially possible agent, the fetus has some respect accorded to it because, barring intervention, it will become a possible agent (protected by precautionary reason) and eventually, a full-blown agent (protected by most theories of morality).

This interpretation would invalidate the given form of the pro-abortion argument because it would suggest that the "at will" provision is incorrect. One may only eliminate some entity "at will" when there is no justifiable respect owed to it. Under the interpretation outlined above, there is always some level of respect due to potentiality tied to precautionary reasoning. It is up to the agent involved to determine the *level of respect*. This is a personal assessment. But to say so does not imply relativism. Rather, it is the proper expression of the PWI in which one legislates a universal interpretation of reality (which would include valuing this level of respect).

I do not feel one may abort a fetus at will. One must have a threat that supersedes the level of respect one has assigned to the fetus. In the above examples, I would say that the sort of threat represented by cases F and G does not meet this standard. Thus, abortion for the sake of the baby's sex or due to some eugenics desire would be impermissible at any stage of pregnancy.

The level of respect due to the fetus as a mere potential possible agent is greater than that level of maternal threat.

I would assess cases A through E as meeting this standard of threat during the first trimester of pregnancy. Others might demur because they would quarrel with me about balancing of threats.

I would always view case A as meeting a sufficient standard of threat throughout the pregnancy, as well as those cases between A and B (covering rape and incest—and all other cases of involuntary sex that has resulted in a pregnancy). However, in third-trimester abortions, there may be an opportunity to remove the fetus without destroying it. The right to an abortion is not a right to have the embryo destroyed, but merely a right to have it removed from one's body.

Cases B and C and D and E both form units that revolve around similar themes (self-defense for the sake of another, and severe disruption to one's personal life plan, respectively). Since averting death is more disastrous to agency than mere roadblocks (no matter how disruptive), I would assess B and C as being higher-order threats than D and E. This differentiation must make itself felt in different stages of pregnancy in which an abortion may be permissible. For example, I would lean toward D and E as being permissible during the first trimester, and B and C as being permissible during the first two trimesters.

The general principle in operation is how to weigh "threat" and "response." In the latter case the nature of the response changes as the fetus develops. Thus, a response to a fetus in the first trimester is different from a response in the second trimester, and is different from a response in the third trimester. This is because in the first trimester one has merely the principle of potentiality by which to refer.

After the first trimester I believe the principle of precautionary reason kicks in and becomes proportionally more relevant until the minimal stages of operationally verifiable agency are evidenced (thirty months after birth—or less). After thirty months (or whatever time frame is chosen), it would be absolutely impermissible to kill the entity unless it were materially threatening the life of the mother. Such a situation would be bizarre and one would have to stretch his/her imagination to come up with a plausible case. Unfortunately, in my volunteer work experience, it is all too frequently the case that adults feel threatened by children. "They cry too much," or "They keep needing to have their diaper changed," or "They drive me nuts with their fussiness," etc. Far too often the "threat" threshold is far too low for these adults. Beating, abusing, and even killing infants is justified in the minds of these adults because the needs of the child interfered with their life plans (as per cases F and G above). Such a response to the perceived threat is far too great, and is therefore morally impermissible.

Conclusion to Part One

Part one of this chapter has aspired to be suggestive rather than definitive on the question of abortion. To this end I have suggested criteria that can be used by different people to set the universal limits of permissibility and impermissibility. This variation is due to the variation in personal worldviews, in which one may weigh maternal threats and fetal respect differently. Instead of focusing on the definition of personhood or the expression of autonomy, I would suggest that it is more productive to focus on "maternal threats versus fetal respect."

This approach suggests there are three levels that should be considered when evaluating how much respect anyone deserves:

A. Full personhood (at some time in the first few years of development)
B. Possible personhood (protected by precautionary reason from some base level to personhood—I would put this moment at the end of the first trimester of pregnancy)
C. Potential possible personhood (from the moment of conception to possible personhood)

Full moral rights obtain necessarily to those enjoying full personhood (since they are actual deliberating agents). Something proportionally approaching full moral rights may be claimed for the possible agent. And some proportionally lesser level of respect (with its associated rights) should be granted to those on the lowest level.

Contra the traditional anti-abortionists who generally argue for full moral rights for the fetus from conception, this theory creates three levels of respect that move well past birth in order to be complete. Contra the traditional pro-abortionists, who generally argue for the right of abortion at will, this theory denies abortions at will. What is requisite is demonstrating a level of maternal threat that is greater than the level of respect we ought to give the developing (though not yet actual) person.

The levels that one sets for threats versus respect will follow from one's complex web of values that I call the worldview. Through a dialectical interaction between the question at hand and these values emerges personal ownership of a universal theory dealing with "if, when, and under what conditions" an embryo may be separated from its biological mother.

The question of abortion has stayed with us so long in the public square because it addresses so many key issues about the rights of others versus our own individual expressions of autonomy. I believe that total consensus on this issue will never occur in the present framework because consensus is a derivative property of one's worldview. And since worldviews differ, so will the imperatives they endorse. This is not a statement of relativism, but a factual description of various people working on a common problem (each thinking s/he has *the* correct answer).

However, on the optimistic side, I believe that if the abortion question is viewed from the personal worldview imperative, at least their will be more understanding of a) where the other side is "coming from"; and b) a vocabulary structured so that it does not prejudge the issue (viz., the vocabulary of maternal threat vs. fetal respect). These sorts of understanding will be essential if there is to be any real progress in the public debate on abortion.

Part Two

The discussion in part two moves to the legal parameters of the United States and a reaction to *Dobbs v. Jackson Women's Health Organization* (2022). This decision overturned *Roe v. Wade* that set abortion as a legal right in the United States, based upon the principle of recognizing the right of privacy understood as personal autonomy that began with *Griswold v. Connecticut* (1965). Consideration of the status of the fetus in *Roe* followed the standard of fetal viability. Using *actual* viability (as opposed to artificial viability), Roe would move the acceptable period of an abortion into the end of the second trimester of pregnancy (giving some leniency to states to set the exact date). The standard of "separability," aka, "viability," is used in zoology as a key distinction to identify between two separate organisms that were biologically connected as opposed to being one organism and a parasitic appendage. (For more on these biological relations, see Gardner and Diamond.)

In *Dobbs*, Justice Samuel Alito's opinion and Brett Kavanaugh's concurring opinion presented two arguments that were set out to overturn the existing law of fifty years. First, it was argued that the Constitution does not set out a right to abortion in its contents. Because it was not included, the contention is that it is not a civil right (since, they contend, the Constitution is the explicit source of all civil rights). Second, because the Constitution does not validate a civil right to abortion, the only body left to do so is at the state level. In this way the "civil right to an abortion" devolves to the state level. If there is any possibility for a civil right to an abortion, it must be recognized at the state level.

There are at least two problems with this argument; first, the due process clauses of the Fifth and the Fourteenth Amendments, which state that individuals residing in the United States will "not be deprived of life, liberty, or property, without due process of law" (Fifth Amendment) and that "No state shall make or enforce any law which shall abridge the privileges or immunities of citizens of the United States; nor shall any state deprive any person of life, liberty, or property, without due process of law; nor deny to any person within its jurisdiction the equal protection of the laws" (Fourteenth Amendment). These are taken in concert with the Tenth Amendment, which states: "The powers not delegated to the United States by the Constitution, nor prohibited by it to the States, are reserved to the States respectively, or to the people."

A second line of argument against Alito's opinion in *Dobbs* (as per the Tenth Amendment) is a clear sense that *unless* a liberty right is prohibited by the Constitution or the states, it resides with the people. This is sometimes called *substantive due process.* Putting Alito on his head, this could be set that unless the Constitution or the states *prohibit* abortion (and some states do—but not the Constitution), there is *at best* a particular state prohibition against abortion. Since the Constitution is *silent* on abortion, this means that there is a *lack of a prohibition.* Given this lack of a prohibition, there is no federal prohibition. Unless there is a state prohibition, then there is a general *permission* for abortion; meaning, one has a natural civil right unless the state intervenes to create a prohibition. According to Boylan (2014), such permissions follow from the autonomy that is expected to flow from ethical action theory as a claims right, according to Hohfeld.

In the United States today (2023), there are thirteen states that ban abortion. On the above argument, since there are no state prohibitions in the other thirty-seven states, abortion in those states is legal and viable.

But going further into substantive due process, the Fifth, Fourteenth, and Tenth Amendments together protect fundamental rights from any governmental interference against "life, liberty, or property without due process of law." It is generally recognized that this is at least a procedural protection, but there is some disagreement on the extent of the substantive rights claims (Wurman). As suggested in Boylan (2014) and Gewirth (1984), an action-theory approach to human rights emphasizes the autonomy of the principal agent, who would in this case be the carrier of the embryo. In a balance between any "action-based" claims right, the principal agent's claim would take precedence over a dependent's rights, according to the level of "threat" (as set out in part one). If, indeed, substantive due process supports a general federal recognition of the right to abortion as part an individual's expression of life and liberty, then Alito's general premise is overturned.

Such a strategy of discovering "life, liberty, and property" rights through action-theory-based autonomy has been done before with LGBTQIA+ (Cohen & Bostock). There is no consistent logical reason that it cannot also be applied here (as argued by Frank, McLachlan).

Conclusion to Part Two

Part two suggests that there is no good reason to accept Alito's *Dobbs* reasoning. The practical disadvantages will probably return women to the "back-alley" abortions of the past that are not safe or hygienic (Steinbock, Reagan, Warren). Let us not make this mistake going forward. There is not a good reason to get rid of the established law of fifty years in the United States and the general practice of many other democratic countries elsewhere in the world.

Legal and social systems should support a woman's right to choose her reproductive future on the basis of autonomy (subject to any caveats in part one of this chapter). Everyone should press strongly in support of this natural right becoming a civil right, as well. Substantive due process, supported by a conception of autonomy based upon action theory, demands no less.

References

Allen, Anita. "'*Dobbs v. Jackson Women's Health*' Interview with Michael Boylan." YouTube, https://www.youtube.com/watch?v=FMoMFeGQj6M&t=2s (accessed April 6, 2023).

Beyleveld, Deryck, and Shaun Pattinson. "Precautionary Reason as a Link to Moral Action." In Michael Boylan, ed., *Medical Ethics*. Upper Saddle River, NJ: Prentice Hall, 2000: 39–52.

Boonin-Vail, David. "A Defense of 'A Defense of Abortion': On the Responsibility Objection to Thomson's Argument." *Ethics* 107 (January 1997): 286–313.

Boylan, Michael. *A Just Society*. New York and Oxford: Rowman & Littlefield, 2004.

———. *Natural Human Rights: A Theory.* Cambridge: Cambridge University Press, 2014.

———. *Basic Ethics,* 3rd ed. London and New York: Routledge, 2020.

———. *On Nature: A Philosophical History of Western Medicine.* London and New York: Routledge, forthcoming.

Cohen, Susannah. "Redefining What it Means to Discriminate Because of Sex: Bostock's Equal Protection Implications." *Columbia Law Review* 122 (2) (2022): 407–48.

Comstock v. Clayton County. 590 U.S. (2020).

Donagan, Alan. *The Theory of Morality.* Chicago: University of Chicago Press, 1977, 154, ff.

Frank, Matthew J. "What Happened to the Due Process Clause in the Dred Clause Case? The Continuing Confusion over 'Substance' versus 'Process.'" *American Political Thought* 4 (1) (2015): 120–48.

Gardner, Scott Lyell, and Judy Diamond, et al. *Parasites: The Inside Story.* Princeton, NJ: Princeton University Press, 2022.

Gewirth, Alan. "Replies to My Critics." In Edward Regis Jr., ed. *Gewirth's Ethical Rationalism: Critical Essays with a Reply by Alan Gewirth.* Chicago: University of Chicago Press, 1984: 228–29.

Hart, H. L. A., and A. M. Honoré. *Causation in the Law.* Oxford: Clarendon Press, 1959, 129 ff., cf. 127, 292–96.

Hohfeld, W. *Fundamental Legal Conceptions.* New Haven, CT: Yale University Press, 1919.

Kant, Immanuel. *Grundlegung zur Metaphysik der sitten.* 1st ed. 1785; 2nd ed., 1786, Prussian Academy Edition, Vol. 4. Berlin: G. Reimer, 1902–1942, 421.

Lewis, Thomas Tandy. "The Ironic History of Substantive Due Process: Three Constitutional Revolutions." *International Science Review* 76 (1) (2001): 21–35.

McLachlan, Hugh V. "Bodies, Rights and Abortion." *Journal of Medical Ethics* 23 (3) (1997): 176–80.

Pavlischek, Keith J. "Abortion Logic and Paternal Responsibility: One More Look at Judith Thomson's 'A Defense of Abortion.'" *Public Affairs Quarterly* 7 (1993): 341–61.

Reagan, Leslie J. *When Abortion Was a Crime: Women, Medicine, and Law in the United States, 1867–1973.* Berkeley: University of California Press, 1997.

Steinbock, Bonnie. *Life Before Birth: The Moral and Legal Status of Embryos and Fetuses.* Oxford: Oxford University Press, 1992.

Thomson, Judith Jarvis. "A Defense of Abortion." *Philosophy and Public Affairs* 1 (1971): 47–66.

Warren, Mary Anne. "On the Moral and Legal Status of Abortion." In Lewis M. Schwartz, ed., *Arguing about Abortion.* Belmont, MA: Wadsworth, 1993: 227–24.

Wennberg, Robert N. *Life in the Balance: Exploring the Abortion Controversy.* Grand Rapids, MI: Eerdmans, 1985.

Wilcox, John T. "Nature as Demonic in Thomson's Defense of Abortion." In Robert M. Baird and Stuart E. Rosenbaum, eds., *The Ethics of Abortion: Pro-Life vs. Pro-Choice,* rev. ed. Buffalo, NY: Prometheus, 1993: 212–25.

Wurman, Ilan, "The Origins of Substantive Due Process." *University of Chicago Law Review* 87 (3) (2020): 815–81.

CHAPTER 15

The Future of Reproductive Justice in the United States after *Dobbs*

Kimberly Mutcherson

Abstract

The reproductive justice (RJ) movement rests on three central human rights: the right to have a child, the right to not have a child, and the right to parent one's children in safe and healthy environments. The US Supreme Court decision in *Dobbs*, which ended federal constitutional protection for the right to an abortion, has created a seismic shift in the reproductive futures of women and other people capable of pregnancy with particularly harsh outcomes for the most vulnerable women. This chapter focuses on the collateral consequences of the loss of abortion access, including increased maternal mortality and morbidity as more women are forced to carry pregnancies to term without concomitant attention to the need for expanded access to high-quality prenatal care; miscarriage mismanagement as health-care providers attempt to navigate an uncertain landscape of exceptions to bans; criminalization of pregnancy for suspected self-managed abortions or for behavior by a pregnant woman thought to create risk for a fetus; and potential changes to the regulation of infertility care as states shift the line of personhood closer to the point of fertilization.

Introduction

In June 2022, the abortion landscape in the United States changed radically. This is not to say that abortion access had not been eroded in significant ways in the almost fifty years since the Court decided *Roe v. Wade* in 1973, but the federal constitutional right to abortion had long been a bulwark against the most egregious excesses by state legislators eager to make abortion wholly inaccessible in their jurisdictions and, for many, in the United States as a whole. The *Dobbs* decision removed the impediment that had made it possible for thousands of women each year to terminate pregnancies because they were not ready to have a child, because they did want to have a child with a particular person, because they felt too young or too old, because the pregnancy was a result of sexual assault or incest, because the pregnancy posed a risk to their own health or safety, because of a fetal anomaly, or just because they did not want to be pregnant. Women in the United States now find themselves living in a divided nation where crossing a border can be the difference between being able to make autonomous decisions about one's reproductive life or being obligated to remain pregnant against one's wishes.

This chapter uses the reproductive justice (RJ) paradigm to analyze the myriad ways in which the *Dobbs* decision violates the basic human rights of women and other people capable of pregnancy and creates deeply problematic ethical conundrums for health-care providers and others. In addition to describing the present landscape for abortion access in the United States, an ever-moving target due to new legislation and copious amounts of litigation, this chapter focuses on the collateral consequences of the loss of abortion access, including increased maternal mortality and morbidity as more women are forced to carry pregnancies to term without concomitant attention to the need for expanded access to high-quality prenatal care; miscarriage mismanagement as health-care providers attempt to navigate an uncertain landscape of medical exceptions to abortion bans; criminalization of pregnancy for suspected self-managed abortions or for behavior by a pregnant woman thought to create risk to a fetus; and potential changes to the regulation of infertility care as states shift the line of personhood closer to the point of fertilization. All of these consequences move the United States further away from the promise of creating a nation in which reproductive justice is a reality for all people.

The End of the Federal Right to an Abortion in the United States

After an explosive leak of a draft opinion in May of the same year, in June 2022, the US Supreme Court issued its final opinion in *Dobbs v. Jackson Women's Health Organization* (*Dobbs v. Jackson Women's Health Organization* 2022). Jackson Women's Health Organization and other plaintiffs filed the case against Dobbs, the State Health Officer of Mississippi, to challenge the state's Gestational Age Act. That act made it illegal to perform an abortion past fifteen weeks of gestation in the absence of a medical emergency or a severe fetal anomaly. The legislature chose to fix the gestational age at fifteen weeks as a deliberate attack on existing US Supreme Court precedent in *Planned Parenthood v. Casey* (*Planned Parenthood v. Casey* 1992). In *Casey*, the Supreme Court severely curtailed the abortion right that it had previously rooted in the federal Constitution in *Roe v. Wade* in 1973.

The justices who embraced the prevailing opinion in *Casey* jettisoned the trimester framework created in *Roe* to demarcate when abortion could be curtailed or even banned by states. Under Roe's rules, states could not regulate abortion in the first trimester. In the second trimester, states could regulate abortion in order to safeguard the health of the pregnant woman but could not ban abortion. In the third trimester, because the Court felt states did have an interest in potential life at some point during a pregnancy, states could go so far as to ban abortion, but only if those bans included an exception for the life and health of the pregnant woman. This was the most protective the US Supreme Court would ever be of abortion rights.

By 1992, the Court decided that its previous decisions had given insufficient weight to the state interest in potential life. That interest, declared the Court, began at the very start of a pregnancy. As such, the Court determined that the trimester framework could not stand and shifted to a viability standard. Under this new standard, states could limit or ban abortion access at the point of viability, again, as long as those bans included an exception for the life or health of the pregnant person. Viability for these purposes was fixed around the twenty-third or twenty-fourth week of gestation, so Mississippi's fifteen-week-ban was a direct assault on what was then existing law. The conservative majority of the Supreme Court wasted no time in using the *Dobbs* case to overrule *Roe* and *Casey*, which immediately ended federal constitutional protection for the right to an abortion.

When the Court's decision came down, there were patients sitting at Jackson Women's Health Organization, the last abortion clinic in Mississippi, waiting to receive abortions. These women had already decided whether to remain pregnant or abort their pregnancy, but staff at The Pink House, the nickname for the clinic, which was located in a large pink building, had to share the difficult and likely shocking news that Jackson Women's Health could no longer provide them with the reproductive health care they desired that day (Crowe). Instead, they would need to remain pregnant, find the resources and wherewithal to leave the state for an abortion, attempt to self-manage an abortion, or find an abortion provider in the state who was willing to break the law. Later, the clinic reopened briefly to continue to provide abortions in a short window before the state's ban went into full effect. Unfortunately, for those women who were unable to find an alternative source of abortion care, there were potentially many consequences of losing access to legal abortions.

The hours, days, weeks, and months after *Dobbs* brought a seismic shift in the reproductive futures of women and other people capable of pregnancy in the United States, with particularly harsh outcomes for the most vulnerable women. It is not necessary to speculate on what outcomes might befall a woman unable to get a desired abortion because a significant study was already conducted that shows what it can mean in a woman's life to bear a child because of a lack of access to abortion care. The Turnaway study—a ten-year study of women who wanted an abortion and got one as compared to women who wanted an abortion and were turned away—revealed several negative outcomes for those women who remained pregnant despite their desire for an abortion.

As described by the study author, "Continued pregnancy and childbirth is associated with large physical health risks, so great that two women in [the] study died from childbirth-related causes [and] [m]any others experienced complications from delivery and, extending over the next five years, increased chronic head and joint pain, hypertension, and poorer self-rated overall health" (Foster 2020, 22). Unsurprisingly, the consequences of being turned away from an abortion were not just the physical manifestations of pregnancy and its discomforts and risks. Women denied wanted abortions also "experienced increased anxiety and loss of life satisfaction . . . and those with violent partners found it difficult to extricate themselves after the birth" (Foster 2020,

22). Similarly, being denied an abortion had predictable economic consequences for women in the Turnaway study, as "[o]ver the next several years, [these women] experienced economic hardships not experienced by women who received their wanted abortions" (Foster 2020, 22).

What happens to women who are unable to have wanted abortions is crucial to considerations about the ethics of abortion access in the United States and beyond. The implications of abortion bans are physical, psychological, and economic, and should not be understated in favor of rhetoric about the joys of pregnancy or parenthood. It is vital to understand these implications not in a hypothetical world, in which every pregnancy is wanted, every pregnant person has an easy pregnancy, all new parents are financially and emotionally stable and adequately housed, and every new mother has a deep network of support upon the birth of her child. Instead, understanding the ethical implications of radically restricting access to abortion in the United States demands an analysis steeped in the realities of the lives of women in the United States, especially women of color, poor women, adolescents, undocumented immigrants, incarcerated women, and others whose life circumstances may be deeply incompatible with having a child. For these and other especially vulnerable pregnant people, any examination devoid of the conditions under which they make decisions about pregnancy, childbearing, and parenting fails them and those who seek to understand and theorize about the broad ethical implications of abortion law and policy.

Analyzing the Impact of *Dobbs* through a Reproductive Justice Lens

Several ethical schools of thought can be brought to bear on a discussion about abortion politics and practice in the United States, but this chapter will be framed around the concept of reproductive justice (RJ). Black women founded the RJ movement in the mid-1990s as a corrective to the mainstream reproductive rights movement. That mainstream movement, typically led by white women with class privilege, was deeply fixated on issues of "choice," especially in the context of abortion, but much less focused in any sustained way on the needs and experiences of marginalized women, including low-income Black women (Ross and Solinger 2017). The RJ movement was deliberately created to be more expansive, more inclusive, and more grassroots than the large national organizations that so often set the agenda for the entirety of the reproductive rights movement in the United States.

The RJ frame implicitly and explicitly draws on many schools of ethical and critical legal thought that are relevant to the conversation about regulating reproduction, including access to reproductive health care, and family life. In its most capacious form, Loretta Ross, a founding mother of the movement, defines RJ as "the complete physical, mental, spiritual, political, social and economic well-being of women and girls, based on the full achievement and protection of women's human rights" (Ross 2006). That RJ is a human rights–based movement is deeply meaningful in a constitutional order like the United States, in which human rights are not thought to bear much relevance to constitutional rights. By steeping RJ in human rights, its founders ensured that their movement would be concerned with what is owed to human beings simply by virtue of their existence rather than as a benefit or burden of citizenship, place of birth, or present location.

In addition to being based on human rights, RJ is explicitly intersectional, as law professor Kimberlé Crenshaw originally defined it. Crenshaw's articulation of intersectionality is a logical extension of work that has long been done by Black feminist scholars, focusing on the unique positioning of Black women in a world in which discussions about race have typically focused on men, and discussions about sex or gender have typically focused on white women. Intersectionality—and RJ, by extension—focuses on ways in which intersecting identities have an impact on how an individual or community experiences reproductive oppression (Crenshaw 1989).

As used in this chapter, "reproductive oppression" broadly refers to ways in which the government and private actors use and have used reproduction and parenting as sites for pursuing discriminatory, degrading, and dehumanizing treatment of people of color, especially Black and brown people in general, and, specifically, women of color. Forms of reproductive oppression include the sexual violence and loss of control of childbearing and child raising perpetrated against Black women during slavery in the United States; forced or coerced sterilizations of poor Black women and girls in the American South and Chicanas on the West Coast; the dehumanizing and dangerous shackling of incarcerated pregnant women during labor; criminal punishment for women accused of using illicit drugs during pregnancy or of attempting to self-abort; and overutilization of the child welfare system to break up Black families. There are many more examples of reproductive oppression, but the preceding list gives a sense of the breadth of attacks against parenting and procreation by those who the white majority in the United States deem inferior.

The RJ movement rests on three central human rights: the right to have a child, the right to not have a child, and the right to parent one's children in safe and healthy environments (Ross and Solinger 2019, 9). As such, the portfolio of issues that fall within the purview of RJ is broad, including: housing justice, because one cannot parent children safely without secure and affordable housing; criminal justice reform, because Black and brown communities cannot survive when they are over-policed and over-incarcerated; environmental justice, because the health of children, parents, and their communities is compromised when environmental hazards disproportionately appear in communities made up of a majority of people of color and/or low-income; restructuring of the deeply biased child welfare system in the United States, in which Black and brown children are starkly overrepresented and parents are often punished for poverty rather than the abuse or neglect of their children; and the end of coercive sterilization practices that were used in the past, and, unfortunately, into the modern moment, to support eugenics goals related to who "deserves" to procreate or parent; and much more.

While rights are a necessary component of RJ, they are not the single or central locus of the movement, because rights without more typically benefits those who already have power (Mutcherson 2017). Within the RJ frame, rights are instrumental and integral, but they cannot stand alone. RJ fights for the ability to actually benefit from rights in one's lived experience, which means demanding access to the tools that allow people to exercise agency in parenting and procreation, which often requires government support, including financial support. RJ activists also engage in the vital work of empowering communities and individuals to be their own advocates, and to build the living and work spaces that allow them to raise children in safe and healthy environments, in keeping with RJ's primary tenets. Even while recognizing the limitations of rights, those fighting for RJ cannot afford to completely jettison the need for rights. As one legal scholar explained, "Our scholarship as politics must be engaged at a practical, immediate level. . . . We have no choice but to take rights aggressively while we buy the time needed to perfect new weapons out of the materials at hand provided by our insurrectionist discursive traditions" (Williams 1987).

The justice and human rights components of RJ recognize both the expansiveness of rights related to procreation and the need to shift away from a paradigm of choice that assumes that the only barrier to exercising choice is governmental interference. This notion of rights is in keeping with the US Constitution, which is primarily focused not on what the government owes to its people, but what the government cannot do to its people. RJ, however, recognizes the crucial need for positive obligations for those who sit in positions of power. In the case of RJ, those positive obligations could include providing clean and safe affordable housing; high-quality child care; access to expensive infertility treatments; funding for abortions for poor women; protection against pregnancy discrimination in workplaces and educational institutions; and radical reform of the criminal justice system. These, of course, are but a small slice of what a government could or should do to help people realize their reproductive and familial desires, but any one of them would be a good start.

RJ discourse also incorporates feminist theory by surfacing and explaining how law and policy subordinate women, while still recognizing that law is part of the quest for sex equality (West 2019, 1). Also, like feminist theory, RJ is "both descriptive and critical on one hand, and normative and aspirational on the other" (West 2019, 1). It shines a light on the reproductive wrongs that have long plagued the United States, and how law and policy have been integral to, but not solely responsible for, those wrongs. At the same time, RJ imagines a better world in which by using a variety of tools, including law, those who are without power can come to wield it, and those who wield power can use it to right the wrongs of the past and present and build a future free of reproductive oppression. Importantly, by its commitment to intersectionality and looking to the bottom, RJ avoids the trap of feminist theory being synonymous with discussions of the experiences of white women (Lorde 1989, 94–101).

Further, RJ operates on the same plane as movements to bring many more voices to the forefront of discussions of health law, public health, and bioethics in the United States. RJ, like other movements for diversifying scholarly voices, recognizes that law is a central site of both resistance to racism and its perpetuation. As Goodwin and Lynch explain, "[L]aw and racism are deeply intertwined, with legal tools bearing the potential to be wielded as both instruments of racial oppression and [a] means to promote racial equity" (Goodwin and Lynch 2022). Thus, law reform must be a part of any discourse on RJ.

Laying out the expectations and contours of RJ is necessary in order to describe how an RJ-centered analysis considers what has happened in the United States in the wake of *Dobbs*. While the immediate impacts on abortion access are deeply concerning and problematic, RJ provides a wider lens through which to see how abortion is one spoke in a wheel of reproductive impacts that flow from *Dobbs* and what has followed that decision.

Dobbs as an Obstacle to Reproductive Justice

The US Supreme Court's *Dobbs* decision has been a disaster for RJ. In a single decision in which the majority of justices barely acknowledged the reality of pregnancy or the realities of women's lives, the Supreme Court blithely discarded a right that it had established as fundamental in 1973. The decision returned the issue of abortion legality to the states, giving state legislators essentially free rein to regulate abortion as each state legislature saw fit, and in keeping with their own state constitutions, which inevitably led to a patchwork of legality that has bred chaos and confusion for patients and health-care practitioners (Fuentes 2023). In the short term, in some states trigger laws already on the books went into effect, making abortion immediately, or almost immediately, illegal (Fuentes 2023). In other states, the path to blocking access has been more circuitous, but the flurry of legislation and litigation that was certain after *Dobbs* has had the wholly foreseeable impact of making life even more difficult for the already most vulnerable among us, as proven by data.

According to the Guttmacher Institute, in the first one hundred days after *Dobbs*, "at least 66 clinics in 15 states stopped providing abortion care, many closing down altogether. That means 29 percent of the total US population of women of reproductive age [were] living in states where abortion is either unavailable or severely restricted. And more than 10,000 people were unable to access abortion care at a facility in just the first two months after the decision" (Fuentes 2023). The researchers estimate that half of the states are "certain or likely to eventually enact abortion bans now that *Roe v. Wade* has been overturned" (Fuentes 2023). This means that an enormous number of women of reproductive age will not have abortion access in their home states.

At the most basic level, *Dobbs* strips autonomy from a huge swath of women and other pregnant people who do not wish to carry pregnancies to term. The autonomy in this context is relational autonomy rather than the cramped, male-centric notion of autonomy that long dominated the worlds of ethics, philosophy, and law (Nedelsky 2012, 118). Relational autonomy as used in this chapter is "not to be equated with independence" (Nedelsky 2012, 118). Rather, "Autonomy is made possible by constructive relationships—including intimate, cultural, institutional, national, global, and ecological forms of relationship—all of which interact" (Nedelsky 2012, 118). To be more specific in the context of health-care access, "relational autonomy allows us to look beyond formal informed consent and acknowledge the reality that each individual choice—about reproductive healthcare, healthcare more generally, and other matters related to health—occurs within a complex web of personal and societal relationships, pressures, and obligations" (Mohapatra and Wiley 2019).

For this reason, a discussion about abortion is never just about abortion. It is about relationships between partners and between health-care providers and patients. It is about economic realities and porous social safety nets. It is about the lack of paid parental leave in the United States and the difficulty of finding affordable, high-quality child care. It is about pregnancy discrimination and thwarted life plans. It is about controlling the size of one's family and reproductive coercion and control by abusive partners. To understand the decisions that women make about abortion, one must also seek to understand the networks of connectivity that drive that decision-making.

To the extent that an element of autonomy is synonymous with the idea of individuals being able to make their own considered choices about their bodies and reproductive futures, understanding that those decisions are not made in a vacuum, *Dobbs* was impactful; however, the shift that it created was not seismic in the sense that choice had long been constrained for many women and pregnant people in the United States. The long-standing Hyde Amendment meant that poor women on Medicaid, except in a narrow set of circumstances, could not use government dollars to pay for abortions (Congressional Research Service 2023). Many states passed laws that increased the burdens on those seeking abortion care, called TRAP laws, or Targeted Regulation of Abortion Providers. These laws included unnecessary requirements like waiting periods, multiple visits to clinics, mandatory ultrasounds, biased informed consent, admitting privilege requirements for providers, and onerous regulation of the physical spaces in which abortions could be performed (Gold and Nash 2013). Lawmaking of this sort has predictably ramped up since *Dobbs*, with states creating gestational limits on abortion that, in some cases, will mean that a woman has almost no opportunity to access abortion even if it is ostensibly available and legal in her state (Kaiser Family Foundation 2023).

The importance of recognizing relational autonomy in abortion care is especially crucial given the demographics of women who have abortions in the United States. Most of those women are young (in their twenties), most already have a child or children at home, and women of color, especially Black women, are overrepresented in the statistics on those who seek abortion care (Kaiser Family Foundation 2023). Abortion in the United States also tends to be concentrated among women who are low-income (Boonstra 2016). Thus, the decision-making around abortion happens not in a void, but often in consultation with family and friends who create a support network, and takes into account how a pregnancy and another child will impact am existing child or children and the stability of a family; how or whether there is access to an adequate social safety net if the pregnant person will need some sort of assistance, often financial, from the government in order to sustain herself and her children; and whether access to abortion care is feasible given the laws in place in any given jurisdiction.

There is also overlap between autonomy and beneficence/nonmaleficence in this context because of the ways in which post-*Dobbs* rules impact the provider–patient relationship. Some, but not all, abortion bans or laws severely restricting abortion contain an exception for medical emergencies that creates a need to act to save the life of the pregnant person. This should allow medical providers, not state legislators, to use their discretion in deciding when they should provide needed abortion care in spite of a general ban on the procedure. In practice, however, the meaning of those exceptions has been unclear to many of the health-care providers who should be able to use them to provide needed abortion care to their patients. Faced with the risk of losing their license to practice medicine, or even receiving a prison sentence for performing an abortion not authorized by law, since *Dobbs*, there have been several heart-wrenching stories reported in media outlets about women denied standard abortion care to manage miscarriages due to fears about liability for providers (McCammon 2023). Rather than being offered a D&C to empty their uterus of a nonviable fetus, women are being sent home to bleed and deal with painful miscarriages causing them both physical and emotional damage. Some women are being kept in hospitals until no fetal cardiac activity can be detected, even as the women themselves risk harm from potential infections.

The consequences of ill-defined medical exceptions go beyond miscarriage mismanagement. For instance, as a direct consequence of opaque medical exceptions in existing state abortion statutes, physicians and other health-care providers must understand whether a woman who needs cancer treatment can terminate a pregnancy in order to begin the treatment that might save her own life, or whether preserving a patient's fertility is an adequate reason to move forward with an abortion of a fetus that cannot survive. Some physicians may be met with the dilemma of whether they can perform a selective reduction, a procedure that terminates some fetal life in a multifetal pregnancy in order to preserve the life or health of the fetus and/or the pregnant woman.

In these scenarios, rather than acting based solely on the professional standard of care and in consultation with patients, health-care providers feel forced to make decisions based on consultations with lawyers. This kind of interference with the provider–patient relationship would seldom, if ever, be tolerated in other circumstances. In such cases, a health-care provider who seeks to act in the best interest of her patient or to avoid doing harm to her patient is, instead, obliged to choose between violating a criminal law or violating her professional obligation to her patient—a choice for which there are no easy answers, and one that no health-care provider should have to make.

The relationship between provider and patient is potentially compromised in other ways as well. For instance, a provider might feel compelled to recommend long-acting or even permanent forms of birth control to patients in a state where abortion will not be an option if a woman becomes pregnant. Providers may find themselves struggling with whether they have an obligation to report a patient to the police if she presents for care and the provider suspects that she has attempted to self-manage an abortion (Aspinwall, Bailer, Yurkanin 2022). The carceral and child welfare implications of physicians and other health-care providers acting as agents of the state to turn in their patients for suspected criminal behavior has deep implications for whether and with whom patients access care, and, in turn, can have negative consequences on a fetus when a pregnant woman avoids prenatal care for fear of adverse treatment by her health-care provider.

Similarly, when an abortion is followed by criminal punishment for the formerly pregnant woman, or when her health-care team reports her to child welfare authorities, the collateral consequences for her, her family, and her community can be significant.

She could spend time in prison or jail. She could lose custody of her existing children and see them sent to foster care. She could lose her job because of absences. She could lose her housing because she cannot pay bills without a job. If she is an immigrant, she could lose her lawful status in the United States, and if she is an undocumented immigrant, she could be deported to a country where she would not be safe. The ability to control reproductive futures is about so much more than just being able to access safe and legal abortion care.

Concerns about maternal morbidity and mortality are also relevant to the ability to make autonomous choices and to the relationship between provider and patient. The United States has the highest maternal mortality rate of all developed nations (Gunja, Gumas, and Williams 2022). That rate is even higher for Black women (Hoyert 2023). Given this reality, the inability to make choices about continuing a pregnancy is even more invasive. Sadly, but not surprisingly, the states with the highest rates of maternal morbidity and mortality and infant mortality tend to be the same states that have already effectively banned abortion or are working toward such a ban in the near future (Vilda, Wallace, Daniel, Evans, Stoecker and Theall 2021). These states also have high rates of poverty, weak access to health care, dreadful public education outcomes, and high rates of unemployment. It is hypocrisy of the highest order to claim an allegiance to life given these concrete examples of life—or at least a life with a basic level of quality—not being prioritized or pursued at all.

The resurgence of fetal personhood in the wake of *Dobbs* is also crucial because of its implications for the lives of women and other pregnant people, as well as their families and communities. The goal of treating fetuses as persons has long been a not-so-secret part of the anti-choice agenda in the United States (Ziegler 2022). Often, those who espouse fetal personhood fail to take serious account of the reality of "fetal geography" (Little 1999). Rather, these actors focus on the fetus as though it is atomistic. In their reality, the survival of a fetus is paramount to the consequences of pregnancies for those women, whose bodies must be conscripted into any project that seeks to ban access to abortion. Those consequences include the physical and emotional toll that pregnancy takes on a body, the potential for loss of employment or wages, the risk of violence or manipulation for women in relationships in which there is intimate partner violence, or the interruption of other life plans like pursuing higher education or other forms of training.

Justice Amy Coney Barrett made manifest this belief of a fetus as a separate individual and pregnancy as not burdensome or, at worst, a slight burden during the oral argument of *Dobbs*, during which she pursued a line of questioning positing that safe haven laws and adoption were viable alternatives that should lessen the need for a pregnant woman to choose abortion. As one commentator succinctly explained, "For Barrett, because safe-haven laws allow women to terminate parental rights, they 'take care of the problem.' The safe-haven laws, Barrett claims, allow women to participate in the full life of society in the same manner as men. Parenting is the burden in need of relief rather than pregnancy" (Phelan 2022).

Barrett's bizarre line of questioning raised serious concerns about her understanding of the risks of pregnancy and her knowledge about the pros and cons of adoption in a country where thousands of Black and brown children languish in foster care.

First, as already described, pregnancy can be filled with peril in the United States, especially for Black women. Further, even the best pregnancies will be disruptive to the pregnant person's life. Second, the choice to place a child for adoption is not one that pregnant women make easily. In fact, over 90 percent of women who carry a pregnancy to term despite a desire to have an abortion will keep the child to whom they give birth (Trent 2022). Barrett not only fundamentally and inexcusably "underestimates the legal, emotional, and psychological complexities of terminating parental rights" (Phelan 2022), she also seems to lack any sense of the social and psychological impact that adoption can have on children who are not raised in their families of origin (Smit 2002).

Conclusion

As described by Ross and Solinger, "At the heart of reproductive justice is this claim: all fertile persons and persons who reproduce and become parents require a safe and dignified context for these most fundamental human experiences" (Ross and Solinger 2017, 9). Reproductive justice cannot be obtained without a concerted and sustained commitment to supporting the conditions that must be met in order for justice to exist. Women and others with the capacity for pregnancy must be able to make and effectuate choices about their reproductive futures based on their wants and desires; their access to resources, including resources provided by the state; and their existing responsibilities. Women and the children they bring into the world deserve better than to be pitted against each other when a viable path forward, rooted in RJ, is available to policymakers willing to think more deeply about what it means to choose life.

References

"Abortion Policy Tracker." Accessed May 13, 2023. https://www.kff.org/other/state-indicator/abortion-policy-tracker/?currentTimeframe=0&sortModel=%7B%22colId%22:%22Location%22,%22sort%22:%22asc%22%7D.

Aspinwall, Cary, Brianna Bailey, and Amy Yurkanin. "They Lost their Pregnancies. then Prosecutors Sent them to Prison." *The Marshall Project*. September 1, 2022. https://www.themarshallproject.org/2022/09/01/they-lost-their-pregnancies-then-prosecutors-sent-them-to-prison.

Boonstra, Heather. "Abortion in the Lives of Women Struggling Financially: Why Insurance Coverage Matters." Accessed May 2023. https://www.guttmacher.org/gpr/2016/07/abortion-lives-women-struggling-financially-why-insurance-coverage-matters.

Crenshaw, Kimberlé. "Demarginalizing the Intersection of Race and Sex: A Black Feminist Critique of Antidiscrimination Doctrine, Feminist Theory and Antiracist Politics." *University of Chicago Legal Forum* 1989, no. 1: 139–67.

———. "Demarginalizing the Intersection of Race and Sex: A Black Feminist Critique of Antidiscrimination Doctrine, Feminist Theory and Antiracist Politics." *Living with Contradictions* 1989 (March 8, 2018): 39. doi:10.4324/9780429499142-5.

Crow, Maise. "The Pink House at the Center of the World." Accessed May 13, 2023. https://www.thisamericanlife.org/774/the-pink-house-at-the-center-of-the-world.

Dobbs v. Jackson Women's Health Organization, 597 U.S. (2022).

Foster, Diana Greene. *The Turnaway Study: Ten Years, a Thousand Women, and the Consequences of Having—Or Being Denied—an Abortion*. New York: Scribner, 2020.

Fuentes, Liza. "Inequity in US Abortion Rights and Access: The End of *Roe* is Deepening Existing Divides." Accessed May 13, 2023. https://www.guttmacher.org/2023/01/inequity-us-abortion-rights-and-access-end-roe-deepening-existing-divides.

Gold, Rachel Benson, and Elizabeth Nash. "TRAP Laws Gain Political Traction while Abortion Clinics—and the Women they Serve—Pay the Price." *Guttmacher Policy Review* 16, no. 2 (June 25, 2013). https://www.guttmacher.org/gpr/2013/06/trap-laws-gain-political-traction-while-abortion-clinics-and-women-they-serve-pay-price.

Goodwin, Michele, and Holly Fernandez Lynch. "Introduction: Health Law and Anti-Racism: Reckoning and Response." *Journal of Law, Medicine & Ethics* 50, no. 1 (2022a): 10–14. doi:10.1017/jme.2022.3. https://www.cambridge.org/core/article/introduction-health-law-and-antiracism-reckoning-and-response/763FF7FD2DA62935B208D504613FB940.

———. "Introduction: Health Law and Anti-Racism: Reckoning and Response." *The Journal of Law, Medicine & Ethics* 50, no. 1 (2022b): 10–14. doi:10.1017/jme.2022.3. https://www.ncbi.nlm.nih.gov/pubmed/35243994.

Gunja, Munira Z., Evan D. Gumas, and Reginald D. Williams II. *The U.S. Maternal Mortality Crisis Continues to Worsen: An International Comparison.* Commonwealth Fund, 2022. https://www.commonwealthfund.org/blog/2022/us-maternal-mortality-crisis-continues-worsen-international-comparison

Hoyert, Donna L. "Maternal Mortality Rates in the United States, 2020." Accessed May 13, 2023. https://www.cdc.gov/nchs/data/hestat/maternal-mortality/2020/E-stat-Maternal-Mortality-Rates-2022.pdf.

Little, Margaret Olivia. "Abortion, Intimacy, and the Duty to Gestate." *Ethical Theory and Moral Practice* 2, no. 3: 295–312. doi:10.1023/A:1009955129773. https://www.jstor.org/stable/27504096.

Liu, Edward C., and Wen W. Shen. *The Hyde Amendment: An Overview*. Washington, DC: Congressional Research Service, 2022.

McCammon, Sarah. *5 Texas Women Denied Abortions Sue the State, Saying the Bans Put Them in Danger*. Washington, DC National Public Radio, Inc., 2023.

Mohapatra, Seema, and Lindsay F. Wiley. "Feminist Perspectives in Health Law." *Journal of Law, Medicine & Ethics* 47, no. S4 (2019): 103–15. doi:10.1177/1073110519898047. https://www.cambridge.org/core/article/feminist-perspectives-in-health-law/8E96686E000BC9933E8B6825A1152BB8.

Mutcherson, Kimberly. "Reproductive Rights without Resources or Recourse." *Hastings Center Report* 47 (2017): S12–S18. doi:10.1002/hast.790. https://doi.org/10.1002/hast.790.

Nedelsky, Jennifer. *Law's Relations: A Relational Theory of Self, Autonomy, and Law*. New York: Oxford University Press, 2012.

Phelan, Peggy. "The *Dobbs* Decision: Abortion, Adoption, and the Supreme Court." *Adoption & Culture* 10, no. 2: 171–83. doi:10.1353/ado.0.0001. https://muse.jhu.edu/article/881455.

Planned Parenthood v. Casey, 505 U.S. 833 (1992).

Ranji, Usha, Karen Diep, and Alina Salganicoff. *Key Facts on Abortion in the United States.* Kaiser Family Foundation, 2023.

Ross, Loretta. "Understanding Reproductive Justice: Transforming the Pro-Choice Movement." *Off Our Backs* 36, no. 4 (2006): 14–19.

Ross, Loretta, and Rickie Solinger. "A Reproductive Justice History." In *Reproductive Justice.* 1st ed. Vol. 1, 9. Oakland: University of California Press, 2017. doi:10.1525/j.ctv1wxsth.4. https://www.jstor.org/stable/10.1525/j.ctv1wxsth.4.

Sister Song. "The Herstory of Reproductive Justice (RJ)." Accessed May 13, 2023. https://www.sistersong.net/reproductive-justice.

Sister Song. "What Is Reproductive Justice?" Accessed May 13, 2023. https://www.sistersong.net/reproductive-justice.

Smit, Eileen M., MSN, RN. "Adopted Children: Core Issues and Unique Challenges." *Journal of Child and Adolescent Psychiatric Nursing* 15, no. 4 (October 2002): 143–50. doi:10.1111/j.1744-6171.2002.tb00389.x. https://api.istex.fr/ark:/67375/WNG-FPZ0D55T-F/fulltext.pdf.

Supreme Court of the United States. *Dobbs v. Jackson Women's Health Organization* (June 24, 2022). https://www.supremecourt.gov/opinions/21pdf/19-1392_6j37.pdf.

This Bridge Called My Back, Fortieth Anniversary Edition: Writings by Radical Women of Color, edited by Cherrie Moraga and Gloria Anzaldúa. Albany: State University of New York Press, 2021. http://ebookcentral.proquest.com/lib/rutgers-ebooks/detail.action?docID=6925936.

Trent, Sydney. "Women Denied Abortion Rarely Choose Adoption. That's Unlikely to Change." *Washington Post.com*, July 25, 2022. https://global.factiva.com/en/du/article.asp?accessionno=WPCOM000202207 18ei7i0018h.

Vilda, Dovile, Maeve E. Wallace, Clare Daniel, Melissa Goldin Evans, Charles Stoecker, and Katherine P. Theall. "State Abortion Policies and Maternal Death in the United States, 2015–2018." *American Journal of Public Health (1971)* 111, no. 9 (September 1, 2021): 1696–704. doi:10.2105/AJPH.2021.306396. https://search.proquest.com/docview/2577535328.

West, Robin, and Cynthia Grant Bowman. *Research Handbook on Feminist Jurisprudence.* Cheltenham, UK: Edward Elgar Publishing Limited, 2019.

Williams, Robert A., Jr. "Taking Rights Aggressively: The Perils and Promise of Critical Legal Theory for Peoples of Color." *Law & Inequality* 5, no. 1 (May 1, 1987): 103. https://search.proquest.com/docview/1311903657.

Ziegler, Mary. "The Next Step in the Anti-Abortion Playbook is Becoming Clear." *New York Times* (Online), August 31, 2022. https://www.nytimes.com/2022/08/31/opinion/abortion-fetal-personhood.html?auth=login-google1tap&login=google1tap.

CHAPTER 16

Euthanasia Could Be a Medical Duty

Carlos Verdugo-Serna

Abstract

Most people, including philosophers and physicians, would be willing to accept that human beings have some sort of moral rights to live not only with the highest possible level of autonomy, dignity, liberty, and well-being, but also with the minimum level of unnecessary pain, suffering, distress, anguish, and physical or mental degrading conditions.

By accepting those rights, we can also claim that we have some duties to respect them and behave accordingly. In addition, since it is a fact that dying is part of the process of living, it is reasonable to believe that the rights and duties acknowledged above apply also to the process of living.

I will attempt to show that, when physicians, under some restricted conditions, bring about a patient's death, they are acting in compliance with the moral rights and duties mentioned earlier.

Introduction

In his influential paper "The Scientist qua Scientist Makes Value Judgments" (1953), the late American philosopher Richard Rudner said:

> The question of the relationship of making of value judgments in a typical ethical sense to the method and procedures of science has been discussed in the literature at least to that point which E. E. Cummings somewhere refers to as "The Mystical Moment of Dullness." Nevertheless, albeit with some trepidation, I feel that something more may fruitfully be said on the subject. (540)

I have to confess that I am in a similar position writing about the morality of euthanasia. Nevertheless, with some trepidation, I think I can add (hopefully) something relevant and fruitful to the age-old and still-vigorous euthanasia debate. Of course, I am fully aware that the very nature of philosophy and logic impedes giving conclusive arguments in "pro" or "con" of the morality of any form of assisted dying.

I also agree with Popper's idea that the method for dealing with philosophical problems, including, of course ethical problems, is the method of stating a problem as clearly as possible and then assessing any solutions critically. But this method does not allow us to reach definite and conclusive true answers to our problems. In philosophy and science, all of our intended solutions are conjectural and can never be proved to be true.

Nevertheless, this does not imply that we have to abandon our search for truth in philosophy or science. We have only to accept, following Popper, that we do not have criteria for truth (i.e., for proving that we have reached truth), and that for logical reasons we can never prove that we are justified claiming that we have the right answers to some questions, especially in the field of philosophy. According to Popper, there exist no general criteria of truth, not only in the realm of facts, but also in the realm of values and standards or proposals, including moral ones:

> For though we should seek for absolutely right or valid proposals, we should never persuade ourselves that we have definitely found them, for clearly, there cannot be a *criterion of absolute rightness*—even less than a criterion of absolute truth. . . . But although we have no criterion of absolute rightness, we certainly can make progress in this realm. As in the realm of facts, we can make discoveries. That cruelty is always "bad"; that it should always be avoided where possible; that the golden rule is a good standard which can perhaps even be improved by doing unto others, wherever possible, as *they* want to be done by: these are elementary and extremely important examples of discoveries in the realm of standards. (2013, 501)

I also want to indicate that we cannot simply abandon the use of arguments in dealing with some moral questions, but only that it is very important to learn what are the functions, possibilities, and limits of arguments or inferences in general. The next section will be devoted to expanding briefly these working observations.

Logical–Methodological Preliminaries

Let's start by first remembering that, as a matter of simple elementary logic, we know that, in any valid deductive arguments, if the truth of a conclusion R logically follows from assuming the truth of premises P and Q, then we have to also accept that, if R is false (-R), then it is not possible that all premises are true.

For example, if we accept the truth of the following premises:

> P: All forms of intentionally killing firstborn children by humans or God are inherently morally wrong.
>
> Q: God killed all the firstborn Egyptians.

We can therefore conclude:

> R: God did something inherently morally wrong.

Now, if someone does not want to accept the truth of the conclusion, he/she could also formulate the following valid deductive argument:

> -R: It is false that God did something inherently morally wrong.
>
> Q: God killed all the firstborn Egyptians.

Therefore:

> -P: It is false that all forms of killing newborn children are inherently morally wrong.

An additional and deeper difficulty with giving conclusive arguments in general is the known fact that it can be shown that valid deductive arguments are circular: The truth of the conclusion has already been accepted in the premises; that is, they assume what they are trying to prove or are supposed to prove.

This important logical point has been noted by David Miller (2006) in *Out of Error: Further Essays on Critical Rationalism*:

> Since, as Mill noted, the conclusion of every valid syllogism, indeed of every valid argument, is included entirely within its premises, the premises cannot lend any weight at all to the conclusion. At an everyday level we may say that any purported proof or justification is *circular*, that is, *begs the question at issue*, or in a more philosophical jargon, commits the fallacy of *petitio principia* . . . if the premises of a deductive valid argument are not already proved, the argument will be insufficient to prove the conclusion (this is the objection of classical scepticism); but if the premises are already proved, then the conclusion, being a part of the premises, is also proved (though admittedly we need an argument to make this obvious to us). (70)

Nevertheless, there are two uses of arguments that will be relevant and fruitful for the ensuing discussion on the morality of euthanasia: Valid deductive arguments or inferences, as in formal and empirical theories, allow us to identify the logical consequences of what we assume to be true. Another use of arguments in deductive logic has been remarked on by Popper (1975):

> We can say: if all the premises are true and the inference is valid, then the conclusion *must* also be true; and if, consequently, the conclusion is false in a valid inference, then it is not possible that all the premises are true. In this way deductive logic becomes the theory of rational criticism. For all rational criticism takes the form of an attempt to show that unacceptable conclusions can be derived from the assertion we are trying to criticize. If we are successful in deriving, logically, unacceptable conclusions from an assertion, the assertion may be taken to be refuted. (98–99)

In other words, the role of logical arguments in deductive logic is to be the *organon* of criticism and should not to be taken as an instrument allowing us to prove or justify our theories in science or philosophy.

All of these considerations will show their importance in the analysis and assessment of arguments against or in favor of the morality of euthanasia.

Arguments against Euthanasia

In an article entitled "The Wrongfulness of Euthanasia," bioethicist J. Gay-Williams gives three arguments to show that euthanasia is morally wrong: a) the argument from nature; b) the argument from self-interest; and c) the argument from practical effects. Even though I think there are serious flaws in these arguments, I will concentrate my criticism on the first one.

THE ARGUMENT FROM NATURE

This argument is an attempt to show that euthanasia is inherently wrong and should be rejected because it violates the natural propensity to preserve our life (i.e., it is unnatural). Let's quote the argument:

> Every human being has a natural inclination to continue living. Our reflexes and responses fit us to fight attackers, flee wild animals, and dodge out of the ways of trucks. In our daily lives we exercise the caution and care necessary to protect ourselves. Our bodies are similarly structured for survival right down to the molecular level. When we are cut, our capillaries seal shut, our blood clots, and fibrogen is produced to start the process of healing the wound. When we are invaded by bacteria, antibodies are produced to fight against the alien organisms, and their remains are swept out of the body by special cells. Euthanasia does violence to this natural goal of survival. It is literally acting against nature because all the processes of nature are bent towards the end of bodily survival. . . . By reason alone, then, we can recognize that euthanasia sets us against our own nature. (Gay-Williams 1987, 57–58)

It seems that, according to this quotation, Gay-Williams is formulating the following argument:

1. Every human being has a natural inclination to preserve their life or to continue living (premise).
2. Euthanasia acts against nature and sets us against our own nature (premise).
3. Therefore, euthanasia is morally wrong.

But this argument cannot be accepted. First, clearly, this argument is not an instance of a valid deductive argument. Even if the premises were true, the conclusion would not necessarily be true. Why? Because the information content of the conclusion is wider than the content of the premises. To imply the conclusion, you need to add another premise, such as

4. Everything that acts against nature and sets us against our own nature is morally wrong.

However, if Gay-Williams wants to claim that this premise is true, he would have to accept very undesirable consequences, among them that all self-sacrificial deaths would be morally wrong. It seems awkward to claim that firemen, soldiers, and policemen, when putting their lives at risk and thereby acting against their natural inclination to preserve their own lives and to continue living, are doing something morally wrong.

On the other hand, if he were trying, on the basis of premises 1 and 2, to infer the normative conclusion "We should not practice euthanasia" or "We have the moral duty to reject euthanasia" or "We ought not to perform euthanasia," he would be guilty of deriving a normative conclusion from descriptive premises (i.e., from premises stating facts). (Hume in the eighteenth century made the straightforward logical remark that no ought-statements are logically deducible from only factual are-statements.)

A similar criticism concerning the problem of *prima facie* unacceptable consequences of some premises can be applied to an argument against euthanasia put forward by the late Chilean philosopher Dr. Alfonzo Gomez-Lobo (1940–2011), who held the Ryan Chair in Metaphysics and Moral Philosophy at Georgetown University, USA.

In his book entitled *Morality and the Human Goods: An Introduction to Natural Law Ethics* (2002), we find the following:

> For there to be a genuine case of euthanasia (or "mercy killing," as it used to be called), the agent must first intend the death of the person; this is the main immediate goal or point of his action. The agent also must have the further goal, however, of relieving a dying person of great suffering. Without this further goal, the action would be classified as murder. If a patient is in severe pain but is likely to recover soon, or terminally ill but not suffering pain, killing such a patient will hardly count as causing a good death. The alleged mercy is simply misplaced.
>
> In plausible cases of euthanasia, then, there is a conflict that becomes all the more acute if the pain becomes unbearable. Is that sufficient, however, to justify intentional killing? I argue that it is not. Here is the fundamental argument against active euthanasia (voluntary or otherwise):
>
> (Premise 1): Any act whose goal is intentionally to attack, harm, destroy an instance of a basic human good is irrational and morally wrong. (This is the guideline of respect for basic goods under the Formal Principle of practical reason. How seriously wrong the act is will depend on the prudentially determined importance of the good under attack.)
>
> (Premise 2): Life is a basic human good (the first supplementary principle of practical rationality).

(Premise 3): Active euthanasia is an action whose goal is intentionally to take the life of a terminally ill patient to alleviate great pain (definition of active euthanasia).
Conclusion: Active euthanasia is irrational and morally wrong.

Before evaluating this argument, it is important to understand exactly what he is asserting in premise 2, especially his use of the word "life." Here is Gomez-Lobo's (2002) definition:

> By "life" I mean here human life at the basic biological level, manifesting itself in the typical functions of a human organism (taking nourishment, growing, etc.). Whether a certain organism is human depends on whether it has the complete set of standard human chromosomes or a deviation therefrom that counts as a human genetic abnormality. An egg or a sperm by itself does not qualify. Neither of them, as we now know, has the complete set. (10, 101)

What can be said about this argument?

First, this argument is an instance of a valid deductive inference. If somebody accepts that the premises are true, then he/she has to accept that the conclusion is also true. (Although, as we know, a big debate still exists about the alleged truth or falsity of moral sentences; for the sake of our discussion, let's also agree that the argument is not valid but that it is sound.) As we emphasized before, a valid deductive argument is circular; therefore, you are assuming the truth of the conclusion has already been included in the premises. Thus, the truth of the premises cannot "justify" the truth of the conclusion.

Actually, we can formulate, as we also showed above, that we could put forward another instance of a valid deductive inference by affirming instead the falsity of the conclusion and therefore the falsity of at least one of the three premises accepted by Gomez-Lobo. In this case, I would claim that the first premise is false. Or, as we did before with the argument given by Gay-Williams, we can show that the first two premises seem to imply some consequences that are very difficult to accept.

Among these undesirable commonsense consequences we find that, according to these premises, war is irrational and morally wrong because it necessarily involves soldiers intending to kill human beings and, therefore, harming and destroying a basic good (i.e., life). Thus, it seems that we are obliged to be "absolute pacifists" for whom human life has an absolute value and therefore must not be destroyed. From this follows that we could not defend at all the moral justifications in favor of going to war, not even in the case of national self-defense.

A similar problem would face someone adopting a less extreme view about the morality of war. One of them, known as "limited pacifism," considers as morally wrong only wars involving the killing of innocent "noncombatants" (i.e., people who are not members of the armed forces). We have to also point out that just-war theorists, while strongly defending the value of human life, are at the same time willing to accept that, under some conditions, a country has a moral right to go to war. Additionally, certain police actions, self-defense, and capital punishment would also have to be rejected as immoral.

All of these consequences show that the first two premises of Gomez-Lobo's argument against euthanasia—claiming that life is a basic good and that any act whose goal is intentionally to attack, harm, or to destroy an instance of a basic good is irrational or morally wrong—should be rejected. I will argue later that euthanasia should also be seen as another important exception or example of *force majeure*.

Now, let's critically examine another rejection of voluntary active euthanasia based on the doctrine that putting to death is always wrong because all human life has an especial worth, or dignity (or sanctity), and should be preserved.

This doctrine, called "the inviolability of human life," seems to be behind the claim that doctors have an absolute prohibition against killing patients. An illustrative example of this strong position is Leon R. Kass's (2014) article "Why Doctors Must Not Kill." Therein, he says:

> In forswearing the giving of poison, *when asked for it*, the Hippocratic physician rejects the view that the patient's choice for death can make killing him—or assisting his suicide—right. For the physician, at least, human life in living bodies commands respect and reverence—*by its very nature*. As its respectability does not depend upon human agreement or patient consent, revocation on one's consent to live does not deprive one's living body of respectability. The deepest ethical principle of restraining the physician's power is not the autonomy or freedom of the patient; neither is its own compassion or good intention. Rather, it is the dignity and mysterious power of human life itself, and, therefore, also what the oath calls the purity and holiness of the life and art to which he has sworn devotion. (181–82)

We cannot in this short space deal in depth with the issue of the sanctity of life or the principle of the inviolability of human life. Nevertheless, I want to make a couple of short comments on this subject. It is rather difficult to understand what Kass means by "the dignity and mysterious power of human life itself." How do we understand the phrase "the dignity of human life itself"? What does he mean by "life"? And why "For the physician, at least, human life in living bodies commands respect and reverence—*by its very nature*"? Is he using this term in the same, or close to the same, sense that was used by Gomez-Lobo in his argument that we examined above (i.e., meaning the more basic biological functions)?

I think he does. Actually, Kass claims that our highest mental life and functions "are held up by, and are inseparable from, lowly metabolism, respiration, circulation, excretion" (Kass 2014, 182). Unfortunately, he did not provide any philosophical reasons for his claim on the "dignity and mysterious powers of human life itself."

Nevertheless, what is really surprising and difficult to understand is the fact that most of the people who strongly support the thesis or the principle of an intrinsic, inviolable value, dignity, sacredness of life, or a right to life principle, normally stress just the wrongfulness of killing. The question is, why stress only or mainly the medical duty of not killing, instead of the duty to do everything possible to save a patient's life? If life is so precious, it is a basic human good, has an intrinsic value, and is inviolable and even sacred. Why not act to protect and save it under all conditions and circumstances, or to prolong it by all possible means?

This is the way that Gomez-Lobo and Keown (2015) answer this question when dealing with patients in a persistent vegetative state:

> So, if the "right to die" means a right to end one's life, to commit suicide by refusing life-prolonging treatment, it should be rejected. Or does the phrase connote a right to resist medical obstinacy or vitalism? Does it mean a right to resist doctors who, forgetful that the core purpose of medicine is to restore patients to health, practice "meddlesome medicine" and try to preserve life at all costs, even by way of clearly disproportionate treatments that impose excessive burden on the patient or her family? If this is what the "right to die" means, it is a legitimate right. (85)

Both philosophers support a natural law perspective on bioethics, and they emphasize that their ethical claims and arguments are based on reason alone. A similar position has been defended by the Catholic Church. Talking about the Bland case, the late Cardinal Winning said in an interview in 1999 that "To give someone antibiotics in a vegetative state, with no prospect of recovery, was extraordinary and, one would say, unnecessary. Perhaps he could have been left to die on several occasions."

Thus, it is clear that concerning bioethics, a natural law perspective is common to some philosophers and religious people, such as the Catholic Church. But it is more important for our discussion to realize that some of those who defend the principle of the sanctity and inviolability of life also admit additional limitations in its application.

First, even though life can be considered a basic good and human life is invaluable, doctors are not morally obliged to maintain this good at all cost. Second, according to the Catholic Church, sometimes, killing a human being can be morally legitimate, as in Cardinal Winning's (1999) words: "Human life is invaluable, innocent human life is inviolable and the only time the state can take human life is to right an injustice—in other words when somebody's committed a crime where the punishment is death" (142).

Clearly, according to Cardinal Winning, killing somebody can be a morally legitimate means "to right an injustice." We also have to remember that there is another morally justified killing, not only for the Catholic Church, but also for very important supporters of natural law ethics, such as Thomas Aquinas. He is often cited as saying, "He who kills a tyrant to free his country is praised and rewarded" (Aquinas, *II Sentences*, 44.2.2., cited by Harty 2012).

With all these exceptions, it seems odd that many people, including doctors, religious believers, and lawyers, who defend normative moral claims such as "We have the moral duty to reject euthanasia," "We ought not to perform euthanasia," "Doctors must not kill," or "We are always morally culpable for killing someone," could support those claims appealing to a strict and absolute understanding of the principles of the "sanctity of life" or the "right to life."

Following, I argue that, contrary to the claim that a right to life makes euthanasia morally wrong, the right to life principle—when human life is understood far beyond the basic biological level—actually makes euthanasia not only a morally permissible medical act, but, more importantly, under certain conditions, it could be considered a medical duty.

Arguments for Euthanasia

One of the most common arguments advanced in favor of euthanasia is the existence of a "right to die," or a right to choose death. Thus, it is argued that, if we have such rights, euthanasia and physician-assisted suicide are morally permissible. Now, due to the empirical biological fact that death is an inevitable event for any living animal, including human animals, it seems to be quite odd to fight or defend this right. We are going to die anyway.

On the other hand, there are not many possibilities of how to die to choose from, with the exception of a few cases, such as committing suicide; sacrificing your life for your family so they can access a lifeboat (as we saw in the movie *Titanic* as it was sinking); or, in some war scenarios, such as leading an assault on a fortified enemy position. Nevertheless, you can sometimes choose how you want to go through the process of dying, the ending of one's life by death. In this case, you can claim that other people have the moral obligation to respect your autonomous and deliberate decision about some form of dying; for example, if you want to die without receiving a blood transfusion that would save your life.

What I want to claim is that such a right to choose how to die should be included within the right to live (i.e., with the right to choose how we should live our own life).

I think that most people would accept that we have a right to live with the highest possible level of self-determination or autonomy; of freedom from any kind of unlegitimate or unjustified coercion; and with the best possible functioning of our physical, psychological, emotional, and intellectual capacities. Of course, we also firmly believe that we have a right to live without unnecessary pain, suffering, and anguish, and also with the least degrading and humiliating conditions.

Thus, I want to propose accepting that, if we believe that we are obliged to promote this kind of life, or we have a right to live under the conditions mentioned above, this also applies to the process of dying. I also want to claim that any physician involved in an act of euthanasia is fulfilling this important duty.

All of the assertions made above can be formulated in the following arguments:

1. Every human being has the right to live with the highest possible level of autonomy or self-determination, freedom from any kind of unlegitimate or unjustified coercion, and with the best possible functioning of our intellectual capacities. We also have the right to live with the minimum level of pain, suffering, and anguish and without any form of degrading and humiliating conditions.
2. Dying is a process included in the process of living.
3. Therefore, every human being has the right to die with the rights mentioned in premise 1.

Now, if we accept the conclusion (premise 3 above) as a premise, and then we add this new additional premise:

4. Euthanasia allows human beings to die with the rights mentioned in premise 3.

We can conclude,

5. Therefore, any human being has a right to euthanasia.

Of course, those who are opposed to the morality of killing will claim that taking the life of a patient even when the patient is asking to end his life is wrong. But, as shown before, there are exceptions to the absolute principle of the sanctity of life or to the absolute inviolability of the right to live principle.

What are the reasons for not considering euthanasia as a case of *force majeure* (i.e., as a reasonable and plausible exemption benefiting some patients)?

A logical objection has been formulated by some authors, including Kass (2014), who, in his article cited above, asks: "Can one benefit the patient as a whole by making him dead? There is, of course, a logical difficulty: how can any good exist for a being that is not? But the error is more than logical: to intend and to act for someone's good requires his continued existence to receive the benefit."

I think that this logical criticism is unfounded. First, many people believe that they are morally obliged to take care of our environment for future generations, to the benefit of beings that are not existing today. They will think that they are doing something good for their future descendants. Of course, to enjoy some common goods (e.g., a healthy condition), you have to be alive. Neither can any bad exist for a being who is not.

But, in the case of euthanasia, we are talking of human beings who are alive and going through the process of dying. Thus, "making a patient dead" is a process and not an event. The good here is to relieve the unbearable and unnecessary pain while the patient is alive. And this is exactly the good that a patient enjoys as a benefit while still alive and conscious. Of course, it will be nonsense to try to relieve pain in a dead patient. Thus, it seems to me that Kass is ignoring the distinction between dying and death, and that we do not have to solve his problem but rather just dissolve it.

Now, I would like to show that our argument can, with some modifications, be applied by some doctors who claim that it is not only a right for them to perform euthanasia, but even a duty to do it. This is the case of Pieter V. Admiraal (2014), who, in his article "Euthanasia in The Netherlands: Justifiable Euthanasia," says:

> It is my opinion that every doctor has the right and the duty after prolonged and thorough deliberation to carry out euthanasia; at the request of the other person and in its interest, knowing that he is responsible to himself, to the others, and to the law. Similarly, every doctor has the unassailable right under any circumstances to refuse to carry out euthanasia, knowing that he is responsible to himself and to the other. (176)

Earlier, in 1999, in Admiraal's defense of the morality and legality of euthanasia, he had already stated: "It is my intention that the patient will die and his suffering will come to an end. It is my intention, my right and my duty to stop the suffering of a patient who has unbearable suffering" (2014, 129).

I think that Admiraal's claim that doctors have a duty to stop the unbearable suffering of their patients by carrying out euthanasia clearly demonstrates that, if doctors believe that they have the same rights mentioned in premise 1 above, then it is also their duty to see that other human beings also enjoy them.

In sum, it seems that, after all, euthanasia can be considered a doctor's duty.

Conclusion

Surely the contemporary debate concerning euthanasia will continue in the future as long as we have to admit that the nature of any rational discussion on philosophical issues, and especially on ethical problems, cannot be resolved once and for all. The use of arguments can only help us to establish the logical consequences of some premises that are, in principle, always conjectural and subject to criticism.

I have tried to show that the ethical problem of euthanasia can be seen and examined from a new perspective when the basic fact has been accepted, being that the process of dying is part of the process of living, together with a set of conditions and values that seem reasonable to be proposed as belonging to a desirable human life.

Insofar as they have been accepted, euthanasia can be considered by doctors as a medical duty to carry out to the extent that one of the principal aims of medicine is to reduce and eliminate human suffering. Thus, euthanasia has to be seen as another important exception to the sanctity of life or a right to life principle.

Acknowledgments

I am indebted to David Wayne for his helpful comments on the accuracy of my English translation of a previous presentation in Spanish. I am heavily indebted also to Rodrigo Lopez for his invaluable help in presenting my work according to international edition standards. I want also to thank Professor Michael Boylan for some valuable comments on a lecture given under the title "A Defense of Euthanasia," held at Marymount University in 2014.

References

Admiraal, P. V. 2014. "Euthanasia in The Netherlands: Justifiable Euthanasia." In *Medical Ethics*, edited by M. Boylan, 171–78. West Sussex, UK: Wiley-Blackwell.

Gay-Williams, J. 1987. "The Wrongfulness of Euthanasia." In *Social Ethics: Morality and Social Policy*, edited by T. A. Maples and J. S. Zembaty, 55–60. New York: McGraw-Hill.

Gomez-Lobo, A. 2002. *Morality and the Human Goods: An Introduction to Natural Law Ethics.* Washington, DC: Georgetown University Press.

Gomez-Lobo, A., and J. Keown. 2015. *Bioethics and the Human Goods: An Introduction to Natural Law Bioethics.* Washington, DC: Georgetown University Press.

Harty, J. 2012. "Tyrannicide." In *The Catholic Encyclopedia*, Vol. 15. New York: Robert Appleton Company. Accessed July 3, 2019. http://www.newadvent.org/cathen/15108a.htm.

Kass, L. R. 2014. "Why Doctors Must Not Kill." In *Medical Ethics*, edited by M. Boylan, 179–84. West Sussex, UK: Wiley-Blackwell.

Miller, D. W. 2006. *Out of Error.* Burlington, VT: Ashgate Publishing Company.

Popper, K. R. 1975. "The Logic of the Social Sciences." In *The Positivist Dispute in German Sociology*, edited by Th. W. Adorno et al., 87–104. London, UK: Heinemann Educational Books.

Popper, K. R. 2013. *The Open Society and Its Enemies.* First single volume of Popper (1945). Princeton, NJ: Princeton University Press.

Rudner, R. 1953. "The Scientist qua Scientist Makes Value Judgments." *Philosophy of Science* 20, no. 1: 1–6.

Winning, C. 1999. "Interview." In *Euthanasia: The Heart of the Matter*, edited by A. Dunnett, 141–54. London, UK: Hodder & Stoughton.

CHAPTER 17

Is There a Global Bioethics? End of Life in Thailand and the Case for Local Difference

Scott Stonington and Pinit Ratanakul

Abstract

The twenty-first century has seen a debate over whether there should be international standards in medical ethics and human rights. Critics worry that such standards risk overlooking important cultural differences in the way people conceptualize medical decision-making. The question for a global bioethics then is what bioethical guidelines and framework should guide developing countries that are building allopathic medical systems. This chapter examines the issue—including the presumed universality of Western bioethics values like autonomy, beneficence, nonmaleficence, truth-telling, and justice. It concludes that Western bioethics is inadequate to solve the problems in non-Western societies.

Introduction

Over the past decade, several scholars have advocated for international standards in medical ethics and human rights [1–3]. Others have countered that such standards risk ignoring important cultural differences in the way people conceptualize medical decision-making [4–8]. Within this debate hangs a question for international bioethics: As developing countries build allopathic medical systems, what should their bioethics be? In this chapter, we explore possible answers to this question, ultimately arguing that Western bioethics is insufficient to solve the problems that arise in the practice of allopathic medicine in non-Western contexts.

As an example, we discuss recent conflicts over the use of mechanical ventilators in Thailand. Thailand is a center of cutting-edge allopathic medical care in Asia. It has a universal health-care system, which provides many Thais with access to mechanical ventilation. So many Thais are placed on mechanical ventilators at the end of life that it has become one of the largest drains on Thailand's universal health-care system [9]. Furthermore, the use of ventilators has become a source of vehement national debate, mostly as a result of several prominent political figures who received overly aggressive medical care at the end of life [10, 11]. As in Western hospitals, the ascension of mechanical ventilation has introduced a host of difficult ethical dilemmas for doctors, families, and patients [12, 13]. How will Thais go about solving these dilemmas? On which principles of bioethics will they rely?

To answer these questions, we start with a case that illustrates a common ethical dilemma about withdrawal of mechanical ventilation in Thai intensive care units. We then explore some concepts from Western bioethics to see if they help resolve this dilemma. Finally, we explain some of the local ethics behind the case and discuss the concept of a Thai bioethics to address the use of ventilators in Thailand.

A Case Scenario

The following fictional case is based on thirty ethnographic interviews and two months of participant-observation fieldwork by one of us (SS) in 2005. The case contains themes that arose frequently during this research.

Gaew, a thirty-nine-year-old Thai construction worker, falls from a scaffold and hits his head on the pavement. He is unconscious by the time he arrives at one of Bangkok's cutting-edge emergency rooms. He is intubated and placed in the intensive care unit. Gaew's physician, Dr. Nok, informs Gaew's brother, Lek, that Gaew has little chance of recovery due to his lack of brain activity.

Lek does not know what to do; he wants to give his brother the best care possible, but he knows his brother is suffering. He would like to remove Gaew's ventilator. Dr. Nok replies that this is impossible because it is unethical to remove ventilators. Very few physicians in Thailand withdraw ventilators from patients [10]. They have a complex array of reasons for declining to withdraw ventilator support, including their medical training, fear of litigation, and belief in the sanctity of life.

As with most Thai physicians, Dr. Nok's refusal to withdraw the ventilator is explicitly Buddhist. The first precept of Buddhism forbids killing. Other Buddhist doctrines teach that the last part of the body to die is the breath. For a Thai Buddhist physician, pulling out a patient's ventilator may feel like pulling out the patient's soul. If Dr. Nok withdraws Gaew's ventilator, she will necessarily have "ill-will" or "repugnance" in her mind [14, 15].

In Buddhist terms, Dr. Nok's own karma is at stake. Karma is a moral law, central to lay Thai Buddhism, which describes chains of cause and effect that result from individual behavior.

Actions generate either merit or demerit, and the balance of these two currencies determines one's spiritual future [10, 15, 16]. If Dr. Nok's mind contains ill-will or repugnance, she will accrue demerit, and this will negatively affect her in this and future lifetimes.

Neither Lek nor Dr. Nok asks what Gaew would have wanted in his current situation. They do not ponder this question because in lay Thai Buddhism, the self is seen as different from moment to moment—so Gaew is not the same person now as he was ten days ago. To Dr. Nok and Lek, an advance directive seems ludicrous. How could a person know what he would want years later, in a different state of consciousness [10]?

Dr. Nok is ready with a strategy for circumventing their dilemma. She tells Lek that together they must help Gaew "let go." She explains that it is Gaew's mental attachments that are keeping him alive and suffering on the ventilator. When Dr. Nok says "attachments," she uses the Thai word for "knot of problems" (*bpom bpan ha*), implying a gnarled set of worries tangling Gaew's mind and keeping him from achieving mental clarity and letting go of life. She asks Lek what Gaew might be worried about. Lek replies that Gaew wanted to be ordained as a monk before dying. Although they cannot know what is in Gaew's mind in his new state of consciousness, this is a possible element in his "knot."

Dr. Nok suggests that Lek go to Bangkok and ordain as a monk for several days in Gaew's stead, then return to tell Gaew what he has done. She explains that even though Gaew has little brain activity, when all of the senses subside, the spirit may still take in sound [15]. She hopes that when Gaew hears about his brother's ordination, he may let go and die with the ventilator still attached and running. This way, she and Lek can relieve Gaew's suffering without compromising their karma.

How Would Western Bioethics Handle This Case?

There has been a recent fervor of discussion in many Western medical schools about culture and bioethics [8]. Medical students and physicians are being trained in "cultural competence" to help them handle a culturally diverse society. This training usually focuses on prototypic cases meant to exemplify particular cultural or ethnic groups. In general, it is assumed that the principles of Western bioethics—autonomy, beneficence, nonmaleficence, truth-telling, and justice—are universal. Different cultures are seen as emphasizing these principles differently, rather than as operating on unique principles of their own.

A classic example, taught in many United States medical schools, is the story of the "Asian" elder who comes into the hospital and whose son says "Please, do not tell my father that he has cancer." Most Western physicians would analyze this situation as follows: The son believes that knowing about the illness will hurt his father; the son values beneficence (doing what is best for the patient) over autonomy (the patient's prerogative to make decisions for himself), and thus wants to conceal the illness from his father. In this analysis, the principles of bioethics are held to be universal—the son's culture simply makes him value these principles in a unique proportion.

This approach proves unhelpful in understanding Gaew's case. Dr. Nok's refusal to remove the ventilator is not based on Gaew's wishes; it is not based on what is best for Gaew; and it is not about what is most truthful, or what is best for Thais as a whole. None of these fundamental principles of Western bioethics—autonomy, beneficence, nonmaleficence, truth-telling, or justice—sufficiently explain Lek and Dr. Nok's dilemma. Even though the hospital taking care of Gaew is a center of allopathic medicine—a form of medicine grown out of the West—it is nonetheless a zone governed at least partially by non-Western bioethical principles.

A tool central to the practice of bioethics in Western hospitals is delineating between different kinds of dilemmas. The most widely read textbook of bioethics in the West, by Beauchamp and Childress, distinguishes between at least three kinds of dilemmas: 1) ethical dilemmas, where two ethical principles dictate opposite actions; 2) self-interest dilemmas, where the decision-maker's own self-interest conflicts with a decision dictated by an ethical principle; and 3) practical dilemmas, where something logistical prevents an ethical decision from being enacted [17]. Making these distinctions is often the first task that a physician must complete during an ethics consult. One must separate the entangled needs of doctors and family members from the ethical principles that determine how to treat a patient.

So what kind of dilemmas are Lek and Dr. Nok confronting? Are the principles governing their behavior ethical, practical, or self-interested? Take, for example, Dr. Nok's reason for not withdrawing the ventilator: to do so would be revoking a patient's life. At first, this sounds like an ethical principle, a kind of nonmaleficence. But on closer inspection, the principle beneath her action diverges significantly from nonmaleficence.

In a Buddhist framework, killing is ethically wrong because it defiles the mind of the killer. Even if Dr. Nok thinks that withdrawing the ventilator is the most compassionate thing for Gaew, it would be spiritually disadvantageous for her. As one Thai physician explained, "It may be the best thing for the patient [to withdraw the ventilator], but how could you find someone who would do it?" A Thai physician would not want to take the risk of acquiring spiritual demerit.

It would then be tempting to say that Dr. Nok's situation represents a self-interest dilemma. An ethical decision—compassionately relieving suffering by removing the ventilator—is in conflict with Dr. Nok's concern for her own spiritual fate. But this interpretation also breaks down because the precise thing that would generate demerit for Dr. Nok is ill-will toward Gaew.

In a Buddhist ethical framework, it is impossible to withdraw a ventilator with beneficent intent. In Dr. Nok's case, self-interest and ethical duty are so intertwined as to be indistinguishable. The distinction made between self-interest and ethical dilemmas collapses. The first task of a Western ethicist—to determine the type of dilemma at work—proves to be an impasse in Gaew's case.

The fact that a Western bioethical approach fails in Gaew's case may be an indication of the limitations of the "one-size-fits-all" bioethics used in Western hospitals as much as it is an illustration of local differences in ethical reasoning (Damien Keown, personal correspondence). Western bioethics is a young discipline, and draws on only a minority of the rich history of Western ethical philosophy [18]. Nonetheless, the conceptual tools of Western bioethics dominate policy, law, bureaucracy, and physician decision-making in Western hospitals. These concepts are beginning to have weight in policymaking in Thailand [19]. Gaew's case makes it clear that one must examine local ethical concepts before uncritically importing Western bioethical tools.

Does Thailand Need a Thai Bioethics?

Dr. Nok's solution to Gaew's end-of-life is instructive as an introduction to what a Thai bioethics might look like. Dr. Nok and Lek cannot remove Gaew's ventilator, and yet their compassion and duty demand that they relieve his suffering. They circumvent this dilemma by helping Gaew to let go of his life peacefully. This strategy has a positive effect on the karmic fate of everyone involved. They relieve Gaew's suffering. Lek acquires merit by ordaining as a monk.

These decisions are based on the logic of karmic morality. They also illustrate the Buddhist principle of interdependence. Interdependence means that doctors, patients, and relatives must think about the emotions and interests of all parties involved in a medical decision. This is in contrast to the Western concept of autonomy, which allows a patient to make decisions without consideration of the feelings and responsibilities of other people concerned. Dr. Nok's solution to Gaew's end-of-life is not just for Gaew, it is also for herself and for Lek. It is an ethics of compassion that must relieve the suffering of all people concerned.

One of us (PR), as a member of a team of Thai scholars, has worked for the last ten years to develop an applied ethics using principles such as karma, compassion, and interdependence [20–23]. In the West, the main purpose of a countrywide policy is to resolve conflicts between individuals over medical decisions. However, because the concept of interdependence is so central for most Thais, Thailand's bioethical policies may differ dramatically from those found in the West.

Conclusion

The purpose of this exploration has been to illustrate the need for Thailand and other countries to develop bioethical systems using local concepts. It would be a mistake, however, to leave our analysis of Thai bioethics without considering the term "Thai." This has long been a problem with writings on "Asian values" or "Asian thinking."

In this article, we have emphasized Buddhism as a major ethical system, but it is one of many such systems engaged in decisions about the end-of-life in Thailand. Buddhist monasteries, lay Buddhist organizations, advocates of medical technology, public health officials, and lobbyists for the booming medical tourism industry are all engaged in vehement debate over what should guide Thailand in making medical decisions [10, 11]. As with other countries, Thailand is not a place with a single ethics. In the same way that one cannot import concepts from the West to solve dilemmas in Thailand, one cannot haphazardly select a view within Thailand and label it as "Thai."

Nonetheless, there is an urgent need for solutions to the "ventilator problem"—both to patch the failing universal health-care system, and to help Thais make difficult decisions about intervention at the end-of-life. Thailand is just beginning the long process of integrating its multitude of local voices and concepts into nationwide ethical standards. This new Thai ethics promises to be much more effective at solving Thailand's ethical problems than tools imported uncritically from the West.

Acknowledgments

This research was made possible by the University of California Pacific Rim Research Program and the University of California San Francisco Office of International Programs. I would like to thank Warapong Wongwachara for translation, insight, and comments in all phases of fieldwork. I would like to thank Gay Becker, Vincanne Adams, China Scherz, Olivia Para, Sherry Brenner, and Damien Keown for help with this manuscript.

References

1. Benatar SR (2005). Achieving gold standards in ethics and human rights in medical practice. PLoS Med 2: e260. DOI: 10.1371/journal.pmed.0020260
2. Kim JY (2000). Dying for growth: Global inequality and the health of the poor. Monroe (ME): Common Courage Press. 584 p.
3. Farmer P (2001). Infections and inequalities: The modern plagues. Berkeley: University of California Press. 419 p.
4. Adams V (2002). Randomized controlled crime: Post-colonial sciences in alternative medicine research. Soc Stud Sci 32: 659–90.
5. Butt L (2002). The suffering stranger: Medical anthropology and international morality. Med Anthropol 21: 1–24; discussion 25–33.
6. Cohen L (1999). Where it hurts: Indian material for an ethics of organ transplantation. Daedalus 128: 135–65.
7. Pellegrino ED, Mazzarella P, Corsi P (1992). Transcultural dimensions in medical ethics. Frederick (MD): University Publishing Group. 221 p.
8. Turner L (2005). From the local to the global: Bioethics and the concept of culture. J Med Philos 30: 305–20.
9. Alpha Research (2005). Thailand public health 2005–2006. Nonthaburi (Thailand): Alpha Research. pp. v.
10. Ratanakul P (2000). To save or let go: Thai Buddhist perspectives on euthanasia. In: Keown D, editor. Contemporary Buddhist ethics. Richmond, Surrey (United Kingdom): Curzon. pp. 169–82.
11. Jackson PA (2003). Buddhadasa: Theravada Buddhism and modernist reform in Thailand. Chiang Mai (Thailand): Silkworm Books. 375 p.
12. Kaufman SR (2005). And a time to die: How American hospitals shape the end of life. New York: Scribner. 400 p.
13. Klessig J (1992). The effect of values and culture on life-support decisions. West J Med 157: 316–22.
14. Keown D (1998). Suicide, assisted suicide and euthanasia: A Buddhist perspective. J Law Relig 13: 385–405.
15. Keown D (2005). End of life: The Buddhist view. Lancet 366: 952–55.
16. Keown D (1995). Buddhism and bioethics. New York: St. Martin's Press. 208 p.
17. Beauchamp TL, Childress JF (2001) Principles of biomedical ethics. New York: Oxford University Press. 454 p.
18. Jonsen AR (1998). The birth of bioethics. New York: Oxford University Press. 431 p.

19. Lindbeck V (1984). Thailand: Buddhism meets the Western model. Hastings Cent Rep 14: 24–26.
20. Ratanakul P (1988). Bioethics in Thailand: The struggle for Buddhist solutions. J Med Philos 13: 301–12.
21. Ratanakul P (1990). Thailand: Refining cultural values. Hastings Cent Rep 20: 25–27.
22. Ratanakul P (1999). Love in Buddhist Bioethics. Eubios J Asian Int Bioeth 9: 45–46.
23. Boyd A, Ratanakul P, Deepudong A (1998) Compassion as common ground. Eubios J Asian Int Bioeth 8: 34–37.

CHAPTER 18

Confucianism and Killing versus Letting Die

Cecilia Wee

Abstract

Much of the Western contemporary debate on the permissibility of active euthanasia centers on whether there is any morally significant distinction between killing and letting die. Those who would prohibit active euthanasia but permit passive euthanasia point out that the former involves a direct *act* of killing, whereas the latter involves an *omission* (i.e., omitting to do that which may prolong life). This argument turns on a commonly accepted view in the West that there is a morally significant difference between an act and an omission (even in contexts where the eventual outcomes are the same).

I will argue that this distinction between act and omission may not carry the same moral weight in Confucianism. I begin with an outline of Confucian role-morality. Drawing in part from classical Confucian texts, I then argue that, on such a role-based morality, the distinction between acting and omitting to act may be largely irrelevant to moral decision-making. This is then brought to bear on end-of-life decisions: I suggest that, to the Confucian, the distinction between killing and letting die may not play the same role in end-of-life decisions that it has in the West.

Introduction

Medical ethics, particularly in Western countries, has traditionally held that there is a clear distinction between passive and active euthanasia, that is, between withholding treatment from a patient so as to allow her to die and taking direct action aimed at killing the patient. While the former is held to be permissible in certain circumstances, the latter has been seen as wholly impermissible. Put another way, while it is acceptable in some cases to let a patient die, it is never acceptable to kill a patient.

The difference in the ethical permissibility of active and passive euthanasia is at least partly rooted in another previously entrenched distinction, namely, the moral (and in many cases also legal) distinction between an action and an omission to act.

Consider Person A who wants to see a person dead and, hence, deliberately shoots and kills that person. Person A would be deemed to have direct moral culpability for that person's death and might well be guilty of murder. In contrast, consider Person B who also wants a particular person dead and accordingly decides to stand by and not save her from being killed, although she could easily have done so without harm to herself. Person B would generally be deemed to be less morally culpable than A (if morally culpable at all) for the death. She would not be seen as having murdered the person. This suggests that there is a moral difference between acting to obtain an outcome and (knowingly) failing to act in order that the outcome obtains. This distinction underpins the permissibility of withdrawal of treatment in end-of-life situations and the nonpermissibility of an act that is designed to directly kill the patient.

In view of these debates (many of which have yet to receive final resolution), it would be helpful to put in some caveats concerning the scope and concerns of this chapter. First, note that the distinction between active and passive euthanasia used here is rather broad. The actual range of options pertaining to end-of-life situations should perhaps more appropriately be classified as follows:

1. Passive euthanasia
2. Indirect euthanasia (namely, pain-relieving treatment under the nonintended risk of abbreviation of life)
3. Abetment to suicide (e.g., procurement and provision of deadly medicine)
4. Active euthanasia

For the purposes of argument, however, this chapter will merely contrast active euthanasia with passive euthanasia, including options 3 and 4 broadly under active euthanasia, and options 1 and 2 broadly under passive euthanasia. Indeed, the primary focus of the chapter will be a contrast of option 1 with option 4.

Second, while the distinction between action and omission is widely (and most likely correctly) accepted as underpinning the distinction between active and passive euthanasia, the two distinctions may not stand in a one-to-one relation with each other. To begin with, suppose that one distinguishes passive euthanasia from active euthanasia on the basis that the former involves an omission and the latter an action. One objection is that the term "passive euthanasia" is a contradiction in terms. This is because euthanasia, by definition, causes death, and omissions, by definition, cannot cause anything. Passive euthanasia would then be that which causes death but cannot cause anything.[1] The viability of this objection hinges on the question of whether omissions can have causative effect. Recent commentators have suggested that omissions in specific contexts can in fact do so.

The discussion above assumes that passive euthanasia always involves an omission to act. Another objection as to why active and passive euthanasia do not stand in a one-to-one correlation with action and omission comes by way of the point that passive euthanasia does not always involve an omission to act. For example, we usually encompass under passive euthanasia the case of "pulling the plug" on a patient's ventilator, which involves an *action* by some agent. A reply here is that pulling the plug and thus allowing the patient to die as she would have done if Nature were allowed to take its course is different from the direct killing that occurs when, say, one stabs someone to death. In the latter case, the outcome would be death regardless of whether the individual in question is healthy or ill. In the former case, the outcome is the death *specifically* of a terminally ill person. Frances Kamm (2008)[2] has likened the case of pulling the plug on a patient whose life is being prolonged solely by the ventilator to a situation where one has been saving someone from drowning and then decides to stop (perhaps by pressing a button on one's side). Both cases thus count as omissions (despite one's action).

Another case where passive euthanasia involves an action would be the case where such euthanasia involves extraordinary treatment (e.g., putting the patient on a ventilator) being discontinued while ordinary treatment (e.g., providing nutrition) is continued. In such a situation, passive euthanasia arguably involves not just pure omission but action (in the provision of nutrition). However, the relevant contrast in the present debate concerning end-of-life situations is that of the action of *killing* versus the omission of letting the patient die. The action of providing nutrition is aimed at the (ordinary) *sustenance* of life and, hence, is not directly germane to the specific action–omission contrast at issue here.

The distinction between active and passive euthanasia may not map directly onto the distinction between action and omission. Nevertheless, there are reasonable grounds, and some intuitive plausibility, to holding that passive euthanasia is an omission, in relevant contrast to active euthanasia, which is an action. In this chapter, I shall take it that passive euthanasia is indeed an omission to act, while active euthanasia is an action.

Let me now come to the third caveat. As can be seen above, it is not always easy to distinguish clearly between actions and omissions. (Pulling the plug on the ventilator that keeps a patient alive can be both an action and an omission.) But, even if one assumes there is a distinction between an action and an omission, there remains the question as to whether there is any significant *moral* difference between action and omission.

The debate here too has been huge. For example, it has been argued that the moral distinction between an action and an omission derives from the fact that an action can cause an outcome but an omission cannot. The agent is causally responsible (and hence morally responsible) for the outcomes of his actions, but he cannot stand in a relation of causal responsibility (and hence of moral responsibility) with respect to his omissions. However, as indicated above, some commentators argue that in fact omissions can be causal as well, and we can thus be morally responsible for our omissions. Whether one accepts that there is a moral difference between an action and an omission to act may also ultimately depend on the ethical theory that one holds. The utilitarian, for instance, would hold that there is no relevant moral difference between an action and an omission to act because utilitarianism enjoins that one should always pursue (whether by action or omission to act) that which maximizes the overall balance of pleasure over pain.[3]

In this chapter, I shall not engage with the recent debate and controversy on the distinction (moral, metaphysical, or both) between actions and omissions. The moral distinction between action and omission is likely a pervasive feature of the moral perspective of the average person, even if he or she is seldom clear about the actual bases for making such a distinction. That the American Medical Association has maintained that passive euthanasia is permissible but active euthanasia is not goes to show how entrenched is the assumption of the moral difference between action and omission.[4]

I shall try to show here that the pervasive Western assumption of moral difference between action and omission is much less likely to obtain in a person who comes from a role-based morality like Confucianism. As a result of this divergence, the distinction between active and passive euthanasia (plausibly taken to be underpinned by this action–omission distinction) continues to play an important role in determining end-of-life medical decisions in the West but would likely not have the same role in such decisions in societies with a strong Confucian background.

Bioethical decision-making in countries influenced by Confucianism differs markedly from that which obtains in Western countries. On this basis, some writers have advocated the development of a distinctive Confucian bioethics that draws on the fundamental metaphysical and moral beliefs of the tradition (see, e.g., Fan 1999; Lee 2007). If indeed there is no morally significant difference between active and passive euthanasia in Confucianism, this can be addressed when developing a Confucian bioethics.

This chapter begins by giving a brief account of Confucian morality as a role-morality. I then discuss role-moralities in the context in which they are most frequently associated in the West, namely, the professions. In contexts where there are well-specified professional role-obligations, there is sometimes no moral distinction to be drawn between an act and an omission to act. Confucianism is then shown to be similar to the professions in having highly specific sets of role-obligations. It is then argued that the distinction between act and omission is similarly absent in such Confucian contexts. This is used to explain why end-of-life decisions in Confucian societies may differ from those in the West.

Confucianism as a Role-Morality

The view that Confucianism is essentially a role-morality is well accepted and pervasive. (Rosemont 1986 and Nuyen 2007 provide succinct accounts of this view.) Apart from this view, various commentators have argued that there are important similarities between Confucianism and Aristotelian virtue ethics (e.g., Sim 2007), feminist care ethics (e.g., Li 2000), and Kantian deontology (e.g., Wawrytko 1982). It is not clear whether the view that Confucianism is a role-morality is ultimately incompatible with any of these other positions (e.g., Roger Ames and Henry Rosemont [2008, 2009] have argued that it is not thus compatible). This issue is evidently one that cannot be settled here. What is certainly true is that the view of Confucianism as a role-morality has considerable textual and historical support and that it is very likely an accurate representation of Confucianism *as it is actually practiced* (see Ho 1998).

According to Confucius, there is one true path ("the Way") that all humans should try to follow and attain. Following this true path has as its crucial component the cultivation and development of the appropriate inward attitudes and feelings toward others, which are then expressed in appropriate outward behaviors. However, unlike the rival Mohist school, which had advocated the development of an attitude of universal and impartial concern toward all mankind, Confucians held that the appropriate attitudes and behaviors toward others should be subject to gradations and should in general differ according to the relation in which one stands to the person in question. Confucianism is well known for emphasizing the importance, indeed the primacy, of the family. More generally, what is accorded to any given person would depend on the *role* one inhabits with respect to that person; what is appropriately accorded to one's father, elder brother, friend, political leader, etc. would thus be quite different.

There are of course certain general virtues or attributes that Confucius and his followers thought the ethical person should possess and should make an effort to cultivate. These virtues would include sincerity (*cheng*), trustworthiness (*xin*), conscientiousness (*zhong*), and especially benevolence (*jen*), held to be the key or overarching virtue, without which one cannot be an effective political leader or attain moral sagehood. But these attributes or virtues may be expressed in different behaviors and may receive somewhat different emphases, depending on the role that one occupies with respect to the person in question. There are also virtues that tend to be role-specific; for instance, the virtue of filiality (*xiao*) obviously applies specifically to sons and daughters.

It has been argued that Confucian role-morality has its roots in the Confucian conception of the self, which sees the self as relational and embedded within a set of social, and more especially, familial relations.[5] This conception of the self differs from the standard Western conception of the self or person as an independent individual with autonomy, choosing freely to enter into the various associations she enters.[6] The Confucian conceives herself primarily as a part of a larger whole(s). She is a *member* of a particular family, a particular institution, a particular society, and, hence, embedded in a wider network of specific relationships. It then behooves her to cultivate the appropriate internal attitudes and outward behaviors in respect of each of these roles.

I now turn to professional ethics, which accepts that how a person should act is to some extent regulated by the specific role that she has undertaken as a professional. It will be argued that, in the context of such professional roles, the moral or ethical gap between act and omission to act is usually less than in ordinary nonprofessional contexts.

Professional Roles and the Moral Difference between Action and Omission

Writers on professional ethics have emphasized the link between the specific role that a professional plays and what is ethically or morally expected of her in virtue of occupying that role. Being in a certain profession generates certain role-obligations, which are often embodied in a code of ethics. While such obligations may include the observance of professional etiquette, they would also, and importantly, include the moral and ethical obligations that a professional has in virtue of being a member of that profession (Beauchamp and Childress 1989, 6).

A substantial portion of the literature on professional role-morality concerns the potential conflicts that might arise between the specific moral obligations that a professional has in her professional role and the (more) universal moral norms that should be observed. We will not be concerned here with how the moral obligations of particular professions stand in relation to the wider set of moral norms, whether genuine conflicts may arise between the two, and if so, what the potential means of resolution are.[7] These issues lie beyond the scope of the chapter. Instead, that these issues arise at all makes evident that the moral obligations of the professional are different from—extend beyond—the broader moral norms that people are expected to observe in the community. In this section, I highlight two ways in which the presence of such professional role-obligations can affect the moral assessment of omissions to act by the professional.

The first is that an omission or failure to observe a professional role-obligation is often taken to be a more significant moral failure than other comparable omissions to act in contexts that do not involve such role-obligations. Consider a doctor who, in the course of treating a patient for a minor problem, discovers a tumor needing urgent excision. The doctor fails to inform the patient of the tumor and the need for urgent surgery. Compare this with someone who notices that there are some loose tiles on their neighbor's roof, which should be fixed urgently, as they could be dislodged and cause serious injury. The person fails to inform the neighbor of the loose tiles.

We would tend to assign the doctor a higher degree of moral culpability for her failure to inform than we would the neighbor. This is because the doctor in her professional role has well-specified role-obligations toward her patients. The same does not apply to neighbors, where the issue of what one owes to, or ought to observe in respect of, a neighbor is much less specific. One's attitude toward a neighbor can acceptably range from the stance of "Am I my brother's keeper?" to one of some degree of concern and responsibility. This contrasts with the doctor, who, in embarking on her profession, is required to have a reasonably clear idea of what is or is not morally acceptable in a doctor–patient relationship.

The second way in which omissions to act by professionals differ from omissions in a nonprofessional context can be made clear through the following example. Suppose Doctor C conspires with a patient's relative to ensure the patient's demise so that the latter can inherit her vast wealth. To bring about this demise, she deliberately prescribes a drug that she knows full well will, given the patient's condition, result in the latter's certain death. Now, Doctor D is similarly in conspiracy with a patient's relative to ensure the patient's demise. To bring about this demise, she deliberately withholds a drug, knowing full well that, given the patient's condition, this will result in her certain death.

In the situation outlined above, *both* doctors would be seen to be morally culpable for their respective patients' deaths. Moreover, it is not intuitively evident that there is any clear difference in the *level* of moral culpability in the two doctors, although one doctor brings about the death by deliberately acting and the other by deliberately omitting to act. While physicians are bound by the obligation to not kill, but are allowed to let die in end-of-life contexts, they are also bound by the obligation to prolong the life and well-being of the patient. All other things being equal, the deliberate transgression of this obligation, whether by omission or commission, would be counted as a moral failure.

The cases of Doctors C and D thus stand in some contrast to the cases mentioned in the introduction, where the level of moral culpability between A and B is intuitively judged to be quite different. What underpins the difference in our intuitions in the two cases is again that the doctors here are acting in their professional roles, and in that capacity have a particular set of obligations that A and B, judged to be acting in their personal capacity, do not.

"Ordinary" morality, underpinned by "ordinary" intuitions, generally assigns less culpability to one who fails to act to bring about an outcome than one who acts to bring it about. A direct action aimed at a negative outcome is a much more serious overall threat to the peace and security of humans in a society than an omission to act to bring about that outcome (see Nesbitt 1999).[8] However, matters are different when one is acting in a professional capacity and hence is governed by well-specified role-obligations. In such contexts, transgressions of such obligations, whether by omission or commission, are, *ceteris paribus*, regarded quite equally as transgressions.

In sum, professional roles generally come with specific obligations embodied within and emphasized by a code of ethics. In such a context, an omission to act would clearly count as an ethical failure, where an omission in ordinary, nonprofessional contexts might not.

Professional Role-Morality and Confucian Role-Morality

I now turn back to the role-based ethics of Confucianism, which enjoins the cultivation of the appropriate inward attitudes, which will then be expressed as appropriate outward behaviors. These appropriate attitudes and behaviors would differ according to the specific relationship that obtains between oneself and the person in question.

Suppose that Mei-ling is both a daughter and a sister. As a daughter, she would be expected to cultivate certain attitudes and behaviors in respect of this role; they would not be quite the same as the attitudes and behaviors that should be cultivated in her role as a sister. Moreover, the respective behaviors by which Mei-ling expresses her filiality and sisterhood would include not only general sorts of behaviors that manifest concern for parent and sibling. Confucianism also indicates that her appropriate inward attitudes would also be expressed by the fulfillment of some well-specified requirements, including the observance of various rituals and rites.

There are thus similarities between professional role-morality and Confucian role-morality. First, both emphasize the role that an individual inhabits in relation to another and on the role-obligations that obtain as a result. Second, these role-obligations are well-specified in Confucianism, as in professional role-morality.

These features suggest that Confucian morality would differ significantly from "ordinary" morality in the West. Consider the question of what a son should morally owe to his father. In "ordinary" morality, there seems to be relatively wide latitude for one's answers to this question, just as there is for one's answers to what one owes to a neighbor. One son may maintain that he owes it to his father to turn up annually for Thanksgiving; another might think he is obliged to regularly visit his parent once a month; and so on.

In contrast, the role-obligations of a son are quite clearly specified in the Confucian tradition. As Ho notes, the "stringent demands" that must be fulfilled for one to be filial include "providing for the material and moral well-being of one's aged parents, performing the ceremonial duties of ancestral worship . . . ensuring the continuity of the family line, and in general conducting oneself so as to bring honor and avoid disgrace to the family name" (Ho 1998, 11). Inhabiting the role of son thus brings with it very specific role-obligations, and the tradition is quite emphatic on the need to observe these specific obligations. In these respects, Confucian morality is more akin to professional morality than "ordinary morality."

There is also a degree of latitude as to how a Confucian child should manifest filiality, just as there is a degree of latitude as to how a professional, such as a doctor, should meet her obligation to her patients. For example, a Confucian child may manifest filiality by deciding to take her parents on an overseas holiday; similarly, a doctor may decide on prescribing one specific course of treatment for a patient rather than another. Also, specific obligations that a Confucian child is expected to fulfill to her parents could change over time in accord with changes in tradition, just as a doctor's specific obligations can change over time in accord with changes in the accepted code of medical ethics. Nevertheless, both the Confucian child and the doctor are subject, at any given point in time, to very specific obligations in many areas in which "ordinary" (Western) morality does not enjoin any specific obligation.

Given these similarities, one might expect to find that there is less of a moral distinction in Confucianism between actions and omissions to act, particularly in contexts where these are transgressions of a particular role-obligation. And, indeed, there is textual evidence in classical Confucian texts that this is the case. While there are certainly examples of moral transgression that involve a specific action in Confucian texts, there are a number of texts in which an *omission to act* is treated as moral failure. In 4A:26 of the *Book of Mencius*, Mencius notes: "There are three ways of being a bad son. The most serious is to have no heir."

Here, it is the *omission* of providing an heir that is considered a transgression of one's role-obligation as a son. Again, Mencius also notes that: "No one considers the *neglect* of parents and the *denial* of relationships between prince and subject, and between superior and inferior as laudable" (*Mencius* 7A:34, emphasis mine).

Once again, moral transgression is expressed in terms of what one has omitted or failed to do. The failure to look after one's parents and to observe the role-obligations that obtain in the relations between prince and subject and superior and inferior are deplored because one has *omitted* to behave in the morally appropriate way. Confucius notes: "Faced with what is right, to leave it undone shows a lack of courage" (*Analects* 2:24). This encapsulates the general Confucian position that an *omission* to do what is right (which of course includes what is demanded by one's various role-obligations) is morally wrong.

There are significant similarities between professional role-morality and Confucian role-morality. Both emphasize role-obligations that pertain to the particular role one inhabits, and in both cases, these role-obligations are fairly well specified. Finally, both would hold that transgression of these role-obligations constitutes a moral breach, whether the transgression is caused by a direct action or an omission to act.

In the next section, because the Confucian sees no moral distinction between a transgression of one's role-obligation by omission and one by direct action, she will not see any moral difference between letting die and killing in end-of-life situations. Letting die in this context is quite as bad as killing for the Confucian.

End-of-Life Issues and the Confucian Moral Person

Empirical studies have suggested that, in countries with a strong Confucian background, families are often reluctant to withdraw life support for family members in end-of-life situations (Hui 1999). To understand why this may be so, we need to take into account not just the role-obligations of family members but the overall Confucian attitude toward the body.

The Confucian, and more generally East Asian, understanding of "body" is shaped by a different metaphysical framework than that which obtains in the West. The predominant conception of the person in the latter as an autonomous individual rests on a dichotomy between mind and body. After all, the autonomous decisions by the individual are often seen as *mental* decisions, as taking place in the individual's mind, and this is seen as (at least) conceptually distinct from what takes place in the body. This distinction does not obtain in Confucianism. There is no corresponding concept in Confucianism of what we would call the individual "mind" insofar as that is seen as the locus not only of one's autonomous choices, but also as the repository of a lifetime of thoughts, feelings, experiences, and memories (Rosemont 2007).

Part of what underwrites the movement to define "death" as brain death is the assumption that, with the cessation of brain function is a cessation (or, if one believes in an afterlife, a departure from the body) of the *ego*, or "I." That is, there is an end or departure of a particular consciousness with its own specific thoughts, choices, life experiences, memories from the body, and, therefore, for all intents and purposes, an end to a *lived* life in that particular body.

But Confucians do not have an equivalent concept of mind *qua ego*, or discrete experiencing "I," conceptually distinct from body. Thus, brain death, commonly seen as concomitant with the end or departure of a consciousness in the West, may not be accorded the significance that it holds in the West. Absent the contrast of mind and body, the individual live body of someone in a vegetative state is not seen as an empty husk; it remains significant despite this cessation of brain function. Confucianism also enjoins in general a reverent attitude toward the body: "Being reverent about the body (*shen*) is of the greatest importance. The body is a branch of one's parents, so how could one be irreverent in this regard?"[9]

The Confucian body is seen as a branch whose foundational trunk are the parents. The reverence for one's body is seen implicitly as a form of family reverence. Failure to take care of one's body is a dishonoring of one's parents. Failure to take care of one's parents' bodies might well be seen as a dishonoring of one's ancestors or family line. Given this Confucian attitude toward the body, we can now come back to the role-obligations of the Confucian family member.

Confucianism emphasizes the primacy of family; patient autonomy does not receive the same emphasis that it does in the West (Fan and Tao 2004). Many significant medical decisions, including end-of-life decisions, are made by family members rather than the patients (Fielding and Hung 1996; Li and Chou 1997). Patient confidentiality also takes a back seat. Bad medical news is usually conveyed by the doctor—first, to family members, who then decide whether the patient should be told of her condition. In the context of such medical decisions, a family member is expected to honor her role-obligations to the patient. Thus, if one is making a decision for a parent, the attitude that one should bear when deciding is that of filiality, or *xiao*.

One significant role-obligation of a Confucian child (especially a son) is to ensure his parents' well-being and to take care of them in their old age. This is often held to include keeping one's parents alive for as long as possible. For example, *The Twenty-Four Paragons of Filial Piety*, written by the Yuan dynasty scholar Guo Jujing, abounds with stories of paragons who went to extreme lengths to prolong their parents' or in-laws' lives.[10] To keep one's parents, and, more specifically, parents' bodies, alive on life support is an expression of filiality (Hui 1999; Tse and Tao 2004).

For the Confucian (as for the professional), an omission to meet one's role obligation is a significant moral transgression. Given that the Confucian's primary obligation is to her parent or other family member, *not* keeping the latter alive is a serious moral transgression, even if the family member is brain dead or in a persistent vegetative state. This is because there is, first, no clear conception here that the family member's life is over because her lived, experienced life is over, and, second, because of the general Confucian reverence for body. Withdrawal of a ventilator or life-support system—the letting die of one's family member—would be seen as a failure or omission to keep that member alive. This would be a transgression of one's role-obligation and might indeed be almost as bad as if one were directly to kill a family member in similar circumstances.

Where the West has had a tendency to assume that there is a morally significant difference between killing and letting die, the tendency in Confucianism is to see no difference in the two in such contexts. Moreover, in the West is the line of argument that, if it is morally permissible to let die in appropriate contexts, it should also be morally permissible to kill in those contexts. In Confucianism, the assimilation apparently goes in the other direction. The Confucian assimilates letting die to killing, maintaining that, inasmuch as it is morally impermissible to kill one's parents, it is also impermissible (given one's role-obligations) to let them die.

In November 2008, a Seoul Western District Court ordered doctors to remove life support from a woman who was "in a persistent vegetative state." This made international news because, prior to this, South Korean courts, and indeed, the general populace, had generally been against the withdrawal of life support for such patients. This in turn has been widely attributed to the Confucian background of South Koreans. This was thought to be similar to a 1997 case in which a father had requested the removal of a ventilator, an extraordinary means of life support, from his son, who was similarly in a vegetative state. The doctors who acceded to his request and took the patient off life support were subsequently convicted of "abetment to murder."

The withdrawal of life support, and the consequent *letting die*, of the patient, was deemed to be a (direct) act of *murder*, and the doctors were guilty of abetting the father in murder. While none of the parties involved were jailed, the very conviction of "abetment to murder" does at least suggest the lack of a clear-cut distinction between omission to keep alive and direct action to kill in respect of this particular end-of-life decision. Confucianism, as I showed, is a role-morality with well-specified moral obligations in respect of end-of-life situations. In such contexts, an omission to preserve life could be seen as impermissible as, and not entirely distinguishable from, a direct killing.[11]

Notes

1. See, for example, Garrard and Wilkinson (2005) for a discussion of this particular claim. McLachlan (2008) provides a response.
2. See also McMahan (2002). McMahan provides some fine-grained distinctions with respect to the question of whether withdrawal of ventilator support counts as a killing or a letting die.
3. See, e.g., Singer 1979, 147–53. It is also likely that adherents of other moral theories, such as Kantians and virtue ethicists, would accept that (at least under specific conditions) there may be no relevant moral difference between an action and an omission. I thank an editor for this point.
4. Helpful further readings on the issues I have discussed above can be found in Beauchamp and Childress 1996, Foot 2002, Rachels 1999, and Singer 1979.
5. Confucian scholars argue that the Confucian self is *metaphysically constituted* by the roles that she inhabits with respect to the various others in her life (see, e.g., Rosemont 2007).
6. This conception of the self is also being reevaluated in the West (see Mackenzie and Stoljar 2000).
7. See, e.g., Andre 1991, Bowie 1982, Gibson 2003, and Veatch 1972.
8. Nesbitt's point here occurs in a response to Rachels (1999). Rachels's seminal paper uses a specific example (usually called the example of the "nasty cousins") to argue that, under appropriately specific conditions, there is no moral difference between killing and letting die. Nesbitt responds by revisiting the example and arguing that the example does not show that there is no moral difference between killing and letting die. A response to Nesbitt is to be found in Kuhse (1999). Kuhse argues that Nesbitt's conclusions from the example are not germane to the case of active versus passive euthanasia, and she provides other examples that she thinks are more closely analogous to the latter.
9. See Legge (1894, 288).
10. These include the Emperor of Han, who unfailingly tasted the daily prescriptions for his sick mother himself, and Lady Tang, who saved her ailing mother-in-law from death by daily expressing her own milk for the latter.

11. I would like to thank C. L. Ten, Henry Rosemont Jr., and the editors of this volume for their very helpful comments on earlier drafts of this chapter.

References

Ames, R., and H. Rosemont. (2008). "Family Reverence (*xiao*) as the Source of Consummatory Conduct (*jen*)." *Dao* 7, 9–19.

———. (2009). *Xiaojing: The Chinese Classic of Family Reverence.* Hawai'i: University of Hawai'i. (See esp. 34–59.)

Andre, J. (1991). "Role Morality as a Complex Instance of Ordinary Morality." *American Philosophical Quarterly* 28, no. 1: 73–80.

Beauchamp, T. L., and J. F. Childress. (1996). "Rachels on Active and Passive Euthanasia." In *Ethical Issues in Death and Dying.* 2nd ed. Edited by T. L. Beauchamp and R. M. Veatch Upper Saddle River, NJ: Prentice Hall.

———. (2001). *Principles of Biomedical Ethics.* New York: Oxford University Press.

Bowie, N. E. (1982). "Role as a Moral Concept in Health Care." *Journal of Medicine and Philosophy* 7: 57–63.

Confucius. (1979). *The Analects.* Edited by D. C. Lau. Harmondsworth: Penguin.

Fan, R., ed. (1999). *Confucian Bioethics.* Dordrecht: Kluwer.

Fan, R., and J. Tao. (2004). "Consent to Medical Treatment: The Complex Interplay of Patients, Families and Physicians." *Journal of Medicine and Philosophy* 29: 139–48.

Fielding, R., and J. Hung. (1996). "Preferences for Information and Involvement in Decisions during Cancer Care among a Hong Kong Chinese Population." *Psycho-Oncology* 5: 231–329.

Foot, P. (2002). "Killing and Letting Die." In *Moral Dilemmas.* Oxford: Clarendon Press.

Garrard, E., and G. Wilkinson. (2005). "Passive Euthanasia." *Journal of Medical Ethics* 31: 64–68.

Gibson, Kevin. (2003). "Contrasting Role Morality and Professional Morality: Implications for Practice." *Journal of Applied Philosophy* 20, no. 1: 17–29.

Ho, D. Y. F. (1998). "Interpersonal Relationships and Relations Dominance: An Analysis Based on Methodological Relationalism. *Asian Journal of Social Psychology* 1, no. 1–16.

Hui, E. (1999). "A Confucian Ethic of Medical Futility." In *Confucian Bioethics,* edited by R. Fan. Dordrecht: Kluwer.

Kamm, F. (2008). "Physician Assisted Suicide, Euthanasia and Intending Death." In *Physician Assisted Suicide: Expanding the Debate,* edited by M. Battin, R. Rhodes, and A. Silver. New York: Routledge.

Kuhse, H. (1999). Why Killing Is Not Always Worse—and Sometimes Better—than Letting Die. In *Bioethics: An Anthology* , edited by H. Kuhse and P. Singer, 227–30. Oxford: Blackwell.

Lee, S. C. (2007). *The Family, Medical Decision-Making and Biotechnology: Critical Reflections on Asian Moral Perspectives.* Dordrecht: Netherlands.

Legge, J. (1894). *The Chinese Classics.* University of Hong Kong reprint of Shanghai edition.

Li, C. (2000). *The Sage and the Second Sex: Confucianism, Ethics and Gender.* Chicago: Open Court.

Li, S., and J. L. Chou. (1997). "Communication with the Cancer Patient in China." *Annals of New York Academy of Sciences* 809: 243–48.

Mackenzie, C., and N. Stoljar, eds. (2000). *Relational Autonomy: Feminist Perspectives on Autonomy, Agency and the Social Self.* New York: Oxford University Press.

McLachlan, H. V. (2008). "The Ethics of Killing and Letting Die: Active and Passive Euthanasia." *Journal of Medical Ethics* 34: 636–38.

McMahan, J. (2002). *The Ethics of Killing*. New York: Oxford University Press.

Mencius. (1970). *Mencius*, translated by D. C. Lau. Harmondsworth: Penguin.

Nesbitt, W. (1999). "Is Killing No Worse than Letting Die?" In *Bioethics: An Anthology*, edited by H. Kuhse and P. Singer, 231–25. Oxford: Blackwell.

Nuyen, A. T. (2007). "Confucian Ethics as Role-Based Ethics." *International Philosophical Quarterly* 47, no. 3: 315–28.

Rachels, J. (1999). "Active and Passive Euthanasia." In *Bioethics: An Anthology*, edited by H. Kuhse and P. Singer, 227–30. Oxford: Blackwell.

Rosemont, H. (1986). "Kierkegaard and Confucius: On Finding the Way." *Philosophy East and West* 36, no. 3: 201–12.

———. (2007). "On the Non-Finality of Physical Death in Classical Confucianism." *Acta Orientalia Vilnensis* 8: 2.

Sim, M. (2007). *Remastering Morals with Aristotle and Confucius*. Cambridge: Cambridge University Press.

Singer, P. (1979). *Practical Ethics*. Cambridge University Press.

Tse, C., and J. Tao. (2004). "Strategic Ambiguities in the Process of Consent: Role of the Family in Decisions to Forgo Life-Sustaining Treatment for Incompetent Elderly Patients." *Journal of Medicine and Philosophy* 29: 207–23.

Veatch, H. (1972). "Models for Ethical Medicine in a Revolutionary Age." *Hastings Center Report* 2: 5–7.

Wawrytko, S. (1982). "Confucius and Kant: The Ethics of Respect." *Philosophy East and West* 32, no. 3: 237–57.

CHAPTER 19

Global versus Local: The Use of Lethal Injection in China

Cher Weixia Chen

Abstract

This chapter seeks to expand the existing literature by focusing on one of the most recent developments of the death penalty in China—lethal injection, which scholars have, for the most part, failed to examine. I will look at its use from the perspectives of human rights and bioethics, for which both are intimately entwined with respect to lethal injection. Two concerns will be given particular consideration: the participation of medical personnel—in lethal injection, and in the harvesting of organs from executed prisoners. I will also offer some recommendations as to the need for guidelines.

Introduction

In the past two decades, China has accounted for a large portion of executions throughout the world. For example, in 2008, China carried out 1,718 out of 2,390 executions (72 percent) worldwide (Amnesty International 2008). The exact number of executions in recent years remained a state secret (Smith 2020), but it is estimated that China executes "thousands each year" (OHCHR, 2021). China's death penalty system has always been seen as a violation of human rights. Its socialist government is said to utilize capital punishment to maintain its social order, oppress its political opposition, and curb the rising crime rate (Lim 2013; Miao 2013).

There is truth to these reports. Nevertheless, Western media reports and academic research on the death penalty in China tend to be one-dimensional and oversimplified. They typically lack sufficient detail and overlook the complex nature of the issue. In addition, Western legal academics pay little attention to the most recent developments in China's practice of capital punishment.

Lethal injection has not yet been examined in China to the extent it has in the West. It merits a much more thorough analysis than it has received. In this chapter, I seek to expand the existing literature by focusing on one of the most recent developments of the death penalty in China: the use of lethal injection. In particular, I will discuss its use from the perspectives of human rights and bioethics.

Lethal Injections and Human Rights

In the twentieth century, lethal injection was considered a relatively humane method of execution by the international human rights movement. This movement has been a restraining influence on China, a country that has frequently been cited as a violator of human rights because of its extensive use of the death penalty. It is the concern for a better global image that propelled China to research lethal injection as a preferable method of execution, leading China to adopt it in 1997 (Li 2008). The use of lethal injection in China shares many elements with other countries, while also having some distinctive local peculiarities. Given that the United States regularly uses lethal injection to execute convicts, its use will be addressed as a point of reference.

China previously used shooting as the sole legal method of execution, but added lethal injection in 1997. A key contrast to shooting or other methods of execution is that lethal injection simulates a medical procedure. This has fundamentally transformed the practice. The introduction of lethal injection entails the involvement of medical personnel on a regular basis. To undergo lethal injection, the inmate is typically put in an environment like an "operating" room. Medical or designated personnel are present to place a needle in the arm of the prisoner to induce sleep. The next step in the process is a drug-induced cardiac arrest, followed by the inmate's death (Maggio 2005).

China developed its own combination of drugs that would be used in lethal injection (Li 2008), similar to that used in the United States. It is composed of three ingredients: The first is to cause loss of consciousness (pentothal); the second is to paralyze the heart and suspend pulmonary activities (Pavulon); and the third (potassium chloride) is to induce cardiac arrest (Yang 2008).

I should note, however, that there are differences between China and the United States with regard to the use of lethal injection. One major distinction is that lethal injection in China takes place in an "execution van" or "mobile execution chamber." In 1997 these windowless execution vans were developed and utilized for the first time in Yunnan. Amnesty International (2004) gives this report:

> The windowless execution chamber at the back contains a metal bed on which the prisoner is strapped down. Once a technician attaches the needle, a police officer presses a button and an automatic syringe injects the lethal drug into the prisoner's vein. The execution can be watched on a video monitor next to the driver's seat and can be recorded if required (p. 76).

The Human Rights Committee has urged that "The death penalty . . . must be carried out in such a way as to cause the least possible physical and mental suffering" (The Human Rights Committee 1992, 6). It has been argued that lethal injection inflicts less physical and mental pain than its alternatives (Lifton and Mitchell 2000).

In this sense, China's use of lethal injection is in conformity with international human rights standards, although its implementation of such standards concerning the method of execution is rather localized.

To some degree, the notion of an execution van is used by China to balance its international obligations and local realities. On the one hand, China sought to humanize its method of execution. Because of the influence of the global human rights movement, it adopted the method of lethal injection. On the other hand, the cost of building execution grounds for lethal injection could put a financial strain on the local courts. Thus, execution vans were developed in part to relieve the local courts of such financial burdens (Yang 2008).

Though there is a concern among human rights activists that execution vans and their secrecy may cause the process to be less transparent, they are preferred over conventional execution grounds for at least three reasons. First, execution vans elicit much less resistance from the public than execution grounds. Most people do not want to be living close to an execution ground, as it is deemed inauspicious in Chinese culture (Xu and Tang 2003). Second, execution vans are windowless, and thus do not involve a public spectacle. The vans prevent the widely condemned public executions that were rampant in the 1980s and 1990s (Amnesty International 2004).

Finally, execution vans are more cost-effective. They require less manpower and allow local courts to share and save on the cost. In light of the fact that execution grounds are expensive to be built, the lower-priced execution vans find favor in financially stricken local courts. Even so, execution vans pose a fiscal burden on local communities, and as a result, some experts have called for a special fund to assist local courts in building them (Yang 2008).

For these reasons, execution vans are more suitable than the conventional execution grounds for the local settings in China and have, therefore, been encouraged.

Historically speaking, embracing the global human rights movement and adopting lethal injection signify a philosophical shift in the domestic criminal justice system in China. It is fair to say that the imperial law in China was primarily a prescription of punishments. For example, under the Code of Qing, there were 3,987 punishable offenses (Da Qing Hui Dian). By performing physical torture and mutilation, and very often in public, the state ensured that law was literally implicated into the body politic. When convicts were decapitated, mutilated, or disemboweled, pain was inflicted, and it was thought that justice was served.

Lethal injection, in contrast, is viewed as painless (Pan and Wang 2008). It is intended to be more humane and to minimize the suffering of both inmates and executioners (Zheng, 2008). Not only have policy-makers found value with painless lethal injection, the public has also agreed that humane methods of execution are preferable. For this reason, it was concluded that lethal injection should replace traditional execution methods (Yuan 2009). From this standpoint, using less painful lethal injection is a historic landmark in the evolution of the Chinese criminal justice system.

China is seeking to expand the use of lethal injection on a nationwide basis. In 2008 about half of the 404 intermediate courts were using lethal injection. One major obstacle to the expansive use of lethal injection is cost considerations. Consequently, in order to lower the cost and expedite the reform, the Supreme People's Court took a bold step, deciding to provide the lethal cocktail to local courts at no expense (Bezlova 2008).

The next step for China's death penalty is to legalize lethal injection as the sole lawful method of execution. There are various reasons to recommend this reform. First, it results in less suffering. Compared to shooting and other methods of execution, lethal injection inflicts much less pain (LeGraw and Grodin 2002). It is the method of execution least likely to constitute "cruel and unusual punishment."

Second, there are human rights concerns. Lethal injection conforms to international human rights standards. As far as prisoners' rights, it is in accordance with inmate preferences. According to a Supreme Court poll, death row inmates overwhelmingly prefer lethal injection (Yang 2008). In this sense, to use lethal injection—a more humane method of execution favored by prisoners—is to respect prisoners' rights.

Third, the invention of execution vans has effectively addressed local concerns throughout China. That is to say, they have provided a unique approach for China to implement global human rights standards within its own social context. For this reason, China should discontinue the use of shooting and establish lethal injection as the sole method of execution.

Lastly, by making lethal injection the only form of capital punishment, discrimination and corruption among officials will be reduced. Public opinion polls indicate a concern about the fair use of lethal injection. Several media reports indicate that lethal injection has become the "privilege" of wealthy convicts, while others receive shooting instead. Some experts argue that this phenomenon is not because of corruption but rather an "economic" reason instead. Since the use of lethal injection proves to be too costly for many less developed areas, it is plausible that corrupt officials allow lethal injection more often for wealthy criminals than those who are more disadvantaged (Bezlova 2008). Nonetheless, consistent and detailed implementation guidelines that explicitly prescribe who receives lethal injection and how it should be carried out are imperative (Yang 2008; Zou 2012). This is not simply a matter of honoring the last wishes of convicts, but an issue of fairness and integrity of the criminal justice system as a whole.

Lethal Injections and Bioethics

In general, the use of lethal injection is a positive step forward in China's reform of its death penalty system. Its "humane" feature identifies with the spirit of international human rights standards. Nevertheless, the "medical" nature of lethal injection demands that any discussion of its use should involve bioethics.

In China, the implementation of lethal injection has raised several bioethical concerns with some distinctive local features. Currently, there are two key bioethical issues that need to be attended to. These are the role of the medical profession, and the harvesting of organs from executed prisoners. Let us look at both of these concerns.

THE ROLE OF MEDICAL PROFESSIONALS

One source of the controversy surrounding lethal injection is the involvement of medical professionals. Before 1997, China used shooting as the sole legal method of execution. No other medical personnel other than forensic officers took part in the process. But to carry out lethal injection, medical knowledge is essential, which means medical professionals, or personnel with medical training, have to take part in the implementation. Whether such involvement violates medical ethics is subject to debate (Amnesty International 1994).

In the United States, the medical profession has expressed mixed views on participating in the process of lethal injection (Maggio 2005). One argument is that it violates the Hippocratic Oath, of "first do no harm." Yet, there is no agreement as to what exactly constitutes "participation" in an execution, even though physicians, nurses, and other medically trained personnel "play a vital role" in lethal injection, at least in the United States (LeGraw and Grodin 2002, 384). The participation of medical professionals in lethal injection is considered to be morally impermissible by some scholars (Nelson and Ashby 2011). They are accused of using their medical knowledge to assist in state-sanctioned killing—"judicial homicide." Furthermore, it is argued that they facilitate the process and glorify the death penalty by taking part. One concern is that this may shield capital punishment from legal challenges (LeGraw and Grodin 2002).

Some scholars in China have argued that "do no harm" is a relative concept. It does not necessarily entail humanitarianism. Under certain circumstances, only relative humanitarianism can be achieved (Zhou 1997). Generally speaking, the role of medical professionals in the process of lethal injection has yet to become as much a source of debate in China as it is in the United States. One way to end the ethical dilemma for the medical profession is to abolish the death penalty so that lethal injection will not be needed. After all, the death penalty itself has long been challenged as a violation of human rights (Méndez 2012).

There has been a worldwide movement toward ending capital punishment (Schabas 2002). Such international trends have pressured the Chinese government to compromise (Cohen 1987). While acknowledging the international trend toward the abolition of the death penalty, it is crucial to be aware of the important role that local culture can play.

Overall, the death penalty law in China is headed in the right direction, namely, toward conforming to international human rights law. With ongoing reform, China will abolish the death penalty altogether ("China Questions Death Penalty" 2005). Until then, it appears that "killing fewer and killing carefully" will be the dominant policy. If so, this will be a step closer toward the ultimate abolition of capital punishment, and is more applicable to the social reality of China (Stetler 2008).

It helps to look at the issue in a historical context. The use of capital punishment, constituting "cruel and unusual punishment," is a fairly new and modern concept. There had been general acceptance of the necessity of harsh punishments for thousands of years in China (Moore 2001; Zhang 2008). Drastic change might be counterproductive. Nonetheless, among Chinese policymakers and academics is an increasing willingness to reconsider the use of the death penalty and eagerness to reform their death penalty system.

We can see a dramatic rhetorical change by examining the discussion on the death penalty among Chinese policymakers since the economic reform took place in 1978 (Hood 2009). This change indicates less and less emphasis on the local context over time. In 1987, Gao Mingxuan, a prominent legal scholar and public official, claimed that the death penalty was indispensable to China, "to protect the fundamental interests of the state and people, to safeguard our socialist construction and to secure and promote the development of productive forces" (Fitzpatrick and Miller 1993, 278). In 1993, a top Chinese official asserted at the World Conference on Human Rights that "countries at different development stages or with different historical traditions and cultural backgrounds . . . have different understanding and practice of human rights" (Wyman 1997, 561).

But in 2008, Xiao Yang, the former chief justice of the Supreme People's Court, in his report to the National People's Congress, stated that executions in China were now limited to an "extremely small number of extremely serious and extremely vile criminals posing a grievous threat to society" (Scott 2010, 66). Evidently, there is a growing interest in the issue of the death penalty among Chinese authorities. They have become more receptive to the global trend of an abolitionist movement and have adjusted their local policies accordingly. It seems that the death penalty in China will continue to be reformed, and it will be abolished in the future.

The debates on the death penalty among Chinese legal scholars have shifted the focus from the justification of its use to how to eventually abolish it (Sun 2009). With the global abolitionist movement in mind, fewer Chinese legal scholars believe in the permanent necessity of capital punishment in China. More and more agree that it is just a matter of when and how to abolish it. They have proposed a strategy of "the gradual abolition of the death penalty" in an attempt to maintain a balance between the international trend and the local reality (Wei 2008, 57). To a large extent, a gradual abolition is a workable and realistic proposal. It could be dangerous to become an abolitionist overnight, especially if that country is known for its overuse of the death penalty (Sharoni 2001). "Killing fewer and killing carefully," as a transitional policy toward the ultimate abolition of capital punishment in China, should be allowed. Until China abolishes the death penalty, lethal injection is a relatively humane method of execution to use. Thus, as long as lethal injection is used in capital punishment, the ethical dilemma for the medical profession remains.

China has found an uncommon way to moderately solve this ethical dilemma by sheltering the entire medical profession, including physicians and nurses, from the process. In China, local prison officers are trained to carry out lethal injection, and forensic officers are present only to pronounce the death of prisoners (Zhuang 2005). Essentially, this practice minimizes the involvement of medical personnel and, to a certain extent, frees them from the ethical predicament. Undoubtedly, it will require strict protocols to avoid any botched executions. But at least the medical profession can be somewhat exempt from the ethical dilemma that their American colleagues face with lethal injection.

Nonetheless, even though, according to the current practice in China, the medical profession does not have to participate directly in the process of actual lethal injection, other issues arise. They still have to be involved in the process, such as training prison officers and developing a safe formula for drugs to be used in lethal injection. The latter two activities may or may not constitute "participation in execution."

According to the AMA (American Medical Association) definition, training prison officers to carry out lethal injection is "an action which would assist, supervise, or contribute to the ability of another individual to directly cause the death of the condemned." Developing a safe drug formula to be used in lethal injection could also constitute "participation in execution" (AMA Code of Medical Ethics, Opinion 2.06). In this sense, the current practice in China has not completely excused the medical profession from the ethical dilemma.

HARVESTING THE ORGANS OF DEATH ROW INMATES

In addition to the ethical predicament of the medical profession, harvesting the organs of death row inmates is another major bioethical issue associated with lethal injection. Both shooting and lethal injection offer the opportunity to harvest the organs of prisoners, as these two methods of execution allow most organs to remain intact. There has been an outcry that China practices harvesting prisoners' organs without their consent (Brown 1996; Gittings 1998). Human rights activists worry that the use of lethal injection and execution vans ensures that the body remains undamaged and, therefore, might promote the actual organ harvesting of prisoners in China (Bezlova 2008).

The issue of harvesting the organs of prisoners is multifaceted. First, death row inmates should be allowed the opportunity to donate their organs. When an organ is transplanted, the donor may perceive that his/her life has been continued in the recipient (Shen 1997). This act of altruism is the ethical foundation for organ transplants (Guan and Li 2001). As members of society, death row inmates should be granted the opportunity to donate their organs if they explicitly express that wish. Conversely, death row inmates should have the right to refuse to donate their organs. Because the practice of harvesting prisoners' organs without their consent has occurred in China, this side of the argument should be emphasized to prevent any injustice.

Second, if prisoners do not give consent, harvesting their organs is morally wrong and should be illegal. The percentage of the Chinese favoring organ transplants is around 70 percent, but the donation rate is much lower (Wang, Su, and Liu 2002). Such discrepancy reflects the impact of the traditional culture. According to Confucianism, our bodies are given to us by our parents, and donation is the most unfilial act. Many people still think that keeping a dead body intact is a respectful act and hope they can have an unbroken body after death (Xie, Huang, and Liu 2000). This is to say that a significant number of Chinese people culturally oppose the idea of donating their organs. Thus, to lure or force death row inmates to donate their organs or to harvest their organs without their consent is considered repugnant (Caplan 2011).

Third, harvesting organs requires medical knowledge. One way to thwart illegal harvesting is to have a strict ethical code prohibiting medical professionals from engaging in any illegal harvesting of the organs of executed prisoners (Brown 1996). In response to such concern, the Ministry of Health in China issued a ban on the sale of organs ("Execution Van" 2009). In addition, the People's Supreme Court issued an order in 2011 stipulating that only with the consent of death row inmates or their families can their organs be harvested. There is also the Interim Provisions on Human Organ Procurement and Allocation issued by National Health and Family Planning Commission in 2013 (Huang 2017). The effect of these orders remains to be seen.

In order to address those two bioethical dilemmas—medical personnel participating in lethal injection, and the harvesting of executed prisoners' organs—detailed implementation guidelines on lethal injection are imperative. These guidelines ought to be based on widely accepted principles of bioethics, such as those proposed by Beauchamp and Childress (2008). Their transformative four principles are autonomy, nonmaleficence, beneficence, and justice. All are strongly relevant to the issues described above. For example, their theory of "autonomy" could be useful for examining the meaning of consent with respect to condemned prisoners donating their organs in China. How to apply these principles to specific policies is challenging, but would appear to be very fruitful.

China has incorporated international standards into its major national bioethics regulations that explicitly refer to international bioethics documents, such as the Declaration of Helsinki (WMA 2004). Nevertheless, the principal concern is that these regulations lack specifics, a problem that the new guidelines on lethal injection should overcome (Hennig 2006). Guidelines with specifics will also help to prevent the occurrence of botched lethal injection, as has happened in the United States. In particular, the administering of drugs in the United States has been found to be problematic. The botched executions of Raymond Landry, Stephen McCoy, and Billy Wayne White have raised questions on how to improve the safety of administering lethal injection and how to minimize the pain inflicted on prisoners (Maggio 2005). So far, in China, no such cases have been reported.

Nevertheless, China could learn from what has occurred in the United States. In particular, some have raised concerns over the questionable death determination criteria in execution by lethal injection in China (Paul et al. 2018). The People's Supreme Court of China issued the Notice on Using Lethal Injection in Executions in 2001 to standardize the procedures (Liu 2006), but the notice itself lacks details and lags behind in addressing some critical issues, such as the role of the medical profession and organ transplants.

It is worth mentioning that the psychological impact on executioners has been duly noted in China. In Chinese culture, it is normally considered inauspicious to administer an execution. Because of such a heavy psychological burden, some prison officers have been reluctant to carry out lethal injection (He and Li 2008). How to seek aid from professional psychologists for those involved in administering lethal injection should also be included in the guidelines (Yang 2008). If lethal injection is to be effectively applied in China, there needs to be a satisfactory implementation of global human rights and bioethical norms, as well as the cultural considerations noted above.

Conclusion

To sum up, the use of lethal injection represents a progressive development of the death penalty in China. It is an attempt to balance China's international obligations with its own social and cultural realities. The practice of lethal injection in China indicates that when abstract international human rights and bioethical norms are implemented in local contexts, there exists a degree of variation. Such variation is inevitable and ought to be tolerated. The use of execution vans is a case in point. As the Universal Declaration on Bioethics and Human Rights justly puts it, "the importance of cultural diversity and pluralism should be given due regard" (UNESCO 2005, Art. 12).

Lethal injection requires continuous reform to ensure its safe and fair use. Such reform should consider local details while incorporating global standards. Practical application of global norms necessitates a deep knowledge of local conditions. Neglecting local conditions and cultural factors influencing values and perceptions could be disastrous.

Two major related bioethics challenges—the role of the medical profession, and organ harvesting of condemned prisoners—call for legislative and judiciary action. Detailed implementation guidelines for lethal injection based on local specifics should be developed to adequately address these challenges. It is not easy to find a balance between global norms and local reality, especially when the global norms are new to the local culture. But it is not impossible.

Note

1. © Springer Nature Switzerland AG 2019. Wanda Teays, "Doctors and Torture: Medicine at the Crossroads," International Library of Ethics, Law, and the New Medicine 80: 95–107. Used with permission

References

American Medical Association. *AMA Code of Medical Ethics 9.7.3 Capital Punishment*. 2022. https://code-medical-ethics.ama-assn.org/sites/default/files/2022-08/9.7.3.pdf.

Amnesty International. *Undermining Global Security: The European Union's Arms Exports*. 2004. https://www.amnesty.org/en/wp-content/uploads/2021/08/act300032004en.pdf.

———. *Death Sentences and Execution*. 2008. http://www.amnesty.org/en/death-penalty.

Beauchamp, Tom, and James F. Childress. *Principles of Biomedical Ethics* (6th ed.). Oxford: Oxford University Press, 2008.

Bezlova, Antoaneta. "China: Will the People Choose the Death Penalty?" Inter Press Service. June 14, 2008. https://www.ipsnews.net/2008/06/china-will-the-people-choose-the-death-penalty/

Brown, Kelly M. "Execution for Profit? A Constitutional Analysis of China's Practice of Harvesting Executed Prisoners' Organs." *Seton Hall Constitutional Law Journal* 6 (1996): 1029–82.

Caplan, Arthur. "The Use of Prisoners as Sources of Organs: An Ethically Dubious Practice." *American Journal of Bioethics* 11, no. 10 (2011): 1–5.

China Questions Death Penalty. *China Daily*. 2005. http://www.chinadaily.com.cn/english/doc/2005-01/27/content_412758.htm.

Cohen, Roberta. "People's Republic of China: The Human Rights Exception." *Human Rights Quarterly* 9, no. 4 (1987): 447–549.

Da Qing Hui Dian (Collected Institutes of the Great Qing Dynasty), 54:1a-b.

Fitzpatrick, Joan, and Alice Miller. "International Standards on the Death Penalty: Shifting Discourse." *Brooklyn Journal of International Law* 19 (1993): 273–366.

Gittings, John. "Amnesty Expresses Concern as China Adopts Lethal Injection Law." *The Guardian*, January 30, 1998, 17.

Guan, Wenxian, and Kaizong Li. "Kaizhan Huoti QiguanYizhi de Lunli Xue Sikao." Yixue yu Zhexue (*Medicine and Philosophy*) 22, no. 6 (2001): 8–13.

He, Chengbing, and Jiaxian Li. "Kaowen Zhushe Sixing de Sandananyan Zhiyin." *Fazhi Yanjiu* (*Legal Research*) 10 (2008): 75–79.

Hennig, Wolfgang. "Bioethics in China: Although National Guidelines Are in Place, Their Implementation Remains Difficult." *EMBO Reports* 7, no. 9 (2006): 850–54. https://doi.org/10.1038/sj.embor.7400794.

Hood, Roger. "Abolition of the Death Penalty: China in World Perspective." *City University of Hong Kong Law Review* 1 (2009): 1–21.

Huang, Jiefu. "The 'Chinese Mode' of Organ Donation and Transplantation." *Hepatobiliary Surgery and Nutrition* 6, no. 4 (2017): 212–14. https://doi.org/10.21037/hbsn.2017.07.08.

Human Rights Committee. *General Comment 20*, UN HRC, 44th Session, UN Doc ccpr/c/21/Add.3. 1992.

LeGraw, Joan M., and Michael A. Grodin. "Health Professionals and Lethal Injection Execution in the United States." *Human Rights Quarterly* 24, no. 2 (2002): 382–423.

Li, Jingrui. "Zhushe Sixing" (Lethal Injection). *The Beijing News*, 2008. http://www.thebeijingnews.com/news/reform30/2008/11-03/011@10043 8.htm.

Lifton, Robert, and Greg Mitchel. *Who Owns Death? Capital Punishment, The American Conscience, and the End of the Death Penalty*. New York: William Morrow, 2000.

Lim, Zi Heng. "Why China Executes So Many People?" *The Atlantic*. May 9, 2013. https://www.theatlantic.com/china/archive/2013/05/why-china-executes-so-many-people/275695/.

Liu, Xiaoxiao. "Zhejiang Jiuyue Yiri qi Zhushe Daiti QiangjueZhixing Sixing." *Legal Daily*, 2006.

Maggio, Edward J., Esq. "A Violent Roman Tradition." *Digest* 13, no. 35 (2005): 35–49.

Méndez, Juan E. "The Death Penalty and the Absolute Prohibition of Torture and Cruel, Inhuman, and Degrading Treatment or Punishment." *Human Rights Brief* 20, no. 1 (2012): 2–6.

Miao, Michelle. "Capital Punishment in China: A Populist Instrument of Social Governance." *Theoretical Criminology* 17, no. 2 (2013): 233–50.

Moore, Barrington, Jr. "Cruel and Unusual Punishment in the Roman Empire and Dynastic China." *International Journal of Politics, Culture, and Society* 14, no. 4 (2001): 729–72.

Nelson, Lawrence, and Brandon Ashby. "Rethinking the Ethics of Physician Participation in Lethal Injection Execution." *Hastings Center Report* 41, no. 3 (2011): 28–37.

OHCHR. *UN Universal Periodic Review of China: Mid-Term Report*. 2021. https://www.ohchr.org/sites/default/files/2021-11/TheRightsPractice_UPR_of_China_Mid-term_Report_November2021.pdf.

Pan, X., and X. Wang. "Zuihou Yiqiang-Zhongguo Jiasu PujiZhushe Sixing." *Nanfang Zhoumo* (*Southern Weekend*), April 10, 2008, A03.

Paul, Norbert W., Arthur Caplan, Michael E. Shapiro, Charl Els, Kirk C. Allison, and Huige Li. "Determination of Death in Execution by Lethal Injection in China." *Cambridge Quarterly of Healthcare Ethics* 27, no. 3 (2018): 459–66.

Schabas, William A. *The Abolition of the Death Penalty in International Law* (3rd ed.). Cambridge, UK: Cambridge University Press, 2002.

Scott, Kandis. "Why Did China Reform Its Death Penalty." *Pacific Rim Law and Policy Journal* 19 (2010): 63–80.

Sharoni, Michelle M. "A Journey of Two Countries: A Comparative Study of the Death Penalty in Israel and South Africa." *Hastings International Comparative Law Review* 24, no. 2 (2001): 257–84.

Shen, Mingxian. "Shengsi Jushan, Rendao Biyi." Shanghai Shehui Kexue Yuan Xueshu Jikan. *Academic Seasonal Journal of Shanghai Academy of Social Science* (1997): 2.

Smith, Tobias. "Body Count Politics: Quantification, Secrecy, and Capital Punishment in China." *Law & Social Inquiry* 45, no. 3 (2020): 706–27.

Stetler, Russel. "Killing Fewer, and Killing Carefully: Death Penalty Defense in China on the Eve of the Beijing Olympics." *Champion*, 32, no. 22 (July 2008): 27.

Sun,W. "Sixing Cunzai de Beilun yu Feizhi de Genben Dongle." Huadong Zhengfa Daxue Xuebao. *Journal of the East China University of Political Science and Law* 2 (2009): 106–12.

UNESCO. *Universal Declaration on Bioethics and Human Rights*. 2005. http://portal.unesco.org/en/ev.php-URL_ID=31058&URL_DO=DO_TO PIC&URL_SECTION=201.html.

Wang, Hua, Bo Su, and Jianwen Liu Guanyu. "Woguo QiguanYizhi de Youguan Falv he Lunli Wenti." *Zhongguo Yixue LunliXue* (*Chinese Medical Ethics*) 4 (2002): 21.

Wei, Y. "Qiu Xinglong he 96ming Sixingfan Tongjian." *Nanfang Renwu Zhoukan* (*Southern People Weekly*) 12 (2008): 57–59.

WMA. *Declaration of Helsinki: Ethical Principles for Medical Research Involving Human Subjects.* Ferney-le-Voltaire, France: World Medical Association, 2004.

Wyman, James H. "Vengeance Is Whose? The Death Penalty and Cultural Relativism in International Law." *Journal of Transnational Law and Policy* 6 (1997): 543–67.

Xie, Miao, Chun Huang, and Xingchun Liu. "Guanyu WoguoQiguan Yizhi yu Qiguan Juanxian de Sikao." Zhongguo YixueLunli Xue (*Chinese Medical Ethics*) 6 (2000): 9.

Xu, R., and J. Tang (2003). Yunnan Tuiguang Zhushe Sixing: Guannian Zuai. *Xinwen Zhoukan* (*News Weekly*) 9 (2003): 32–33.

Yang, Xi. "Expert: China Is Fit for Lethal Injections." *China.org.cn*. January 3, 2008. http://www.china.org.cn/english/GS-e/237842.htm.

Yuan, B. "Woguo Minzong Sixing Jinben Guannian ShizhengFenxi." *Xingfa Luncong* (*Criminal Law Review*) 1 (2009): 36.

Zou, Bing (2010). "On the Standardization of Lethal Injections in China." *Asian Social Science* 8, no. 6 (2010): 82–85.

Part III Internet Resources

LIFE AND DEATH

The Hastings Center
https://www.thehastingscenter.org/

Center for Reproductive Justice
https://reproductiverights.org/

Abortion Laws by State | Center for Reproductive Rights
https://reproductiverights.org/maps/abortion-laws-by-state

Where is Abortion Illegal? | Abortion Limits by State
https://www.plannedparenthoodaction.org/abortion-access-tool/US

An Overview of Abortion Laws | Guttmacher Institute
https://www.guttmacher.org/state-policy/explore/overview-abortion-laws

Focus | Death: Pros and Cons of Physician Aid in Dying
https://www.ncbi.nlm.nih.gov/pmc/articles/PMC6913818

Doctors' Opinions on Euthanasia, End-of-Life Care, and Doctor–Patient . . .
https://www.bmj.com/content/327/7415/595

Euthanasia and Assisted Dying: What Is the Current Position | PubMed
https://pubmed.ncbi.nlm.nih.gov/30427291

Not Dead Yet (Grassroots Disability Rights Group)
https://notdeadyet.org/

So Long as They Die: Lethal Injections in the United States | HRW
https://www.hrw.org/report/2006/04/23/so-long-they-die/lethal-injections-united-states

World Federation of Right to Die Societies
https://wfrtds.org/

Suicide Tourism and Understanding the Swiss Model of the Right to Die
https://theconversation.com/suicide-tourism-and-understanding-the-swiss-model-of-the-right-to-die-96698

Part III Discussion Topics

LIFE AND DEATH

1. How can we balance the needs of the aging with the needs of pregnant women, infants, and children?
2. Should children be able to participate—if not decide treatment—in life/death medical decisions?
3. Should parents be able to use the sperm of their dead son to have grandchildren? Set out your position in response to this case: *In the Matter of Zhu* (https://law.justia.com/cases/new-york/other-courts/2019/2019-ny-slip-op-29146.html.
4. Consider the case of the NASA scientist who used in vitro fertilization [IVF] with a nineteen-year-old embryo in her quest for a child. Denise Lineberry (2013) reports:

> After three years of trying to conceive, accompanied by two miscarriages, [NASA scientist] Kelly Burke headed in the direction of adoption. Her adoption lawyer called her with an unexpected opportunity: A couple from Oregon was donating their frozen embryos—four of them, to be exact. When Burke heard that the embryos [had been] frozen for nineteen years, she was initially worried and began to research the viability of frozen embryos and have discussions with her fertility doctors. "What I found was that they were still very viable," says Burke. Her research proved true when Liam, who is now nine months old, is believed by her doctors to be the second-oldest cryopreserved embryo to result in a live birth (www.nasa.gov/lare/center-snapshot-kelly-burke).

- What sorts of limits—if any—do you think should be put in place?
- Given the unknown risks of using embryos, eggs, and sperm that have been frozen for years, or even decades, at what point should societal interests be factored into policies regarding such assisted reproduction?

5. Do you think it is right to restrict or even prohibit egg donation or sales? Read the following excerpt from the *Science Daily* (2011) and then share your thoughts:

> Women who have become pregnant after egg donation should be categorized as high-risk patients. . . . Ulrich Pecks and co-authors . . . support their assessment with data from recent publications and with a case series they

> encountered in their own hospital. . . . [T]hey found that within the past four years, eight women who had received donated eggs had to be treated for pregnancy-induced hypertension. Three of these pregnancies had to be terminated prematurely because of the threat to the mother's life. The other five cases showed a milder course of pregnancy-induced hypertension.
>
> Egg donation has been in use for more than twenty-five years to treat unwanted childlessness. Since the German law on the protection of embryos explicitly forbids the procedure, couples often use medical institutions in neighboring European countries. After successful embryo transfer, the pregnant women are subsequently cared for in Germany in accordance with statutory maternity provision. Because of the risk of a hypertensive disorder of pregnancy, the authors recommend that patients are closely monitored by doctors with a specialization in maternofetal medicine. ("Egg Donation: The Way to Happy Motherhood, With Risks and Side Effects," *Science Daily,* January 25, 2011).

6. Share your thoughts and concerns regarding the autonomy of minors seeking an abortion.
   - A 2013 report on the state of Arizona stated that 25 percent of abortion requests by minors that go before the Juvenile Court are denied (e.g., because of her "maturity"). Should the minor woman's maturity be a factor in deciding this issue?
   - An example is the August 2022 decision by a Florida court. CNN reports: "A pregnant sixteen-year-old in Florida was denied a waiver to get an abortion in the state without legal guardian notification and consent, after a court deemed that she did not prove that she is mature enough to make the decision" (Veronica Stracqualursi, "Florida Court Denies Pregnant Teen's Request to Waive Legal Guardian Consent for Abortion," *CNN*, August 17, 2022).
7. To what degree should the abortion debate focus on the personhood of the fetus?
   - If the fetus can be considered a person, should it have equal or greater rights than the woman whose body is gestating that person?
   - If the fetus cannot be considered a person, should it have fewer rights than the woman whose body is gestating that entity (nonperson)?
8. If a patient cannot speak for him- or herself and has no advance directives, but the hospital knows the patient's religious affiliation, should doctors be allowed to turn to a representative (priest, minister, imam, rabbi, etc.) about the patient's medical care in end-of-life decisions?
9. If people have a right to life and liberty, does it follow that they also have a right to die in terms of obtaining assistance in dying?
10. In their chapters, Scott Stonington and Pinit Ratanakul and Cecilia Wee examine cultural issues around euthanasia.
    - How might we factor in cultural considerations when medical issues center on the end of life?
    - Would some form of sensitivity or mediation help to bridge the differences between caregivers and the patient and his or her family? If not, what else could be put in place—for example, in terms of cultural protocols?

11. Should doctors participate in lethal injections?
12. Amnesty International objects to lethal injections in capital punishment and raises concerns on its website about the involvement of medical personnel when it comes to harvesting organs from condemned prisoners.
    - State *one* argument for and *one* argument against harvesting organs from executed prisoners.

Part IV

PUBLIC HEALTH

CHAPTER 20

A Bioethics for Global Mental Health

Zenon Culverhouse

Abstract

Global mental health (GMH) is a rapidly growing movement supported by the World Health Organization that aims "to improve treatments . . . and reduce human rights abuses of people experiencing mental disorders," particularly among the most vulnerable populations in the Global South (Patel et al. 2014, 3). Because of GMH's reliance on Western psychiatry, this movement is criticized for engaging in a form of colonialization by imposing Western concepts and treatments of mental disorder on "other" cultures, often on the assumption that local cultural norms of disorder are inferior to the scientifically rigorous concepts of psychiatry. There is, therefore, a great need to reassess the moral principles that guide psychiatric interventions in non-Western cultures. Yet bioethics as a profession has paid relatively little attention to mental health, much less to mental health in a global context. In addition, the values of mainstream bioethics are the very values encoded in GMH and criticized by its opponents. I argue that a bioethics for GMH must avoid the twin horns of colonialization and ethical relativism. While proposed solutions from GMH and bioethics are on the right path by incorporating guidelines for culturally sensitive treatment, they do not go far enough. To make up for this, I utilize the framework of epistemic injustice, which identifies a fundamental harm that other solutions miss and offers a solution for avoiding it.

The Promise and Peril of Globalized Medicine

GMH developed as a movement as a result of several alarming statistics on the burden of mental health worldwide. The World Health Organization's (WHO's) *World Health Report* stated in 2001 that approximately 7.5 percent of the world's population suffers from mental disorders, with increases projected (2001, 23, 26).

It also indicates that poverty-, war-, or disaster-stricken populations bear a disproportionate burden of mental disorder (2001, 40). This report spurred the creation in 2008 of the Mental Health Gap Action Programme (mhGAP).[1] Given that low- and middle-income countries, particularly in the Global South, are especially burdened by mental disorder due to a relative shortage or outright lack of resources, the primary objective of WHO was, and still is, to close the "treatment gap." Providing adequate treatment in countries with limited resources has the added challenge of having to rely on "*task-sharing,* whereby non-specialist health workers are trained to take on the more routine aspects of interventions" (Cohen et al. 2014, 16).

GMH is not without its critics. While the work of psychiatrists is well intentioned and often helpful, there is a concern that as a field dominated by Western values, psychiatry imposes these values on cultures and persons as though they are the only correct values. GMH is accused of a form of colonialism, or "psychiatric imperialism" (Summerfield 2013, 1), by "exporting Western illness categories and treatments that would ultimately replace diverse cultural environments for interpreting mental health" (Bemme and D'Souza 2012). Many of the examples of testimony from those involved with GMH echo the complaints of psychiatric patients in the West: Psychiatrists favor objective, scientifically verifiable evidence to make a diagnosis and therefore do not take seriously the patients' own subjective assessments of their distress (Mills 2014, 1).

Excessive reliance on pharmacological treatments is also problematic, especially when it supersedes or negates religious, spiritual, or culturally specific treatments (Fernando 2010; Mills 2014, 3). Most damning is the claim that psychiatry not only undermines a person's agency but is a threat to their very identity: "Western psychological discourse is setting out to instruct, regulate, and modernise, presenting as definitive the contemporary Western way of being a person" (Summerfield 2008, 992).

Framing these criticisms of GMH in terms of principle-based bioethics, the problem is that medical practitioners override a patient's autonomy in the name of beneficence, on the assumption that the two principles conflict. If these efforts at diagnosis and treatment are harmful, then GMH is really just paternalism in disguise. The problem is made more difficult given the cross-cultural context of GMH work. The right to autonomy (i.e., the right to self-determination and individual freedom) is arguably a distinctly Western value of liberal individualism, rather than a principle universal to all persons.

Many cultures that receive aid from GMH prioritize communal decision-making over individual autonomy. In effect, GMH is accused of failing to respect individual autonomy, on the one hand, and on the other, failing to acknowledge the relevance of cultural norms in diagnosing and treating mental disorders. A bioethics for GMH will therefore have to adapt its expertise to ensure that the individual patient has a voice in managing her own mental health and that the beliefs and practices of the culture in which that patient lives are given due respect.

However, anyone looking for a thorough assessment of the ethics of global mental health will not find it in mainstream bioethics alone. The Hastings Center series produced *What Price Mental Health?* in 1995. Though this work briefly acknowledged the unique difficulties that set mental health apart from general medicine, it mainly focused on how to allocate limited health-care resources between the two in the United States (Boyle and Callahan 1995, 4–5). At the same time, there was a proliferation of entries on mental health in the second edition of the *Encyclopedia of Bioethics*, with updates and additions to the third edition (Post 2003). In spite of this, as well as several publications urging the profession to devote more attention to mental health, a survey of popular bioethics texts published over the past decade contain very little devoted to ethical issues in mental health, much less in GMH.[2] To get a clearer picture of the potential challenges to a bioethics of GMH, it is necessary to consider the ethical decision-making tools currently utilized in mainstream bioethics.

Autonomy-Driven Bioethics of Mental Health, Past and Present

When the Hastings Center began to establish itself as a premier center for bioethics, mental health (at the time labeled "behavioral control") was one of five areas of focus. This focus was short-lived due to bioethics' prioritization of autonomy and its preoccupation with physical medicine and technology. One of the center's cofounders, Daniel Callahan, writes that "bioethics is a child of American individualism," favoring "principlism," which prizes respect for individual freedom and autonomy above all (Callahan 1999, 58). Emphasis on the right to self-determination and resistance to paternalism in medicine was not balanced with attention to the ways in which society and culture shape individual experience (Callahan 1999, 59). In other words, the focus on autonomy neglected the fact that an individual's values are embedded in a cultural context and are given meaning by that context.

Drawing from her review of bioethics literature from this time period, Janet Nelson states that the conception of autonomy that emerges is a "rationalistic model of decision making," in which the patient is viewed as "an independent agent faced with essentially either/or choices to be made in the context of health care" (Nelson 2003, 186). This is implied by Callahan when he laments that the focus on autonomy marginalized the value of beneficence. When it comes to medical decisions that could override a person's own desires, beneficence looks like a crude form of paternalism or, as Callahan puts it, "deciding what's good for others" (Callahan 1999, 58). At the same time that bioethics was emerging, the public was reminded of horrific conditions in mental health institutions, accelerating the move from institutionalization to community-based mental health services precisely because outpatient care was deemed more conducive to autonomy.[3]

Given that the psychiatric community moved on its own toward a more autonomy-friendly model of mental health care, bioethics left psychiatry to its own devices in determining the ethics of mental health care and turned its attention back to emerging issues in physical medicine and technology (Nelson 2003, 183; Williams 2016, 224). Given all of this, it is easy to see how ethical issues regarding mental health in other countries and cultures were even less of a priority. Furthermore, it is clear that the accusation of medical colonialization against GMH could not be countered by the principlism of bioethics. Bioethics' prioritization of individual autonomy could serve as a counter to GMH's medical paternalism, but, given the neglect of social and cultural factors, bioethics would have had little to say to critics of GMH who maintain that liberal individualism is among the values dogmatically imposed on other cultures.

More recent assessments of bioethics for mental health echo this prioritization of autonomy, despite their sensitivity to ethical challenges to medicine in a global context. Nelson argues that one of the reasons bioethics has not paid enough attention to mental health is professional isolation from those who work in the mental health profession, and suggests that, in engaging with them, bioethicists ought to "educate themselves, not only on the medical techniques and practices involved, but on the full range of legal, political, cultural, and, above all, social aspects of mental health care. [Bioethicists] need to develop a social bioethics rather than a narrowly analytic one" that disregards a person's social identity (Nelson 2003, 192–93).

In spite of this call for "social bioethics," Nelson ultimately prioritizes autonomy in spite of her criticisms of it: "Bioethics discourse, drawing upon a richer conceptual framework of . . . autonomy, and self-determination in relation to recovery and inclusion, could significantly contribute to a deeper understanding of the stigma surrounding mental illness" (2003, 193). Williams, who draws from Nelson, also suggests that "such a union [of bioethics and mental health] may have the greatest implications for international human rights if American bioethicists can re-energize an understanding of autonomy" (Williams 2016, 225). Again, this may serve as a counter to medical paternalism, but this alone is insufficient to meet all the charges of medical colonialization. For that, it is necessary to have a bioethics that is more culturally sensitive.

A bioethics that is culturally sensitive must address the following dilemma. When faced with conflicting cultural values, one is often caught between two possibilities, namely, that there are universal moral principles that underlie some cultural variances but are at odds with others, or that there are no such universals: Morality is relative to a given culture or society. There are pitfalls in both possibilities. Ethical relativism renders impossible cross-cultural judgments of harmful practices, such as female genital mutilation. Insistence on universal moral principles runs the risk of colonialism. One need not commit to either. In her work on culture and bioethics, Gbadgesin advocates for "cultural pluralism" (Gbadgesin 2012, 32).

To avoid the twin horns of paternalism and relativism, she argues that the pluralist ought first to seek out a "consistent and intelligible" standard that may underlie various beliefs and practices. To do this, Gbadgesin proposes that one make a serious effort to understand a culture by engaging in intercultural dialogue to identify potential commonalities. In so doing, she says, cultures can establish shared moral principles that may serve as the basis for intercultural bioethics. Only then can some judgment be made about whether or not to accept the belief or practice across cultures.

Gbadgesin's pluralism is not quite *moral* pluralism. Moral pluralism, for present purposes, is the view that there is no shared, universal moral foundation that underlies diverse moral practices and beliefs (Chang 2015). For Gbadgesin, by contrast, moral practices ultimately rest on an objective foundation, namely, a "principle of human flourishing" in which "the moral weight of culture in ethics and bioethics is *relative* to its effect on human flourishing," where flourishing is fundamentally "when an individual . . . is capable of participating in the affairs of the community as a free person with human dignity" (Gbadgesin 2012, 33–34). Should a cultural norm violate that dignity, then one is justified in rejecting it.

A bioethics for mental health in a global context, by extension, should examine the practices of mental health providers to ensure that they are sensitive to cultural norms while also steering clear of those that hinder human flourishing. Again, however, Gbadgesin's notion of human flourishing prioritizes individual autonomy and implies that the person be left alone to pursue her own interests without interference from society, a hallmark of liberal individualism. If a non-Western culture does not share this value, then to avoid the risk of colonialization, it is necessary to revise what "human flourishing" is. Furthermore, Gbadgesin's argument is aimed at a bioethics of physical illness. If flourishing requires having a sound mind, a diagnosis of mental disorder may carry with it an implicit and misguided conception of human flourishing, or, worse, the view that the afflicted lacks the capacity to flourish at all.

Ethical Challenges in Global Mental Health

Advocates of GMH see little controversy in their aims and methods. Vikram Patel, one of the leaders in the GMH movement, says that the cross-cultural work of GMH has "put to rest any notion that mental disorders were a figment of a 'Western' imagination and that the imposition of such concepts . . . amounted to little more than an exercise in neocolonialism" (Patel 2010, 1976; Patel 2012, 6–7). Framing the notion of mental disorder as a "figment of . . . imagination" is a straw man argument. Despite strenuous efforts by Thomas Szaz and others, very few today think that mental disorder is a complete fiction designed to pathologize normal life challenges (Szaz 1961). But there is significant resistance to the idea that mental disorders are uniform across cultures, and much more to the idea that the Western concept of mental disorder is the right one (e.g., Mills 2014).

Patel states that there is consensus on a middle ground: "Despite the important contextual influences on how mental disorders were experienced, explained, and acted upon, these health conditions affected people in all cultures and societies" (Patel 2012, 8). In other words, mental disorders are fixed or universal in their ontology, though diverse in their expression. For Patel, this claim has normative implications: If mental disorders are universal, then the psychiatric community is justified in locating them across cultures and basing their treatment plans on them.[4] A corollary is that the rejection of any universally valid distinction between mental disorder and health runs the risk of ethical relativism: There is no justification for favoring Western modes of psychiatric diagnosis and treatment over a culture's own, ostensibly harmful practices.

To address this problem, GMH advocates have proposed some guidelines for interacting with patients from cultures different from the provider's own that avoids appropriating local medical practices and imposing Western ones. Kirmayer and Swartz (2014), for instance, acknowledge that human beings "live within culturally constructed systems of meaning that are shared by local and global communities" (41). Thus, they also acknowledge "the central role of culture in providing local explanations for suffering and impairment" (2014, 42). They propose an "ecosocial approach that characterizes mental health problems in terms of interactions with the local social environment" that aims to "translate interventions into culturally appropriate language" and "use[s] specific intervention methods that draw from local cultural traditions," among other things (2014, 50).

This approach is promising. It is closely parallel to Nelson's call for "social bioethics," discussed above, and the guidelines mirror Gbadgesin's suggestions to understand a given culture's values, promote intercultural dialogue, and find common ground on which to establish ethical principles for medical treatment.

These guidelines address many of the charges of colonialism made by critics of GMH, particularly its lack of sensitivity to cultural norms and practices. But, if we attend closely to the language of the guidelines, it is clear that the fit between pathology and its cultural expression is a one-way street: Rather than questioning the validity of core concepts of mental disorder in light of cultural idiosyncrasies, these concepts are imported—"translated" into or characterized in terms of culturally specific language. In doing so, the dilemma posed by bioethics between ethical relativism and paternalism rears its head again. Kirmayer and Swartz (2014) and many advocates of GMH *reject* the view that mental disorders—at least the more severe ones—are entirely "culture-bound" (45).

What emerges is a form of pluralism parallel to that proposed by Gbadgesin. In this case it is primarily ontological pluralism of mental disorder that is nonfoundational. Mental disorders are diverse in their expression but universal in their pathology. That is, these interventions assume that understanding the plurality of experience of mental disorders ultimately aims to reduce them to their underlying, universal pathology in order to prescribe appropriate treatment. If they did not, the practice of psychiatry may have to give way to ontological relativism, or the view that there is no universal pathology by which to diagnose and treat an individual.

Given the ethical implications of diagnosis and treatment, ontological pluralism of this sort can also avoid ethical relativism: There are grounds to justify treatment in opposition to cultural norms. But in doing so, it risks being impaled by the other horn: In attempting to preserve objectivity, culturally sensitive interventions that rely ultimately on Western psychiatric concepts still risk colonialization. For instance, Kirmayer and Swartz rely ultimately on the view that cultural beliefs and practices—as well as disorders—are "inscribed in the brain" (2014, 43–45), which fits squarely in the dominant, Western view of mental disorders that characterizes psychiatry today.

Even if it is not disputed whether mental disorders are fixed or universal, problems can still arise in how mental disorders are conceived by the psychiatric community at large and endorsed by GMH. The effort to "translate" psychiatric interventions into cultural idioms of distress does little to address problems at the source. Some explanation is needed to show that attention to cultural idiosyncrasies in the diagnosis and treatment of mental disorder is not simply a reductive exercise, in which cultural differences are stripped away to get at the underlying, universal pathology. This effort is rendered moot if the *proposed* universal pathology turns out not to be universal after all. It is therefore necessary to consider GMH's conception of mental disorder and its underlying values.

GMH is dominated by Western psychiatry, as is evident from the definition of mental disorder stated at the start of WHO's trend-setting *World Health Report* (2001, 21): "Mental and behavioural disorders are understood as clinically significant conditions characterized by alterations in thinking, mood (emotions) or behaviour associated with personal distress and/or impaired functioning."

Though this report explicitly refers to WHO's (1992) standard manual for diagnosis of mental disorders, namely the *International Classification of Diseases* (*ICD*), the phrase "clinically significant" also echoes the definition of mental disorder found in all editions of the American Psychiatric Association's (1994) *Diagnostic and Statistical Manual of Mental Disorders* (*DSM*).[5] The phrase effectively makes the medical practitioner the sole arbiter of what counts as a mental disorder. Put in a global context, this problem is compounded by conflicts between the *DSM* and the *ICD*, now in its eleventh edition (2018). Fulford highlights one such conflict, in which a person receives a diagnosis of schizophrenia from the *ICD-10*, but not the *DSM-4*, precisely because the latter, and not the former, requires that the symptoms of schizophrenia significantly impair social functioning (Fulford 2003, 1790–91). While the person in question suddenly behaved in ways that were unusual, he thrived in his work and life.

In light of such an example, which is by no means rare, it is difficult to accept Patel's dismissal of the idea that mental disorders as defined by the *DSM* and *ICD* are not constructs imposed on individuals and societies. Furthermore, while Patel may be right to claim that there is a universal ontology of mental disorder, it does not follow that the *DSM* or the *ICD* provides the correct one. The values that inform psychiatric approaches to mental disorders in these manuals suggest it is not.

The discipline of psychiatry is still embroiled in controversy over whether mental disorder is a natural kind or a social construct. Both the *DSM* and *ICD*, despite efforts to acknowledge the role culture plays in shaping the experience of mental disorder, are mainly reductive. Particularly relevant is the *DSM*'s "hyponarrativity" of a given syndrome. In his analysis of values in the *DSM*, Sadler observes that "[t]o diagnose a person under the *DSM* is to reveal little of the person's biography . . . and, most importantly, how the illness experience interacts with these narrative aspects" (Sadler 2005, 177). To treat a person's disorder solely in terms of a set of symptoms marginalizes that person's own voice and effectively strips the patient of agency: The patient's subjective assessments of her own distress add little of value to an accurate diagnosis that relies on a general classification of symptoms (e.g., "distressing thoughts" or "avoidance"), or, as psychiatrist Jonathan Shay puts it, "sorting the patient's words into mental bins" (Shay 1995, 10). This makes provider–patient interaction and any subsequent treatment plan effectively paternalistic. While practitioners may acknowledge shortcomings of their practice, the *DSM* and *ICD* do not provide—nor are they intended to provide—any guidance on the role of patient agency and voice in diagnosis.

Hyponarrative assessments of mental disorders are largely due to the psychiatric profession's adherence to values that Sadler describes as "disease naturalism," "individualism," and "empiricism" (Sadler 2005, 177–78). Put roughly, mental disorders are universal, neurobiological pathologies that occur in an individual and are subject to scientific verification. The phenomenology of a disorder, particularly how an individual perceives her own experience, is deemed less important than the underlying ontology of the disorder, given that the underlying ontology is identified via empirical science.

On this model, treatment again focuses on the individual alone, rather than familial, societal, and otherwise shared aspects of disorder. Again, the standard manuals for diagnosis and treatment are not sufficient to address the concerns of critics of GMH. They are in fact counterproductive by advancing a concept of mental disorder that rules out the way in which mental disorders are at least partly socially constructed.

Psychiatry is rationalistic in the sense that both diagnosis and treatment are limited to the language of empirical science. It is also rationalistic insofar as mental disorder is linked to the status of the patient's own rationality—another important mark of autonomy. If a mental disorder disrupts a person's ability to make rational choices, then mental disorder is associated, if not equated, with irrationality. If a person's autonomy depends on being able to make rational choices about their own treatment (the very criterion of autonomy present in mainstream bioethics), then those afflicted with mental disorders lack autonomy. But rationality, too, is a normative concept that carries certain assumptions about what standards of rationality count most.

In her work on mental disorders, philosopher Lisa Bortolotti argues that irrationality is neither necessary nor sufficient for diagnosis of a mental disorder. It is not sufficient since many instances of irrationality (e.g., beliefs that a person maintains contrary to counterevidence, such as racist beliefs), are not typically considered pathologies (Bortolotti 2015, 73). Nor is it necessary, given evidence that depressed persons make more accurate predictions as opposed to the more optimistic person (Bortolotti 2015, 74). This is relevant to the problems facing GMH for several reasons. First, if the person diagnosed with a mental disorder is not by definition irrational, then the patient is also not necessarily lacking agency and autonomy. Second, and more importantly, the practitioner is just as prone to irrationality as the patient, so proper treatment not only requires attending to the patient, but to one's own biases.

Thus far, it looks as though GMH and mainstream bioethics are moving on separate but parallel tracks. Both fields see the need to revise their fundamental principles in light of culturally specific practices without lapsing into relativism. In advocating for a "social bioethics," Nelson and Williams suggest that bioethics involve itself in the mental health field to learn its aims and practices. But given the specific problems associated with psychiatry's conception of mental disorder, looking to beliefs and practices of psychiatry for guidance will reveal only the same sorts of problems that beset bioethics in the first place, namely, prioritization of an individualistic conception of autonomy and the dilemma of colonialization and moral relativism. Where, then, might bioethics look for guidance?

Accounting for Epistemic Injustice in Global Mental Health

The threat of medical colonialization is not just an ethical problem, but also an epistemological problem. The values and concepts endorsed by the GMH movement can conflict with the beliefs and knowledge systems of the populations they treat. In failing to take seriously those knowledge systems—either by ignoring them, overriding them, or "translating them" into psychiatric concepts—GMH is effectively committing what philosopher Miranda Fricker terms "epistemic injustice" (Fricker 2007). Framing the problems facing GMH in terms of epistemic injustice illuminates the specific harm that is caused when these problems go unacknowledged. This framework also provides substantive guidelines for avoiding harm that complement the guidelines for ethical cross-cultural mental health advocacy.

Epistemic injustice in general occurs when "someone is wronged specifically in her capacity as a knower" (Fricker 2007, 20). Fricker identifies two forms of epistemic injustice: testimonial injustice and hermeneutical injustice. *Testimonial injustice* occurs when a person does not take a speaker seriously, owing to a prejudice or negative stereotype that person has regarding the speaker's social identity (Fricker 2007, 28). The example Fricker gives is of a Black person not being believed by the police when reporting a crime against her due to the police officer's prejudice toward people of color. This is easily applicable to a person suffering from a mental disorder: Their community and care providers do not grant them credibility due to prejudices about their identity as a patient with a mental disorder. A physician ignoring a patient's subjective experience and looking only to objective, empirical evidence for a diagnosis is one such example.[6]

An important aspect of this type of injustice is that it is *systematic*. That is, the prejudice consists of a false or distorted belief about a person's membership in a group that is endemic to the society in which one lives, particularly the web of beliefs, practices, and attitudes that perpetuate negative stereotypes. In the psychiatrist's case, the web of beliefs consists of the discipline-specific conception of mental disorder, which may very well harbor prejudices about the value of a patient's own input. In Fricker's example, the particular instance of testimonial injustice occurs among members of one society.

In a cross-cultural context, things are somewhat more complicated, for there can be two systems of prejudice at work—that of psychiatry's biases about a patient's agency and rationality, and the beliefs of the local culture in which the afflicted person lives—that cause the person to be isolated or even institutionalized. In addition, a person's credibility could be deflated not just because of negative stereotypes about mental disorders, but also about that person's race, gender, or ethnicity. GMH must contend with all of these potential biases.

Hermeneutical injustice "occurs at a prior stage, when a gap in collective interpretive resources puts someone at an unfair disadvantage when it comes to making sense of their social experiences" (Fricker 2007, 1). Fricker gives several examples, but most germane is her example of a woman who is disadvantaged because she, and society at large, lack an understanding of the concept of postpartum depression. Fricker relates Susan Brownmiller's report of a woman who blamed herself (and was blamed by her husband) for her feelings of worthlessness, lack of energy, and poor concentration after childbirth, until she learned about postpartum depression. Only then did she recognize that her condition was not simply a personal failure (Fricker 2007, 149). Fricker's example may oversimplify matters given the problems already identified for the values and beliefs of psychiatry.

While psychiatric categories can help to make sense of one's experience in ways more beneficial than society's tendency toward moral blame, it can still hinder full credibility if it relies on the psychiatric conception of mental disorder as hyponarrative, individualistic, empirically based, and irrational. This in and of itself can be a misguided or insufficient hermeneutical resource for making sense of a person's disorder. In the context of cross-cultural psychiatry, where the patient's subjective experience is embedded in norms of her culture, the "gap" in hermeneutical resources can exist between patient and psychiatrist or others within the patient's own society. This gap is precisely the source of the dilemma between medical paternalism and moral relativism: GMH is caught between imposing negative prejudices encoded in psychiatric values and giving way to potentially negative prejudices of a local culture.

Being subject to epistemic injustice opens the door to a variety of other injustices, such as the sorts of harms that are typically identified by critics of GMH that result from not taking the afflicted person seriously (e.g., misdiagnosis, stigmatization, and further decline of health). But the fundamental harm of epistemic injustice is that it undermines its victim's very *identity* as a human being: "To be wronged in one's capacity as a knower is to be wronged in a capacity essential to human value. . . . [O]ne suffers an intrinsic injustice" (Fricker 2007, 44). Systematically having one's capacity as a knower undermined erodes confidence in oneself, one's ability to know oneself and the world, and one's courage in standing up for one's beliefs (Fricker 2007, 49).

In other words, being subject to epistemic injustice undermines a person's agency and autonomy. It also shows that autonomy and agency are fundamentally relational. A person's self-determination depends on their self-confidence, which, in turn, depends on the level of credibility they are afforded as a knower *by others*. This harm is more fundamental than Gbadgesin's autonomy-based principle of human flourishing. Flourishing depends on the hermeneutical situation: If a society lacks the proper resources to make sense of their experience, no amount of self-determination or freedom is going to overcome that.

Identifying the nature and harm of epistemic injustice also reveals ways to correct for it and develop the virtue of epistemic justice. Fricker (2007) argues that "responsibility requires a distinctly *reflexive* critical social awareness" (91). The hearer must not only attend to what the speaker is saying, but also attend to her own moments of cognitive dissonance, where her prejudice conflicts with what she is actually experiencing with the speaker. This should prompt reflection on whether prejudice has influenced her attitude toward the speaker.

The practice of epistemic justice in GMH therefore requires care providers to reflect on the impact that interactions with members of local cultures have on her own beliefs and revise accordingly. Recent work on addressing epistemic injustice in psychiatry applies this line of thought more generally, and in so doing, it echoes many of the suggestions made by advocates of a culturally sensitive approach to GMH. Crichton et al. (2017), for instance, suggest that psychiatric training include rounds "which allow health professionals to focus on the existential, ethical, and personal aspects of a medical case" (67). Kurs and Grinshpoon (2018), too, advocate prioritizing the voice of the patient as well as sensitivity to the social and environmental factors that influence the patient's affliction (340). It is not enough, however, to understand another culture and incorporate that into one's perspective. Gathering evidence of another's status as a knower is half of the work, to be sure. But doing this alone sounds a lot like GMH's reductive exercise of translating or reducing cultural idioms to their underlying pathology.

This does little to solve the problems inherent in psychiatric concepts of mental disorders. For that, there needs to be reflection on whether conflicts between the two reveal prejudices in the collective hermeneutical resources of psychiatry. The *DSM* and *ICD* do not offer guidance for navigating the existential, ethical, and personal aspects of a person's experience of a disorder, much less reconcile them with its psychiatric conception. In fact, these manuals may resist such efforts. To get beyond this, guidance is needed from philosophy.[7]

Epistemic injustice is a valuable framework for avoiding the twin horns of paternalism and moral relativism facing GMH. Gbadgesin's principle of flourishing is meant to resolve this dilemma by offering a principle that could determine the moral value of beliefs and practices across cultures. But as I point out above, it relies on an individualistic notion of autonomy, when the harm of epistemic injustice that the principle should identify is more fundamental. Autonomy is possible only if the individual is not subject to epistemic injustices that affect her identity and self-worth.

Because of this, autonomy is also relational. Respecting autonomy is not simply a matter of counseling someone on their diagnosis and allowing her to decide what treatments to undergo, given the gap in hermeneutical resources of psychiatry. It is a collaborative effort between the care provider and patient to engage in reflection about potential prejudices that conflict with the lived experience of the patient.

While epistemic injustice helps overcome a dilemma facing GMH, it is not a failsafe solution given the unique complexities of providing mental health services in a variety of diverse contexts. For one thing, accounting for prejudices in the care provider may not be sufficient, given that the patient may be subject to additional prejudices from her community. Nevertheless, psychiatry alone is not sufficient to address these prejudices, which underscores the need for bioethics to fill the gap, particularly a bioethics that draws from rich philosophical resources such as epistemic injustice. Epistemic justice is both an intellectual and moral virtue (Fricker 2007, 120). As such, it is not an act- or duty-based moral theory, but one that is grounded in a person's disposition. As I mentioned at the start, GMH relies on "task sharing" or training nonspecialists as primary care providers. This training cannot come from psychiatry alone, nor can it come in the form of guidelines or rules that satisfy a duty-based ethics.

The challenge, then, is especially great if there is a need to develop or identify affective dispositions, as well as cognitive ones. In many ways, the problem facing GMH recalls the ancient quarrel between medicine and philosophy, each with its own claim to human flourishing. It also recalls Socrates's point in Plato's *Gorgias*: While medicine may know how to heal, it is up to the moral expert to determine when and why.

Notes

1. "WHO Mental Health Gap Action Programme (mhGAP)," World Health Organization, accessed October 25, 2019, https://www.who.int/mental_health/mhgap/en/; see also Cohen et al. (2014), 15.

2. For instance, the most widely used text in bioethics, *The Principles of Biomedical Ethics*, by Beauchamp and Childress (5th edition, 2001), makes only cursory mentions of mental illness and "mental retardation." More recent papers addressing this neglect are Janet R. Nelson (2003) and A. R. Williams (2016).

3. The impetus toward community-based outpatient care had already been made by the federal government through the National Mental Health Act of 1946, but the proliferation of especially cruel treatments, such as electroshock therapy and lobotomies, returned the spotlight to mental asylums.

4. This is explicit in Patel et al. (2006, 1312), where he argues that the scientific basis of diagnosis being settled, it is "unethical to deny effective, acceptable, and affordable treatment."

5. WHO *World Health Report* references the *ICD-10*, which uses the phrase "clinically recognizable." The newest version, the *ICD-11* (2018), uses the phrase "clinically significant." The phrase was moved later to the definition for the most recent version of the *DSM* (*DSM-V*, 2013).

6. Crichton et al. (2017); Kurs and Grinshpoon (2018).

7. Kurs and Grinshpoon (2018) suggest that patients be involved in the revision process of the *DSM*, which has the potential to address problems within psychiatric nosology (341), but without the guidance of philosophical analysis of mind/body, ethics, and related areas, psychiatry does not have the resources to address these problems.

References

American Psychiatric Association. 1994. *Diagnostic and Statistical Manual of Mental Disorders.* 4th ed. Washington, DC: American Psychiatric Association.

Bemme, D., and N. D'Souza. 2012. "Global Mental Health and Its Discontents." *Somatosphere.* Published July 23, 2012, http://somatosphere.net/2012/07/global-mental-health-and-its-discontents.html.

Bortolotti, Lisa. 2015. *Irrationality.* Cambridge, UK: Polity.

Boyle, Philip J., and Daniel Callahan. 1995. *What Price Mental Health? The Ethics and Politics of Setting Priorities.* Washington, DC: Georgetown University Press.

Callahan, Daniel. 1999. "The Hastings Center and the Early Years of Bioethics." *Kennedy Institute for Ethics* 9, no. 1: 53–71.

Chang, R. 2015. "Value Pluralism." In *International Encyclopedia of the Social and Behavioral Sciences*, Volume 25, 2nd ed., edited by James Wright, 21–26. Amsterdam: Elsevier.

Cohen, Alex, Vikram Patel, and Harry Minas. 2014. "A Brief History of Global Mental Health." In *Global Mental Health: Principles and Practice*, edited by Vikram Patel, Harry Minas, Alex Cohen, and Martin J. Prince, 3–26. New York: Oxford University Press.

Crichton, Paul, Havi Carel, and Ian Kidd. 2017. "Epistemic Injustice in Psychiatry." *British Journal of Psychiatry Bulletin* 41: 65–70.

Fernando, Suman. 2010. *Mental Health, Race, and Culture.* London: Palgrave.

Fulford, K. M. W. 2003. "Mental Illness." In *Encyclopedia of Bioethics*, Volume 3, 3rd ed., edited by Stephen G. Post, PAGES. New York: Macmillan.

Fricker, Miranda. 2007. *Epistemic Injustice: Power and the Ethics of Knowing*. New York: Oxford University Press.

Gavey, Nicola. 2005. *Just Sex? The Cultural Scaffolding of Rape*. New York: Routledge.

Gbadgesin, Segun. 2012. "Culture and Bioethics." In *A Companion to Bioethics*, 2nd ed., edited by Helga Kuhse and Peter Singer, 24–35. Oxford, UK: Wiley-Blackwell.

Kirmayer, Laurence J., and Leslie Swartz. 2014. "Culture and Global Mental Health." In *Global Mental Health: Principles and Practice*, edited by Vikram Patel, Harry Minas, Alex Cohen, and Martin J. Prince, 41–62. New York: Oxford University Press.

Kurs, Rena, and Alexander Grinshpoon. 2018. "Vulnerability of Individuals with Mental Disorders to Epistemic Injustice in Both Clinical and Social Domains." *Ethics & Behavior* 28, no. 4: 336–46.

Mills, China. 2014. *Decolonizing Global Mental Health*. New York: Routledge.

Nelson, Janet. 2003. "Bioethics and the Marginalization of Mental Illness." *Journal of the Society of Christian Ethics* 23, no. 2: 179–97.

Patel, Vikram. 2006. "Beyond Evidence: The Moral Case for International Mental Health. *American Journal of Psychiatry* 163, no. 9: 1312–15.

———. 2010. "Global Mental Health: A New Global Health Field Comes of Age." *Journal of the American Medical Association* 303, no. 19: 1976.

———. 2012. "Global Mental Health: From Science to Action." *Harvard Review of Psychiatry* 20, no. 1.

Sadler, John Z. 2005. *Values in Psychiatric Diagnosis*. Oxford, UK: Oxford University Press.

Shay, Jonathan. 1995. *Achilles in Vietnam: Combat Trauma and the Undoing of Character*. New York: Simon & Schuster.

Szaz, Thomas. 1961. *The Myth of Mental Illness*. London, UK: Harper.

Summerfield, Derek. 2008. "How Scientifically Valid Is the Knowledge Base of Global Mental Health?" *British Medical Journal* 336: 992–94.

Williams, Arthur R. 2016. "Opportunities in Reform: Bioethics and Mental Health Ethics." *Bioethics* 30, no. 4: 221–26.

World Health Organization. 1992. *The ICD-10 Classification of Mental and Behavioural Disorders: Clinical Descriptions and Diagnostic Guidelines*. Geneva: World Health Organization.

———. 2001. *World Health Report 2001: Mental Health: New Understanding, New Hope*. Geneva: World Health Organization.

CHAPTER 21

Long-Term Care for Elderly People Globally: A Feminist Perspective

Rosemarie Tong

Abstract

Global aging will increase the need for long-term care (LTC) worldwide. Social critics have raised serious questions about whether it is primarily the responsibility of governments, individuals, or families to provide for the requirements of elderly people. In this chapter, I speculate that families will more and more be asked to care for their elderly members. From a feminist point of view, this situation would be less worrisome if, contrary to fact, most countries were not tempted to turn to women to meet their need for more unpaid family caregivers. Asking women to leave the paid workforce to do unpaid family care work may weaken women's recent economic and social gains and jeopardize their physical and psychological health status. Therefore, I propose another solution to the family care problem, namely, a thorough deconstruction of ingrained notions about who should do paid work (men) and who should provide unpaid care work (women).

Introduction: The Global Phenomenon of Aging

Aging is a global phenomenon. People are living longer in both developed and developing countries. Worldwide, approximately 703 million people were age 65 or older in 2019. This number will swell to 1.5 billion in 2050 (Kochhar 2014, 1), when, in the United States, the population of people older than 65 will surpass that of people younger than 15 (Kochhar 2014, 3). Also by 2050, the majority of people in Japan, South Korea, and Germany are likely to be older than 65 (Weisman 2060, A01). Moreover, many developing countries are aging at a faster rate than developed countries. It took the United States sixty-nine years to increase the size of its over-age-65 population from 7 to 14 percent (Department of State 2007, 15), but Singapore accomplished this same feat in only nineteen years (Department of State 2007, 7).

The primary reasons for global aging are twofold. First, fertility rates are decreasing in most developing countries, as well as in most developed countries. Up to 1965, the global fertility rate was 5.0 children per woman, but since then the global fertility rate has halved, to 2.5 children per woman (Brilliant Maps 2015, 3). Given that the ideal replacement level is 2.0 children per woman, particularly striking is Singapore's replacement rate, where it is just 0.8 percent (Brilliant Maps 2015, 3). Nearly all of Europe (except France, Ireland, and Turkey), three of the four BRIC countries (China, Russia, and Brazil), and all of Japan, Canada, and Australia are also below replacement level (Brilliant Maps 2015, 3). It is theorized that low replacement levels are largely due to strides in women's "empowerment" (Roser 2017, 10).

Among the factors said to lower people's interests, especially women's interest, in having a large number of children are 1) better education, especially education for women; 2) women's increased participation in the paid workforce; 3) lower child mortality rate; 4) decreased need for child labor in most nonagrarian countries; 5) increased prosperity in many developing—as well as developed—countries (the richer people are, the more choices they have, including the choice to remain child-free); 6) declining religiosity in many countries that previously espoused a biblical "be-fruitful-and-multiply" ethos; and 7) growing availability of family planning counseling and contraceptive services (Roser 2017, 10–32).

The other primary cause of global aging is the simple fact that people are living longer in many developing countries, as well as in most developed countries. Between 1960 and 2000, life expectancy at birth grew from 50.4 to 71 in East Asia (Shrestha 2000, 207), from 56.8 to 70.4 in Latin America and the Caribbean (Shrestha 2000, 207), and from 69.7 to 76.9 in the United States (Arias 2002, 33). Especially noteworthy is that by 2030, South Korean women and men are expected to live to slightly more than ages 90 and age 84, respectively (Senthilingam 2017).

On the face of it, increased life expectancy and lower fertility rates would seem to be an occasion for global celebration (Kinsella and Phillips 2005, 1–42). But when human beings fail to produce enough children at the very same time they begin to live far longer lives than before, a crisis situation can be produced relatively rapidly. First, there is the most obvious problem: How do young people support elderly people, if the number of elderly people significantly exceeds the number of young people?

For example, in 2010 there were one hundred US working-age people for every forty-nine dependents (people younger than 15 and older than 65) (Kochhar 2014, 5). By 2015, that same number of US workers will need to support sixty-six dependents (Kochhar 2014, 5). Moreover, also by 2050, in the seven most developed countries, there will be only two workers for every one retiree in need of support (Department of State 2007, 3), and in Japan only one hundred working-age people for every ninety-six dependents (Angel 2018, 19–23).

Throughout the world, there will be a "great-grandparent boom" (Department of State 2007, 11). Working-age people will find themselves simultaneously responsible for supporting more than one generation of elderly people. In China, this state of affairs is termed the "four-two-one" problem. As the first cohort of China's now-abandoned one-child policy reach adulthood, they may find themselves singly responsible for both their parents' and grandparents' LTC (Green 2014). There has even been alarmist talk in China about the "eight-four-two-one" problem: one adult Chinese child responsible for the LTC of two elderly parents, four elderly grandparents, and eight elderly great-grandparents (Liu 2008, 29).

Second, the costs of caring for large numbers of elderly people are probably greater than the costs of caring for large numbers of young people. Increasingly, chronic diseases such as diabetes, hypertension, coronary heart disease, arthritis, and dementia account for a higher percentage of the overall global disease burden (National Institute on Aging 2011, 13–15). According to the Global Burden of Disease Project, in 2008, noncommunicable diseases accounted for an estimated 86 percent of disease in high-income countries, 65 percent in middle-income countries, and a "surprising" 37 percent in low-income countries (National Institute on Aging 2011, 1). In India, where the battle against death from diarrhea, malaria, pneumonia, and other infectious diseases continues, stroke, coronary heart disease, and lung disease are the three top killers of people (World Life Expectancy 2015). Moreover, people in developing countries constitute two-thirds or more of dementia sufferers worldwide (Alzheimer's Disease International 2010).

Third, and related to the growing population of elderly people with costly chronic diseases, is the fact that, worldwide, there are not nearly enough health-care workers, let alone health-care workers who specialize in geriatrics. In 2012, for example, there were only 7,356 geriatricians in the United States, and there was only about 1 geriatric psychiatrist for every 23,000 elderly people, a number that is going to increase to 1 geriatric psychiatrist for every 43,000 elderly people in 2030 (Chernof and Warshawsky 2013, 19).

Moreover, as of 2020, the number of available US skilled nurses became insufficient to tend to the needs of elderly US people, a reality exacerbated by a very high turnover rate for home-care workers (44 to 46 percent) and certified nurse assistants (48 percent), the workers who do the bulk of hands-on US eldercare (Chernof and Warshawsky 2013, 19–20). Among the factors explaining this turnover rate are low wages, poor employment benefits, lack of promotion opportunities, inadequate training, negative public image, lack of respect, and little direct involvement in patient-care decisions (Maun 2007).

Not surprisingly, high-income developed countries have sought to secure extra health-care workers from low-income developing countries, where hard labor is typically compensated with low wages. In a 2010 study, Martha Hill found that in the United States and United Kingdom, there were about 1,000 nurses per 100,000 people, while there were only 20 nurses per 100,000 people in poor countries like Chad, Gambia, and Uganda (Hill 2010). The situation was particularly bad in Chad, where there is less than 1 physician for every 20,000 people, and just four hospital beds for every 10,000 people. Because of increased health-care needs and a "noticeable reduction in the number of healthcare workers due to HIV/AIDS related deaths," (Tankwanchi et al. 2015), Chad will need 300 percent more health-care workers over the next few years. This statistic is especially worrisome given the large number of physicians and nurses who emigrate from low-income sub-Saharan African countries to high-income developed countries (Tankwanchi et al. 2015).

Government as Primary LTC Provider

Given the state of affairs sketched above, people may think their respective governments should have the primary responsibility for providing individuals with LTC, but as it turns out, an increasing number of governments are seeking to privatize health-care services. In Russia, state-sponsored health-care services are on the verge of collapse due to Russian's poor economy, low birth rate, and corruption among health-care workers (Ostrousky 2005), and in China and India, ever-burgeoning populations make government-funded health-care services elusive (Lum 2012, 563–69). Moreover, many European countries, including some of those that had been lauded for the health-care benefits they provide to citizens (Walker 2000, 83), now question whether their public programs can be sustained as their populations gray. Retrenchments in LTC are noticeable in Belgium, France, Greece, Italy, Portugal, Luxembourg, Germany, Netherlands, and the United Kingdom (Walker 2000, 83). Still, the Nordic countries resist the privatization of long-term health-care insurance and/or services. For example, Norway and Denmark remain especially committed to providing public-subsidized LTC to their citizens for two reasons: 1) Their populations remain willing to pay very high taxes for social welfare programs (Blackman 2001, 185–88); and 2) Their populations are decidedly opposed to marginalizing care work (Williams 2000, 57–58). Indeed, the Danish state "is based on the explicit principle of social inclusion for both older people and women of working age who are relieved of any duty to provide unpaid care work" (Blackman 2001, 184).

Other countries that have inaugurated or continue to subsidize LTC for their citizens are Japan and Israel. In 1996, the Japanese Ministry of Health and Welfare proposed and subsequently passed a publicly subsidized LTC bill for all of its elderly people (Hong and Liu 2000, 221). In 1988, Israel made LTC care in one's home a legal right (Schmid 2005, 191). Israel provides for two levels of benefits: 1) a 100 percent disability allowance for citizens who are highly dependent on help from others to carry out some activities of daily living; and 2) up to a 150 percent disability allowance for citizens who are completely dependent on others to carry out most activities of daily living (Schmid 2005, 192). Eligibility is means-tested, but not in the stringent ways it is tested in the United States, for example.

The United States is conspicuous among developed countries for not providing much in the way of long-term, government-subsidized LTC services. Established in 1965, the Medicare program provides US people over the age of 65 with only limited in-patient hospital costs, out-patient hospital costs, physicians' fees, medical supplies, surgical services, diagnostic tests, and prescription drug benefits. Contrary to many Americans' general belief, Medicare does not provide for any more than one hundred days of care in a skilled nursing home following an at least three-day hospital stay. Moreover, the services must be related to acute health-care needs, and the recipient must be "expected to recover" (Eisenberg 2017, 3–4). Because Medicaid does not provide funds to assist elderly US people with activities of daily living (ADLs), such as toileting, bathing, dressing, getting in and out of bed, money management, meal preparing, shopping, and housecleaning, elderly US people who need this type of help must pay for it themselves from savings, private LTC insurance, or assistance from charities, or by qualifying for the US Medicaid program (Paying for Senior Care 2018).

Established in 1964, the Medicaid program is the "default" program for LTC in the United States. It covers "functionally eligi[ble]" individuals (unable to perform at least one of six ADLs on their own) who are also very poor (without assets exceeding around $2,000, excluding a home and car). If the individual is married to someone who is living in the community, the spouse can keep roughly $120,000 in assets, plus a home and car (Eisenberg 2017, 4–5). Because poverty is the entry condition for the Medicaid program, some elderly US people try to hide their assets in protected investments and/or transfer them to family members or even friends ahead of time, making themselves look like indigent people. These people are acting illegally, if not also immorally, says Binstock, because they "take advantage of a program for the poor without actually being poor themselves" (Binstock 1998, 10). Therefore, if the US government determines "that you have given away or transferred your assets within the five years of the date you are applying (two and a half in California), you will be ineligible for Medicaid benefits for a period of time" (Eisenberg 2017, 5). While the asset maximum for Medicaid sounds very low, Janet Grant, regional vice president for the Great Plains Region at Aetna Medicaid says, "almost everyone has depleted their funds after a couple of years of long-term care" (Eisenberg 2017, 4, 5). The average rate in 2012 for a private room was $4,466 to $9,375 per month in a skilled nursing home, and $2,414 to $5,713 per month in an assisted living residence (Consumer Reports Money Advisor 2012, 3).

Slowly the US population, like populations throughout the world, is being educated about the high cost of LTC and the fact that governments may lack sufficient funds to pay for not only LTC, but also other traditional benefits. Specifically, the US government may require US workers to work until they are age 70 instead of 65 before receiving the first of their Social Security checks. It is estimated that this change in Social Security alone would cut public debt by $6.2 trillion by 2085 (Fabian 2011).

In addition to the United States, many European countries and the United Kingdom have similar plans to reduce social security benefits to offset rising LTC costs. In particular, in Italy, "historically one of the most generous welfare states," men's retirement age will be raised from 62 and 60 for women to ages 69 and 70, respectively, by 2050. Even more noteworthy is the fact that Greece will raise its retirement age for men from 55 to 67 (Brown 2012). Both of these countries claim that they simply cannot fund their people's retirement years as generously as they traditionally have.

The belief that individuals should finance their own LTC is growing not only in Western countries but also in Eastern countries (Tao et al. 2007; Chan and Pang, 2007; Zhai and Qiu, 2007; Borsaubin et al. 2007; and Engelhardt 2007). For example, a sample study of Hong Kong families, health-care professionals, and health-care administrators showed support for the view that individuals should either save funds for their own LTC voluntarily or be required by the government to do so (Chan and Pang 2007, 422). In a similar study conducted in Beijing, there was also support for compulsory saving for LTC (Zhai and Qui 2007, 442). Moreover, Singapore already requires individuals to save for their own LTC needs (Engelhardt 2007, 520). But requiring people to work longer to finance their own LTC needs is reasonable only if the people in question are relatively healthy. Similarly, requiring people to save money for their own LTC needs is reasonable only if they can do so without jeopardizing their ability to meet their other basic needs, such as food, clothing, and shelter.

So, too, it may not be reasonable to expect elderly people to purchase their own private LTC insurance. Such policies are expensive, especially if people hold them twenty years or more and never need to make a claim on them (Chernof and Warshawsky 2013, 26–29). In 2015, between seven and nine million Americans had a private LTC insurance policy, approximately 8 percent of the age-45-and-older US population (Logeland 2015). That percentage has not increased appreciably in recent years despite the increase in numbers of elderly US people. Slow growth in the number of LTC insurance policyholders is not surprising given not only the high cost of LTC insurance (e.g., in New York a 70-year-old person might pay between $2,650 and $9,900 a year) but also because LTC insurance companies frequently hike their rates (130 percent in some cases) (LaPonsie 2016), deny claims, and, even worse, simply go out of business (Kristof 2009). According to Howard Gleckman, in 2015, sales of new LTC insurance policies fell by 75 percent as compared to sales in 2005, and 90 percent of the carriers that were offering LTC insurance in 2005 had stopped selling them by 2015 (Gleckman 2015).

Families as Primary LTC Providers

Given that many individuals may neither be able to work into their 70s and 80s nor be able to save enough funds from their low pay to meet their own LTC needs, governments are increasingly asking and, in some instances, requiring families to financially assist them (Parker and Dickerson 2001, 247). Families all over the world already do a lot of eldercare. The United States is a case in point, where the value of family caregiving exceeds the total value of all paid long-term services and support. Does there come a point in time when it becomes simply unfair to ask family caregivers to provide for their elderly members? With respect to this sensitive issue, bioethicist Daniel Callahan had this to say over thirty years ago when the burden of eldercare was much lower:

> [I]t is an old and hard moral question to know what we should make of demands for self-sacrifice. Most moral rules have common sense and practicality to commend them. Murder, lying, and theft ordinarily have tangibly bad consequences for those who commit such acts. Even our self-interest commends us to avoid them. Matters are otherwise when we are morally asked to give up our lives, or personal hopes, for the sake of another. Only under special circumstances can that seem to make any sense of all from the viewpoint of self-interest, even of the most benign sort. It is not for nothing that almost all Western moralities have been careful to distinguish between duty and supererogation. They all recognize that everyone cannot be a saint or a selfless paragon of altruism. The notion that we might as a matter of social policy burden families with the heroic duty of caring for the chronically ill or those in need of a course of rehabilitation that may fail and render

> them chronically ill or disabled ought at least to raise a red flag of warning (Callahan 1991, 157–58).

To be sure, questioning young people's obligations to elderly people is disconcerting. If people worldwide believe that parents have the primary responsibility to care for their young children, then, why should there be any question about whether adult children should have the primary responsibility to care for their elderly parents? Why should children who take care of an elderly parent view themselves as "heroes" or "saints" rather than persons simply discharging a duty? Why should children, as in contemporary China, be legally and not simply morally required "to provide for the emotional and physical needs of their parents, which includes visiting them often or facing fines and potential jail time"? (Russo 2013).

In addressing these questions it is important to stress that although all cultures explain children's obligations to elderly parents in terms of some duty or affection for them, some cultures emphasize duty and others emphasize affection. For example, in those Asian countries with a still intact Confucian tradition, all children, but especially the oldest son, still believe it is their moral duty to take care of their elderly parents (Li 1994, 71–72).

Because parents give life to their children and take care of them until they are adults, children reason that they owe their parents a debt of gratitude. Therefore, not to take care of one's elderly parents in their years of need is shameful and enough to warrant society's condemnation (Hong and Liu, 2000, 165–82; Liu 2000, 183–99; Koyano 2000, 200–23; Hi and Chou 2000, 224–48; Lee et al. 2000, 269–96; Wong 2000, 297–21; Yu et al. 2000, 322–38).

The need to reciprocate one's parents for the gift of life, and more, is felt by most adult children in the West, although the emphasis seems to be on affection rather than duty. In fact, in a now-classic article, philosopher Jane English (1991) has claimed that affection, not duty, is the primary basis for adult children's obligations to parents. She comments that:

> Although I agree that there are many things that children *ought* to do for their parents, I will argue that it is inappropriate and misleading to describe them as things "owed." I will maintain that parents' voluntary sacrifices, rather than creating "debts" to be "repaid," tend to create love or "friendship." The duties of grown children are those of friends, and result from love between them and their parents, rather than being things owed in repayment for the parents' earlier sacrifices. . . . Seen in this light, parental requests for children to write home, visit, and offer them a reasonable amount of emotional and financial support in life's crises are well founded, so long as a friendship still exists (147, 152–53).

But whether filial obligation is based mostly on duty or mostly on affection, worrisome issues still remain. For example, who has the responsibility to care for individuals who have no children or who are totally estranged from the children they do have? In modern societies, about 20 percent of women do not give birth, and this percentage is growing more rapidly than previously expected (Department of State 2007, 16). In addition, many women and men are childless because they lose their children to disease, war, or other violence. Childless single men and women are particularly vulnerable in their old age if they are poor (Lee et al. 2000, 292). Still another issue is simply that as the world ages, young people's well-being and their children's well-being are being mortgaged to provide for elderly people's well-being. In the United States, for example, a recent American Association of Retired People study "projected a dramatic decline over the next 20 years in the caregiver support ratio: from 7 potential caregivers for every person in the high-risk years of 80-plus in 2010 to 4 for every person 80-plus in 2030" (Chernof and Warshawsky 2013, 19–20).

Is it fair that an only child should have to shoulder the entire burden of caring for one or two elderly parents, whereas a child with siblings can share this duty? Similarly, is it fair for siblings to expect whichever one of them feels most obligated to help their parents to do so? Why should the most generous sibling be burdened in ways that his or her ungenerous siblings escape? Finally, is it fair to ask children in their 60s who have looked forward to their retirement as a responsibility-free time to become the primary caregivers for their elderly parents? (Montgomery, Borgatta, and Borgatta 2000, 33–35).

Emphasizing that caring for one's elderly parents can be burdensome is troubling. Yet it is not necessarily wrong for adult children to have reservations about being primarily responsible for their parents' LTC. Economist Carroll Estes has stressed that women in particular should think carefully before leaving their paid jobs to care for a family member. Importantly, she notes that elderly US women are not nearly as well off as elderly US men because US benefits for the elderly are gender-biased against women in at least three ways. Specifically, Estes (2006) observes that:

1. Retirement income is linked to waged labor, which is itself gendered;
2. Nonwaged reproductive labor, performed predominantly by women, is not recognized or counted under state policy as labor; and
3. Retirement policy is based on a model of family status as married with male breadwinner (and with marital status as permanent rather than transient) (88–89).

Because of these three factors, says Estes, state policy "sustains the subordination of women by imposing a normative and preferential view of a particular family form with a male breadwinner and a dependent wife that is inherently disadvantageous to the majority of older women (the majority of whom are not married, especially among women of color and the very old)." In sum, elderly US women are often poorer than elderly US men largely because they have not worked long enough in the paid workforce, instead devoting their energies to unpaid family work (Estes 2006, 89).

Caregiving does not only take a disproportionate toll on women as compared to men; it takes a toll on them health-wise. According to the Family Caregiver Alliance in the United States, "[t]he impacts of . . . women's intensive caregiving can be substantial" (Family Caregiver Alliance 2015). Various studies have found that "hallmarks" of women's caregiving experience include "a higher level of hostility and a great decline in happiness for caregivers of a family member; greater increase in systems of depression; less personal mastery and less self-acceptance; less high caregiving-related stress"

(Marks et al. 2002). In addition, a 2003 study found that 26 percent of female caregivers reported fair to poor health compared to 12 percent of women generally (Australian Bureau of Statistics 2004). This is not to say that being a caregiver has no positive effects. Often women caregivers report that they feel "more purpose in life than their noncaregiving women peers" (Marks et al. 2002, 657–61). But this advantage does not negate the negative toll of eldercare on women, especially minority and low-income female caregivers. One telling study found "that the caregiving time burden falls most heavily on lower-income women: 52 percent of women caregivers with incomes at or below the national median of $35,000 spend 20+ hours each week providing care" (The Commonwealth Fund 1999).

Conclusion

As the world's population ages, new arrangements will need to be made between governments, individuals, and families to meet elderly people's LTC requirements. No matter how the responsibilities for elderly people's LTC are allocated, however, families will continue to be called on for major help.

To be sure, many elderly people will not need much in the way of family-provided LTC. They will remain healthy enough to care for themselves (Choi and Dinse 1998, 159) or wealthy enough to hire nonfamilial caregivers (Rosen 2007, 13). Moreover, a good measure of elderly people will find government-provided LTC benefits sufficient to meet their needs. But there will still be millions of elderly people who will look to their families or family-like persons (close friends, charitable individuals/groups, people who share the same plight) for help to meet their LTC needs, and many societies will automatically call on women to provide this help.

For example, after decades of sex-selecting males for their one and only child, a practice that has resulted in a dramatic sex-ratio imbalance of 119.6 males for every 100 females in China (Hudson and Boer 2008, 186), the Chinese are now starting to sex-select for girls (Liu 2008, 28). Apparently, many young Chinese couples believe that daughters are more likely than sons to minister to them in their old age. Moreover, some elderly Chinese couples that do not have a daughter or are childless are trying to acquire "a daughter" through a process akin to adoption. Advertisements for "daughters" now appear in Chinese newspapers, some of them promising ample reward to the women who answer them (Liu 2008, 29).

Clearly, unless developed and developing countries explode the gender system that captures their collective imaginations, they will run the risk of not having enough caregivers to meet their needs. The challenges of global aging present a unique opportunity to weaken the two norms that uphold the world's gender systems, namely, the ideal worker norm, theorized by Joan Williams (Williams 2000, 1), and the ideal care worker norm, alternately celebrated and criticized by feminist care ethicists (Gilligan 1982; Held 2006; Kittay 1999; Noddings 1984).

Williams (2000) reasons that "domesticity" is a rigid gender system that separates market work from family work and then structures market work "around the ideal of a worker who works full time and overtime and takes little or no time off for childbearing or child rearing." As Williams sees it, "though the ideal worker norm does not define all jobs today, it defines the good ones; full-time blue-collar jobs in the working-class context, and high-level executive and professional jobs for the middle class and above" (Williams 2000, 1). Structured in this way, market work has no patience for caregivers who are distracted by family work. Workers who put their families above their work commitments are punished with marginalization in the workforce. But this state of affairs has negative consequences for caregivers. Their marginalization disqualifies them from the rewards of market work, including not only "responsibility and authority," but also the extra money they need to care for themselves and others. The only way to change this inequitable state of affairs, argues Williams, is to make the workplace conform to the family rather than the family to the workplace. The ideal worker would then become someone who has time for both family and work and is able to care because of the way the workplace is structured.

US women continue to be the ones who worsen their social, economic, and physical/psychological health to meet their elderly relatives' LTC needs (The Swaddle Team 2018). Countries that are really serious about gender equity realize that the only way not to marginalize care work is not to tweak but to destroy both the ideal care worker norm and the ideal worker norm. These countries do not aim to pull women out of the paid workforce so men can stay in it. Instead, they will not simply permit but also require men to take time off for family matters. For example, in Iceland, both women and men get three months' post-childbirth leave at 80 percent of their salary, plus another three months they can split any way they want. Neither the man nor the woman can transfer their three months' paternity or maternity leave to each other. Weller (2016) says "the government wants to ensure both parents can work and that kids get to spend time with both."

Significantly, most workplace family-care leave and benefit policies still emphasize child-care leaves. But, in the future, they will probably have to emphasize eldercare leaves just as much, if not more. This shift in emphasis from child care to eldercare may, in my estimation, present new opportunities for society to view men as just as able as women to deliver care. Because women give birth to children, they have been assigned the duty to rear them (Tong 2009, 85–86). But there is no equivalent "natural" reason for women to care for elderly people, and so the rationale for men not caring for elderly people is not as plausible as the rationale for men not taking caring of infants and children. Thus, men as well as women should be equally obligated to be caregivers for elderly people.

To be sure, most men have not actually done the care work assigned to them. Their wives, sisters, and daughters have done it for them. Consider Japan, where daughters-in-law have done the majority of eldercare, even though their husbands were officially in charge of taking care of their aged parents (Care of the Elderly 2016). But in the face of a burgeoning aging population, now may be the ideal time to ask men to develop their caregiving skills. There are too many elderly people with too many needs. Women cannot be expected to meet all of the world's increasing caregiving needs. Men will have to help women care for elderly people, or elderly people will need to fend for themselves.

Men have started to care for children more than in the past (Yogman and Garfield 2016). There is simply no compelling reason they cannot also care for elderly family members' needs (Belkin 2008). To be sure, eldercare may be particularly frightening for men. The bodies of elderly people speak of diminishment, disintegration, and death—threats to the autonomous self who charts the course of *his* destiny. They speak of nature, materiality, and that which cannot be controlled but must instead be accepted. But it is precisely by coming to terms with the reality of aging that men could join with women to overcome the dichotomies that are at the root of job segregation and gender inequity. Vulnerability is our common fate as human beings. We need to construct our workplaces and families in ways that acknowledge our dependence on each other. In order for us to be properly autonomous, men as well as women need to do care work. Only then will women's old age be as good as men's (Dodds 2007, 500–510).

References

Agich, G. J. (2007). Reflections on the function of dignity in the context of caring for old people. *The Journal of Medicine and Philosophy* 32(5), 483–94.

Alzheimer's Disease International. (2010). *World Alzheimer's Report.* Retrieved on April 9, 2018, from http://www.alz.co.uk/research/files/WorldAlzheimerReportpdf.

Angel, J. L. (2018). Aging policy in a majority-minority nation. *Public Policy & Aging People* 28(1), 19–23. Retrieved on April 6, 2018, from https://doi.org/10.1093/ppar/pry005.

Arias, E. (2002). National vital statistics reports: United States life tables, 2000. *National Center for Health Statistics* 51(3), 33.

Binstock, R. H. (1998). The financing and organization of long-term care. In L. C. Walker, E. H. Bradley, and T. Wetle, (eds.), *Public and private responsibilities in long-term care.* Baltimore: Johns Hopkins University Press.

Blackman, T. (2001). Conclusion: issues and solutions. In T. Blackman, S. Brodhurst, and J. Convey, (eds.), *Social care and social exclusion.* New York: Palgrave Publishers.

Borsaubin, E. V., Chu, A., and Catalano, J. M. (2007). Perceptions of long-term care, autonomy, and dignity, by residents, family, and care-givers: the Huston experience. *The Journal of Medicine and Philosophy* 32(5), 447–64.

Brilliant Maps. (2015). The astounding drop in global fertility rates between 1970 and 2014. Retrieved on April 2, 2008, from https://brilliantmaps.com/fertility-rates/.

Brown, E. N. (2012). The takeaway: 14 countries raising retirement age. *The American Association for Retired People (AARP).* Bulletin Today.

Callahan, D. (1991). Families as caregivers: *The Limits of Morality.* In N. S. Jecker (ed.), *Aging and ethics: philosophical problems in gerontology.* Totowa, NJ: Humana.

Chan, H. M., and Pang, S. (2007). Long-term care: dignity, autonomy, family integrity, and social sustainability: the Hong Kong experience. *The Journal of Medicine and Philosophy* 32(5), 401–24.

Chernof, B., and Warshawsky, M. (2013). *Commission on long-term care:* report to the Congress, 1–58.

China Population Association. (2010). Are "four-two-one" families really a problem? (in Chinese). Retrieved on April 7, 2018, from the original article on 2011-07-07.

The Commonwealth Fund. (1999). Informal caregivers (Fact Sheet). https://www.commonwealthfund.org/sites/default/files/documents/___media_files_publications_data_brief_1999_may_informal_caregiving_caregiving_fact_sheet_pdf.pdf

Consumer Reports Money Advisor. (2012). Long-term-care insurance: insurers of funding to boost premiums or stop selling policies, 3. Retrieved on April 13, 2018, from https://www.consumers-reports.org/cro/2012/081/long-terminsurance/index.htm.

Department of State and the Department of Health and Human Services, National Institute on Aging, National Institutes of Health. (2007). *Why population aging matters: a global perspective.* US Department of State.

The Economist. (2017). The Economist: longevity in rich countries. *Kyiv Post.* Retrieved on April 4, 2018, from https://www.kyivpost.com/world/economist-longevity-rich-countries.html.

Eisenberg, Richard. (2017). "Medicare, Medicaid, and long-term care: your questions answered." *Forbes.* Retrieved on April 12, 2018, from https://www.forbes.com/sites//2017/ 11/21/medicare-medicaid-and-long-term-care-2017/11/21/medicare-medicaid-and-long-term-care-your-questions-answered/a3e22d17699.

Engelhardt, H. T. Jr. (2007). Long-term care: the family, post-modernity, and conflicting moral life-worlds. *The Journal of Medicine and Philosophy* 32(5), 519–36.

English, J. (1991). What do grown children owe their parents? In N. S. Jecker (ed.), *Aging and ethics: philosophical problems in gerontology.* Totowa, NJ: Humana.

Estes, C. (2006). Critical feminist perspectives, aging, and social policy. In J. Baars, D. Dannefer, C. Phillipson, and A. Walker (eds.), *Aging, globalization and inequality: the new critical gerontology.* Amityville, NY: Baywood Publishing Co., Inc.

Fabian, Jordan. (2011). GOP senators: raise retirement age to 70. Retrieved on April 14, 2018, from https://thehill.com/blogs/blog-briefing-room/news/155715-gop-senators-raise-retirement-age-to-70.

Family Caregiver Alliance. (2015). Women and caregiving: facts and figures. https://www.caregiver.org/women-and-caregiving-facts-and-figures.

Fields, S. (2008, June 19). Death, be not proud. *The Washington Times*, A17.

Fran, R. (2007). Which care? whose responsibility? and why family? A Confucian account of long-term care for the elderly. *The Journal of Medicine and Philosophy* 32(5), 495–518.

Gilligan, C. (1982). *In a different voice.* Boston: Harvard University Press.

Gleckman, Howard. (2015). The long-term care insurance industry ponders its future. Retrieved on April 13, 2018, from https://www.forbes.com/sites/howardgleckman/2015/04/09/the-long-term-care-insurance-industry-ponders-its-future-seven-trends-to-watch/#4d6d88dcf6fe.

Green, Denis. (2014). Elderly care—coping with the 4:2:1 problem. *China Outlook.*

Held, V. (2006). *The ethics of care: personal, political and global.* New York: Oxford University Press.

Hill, Martha. (2010). Nursing shortage knows no boundaries. *Baltimore Sun*, September 13, 2010.

Hong, Y., and Liu, W. T. (2000). The social psychological perspective of elderly care. In W. T. Liu and H. Kendig (eds.), *Who should care for the elderly?* Singapore: Singapore University Press.

Hudson, V. M., and Boer, A. D. (2008). China's security, China's demographics: aging, masculinization, and fertility policy. *Brown Journal of World Affairs* 14(2), Spring/Summer 2008, 185–200.

Kinsella, K., and Phillips, D. R. (2005). Global aging: the challenge of success. *Population Bulletin* 6(1), 1–42.

Kittay, E. F. (1999). *Love's labor: essays on women, equality, and dependency.* New York: Routledge.

Kochhar, R. (2014). 10 projections for the global population in 2050. *Pew Research Center.* Retrieved on April 1, 2018, from https://www.pewresearch.org/fact-tank/2014/02/03/10-projections-for-the-global-population-in-2050/.

Kristof, Kathy. (2009). Long-term-care insurance: 4 biggest risks to avoid. Retrieved on April 15, 2018, from https://www.cbsnews.com/news/long-term-care-insurance-4-biggest-risks-to-avoid.

LaPonsie, Maryalene. (2016, March 10). The high cost of long-term care insurance (and what to use instead). *US News & World Report.* Retrieved on April 14, 2018, from https://money.usnews.com/money/personal-finance/family-finance/articles/the-high-cost-of-long-term-care-insurance-and-what-to-use-instead.

Lee, R. L., Lee, J., Yu, E. S. H., Sun, S., and Liu, W. T. (2000). Living arrangements and elderly care: the case of Hong Kong. In W. T. Liu and H. Kendig (eds.), *Who should care for the elderly?* Singapore: Singapore University Press.

Li, C. (1994). The Confucian concept of Jen and the feminist ethics of care: A comparative study. *Hypatia* 9(1), 70–89.

Liu, M. (2008, March 17). Playing with the old blood rules. *Newsweek*, 27–29.

Liu, W. T. (2000). Values and caregiving burden: the significance of filial piety in elder care. In W. T. Liu and H. Kendig (eds.), *Who should care for the elderly?* Singapore: Singapore University Press.

Logeland, Denise. (2015). Can long-term care insurance work for more people? *Forbes.* Retrieved on April 26, 2018, from https://www.forbes.com/sites/nextavenue/2015/12/03/can-long-term-care-insurance-work-for-more-people/#3f5573ea3b35.

Lum, Terry. (2012). Long-term care in Asia. *Journal of Gerontological Social Work* 55(7), 563–69.

Marks, N., Lambert, James David, and Choi, Heejong. (2002). Transitions to caregiving, gender, and psychological well-being: a prospective U.S. national study. *Journal of Marriage and Family* 64(3), 657–67.

Mason, Barry. (2004). World health report: life expectancy falls in poorest countries. *World Socialist Web Site.* Retrieved on April 11, 2018, from https://www.wsws.org/en/articles/2004/01/whor-j12.html.

Maun, Clint. (2007). Turnover rates and statistics in long-term care and hospitals. Retrieved on April 10, 2018, from http://clintmaun.com/index.php5?cID=265.

Montgomery, R. J. V., Borgatta, E. F., and Borgatta, M. L. (2000). Societal and family change in the burden of care. In W. T. Liu and H. Kendig (eds.), *Who should care for the elderly?* Singapore: Singapore University Press.

National Institute on Aging and World Health Organization. (2011). Global health and aging. https://www.who.int/ageing/publications/global_health.pdf.

Noddings, N. (1984). *Caring: a feminine approach to ethics and moral education.* Berkeley: University of California Press.

Ostrousky, Arkady. (2005). Bribery in Russia up tenfold to $316 bn in four years. *Financial Times.*

Parker, M., and Dickerson, D. (2001). Resource allocation. In M. Parker and D. Dickerson (eds.), *The Cambridge medical ethics workbook: case studies commentaries and activities.* Cambridge, UK: Cambridge University Press.

Paying for Senior Care. (2018). How to pay for nursing home care/convalescence care. Retrieved on May 15, 2018, from https://www.payingforseniorcare.com/longtermcare/paying-for-nursing-homes.html.

Rosen, R. (2007). The care crisis. *Nation* 284(10), 11–16.

Roser, Max. (2017). Fertility rate. *Our World in Data.* Retrieved on April 3, 2018, from https://ourworldindata.org/fertility-rate.

Russo, F. (2013). Caring for parents: should there be a law? *Time,* July 22, 2013.

Schmid, H. (2005). The Israeli long-term care insurance law: selected issues in providing home care services to the frail elderly. *Health and Social Care in the Community* 13(3), 191–200.

Schmid, R. E. (2008). Health care system not ready for Boomers, report says. *SFGate.* Retrieved July 1, 2008, https://www.sfgate.com/business/article/Health-care-system-not-ready-for-Boomers-report-3217790.php.

Senthilingam, Meera. (2017). South Korea will take lead in life expectancy by 2030, study predicts. CNN.

Shrestha, Laura B. (2000). Population aging in developing countries. *Health Affairs* 19(3), 207.

The Swaddle Team. (2018). The key to being a couple with equitable, dual careers. Retrieved on April 29, 2018, from https://theswaddle.com/couple-equitable-dual-careers-long-term-planning/.

Tankwanchi, A. B. S., Vermund, S., and Perkins, D. (2015). Monitoring sub-Saharan African physician migration and recruitment post-adoption of the WHO code of practice: temporal and geographic patterns in the United States. Retrieved on April 27, 2018, from https://doi.org/10.1371/journal.pone.0124734.

Tao, J., and Wah, L. (2007). Dignity in long-term care for older persons: A Confucian perspective. *The Journal of Medicine and Philosophy* 32(5), 465–82.

Tao, J., Wah, L., Chan, H. M., and Fan, R. (2007). Exploring the bioethics of long-term care. *The Journal of Medicine of Philosophy* 32(5), 395–400.

Tong, R. (2009). *Feminist thought: a more comprehensive introduction.* 3rd edition. Boulder, CO: Westview.

Walker, A. (2000). Sharing long-term care between the family and the state—a European perspective. In W. T. Liu and H. Kendig (eds.), *Who should care for the elderly?* Singapore: Singapore University Press.

Williams, J. (2000). *Unbending gender: why family and work conflict and what to do about it.* New York: Oxford University Press.

World Life Expectancy. (2015). World health review: China vs. India. Retrieved on April 8, 2018, from https://www.worldlifeexpectancy.com/world-health-review/china-vs-india.

Yogman, M., and Garfield, C. F. (2016). Fathers' roles in the care of development of their children: the role of pediatricians. Retrieved on April 30, 2018, from https://pediatrics.aappublications.org/content/138/1/e20161128.

Zhai, X., and Qiu, R. Z. (2007). Perceptions of long-term care, autonomy, and dignity, by residents, family, and caregivers: the Beijing experience. *The Journal of Medicine and Philosophy* 32(5), 425–46.

CHAPTER 22

Reconsidering Acoustic Attacks

Alison Dundes Renteln

Abstract

This chapter focuses on the use of sound as a weapon and the implications of its impact for principles of international law and global bioethics. I examine various acoustic attacks, including loud music as torture, the "Havana Syndrome" (or anomalous health incidents) and long-range acoustic devices. These sonar weapons cause fear and trauma and have serious consequences for global health. This is an example of when technology has outpaced our ability to formulate proper policies based on established principles of law and ethics. Inspired by the original scholarship of James Parker on acoustic jurisprudence and sonar warfare, as well as others, this study also draws on scholarship in sensory studies (e.g., David Howes and Constance Claussen) to reassess malevolent uses of sound. I analyze the use of sound as a weapon and consider whether and to what extent international law instruments apply to this newly recognized phenomenon, namely nonlethal weapons. Ultimately, it may be crucial to determine whether a new treaty is needed to control the potentially devastating consequences of weaponized sound.

Introduction

In the twenty-first century, the prospect of new weapons systems is frightening. Although some forms of technology have been under development since the 1970s, we are witnessing much greater use of them in the United States and abroad. In this chapter, I discuss the malevolent uses of sound, including loud music as torture, weaponized sound against diplomats, and police techniques such as long-range acoustic devices (LRADs) or crowd dispersal. I advance the argument that they should be banned entirely given the current state of knowledge about their adverse health consequences, or at the very least, be subject to a moratorium. Acoustic bombardment violates principles of international law and global bioethics, as I will show.

This analysis draws on the scholarship in sensory studies, international law, and public policy. The discipline of sensory studies is an important part of anthropology, although not limited to it. Regina Bendix, a leading scholar based in Germany, makes the case for including sensory studies in anthropology. She argues: "Ethnography can contribute to an understanding of the sensorium's role in human experience as well as its culturally divergent deployment and valuation" (Bendix and Brenneis 2005, 3). A journal titled *The Senses and Society* was launched in 2004 that helped raise the profile of sensory studies.

Other significant contributions to the field are those of legal scholars who bring together sensory research and jurisprudence (Bently and Flynn 1996). A pioneer in this area, Desmond Manderson, is known for his brilliant contributions to the study of visual and olfactory matters. The researcher whose work is most relevant to this inquiry is that of James Parker, inspired by Manderson, who is the preeminent authority on acoustic jurisprudence. He analyzes malevolent uses of sound (Parker 2018, 2019). While his research has been central to the question of weaponizing sound, he has not explicitly advanced a normative argument regarding weapons of the twenty-first century. I intend to advance this argument here: I contend that the use of sound as a nonlethal weapon should be prohibited entirely, just as lethal weapons such as mustard gas have historically been considered contrary to the long-established rules of international law.

This chapter examines how international law applies to relatively new acoustic weapons, shows why sensory studies are important for jurisprudence, and advances an argument to ban altogether, or at least delay the use of, some nonlethal weapons. I will now consider some of the behavior that should be prohibited under existing international legal standards and that is incompatible with bioethics principles. Let us begin with raucous music.

Loud Music as Torture

Sound is the neutral term, and according to experts, unwanted sound is considered noise. In this context I am speaking about the use of loud music as a form of torture. Although music has long been used in armed conflict (Hirsh 2012, 111), one type of sound that has received widespread condemnation in the context of detention centers is loud rock music (Cusick 2006). Suzanne Cusick explains as follows: "While few narratives offer much musical detail, they constitute ample evidence, and music and sound have been systematically used to harass, discipline, and in some cases 'break' detainees for the entire duration of the so-called global war on terror" (2006).

Scholars who discuss music as torture in a historical perspective suggest that certain songs are more likely to cause harm; for example "[t]he sexual explicitness of Christina Aguilera, the demonic chromaticism of Metallica, [and] the blatant force of hard-core rap" (Hamilton 2008, 152). Loud music is also played to prevent sleep, and sleep deprivation is itself another method of torture. During the past two decades, the US government was notorious for its use of rock music to torture those detained in Guantanamo Bay, Cuba ("Gitmo"), the so-called enemy combatants. The BBC reported that the US Army had played music such as Metallica's "Enter Sandman" and Barney the Purple Dinosaur's "I Love You" at high volume during the interrogation of Iraqi detainees (Cusick 2006). Cusick describes music used only for harsh interrogation in certain military cases. In these deplorable conditions: "Detainees typically spent their first twenty-four hours there standing blindfolded and naked, their hands bound behind their backs, without access to food, water, or the toilet, in a metal shipping container where, in summer 2003, the temperatures rose to between 135 and 145 degrees Fahrenheit" (Cusick 2008, 9, citing Human Rights Watch report "No Blood, No Foul," 30–31). She notes further that "the music was often so loud that soldiers standing thirty feet away, guarding the metal shipping containers, had to yell at each other to be heard" (2008, 9).

The practice was so distressing to the musicians whose songs were played there that they filed lawsuits to force the US government to cease and desist. Furthermore, professional associations of musicians issued statements condemning the use of music as torture.

Excessively loud music has repeatedly been interpreted as a form of torture contrary to some of the important international legal standards. In international law some rights are considered fundamental and therefore are characterized as *jus cogens*, or peremptory norms. This means that these particular rights cannot be violated under any circumstances, even if there is a national emergency threatening the life or existence of the state. According to the jurisprudence of emergencies, such norms are said to be "non-derogable," meaning that states may not derogate from their responsibilities to guarantee these rights. This set of rights includes the right against genocide, the right against slavery, the right against piracy, and central to this analysis, the right against torture.

The right against torture is broader in scope than many may realize. The precise formulation is the right against torture and cruel, inhuman, or degrading treatment or punishment. This is significant, because it prohibits state-sponsored actions that may not rise to the level of torture but nevertheless constitute impermissible harms. Also noteworthy is that the standard applies not only to punishment or penal institutions, but to other types of institutions. Cruel, inhuman, or degrading treatment unfortunately occurs in a wide variety of settings, such as schools, mental health facilities, jails, and many others. It would be a mistake to think that this normative framework applied only to prisons.

Some of the other most highly publicized examples include bombarding embassies to try to compel those who have received political asylum there to exit the premises. This included aural assaults to compel Noriega to leave the Vatican's embassy in Panama (Anon. 2021) and Honduran president Zelaya to leave the Brazilian embassy in Honduras (Carroll 2009).

The FBI also used weaponized sound to force members of the Branch Davidian cult compound in Waco, Texas (Johnson 1993), to surrender. Their tactics included blaring recorded music ("These Boots Were Made for Walking" by Nancy Sinatra and Tibetan chants) as well as recordings of squealing rabbits and jet planes (Davidson 1995; Yearsley 2009).

The long-term consequences of enduring excessively loud music are manifold: loss of hearing, trauma, balance disorders, and other health problems. Studies of noise pollution have documented a relationship between excessive noise and mental disorder (Anon. 1968, 106). Often, the use of music as a weapon has been deployed through amplification systems. In this context it is clearly illegal to use music as a form of torture, because torture is per se a violation of international law. Still, it is even more devastating that something that is a means of human flourishing—listening to music—could be ruined for those subjected to this particularly obnoxious treatment.

I now turn now to an analysis of the deliberate use of sound as an acoustic weapon.

The "Havana Syndrome"

Diplomats from the United States and Canada based in embassies in Cuba reported that they experienced unusual health problems between 2016 and 2018. Although the media coverage suggested this was a new phenomenon, other acoustic attacks on internationally protected persons have been documented for decades. One scholar claims to have coined the term "Havana Syndrome" to describe the experience. Those afflicted with the syndrome describe having incessant headaches, tinnitus, balance disorders, loss of memory, and other debilitating conditions.

Although relatively little has been written about this phenomenon, in the material that does exist, commentators debate whether or not it is real. Some have suggested it is actually hysteria, a figment of the imagination of hypochondriacs. Some consider it a paranoid conspiracy theory, a ruse to attack Communists, because it has been attributed to the Russians and occurred in countries such as China and Cuba, against American officials. Much of the debate turns on who is responsible for inventing and developing acoustic weapons. While some contend they were originally developed by Americans, others say Russians took the lead. In a podcast by Nicky Woolf, he suggests that the Trump administration asserted in bad faith that Russians were responsible, and that this was an attempt by Trump to undermine the Obama administration's decision to reverse sanctions on Cuba. It may well be that they discovered it simultaneously.

To ascertain what the phenomenon is and how it ought to be characterized, the CIA wrote a report that has been declassified. So much has been redacted, however, that it says virtually nothing. A whitewash, it basically blames crickets for the Havana Syndrome. A report by the National Academy of Sciences, however, takes a different tack: "[T]hese mysterious manifestations are consistent with the use of directed, pulsed radiofrequency energy. In addition . . . the persistent postural-perceptual dizziness, a functional vestibular disorder, could also be considered a secondary reinforcing mechanism, along with the possible effects of psychological conditions" (Nelson 2019).

A few reports have been published in medical journals. For instance, the *Lancet* reported the findings of the National Academy of Sciences. Media coverage references several studies conducted at universities that reach contradictory conclusions.

While it is fair to say that no publicly available explanation is entirely credible, the most likely account is that acoustic weapons were developed as a surveillance technique that ran amok. In the absence of clearly established evidence regarding acoustic weapons and their long-term consequences, the real question iswhat sort of regulations should be imposed?

It is common practice for scientists to conspire with the military to devise new weapons systems. Technological innovations emerge before society has time to consider the ethical implications of their use. Ideally there would be no desire to create new weapons systems. However, as there is always fear of "the other," the quest to protect "us" against "them" fuels this insane competition. As it is not realistic to ban war entirely, I turn now to a discussion of how international law applies to the Havana Syndrome.

If empirical evidence substantiates claims of the adverse health effects of targeted sound, then it is important to determine how to handle accountability for the attacks. While it might be possible to prosecute those responsible for launching them, if they could be identified, that does not settle the question. Insofar as the host countries are responsible for protecting the embassy and internationally protected persons, litigation might prove successful.

Mark Zaid, who specializes in international legal matters, filed lawsuits on behalf of individuals claiming they were harmed by the sonic attacks. These cases were pending in US courts as of this writing. Furthermore, Foreign Service officers have published articles attacking the CIA and the US government generally for failing to take the attacks seriously.

Not only could accountability be pursued in domestic courts, but it may be possible to prosecute perpetrators of the attacks in international criminal tribunals, manufacturers of the technology, and government officials who failed to take precautions to protect diplomats. It remains to be seen whether jurists will construe Article 5 (below) as covering this as an international crime subject to the jurisdiction of the International Criminal Court:

> **Article 5**
> Crimes within the Jurisdiction of the Court
> The jurisdiction of the Court shall be limited to the most serious crimes of concern to the international community as a whole. The Court has jurisdiction in accordance with this Statute with respect to the following crimes:
>
> a) The crime of genocide;
> b) Crimes against humanity;
> c) War crimes; and
> d) The crime of aggression.

International Legal Frameworks

In this section I discuss how the Havana Syndrome may be construed within the context of several distinct international law frameworks. I begin with diplomatic law, an ancient branch of international law, designed to guarantee safe passage for internationally protected persons as well as safe working conditions, enabling them to fulfill their official functions.

The main treaty that protects diplomats is the Vienna Convention on Diplomatic Relations. While the entire instrument is important, specific provisions directly pertain to this question. Article 29 states:

> The person of a diplomatic agent shall be inviolable. He shall not be liable to any form of arrest or detention. The receiving state shall treat him with due respect and shall take all appropriate steps to prevent any attack on his person, freedom, or dignity.

This protection also covers the premises of the embassy and the private residence of diplomats (Article 30). Similarly, the embassy is supposed to be inviolable, and those employed in the embassy should not be attacked, should enjoy some degree of immunity (McClanahan 1989; Wilson 1967), and are entitled to other protections concerning their health and access to medical care. Clifton Wilson discussed the protections afforded diplomatic agents from assault and attack (51–61). A similar treaty, the Vienna Convention on Consular Relations, affords protections to those who work in consulates, the location of the state's officials outside the capitol. As well in these provisions, the Convention on Internationally Protected Persons expressly forbids inflicting harm on individuals representing their countries abroad.

Concern about protecting diplomats is hardly new. How best to ensure their safety from political violence has been subject to much commentary (Hargrove 1986). There is unquestionably an obligation on the part of the "host" state to protect diplomats and staff members. Regardless of the source of the sonic attacks, the host country is responsible for ensuring the safety of the embassy and those who work within it. As explained, the importance of protecting diplomats is clear in international law (Hevener 1986). Even individuals who do not have the status of diplomats are entitled to protection under international law (Advisory Opinion 1999).

The Havana Syndrome is obviously incompatible with the legal obligations of the "host" states, insofar as they must protect diplomats, but to date this body of law has proven to be insufficient, as well. Others, in different sorts of conditions and institutions, have also been attacked and could be harmed in the future, so we must consider other legal frameworks.

Humanitarian International Law

Another branch of public international law that dates to antiquity concerns the treatment of individuals during armed conflict. In the twentieth century this came to be known as international humanitarian law (the law of war), or the Geneva Conventions and the Hague Conventions. Increasingly, scholars refer to both collectively under the rubric of international humanitarian law. In this body of law, the principle of distinction is critical—namely, that weapons must not be indiscriminate; military operations must use weapons systems in such a way that they distinguish between combatants and civilians. This is perhaps the most basic principle here.

Under the United Nations Charter, the use of force is forbidden, with few exceptions. These include authorization by the Security Council to protect peace and security and self-defense. Under Article 51, self-defense—collective or individual—is only permissible in response to an "armed attack." Much ink has been spilled over the question of whether an acoustic attack would constitute an "armed attack." Inasmuch as 9/11 forced jurists to reconsider what counts as a weapon (i.e., the use of an airplane to kill thousands), nowadays analysts often accept the proposition that a cyberattack could constitute an "armed attack" under some circumstances, and therefore a hacker could be considered a combatant under the law of war. An overview of this subject may be found in the Tallinn Manual.

It is conceivable that acoustic weapons were designed to target particular locations. Nevertheless, it is probable that they cannot avoid harming others who are near the designated targets. One objection to the use of acoustic weapons, then, is that they may well be incapable of being limited, so as to avoid civilians. (A similar objection is often made to the use of drones or killer robots.) Hence, the use of these so-called nonlethal weapons will inevitably violate the principle of distinction, avoiding civilians and civilian institutions.

As international humanitarian law applies only when there is an armed conflict, recognized as such under international law, one question to consider will be whether there is sufficient violence to trigger the application of the law. Does the intensity and magnitude of the acoustic attacks make this body of law applicable? Another limitation is that it applies for the most part to interstate conflict and not internal armed conflicts. This is problematic, because most of the conflicts in the world during the twentieth century were within a state's borders, and hence, non-international armed conflicts. This remains mostly true in the twenty-first century (although arguably not in the current conflict between Russia and Ukraine).

International humanitarian law does cover non-international conflicts, i.e., civil wars or internal conflicts, through the important Common Article 3, as well as the two additional Protocols to the 1949 Geneva Conventions. The notion is that there exists a minimum set of standards governing the conduct of military forces that they must recognize during non-international conflicts. This is the Magna Carta for civilians during non-international conflicts. The use of acoustic weapons, if construed as an "armed attack," might implicate Common Article 3.

Having considered how international humanitarian law applies to acoustic attacks, we turn now to international human rights law.

International Human Rights Law

The use of acoustic weapons also violates human rights. As with loud music, the use of this technology violates the right against torture or cruel, inhuman, or degrading treatment or punishment guaranteed in Article 7 of the International Covenant on Civil and Political Rights (ICCPR) and the Convention Against Torture (CAT).

If we accept the reports of those who say they are afflicted with Havana Syndrome and suffer the effects of insomnia, nausea, and other adverse health conditions, this would infringe upon their right to health guaranteed in Article 12 of the International Convention on Economic, Social, and Cultural Rights. The General Comment on Article 12 guarantees the right to the highest attainable standard of health and makes reference to mental health.

If acoustic weapons should turn out to be part of a system of mass surveillance, then that violates the right to privacy. This is guaranteed in several human rights instruments, for example, ICCPR, Article 8, of the European Convention on Human Rights.

The European Court of Human Rights elaborates on the importance of privacy. The use of acoustic weapons certainly implicates international human rights law. To begin, it is contrary to the right against arbitrary killing and the right to life (Casey-Maslen 2021). The use of ostensibly nonlethal weapons does not guarantee that they will not result in the demise of those targeted.

Lethal Weapons

Some weapons, such as mustard gas, are deemed too devastating to be used under any circumstances. If the impact causes excessive suffering, then it should be banned. This question has arisen as to whether the use of nuclear weapons can ever be justified. After the horrendous death and suffering caused by dropping two bombs on the Japanese cities of Nagasaki and Hiroshima during World War II, one would have thought the answer was obvious. Despite the existence of empirical evidence of the devastation they cause, the Advisory Opinion of the International Court of Justice ruled that the use of nuclear weapons is neither permitted nor prohibited under international law. The ICJ recognized that a state, when faced with a threat to its very existence, might, as a last resort, feel compelled to use nuclear weapons. This was a missed opportunity to condemn their use.

The logic is that weapons that are lethal and cause excessive suffering should be forbidden. I maintain that some nonlethal weapons should also be prohibited, particularly if full knowledge of their effects is still to be determined.

Solutions

I now turn to possible solutions to the threat posed by acoustic weapons in the twenty-first century. One question is whether existing international law is adequate to the task of blocking this. I showed above that some provisions in treaties could be invoked to challenge their deployment. As there appears to be a need for a more comprehensive assessment of acoustic devices, it would be advisable for the International Law Association to establish a working group to draft a new treaty devoted to this subject. It could incorporate text from other instruments and expand the coverage. For instance, if acoustic devices require particular constituent parts, production and sale of those could be banned and defined as international crimes.

If the international community were to reach a consensus on the potential damage they could cause, the jurisdiction of the International Criminal Court could be interpreted to cover use of these weapons as a crime against humanity, a war crime, or a crime of aggression. Insofar as loud music is used as torture during armed conflict, it would already appear to be subject to the jurisdiction of the ICC.

Under diplomatic law, if the "host" country is obligated to protect the premises of the embassy, then it is not crucial to determine the origin of the acoustic attacks. There is, regardless of the source, a responsibility to safeguard the premises of the embassy with proper shielding of those inside, with Faraday cages or the like.

Long-Range Acoustic Devices (LRADS)

Another problematic use of sound as a weapon is what has been termed long-range acoustic devices (LRADS). Originally developed to help military forces handle situations at sea, they facilitate communication between military personnel: "The Long-Range Acoustic Device (LRAD) was designed primarily to 'hail, warn, and notify' vehicles and sea vessels at a distance and was developed to assist service members with difficult scenarios" (Schrantz 2010, 53). One commentator states that the LRAD was developed specifically in response to the attack on the US vessel, the USS *Cole*, in October 2000 (Wood 2014).

While there may be issues with its use by military forces, even more worrisome has been its appropriation by law enforcement in civilian contexts. This use by police of weaponized sound is a fairly common technique for crowd dispersal. Commentators discuss how police use LRADs when they are dealing with protests as part of "strategic incapacitation" (Wood 2014, 26). Protesters in cities across the United States have been subjected to this form of weaponized sound, which they say causes severe migraines and other adverse health consequences.

Use of LRADs by law enforcement should certainly be evaluated. Some contend their deployment constitutes a violation of international human rights law. If it is considered torture, or at least cruel, inhuman, or degrading treatment, then use of acoustic devices for crowd dispersal or any other purpose should be prohibited.

A high-profile lawsuit in New York City called the use of LRADs into question (Moynihan 2018). In this case, the Court of Appeals for the 2nd Circuit affirmed Judge Sweet's opinion, saying the defendants violated "plaintiffs' Fourteenth Amendment right against excessive force when they used a long-range acoustic device (LRAD), which did rise to the level of "shock[ing] the conscience." In a settlement the police agreed to "stop using the shrill beeping—referred to as the deterrent and alarm tone" (Moynihan 2021). The trend in US jurisprudence appears to be in the direction of banning the use of acoustic weapons, at least in this context.

If a norm of customary international law should emerge that condemns the use of acoustic attacks, this could be the basis for lawsuits brought under two federal statutes: the Alien Tort Claims Act (ATCA) and the Torture Victim Protection Act (TVPA).

Whereas the first authorizes only those from outside the United States to file lawsuits, the TVPA allows US citizens to bring actions against foreign governments. Given the proclivity of police to use LRADs, we will likely witness many more lawsuits to attempt to limit or ban their usage.

Global Bioethics and Human Rights

Although bioethicists have not devoted much attention to acoustic attacks, the potential for their misuse is cause for alarm. There is no question that the trauma and suffering resulting from these attacks violates the principle of nonmaleficence. States have the obligation not to harm individuals, so the use of weaponized sound is incompatible with the fundamental principles of bioethics.

Some might retort that the evidence documenting the magnitude of harm is inconclusive. Even if that is the case, absent proof that such weapons will not cause harm, they should not be deployed. When in doubt of the potential for causing great harm, leaders should be advised to delay their deployment. The principles of bioethics are powerful, and can be cited along with international law to exert pressure for a moratorium on acoustic attacks until such time as their safety can be assured.

Final Reflections

The use of acoustic weapons deserves far greater consideration insofar as they violate international law and principles of global bioethics. The powerful scholarship of James Parker and other analysts documents the potential devastating consequences that these understudied weapons of the twenty-first century may cause. Even though the weapons are technically nonlethal, they nevertheless should receive much greater scrutiny before they are deployed.

It may be that a new treaty focused on acoustic weapons should be developed. hether they should be rendered more targeted and less devastating, or whether they should be banned altogether remains to be seen.

References

Advisory Opinion on the Applicability of Article VI, Section 22, of the Convention on the Privileges and Immunities of the United Nations.

Anon. (1968). "Urban Noise Control." *Columbia Journal of Law and Social Problems* 4, 105–19.

Anon. (2017, May 30). "Music Torture: How Heavy Metal Broke Manuel Noriega." *BBC.* https://www.bbc.com/news/world-latin-america-40090809, accessed April 28, 2023.

Aramova, Nina (2019, February 19). "The Dark Side of Music: Using Sound as Torture." CNN. https://www.cnn.com/2019/02/08/health/music-in-torture-intl, accessed April 28, 2023.

Baloh, Robert W., and Robert E. Bartholomew (2020). *Havana Syndrome: Mass Psychogenic Illness and the Real Story Behind the Embassy Mystery and Hysteria.* Cham, Switzerland: Springer Nature, 2020.

Bartholomew, Robert (2022, February 3). "The Real Danger 'Havana Syndrome' Poses to Society." *Psychology Today.* https://www.psychologytoday.com/us/blog/its-catching/202202/the-real-danger-havana-syndrome-poses-society, accessed April 28, 2023.

Bendis, Regina (2005). "Introduction: Ear to Ear, Nose to Nose, Skin to Skin: The Senses in Comparative Ethnographic Perspective." *Ethnofoor* XVIII (1), 3–14. [Special issue coedited with Don Brenneis, "The Senses."]

Bentley, Lionel, and Leo Flynn (eds.) (1996). *Law and the Senses: Sensational Jurisprudence.* London, UK: Pluto Press.

Carroll, Rory (2009). "Honduran Forces Blast Recordings of Sound Effects Outside Brazilian Embassy." *The Guardian* online.

Convention on the Prevention and Punishment of Crimes against Internationally Protected Persons, including Diplomatic Agents. 1973.

Cusick, Suzanne G. (2006). "Music as Torture / Music as Weapon." *Trans* 10. https://www.sibetrans.com/trans/articulo/152/music-as-torture-music-as-weapon, accessed April 28, 2023.

——— (2008). " 'You Are in a Place that Is Out of the World . . .': Music in the Detention Camps of the 'Global War on Terror.' " *Journal of the Society for American Music* 2, 1–26.

Davidson, Lee (1995, November 2). "Hatch Blasts Use of Rabbit Scream Tapes." *Deseret News.* https://www.counterpunch.org/2009/03/13/music-torture/.

Entous, Adam. and Jon Lee Anderson (2018, November 19). "The Mystery of the Havana Syndrome." *The New Yorker* 94 (37), 34–48.

Hamilton, John T. (2015). "Torture as an Instrument of Music." In Sander van Mass (ed.)., *Thresholds of Listening: Sound, Technics, Space.* New York: Fordham University Press, 143–52.

Hamilton, Jon (2019, July 23). "Brain Scans Find Differences But No Injury in U.S. Diplomats Who Fell Ill In Cuba." *All Things Considered,* National Public Radio.

Hargrove, John Lawrence (1986). "Security of Diplomats as a Problem of International Community Policy." In Natalie Kaufman Hevener (ed.), *Diplomacy in a Dangerous World: Protection for Diplomats Under International Law.* Boulder: Westview Press, 15 –44.

Hevener, Natalie Kaufman (1986). Reflections on the Interpretation and Application of the Law of Diplomatic Protection. In Natalie Kaufman Hevener (ed.), *Diplomacy in a Dangerous World: Protection for Diplomats Under International Law.* Boulder: Westview Press, 45 –71.

Hirsh, Lily E. (2012). "Music as Torture." In *American Crime Prevention and Punishment.* Ann Arbor: University of Michigan Press, 110–31.

Johnson, Dirk (1993, April 26). "Last Hours in Waco: A Special Report—Inside the Cult: Fire and Terror on Final Day." *New York Times.* https://www.nytimes.com/1993/04/26/us/last-hours-in-waco-a-special-report-inside-the-cult-fire-and-terror-on-final-day.html.

Kirk, John M. (2019). "The Strange Case of the Havana Sonic Attacks." *International Journal of Cuban Studies* 11 (1), 24–42.

Lin, James C. (2021). *Auditory Effects of Microwave Radiation.* Cham, Switzerland: Springer Nature.

Moynihan, Colin (2021, April 19). "N.Y.P.D. to Limit Use of 'Sound Cannon' on Crowds After Use on Protesters' Lawsuit." *New York Times* online.

Parker, James E. K. (2019). "Sonic Lawfare: On the Jurisprudence of Weaponized Sound." *Sound Studies* 10, 1–25.

——— (2018). "Towards an Acoustic Jurisprudence: Law and the Long-Range Acoustic Device." *Law, Culture, and the Humanities* 14, 202–18.

——— (2015). *Acoustic Jurisprudence: Listening to the Trial of Simon Bikindi*. Oxford, UK: Oxford University Press

——— (2011). "The Soundscape of Justice." *Griffiths Law Review* 20, 963–93.

Robles, Frances (2018, December 13). "'These People Were Injured,' Doctors Conclude, After Studying U.S. Diplomats." *New York Times*, A10.

Schrantz, Major Joe (2010, August). "The Long-Range Acoustic Device: Don't Call It a Weapon—Them's Fightin' Words." *Army Lawyer*, 53–59.

Wilson, Clifton E. (1967). *Diplomatic Privileges and Immunities*. Tucson: University of Arizona Press.

Woolf, Nicky (2023, January 25). "The Sound Mystery of the Havana Syndrome." https://www.npr.org/2023/01/25/1151421770/the-curious-case-of-havana-syndrome.__Podcast: https://www.youtube.com/watch?v=_eALY8MFFQU._

Wood, L. J. (2014). *Crisis and Ccontrol: The Militarization of Protest Policing*. Pluto Press.

Yearsley, David (2009, March 13). "Music Torture." *Counterpunch*. https://www.counterpunch.org/2009/03/13/music-torture/.

Zimmer, Carl (2017, October 6). A 'Sonic Attack' on Diplomats in Cuba? Experts on Acoustics Are Doubtful." *New York Times*, A6.

CHAPTER 23

Climate Change and Bioethics

Peter Tagore Tan

Abstract

Anthropogenic climate change constitutes an existential threat to human health and thriving. That it is a pressing issue for bioethics seems beyond argument, and yet the connections between climate change and human health have largely been the work of international organizations, nonprofit organizations, researchers, atmospheric scientists, biologists, and so on. Conspicuously missing from this list is the bioethicist. But there are at least three overlapping ways in which anthropogenic climate change and human health interact: Climate change worsens natural disasters; it worsens preexisting health problems; and it creates the conditions for the possibility of further collapse. Given this, the question is why bioethics is unable to properly address climate change. Combining sociological and climatological analyses of bioethics' origin story show a discipline formed during an explosive growth in medical technology and interventions, along with a fortunate stability of the climate. The result is a version of bioethics that had the luxury of identifying the main existential threats to humanity as natural diseases that could be addressed through technological interventions, without having to consider the existential threat that anthropogenic climate change poses. An axiological analysis further shows that the values of an anthropocentrism do not neatly line up with those of an anthropogenic event. The task at hand is to recast bioethics with these analyses in mind. Doing so requires a revisitation of the original meaning of "bioethics," something that is but in its nascent stages.

Introduction

This chapter is dedicated to answering this question: How does climate change affect bioethics? The short answer is that it hasn't really. Yet. But when (not if—bioethics cannot afford to entertain the conditional) it does, it will come with a larger-scale reevaluation of what bioethics must be. The longer answer is not so simple. In the past decade there has been a growing awareness that bioethics must be engaged with the existential problem of anthropogenic climate change, but just what that engagement was supposed to look like was left unstated. I want to delve into giving the longer answer by analyzing three separate but related questions, one giving rise to the next:

1. How does anthropogenic climate change affect bioethics?
2. Why has bioethics been unable to substantively engage with climate change?
3. What does bioethics need to look like in order to address climate change?

Of these, the second question demands the most attention. The first one is straightforwardly driven by empirical data, and the question is included because it is instructive to note how anthropogenic climate change has affected bioethics. It goes far beyond, for example, the destruction of a hospital in a hurricane fueled by warming waters. Climate change events have many downstream effects that deny or alter the delivery of medicine, medical care, and medical research. The answer to the third question is still in the making, and while recent work has given shape to how bioethics should look with anthropogenic climate change in mind, we can expect alternate iterations and competing visions in the future.

The second question is the most difficult to address. Why has bioethics taken such a long time to address anthropogenic climate change? It isn't because bioethicists have been blind to the effects. Several have in fact argued that something needed to be done by bioethics as a discipline not long after anthropogenic climate change became a publicly known issue. Bioethics is based on medical science, and the respect it has for science is reflected by the fact that bioethics literature does not include (except as a repudiation of it) climate skepticism. So why the difficulty in addressing climate change?

My argument will be that bioethics has been hindered by its own understanding of itself. Meant by its founder to be an interdisciplinary practice combining biology, medicine, and ecology, bioethics quickly jettisoned the ecological third leg and has come to mean something more limited than originally intended. Developed during a time when global temperature variations could be (if they were even known by more than atmospheric scientists) passed off as natural fluctuations, bioethics never had to consider that without the ecological aspect to properly situate the biology and medicine, the principlism that came to define bioethics was unable to navigate how medicine and health care should adapt to a changing environment. Unbeknownst at the time, a principlistic bioethics was in fact dependent on a stable environment in which to secure and maintain human health. The difficulty involved in answering this second question in turn is reason enough why bioethics, despite a smattering of promising starts, has yet to address the third question in earnest.

Climate Change and Bioethics

Even if we were to accept the current definition of bioethics as part of a narrower analysis of medical and biomedical ethics, apart from ecology, the relationship between climate change and bioethics is impossible to ignore. Given that climate change adversely affects the physician–patient relationship; disrupts or makes impossible proper medical interventions; frustrates methods of health-care delivery; redirects funding from medical care to emergency services; and damages or destroys the medical infrastructure, climate change literally has everything to do with what bioethics has charged itself with.

There are three main categories that climate change affects: It increases the likelihood of extreme natural disasters; it exacerbates existing health and medical problems; and it creates the conditions for further human suffering. These are not exclusive of one another, as there can be significant overlap between these categories, but it is helpful to get a sense of the breadth and temporal depth of the problems climate change brings to bioethics.

THE WORSENING OF NATURAL DISASTERS

Perhaps the most visible effect is the increase in the likelihood of extreme natural disasters that directly affect human health and health-care delivery. Our cultural idioms have expanded to include terms such as explosive cyclogenesis (bombogenesis) and ARkStorm (atmospheric rivers), joining better-known events such as droughts, hurricanes/typhoons/cyclones, and firestorms. Explosive cyclogenesis occurs when a severe and rapid drop in air pressure occurs in a twenty-four-hour span (NOAA 2023); ARkStorm is the USGS's abbreviation and portmanteau for a 1,000-year flooding from an atmospheric river event that is patterned after a US West Coast winter storm (USGS 2018).

Both these and other examples of extreme weather can occur without human causation, but anthropogenic climate change makes these destructive events more likely to occur. The statistical evidence is clear on this. "[2022's] warming trend is alarming," says NASA administrator Bill Nelson. "Forest fires are intensifying; hurricanes are getting stronger; droughts are wreaking havoc; and sea levels are rising" (NASA 2023).

The bioethical effects of these events have been drastic:

- Wildfires have normalized hospital evacuations to the point that it has altered the practical meaning of what it means "do no harm" to patients (Parodi 2019). Nearly 250 hospitals "simultaneously lost power in intentional power outages in California because of wildfire prevention measures (Salas et al. 2020). State law requires health facilities to have three days' worth of emergency power, but a survey during the 2019 California fire season found that only 44 percent have a backup energy source (Sherer 2019).
- Floods from atmospheric river events routinely outstrip wastewater treatment operators' ability to provide potable water. Tens of millions of gallons of untreated sewage have escaped containment and spilled into neighborhoods and the environment during the California storms in 2023 (McClurg 2023). Similar events have caused public health and human services to issue warnings that "exposure to contaminated floodwater can cause wound infections, skin rash, or tetanus" (MDPHHS 2022).
- Prolonged drought directly affects the availability of potable water, decreases air quality, and stresses sanitation, hygiene, and food and nutrition infrastructures

(CDC 2020). Drought also impacts health-care facilities: 7 percent of total commercial water is used by hospitals for heating, cooling, medical equipment, and sanitation (Fink 2022).

- The marked increase in wildfires has exposed population centers to unhealthy levels of $PM_{2.5}$, or particulate matter less than 2.5 micrometers in diameter, resulting in air that is likened to a "toxic soup" (Kozlov 2021). Air pollution researchers in Australia estimate that 417 deaths and 1,305 emergency admissions for asthma were caused by excessive smoke during the 2019–2020 wildfire season (Pickrell 2020). In California, almost 7,000 preterm births were "attributable to wildfire smoke exposure [from] 2007–2012" (Heft-Neal et al. 2022).
- The mental health of individuals and communities is often overlooked in bioethical analyses, but natural disasters especially have been linked to higher rates of PTSD, depression, and anxiety as survivors grapple with injury, deaths of loved ones, displacement from home, loss of property, lack of food, economic disruption, loss of employment, and having to manage claims for insurance companies and social services (Lieberman-Crib et al. 2017).
- According to the Commonwealth Fund, "health care professionals experience the physical and mental health risks of climate change more acutely than the general population[,] raising the risk of burnout" (Commonwealth Fund 2022). In Australia, climate change has been linked to contributing to health-care worker shortages in underserved populations (Pendrey et al. 2021).

These bioethical effects are of course not unique to the particular events mentioned. We should be sensitive to the fact that the examples above are from the United States, Australia, and Canada. Places with less developed health infrastructure are especially affected. I have chosen these examples precisely because they are well documented with effects and damages that have been quantified. I have also focused on more recent examples of extreme weather occurrences because these are clearly 400 ppm events—in other words, they occurred when CO_2 levels were around or had surpassed the 400 parts per million of carbon dioxide mile marker that is used as a measure and symbol of human involvement in the release of carbon into the atmosphere.

WORSENING PREEXISTING HEALTH PROBLEMS

Anthropogenic climate change also affects bioethics because it worsens already-existing health problems. This is in part because it adds to the downstream problems of displacing health-care workers and health-care facilities. The final report by the American College of Emergency Physicians on the effects of Hurricane Sandy, for example, states that "6,400 patients were evacuated, and six hospitals and 26 residential care facilities in New York City alone were closed. Estimates indicate that 75,000 people with significant health issues lived in areas inundated by the surge of water" (ACEP 2015). The result is that "climate change increasingly threatens the ability of the US health-care system to deliver safe, effective, and efficient care to the American people" (Salas et al. 2020).

Climate change also worsens preexisting inequalities already present in the delivery of health care itself. According to the World Health Organization (in language adopted by the CDC), the social determinants of health (SDH) "are the non-medical factors that influence health outcomes," which include where people live and work, and in what conditions they grow and age. The SDH is very telling of health inequities, "the unfair and avoidable differences in health status between [communities]." WHO further notes that "in countries at all levels of income, health and illness follow a social gradient: the lower the socioeconomic position, the worse the health" (WHO 2023).

When climate change enters into the equation, we can refine this even more: The lower the socioeconomic position, the more people will be adversely affected by climate change events, which then results in worsening health. This is the finding that drives the concept of "climate justice," a term "that acknowledges climate change can have differing social, economic, public health, and other adverse impacts on underprivileged populations" (Simmons 2020). This inequity is, if anything, even worse outside of the developed world, where people, especially "people of colour across the Global South are those who will be most affected by the climate crisis, even though their carbon footprints are generally very low" (Williams 2022).

A warming climate also increases the spread of disease vectors beyond their historic geographic distribution. A recent study has found that the observed range of Anopheles mosquitoes over a 120-year span increased 6.5 meters of elevation per year, and 4.7 km per year polewards. "These shifts would be consistent with the local velocity of recent climate change, and might help explain the incursion of malaria transmission into new areas over the past few decades" (Carlson et al. 2023). Other ectotherms such as ticks and fleas have also expanded their range.

According to the EPA, deer tick distribution has now spread in areas of Canada where they were previously unable to survive, exposing new and more northern populations to Lyme disease. Cases of tularemia spread by ticks, biting flies, and fleas have similarly spread (Rydén 2009), and there is, according to studies, "consistent evidence for a temperature-related process influencing the epidemic peak timing and growth of plague epidemics" (Krauer et al. 2021).

CREATING THE CONDITIONS FOR THE POSSIBILITY OF WIDESPREAD COLLAPSE

The third category of climate change effects on bioethics is by far the largest one, since they are global in scale. These events are not preexisting, nor do they exacerbate bioethical challenges; they are caused by anthropocentric climate change and cause a further cascade of debilitating events that result in greater human suffering. There are four main concerns, any one of which presents enormous health consequences for humans.

The best known among these is *sea-level rise*. Rising oceans are not just caused by melting glaciers or icebergs, but also because seawater expands as it absorbs thermal energy from the atmosphere (NOAA 2023). The ocean absorbs 90 percent of the Earth's heat (Lindsey and Dahlman 2020). The UN has called sea-level rise a direct health and existential threat to the 900 million people living in coastal zones around the world. The UN Secretary-General describes "sea-level rise as a threat multiplier, [jeopardizing] access to food, water, and healthcare" (UN 2023). A one-meter rise in sea level that is expected by 2100 would bring infrastructure destruction, population disruption and displacement, loss of arable land, and the salination of freshwater (McMichael et al. 2020). This is already an immediate and pressing issue. According to a 2022 study of the eastern and southern United States, 44.2 percent of the 682 acute-care hospitals located within ten miles of the Atlantic or Gulf Coasts were at risk of seawater inundation during a Category 4 storm; 22.2 percent were at risk with a weaker Category 1 storm (Tarabochia-Gast et al. 2022).

Glacial melt does not just increase sea-level rise; it also leads to drought conditions along the rivers that are formed by the diminishment and retreat of long-standing glaciers that have defined waterways and cultural identities. The Tibetan Plateau, called the "Third Pole" because it has the greatest reserves of snow and ice after the Arctic and Antarctic (Vince 2019), is the source for water and food for much of Southeast Asia and China. More than a billion people depend on the Indus, Ganges, and Brahmaputra rivers (Chandrashekhar 2022), and the nearby Qinghai glaciers feed the Yangtze and Yellow rivers that support 800 million (Cardascia 2022; Davidson 2022). All five of these rivers and their subsequent river basins experienced severe droughts in 2022 due to glacial retreat. Retreating Alpine glaciers similarly caused the Rhine and Danube rivers to significantly shrink in volume in 2022 (Gross 2022). The loss is not just to physical health. China and India are river cultures, the loss of which also adds to the mental health toll as the passing of a way of life is added to the other concerns of displacement, and food and water insecurity.

Ocean acidification has been called "global warming's evil twin" because the burning of hydrocarbons has the secondary effect of releasing excess CO_2, which is then absorbed by the ocean. Seventy percent of the Earth's surface is covered by the ocean, and 97 percent of the Earth's water is oceanic. It is estimated that 525 billion tons of CO2 has been absorbed by the ocean since the beginning of the Industrial Revolution (Climate Reality Project 2016). Increasing concentrations of carbonic acid in ocean water negatively impact the development and growth of a wide range of oceanic organisms. "As acidification progresses," states a recent study, "many organisms must invest additional energy to maintain their acid–base balance, metabolic processes, or other biological functions, with consequences for their growth, reproduction, and survival" (Falkenberg et al. 2020).

Other research links acidification with both promoting the growth and increasing toxicity of red tidal algal events, as well as brown tide species, both of which "promote their blooms at the expense of benign phytoplankton" (NCCOS 2014). Ocean acidification disrupts the entire oceanic food chain, from autotrophs to consumers to apex predators. The threat to humans is especially keen: The UN estimates that 600 million people "rely on the fisheries and aquaculture sector for their livelihoods" (FAO 2022), and more than 3 billion people rely on seafood as a significant source of protein (WWF 2023). Not only are the traditional target-species' numbers affected, but "the higher-level species that we rely on for sustenance [have decreased] nutritional value," while having increased heavy metal contents like mercury and cadmium, which are "often more bioavailable in acidified aquatic habitats" (Falkenberg et al. 2020).

There are other anthropogenic changes to the environment that we can predict from available data, the effects on human health we do not quite know because they do not have precedent in recorded human history. The recent *instability of the Gulf Stream*, more formally known as the Atlantic Meridional Overturning Circulation (AMOC henceforth), is the best-known example. The AMOC is known as "the ocean's great conveyor belt" (Velasquez-Manoff and White 2021), a current that shuttles warm water from the Caribbean to the North Atlantic, only to be returned when the cold water from the North Atlantic flows beneath the warm current flowing north. "The AMOC is driven by dense, salty seawater sinking into the Arctic Ocean" (Carrington 2021), but the warmer oceanic temperatures melting the Greenland icecaps not only increase sea-level rise, but also have the effect of destabilizing the AMOC. This has potentially catastrophic effects: "a drastically altered AMOC could . . . shift rainfall patterns[,] making parts of Europe and Northern Africa drier, and areas in the Southern hemisphere wetter."

Changing ocean currents might affect marine ecosystems that people rely on for food and livelihood (Velasquez-Manoff and White 2021). As is the case with areas now vulnerable to extended droughts, floods, sea-level inundation, hurricanes, and firestorms, where there is mass displacement of populations, and where food and water supplies and livelihoods are threatened, human health, both physical and mental, suffers, as does the means to systemically deliver health care to address those needs.

Where Is Bioethics in the Climate Change Discussion?

Given that anthropogenic climate change has everything to do with patients, medical professionals, medical researchers, biomedical corporations, health-care organizations, and the delivery of health care, the question isn't *how* bioethics is related to climate change, but *why* it has remained so silent about climate change. Why hasn't it squarely addressed this existential threat? There are, of course, happy exceptions to this rule. Susan Sherwin argues that bioethics is due for a serious reorientation. "[The] various approaches to ethics that bioethicists rely on are not adequate to provide effective moral guidance in how to avoid a series of looming human catastrophes" (Sherwin 2008), she writes, arguing that a feminist framework of relational autonomy can be used to rectify this issue.

David Resnick claims that "bioethics, for the most part, have remained on the sidelines of the [climate change] debate[.] Because global climate change is likely to have substantial impacts on the environment and human health, bioethicists should take part in the discussion about global warming and contribute their perspective to these urgent issues" (Resnick 2009). Cheryl Cox Macpherson states that "Climate change is a bioethics problem because it harms everyone and involves health, values, and responsibilities" (Macpherson 2013), and Sean A. Valles extends Macpherson's central claim in the effort to reframe both bioethics and climate change discourse (Valles 2015). What all these articles have in common is the fact that while it would seem to be easily within the wheelhouse of bioethics to consider existential issues, bioethics as a discipline has resisted actually dealing with them.

We have of course heard how climate change poses a serious challenge to human health long before this current spate of formal awareness. It has been more than three decades since the US Senate climate hearings. So why has it taken so long for bioethics to catch up? That alone is puzzling. On the face of it, if bioethics is about human flourishing and health, clearly climate change frustrates both of these outcomes, and thus ought to be a central issue addressed according to bioethical analyses. But the investigation into the health effects of climate change is driven by intergovernmental organizations, atmospheric researchers, medical professionals, and governmental agencies. They are not being driven by bioethics. The reason for this is that what the question asks is hardly simple, in part because climate change and bioethics are two very different things.

There are three issues to be unpacked to arrive at a satisfying answer to why bioethics has difficulty facing anthropogenic climate change.

A QUESTION OF HISTORY

According to Cristina Richie, there are two branches that define the developmental history of bioethics (Richie 2019). There is the first mention of the term in 1927, by Fritz Jahr, and the first mention of it in the English language in 1971, by Van Rensselaer Potter. Working independently, they both came up with a concept that emphasizes the βίος in bioethics, which is to say life as understood in holistic terms, which includes other forms of life and the environment at large. Human health, in other words, is tied directly to the health of the environment, and in Potter's understanding of the term, bioethics rested on health, medicine, and ecological conservation working together.

The other branch retrained the focus of bioethics to consider the life of humans alone, conflating human life with human health, and the technical means to attain such health. Scher and Kozlowska's historic overview of bioethics states that this branch began in 1966, five years prior to Potter's 1971 *Bioethics: Bridge to the Future*, developed by Henry Beecher, a medical doctor who wrote about the failure to inform patients of risky medical procedures (Scher and Kozlowska 2018). Beecher, however, never mentions the term "bioethics," and his articles can be read as offering concrete examples of the issues brought up in the World Medical Association's 1964 Declaration of Helsinki, and the 1946 International Military Tribunal's judgment at Nuremberg.

Of these two branches, it was the latter that won out. Potter's threefold criteria for bioethics lost out, as the third leg of ecological conservation was removed. What was left was bioethics understood as strictly a biomedical ethics. There was certainly significant pressure to do so. Sociologically, this version of bioethics was created in the context of a society that had the ability to direct technologies toward medical interventions combined with the inability to direct them intentionally as ethical or responsible. In the words of Scher and Kozlowska (2018):

> New problems were emerging faster than the medical profession, without an immediate, large-scale, and immediate effort, could itself address. The result was a developing, and growing, gap between the profession's established practices, ethical and otherwise, and the public's need to address the problems that emerged as modern medicine extended its scientific and clinical powers.

This gap was addressed by trading βίος for υγεία (bios for hygieia, or life for health), which meant that the ethics of life became the ethics of health, specifically human health and the technological interventions that drove (and problematized) its disbursement. This is the bioethics of the Hastings Center of 1969, and Georgetown's Kennedy Institute of Ethics of 1971, a version that its critics (mostly in, but certainly not limited to, the UK and Europe) refer to as the "Georgetown mantra" because of the fourfold principles of beneficence, nonmaleficence, autonomy, and justice.

This sociological analysis may give insight as to why bioethics has been unable to effectively address anthropogenic climate change. It readily defined itself as the product of medical technology such that the problems and solutions on its immediate horizon are of the medically technological sort. This made the practice of bioethics the business of developed societies that had access to such technologies. And while this points to the implicit privilege behind bioethical principlism (especially highlighting its criterion of justice), in the context of climate change, bioethics finds itself unable to address environmental problems. Absent Potter's third leg of ecological conservation, a bioethical prescription to climate change is literally outside its zone of specialization. The Georgetown mantra can give very little other than the platitude that we really ought to do something about it.

It is also instructive to analyze this branch of bioethics in terms of the changing climate itself. We note that the medical and cultural contexts under which bioethics developed occurred during a period of relative climatic stability. The rise in CO_2 emissions was noted in the 1950s only by atmospheric scientists, and when the Hastings Center Report came out, the slight increase in global temperatures could still be attributed to natural fluctuations. By the time James Hansen's testimony before Congress in 1988 raised public awareness of anthropogenic climate change, bioethics had already established itself in much the form we know it today.

The fact that bioethics developed during a time of relative climatological quiescence is important: Ensconced in a barely perceptible warming climate that they could not perceive as dangerous, bioethicists had the luxury of not having to think of existential threats other than those already known or discovered, addressed, and treated by expert medical interventions and health-care delivery. The health and health-care challenges brought about by anthropogenic climate change did not and could not register as a bioethical concern.

A QUESTION OF VALUES

The difference between climate change science and bioethics is most apparent when we consider their larger disciplines. Ethics falls under a category of philosophy known as axiology, and bioethics as a profession has developed its own principlistic axiological criteria by which to pass value judgments on events. The fourfold principles held in highest value are deontological by lineage, as they have been determined to have the highest degree of logical universality and applicability. Climate change is of course the subject of science, and it, too, has its own method by which it makes sense of the world. Unlike bioethics, its findings are inductively verified and are iterative, and thus subject to empirical verification.

So why can't bioethics successfully address climate change? If we want to say that the Georgetown mantra has applications to anthropogenic climate change, we would need to transpose the values that bioethics has developed onto the quantified data of science. Is such a thing possible? While that initially sounds like nothing but a detail to be ironed out, it is actually based on the demand that the scientific understanding of anthropogenic climate change interface neatly with the axiology of bioethics.

But what exactly is the relationship between anthropogenic climate change and the anthropocentric principles of autonomy, beneficence, nonmaleficence, and justice of bioethics? Answering it invites a more unsettling question: Is even asking it not a practical example of a category mistake?

Bioethics and climate change are not the same type of thing. Ethics as traditionally developed is anthropocentric. We are meant to imagine that those are real human beings in the way of the trolley car. This is not the case with climate change. The climate change referred to in this chapter is anthropogenic; it is not anthropocentric. It is, if anything, pancentric in that it is a concern for the entire planet. Anthropogenic climate change affects all organisms, even—or rather, especially—nonliving things: earth, water, air. How can the Georgetown mantra derive an adequate prescriptivism regarding anthropogenic ecological collapse? Analyzing the relationship between bioethics and climate change assumes parity in what is in fact an asymmetry of human involvement, where the empirically derived fact of anthropogenic climate change leads to human health crises that are of anthropocentric concern. However, those anthropocentric principles of bioethics cannot lead to strategies meant to address climate change.

The etiology of climate change may indeed feature patient autonomy and justice somewhere down the line, but that causal chain is long and tangled. How beneficence and nonmaleficence are related to climate change is even more complicated because many medical interventions needed to prolong human health necessarily partake in the resource depletion, carbon emissions, and energy consumption that go into the production and storage of pharmaceuticals, and the sustained operation of medical equipment and health-care services. In terms of climate change, the long-standing principles of bioethics may well be harming human health on the macroscopic level while attempting to better it on the microscopic.

HOW OUGHT ANTHROPOGENIC CLIMATE CHANGE AFFECT BIOETHICS?

At present, the question is not really whether bioethics ought to respond to anthropogenic climate change, but how it can possibly do so. As the sociological, climatological, and axiological analyses above indicate, I do not believe the present practice of bioethics can. It simply was not meant to respond to such an existential threat of our own making.

Fortunately there is another version of bioethics already established in the literature that can respond to environmental threats. This is the first iteration proposed by Fritz Jahr and developed by Van Rensselaer Potter. Rehabilitating this version would reestablish the ecological third leg that Potter found central to bioethics. Cristina Richie's Principles of Green Bioethics: Sustainability in Health Care (2019) is one such attempt. Richie develops it in the familiar principlistic language of bioethics currently practiced. It even has the same number of principles as the Georgetown mantra, albeit with distributive justice, resource conservation, simplicity, and ethical economics replacing the usual bioethical quartet.

A thorough reworking of bioethics would require a fundamental restructuring of ethics. Potter's intellectual mentor, Aldo Leopold, whose name is in Potter's second book of bioethics, develops an ecocentric ethics instead. I have written about this in the previous edition of this text (Tan 2020). Such a turn would necessitate a different metaphysical outlook as well. Arne Næss's *Deep Ecology* is inspired by Spinoza's monism, which allows Næss to understand ethical agents in non-substantive relational terms absent from the species or individual egoism that accompanies ethical ends, utility, rights, and duties.

The point of this is of course not to engage with this other version of bioethics, but to underscore that one does not need to be created out of whole cloth. It need not even replace the more familiar formulation of bioethics; it is not claiming that principlism's conflation of life and human health is ill-advised, just that it is inherently limited in its ability to contextualize human health in the environmental milieu that it thought unnecessary to include at the outset of its formation.

It is, however, meant to show the philosophical depth that an ecocentric bioethics can have. It has an interpretive richness and intellectual thickness that has yet to be applied to ethical ends. If we are serious about applying a viable bioethical response to anthropogenic climate change, we can do no better than to explore this new old version of bioethics.

References

American College of Emergency Physicians. "Lessons Learned from Hurricane Sandy and Recommendations for Improved Healthcare and Public Health Response and Recovery for Future Catastrophic Events: Final Report." December 22, 2015. Accessed February 5, 2023.

Cardascia, Sylvia. "Protecting the Yellow River Basin in the People's Republic of China." *Asian Development Blog.* January 17, 2022. https://blogs.adb.org/blog/protecting-yellow-river-basin-people-s-republic-china. Accessed February 20, 2023.

Carlson, Colin J., Ellen Bannon, Emily Mendenhall, Timothy Newfield, and Shweta Bansal. "Rapid Range Shifts in African *Anopheles* Mosquitoes over the Last Century." *Biology Letters,* vol. 19, no. 2, February 15, 2023. https://royalsocietypublishing.org/doi/10.1098/rsbl.2022.0365. Accessed February 18, 2023.

Carrington, Damian. "Climate Crisis: Scientists Spot Warning Signs of Gulf Stream Collapse." *The Guardian.* August 5, 2021. https://www.theguardian.com/environment/2021/aug/05/climate-crisis-scientists-spot-warning-signs-of-gulf-stream-collapse. Accessed March 2, 2023.

Centers for Disease Control and Prevention. "Health Implications of Drought." *CDC: Drought and Health.* January 16, 2020. https://www.cdc.gov/nceh/drought/implications.htm. Accessed February 7, 2023.

Chandrashekhar, Vaishnavi. "As Himalayan Glaciers Melt, a Water Crisis Looms in South Asia." *Yale School of the Environment.* October 3, 2022. https://e360.yale.edu/features/himalayas-glaciers-climate-change. Accessed February 19, 2023.

Climate Reality Project. "Global Warming's Evil Twin: Ocean Acidification". https://www.climaterealityproject.org/blog/global-warming-ocean-acidification. June 21, 2016. Accessed February 21, 2023.

Commonwealth Fund. "The Impact of Climate Change on Our Health and Health Systems." *The Commonwealth Fund.* May 4, 2022. https://www.commonwealthfund.org/publications/explainer/2022/may/impact-climate-change-our-health-and-health-systems. Accessed February 18, 2023.

Davidson, Helen. "China Drought Causes Yangtze to Dry Up, Sparking Shortage of Hydropower." *The Guardian.* August 2022. https://www.theguardian.com/world/2022/aug/22/china-drought-causes-yangtze-river-to-dry-up-sparking-shortage-of-hydropower. Accessed February 20, 2023.

Environmental Protection Agency. "Climate Change Indicators: Lyme Disease." *EPA.* April 2021. https://www.epa.gov/climate-indicators/climate-change-indicators-lyme-disease. Accessed February 18, 2023.

Falkenberg, Laura J., Richard G. J. Bellerby, Sean D. Connell, Lora E. Fleming, Bruce Maycock, Bayden D. Russell, Francis J. Sullivan, and Sam Dupont. "Ocean Acidification and Human Health." *International Journal of Environmental Research and Public Health,* vol. 17, no. 12, June 24, 2020. https://www.ncbi.nlm.nih.gov/pmc/articles/PMC7344635/. Accessed February 21, 2023.

Fink, Camille. "Record Drought Conditions Pose Serious Challenges to Hospitals." *American Society for Health Care Engineering.* March 4, 2022. https://www.hfmmagazine.com/articles/4405-record-drought-conditions-pose-serious-challenges-to-hospitals. Accessed October 15, 2022.

Food and Agriculture Organization of the United Nations. *The State of World Fisheries and Aquaculture 2022: Towards Blue Transformation.* https://www.fao.org/documents/card/en/c/cc0461en. Accessed February 21, 2023.

Gross, Jenny. "Low Water Levels Disrupt European River Cruises, A Favorite of US Tourists." *New York Times.* August 29, 2022. https://www.nytimes.com/2022/08/29/travel/river-cruises-drought-europe.html. Accessed February 20, 2023.

Heft-Neal, Sam, Anne Driscoll, Wei Yang, Gary Shaw, and Marshall Burke. "Associations between Wildfire Smoke Exposure during Pregnancy and Risk of Preterm Birth in California." *Environmental Research,* vol. 203, January 2022. https://www.sciencedirect.com/science/article/abs/pii/S001393512101166X?via%3Dihub. Accessed February 17, 2023.

Kozlov, Max. "How Record Wildfires Are Harming Human Health." *Nature*. November 24, 2021. https://www.nature.com/articles/d41586-021-03496-1. Accessed February 16, 2023.

Krauer, Fabienne, Hildegunn Viljugrein, and Katherine R. Dean. "The Influence of Temperature on the Seasonality of Historical Plague Outbreaks." *Proceedings of the Royal Society II*, vol. 288, no. 1954. https://royalsocietypublishing.org/doi/10.1098/rspb.2020.2725. Accessed February 19, 2023.

Lieberman-Cribbin, Wil, Bian Liu, Samantha Schneider, Rebecca Schwartz, and Emanuela Taioli. "Self-Reported and FEMA Flood Exposure Assessment after Hurricane Sandy: Association with Mental Health Outcomes." *PLOS One*. January 27, 2017. https://stacks.cdc.gov/view/cdc/44742. Accessed February 14, 2023.

Lindsey, Rebecca, and Luann Dahlman. "Climate Change: Ocean Heat Content." *National Oceanic and Atmospheric Administration*. August 17, 2020. https://www.climate.gov/news-features/understanding-climate/climate-change-ocean-heat-content. Accessed February 19, 2023.

Macpherson, Cheryl Cox. "Climate Change Is a Bioethics Problem." *Bioethics*, vol. 27, no. 6: Special Issue—International Association of Bioethics 11th World Congress, 305–8. https://onlinelibrary.wiley.com/doi/epdf/10.1111/bioe.12029. Accessed 1/26/23.

McClurg, Lesley. "Storms in Bay Area Have Unleashed Millions of Gallons of Untreated Sewage Water." *National Public Radio*. January 14, 2023. https://www.npr.org/2023/01/14/1149245154/storms-in-the-bay-area-have-unleashed-millions-of-gallons-of-untreated-sewage-wa. Accessed February 7, 2023.

McMichael, Celia, Shouro Dasgupta, Sonja Ayeb-Karlsson, and Ilan Kelman. "A Review of Estimating Population Exposure to Sea-Level Rise and the Relevance of Migration." *Environmental Research Letter*, vol. 15, no. 12, November 27, 2020. https://iopscience.iop.org/article/10.1088/1748-9326/abb398. Accessed February 18, 2023.

Montana Department of Public Health and Human Services. "Flooding Creates Potential Human Health and Recreational Risks in Rivers Across Montana." https://dphhs.mt.gov/News/2022/June/Flooding. Accessed October 14, 2022.

National Aeronautics and Space Administration. "NASA Says 2022 Fifth Warmest Year on Record, Warming Trend Continues." January 12, 2023. https://climate.nasa.gov/news/3246/nasa-says-2022-fifth-warmest-year-on-record-warming-trend-continues/. Accessed February 5, 2023.

National Centers for Coastal Ocean Research. "Ocean Acidification Promotes Disruptive and Harmful Algal Blooms on Our Coasts." *NOAA*. January 13, 2014. https://coastalscience.noaa.gov/news/ocean-acidification-promotes-disruptive-and-harmful-algal-blooms-on-our-coasts/. Accessed February 21, 2023.

National Oceanic and Atmospheric Administration. "Is Sea Level Rising?" *NOAA*. https://oceanservice.noaa.gov/facts/sealevel.html. Accessed February 19, 2023.

———. "What Is Bombogenesis?" https://oceanservice.noaa.gov/facts/bombogenesis.html. Accessed February 4, 2023.

Parodi, Stephen. "When 'Do No Harm' Means Evacuating Hospitals in California." *New York Times*. November 1, 2019. https://www.nytimes.com/2019/11/01/opinion/california-kincade-hospital-wildfire.html. Accessed February 6, 2023.

Pendrey, Catherine G; Russell L. Gruen, Robyn M. Lucas, Simon Quilty, and Tarun Weeramanthri. "Is Climate Change Exacerbating Health-Care Workforce Shortages for Underserved Populations?" *The Lancet*, vol. 5, no. 4. https://www.thelancet.com/journals/lanplh/article/PIIS2542-5196(21)00028-0/fulltext. Accessed February 18, 2023.

Pickrell, John. "Bush-Fire Smoke Linked to Hundreds of Deaths." *Nature*. March 24, 2020. https://www.nature.com/articles/d41586-020-00886-9. Accessed February 16, 2023.

Resnick, David B. "Bioethics and Global Climate Change." *Bioethics Forum*, vol. 39, no. 3, 2009. https://www.ncbi.nlm.nih.gov/pmc/articles/PMC2688386/. Accessed October 13, 2022.

Richie, Cristina. *Principles of Green Bioethics: Sustainability in Health Care*. East Lansing, MI: Michigan State University Press, 2019.

Rydén, Patrik, Anders Sjöstedt, and Anders Johansson. "Effect of Climate Change on Tularemia Disease activity in Sweden." *Global Health Action*, vol. 2, no. 1. https://www.tandfonline.com/doi/full/10.3402/gha.v2i0.2063. Accessed February 18, 2023.

Salas, Renee N.; Tynan H. Friend, Aaron Bernstein, and Ashish K. Jha. "Adding a Climate Lens to Health Policy in the United States." *Health Affairs*, vol. 39, no. 12, December 2020. https://www.healthaffairs.org/doi/10.1377/hlthaff.2020.01352. Accessed February 18, 2023.

Scher, Stephen, and Kasia Kozlowska. "The Rise of Bioethics: A Historical Overview." *Rethinking Health Care Ethics*, August 3, 2018. https://www.ncbi.nlm.nih.gov/books/NBK543570/ doi: 10.1007/978-981-13-0830-7_3. Accessed December 26, 2022.

Scherer, Paul M. "California Power Blackouts Reveal Widespread Vulnerability in Health Care System." *Direct Relief.* October 17, 2019. https://www.directrelief.org/2019/10/california-power-blackouts-reveal-vulnerability-in-healthcare/. Accessed February 5, 2023.

Sherwin, Susan. "Whither Bioethics? How Feminism Can Help Reorient Bioethics." *International Journal of Feminist Approaches to Bioethics*, vol. 1, no. 1 (Spring 2008), 7–27. https://www.jstor.org/stable/40339210. Accessed January 26, 2023.

Simmons, Daisy. "What Is 'Climate Justice?' " *Yale Climate Connections*. July 29, 2020. https://yaleclimateconnections.org/2020/07/what-is-climate-justice/. Accessed February 18, 2023.

Struzik, Ed. "Fire-Induced Storms: A New Danger from the Rise in Wildfires." *Yale School of the Environment*. January 24, 2019. https://e360.yale.edu/features/fire-induced-storms-a-new-danger-from-the-rise-in-wildfires. Accessed February 5, 2023.

Tan, Peter Tagore. "Bioethics as Environmental Ethics: Ontogeny Recapitulates Environment." In *Global Bioethics and Human Rights: Contemporary Perspectives*, edited by Wanda Teays and Alison Dundes Renteln, 52–63. Lanham, MD: Rowman & Littlefield, 2020.

Tarabochia-Gast, A. T., D. R. Michanowicz, and A. S. Bernstein. "Flood Risk to Hospitals on the United States Atlantic and Gulf Coasts from Hurricanes and Sea Level Rise." *GeoHealth*, vol. 6, no. 10. https://agupubs.onlinelibrary.wiley.com/doi/10.1029/2022GH000651. Accessed September 29, 2022.

United Nations. "Sea-Level Rise Poses 'Unthinkable' Risks for the Planet, Security Council Hears." *United Nations Climate and Environment*. February 14, 2023. https://news.un.org/en/story/2023/02/1133492. Accessed February 19, 2023.

United States Geological Survey. "ARkStorm Scenario." https://www.usgs.gov/programs/science-application-for-risk-reduction/science/arkstorm-scenario. January 23, 2018. Accessed February 4, 2023.

Valles, Sean A. "Bioethics and the Framing of Climate Change's Health Risks." *Bioethics*, vol. 29, no. 5, 334–41. https://onlinelibrary.wiley.com/doi/full/10.1111/bioe.12110. Accessed January 26, 2023.

Velasquez-Manoff, Moises, and Jeremy White. "In the Atlantic Ocean, Subtle Shifts Hint at Dramatic Dangers." *New York Times*. March 2, 2021. https://www.nytimes.com/interactive/2021/03/02/climate/atlantic-ocean-climate-change.html?searchResultPosition=3. Accessed March 2, 2023.

Vince, Gaia. "The World Has a Third Pole—and It's Melting Quickly." *The Guardian*. September 15, 2019. https://www.theguardian.com/environment/2019/sep/15/tibetan-plateau-glacier-melt-ipcc-report-third-pole. Accessed February 19, 2023.

Williams, Jeremy. "Why Climate Change Is Inherently Racist." *BBC.* January 26, 2022. https://www.bbc.com/future/article/20220125-why-climate-change-is-inherently-racist. Accessed February 18, 2023.

World Health Organization. "Climate Change and Health." *World Health Organization Health Topics.* October 30, 2021. https://www.who.int/news-room/fact-sheets/detail/climate-change-and-health. Accessed February 8, 2023.

———. "Social Determinants of Health." *World Health Organization.* https://www.who.int/health-topics/social-determinants-of-health#tab=tab_1. Accessed February 18, 2023.

World Wildlife Fund. "Sustainable Seafood." https://www.worldwildlife.org/industries/sustainable-seafood. Accessed February 23, 2023.

CHAPTER 24

Immigration Detention and the Right to Health Care in Light of the COVID-19 Pandemic

Rita Manning

Abstract

There are now over 300,000 people overseen by Immigration and Customs Enforcement (ICE), with about 26,000 detained in jails and federal detention centers around the country at any particular time. The vast majority are supervised through the Alternatives to Detention Program, which relies on various technologies. The average detention time is two months, but some are detained for much longer periods. Since 2016, 80 deaths have occurred in ICE detention. Given its secrecy, and lack of accountability and oversight, it is not clear how many of these deaths are the result of inadequate medical care. ICE is a branch of a government agency in a democratic country; thus, the citizens on whose behalf it allegedly operates have an obligation to ensure that it operates in conformity with the fundamental principles of justice on which this nation was founded. ICE is a young and rapidly growing bureaucracy with little oversight. It operates using a mix of federal, state, local, and private centers, many of which are penal institutions. It has a history of serious abuse, and even when it operates in conformity with its penal standards, it inflicts additional harm onto vulnerable people, especially asylum seekers and parents of minor children. It thus requires our constant vigilance and concern. Our immigration policies and detention practices are deeply troubling, but until we elect to reform them, we have a special obligation to the vulnerable populations that we house in ICE detention.

Introduction

Francisco Castaneda came to the United States when he was ten years old, a refugee from the civil war in El Salvador. His mother died before she could apply for refugee status for the family, and Francisco ended up in ICE detention following his arrest for minor drug charges. Francisco repeatedly requested medical attention for a lesion on his penis but was repeatedly denied care until the settlement of an ACLU lawsuit on his behalf. He subsequently died of penile cancer in 2008, at the age of thirty-five (Mooty 2010).

Victoria Arellano, a transgender woman from Mexico with AIDS, was detained in 2007. During detention, she was given her AIDS medication on a very random schedule. Despite repeated requests for help, and symptoms ranging from nausea, vomiting blood, and fever, ICE denied her medical care until a week before her death. She died from pneumonia and meningitis at the age of twenty-three (Papst 2009).

In the early days of the COVID-19 pandemic, immigration detention centers were especially dangerous breeding grounds for this deadly virus. Between April and August of 2020, the rate of COVID-19 among ICE detainees was 13.4 times that of the general US population (Erfani 2020).

As early as 2019, the CDC standards for COVID-19 policy in detention centers required that all immigration detention centers provide, among other things, the ability to socially distance, adequate hygiene supplies and personal protective equipment including masks, cleaning materials, soap and toilet paper, and appropriate testing and isolation protocols (CDC 2019). Prevention for vulnerable populations was especially stressed (ICE, ERO 2020). In spite of this guidance, immigration detention centers continued to be deadly, especially to persons who were medically vulnerable. Cipriano Alvarez, a sixty-three-year-old cancer survivor, was one of the early victims of the indifference of immigration detention centers to the danger of COVID-19. When he was transferred to Stewart Detention Center in Lumpkin, Georgia, in August 2020, he had only the mask he had been given from the federal prison he had been released from in July. Ten days after arriving at Stewart, he tested positive for COVID-19 and died after spending more than a month on a ventilator (Rayasam 2022).

In *Roman v. Wolf* (2020), plaintiffs brought a class action on behalf of noncitizens being held in the Adelanto ICE Processing Center. Their complaint alleged that Adelanto's failure during the COVID-19 pandemic to implement necessary protective measures—including social distancing, sanitation, and the provision of sufficient masks and soap—violated detainees' due process rights under the Fifth Amendment. The Ninth Circuit Court recognized the district court's "broad equitable authority to grant provisional relief to remedy a likely constitutional violation" and remanded the case to the district to address these violations at Adelanto.

Zepeda Rivas v. Jennings (2020) challenged ICE's failure to address COVID-19 by delaying testing during an outbreak and knowingly leaving people with COVID-19 symptoms in a crowded dormitory. Judge Chhabria, in a December 2020 order, described "the conduct of the key ICE and GEO officials in charge of operations" as "appalling."

COVID-19 remains a serious health crisis in ICE detention centers. COVID-19 infections increased by more than 940 percent in January 2022 alone, and approximately 14 percent of people in ICE detention tested positive for COVID-19 (ACLU, *Shaikh v. ICE* 2022). The plaintiffs in this case challenged ICE and DHS for failure to provide them with booster shots in light of the plaintiffs' medically vulnerable status. This case was dismissed without prejudice (February 24, 2022) after ICE provided booster shots to all detainees.

Global Background

While there is no universal definition of "migrant" in international law, the UN International Organization for Migration (IOM) defines it as "a person who moves away from his or her place of usual residence, whether within a country or across an international border, temporarily or permanently, and for a variety of reasons" (IOM 2019). IOM adopts a similarly broad definition of "detention" as "The deprivation of liberty for migration-related reasons" (International Detention Coalition 2015). In 2000, the estimated number of international migrants was 173 million, about 2.8 percent of the world population. By 2022, this number grew to 281 million, approximately 3.6 percent of the world's population (World Migration Reports 2000 and 2022). Europe and Asia were home to the largest number of international migrants in 2020. The United States, with nearly 51 million migrants in 2020, has more international migrants than any other single country (Natarajan 2022).

The Global Compact for Safe, Orderly and Regular Migration is an agreement adopted by the UN General Assembly on December 19, 2018. While the compact is not legally binding, it expresses a set of commitments that extend to all international migrants. These commitments include "respect for and protection and fulfilment of the human rights of all migrants, regardless of their migration status, across all stages of the migration cycle" (Global Compact 2018, 5).

The Global Detention Project, a nonprofit organization based in Geneva, supports a database on detention related to migration around the world. The countries that still use migration-related detention include, in Europe: Greece, Denmark, Switzerland, Turkey, Russia; the Americas: the United States, Mexico, Guatemala, Panama; the Middle East: Morocco, Libya, Yemen, Egypt, Bahrain, Tunisia, United Arab Emirates, Jordan, Saudi Arabia; Asia-Pacific: India and Australia.

Morocco, Turkey, and Mexico are the three gateway countries to the Western world (Rodriguez 2022). Morocco provides no data on the number of detained migrants. Turkey has about twenty-five detention centers with a capacity of 16,000 (Rodriguez 2022). Mexico has one of the largest detention centers in the world (Immigration Detention in Mexico 2021). More than forty migrants died in a fire in Ciudad Juárez Detention Center on March 28, 2023, while locked in a cell holding sixty-eight people (Deaths in Ciudad Juárez Detention Centre 2023). Mexico's extensive detention system is largely a result of its agreement with the United States to detain migrants who are attempting to enter the United States. In what follows, I will largely focus on the migration system in the United States.

US Immigration Detention Policies

There are now over 300,000 people overseen by Immigration and Customs Enforcement (ICE), with about 26,000 detained in jails and federal detention centers around the country as of April 2023 (ICE 2023). Of this number, 281,613 are supervised through ICE's Alternatives to Detention (ATD) program, which uses three different types of technology to ensure compliance with release conditions: telephonic reporting, where phone calls are compared against voiceprints to ensure identity verification; Global Positioning System (GPS) ankle monitoring; and SmartLINK, which involves a range of technology (e.g., facial recognition), and can be used through a personal cell phone or to a SmartLINK mobile device (ICE Alternatives to Detention 2023).

For those who are detained, the average time is two months, but some are detained for much longer periods. Some detainees from the Mariel boatlift from Cuba were detained for thirty years until the Supreme Court ordered their release (*Clark v. Martinez* 2005). ICE currently houses detainees in ninety-nine detention facilities (ICE Detention Facilities 2023). This is a constantly shifting number because ICE operates three different kinds of centers: Service Processing Centers (SPCs) that are run by ICE; Contract Detention Facilities (CDFs) that are run by private prison companies, like Corrections Corporation of America and GEO; and centers run under contract with state or local government correctional agencies.

ICE reports that forty-five deaths occurred in ICE detention centers from 2018 to 2023, with twenty of those deaths occurring in 2019 (ICE, Detainee Deaths 2023). Thirty-five deaths in ICE detention between 2016 and 2018 were reported by the American Immigration Lawyer Association (Deaths in Adult Detention Centers 2022). Given ICE's secrecy, and lack of accountability and oversight, it is not clear how many of these deaths are the result of inadequate medical care.

Legal Background of US Migration Detention

One of the most significant laws governing immigration is the Immigration and Nationality Act (INA), which was first passed in 1952 (INA 1952). In that Act, Congress distinguished between aliens physically arriving in the United States and those who had already entered. Aliens who were found ineligible for entry were subject to "exclusion," and those already present in the United States who were subject to expulsion were deemed "deportable."

Congress expanded federal immigration law with the 1996 Illegal Immigration Reform and Immigrant Responsibility Act (IIRIRA 1996). Among its provisions are:

1. Most criminal offenses are grounds for mandatory, permanent deportation, and this provision applies even to offenses committed before the enactment of this legislation.
2. Mandatory detention is the norm for those in deportation proceedings.
3. The elimination of the right to federal review of INS decisions. (The Homeland Security Act of 2002 replaced INS with Immigration and Customs Enforcement, ICE; United States Citizenship and Immigration Services; and Bureau of Customs and Border Protection.)
4. Expedited removal procedures that allow INS (now ICE) employees broad discretion to deny admission, even to asylum seekers.
5. Evidence not available to immigrants or their lawyers can be used in deportation proceedings.

While ICE's emphasis on deporting immigrant "criminals" suggests that these are the only persons in ICE detention, this is far from the case. The categories of persons in ICE detention include asylum seekers; undocumented persons who are not asylum seekers, but who are not accused of any crime; undocumented persons who are accused of trivial offenses, including identity theft or felonious reentry; undocumented persons accused of serious offenses; and legal permanent residents who have committed a deportable offense. Until 2009, ICE also detained the children of undocumented adults, most of whom were American citizens. The practice of detaining "unaccompanied alien children" ended in 2003 with the transfer of these children to the Office of Refugee Resettlement.

The INA currently authorizes the Department of Homeland Security (DHS) to detain non-US nationals under certain conditions. The INA uses "aliens" to refer to migrants who are removable from the United States.

1. INA Section 236(a) generally authorizes the detention of aliens pending formal removal proceedings and permits migrants not subject to mandatory detention to be released on bond or their own recognizance;
2. INA Section 236(c) generally requires the detention of aliens who are removable because of specified criminal activity or terrorist-related grounds;
3. INA Section 235(b) generally requires the detention of applicants for admission who appear subject to removal; and
4. INA Section 241(a) generally mandates the detention of aliens during a ninety-day period after formal removal proceedings.

Constitutional rights are generally seen as applying only to aliens who have entered the United States (*Landon v. Plasencia* 1982). The constitutional challenges by aliens already in the US immigration detention system generally appeal to the Fifth Amendment's Due Process Clause. The Eighth Amendment does not apply because alien detainees are not being "punished" and thus are not subject to the Eighth Amendment.

The Supreme Court in *Zadvydas v. Davis* (2001) held that aliens who have entered the United States, even unlawfully, are "persons" under the Fifth Amendment's Due Process Clause, which limits the detention to "a period reasonably necessary to secure removal."

In *Demore v. Kim* (2003), the Supreme Court held that although the Fifth Amendment entitles aliens to due process in deportation proceedings, detention during such proceedings is constitutionally permissible.

In cases involving claims of inadequate medical treatment of immigration detainees, courts have typically appealed to the "deliberate indifference" standard under the Fifth Amendment. These cases include *Belbachir v. County of McHenry* (7th Cir. 2013), which held that alien detainees were entitled under the Fifth Amendment to "protection from harm caused by a defendant's deliberate indifference to the detainee's safety or health." *Adekoya v. Holder* (S.D.N.Y. 2010) held that "Deliberate indifference to the medical needs of an immigrant detainee in certain circumstances gives rise to a cognizable claim under the Due Process Clause of the Fifth Amendment."

Concerns about ICE Health Care

Well before the challenges raised about ICE's indifference to the dangers of COVID-19, very serious concerns were raised about the lack of adequate health care in ICE detention facilities (Goldstein 2008; Keller 2003; Guzman 2009). Homer D. Venters, MD, an attending physician at the Bellevue/NYU Program for Survivors of Torture, in New York City, said that "after adjusting for average length of detention, the data show that the mortality rate increased 29 percent between 2006 and 2007, from 27 to 34 per 100,000 detention-years" (AMA 2008).

The concerns about ICE immigration detention centers include their distance from the detainee's place of residence, making legal representation very difficult. In the prisons and jails that lease space to ICE, detainees are treated, in most respects, like prisoners, regardless of their status. Though ICE adopted standards for the provision of health care in immigration detention centers in 2008, these standards were developed for penal institutions and are thus inappropriate for civil detention (Papst 2009; Congressional Research Services 2009).

In addition, there are no clear provisions for enforcing these standards, and the number of serious complaints continues to rise. These complaints range from suicide and lack of treatment for mental illness (Tillman 2009) to the denial of abortion services for a detainee who was raped (Walden 2009), to preventable deaths (Ferrell 2008; Florida Immigration Advocacy Center 2009). Because correctional space is committed to other uses, detainees are transferred often and with little notice, making it difficult to find detainees, though ICE recently included a detainee locator device on their website (ICE Detainee Locator 2023).

Even when detainees can be located and are at a facility which allows the possibility of visitation, it is often very difficult and limited. This was especially true during the COVID-19 pandemic. COVID-19-related restrictions on visits lasted for more than two years, and were not lifted until May 2022—far longer than similar restrictions in federal prison (Kim 2022).

Concerns about the lack of translators and health-care staff indifference and incompetence have also been raised (Mooty 2010).

Obligations to Provide Health Care to Detained Migrants

It is useful to begin by distinguishing three categories of medical conditions that arise in immigration detention. The first is preexisting conditions; second, those that occur in detention but have no causal connection to the conditions of detention; and third, conditions that have a causal relationship to detention. All of the arguments I offer for our obligation to provide adequate health care to detainees apply to all three categories of detainees, but the last category of detainees provides an especially compelling case. Here, we are obligated to mitigate the harm created by the detention practices that the

United States chooses to employ. The failure of ICE to adequately address COVID is a striking example of how detention practices are at least part of the cause of the harm.

Many detainees will enter detention with preexisting conditions. This is not surprising, since this is a vulnerable population. Most left their home countries for economic reasons, and their immigration status makes it difficult to obtain care in the United States. The federal Emergency Medical Treatment and Active Labor Act (EMTALA) requires that hospitals treat and stabilize patients who present with emergencies, but at the same time, there are no requirements to offer long-term or curative care. In addition, the Personal Responsibility and Work Opportunity Reconciliation Act (PRWORA) restricts most federal public benefits, including medical care, for all classes of immigrants, legal and undocumented (Personal Responsibility and Work Reconciliation Act 1996). Many hospitals are currently dealing with this conflict by repatriating undocumented patients, often without their fully informed consent (Caruso 2023; Johnson 2009; Bresa 2010; Babu and Wolpin 2010). It is reasonable to suppose that part of the reason why some people enter detention with preexisting conditions is because of the restrictions on access to health care enshrined in federal law.

The second category includes those that occur in detention but which have no causal connection to the conditions of detention.

The final category is conditions that are either exacerbated or caused by the detention itself. COVID-19 is an obvious example of this kind of condition, but mental health problems also deserve our attention.

The psychological effects of detention are profound and long-lasting. Coffee et al. describe some of the mental health problems directly attributable to detention, including isolation and fractured relationships; demoralization and depression; and changes in view of self (Coffey, Kaplan, Sampson, and Tucci 2010). When the detainee is an asylum seeker, these problems are magnified through the lens of their previous mistreatment. Cutler cites problems in this population ranging from "anxiety to features of depressive illness, and features of post-traumatic stress to more serious conditions such as self-harm and suicide attempts" (Cutler 2005). These problems are especially serious for mothers. As one immigration attorney described it,

> It seems to me that there are so many unique issues with [detained] women. It's a higher psychological toll to be separated from their children. It gets to the point where you cannot even communicate with your client at all [because they are so distraught]. With men, there's definitely an impact, but with women, it takes over their entire being. Anybody who works with women detainees who have been transferred away from children will tell you it's so much more emotionally taxing for them (Rabin 2009).

The effect of ICE detention causes collateral damage that extends well beyond the detainee. Communities are undermined by the absence of contributing members. The fear of ICE detection encourages people to stay away from community activities and to endure abusive living and working conditions (Ray 2006; Kim 2009) The children of detained parents often have the parent detained at a distant location, and in the worst case, the child will lose the parent through deportation. If the child is among the approximately 4 million United States–born children with at least one noncitizen parent—and 79 percent of children with undocumented parents were born in the United States (Passel and Taylor 2010)—she may well face a devastating choice: to remain in the United States without the parent, or to move to an unfamiliar country, with prospects that are likely to be exceedingly poor (Rome 2010).

The experience of having one's parent detained in a prison-like facility to which one has little access is similar to the experience of having one's parent incarcerated for a criminal offense in a correctional institution. One would expect that long-term effects on children of parents detained by ICE would be roughly similar to those experienced by children of incarcerated parents. These consequences include severe and trauma-related stress; depression and difficulty forming attachments; difficulty sleeping and concentrating; withdrawing emotionally; cognitive delays; and difficulty developing trust, autonomy, initiative, productivity, and achieving identity (Miller 2006).

The global spread of COVID-19 that was caused by the deportation of migrants who were infected with COVID-19 while detained is an especially egregious collateral damage.

Arguments for Obligations to Detainees

PUBLIC HEALTH

There are a number of arguments for the obligation to provide health services to detainees, and many of these arguments parallel the arguments offered in support of medical care for immigrants generally. The first is public health. Some of the detainees will later be released, and they may pose a threat to themselves or others if their health concerns are not addressed. One of the problems with this argument is that it does not go far enough. One could address this concern by offering services only to those that have a high probability of release into the United States, or to those who have a medical condition that would pose a public health hazard. Of course, defenders of this argument point out that one doesn't know who will constitute a public health hazard until they have been medically assessed. The prevalence of asymptomatic tuberculosis is instructive here (CDC, The Difference between Latent TB Infection and TB Disease).

JUSTICE

The question of justice most often comes up in bioethics in the context of the allocation of health care, and whether—and when—persons are entitled to a minimum standard of health care. Rawls's principle of equal opportunity is often appealed to in this context (Rawls 1999). He argues that, in a fair bargaining situation, all persons would agree that everyone is entitled to equal opportunity. Meaningful equal opportunity requires, among other things, a right to at least a minimum standard of health care.

Defenders of a right to health care, such as Norman Daniels, argue that failure to respect this right is fundamentally unjust (Daniels 1998). This injustice is compounded when we note that people in ICE detention are unable to access health care on their own. Thus, even if one were persuaded that the right to health care is merely a negative right—one that requires only that others refrain from interfering with a person's act of securing health care—one would have to grant that the conditions of detention must either allow health-care providers access to their detainee patients, or, if security requires limiting outside access, that health care be provided by ICE.

Critics might allege that a right to health care is something that society need only respect for its members, and that persons in ICE detention are at best future members. But most defenders of the equal right to health care would base such a right on membership not in any particular political community, but in the human community. Thus, the denial of health care violates a fundamental human right.

PROFESSIONAL RESPONSIBILITY

The third argument appeals to the professional responsibility of detention medical staff. They may be ICE employees or contractors, but I would argue that even in this conflict of dual loyalties, their professional responsibility is primarily as health-care practitioners. We can appeal here to four principles generally recognized in health-care ethics: autonomy, justice, beneficence, and nonmaleficence. I think it is fairly obvious that denying appropriate health care to detainees runs afoul of some of these principles. Presumably no rational person would choose to have their health issues ignored. Beneficence points in the direction of offering care, and nonmaleficence deems cooperation of health-care practitioners in detention practices that exacerbate health problems as professionally irresponsible. This provides another reason for thinking that the dual loyalty conflict must be settled in favor of the detainee patient.

STATE COERCION

The next argument is that state coercion is a sufficient condition for having certain basic rights. These rights include the right to participate in the government in some fashion. Michael Walzer argues that "the processes of self-determination through which a democratic state shapes its internal life, must be open, and equally open, to all those men and women who live within its territory, work in the local economy, and are subject to local law" (Walzer 1984). Following Henry Shue (1996), I would argue that this fundamental political right cannot be meaningfully exercised unless basic subsistence rights are also provided for.

The Supreme Court made a similar argument in *Plyer v. Doe* (1982), where they claimed that undocumented children were persons under the Fourteenth Amendment and thus entitled to protection of their basic rights. One might respond here that no one is coerced into illegally migrating into the United States. There are two problems with this response. The first is that there is indeed an element of coercion here, and I will return to this in the discussion of the US role in causing migration. Second, once a person is in ICE detention, they are subject to substantial state coercion and thus should have some protections against the excessive use of state power. This leads into the next argument.

CRUEL AND UNUSUAL PUNISHMENT

The next argument applies specifically in the case of ICE detention. The Supreme Court has ruled that the denial of health care to incarcerated persons constitutes impermissible cruel and unusual punishment (*Brown v. Plata* 2011). As Justice Kennedy writes in *Plata*,

> As a consequence of their own actions, prisoners may be deprived of rights that are fundamental to liberty. Yet the law and the Constitution demand recognition of certain other rights. Prisoners retain the essence of human dignity inherent in all persons. Respect for that dignity animates the Eighth Amendment prohibition against cruel and unusual punishment. . . . To incarcerate, society takes from prisoners the means to provide for their own needs. . . . A prison that deprives prisoners of basic sustenance, including adequate medical care, is incompatible with the concept of human dignity and has no place in civilized society.

One might argue here that immigration detention is not identical to criminal incarceration and thus that *Plata* does not apply. However, in *Youngberg v. Romero* (1982), the Supreme Court held that persons who are involuntarily committed to a state institution for a mental incapacity are entitled to better treatment than convicted criminals "whose conditions of confinement are designed to punish." Thus one might argue that ICE detainees, who are subject to administrative and not criminal proceedings, are analogous to persons who are involuntarily confined for noncriminal reasons and thus constitutionally entitled to adequate medical care.

FAMILY MEMBERSHIP

Family reunification has been a criterion for immigration since the Immigration Act of 1965. The underlying principle here is that strong family ties are important, both for individuals and for a flourishing national culture. This principle should apply to all families. The difficulty of reentering the United States has resulted in an undocumented population that is increasingly made up of families with minor children (Passel 2006). There are approximately 4 million United States–born children with at least one noncitizen parent, and 79 percent of the children with undocumented parents were born in the United States (Passel and Taylor 2010).

Given these statistics, it is reasonable to assume that a high percentage of people in ICE detention are the parents, siblings, or other relatives of US citizens. This provides a general argument for loosening immigration restrictions on such persons. If such persons are morally entitled to consideration for entry on family grounds, presumably their treatment in detention should reflect their status as members, to some extent, of our society, and this status can ground the obligation to provide adequate health care to them.

COLLATERAL DAMAGE

If ICE detention imposes collateral damage on the innocent children of detainees, and if there is an acceptable alternative to detention, then we have an obligation to mitigate the harm. One simple way to do this it to move away from detention, at least for parents of minor children. There is good reason to think that alternatives to detention will not only mitigate some of the harms caused by detention, but will also be an effective and cost-saving alternative to detention. A program run by the Vera Institute showed an appearance rate of over 90 percent for undocumented immigrants enrolled in its alternative non-detention program (Root 2000).

If the collateral damage undermines the detainee's ability to assert her rights in immigration proceedings, as it seems to do in the case of mothers, then we have an additional reason to adopt alternatives to detention. If this solution is not politically feasible, we are not thereby absolved of all obligation toward detainee parents. One way we can discharge some of our obligation is to offer them the appropriate health services to mitigate the harm that they are suffering in virtue of this collateral damage.

RECIPROCITY

James Dwyer argues that "Most undocumented workers do the jobs that citizens often eschew. They do difficult and disagreeable jobs at low wages . . . they have the worst jobs and work in the worst conditions," and that such work is a "social construction" that forms the basis of our obligation to provide health care (Dwyer 2004).

I would add that in addition to doing this work, undocumented workers pay taxes and receive few comparable benefits in return. They pay Social Security taxes under fake numbers that, according the Social Security Administration, add about $50 billion annually to the system (Porter 2005). In addition, they pay sales taxes, and some are homeowners who also pay property taxes. At the same time, they are prohibited by the 1996 Personal Responsibility and Work Opportunity Reconciliation Act from collecting most public benefits.

US Role in Causing Global Health Problems and/or in Causing Migration

Many theorists have argued that the political and economic policies of the Global North are direct causes of migration. Thomas Pogge offers a global analysis: The existing global order is upheld by powerful governments and international organizations, such as the World Bank and the International Monetary Fund. Privileged citizens of powerful countries have a collective responsibility for their governments' role in designing a global order that results in the impoverishment of the inhabitants of poor and less powerful countries (Pogge 2008).

Whether or not one is convinced of such a global thesis, other theorists offer more local, empirically based accounts. David Bacon, for example, offers a detailed look at how US policies created, and continue to create, tremendous pressures for Mexican illegal migration to the United States (Bacon 2008). If these theorists are correct, then we have reason to assert a negative duty to stop the policies that created the problem and a positive duty of reparation to mitigate the harm that we have caused.

Whether or not one is convinced that US policies are causally implicated in undocumented immigration, there is no doubt that some detention practices are directly implicated in harm to detainees, especially when deadly contagious diseases like COVID-19 are spreading. *Roman v. Wolf* describes COVID-19 practices in an ICE detention facility: an utter failure to implement necessary protective measures—including social distancing, sanitation, and the provision of sufficient masks and soap. *Shaikh v. ICE* demonstrates that even in 2022, ICE was failing to provide the COVID-19 boosters that were by then a standard prevention.

The prison-like detention conditions that detainees are subjected to, especially asylum seekers who are fleeing state torture, are also a direct cause of subsequent mental health problems and exacerbations of such problems (Robjant, Robbins, and Senior 2009). In these cases, the only question is whether the duty of reparation should apply only to those directly wronged or to the larger class of detainees. I would argue that since ICE makes no real attempt to sort out asylum seekers and other vulnerable people from other less vulnerable detainees, it has an affirmative duty to provide appropriate health care for all detainees.

Arguments Against the Obligation to Detainees

DETERRENCE

Brietta Clark discusses some of the standard objections to providing health care to undocumented immigrants in general, and these arguments apply to detainees as well (Clark 2008). First she discusses the deterrence argument—that restricting such benefits would act as a deterrent to illegal immigration, and that providing them would act as an incentive to such immigration. Her response to this argument is that it is employment, not health care, which is the primary motivator for illegal immigration. Given the restrictions on health benefits for immigrants required by PRWORA, and the fact that by 2008, twenty-eight states had also restricted health-care benefits for immigrants (Matthew 2008), it is very difficult to believe that undocumented immigrants come to the United States in search of publicly subsidized health care.

LIMITED HEALTH-CARE RESOURCES

The next argument Clark refers to is the idea that we must restrict health-care benefits because our health-care resources are very limited. Her response is that health care is not an individual but a public good, and that restricting it has overall bad consequences. Presumably one might point to public health here. Dwyer offers an additional response to this objection (Dwyer 2004), arguing that we need not choose between health care for citizens and the undocumented. There are many other possible trade-offs. Secondly he points out that health care is a basic need, and as such, it is inappropriate to distribute it by appeal to a principle of desert.

DENIAL OF BENEFITS IS APPROPRIATE PUNISHMENT FOR LAWBREAKING

The final argument Clark considers is that benefit restrictions are justified as punishment for violations of the social contract. She has two responses here. The first is that not all excluded immigrants are undocumented; the five-year waiting period for Medicaid applies to legal immigrants as well. This first response seems to exclude persons in ICE detention, but I would argue that it does not.

Recall the categories of persons in ICE detention: asylum seekers; undocumented persons who are not asylum seekers, but who are not accused of any crime; undocumented persons who are accused of trivial offenses, including identity theft or felonious reentry; and undocumented persons accused of serious offenses, and legal permanent residents (LPRs) who have committed a deportable offense. Asylum seekers, in particular, are clearly not in violation of any social contract. Presenting oneself for asylum is within the rules of national and international law.

We can make a similar case for LPRs who are detained for committing a deportable offense. First, even if the offense occurred after the 1996 Illegal Immigration Reform and Immigrant Responsibility Act, I would argue that deportation is grossly disproportionate to most of the offenses that are currently classed as deportable offenses (DUI, for example). Second, the law allows for the deportation of LPRs for offenses that occurred in the past, even before the act became law.

The second response Clark gives is that while criminal sanctions might be seen as appropriate for violations of immigration law, this does not imply that denial of health care should be part of the punishment. Indeed, the Supreme Court has explicitly stated this position in *Plata*: Denial of health care is a violation of the Eighth Amendment ban against cruel and unusual punishment.

RIGHT TO EXCLUDE AND RIGHT NOT TO TREAT

Some theorists have argued that legitimate states have a prima facie right to exclude immigrants from their territory (Wellman 2008). If undocumented persons have no right to be in the country, then it might follow that they have no rights to benefits available to legitimate members of the state. But I would argue that even if we accepted this position, such persons would still have a right against harm. The denial of needed medical services for someone who is otherwise unable to procure them in virtue of being detained is a harm, as is the unnecessary infliction of psychological distress on already vulnerable persons, such as asylum seekers. I think there is actually a much stronger case to be made for the obligation to provide health care for all, but the appeal to a right against harm suffices to show that persons who are detained by ICE have at least the right to be protected from the denial of medical services.

INSUFFICIENT RECIPROCITY

Some would argue that undocumented immigrants take more resources than they provide and thus are not entitled to services based on a principle of reciprocity. "They are taking our jobs" is one way this concern is raised. I think there is something right about this objection, but I don't think it accurately fixes the source of the problem. Richard Trumka, AFL-CIO president, states the problem very succinctly: "Too many U.S. employers actually like the current state of the immigration system—a system where immigrants are both plentiful and undocumented—afraid and available" (Trumka 2010).

Too many employers like a system where our borders are closed and open at the same time—closed enough to turn immigrants into second-class citizens, open enough to ensure an endless supply of socially and legally powerless cheap labor. In *Hoffman Plastics* (2002), the Supreme Court ruled that undocumented workers were not entitled to back pay, even if their various employment claims were sustained, since they were not legally available for work. This decision provides a perverse incentive to hire undocumented workers: No matter what you do to them, they cannot be compensated with back pay in any lawsuit against you (Manning 2010). It is thus likely that having a class of exploitable workers does result in fewer jobs for American workers, along with depressing wages in the unskilled sector. But the fault here is with employers and the Court, not with the undocumented workers.

A related objection is that immigrants don't pay enough in taxes to cover all the public benefits they use. This objection rests on an empirical claim about how much undocumented immigrants pay in taxes versus what they use in services. But even if we granted that the balance tilts in favor of the use of services, this is not the end of the story. We can appeal to James Dwyer's response to this objection here. This objection sees society as a private business venture where one benefits on the basis of what one invests, and, as Dwyer writes, "The business model is not an adequate model for thinking about voting, legal defense, library services, minimum wages, occupational safety, and many other social benefits" (Dwyer 2004, 37).

Even If the United States Is Causally Implicated in Migration, the Best Way to Fix the Problem Is in Home Countries

I turn now to the final argument: that even if we accepted all the justifications for providing health care, and the causal role that wealthy countries play in creating migratory pressures, encouraging undocumented immigration is the wrong approach because it exacerbates the problem by encouraging the youngest, most productive workers to emigrate, leaving their home countries even worse off than they already are. While I am convinced that a more comprehensive, global solution is ultimately in order, this simply does not absolve us of our obligation to those who are already within our borders, and especially those within our detention facilities.

Conclusion

ICE is a branch of a government agency in a democratic country; thus, the citizens on whose behalf it allegedly operates have an obligation to ensure that it operates in conformity with the fundamental principles of justice on which this nation was founded. ICE is a young and rapidly growing bureaucracy with little oversight. It operates using a mix of federal, state, local and private centers, many of which are penal institutions. It has a history of serious abuse, and even when it operates in conformity with its penal standards, it inflicts additional harm onto vulnerable people, especially asylum seekers and parents of minor children. It thus requires our constant vigilance and concern. Our immigration policies and detention practices are deeply troubling, but until we elect to reform them, we have a special obligation to the vulnerable populations that we house in ICE detention. Minimally, that includes being attentive to their medical needs.

References

ACLU, *Shaik v. ICE,* 2022. https://www.acludc.org/en/cases/aamir-shaikh-v-us-immigration-and-customs-enforcement-ice-seeking-covid-19-booster-shots.

Adekoya v. Holder, 751 F. Supp. 2d 688, 694 (S.D.N.Y. 2010).

American Immigration Lawyer Association, Deaths at Adult Detention Centers, AILA Doc. No. 16050900 | Dated September 6, 2022. https://www.aila.org/infonet/deaths-at-adult-detention-centers.

Babu, Maya A, Joseph B. Wolpin (2010). Undocumented immigrants, healthcare access, and medical repatriation after serious medical illness. *American Health Lawyers Association, Journal of Health & Life Sciences Law* 3 (3), 83–101.

Bacon, David (2008). *Illegal People.* Boston: Beacon Press.

Belbachir v. Co. of McHenry, 726 F.3d, 979 (7th Cir. 2013).

Bresa, Lindita (2010). Uninsured, illegal, and in need of long-term care: the repatriation of undocumented immigrants by U.S. hospitals. *Seton Hall Law Review*, 1663–96.

Brown v Plata, 563 U.S. 678, 687 (2011).

Caruso, Catherine. A Lehigh Valley hospital is trying to deport an undocumented comatose patient. *Bucks County Beacon*, March 10, 2023. https://buckscountybeacon.com/2023/03/a-lehigh-valley-hospital-is-trying-to-deport-an-undocumented-comatose-patient/.

Centers for Disease Control (CDC). The Difference between Latent TB Infection and TB Disease. https://www.cdc.gov/tb/publications/factsheets/general/ltbiandactivetb.htm#:~:text=Persons%20with%20latent%20TB%20infection,test%20or%20TB%20blood%20test.

———. Interim Guidance on Management of Coronavirus Disease 2019 (COVID-19) in Correctional and Detention Facilities. https://stacks.cdc.gov/view/cdc/100951.

Clark v. Martinez, 543 U.S. 371 (2005).

Clark, Brietta R. (2008). The immigrant health care narrative and what it tells us about the U.S. health care system. Loyola University Chicago School of Law, Beazley Institute for Health Law and Policy. *Annals of Health Law* 17, 229–78.

Coffey, Guy J., Ida Kaplan, Robyn C. Sampson, Maria Montagna Tucci (2010). The meaning and mental health consequences of long-term immigration detention for people seeking asylum. *Social Science & Medicine* 70, 2070–79.

Congressional Research Services, Health Care for Noncitizens in Immigration Detention. https://crsreports.congress.gov RL34556.

Cutler, Sarah (2005). Fit to be detained? Challenging the detention of asylum seekers and migrants with health needs. Report by BID (Bail for Immigration Detainees), based on the findings of a report by Médecins sans Frontières.

Daniels, Norman (1998). Is there a right to health care and, if so, what does it encompass? *A Companion to Bioethics*, eds. Kuhse and Singer. Oxford, UK: Blackwell Publishers, 316–25.

Deaths in Ciudad Juárez Detention Centre Reveal the Brutality of Immigration Control in Mexico, Global Detention Project, 2023. https://www.globaldetentionproject.org/deaths-in-ciudad-juarez-detention-centre-reveal-the-brutality-of-immigration-control-in-mexico.

Demore v. Kim, 538 U.S. 510 (2003).

Dwyer, James (2004). Illegal immigrants, health care, and social responsibility. *The Hastings Center Report*, January/February, 35–40.

Emergency Medical Treatment and Active Labor Act (EMTALA), 42 U.S.C. § 1395dd.

Erfani, Parsa, et al. COVID-19 testing and cases in immigration detention centers, April–August 2020. *JAMA*, 325 (2), 182–84. https://doi.org/10.1001/jama.2020.21473.

Ferrell, John (2008, May 10). Map: a closer look at 83 deaths. *Washington Post.* http://www.washingtonpost.com/wp-srv/nation/specials/immigration/map.html.

Global Compact for Safe, Orderly and Regular Migration, 2018. https://refugeesmigrants.un.org/sites/default/files/180713_agreed_outcome_global_compact_for_migration.pdf.

Goldstein, Amy, and Dana Priest (2008, May 13). Five detainees who took their lives. *Washington Post.* http://www.washingtonpost.com/wp-dyn/content/article/2008/05/12/AR2008051202694.html; Priest and Goldstein (2008, May 11–14), Careless detention: system of neglect, *Washington Post*, http://www.washingtonpost.com/carelessdetention.

Guzman, Esther Morales (2009). Imprisonment, deportation, and family separation: my American nightmare. *Social Justice* 36 (2), 106–9.

Immigration Detention in Mexico: Between the United States and Central America, February 2021. Global Detention Project: http://www.globaldetentionproject.org/home.html.

Hoffman Plastics Compounds, Inc. v. NLRB3, 535 U.S. 137 (2002).

ICE Alternatives to Detention, 2023. https://www.ice.gov/features/atd.

ICE Detainee Deaths, 2023: https://www.ice.gov/detain/detainee-death-reporting.

ICE Detainee Locator, 2023. https://locator.ice.gov/odls/#/index.

ICE Detention Facilities, 2023. https://www.ice.gov/detention-facilities.

ICE Detention Statistics, 2023. https://www.ice.gov/detain/detention-management.

ICE, ERO COVID-19 Pandemic Response Requirements (Version 1.0, April 10, 2020). https://www.ice.gov/doclib/coronavirus/eroCOVID19responseReqsCleanFacilities-v1.pdf.

Illegal Immigration Reform and Immigrant Responsibility Act (IIRIRA) of 1996, Pub. L. No. 104–208, Div. C, § 302(a), 110 Stat. 3009–579.

Immigration and Nationality Act (INA), 8 U.S.C. ch. 12.

International Detention Coalition. There Are Alternatives: A Handbook for Preventing Unnecessary Immigration Detention (rev. ed., 2015), 79. D 48 *International Migration Law* (47).
International Organization for Migration (IOM). Glossary on migration, IML Series No. 34, 2019, 132.
———. World Migration Report, 2022. https://publications.iom.int/books/world-migration-report-2022.
Johnson, Kit (2009). Patients without borders: extralegal deportation by hospitals. *University of Cincinnati Law Review* 78 (2), Winter, 657–97.
Keller, Allen S., MD (2003). The impact of detention on the health of asylum seekers. *Journal of Ambulatory Care Management* 26 (4), 383–85.
Kim, Juliana. ICE lifted its ban on family visits, but relatives still struggle to see loved ones. NPR, November 21, 2022. https://www.npr.org/2022/11/21/1134611341/ice-covid-restrict-social-visits-immigrants-detained-families.
Kim, Kathleen (2009). Civil rights and the low-wage worker: the trafficked worker as private attorney general: a model for enforcing the civil rights of undocumented workers. *The University of Chicago Legal Forum*, 247–310.
Landon v. Plasencia, 459 U.S. 21 (1982).
Manning, Margaret (2010). A mockery of the American dream: how to prevent employers from exploiting immigration status and escaping Title VII liability post-*Hoffman* (unpublished).
Matthew, Dayna Bowen (2010). Race and healthcare in America: the social psychology of limiting healthcare benefits for undocumented immigrants—moving beyond race, class, and nativism. *Houston Journal of Health Law & Policy* 10, Spring, 201–26.
Miller, Keva M. (2006). The impact of parental incarceration on children: an emerging need for effective interventions. *Child and Adolescent Social Work Journal* 23 (4), 472–86.
Mooty, Brianna M. (2010). Solving the medical crisis for immigration detainees: is the proposed detainee basic medical care act of 2008 the answer? *Law and Inequality: A Journal of Theory and Practice* 28, 223–53.
Natarajan, Anusha, Mohamad Moslimani, and Mark Hugo Lopez. Key facts about recent trends in global migration, Pew Research Center, December 16, 2022.
Papst, Kelsey E. (2009). Protecting the voiceless: ensuring ICE's compliance with standards that protect immigration detainees. *McGeorge Law Review* 40, 261–89.
Passel, Jeffrey (2006). The size and characteristics of the unauthorized migrant population in the U.S.: estimates based on the March 2005 Current Population Survey. Washington, DC: Pew Hispanic Center.
Passel, Jeffrey, and Paul Taylor (2010). Unauthorized immigrants and their U.S.-born children. Washington, DC: Pew Hispanic Center.
Personal Responsibility and Work Opportunity Reconciliation Act (PRWORA), 8 U.S.C. ch. 14.
Plyer v. Doe, 457 U.S. 202 (1982).
Pogge, Thomas (2008). *World Poverty and Human Rights*. Cambridge, UK: Polity Press.
Porter, Eduardo (April 5, 2005). Illegal immigrants are bolstering social security with billions. *New York Times*. http://www.nytimes.com/2005/04/05/business/05immigration.html.
Rabin, Nina (2009). Unseen prisoners: women in immigration detention facilities in Arizona. *Georgetown Immigration Law Journal* 23, Summer, 31–32.
Ray, Mohar (2006). Undocumented Asian American workers and state wage laws in the aftermath of *Hoffman Plastic Compounds*. *Asian American Law Journal* 13, 91–114.
Rayasam, Renuka. "Caged . . .for no fault of your own": detainees dread COVID while awaiting immigration hearings. *Kaiser Health News*, December 22, 2022. https://kffhealthnews.org/news/article/immigration-detainees-covid-risk-hearing-delays/.

Robjant, Katy, Ian Robbins, Victoria Senior (2009). Psychological distress amongst immigration detainees: a cross-sectional questionnaire study. *British Journal of Clinical Psychology* 48, 275–86.

Rodriguez, Joshua. Migrant detention in gateway countries to the Western world, 2022. https://www.niskanencenter.org/migrant-detention-in-gateway-countries-to-the-western-world/#:~:text=In%202019%2C%20the%20country%20detained,legal%20assistance%20and%20due%20process.

Roman v. Wolf 977 F.3d 935 (2020).

Rome, Sunny Harris (2010). Promoting family integrity: the Child Citizen Protection Act and its implications for public child welfare. *Journal of Public Child Welfare* 4 (3), 245–62.

Schriro, Dora (2009). Immigration and customs enforcement: rethinking civil detention and supervision. *Arizona Attorney* 45, 26–27.

Shaikh v. U.S. Immigration and Customs Enforcement (US District Court for the District of Columbia) 1:2022cv00231, filed January 31, 2022, NOTICE of Voluntary Dismissal by All Plaintiffs, February 24, 2022.

Shue, Henry (1996). *Basic Rights*. Princeton, NJ: Princeton University Press.

Tillman, Laura (2009, February 19). America's immigration gulags overflowing with mentally ill prisoners. *Brownsville Herald*. http://www.alternet.org/story/127451/.

Trumka, Richard, president, AFL-CIO. Remarks at the City Club of Cleveland (June 18, 2010). Available at http://www.aflcio.org/mediacenter/prsptm/sp06182010.cfm.

UN High Commission on Refugees: http://www.unhcr.org/4cd91dc29.html.

Walden, Alexandria (2009). Abortion rights for ICE detainees: evaluating constitutional challenges to restrictions on the right to abortion for women in ICE detention. *University of San Francisco Law Review* 43, 979–1012.

Walzer, Michael (1984). *Spheres of Justice*. New York: Basic Books, 1984, 60.

Wellman, Christopher Heath (2008). Immigration and freedom of association. *Ethics* 119, 109–41.

Youngberg v. Romeo, 457 U.S. 307 (1982).

Zadvydas v. Davis 533 U.S. 678 (2001).

Zepeda Rivas v. Jennings 445 F.Supp.3d 36 (2020); Settlement 1/2022 District Court of Northern California.

CHAPTER 25

Global Ethics in a Pandemic: A Rights-Centered Foundation

Edward H. Spence

Introduction

This chapter delves into Alan Gewirth's ethical rationalism and his argument for the existence of positive rights based on the Principle of Generic Consistency (PGC).[1] The PGC posits that if an agent claims a right for themselves, they must also accept that others have the same right. Gewirth extends this principle to argue that since freedom and well-being are necessary for action, every agent has a general need for these components and therefore must accept that they have positive rights to freedom and well-being. Consequently, they also have positive duties to assist others in attaining or maintaining freedom and well-being when they are unable to do so on their own.

In this chapter, I will briefly discuss Gewirth's derivation of positive rights from his argument for the Principle of Generic Consistency. I will also address an objection to Gewirth's thesis and explore the connection he establishes between positive rights and community. While I won't provide a justification for Gewirth's argument for the PGC due to space constraints, I will assume its validity and argue that Gewirth's derivation of both negative and positive rights offers a reasonable foundation for global ethics. There are five key reasons for this:

1. The formal structure of the argument renders rights universal and global in scope.
2. The necessary features of action, namely freedom and well-being, also make the derived rights universal and global.
3. Positive rights are essential for establishing a connection between rights and global community.
4. Gewirth's argument is not only rationally justified but also practically motivating, as it addresses actual socially engaged agents.
5. The argument prevents moral relativism and provides a basis for universal rights without imposing moral uniformity.

Gewirth's derivation of positive rights follows a parallel structure to his argument for negative rights, highlighting the logical consistency between the two. The argument establishes that all agents have positive rights to freedom and well-being, and consequently, positive duties to help others achieve these rights when they cannot do so on their own. He argues that the positivity of human rights is crucial for establishing a connection between rights and community. When rights are seen only as negative, focusing on noninterference, it can lead to a view of society as consisting of isolated individuals with little consideration for cooperation or addressing societal inequalities. Positive rights, on the other hand, require not only refraining from harm but also helping one another, fostering equality and mutual aid. Thus, positive rights create a basis for reconciling rights and community. Gewirth emphasizes the importance of positive rights for building a supportive and caring community, both locally and globally. However, objections to positive rights have been raised, often repeating mistakes made in objections to negative rights. In the following analysis, I will explore the motivational aspects of positive rights and argue that they require more effort and motivation compared to negative rights. This motivational asymmetry helps explain objections to Gewirth's derivation of rights, and highlights the importance of addressing concerns about motivation rather than justification.

He argues that the response to justified claims of positive rights should primarily be political and institutional rather than individual, although individual responsibility is still important. In Western democracies, there are five main institutional modes of response: political; professional; semiprofessional voluntary associations; familial; and other social institutions. Political institutions have the broadest scope and provide assistance with basic welfare services like health care, education, employment, and housing. Gewirth's main objective is to justify the protection, preservation, and promotion of these services by political and government institutions. The state functions as a "community of rights," protecting and providing positive rights through services like the police, ambulance, fire department, and legal aid. Professional services are more effective than untrained individuals in dealing with emergencies. Semiprofessional voluntary associations, like lifeguard associations, also play a role in protecting positive rights in specific situations, such as ensuring safety at the beach. These institutions and associations are indirectly justified by the Principle of Generic Consistency (PGC), and should be supported by the state or local government. This network of communal institutions, referred to as the Communal Ethical Institutional Network (CEIN), can overcome the scope and motivation challenges related to positive rights. Global organizations, such as the Red Cross and Oxfam, operate under the CEIN framework to provide global assistance. The PGC justifies the need for this network to meet the demands of positive rights. Cosmopolitanism suggests that community should extend globally, encompassing all purposive agents who have equal rights to freedom and well-being. Under this view, the rights of cosmopolitan agents become the universal rights of "Citizens of the World," based on their rational purposive agency rather than nationality, religion, race, creed, gender, or socioeconomic status.

The Conciliation of Rights and Community

According to Gewirth,[2]

> The positivity of human rights is of first importance for establishing the connection between rights and community. When rights are viewed solely as negative, in that their correlative duties require only non-interference with persons' having the objects of their rights, the adversarial conception of the relation between rights and community is given ready entry. For persons can fulfill their duties by simply not interfering with or intervening in one another's actions or projects . . . Although such interference is itself valuable as an essential part of freedom and of non-infliction of suffering, when it is the sole conception of rights it may lead to a view of society as consisting of atomized, mutually disregarding, alienated individuals with no positive consideration for cooperation in helping to fulfill one another's needs or interests or for rectifying the extreme inequalities of wealth and power that characterize most societies. . . . As a result, a human society based on positive human rights requires not only that persons refrain from coercing or harming one another, but also that they help one another. . . . Thus, positive rights serve to relate persons to one another through mutual awareness of important needs and, as a consequence, affirmative ties of equality and mutual aid. Hence, if there are indeed positive human rights that must be acknowledged as such by every rational agent, then it provides a rational and mandatory basis for the conciliation of rights and community and thus for the mutuality and solidarity of the community of rights (1996, 31–32).

The above quotation provides Gewirth's rationale and argument for both the need and the justification for the conciliation of positive rights and community. Gewirth, of course, is right to emphasize the crucial importance of positive rights for community. Although necessary, negative rights alone are not sufficient for establishing a mutually supportive and caring community. Positive rights are thus essential for community, not merely locally, but globally as well. For Gewirth, the accommodation of those concerns is one of the main theses of *The Community of Rights* (1996, 33).

Objections to Positive Rights: General Remarks

As with Gewirth's argument for negative rights, his arguments for positive rights have equally attracted several objections from various critics.[3] Most of these objections repeat some of the mistakes with regard to Gewirth's argument for negative rights. Yet other objections—as Deryck Beyleveld correctly points out in his comprehensive treatment of those objections—mistakenly treat the argument to the PGC either as establishing, at best, negative rights only, thus interpreting Gewirth's discussion of the duty to rescue (which is part of his argument from the PGC, already a principle of positive rights) as an attempt to derive positive from negative rights via a question-begging theory of negative causal responsibility, or as establishing nondeontic positive and negative "rights," which requires the discussion of the duty to rescue to provide a derivation of positive deontic rights from positive nondeontic "rights" via a similarly question-begging theory of negative causal responsibility (1991, 358–59). In order not to repeat Gewirth's and Beyleveld's competent and, I believe, correct responses to those objections, I shall not comment further on those objections.

In what follows, I will offer an extensive novel analysis of some of the additional motivational aspects that relate more crucially to positive rights than to negative rights. I will argue that although positive and negative generic rights[4] are characterized by a justificatory symmetry, they are by contrast characterized by a motivational asymmetry. Quite simply, more motivation is required to offer active assistance to those in need in accordance with their positive rights to such assistance, than merely to refrain from interfering with the negative rights to their freedom and well-being. All things being equal, noninterference is motivationally less demanding and less costly, and thus easier to respond to, than positive assistance.

This motivational asymmetry underscores and helps explain several of the objections against Gewirth's derivation of both negative and positive rights from the PGC. Those objections, although primarily intended as objections about justification, are in essence objections about motivation. As such, the objections against negative rights fail because of misdirection.[5] Similarly, concerns raised about positive rights, although warranted as concerns about motivation, are nevertheless unwarranted as concerns about justification. By extension, objections based on those concerns fail, as in the case of negative rights, primarily because of misdirection.

The Overload Objection

One objection raised against Gewirth's argument for positive rights is the "overload" objection. Critics argue that the duties associated with positive rights would overwhelm individuals, as they would be required to attend to the positive rights of others at all times and in all places. This objection emphasizes the communal aspect of positive rights and highlights the need for government institutions to fulfill the correlative duties.

Another objection centers around the motivational asymmetry between negative and positive rights. Noninterference, which is associated with negative rights, is less demanding and costly than providing positive assistance. This motivational asymmetry raises concerns about the feasibility of fulfilling positive rights and the potential burden it places on individuals.

In response to these objections, Gewirth argues that positive rights are necessary for establishing a connection between rights and community, both locally and globally. Without positive rights, it would be difficult to establish a global community based on universal rights to freedom and well-being. Gewirth's argument for the PGC provides the theoretical foundation for a global community based on universal rights, although achieving this in practice may be challenging.

To address the "overload" objection, Gewirth suggests that community institutions, such as government and voluntary associations, play a crucial role in fulfilling positive rights. These institutions can help to alleviate the burden on individuals by providing assistance and support. By distributing the responsibility across the community, the overwhelming moral obligations associated with positive rights can be more effectively managed.

Furthermore, Gewirth argues that a global community is necessary to address positive rights on a global scale. The interconnectedness of our world demands a recognition of universal rights and a collective effort to ensure the well-being and freedom of all individuals. This global community would require cooperation and collaboration.

The primary objective of Gewirth's *The Community of Rights* is to provide a comprehensive and sustained argument-based support, through the argument for the PGC, for the justification of the protection, preservation, and promotion of those basic welfare services by the state's political and other government institutions. And it is as protector and provider of positive rights that the state, according to Gewirth, "functions as a community of rights" (1996, 59)—including the police, ambulance service, fire department, and other emergency services, as well as the legal profession through the legal-aid program—can and does provide support for positive rights to individual citizens.

For example, a domestic dispute in a household or a house that's on fire can be attended to more expertly and effectively by the police or fire department than by concerned but professionally untrained neighbors, who could not as effectively deal with such emergencies even if they were kindly disposed to do so. Calling the police or fire department would be useful individual positive assistance in most cases—provided, of course, that those professional services operated adequately and efficiently. To the extent that professional services such as the police, fire department, and ambulance service, along with other emergency services, are essential in providing positive support for protecting and preserving the positive rights of citizens in specific instances—such as violent crime, fire, or road traffic accidents—the state is ethically required by the PGC to ensure that those services are both efficient and effective in meeting the justified demands of those rights, as we saw recently in the case of the COVID-19 pandemic that affected the whole world.

Equally important to the political and professional institutions that can and do provide protection to and preservation of the positive rights of individual agents, are semiprofessional voluntary associations, such as lifeguard associations, which provide positive assistance in protecting people from harm while swimming in the sea. That assistance is provided both proactively—in getting swimmers to swim safely between the flags, for example—and reactively—by going to the rescue of swimmers who may find themselves in a potentially life-threatening situation. Thus, once again, such semiprofessional voluntary institutions can and do provide valuable assistance in protecting and preserving the positive rights of individual agents in very specific situations, as lifeguards do on the beach each summer in Australia.

To the extent that these semiprofessional voluntary associations are essential in providing protection and preservation for the positive rights of citizens in certain specific contexts, those associations and institutions are indirectly justified and thus required by the PGC; hence, they should be adequately supported by either the state, local, or municipal government. I will henceforth refer to this network as a

Communal Ethical Institutional Network (CEIN). This communal network can—and in most cases, does—provide a division of ethical labor that can, at least in principle, if not always in practice, overcome the overload problem of scope and motivation with regard to positive rights. Needless to say, CEINs are not only an effective way of responding to people's positive rights to assistance locally, but globally as well. International charity organizations such as the Red Cross, Oxfam, and World Vision, as well as other similar organizations operating under the auspices of the United Nations, are prime examples of how global CEINs can offer relief and assistance to those in need when local CEINs are not able to do so. The example of the recent pandemic is a case in point of such assistance offered by global CEINs.

The justification of positive rights by the PGC, together with the overload objection that emphasizes the problem of ethical scope and motivation regarding practical compliance with the demands of those rights, has demonstrated the need for such a communal ethical institutional network. Hence, a CEIN is indirectly justified by the PGC as an essential practical means of meeting the justified demands of positive rights of individual purposive agents. Thus, the conciliation of rights and community—Gewirth's thesis that rights and community have a relationship of mutual support—is established on the basis of the PGC. As long as the PGC is capable from within its own dialectical structure to provide adequate motivation to normal rational agents to act according to its requirements, which it is, then the PGC meets the motivational criterion of practical morality. Moreover, the PGC can also, as demonstrated above, account for the practical means of implementing justified claims of positive rights through its indirect justification of CEIN. Therefore, the PGC both directly and indirectly can account for the justification, motivation, and the practical means of compliance with regard to positive rights.

This points toward the direction of cosmopolitanism. That is, that the community should be conceived more broadly as a cosmopolitan community comprising purposive agents who have equal rights to freedom and well-being, as required by the PGC. Under this extended conception of global rights, the generic rights of purposive agents, both negative and positive, become the rights of cosmopolitan agents—the rights that citizens of the world have by virtue of being human purposive agents regardless of their nationality, religion, race, creed, gender, or socioeconomic status. Since rational purposive agency alone is sufficient for having the generic rights to freedom and well-being, then those rights, as universal, are the rights of citizens of the world—the ethical rights of cosmopolitans.

Conclusion

In this chapter I have presented a model for global justice based on positive rights as derived from Alan Gewirth's argument for the PGC. In establishing such a model for global justice, I have followed Gewirth's thesis that there is a close and crucial conciliation between positive rights to assistance on the one hand and community on the other. I then indicated how the "overload objection" can be met, by arguing that positive rights can be effectively addressed and responded to, through CEINs. Such networks can collectively meet duties to assistance with respect to the correlative positive rights of others, without placing an unreasonable and motivationally impractical burden on individual members of the community to respond to every positive right to assistance placed upon them.

Collective communal responses to positive rights to assistance from others, through CEINs, also recognizes and is sensitive and responsive to the motivational asymmetry that exists between positive and negative rights. Significantly, the model of global justice advocated and argued for in this paper, supports not only communal rights locally within existing national and state boundaries, but also supports cosmopolitan rights globally. This is because the positive rights that Gewirth's argument for the PGC supports are universal rights that apply equally to every purposive agent by virtue only of their purposive agency, and not by virtue of their membership in any given nationality, race, or religion, or cultural, social, or familial group. Insofar as these rights are universal and thus global in their application, the model of justice that in turn these positive rights support is also global. It is the justice belonging by right, to citizens of the world, as demonstrated in practice during the recent global pandemic.

Notes

1. This chapter is a reconstructed essay based on my book, *Ethics within Reason: A Neo-Gewirthian Approach* (Lanham, MD: Lexington Books, 2006), chapters 5–7.
2. It is important to note from the outset that the derivation of positive rights from the argument to the PGC is a separate and parallel argument to that of the derivation of negative rights. Some of Gewirth's critics, failing to appreciate the separate derivation of positive rights from the argument to the PGC, mistakenly ascribe to Gewirth a mere entailed derivation of positive rights from the original derivation of negative rights. This is a mistake that has led to unwarranted and misplaced objections against Gewirth's thesis of positive rights: Cf. Jan Narveson; see Edward Regis Jr., ed., *Gewirth's Ethical Rationalism: Critical Essays with a Reply by Alan Gewirth* (Chicago: University of Chicago Press, 1984).
3. For a comprehensive exposition and critical discussion of these objections with corresponding responses, see Gewirth, *The Community of Rights*, 31–70; and Deryck Beyleveld, *The Dialectical Necessity of Morality: An Analysis and Defense of Alan Gewirth's Argument to the Principle of Generic Consistency* (Chicago: University of Chicago Press, 1991), 333–59.
4. The term "generic rights" is Gewirth's general term for referring to rights, both positive and negative, that are derived directly from the PGC.
5. See Spence, *Ethics within Reason*, especially chapters 1 and 2.

References

Beyleveld, Deryck (1991). *The Dialectical Necessity of Morality: An Analysis and Defense of Alan Gewirth's Argument to the Principle of Generic Consistency.* Chicago: University of Chicago Press.

Gewirth, Alan (1978). *Reason and Morality.* Chicago: University of Chicago Press.

——— (1996). *The Community of Rights.* Chicago: University of Chicago Press.

Narveson, J. (1984). "Negative and Positive Rights in Gewirth's *Reason and Morality*," in Gewirth's *Ethical Rationalism: Critical Essays with a Reply by Alan Gewirth*, ed., Edward Regis Jr. Chicago: University of Chicago Press.

O'Neill, Onora (2000). *Bounds of Justice.* Cambridge, UK: Cambridge University Press.

Regis, Edward, Jr. (ed.) (1984). *Gewirth's Ethical Rationalism: Critical Essays with a Reply by Alan Gewirth.* Chicago: University of Chicago Press.

Spence, E. H. (2007). "Positive Rights and the Cosmopolitan Community: A Rights-centered Foundation," *Journal* of *Global Ethics*, vol. 3, no. 2, 2007.

——— (2006). *Ethics within Reason: A Neo-Gewirthian Approach.* Lanham, MD: Lexington Books.

CHAPTER 26

Is There a Duty to Treat in a Pandemic?[1]

Wanda Teays

Abstract

Do physicians, nurses, and other health workers have a moral obligation to care for infected patients in a pandemic? Or is there something that distinguishes it from other medical contexts? In this chapter we will get an overview of the issues and consider what limits, if any, should be set on the duty to treat. A central concern is whether the greater number of those potentially at risk should be factored into the decision. The contagion factor coupled with mortality statistics suggest that there are boundaries on what we can expect. The risks to care for a patient in a pandemic could end up killing the caregiver—not to mention a host of others who might get infected. Consequently, health-care workers should have the right to decide how much risk they are willing to take, particularly when protective equipment is in short supply. The chapter concludes with six foundational rights of health-care workers.

Introduction

There's not a lot that makes health-care workers want to run to the hills, but a pandemic must be near the top of the list. Smallpox, SARS, Ebola, Marburg hemorrhagic fever, H1N1, MERS, COVID-19, and so on test the courage and commitment to treat the infected victims. Some step forward, seeing their assistance as a duty; others weigh the risks and find their participation untenable. As for the general public—and potential victims of highly contagious diseases—the situation is truly a crisis. We understand the concern but need qualified personnel to tend to our medical treatment. There's fear and trembling on all sides.

As the American Medical Association (2020) recognized, these are trying times. In addressing the issue of professional responsibility, they said in the preamble to the Declaration of Professional Responsibility:

> Never in the history of human civilization has the well-being of each individual been so inextricably linked to that of every other. Plagues and pandemics respect no national borders in a world of global commerce and travel. Wars and acts of terrorism enlist innocents as combatants and mark civilians as targets. Advances in medical science and genetics, while promising great good, may also be harnessed as agents of evil. The unprecedented scope and immediacy of these universal challenges demand concerted action and response by all.

And so, we are called to look closely at the responsibilities owed one another in a pandemic. We need to give careful consideration to what we are asking of health-care workers. Simply put, "Is there a duty to treat in a pandemic?"

Consider the case of ten-year-old Rebecca McLester of Rockford, Illinois. In the summer of 2003, she came down with pus-filled sores after playing with her family's two pet prairie dogs. As it turns out, they got infected from a Gambian pouch rat at the pet store that sold exotic animals. The pouch rat, the prairie dogs, and some unsuspecting owners got monkeypox, a relative of smallpox. Rebecca ended up in the parking lot of Swedish American Hospital waiting to get into an ER isolation room.

As Gretchen Reynolds (2004) reports, over the course of the summer, seventy-two cases of monkeypox would be suspected in the Midwest, and thirty-seven would be confirmed. Up to 10 percent of the infected die from the disease.

Who was going to treat Rebecca? How long was she going to be stuck in the hospital parking lot? What terror was unleashed? And what reluctance was set in motion?

> The word "pox" tends to focus the medical mind. [Dr. Michael] Anderson considered for an instant his own daughters, ages six and two. It was most unlikely that he could carry infection home. But it wasn't impossible. They had no immunity against a pox. Still, Anderson agreed to get involved with the case. But he saw that his decision did not please his colleagues . . . None of them had been vaccinated. "My partners told me I had not needed to take the case and I should not have done it without consulting them," he remembered . . . "They were angry," Anderson said (Reynolds 2004).

Anderson's colleagues rightfully concluded that his exposure to monkeypox could just as easily be *their* exposure—that the disease can quickly spread given the right conditions. And, unfortunately, those treating the infected patients could become patients themselves. For example,

> "If you have an outbreak of, say, Ebola," said Dr. Daniel Bausch . . . "the last two or three people to catch the disease were health care workers, and they decide, quite logically, that it's not worth the risk." During an outbreak in 1995, an international team of doctors arrived in Kikwit in Congo to find that Kikwit General Hospital was deserted and silent, except for a half dozen or so patients, including medical staff, lying unattended in a back room, dying of Ebola (Reynolds 2004).

The sight of both patients and caregivers being struck down by a disease would be enough to send shivers down anyone's spine and call into question any sense of duty. How much risk is too great? What are the limits of a doctor or nurse's fiduciary obligations? In the midst of a pandemic, it's no wonder we seek answers.

Kenneth V. Iserson (2018) cuts to the quick: "The moral backbone of medical professionals—a duty to put the needs of patients first—may be tested as they weigh multiple factors to determine whether to stay and carry out their professional roles or to step back and decrease their personal risks."

The truth is that we can't count on all medical staff to hang in there. "Although 80 percent or more of physicians and nurses might respond to mass casualty incidents, only about half would remain to work during an epidemic or radiological disaster or after a terrorist incident involving a chemical, biological, radiological, or nuclear agent" (Iserson 2018). This was borne out on August 7, 2020, when health caregivers in India went on strike, citing inadequate protections against the coronavirus.

> About 900,000 members of an all-female community health workforce began a two-day strike Friday, protesting that they were being roped in to help with contact tracing, personal hygiene drives and in quarantine centers, but were not being given personal protective equipment or additional pay (Associated Press 2020).

And don't forget—there's not an unlimited amount of time to decide where the boundaries lie. Given that the physician workforce is not an unlimited resource, the dilemma is how to address competing needs. When it comes to disaster responses, physicians should balance benefits to current patients with caring for future patients, Iserson suggests (2018). That means assessing risks and apportioning resources.

Decision-making tends to focus on the present—*this* patient at *this* time in *this* context. However, the application of a caregiver's skills extends beyond these constraints and into the foreseeable future. It is of pressing importance that organizations representing health-care workers clearly indicate what standard of care is expected of their members in the event of a pandemic, observe Carly Ruderman et al. (2006). Their advice has merit.

Because expectations around the standard of care may have dire consequences, assessing limits is imperative. An examination of the role of medical personnel will help set guidelines regarding professional rights and responsibilities, as well as ethical duties and obligations (Shaul et al. 2006). In light of an inconsistent response in a pandemic on the part of governments, politicians, and the general public (as seen with COVID-19), a great deal follows from the role health workers play.

Keep in mind that a health-care system requires the participation of all sorts of medical personnel. This includes anesthesiologists, paramedics, X-ray technicians, and other staff, as well as physicians and nurses. In other words, it's an ever-widening circle as to which parties are affected and which ones may have a duty to treat.

Who should stay and who can walk away? "What is clear is that the issue of duty to care has emerged as a matter of paramount concern among health care professionals, hospital administrators, public policy makers, and bioethicists" (Shaul et al. 2006). It is an important and all-too timely matter. Let's see how.

A pandemic like the bubonic plague, SARS, Ebola, or COVID-19 can strike down people of all ages on a global scale, and do so in a matter of days. Daily reports of new cases and death statistics bear this out. In what follows we will look at the debate and examine the pros and cons of the duty to treat, and if it is a *duty*. In so doing, we should remember that the range of those at risk includes many more people than the ones directly caring for patients. The risk factor in a pandemic continues to expand.

Some infections are spread far beyond the doctor's office or hospital. Families, friends, coworkers, strangers sharing elevators, and fellow passengers on an airplane get little say as to whether health-care workers have a duty to treat. It is often too late for them to avoid exposure. Victims may have no idea who passed the infection on to them; the source of transmission could be a complete mystery.

Whereas SARS was primarily a disease within health-care institutions, "an influenza outbreak [or other pandemic] would hit the community at large. The patient surge would be tremendous" (Malm et al. 2008, 5). The number affected would be on a vastly greater scale, as seen with COVID-19. Worldwide cases run into the millions and deaths number in the hundreds of thousands. And, so, what are the ethical obligations of caregivers? Let us consider the extent to which the medical professions have offered guidance.

Oaths and Codes

The "duty" to treat may seem like an open-and-shut case settled by the Hippocratic Oath ("Do no harm") or other professional oaths and codes. However, the matter is not so easily put to rest.

First, it is not obvious that "Do no harm" entails a duty to treat *regardless of risk*. In fact, the proscription not to harm may apply to a greater population than patients; it may be sufficiently large to include physicians and other caregivers as well.

Secondly, if we examine doctors' and nurses' fiduciary duties to patients, one virtue that stands out is beneficence. Its importance rests on the fact that

> The ethical foundations of the duty to provide care are grounded in several long-standing ethical principles. Foremost among these is the principle of beneficence, which recognizes and defines the special moral obligation on the part of HCPs [health-care professionals] to further the welfare of patients and to advance patients' well-being. In modern health care, it is commonly understood and generally accepted that the principle of beneficence constitutes a foundational principle of the patient–provider relationship (Ruderman et al. 2006).

We might see the moral prescription as follows: Let beneficence be your guide, but at least do no harm. Failing possible benefits, nonmaleficence should prevail. However, this prescription focuses on the *doctor–patient* relationship—which leaves out all others in the path of a pandemic. Surely they warrant consideration. Here's where a need to balance competing interests comes in.

Thirdly, as Judith Jarvis Thomson suggests in another context, if we cannot be Good Samaritans, we could at least strive to be Minimally Decent Samaritans. Doctors may stop short of taking all possible steps to help patients when personal sacrifice seems too great. But that doesn't mean they don't take risks in the care rendered. Basically, a degree of risk goes with the territory.

We find an acknowledgment of this in the AMA's Declaration of Professional Responsibility. The AMA (2020) recognizes that physicians may have to take risks and should not shirk from doing so. Adopted by the AMA in 2001, this declaration "is an oath by which twenty-first-century physicians can publicly uphold and celebrate the ideals that have inspired individuals to enter medicine and earn society's trust in the healing profession." In particular,

> We, the members of the world community of physicians, solemnly commit ourselves to . . . treat the sick and injured with competence and compassion and without prejudice [and] apply our knowledge and skills when needed, *though doing so may put us at risk* (AMA 2020, my emphasis).

How much risk is too much? And how many professional oaths and codes settle the question? Contrary to an assumption that the duty to treat would be commonly prescribed, Heidi Malm et al. point out that

> A review of 61 professional codes revealed that 29 had no mention of a duty to [treat], 23 had broad statements (such as the Declaration of Geneva: A physician shall give emergency care as a humanitarian duty unless he is assured that others are willing and able to give such care), and 8 had what could be construed as specific direction to members (Upshur 2006, noted in Malm et al. 2008, 15).

In other words, less than 15 percent of professional codes offer clear guidelines on the duty to treat. This means that more than 85 percent fall short on guidance. Subsequently, "This casts doubt on the idea that the duty is part of the very nature of the professions" (Malm et al. 2008, 15).

Such doubts imply that "Efforts to ground a professional's duty to treat on a code of ethics are fraught with problems." For instance, "The relevant codes of ethics often do not clearly assert a duty to treat, and even when they do, their scope of application and their correct interpretation is open to significant dispute," notes Malm et al. (2008, 16).

If professional codes do not set clear guidelines, health-care workers face a quandary. Where should they look for guidance or an ethical framework with which to justify their actions? They may then infer a right to decide for themselves as to what is an acceptable risk. May we then conclude that treating patients in a pandemic is an act of *altruism* rather than duty? Let's give it a closer look.

Maybe There Is a Duty to Treat: The Pro Argument

When we consider whether there's a duty to treat in a pandemic, it is important to acknowledge the various concerns factoring into the decision. There's more at work than we might realize. Just note the key parameters that come into play:

- Access to information—e.g., on treatment options
- Contagion factors and statistics
- Mortality statistics
- Risks to infected patients
- Risks to health caregivers
- Second-order risks—Risks to others, families, colleagues, other patients, etc.
- Safety concerns—Access to protective equipment, masks, disinfectant
- Quarantine requirements with positive diagnosis or suspected exposure

We should keep these in mind when weighing the pros and cons of the duty to treat.

That said, let's look at the two sides, starting with the affirmative argument.

A major benefit in assuming a duty to treat is the recognition and appreciation of health-care workers from both patients and the greater community. Taking significant risks to help another person is an act of selflessness and heroism in the dire circumstances of a pandemic. The value in that should not be underestimated.

The American Medical Association (2020) shines its light on this pressing issue in stating that

> As physicians, we are bound in our response by a common heritage of caring for the sick and the suffering. Through the centuries individual physicians have fulfilled this obligation by applying their skills and knowledge competently, selflessly, and at times heroically. Today, our profession must reaffirm its historical commitment to combat natural and man-made assaults on the health and well-being of humankind. Only by acting together across geographic and ideological divides can we overcome such powerful threats. Humanity is our patient.

Moreover, looking back at 1847, the AMA code affirms under the Duties of the Profession to the Public: "When pestilence prevails, it is their duty to face the danger, and to continue their labours for the alleviation of the suffering, even at the jeopardy of their own lives." In this proclamation, the AMA sets a high bar.

This standard of personal risk is backed up by societal expectations. Amy Solnica, Leonid Barski, and Alan Jotkowitz (2020) explain: "Regarding healthcare workers, there is agreement for ethical, professional and societal reasons that they are *required* to put themselves in harm's way to care for their patients" (my emphasis).

By this view, not to accept a duty to treat is to pass the buck. If not you, then *who?* The risk refused by a physician or nurse must be assumed by someone else. Isn't it reasonable to expect health caregivers to tend to the sick, even in a pandemic? The rule of rescue prevents abandoning those in need of help and "prompts a certain minimal decency that is expected from all individuals who are in a position to render aid at a time of crisis." Specifically, "The greater the need, the greater is the responsibility to help" (Anantham, McHugh, O'Neill, and Forrow 2008).

As we have seen with COVID-19, when faced with a contagious disease in pandemic proportions, the need is likely to be tremendous. Resources, personnel, and facilities are stretched to the limits, and the need for health-care workers is crystal clear. In addition, "Unqualified personnel without medical capabilities cannot provide services such as diagnosis and treatment of disease" (Anantham et al. 2008).

The bottom line is that we rely on doctors and nurses in a medical emergency. That reliance may be a catalyst for a self-generated sense of duty on the part of doctors in a pandemic—even if the profession lets them off the hook. Plus, we should not overlook the rewards inherent to the medical profession—that the benefits offset the risks. Just think of the respect and prestige attached to the profession. Think also of the "guild-like powers of self-regulation" over and above the remuneration, observe Anantham et al.

It's like having a goose that lays golden eggs, though not without a cost.

> As members of a profession who have taken advantage of its contract with society to reap social rewards, it is then onerous on physicians to commit to the obligations of the profession when called upon to do so. This is the essence of John Rawls' "no free rider" principle (Anantham et al. 2008).

Ezekiel J. Emanuel would agree. He asserts that the devotion to caring for the sick is what distinguishes health professionals from lawyers, teachers, and businesspeople. It defines the core element of being a medical professional. "The obligation is not chosen," he contends. "It is inseparable from the choice to become a doctor. To reject this ethical ideal is to reject the profession" (2003, 590).

If doctors have a duty to treat, they are not alone; others have such duties as well. That has not been given sufficient attention. Looking at rescue-related professions, there is no escape from risk. Firefighters, paramedics, police, and medical personnel implicitly agree to accept a reasonable level of risk when they enter their profession, Malm et al. argue. They say, "No one has any moral obligation to enter any of those social roles" (2008, 8, citing Fleck 2003). The picture is this: Choosing the health profession => acceptance of reasonable risk => moral obligations => duty to treat.

So goes the argument—the links in the chain—that doctors and nurses know what they are getting into when they enter the profession. The duty to treat is part of the bargain. "That is a risk they incur by virtue of their calling," said Justice Robert Sharpe in 2009 when deciding the SARS nurses' lawsuit in Toronto, Canada.

"Nurses were, by virtue of their profession, in the eye of the SARS storm, but they had no higher claim to have their health protected by Ontario than any other resident of the province," he argued. "When dealing with a crisis like SARS, governments must have to consider the public interest as a whole." Consequently, factoring in the economic repercussions to [such matters as] tourism is "not necessarily out of line during a communicable disease crisis," he asserted (Makin 2009).

Not all would agree with Justice Sharpe on the value of tourism in a health crisis. For example, Emanuel reminds us of the reciprocity of duties. In his view, "Affirming health care workers' ethical duty to care for the sick imposes a correlative duty on health care administrators and senior physicians to maximize the safety of frontline physicians and nurses" (2003, 591). In a pandemic this duty may fall short, as when the demands for masks and safety equipment exceed the supply, which was the case with both SARS and COVID-19.

Finally, one other reason supporting the moral obligation to care lies in a comparison of the various professions. No one else can step up to the plate and be trusted to provide medical care. It follows that the physician's expertise and greater skills increases the duty to treat.

On the Other Hand: the Con Argument

Daniel K. Sokol (2006) observes that "Duty of care, in the medical context, is often invoked as a sort of quasi-biblical commandment, akin to 'Do not lie' or 'Do not murder.'" He continues, "The term 'duty of care' (which I take to be synonymous with duty to care) is, at best, too vague and, at worst, ethically dangerous" (1238).

For these reasons, we need to be more precise about the obligations of health-care workers and figure out how far those obligations extend. A central issue turns on the term "reasonable" when asserting that the duty to treat entails a reasonable, and acceptable, risk. Furthermore,

> Nowhere do the laws oblige a mere bystander to take significant risks to aid another. The duty is limited to minimal risk at best . . . The hallmark of special positive duties is the existence of . . . a role-related relationship such as that between lifeguard and swimmer or between custodial parent and child [and, presumably, between doctor and patient] (Malm et al. 2008, 6).

However,

> The fact that the lifeguard can be obligated to incur greater risks does not mean that she can be obligated to incur any and all degree of risk. Lifeguards are not obligated to enter the surf to try to rescue a swimmer from the mouth of a great white shark, for example. Similarly, paramedics are not obligated to enter a building on the verge of collapse to aid someone inside. They can even be obligated not to do so (Malm et al. 2008, 7).

Caring for patients should not entail death-defying acts on the part of doctors and nurses. So too with other rescue workers, though examples of suicidal risk-taking come to mind. "We felt like members of the Tokkotai [the kamikaze pilots of World War II] in that we were prepared to sacrifice everything," observed one of the rescue workers at Fukushima's nuclear disaster of 2011. "The people lined up outside never said as much, but I could tell by their expressions that they didn't think we would return" (McCurry 2013).

Consider also the case of the terrorist attacks on the World Trade Center on 9/11. It stands as the deadliest incident ever for firefighters and law enforcement officers in the United States, when 343 firefighters, 23 police officers, and 37 Port Authority officers lost their lives. The 9/11 FDNY deaths amounted to more than one-third of the emergency personnel at the scene (Kiger 2019). These rescue workers risked—and lost—their lives. But we should not consider that part of the job.

The difficulty is that, in practice, the boundary separating good medicine from suicide is unmarked. Every doctor and nurse may locate it differently, noted Dr. Mark Cheung, who ended up seriously infected with SARS. "I would never blame anybody who decided they couldn't treat infectious patients," he said (Reynolds 2004).

Should we blame doctors who balk at such risks? In the wake of the 9/11 terrorist attacks, the AMA adopted several new ethics policies focused on the medical profession's obligations and responsibilities in a public health emergency. The AMA policy document Physician Obligation in Disaster Preparedness and Response states

> National, regional, and local responses to epidemics, terrorist attacks, and other disasters require extensive involvement of physicians. Because of their commitment to care for the sick and injured, individual physicians have an obligation to provide urgent medical care during disasters. This ethical obligation holds even in the face of greater than usual risks to their own safety, health or life.
>
> The physician workforce, however, is not an unlimited resource; therefore, when participating in disaster responses, physicians should balance immediate benefits to individual patients with ability to care for patients in the future (AMA 2016).

Bioethicist Peter Singer asks, "Do we in medicine have a higher obligation to treat the sick than do passersby on the street?" His answer is "Yes. We accept an added level of personal risk, just as policemen and firemen do. But," he says, "that added risk has limits. We have an expectation that firemen will enter a burning building. We don't have an expectation that they'll jump into a burning pit and self-immolate" (Reynolds 2004).

There are limits to the degree of acceptable risk. As Anantham et al. point out,

> Physicians are not an inexhaustible resource, however, and should weigh the future benefits that a healthy doctor can provide against the good that can be done immediately. Consequently, . . . expected standards of care may be lowered. Resuscitation codes may be even abandoned because the low probability of success may not justify the risk exposure to healthcare professionals (2008).

This is where the issue of widening the boundaries of "risk" comes in. Sokol puts it this way:

> In times of crisis, the duties deriving from doctors' multiple roles may come into conflict. Doctors, for instance, may have a duty to care for their SARS- or avian influenza–infected patients as well as a duty to care for their own

> children by protecting them (and hence themselves) from infection. So, a further problem with the duty to care, aside from its vagueness, is that it fails to consider the holder of the duty as a multiple agent belonging to a broader community (2006, 1239).

The reality is that a pandemic is on a much greater scale—and with a much wider range of risks and those put at risk—than in the case of *this* doctor caring for *that* patient. The parameters are vastly different. Therefore, the typical "duty to treat" arguments are stretched to the breaking point.

When caregivers and their circle of contacts may succumb to the very disease being treated, we might admire their dedication, but we ought not view that dedication as a duty. Their patients are not their only concern. They also have a moral obligation not to spread the infection to others with whom they come into contact and not to shut the door on future patients they may be called to serve.

Let us honor the fact that health workers tend to approach their profession as a calling. It's a special vocation, in *caring* for others whose needs require a host of specialized skills—and the compassion to apply them, even at personal risk. We ask a lot of doctors and nurses, whose dedication deserves our gratitude. Their service to the community calls for protections and limits on what we should expect of them.

Conclusion

Whether there is a duty to treat in a pandemic raises a number of questions, as we have seen in this chapter. Not all are easy to answer. Expectations are put to the test when the numbers are great and the risks considerable.

A central dilemma is what to expect in the event of conflicting duties involving multiple parties. It's not just a matter of what health-care workers owe their patients; it's also a matter of what they owe a host of others who are also at risk in a pandemic. This includes families, coworkers, members of a church choir, attendees at a wedding, shoppers at the grocery store, and so on. Far more people factor into the equation than just the patient and the caregiver.

Sokol (2006) observes, "Defining the limits of the duty of care is a daunting task, strewn with philosophical and logistical difficulties." This duty "is not absolute but, rather, constrained by several factors. First, the limits of the duty should be a function of the normal risk level" (1238). We should not lose sight of that.

Clearly the risk levels vary depending upon the context of contagion potential and the extent of the numbers possibly affected, as well as the mortality statistics. Reluctance to treat will take its toll.

> Pandemic influenza imposes foreseeable high risks to physicians with the potential consequence of mortality. Survey data suggest that 24 percent of physicians find it acceptable to abandon their workplace during such a pandemic in order to protect themselves and their families (Anantham et al. 2008).

Doctors and nurses are a treasured resource in a society facing a health crisis. They deserve to be protected from lethal risks. Health caregivers have foundational rights in a pandemic. Six stand out:

FOUNDATIONAL RIGHTS OF HEALTH-CARE WORKERS

1. *The Right to Institutional Support*
   Although society may have the right to demand service in a pandemic, physicians have the reciprocal right to demand sufficient institutional support (such as protective equipment, staff assistance, and, if available, vaccination) (Ehrenstein 2008, 165).
2. *The Right to Safeguards*
   Many who treated SARS patients raised concerns about the protections to safeguard their own health and that of their family members. Conflicting obligations were another significant concern. [Health-care professionals] are bound by an ethic of care; therefore, obligations to the patient's well-being should be primary (Ruderman et al. 2006).
3. *The Right to Competing Duties*
   Health-care workers have competing obligations to their families and friends, whom they fear infecting, in addition to obligations to their own health. During SARS, some questioned their choice of career, indicating an unwillingness or inability to care for patients in the face of risk (Shaul et al. 2006).
4. *The Right to Minimize—and Justify—Risk*
   It is unrealistic to expect that this obligation to treat should be burdened with unlimited risks. Some limits in the level of risk will be needed for these obligations to be practically binding, and society will need to question the extent to which doctors have to endanger their lives for the public good (Anantham et al. 2008).
5. *The Right to Clear Communication*
   To improve individual response rates, disaster planners and managers must communicate the risks clearly to all members of the health-care system and provide them with as much support and security as possible. "Clinicians need not assume suicidal risks to care for patients" (Iserson 2018).
6. *The Right to Set Limits on the Duty to Treat*
   As dramatic as it may sound, delineating the limits of the duty of care may prevent large numbers of doctors from abandoning their patients in a crisis. Such abandonment has happened in the past and may occur again (Sokol 2006, 1240).

We cannot assume that health workers will (or should) accept a greater occupational risk during a pandemic. We need to acknowledge the competing needs and interests. We need to acknowledge that our expectations of medical professionals should not be boundless. And we need to honor the fact that they are not just creatures of the present. Future patients factor into the equation as well. Otherwise, we may incur a shortage of health workers farther down the road.

We need to trust physicians, nurses, and other caregivers to weigh the risks they are asked to take and decide where to draw the line in the sand. Too many lives figure into the decision for there to be a rigid duty constraining their actions.

Note

1. © Springer Nature Switzerland AG 2022. In: Michael Boylan (ed.), *Ethical Public Health Policy within Disease Pandemics.* The International Library of Bioethics, Vol. 95. Used with permission.

References

American Medical Association. 1847, May. "1847 Code of Ethics of the American Medical Association," 105, accessed August 10, 2020, at https://www.ama-assn.org/sites/ama-assn.org/files/corp/media-browser/public/ethics/1847code_0.pdf.

———. 2016, November 14. "Physician Obligation in Disaster Preparedness and Response." American Medical Association, accessed August 10, 2020, at https://www.ama-assn.org/delivering-care/ethics/physicians-responsibilities-disaster-response-preparedness.

———. Council on Ethical and Judicial Affairs. 2020, March 11. "AMA Declaration of Professional Responsibility," American Medical Association, accessed August 10, 2020, at https://www.ama-assn.org/delivering-care/public-health.

Anantham, Devanand, Wendy McHugh, Stephen O'Neill, and Lachlan Forrow. 2008, June 24. "Clinical Review: Influenza Pandemic—Physicians and Their Obligations," *Critical Care*, vol. 12, no. 3: 217. Accessed August 10, 2020, at https://www.ncbi.nlm.nih.gov/pmc/articles/PMC2481470/.

Associated Press. 2020, August 7. "India Hits 2 Million Coronavirus Cases as Health Workers Go on Strike," *Los Angeles Times*, accessed August 7, 2020, at https://www.latimes.com/world-nation/story/2020-08-07/india-hits-2-million-coronavirus-cases.

Ehrenstein, Boris P. 2008. "Pandemic Influenza: Are We Prepared To Face Our Obligations?" *Critical Care*, vol. 12, no. 4: 165, accessed August 10, 2020, at https://www.ncbi.nlm.nih.gov/pmc/articles/PMC2575555/.

Emanuel, Ezekiel J. 2003, October 7. "The Lessons of SARS," *Annals of Internal Medicine*, vol. 139, no. 7: 589–91, accessed August 10, 2020, at https://pubmed.ncbi.nlm.nih.gov/14530230/.

Iserson, Kenneth V. 2018, August. "Must I Respond if My Health is at Risk?" *Journal of Emergency Medicine*, vol. 55, no. 2: 288–93, accessed August 10, 2020, at https://pubmed.ncbi.nlm.nih.gov/29773480/.

Kiger, Patrick J. 2019, May 20. "How 9/11 Became the Deadliest Day in History for U.S. Firefighters," *History*, accessed August 10, 2020, at https://www.history.com/news/9-11-world-trade-center-firefighters.

Makin, Kirk, 2009, May 8. "Top Court Dismisses SARS Suits against Ontario," *Globe and Mail*, accessed August 10, 2020, at https://www.theglobeandmail.com/news/national/top-court-dismisses-sars-suits-against-ontario/article1202719/.

Malm, Heidi, Thomas May, Leslie P. Francis, Saad B. Omer, Daniel A. Salmon, and Robert Hood. 2008. "Ethics, Pandemics, and the Duty to Treat," *American Journal of Bioethics*, vol.

8, no. 8: 4–19, accessed August 10, 2020, at https://www.tandfonline.com/doi/full/10.1080/15265160802317974.

McCurry, Justin. 2013, January 11. "Fukushima 50: 'We Felt like Kamikaze Pilots Ready to Sacrifice Everything,' " *The Guardian* (UK), accessed August 10, 2020, at https://www.theguardian.com/environment/2013/jan/11/fukushima-50-kamikaze-pilots-sacrifice.

Reynolds, Gretchen. 2004, April 18. "Why Were Doctors Afraid to Treat Rebecca McLester?" *New York Times Magazine*, accessed August 10, 2020, at https://www.nytimes.com/2004/04/18/magazine/why-were-doctors-afraid-to-treat-rebecca-mclester.html.

Ruderman Carly, C. Shawn Tracy, Cécile M. Bensimon, Mark Bernstein, Laura Hawryluck, Randi Zlotnik Shaul, and Ross E. G. Upshur. 2006, April 20. "On Pandemics and the Duty to Care: Whose Duty? Who Cares?" *BMC Medical Ethics*, vol. 7, no. 5, accessed August 10, 2020, at https://www.ncbi.nlm.nih.gov/pmc/articles/PMC1459179/.

Sokol, Daniel K. 2006, August 12. "Virulent Epidemics and Scope of Healthcare Workers' Duty of Care," *Emerging Infectious Diseases*, vol. 12, no. 8: 1238–41, accessed August 10, 2020, at https://wwwnc.cdc.gov/eid/article/12/8/06-0360.

Solnica, Amy, Leonid Barski, and Alan Jotkowitz. 2020, May. "The Healthcare Worker at Risk during the COVID-19 Pandemic: A Jewish Ethical Perspective," *Journal of Medical Ethics*, vol. 46, no. 7, accessed August 10, 2020, at https://jme.bmj.com/content/46/7/441.

Upshur, Ross. 2006. The Role and Obligations of Healthcare Workers during a Pandemic Influenza Outbreak. WHO Working Draft," accessed August 10, 2020, at https://www.who.int/ethics/PI_Ethics_draft_paper_WG3_14Sept06.pdf.

Voo, T. C., and Benjamin James Capps. 2010, April. "Influenza Pandemic and the Duties of Healthcare Professionals, *Singapore Medical Journal*, vol. 51, no. 4: 27–81, accessed August 10, 2020, at https://pubmed.ncbi.nlm.nih.gov/20505904/.

CHAPTER 27

Vaccine Nationalism and Equity: Bioethical Principles

Bradley P. Stoner

Abstract

Global health equity is a fundamental goal of health development agendas and is predicated upon principles of fairness and social justice. In this chapter I explore the ethical implications and disastrous impact of vaccine nationalism, with particular emphasis upon distribution of, access to, and demand for novel mRNA vaccines to prevent SARS-CoV-2 infection. I argue that vaccine nationalism serves market interests of Global North manufacturers and nation-states, but at the expense of global health equity for low- and middle-income countries. The vaccine development process remains primarily a private sector enterprise and is regulated by market forces that prioritize investor risk and reward. The consequent lag time between initial vaccine deployment in developed economies and their widespread distribution in low- and middle-income countries can be many months or years, challenging bioethical principles of beneficence and justice for the Global South. After presenting the circumstances under which vaccine nationalism emerges, I highlight the ways in which governmental failure to guarantee access to vaccines violates principles of bioethics. I elaborate on the conflict between vaccine nationalism and well-established normative commitments, stressing how this trend undermines the fundamental right to health, guaranteed in international law. I discuss possible proposals to address this disturbing phenomenon in a quest for a solution, including COVAX, a possible Global Vaccine Court, and the creation of a consortium of foundations and other nongovernmental organizations. A more humanitarian approach is necessary when the world faces the next pandemic.

Introduction

Ever since the adoption of the World Health Organization Constitution (WHO 1946), global health equity has been a fundamental goal of health development agendas. The WHO Constitution affirms that "the enjoyment of the highest attainable standard of health is one of the fundamental rights of every human being," and that "the health of all peoples is fundamental to the attainment of peace and security." Quite presciently, WHO founders, in the immediate aftermath of World War II, further argued that "unequal development in different countries in the promotion of health and control of disease, *especially communicable disease* (emphasis added), is a common danger." More than sixty years later, the global COVID-19 pandemic threw into high relief the contested nature of these principles by challenging the abilities of all nations to gain access to life-saving personal protective equipment, medical supplies, therapeutic medications, and especially preventive vaccines as they emerged into the global marketplace. This lack of access to vaccines has had dire consequences for communities in the Global South, and particularly children (UNICEF 2023).

In this chapter, I explore the ethics of vaccine nationalism, and the ways in which policies for COVID-19 vaccine development and distribution led to early, aggressive vaccination coverage of populations in wealthy European and North American locales, despite ongoing profound need in low- and middle-income countries (LMICs). I argue that vaccine nationalism subverts principles of bioethics by emphasizing market justice and the interests of vaccine manufacturers and wealthy nation-states, at the expense of social justice and the needs of the poor and disempowered of the Global South.

Vaccines and Vaccine Nationalism

Vaccines are powerful protective agents that can have profound impacts on infectious disease epidemiology at the population level, and on infectious disease outcomes at the individual level. In general, vaccines work by stimulating the immune system to recognize and attack pathogenic infectious agents, typically viruses and bacteria, to prevent their ability to infect the host, or to minimize the severity of disease if infected.

The very first vaccine is credited to Edward Jenner (1798), who observed in the late eighteenth century that milkmaids acquiring the mild skin disease cowpox (vaccinia) rarely contracted the more serious and often fatal smallpox (variola). Jenner inoculated several persons, including his own son, with material taken from blisters of individuals suffering from cowpox, and subsequently demonstrated they were immune to smallpox upon challenge. His discovery arguably set the stage for the modern vaccine era, although it would take another hundred years before widespread acceptance of the germ theory of disease facilitated the development of vaccines for other diseases (Saleh et al. 2021). Globally, vaccines for smallpox, polio, measles, diphtheria, and other scourges have saved untold millions of lives, and the US Centers for Disease Control and Prevention identified vaccination as one of the ten great public health achievements of the twentieth century (CDC 1999a; CDC 1999b).

Late-twentieth-century business models have allowed vaccine development to become primarily a private sector enterprise, building upon basic science proof-of-concept discoveries in the laboratory and scaling them up into clinically testable and ultimately marketable products (Muraskin 1998). The landscape of vaccine development is regulated by market forces that prioritize investor risk and reward in the context of government regulation, review, and oversight. Efficacy and safety are paramount concerns, and rigorous preclinical and clinical testing are required before regulatory bodies will grant provisional approval. As such, successfully bringing a vaccine from initial discovery, through all the necessary investigations, and then into the marketplace for general use, is a costly enterprise borne primarily by investors in these private sector, for-profit multinational corporations. Some estimates place the total cost of vaccine development in the range of US $200–500 million (Plotkin et al. 2017).

One consequence of this arrangement is that once they are developed, the deployment of new vaccines necessarily requires prioritizing markets that can support cost recovery and profit-taking through vaccine sales. The lag time between initial vaccine rollout in developed economies and their widespread distribution in low- and middle-income countries has been cited to be as long as fifteen to twenty years (Binagwaho et al. 2012). This delay serves market interests by maximizing return on investment in wealthy countries before offering the vaccine at lower cost to developing nations. It also prevents residents of poorer nations from reaping the health benefits of vaccine protection as soon as they might. Public-private safety-net initiatives to provide expanded vaccine access, including the Global Alliance for Vaccines and Immunization (now known as GAVI, the Vaccine Alliance) and the Global Vaccine Action Plan (GVAP), have increased access to vaccines for children (Jaupart, Dipple, and Dercon 2019), but have also been criticized for providing targeted, technical solutions that paradoxically serve to weaken the overall health system (Storeng 2014).

Policies that advance vaccine nationalism are logical outcomes of market forces seeking to maximize the return on investment of risky, highly capitalized vaccine candidates in unstable global economies. Riaz et al. (2021) define "vaccine nationalism" as "an economic strategy to hoard vaccinations from manufacturers and increase supply in their own country" in order to "stock up and vaccinate the nation as soon as possible regardless of the limited vaccine manufacturers' distribution for the rest of the world." Typically, advanced in wealthy countries in Europe and North America, such policies are often widely supported as fair and appropriate strategies that provide early vaccine access to domestic constituents.

For example, during the 2009 H1N1 influenza outbreak, developed countries placed advance orders for as much vaccine as manufacturers could provide, virtually locking up global supply, while wealthy nations such as Australia and the United States articulated country-specific vaccination policies to ensure full domestic coverage before any vaccine could be shipped to other countries (Fidler 2010). Such policies, while playing well politically at home, also enable the manufacturers to recoup their research and development costs and earn a profit for the risks they have taken. The operating ethical principle here is market justice, which holds that the vaccine manufacturers are owed a fair return on their investment, having placed their shareholders' capital at risk during the uncertain vaccine development and regulatory approval process (Ruger 2010). An examination of the circumstances surrounding global access to newly developed COVID-19 vaccines in late 2020 and early 2021 further illustrate this trend.

COVID-19 Vaccines, Market Justice, and Social Justice

By March 11, 2020, when the World Health Organization declared the novel coronavirus (COVID-19) outbreak a global pandemic, the race to develop an effective vaccine was already well under way. The genome of the SARS-CoV-2 virus had already been published in January of 2020, and scientists, government officials, policy experts, and manufacturers across the world were collaborating to identify various vaccine candidates using established and newly developed platforms. The goal was to develop a vaccine that was safe, effective, and scalable for rapid production and widespread distribution.

Prior vaccine development has been slow and methodical, using tried-and-true methods of developing vaccine candidates from protein subunits, virus-like particles, or versions of the virus that have been inactivated or attenuated. However, for COVID-19, advances in molecular biology offered the opportunity for scientists to engineer a vaccine using the genetic code of the virus itself. Homing in on the spike protein, seemingly the most immunogenic component of the SARS-CoV-2 virus, scientists developed a way to deliver an mRNA vector that would be taken up by host cells to produce copies of the spike protein. These protein particles would then generate a brisk immune response, characterized by the production of viral antibody by host B-lymphocytes (Park et al. 2021).

The result, proven in several series of rapidly conducted preclinical and clinical trials, was a high level of protection against infection in most persons who received the vaccine, as well as milder cases of clinical disease in those who ultimately became infected. It is also important to note that vaccine development was occurring at a rapid pace around the globe; by one estimate, as of late 2020 there were more than two hundred vaccines under development worldwide (Zhao et al. 2020).

By December 2020, at a pace not previously seen in history, two new mRNA vaccines (Pfizer/BioNTech and Moderna) cleared all US regulatory hurdles and were granted emergency use authorization (EUA) by the Food and Drug Administration (FDA). A third vaccine (Janssen) received EUA for use in the United States just two months later. The approval process proceeded similarly quickly across the globe, including the WHO Emergency Use Listing process, and other different countries endorsing vaccines not yet approved in the United States (for example, AstraZeneca, Sinopharm, Sputnik V).

Unfortunately, by the time the first COVID-19 vaccines came to market, wealthy nations in the Global North had locked up most of the soon-to-be-available vaccines through preorders with the manufacturers. Mullard (2020) reported that the twenty-seven member states of the European Union, together with five other rich countries (United States, Canada, United Kingdom, Australia, Japan), accounting for just 13 percent of the world's population, had preordered more than half of the 5.3 billion vaccine doses to be produced in 2021 by makers of the three vaccines closest to widespread distribution: AstraZeneca, Pfizer, and Moderna. In terms of per capita coverage, Canada reportedly had preordered nearly nine doses per person, much more than needed to cover its entire population. Little was left available under this scheme for LMICs, which were relying on COVAX to secure adequate vaccine supply for their populations. COVAX was established as a joint fund for equitable distribution of COVID-19 vaccines led by GAVI, WHO, and the Coalition for Epidemic Preparedness Innovations (CEPI) (WHO n.d.). As of November 2020, COVAX had only gained a commitment for 700 million doses (Koop 2020). Estimates of widespread coverage for LMICs would not occur until 2023, "if ever," according to one news source ("Vaccine Nationalism" 2021).

One year later, as of October 2021, vaccine sales to COVAX were only 994 million doses, or 12 percent of the total global sales, and wealthy countries had delivered only 260 million vaccine doses, or 14 percent of the amount pledged (Malpani and Maitland 2021). More recent efforts to accelerate COVID-19 vaccine deployment in developing countries have focused on such factors as increasing strong leadership engagement, increasing funding, and reducing vaccine hesitancy (WHO 2022).

Other Barriers to Vaccine Equity

Of course, the complicated issue of achieving global vaccine equity is not just a supply-side issue of hoarding by wealthy nations, but is also dependent on such factors as addressing and overcoming barriers to vaccine acceptance and distribution in developing countries. One important concern is vaccine hesitancy, or the extent to which local communities express resistance to accept vaccination if and when it is offered. An early study by Solís Arce et al. (2021) identified relatively high rates of willingness to be vaccinated against COVID-19 (80.3 percent) across ten LMICs, suggesting that vaccine demand would remain high globally. However, a subsequent systematic review and meta-analysis by Patwary et al. (2022), involving more than 83,000 respondents from thirty-three countries, found a lower pooled-effect size of vaccine acceptance (58.5 percent) and a relatively high pooled vaccine hesitancy rate (38.2 percent). Major contributors to vaccine hesitancy in these studies were concerns about vaccine safety and effectiveness, including the potential for unknown side effects due to the accelerated development process.

Other significant issues include a lack of LMIC vaccine manufacturing capabilities, owing in part to international rules on intellectual property and patent protections (da Fonseca, Shadlen, and Achcar 2023); lack of essential refrigeration capabilities to maintain vaccine potency, particularly in rural areas (Tagoe et al. 2021); and a general erosion of trust as empowered nations use "vaccine diplomacy" to improve relations with, or to ensure concessions from, developing countries through vaccine delivery commitments (Hotez and Narayan 2021).

A sad paradox of early COVID-19 vaccine hoarding has been the development of a global vaccine surplus by 2023. Wealthy nations now struggle to deal with expiring stockpiles, even though nearly 77 percent of residents of the Global South have yet to receive their first vaccine dose (Quan, Anh, and Taylor-Robinson 2023). This mismatch of supply and demand, and the generation and maintenance of global vaccination disparities along gradients of wealth and privilege, represent significant challenges to fundamental bioethical principles of nonmaleficence and social justice.

Risk and Reward in Vaccine Development

Economic risk and reward drive global vaccine development. Wealthy countries, which shoulder the costly burden of vaccine discovery, quickly seize the opportunity to ensure early and widespread access to vaccines for their citizens, advancing the principle of market justice for the entrepreneurs who risked their own capital to achieve an uncertain goal. This is a dominant neoliberal justification for making sure wealthy Western nations achieve early and complete vaccine coverage before shipping any excess doses to poorer countries in need. Market justice calls for attention to the principles of entrepreneurial fairness, and the maintenance of a level playing field for investors to risk capital, and reap rewards in the marketplace.

However, from a bioethical perspective, market justice stands squarely at odds with social justice and the global goal of health equity for all. When lives are at stake, as we have seen throughout the COVID-19 pandemic, the rewards of investment cannot be limited simply to residents of wealthy countries that donated funds for vaccine discovery and development. Governmental failures to guarantee widespread vaccine access to nations across the globe, regardless of wealth, violate the core bioethical principle of nonmaleficence by causing harm to the disempowered.

The practice of wealthy countries stockpiling vaccine doses to ensure national coverage many times over, while poor countries wait in line until their turn arrives, directly leads to increased suffering and loss of life among the unvaccinated. Such gradients of access are also unacceptable violations of the bioethical principle of justice, since social justice is the salient measure rather than market justice when human life is at stake. The appropriate yardstick of success in combating the global COVID-19 pandemic is lives saved and suffering prevented, rather than capital preserved or profits generated.

The focus on market justice furthermore undermines the fundamental right to health, guaranteed in international law and outlined in the WHO Constitution (WHO 1946), as well as the International Covenant on Economic, Social, and Cultural Rights (United Nations 1966). In 2020, the United Nations Office of the High Commissioner for Human Rights affirmed health as a fundamental human right, declaring that vaccines against COVID-19 should be treated as global public goods that should be affordable and accessible to all without discrimination (United Nations 2020a), a call that was echoed by the Committee on Economic, Social, and Cultural Rights of the United Nations Economic and Social Council (United Nations 2020b). And most recently, the World Health Organization announced an initiative to engage member states in a global process to draft and negotiate a convention to strengthen pandemic prevention, preparedness, and response (WHO 2023), one that will undoubtedly affirm equitable vaccine access as a fundamental principle. Human rights scholars and advocates argue that pharmaceutical manufacturers must recognize their responsibilities to make essential medications, including vaccines, available to patients in the Global South based on the principle of a social contract that underpins corporate responsibility (Santoro and Shanklin 2020). In this sense, the right to health should be construed to encompass a right to vaccines that proven safe and effective, without regard to the ability to pay.

The Future of Vaccine Equity

I have argued that vaccine nationalism is an unacceptable strategy that ultimately violates bioethical principles in the pursuit of market justice. Instead, an approach that recognizes humanity's duty to rescue as global Good Samaritans during a pandemic provides a meaningful path forward (Brysk 2005; Renteln 2012). International relations scholars have advanced the idea that wealthier countries have a moral obligation to address poverty and other global inequities through the provision of resources and humanitarian intervention (e.g. Barry 1980)—that is, there is a global responsibility to protect. A global duty to render assistance to those in distress, a duty to rescue, implicitly includes health equity, and the global response must include access to life-saving medications and vaccines during a pandemic.

What alternative strategies for vaccine distribution would serve to counter the prevailing trend toward vaccine nationalism, and instead advance the goal of global health equity? I offer three proposals that are principled, scalable, and likely to achieve measurable results:

1. *Strengthen the global COVAX response.* Vaccine manufacturers should be required to earmark at least 25 percent of production for early LMIC distribution, alongside the allotment of vaccine dedicated for wealthy nations. Locking up current and future vaccine allocation through preordering doses, before production, leads to an unacceptable loss of life in developing countries. Cost of the LMIC vaccine doses can be absorbed by higher prices charged to developed countries. Profits reaped by manufacturers should be capped at reasonable profit margins.
2. *Create and empower a Global Vaccine Court.* Modeled after the International Court of Justice, the Global Vaccine Court would be charged with prosecuting nations for failure to act equitably with regard to vaccine distribution. Hoarding nations would be sanctioned, and vaccine access for those in greatest need would be greatly enhanced.
3. *Incentivize private sector responses by creating consortia of foundations and nongovernmental organizations dedicated to seeking vaccine equity and which promote health system strengthening.* Grassroots mobilization and advocacy in wealthy nations and LMICs alike can bring greater awareness of the need for more equitable global distribution of vaccines. Existing public-private efforts such as GAVI and GVAP can be broadened in scope and focus to allow greater integration with other aspects of national health systems, including child health, maternal health, noncommunicable diseases, and other areas.

Through these efforts, vaccine nationalism can be replaced with global approaches to new and emerging diseases that emphasize health equity and social justice as foundational principles.

References

Barry, Brian. 1980. "Do Countries Have Moral Obligations? The Case of World Poverty." The Tanner Lectures on Human Values. Delivered at Harvard University, October 27.

Binagwaho, Agnes, Claire M. Wagner, Maurice Gatera, Corine Kamera, Cameron T. Nutt, and Fidele Ngabo. 2012. "Achieving High Coverage in Rwanda's National Human Papillomavirus Vaccination Programme." *Bulletin of the World Health Organization* 90, no. 8 (August): 623–28. https://doi:10.2471/BLT.11.097253.

Brysk, Alison. 2005. "Global Good Samaritans? Human Rights Foreign Policy in Costa Rica." *Global Governance* 11, no. 4 (October–December): 445–66.

Centers for Disease Control and Prevention (CDC). 1999a. "Ten Great Public Health Achievements—United States, 1900–1999." *Morbidity and Mortality Weekly Report MMWR* 48, no. 12 (April 2, 1999): 241–43.

———. 1999b. "Impact of Vaccines Universally Recommended for Children—United States, 1990–1998." *Morbidity and Mortality Weekly Report MMWR* 48, no. 12 (April 2, 1999): 243–48.

da Fonseca, Elize Massard, Kenneth C. Shadlen, and Helena de Moraes Achcar. 2023. "Vaccine Technology Transfer in a Global Health Crisis: Actors, Capabilities, and Institutions." *Research Policy* 52, no. 4 (May): 104739. https://doi:10.1016/j.respol.2023.104739.

Fidler, David P. 2010. "Negotiating Equitable Access to Influenza Vaccines: Global Health Diplomacy and the Controversies Surrounding Avian Influenza H5N1 and Pandemic Influenza H1N1." *PLOS Medicine* 7, no. 5: e1000247. https://doi.org/10.1371/journal.pmed.1000247.

Hotez, Peter J., and K. M. Venkat Narayan. 2021. "Restoring Vaccine Diplomacy." *JAMA* 325, no. 23 (June 15): 2337–38. https://doi: 10.1001/jama.2021.7439.

Jaupart, Pascal, Lizzie Dipple, and Stefan Dercon. 2019. "Has GAVI Lived Up to Its Promise? Quasi-Experimental Evidence on Country Immunisation Rates and Child Mortality." *BMJ Global Health* 4: e001789. https://doi:10.1136/bmjgh-2019-001789.

Jenner, Edward. 1798. *An Inquiry Into the Causes and Effects of the Variolae Vaccinae, a Disease Discovered in Some of the Western Counties of England, particularly Gloucestershire, and Known by the Name of the Cow Pox.* London, UK: Samson Low. https://www.gutenberg.org/cache/epub/29414/pg29414-images.html.

Koop, Avery. "Tracking COVID-19 Vaccines Around the World." *Visual Capitalist,* December 11, 2020. https://www.visualcapitalist.com/tracking-covid-19-vaccines-around-the-world/.

Malpani, Rohit, and Alex Maitland. "Dose of Reality: How Rich Countries and Pharmaceutical Corporations Are Breaking Their Vaccine Promises." *The People's Vaccine,* October 21, 2021. https://peoplesvaccine.org/campaigns/g20/.

Mullard, Asher. "How COVID Vaccines Are Being Divvied Up Around the World." *Nature News,* November 30, 2020.

Muraskin, William. 1998. *The Politics of International Health: The Children's Vaccine Initiative and the Struggle to Develop Vaccines for the Third World.* Albany: State University of New York Press.

Park, Jung Woo, Philip N. P. Lagniton, Yu Liu, and Ren-He Xu. 2021. "mRNA Vaccines for COVID-19: What, Why and How." *International Journal of Biological Sciences* 17, no. 6: 1446–60. https://doi:10.7150/ijbs.59233.
Patwary, Muhammad Mainuddin, Md. Ashraful Alam, Mondira Bardhan, Asma Safia Disha, Md. Zahidul Haque, Sharif Mutasim Billah, Md. Pervez Kabir, et al. 2022. "COVID-19 Vaccine Acceptance Among Low- and Lower-Middle Income Countries: A Rapid Systematic Review and Meta-Analysis." *Vaccines* 10, no. 3: 427. https://doi:10.3390/vaccines10030427.
Plotkin, Stanley, James M. Robinson, Gerard Cunningham, Robyn Iqbal, and Shannon Larsen. 2017. "The Complexity and Cost of Vaccine Manufacturing: An Overview." *Vaccine* 35, no. 33 (July 24): 4064–71. https://doi:10.1016/j.vaccine.2017.06.003.
Quan, Nguyen Khoi, Nguyen Le My Anh, and Andrew W. Taylor-Robinson. 2023. "The Global COVID-19 Vaccine Surplus: Tackling Expiring Stockpiles." *Infectious Diseases of Poverty* 12, no. 21. https://doi.org/10.1186/s40249-023-01070-7.
Renteln, Alison Dundes. 2012. "Review: The Duty to Rescue: Approaches to Global Justice." Review of *The Political Responsibilities of Everyday Bystanders* by Stephen L. Esquith, *Globalizing Justice: The Ethics of Poverty and Power* by Richard W. Miller, and *Can Globalization Promote Human Rights?* by Rhoda E. Howard-Hassmann. *Political Theory* 40, no. 5: 663–74.
Riaz, Mehr Muhammad Adeel, Unaiza Ahmad, Anmol Mohan, Ana Carla dos Santos Costa, Hiba Khan, Maryam Salma Babar, Mohammad Mehedi Hasan, Mohammad Yasir Essar, and Ahsan Zil-E-Ali. 2021. "Global Impact of Vaccine Nationalism During COVID-19 Pandemic." *Tropical Medicine and Health* 49, no. 101. https://doi.org/10.1186/s41182-021-00394-0.
Ruger, Jennifer Prah. 2010. *Health and Social Justice*. New York: Oxford University Press.
Saleh, Amr, Shahraz Qamar, Aysun Tekin, Romil Singh, and Rahul Kashyap. 2021. "Vaccine Development throughout History. *Cureus* 13, no. 7 (July 26): e16635. https://doi:10.7759/cureus.16635.
Santoro, Michael, and Robert Shanklin. 2020. "Human Rights Obligations of Drug Companies." *Journal of Human Rights* 19, no. 5: 557–67. https://doi:10.1080/14754835.2020.1820315.
Solís Arce, Julio S., Shana S. Warren, Niccolò F. Meriggi, Alexandra Scacco, Nina McMurry, Maarten Voors, Georgiy Syunyaev, et al. 2021. "COVID-19 Vaccine Acceptance and Hesitancy in Low- and Middle-Income Countries." *Nature Medicine* 27: 1385–94. https://doi.org/10.1038/s41591-021-01454-y.
Storeng, Katerini T. 2014. "The GAVI Alliance and the 'Gates Approach' to Health System Strengthening." *Global Public Health* 9, no. 8 (September 14): 865–79. https://doi:10.1080/17441692.2014.940362.
Tagoe, Eunice Twumwaa, Nurnabi Sheikh, Alec Morton, Justice Nonvignon, Abdur Razzaque Sarker, Lynn Williams, and Itamar Megiddo. 2021. "COVID-19 Vaccination in Lower-Middle Income Countries: National Stakeholder Views on Challenges, Barriers, and Potential Solutions." *Frontiers in Public Health* 9 (August 6): 709127. https://doi.org/10.3389/fpubh.2021.709127.
United Nations. 1966. "International Covenant on Economic, Social and Cultural Rights (ICESCR)." https://www.ohchr.org/EN/ProfessionalInterest/Pages/CESCR.aspx.
———. 2020a. "Statement on Universal and Equitable Access to Vaccines for the Coronavirus Disease (COVID-19)." December 15. Statement by the Committee on Economic, Social and Cultural Rights. https://digitallibrary.un.org/record/3897801?ln=en.
———. 2020b. "Human Rights and Access to COVID-19 Vaccines. Guidance." December 17. Issued by the Office of the High Commissioner for Human Rights. https://www

.ohchr.org/en/documents/tools-and-resources/human-rights-and-access-covid-19-vaccines-guidance.

United Nations Children's Fund (UNICEF). 2023. *The State of the World's Children 2023: For Every Child, Vaccination.* Florence: UNICEF Innocenti—Global Office of Research and Foresight.

"Vaccine Nationalism Means that Poor Countries Will Be Left Behind." *The Economist,* January 28, 2021.

World Health Organization (WHO) n.d. "COVAX—Working for Global Equitable Access to COVID-19 Vaccines." https://www.who.int/initiatives/act-accelerator/covax.

———. 1946. "Constitution." New York: World Health Organization. https://www.who.int/about/governance/constitution.

———. 2022. "Accelerating COVID-19 Vaccine Deployment: Removing Obstacles to Increase Coverage Levels and Protect Those at High Risk." April 20. https://www.who.int/campaigns/vaccine-equity.

———. 2023. "Pandemic Prevention, Preparedness and Response Accord." February 24. https://www.who.int/news-room/questions-and-answers/item/pandemic-prevention--preparedness-and-response-accord.

Zhao, Jing, Shan Zhao, Junxian Ou, Jing Zhang, Wendong Lan, Wenyi Guan, Xiaowei Wu, et al. 2020. COVID-19: Coronavirus Vaccine Development Updates. *Frontiers in Immunology* 11 (December 23): 602256. https://doi:10.3389/fimmu.2020.602256.

Part IV Internet Resources

PUBLIC HEALTH

CDC | About CDC's Public Health Ethics Activities—OSI—OS
https://www.cdc.gov/os/integrity/phethics/index.htm

CDC | Public Health Ethics Resources—OSI—OS
https://www.cdc.gov/os/integrity/phethics/resources.htm

Closing the Public Health Ethics Gap | NEJM
https://www.nejm.org/doi/full/10.1056/NEJMp2207543

Public Health Ethics | Stanford Encyclopedia of Philosophy
https://plato.stanford.edu/entries/publichealth-ethics

Global Health Ethics | WHO
https://www.who.int/health-topics/ethics-and-health

Public Health Ethics: Mapping the Terrain
https://www.cambridge.org/core/journals/journal-of-law-medicine-and-ethics/article/abs/public-health-ethics-mapping-the-terrain/415AE80C221FD84CDF5067898F7F7425

Asia Pacific Journal of Public Health
https://journals.sagepub.com/home/aph

Brookings Institution Public Health Asia
https://www.brookings.edu/research/democracy-and-public-health-in-asia/

Public Health in Africa
https://africacdc.org/news-item/africa-calls-for-new-public-health-order/

Africa Public Health
https://www.csis.org/analysis/public-health-africa

OECD Public Health South America
https://www.oecd.org/health/health-at-a-glance-latin-america-and-the-caribbean-2020-6089164f-en.htm

Part IV Discussion Topics

PUBLIC HEALTH

1. What do you consider the most pressing health-care issues we face? What should be our priorities as a society?
2. What should we do to achieve justice in health care?
   - Set out four steps that could be taken to address some of the major health-care inequities.
3. In light of Zenon Culverhouse's chapter, share three ideas for addressing mental health concerns found in university students—for example, in terms of available health care on campus.
4. Given limited access to health care, should groups form their own health maintenance organizations (HMOs)? And could this be accomplished on an international scale?
5. Rosemarie Tong looks at the fact that care for the elderly often falls on the children, and this can be morally problematic. Equally problematic is the question of who should care for the elderly who have no children to care for them (or whose children refuse to help them).
   - Can you suggest three or four ideas for addressing this situation?
6. Share three ideas for addressing healthcare needs in migrants held in detention.
   - Should they have access to health care in line with that available for US citizen inmates in federal prisons?
7. Experts think it unlikely that the Havana Syndrome was caused by "a foreign enemy using a secret energy weapon," reports the *Washington Post* on March 2, 2023. (https://www.washingtonpost.com/politics/2023/03/02/is-havana-syndrome-settled-now-white-house-wont-say/). However, not all concerns have been put to rest. How might we resolve the following conflicts:
   - An independent panel assembled by the intelligence community said in 2022 that some foreign actor could have developed "pulsed electromagnetic energy that made people sick."
   - And in 2020, the National Academies of Sciences, Engineering and Medicine observed that "directed, pulsed radio frequency energy appears to be the most plausible mechanism in explaining these cases."

- Do you think the Havana Syndrome is psychosomatic—a product of the imagination—or is an enemy using microwaves or other energy weapons?

8. Climate change, as Peter Tagore Tan notes, has resulted in environmental disasters on a global scale. What should governments do to address this? And what sort of resources should be allocated for emergency medicine?
9. With highly contagious diseases like Ebola, SARS, COVID-19, and monkeypox, medical personnel are often as much at risk as the patient. Given that this is the case, what sort of policies should hospitals put in place?
10. Reporting for *The New York Times* on the lab-leak hypothesis regarding the origins of COVID-19, David Wallace-Wells asks, "What would the chances have to be that a lab accident was the origin of the pandemic to justify a broad and public conversation about the safety of that research?" (See "We've Been Talking About the Lab-Leak Hypothesis All Wrong," *The New York Times,* February 28, 2023, https://www.nytimes.com/2023/02/28/opinion/lab-leak-energy-department-covid.html).
    - What do you think? What should we be doing to prevent possible leaks of dangerous viruses?
11. Looking at public health, a number of hospital patients were put at risk from contaminated surgical equipment used on a patient with Creutzfeldt-Jakob disease (aka, "mad cow disease"). Read about the incident in New Hampshire reported on September 21, 2013:

    > Health officials have confirmed that a patient who underwent neurosurgery at a New Hampshire hospital earlier this year had Creutzfeldt-Jakob disease. The death . . . prompted authorities in two states to warn that as many as 13 patients may have been exposed to surgical equipment used during the patient's surgery, thus to the same disease . . . since normal sterilization procedures are not enough to get rid of the disease proteins, known as prions, tied to Creutzfeldt-Jakob disease—thus potentially exposing the other patients to infection (see Greg Botelho, "Case of Creutzfeldt-Jakob Disease Confirmed in New Hampshire," CNN, September 21, 2013).

    - What is an acceptable risk in such cases—though very rare—as here with Creutzfeldt-Jakob disease? Offer some ideas about what should be done to minimize or prevent incidents such as this.
12. How much is your medical privacy worth? Would you accept $50 to allow prying eyes into your medical records? On August 23, 2013, Craig Klugman posted in a blog on Bioethics.net that CVS pharmacies started a program early in 2013 in which "for every ten prescriptions filled, a customer can receive $5 worth of credits to be used at CVS, up to a maximum of $50 per year." That may sound good—but such loyalty means the company acquires information about your health.
    - Is it worth giving up $50 in order to retain your privacy? Should this be a concern?
    - Who is most vulnerable? What ethical questions do you foresee?

Appendix A
ESSAY QUESTIONS

1. Assume that individuals who were subjected to medical experimentation in the United States and in other countries file a lawsuit against the US Public Health Service and the National Institutes of Health alleging that the government-sponsored testing violated their human rights. Select one major case study and write an analytic essay explaining whether the plaintiffs would likely prevail.
2. Assume that you are the surgeon general of the United States. It comes to your attention that an unspecified number of Muslim women are seeking hymen restoration surgery to avoid "honor-related" violence. The National Organization of Women and the American Medical Association advise you to issue a policy statement on behalf of the executive branch strictly prohibiting this surgery. Write a memo in which you discuss whether this operation is compatible with human rights standards and consistent with the principles of global bioethics.
3. In a liberal democracy, individuals are usually permitted the right to make their own life plans. The question of whether women should have the right to decide whether to continue or terminate a pregnancy, however, remains hotly contested. In what ways do basic principles of international human rights law help us to resolve this matter? Consider cases we studied and the film *Vessel* (2014) in your answer.
4. What is the difference between deontological and teleological approaches to moral questions? Describe two controversies associated with the implementation of the Convention against Torture and Other Cruel, Inhuman, or Degrading Treatment or Punishment. How would you suggest modifying the treaty to render it more effective?
5. The World Trade Organization has devoted considerable attention to intellectual property rights and access to medicine. Discuss whether existing international standards have been implemented in a manner that successfully balances concern for both. Analyze the Doha Declaration of the TRIPS Agreement and Public Health. As part of your analysis, consider the merging trilateral cooperation involving the WTO, the World Intellectual Property Organization, and the World Health Organization (https://www.wto.org/english/tratop_e/trips_e/who_wipo_wto_e.htm).

6. Explain the relevance of the TRIPS Agreement and other instruments to efforts improving access to medicine. In your essay, analyze at least two controversies in the context of evaluating the relevant instruments. What policy recommendations can you propose to harmonize these systems and address the problems these various systems seek to regulate?
7. What rights do prisoners enjoy under international law? Can states deny inmates and detainees the right to health including access to medicine, surgery, and clean water? Present a philosophical consideration of the right to health in international law and global bioethics standards. Be sure to consult Nigel Rodley's treatise *Prisoners' Rights Under International Law* (3rd ed., Oxford University Press, 2009).
8. Write an essay on the status of the human rights of transgender persons that would aid advocates of these rights. To what extent do global standards support these newly recognized rights? Analyze key cases that elucidate this question and refer to specific treaty provisions and instruments that afford insight into this matter. How, if at all, might human rights norms and jurisprudence influence domestic political debates about this issue?
9. To what extent does international human rights law afford protection to the rights of the elderly? Discuss current efforts within the United Nations to develop new instruments to protect the aging. One challenge is how best to protect choice for elderly persons with dementia. This concerns the question of legal capacity. After you analyze the scope of the protections afforded by general human rights norms and the Convention on the Rights of Persons with Disabilities regarding this right, and related ones, present a series of possible solutions. What proposals can you offer to improve policies in this area?

Appendix B

CASES FOR ANALYSIS

Cases for Analysis #1

Select *two* of the cases. Set out your answers (1,000–1,100 words each) in three parts: 1) your answer; 2) defense of your answer using any *one* ethicist we've studied; and 3) your reply to a different ethicist who would disagree with you.

1. How can we bring in the different voices and concerns across different groups and socioeconomic levels to help shape policies addressing injustice in health care? And what kinds of changes should occur in universities and hospitals in the training of doctors, nurses, and other caregivers?
2. Movies such as *Outbreak* (1995) and *Contagion* (2011) present ethical dilemmas with epidemics, such as the allocation of resources and medical personnel. Answer the following:
   - How do we decide, and who decides, who should have priority in access to such resources as vaccines, medical care, treatment centers, and so on?
3. What should professional organizations like the AMA and the WMA do when physician members enable or assist in torture or "harsh interrogation"?
4. Should there be a set of restrictions on egg donations or sales? Read the following excerpt from *Science Daily* (2011), and then share your thoughts:

   > Women who have become pregnant after egg donation should be categorized as high-risk patients. Viewing patient files, they found that within the past four years, eight women who had received donated eggs had to be treated for pregnancy-induced hypertension. Three of these pregnancies had to be terminated prematurely because of the threat to the mother's life. The other five cases showed a milder course of pregnancy-induced hypertension ("Egg Donation: The Way to Happy Motherhood, with Risks and Side Effects," January 25, 2011).

5. When the Environmental Protection Agency planned a two-year environmental study using infants and children up to three years old, they offered the families

$970, children's clothes, and a camcorder in exchange for using pesticides in their homes.

- Share your thoughts on this argument for using children in pesticide studies:

> Linda S. Sheldon, acting administrator for the human exposure and atmospheric sciences division of the EPA's office of research and development, said the agency would educate families participating in the study and inform them if their children's urine showed risky levels of pesticides. She said it was crucial for the agency to study small children because so little is known about how their bodies absorb harmful chemicals (see Juliet Eilperin, "Study of Pesticides and Children Stirs Protests," *Washington Post*, October 30, 2004).

Cases for Analysis #2

Select *only one* of the cases to study. Set out your answers (1,700–2,000 words) in three parts. Answer each part, with the parts clearly marked:

- Part One. Major ethical issues and concerns.
- Part Two. Your argument as to what should be done.
- Part Three. Ethical theory or theorist that supports your argument. Set out his/her support.
- Part Four. Ethical theory or theorist that opposes your argument and your reply to that critique.
- Part Five. Your conclusion and reflections, including lessons to be learned from this case.

SELECT ONE OF THE FOLLOWING CASES TO DISCUSS:

CASE #1. NIH lifts ban on research that could make deadly viruses even worse:

> Scientists could soon resume controversial experiments on germs with the potential to cause pandemics, as government officials have decided to finally lift an unusual three-year moratorium on federal funding for the work. The research involves three viruses—influenza, SARS, and MERS—that could kill millions if they mutated in a way that let the germs spread quickly among people (*NPR*, https://www.npr.org/sections/health-shots/2017/12/19/571744856/nih-lifts-ban-on-research-that-could-make-deadly-viruses-stronger).

CASE #2. A man collapsed with "Do Not Resuscitate" tattooed on his chest, and doctors didn't know what to do:

> Doctors in Miami faced an unusual ethical dilemma when an unconscious, deteriorating patient was brought into the emergency room with the words

> "Do Not Resuscitate" [tattooed] across his chest (*Washington Post*, https://www.washingtonpost.com/news/to-your-health/wp/2017/12/01/a-man-collapsed-with-do-not-resuscitate-tattooed-on-his-chest-doctors-didnt-know-what-to-do/).

CASE #3. First digital pill approved, causing worries about biomedical "Big Brother":

> For the first time, the Food and Drug Administration has approved a digital pill—a medication embedded with a sensor that can tell doctors whether, and when, patients take their medicine (*New York Times*, https://www.nytimes.com/2017/11/13/health/digital-pill-fda.html).

CASE #4. A New York hospital's secret policy led to a woman getting a C-section against her will:

> A New York hospital accused of forcing a mother to undergo a caesarean section against her will used an internal policy permitting doctors to overrule a pregnant woman's medical decisions (*The Guardian* (UK), https://www.theguardian.com/us-news/2017/oct/05/new-york-staten-island-university-hospital-c-section-ethics-medicine).

CASE #5. Should a dying five-year-old have the right to choose?

> Julianna Snow is dying of an incurable disease. She's stable at the moment, but any germ that comes her way, even the common cold virus, could kill her. She's told her parents that the next time this happens, she wants to die at home instead of going to the hospital for treatment. Should her parents have let her know how grave her situation is and have asked her end-of-life wishes? Should her parents heed them? What about the doctors? (CNN, https://www.cnn.com/2016/06/14/health/julianna-snow-heaven-over-hospital-death/index.html).

CASE #6. Should we allow pig organs to be transplanted into humans?

> A Maryland man, fifty-seven-year-old David Bennett Sr., died in March [2022], two months after the groundbreaking experimental transplant [of a pig heart into a human being]. University of Maryland doctors said Thursday they found an unwelcome surprise—viral DNA inside the pig heart. . . . [A] major worry about animal-to-human transplants is the risk that it could introduce new kinds of infections to people (CBS News, https://www.cbsnews.com/news/pig-heart-transplant-david-bennett-sr-animal-virus/).

CASE #7. Should nurse Jane Frances Kendall be admonished for failing to perform CPR on a dead man?

> Nurse Kendall described the patient as "waxy, yellow, and almost cold." She asserted that the patient was not breathing and did not have any vital signs

of life. Her decision not to perform CPR was deemed unacceptable. Without a DNR order, when is it okay not to do CPR? (*Nursing Times*, https://www.nursingtimes.net/news/professional-regulation/nurse-cautioned-for-not-doing-cpr-on-dead-patient-07-03-2017/).

Appendix C

BIOETHICS IN FILM

Doctors and Patients

- *The Doctor*
- *Regarding Henry*
- *John Q*
- *Awakenings*
- *Dopesick* (docudrama)

Human Rights

- *Ghosts of Abu Ghraib* (documentary)
- *Taxi to the Dark Side* (documentary)
- *The Mauritanian*
- *Standard Operating Procedures* (documentary)
- *Camp X-Ray*
- *Solitary: Inside Red Onion State Prison*
- *Rendition*
- *The Deadly Deception* (Tuskegee Syphilis Study documentary)
- *Miss Evers Boys* (docudrama)
- *Gattaca*

Pandemics

- *Outbreak*
- *Contagion*
- *The Hot Zone*
- *The Forgotten Plague* (documentary on TB)
- *Plague City* (documentary on SARS)

- *The Coming Pandemic* (documentary)
- *Facing Darkness* (documentary on Ebola)

Life and Death

- *21 Grams*
- *The Descendants*
- *The Sea Inside*
- *Whose Life Is It Anyway?*
- *The Diving Bell and the Butterfly*
- *Amour*
- *Million Dollar Baby*
- *Near Death* (documentary)

Violence and War

- *Eye in the Sky*
- *The Fog of War*
- *The Hurt Locker*
- *Polytechnique* (docudrama)
- *July 22*
- *Paradise Now*
- *Night and Fog* (documentary)

Environmental Disasters

- *Chernobyl*
- *The Wave*
- *The Impossible*
- *Erin Brockovich* (docudrama)
- *Dark Waters* (docudrama)
- *The Devil We Know* (documentary)
- *Deepwater Horizon*

Reproductive Freedom

- *Four Months Three Weeks Two Days*
- *Happening*
- *Never Rarely Sometimes Always*

- *Vera Drake*
- *No Más Bebés*

Organ Sales and Xenotransplants

- *Never Let Me Go*
- *Organ Farm* (documentary)
- *Brain Transplant* (documentary)
- *Dirty Pretty Things*
- *Coma*
- *The Island*

Index

About the Contributors

Robert Baker is the William D. Williams professor of philosophy (emeritus) at Union College and professor of bioethics and founding director (emeritus) of The Clarkson University-Icahn School of Medicine Bioethics Program. He co-edited *The Cambridge World History of Medical Ethics* (with Laurence McCullough). In a later book, *The Structure of Moral Revolutions*, he analyzed the history of changes in moral views on subjects such as abortion. Dr. Baker's most recent book, *Making Modern Medical Ethics: How African Americans, Anti-Nazis, Bureaucrats, and Whistleblowing Moralists Created Bioethics*, focuses on the creation of modern medical ethics and its bioethical turn.

Tom L. Beauchamp is professor emeritus of philosophy and senior research scholar emeritus at the Kennedy Institute of Ethics, Georgetown University. His research interests are in the ethics of human-subjects research, the ethics of animal-subjects research and human uses of animals, the place of universal principles and rights in biomedical ethics, and methods of bioethics.

Michael Boylan is professor of philosophy at Marymount University. He is the author of 43 books and over 150 articles and book chapters on topics ranging from philosophy to literature.

Marlene Brant Castellano is a Mohawk of the Bay of Quinte Band and professor emeritus of Trent University. She held a faculty appointment in Trent's Native Studies Department from 1973 to 1996, providing leadership in the development of the department and in the emerging discipline of Native Studies. She served as co-director of research with Canada's Royal Commission on Aboriginal Peoples (1991–1996), and subsequently (2003–2010) on the expert Panel on Research Ethics charged with revising ethical guidance for research involving humans (TCPS2) conducted by entities receiving federal government funding.

Cher Weixia Chen is an associate professor in the School of Integrative Studies, the founder of the Human Rights and Global Justice Initiative, a senior scholar of the Center for the Advancement of Well-Being, and a faculty fellow of the Institute for a

Sustainable Earth, George Mason University. Dr. Chen co-created the undergraduate and graduate programs in social justice and human rights. She is the recipient of the 2021 GMU Oscar Mentoring Excellence Award. Her scholarship focuses on the issues of human rights (particularly for marginalized groups, such as women's rights and Indigenous rights) and international and comparative legal studies.

Zenon Culverhouse is an assistant professor of philosophy at University of the Incarnate Word in San Antonio, Texas. He specializes in ancient Greek philosophy and the philosophy of psychiatry. He teaches introduction to philosophy as well as upper-division courses in ancient Greek and medieval philosophy, as well as philosophy of trauma.

Bernard Gert was a moral philosopher known primarily for his work in normative ethics, as well as medical ethics. In his book *Morality: Its Nature and Justification*, Gert presents and defends an original account of the nature of morality. In *Bioethics: A Systematic Approach*, he worked with co-authors Charles M. Culver and K. Danner Clouse to apply his moral system to issues in bioethics. His daughter Heather assisted in the revision of his chapter.

Søren Holm is a bioethicist and philosopher of medicine. He holds a chair in bioethics at the Centre for Social Ethics and Policy, part of the School of Law at the University of Manchester and the University of Oslo. He served as co-editor in chief of the *Journal of Medical Ethics* from 2004 to 2011. Holm holds a master's degree in health-care ethics from the University of Manchester and two doctoral degrees in medical ethics.

Ilhan Ilkilic is a medical doctor and a doctor of philosophy. He is a professor at the Department of History of Medicine and Ethics at the Istanbul University, Istanbul Faculty of Medicine. He is a member of many committees, including the German Ethics Council (2012–2020) and the Central Ethics Committee of the German Medical Association (since 2016). His research interests are intercultural medical ethics, end-of-life decisions, Islamic medical ethics, and genetics and ethics.

Akiko Ito is the chief of the Secretariat for the Convention on the Rights of Persons with Disabilities at United Nations.

Rita Manning is a philosopher emerita from San Jose State University. Her specialties include ethics, social and political philosophy, philosophy of law, feminism, business ethics, and bioethics. She is the author of *A Guide to Practical Ethics: Living and Leading with Integrity* (coauthored with Scott Stroud); *Social Justice in a Diverse Society* (co-edited with Rene Trujillo); and *Speaking from the Heart: A Feminist Perspective on Ethics.*

Kimberly Mutcherson is a professor of law at Rutgers Law School in Camden, New Jersey. She is a reproductive justice scholar who writes and teaches in the areas of family law and bioethics. Her work focuses on assisted reproduction and abortion, among other topics. Professor Mutcherson's edited volume, *Feminist Judgments: Reproductive Justice Rewritten*, was published in 2020 as part of the US Feminist Judgments Project. She has won numerous awards over the course of her career, including the 2020 Association of American Law Schools inaugural Impact Award as one of the creators of the Law Deans Antiracist Clearinghouse Project.

Peter F. Omonzejele is a senior lecturer in bioethics and public policy in the Department of Philosophy, University of Benin, Nigeria. He had his bioethics training at the University of Witwatersrand, Johannesburg, South Africa, and at the University of Central Lancashire, Preston, England. He has published extensively in the area of philosophy and bioethics.

Pinit Ratanakul is director of the College of Religious Studies, Mahidol University, Bangkok, Thailand. He co-edited *Cross-Cultural Dialogues about Healthcare Ethics* (1999). His recent research is on Buddhist perspectives on human cloning and cross-cultural bioethics.

Alison Dundes Renteln is professor of political science, anthropology, law, and public policy at the University of Southern California. Her publications focus on international human rights, particularly cultural rights. She has published two single-authored books, six co-edited volumes, and seventy articles. She collaborated with the UN on implementation of the Convention on the Rights of Persons with Disabilities, lectured on comparative legal ethics at ABA-sponsored conferences in Asia, and served on a California committee of Human Rights Watch. She also served on the Law and Society Association Board of Trustees, the Advisory Committee of the Max Planck Institute for Social Anthropology, and the Interdisciplinary Adjudication Committee of the Canadian Research Chairs. She chaired the APSA Committee on Professional Ethics, Rights, and Freedoms (2019–2021), and is the ethics chair of the American Anthropological Association governance committee.

Maya Sabatello is an associate professor of medical sciences at the Center for Precision Medicine and Genomics, Department of Medicine, and Division of Ethics, Department of Medical Humanities and Ethics, at Columbia University, where she also co-directs the Precision Medicine: Ethics, Politics, and Culture Project. She is a former litigator with a trans-disciplinary background and has extensive experience in national and international policymaking relating to human and disability rights. Her mixed-methods and community-based participatory research program focuses on the ramifications of genetic data in nonclinical settings (e.g., schools) for social justice; the psychosocial impact of genomic data and return of genetic results on adolescents and families; issues of trust and inclusion of people with disabilities in precision medicine research; and disability and intersectional biases in AI/ML training datasets. She serves as a member of the American Society of Human Genetics' Professional Practice & Social Implications Committee and the Institutional Review Board (IRB) of NIH's All of Us Research Program.

Udo Schüklenk is professor of philosophy at Queen's University, Kingston, Ontario, Canada; Ontario Research Chair in Bioethics; and honorary professor at both Witwatersrand University, Johannesburg (since 2008) and Wenzhou Medical University, Wenzhou (since 2017). He is the editor in chief of *Bioethics* (since 1997) and the founding editor and editor in chief of *Developing World Bioethics* (since 2000).

Edward H. Spence is the founder and director of the Philosophy Plays project, now in its twenty-fifth year, whose aim is the communication of public philosophy through dramatic performance and audience participation and discussion. He's also an honorary research associate in the Department of Philosophy at the University of Sydney and adjunct senior lecturer at Charles Sturt University, Australia, as well as the senior research fellow at the 4TU Center for Ethics and Technology in the Netherlands.

Bradley P. Stoner is professor and head, department of public health sciences, and professor, department of medicine at Queen's University, Kingston, Ontario, Canada. His research focuses on sociocultural determinants of infectious disease risk in human populations. Prior to his appointment at Queen's, he was an associate professor of anthropology and medicine at Washington University in St. Louis, Missouri. He is a former visiting medical officer at the World Health Organization and has consulted for the US Centers for Disease Control and Prevention. He is board-certified in infectious diseases and internal medicine.

Scott Stonington is associate professor of anthropology and medicine at the University of Michigan, Ann Arbor. His research addresses the globalization of biomedical ethics and expertise. His first book, *The Spirit Ambulance*, documents two years accompanying Thai elders at their deathbeds, their children's attempts to pay back their "debt of life" via intensive medical care, and the ensuing rush for the last breath to be taken at home. His second Thailand project examines global debates over the use of opiates for pain management. His US-based research addresses how health practitioners decide what constitutes true and useful knowledge.

Peter Tagore Tan is the philosophy department chair and director of the bioethics certificate program at Mount Saint Mary's University in Los Angeles, where he has served as faculty president. His research and publications focus on Whitehead's process philosophy, environmental ethics, bioethics and climate change, and ancient philosophy. He is currently working on Petrarch's allegory, "The Ascent of Mont Ventoux."

Wanda Teays is a philosophy professor emerita from Mount Saint Mary's University in Los Angeles. Her research focuses on bioethics, human rights, ethics and film, and critical thinking. She is the author of numerous essays and author or editor of thirteen books, including: *Doctors and Torture: Medicine at the Crossroads*; *Analyzing Violence Against Women*; *Business Ethics Through Movies*; *The Ethical University* (co-edited with Alison Dundes Renteln); *Bioethics, Justice, and Health Care* (co-edited with Laura Purdy); and *Ethics in the AI, Technology, and Information Age* (co-edited with Michael

Boylan). She is co-founder of MSMU's bioethics certificate program, and is currently writing a book on solitary confinement.

Rosemarie Tong is a distinguished professor emerita of health-care ethics in the Department of Philosophy and director of the Center for Applied and Professional Ethics at UNC Charlotte. She is internationally known for her contributions to feminist thought and bioethics. She has authored and co-edited thirteen books, including *Ethics in Policy Analysis*; *Controlling our Reproductive Destiny: A Technological and Philosophical Perspective*; *Feminist Approaches to Bioethics*; *Linking Visions: Feminist Bioethics, Human Rights, and the Developing World* (with Ann Donchin and Sue Dodds); *New Perspectives in Health Care Ethics: An Interdisciplinary and Crosscultural Approach* (2007); and *Feminist Thought: A More Comprehensive Introduction*. She has also published over one hundred articles on topics related to feminist theory, reproductive and genetic technology, biomedical research, global bioethics, aging, and health-care reform.

Carlos Verdugo-Serna is professor of philosophy (emeritus) at the Universidad de Valparaíso, Chile. His main research areas have been the philosophy of science and technology and the philosophy of Karl Popper. More recently his interests and publications have focused on ethical issues in scientific research and also on the influence of Popper's philosophy of science and political philosophy in Latin America.

Virginia L. Warren is professor of philosophy at Chapman University in Orange, California. She has published articles on medical ethics, disability, philosophy of mind, and Kierkegaard. Her current research focuses on developing a new approach to applied ethics, with particular emphasis on autonomy and empowerment, justice, and moral injury. She teaches courses in ethics, medical ethics, environmental ethics, political and legal philosophy, and philosophy of women / women of color. She is a founding member of the ethics committee of the Children's Hospital of Orange County.

Cecilia (Lim) Wee is an associate professor in the Department of Philosophy at the National University of Singapore. Her major research areas are Cartesian philosophy, early modern philosophy, and Chinese philosophy. She has a BA and an MA in philosophy from NUS, and a PhD in philosophy from the University of Pittsburgh. Her current research is on Descartes on self-motion; life and the passions; the liberal arts and Montaigne on education; *The Cartesian Mind* (co-edited with Jorge Secada); and "Mencius and Feminism" (for *Dao Companion to Mencius*).